Lecture Notes in Computer Scien

T0238536

Commenced Publication in 1973
Founding and Former Series Editors:
Gerhard Goos, Juris Hartmanis, and Jan van Leeuwen

Anton Nijholt   Teresa Romão
Dennis Reidsma (Eds.)

Advances in Computer Entertainment

9th International Conference, ACE 2012
Kathmandu, Nepal, November 3-5, 2012
Proceedings

 Springer

Volume Editors

Anton Nijholt
Dennis Reidsma
University of Twente
Human Media Interaction
Drienerlolaan 5, 7522 NB Enschede, The Netherlands
E-mail: {a.nijholt, d.reidsma}@utwente.nl

Teresa Romão
Universidade Nova de Lisboa
CITI, Faculdade de Ciências e Tecnologia
Quinta da Torre, 2829-516 Caparica, Portugal
E-mail: tir@fct.unl.pt

ISSN 0302-9743   e-ISSN 1611-3349
ISBN 978-3-642-34291-2   e-ISBN 978-3-642-34292-9
DOI 10.1007/978-3-642-34292-9
Springer Heidelberg Dordrecht London New York

Library of Congress Control Number: 2012949672

CR Subject Classification (1998): I.2.1, H.5, H.3, H.4, I.4, F.1, I.5

LNCS Sublibrary: SL 3 – Information Systems and Application, incl. Internet/Web
and HCI

Typesetting: Camera-ready by author, data conversion by Scientific Publishing Services, Chennai, India

Printed on acid-free paper

Springer is part of Springer Science+Business Media (www.springer.com)

Preface

These are the proceedings of the 9th International Conference on Advances in Computer Entertainment (ACE 2012). ACE has become the leading scientific forum for dissemination of cutting-edge research results in the area of entertainment computing. Interactive entertainment is one of the most vibrant areas of interest in modern society and is amongst the fastest growing industries in the world. ACE 2012 brought together leading researchers and practitioners from academia and industry to present their innovative work and discuss all aspects and challenges of interactive entertainment technology, in an exciting, cultural, and stimulating environment.

ACE is by nature a multidisciplinary conference, therefore attracting people from across a wide spectrum of interests and disciplines including computer science, design, arts, sociology, anthropology, psychology, and marketing. The main goal of ACE is to stimulate discussion in the development of new and compelling entertainment computing and interactive art concepts and applications. At ACE conferences participants are encouraged to present work they believe will shape the future, going beyond the established paradigms, and focusing on all areas related to interactive entertainment.

This was the 9th ACE conference, and the first time that such an entertainment computing conference was held in the emerging world. The theme of ACE 2012 was "Entertaining the Whole World," and Kathmandu in Nepal ("The Roof of the World,") was chosen as the venue. In line with the theme, ACE 2012 emphasized the use of easily available technology. Technology for entertainment design is becoming cheap or even extremely cheap. Designing interactive entertainment with commercial off-the-shelf technology (cheap sensors, Kinect, Arduino, etc.) is becoming regular business. How can we use this development to invent yet more new ways of harnessing the entertainment power of creating? Can we convert consumers of entertainment into creators of entertainment, where the process of creating is perhaps as important as the resulting product? Young people in emerging markets can become creators as well as consumers of digital entertainment. They can distribute their work through apps and the Internet, and through media creativity benefit their country and economy. We wish to strike up discussions and initiate projects that will benefit the emerging world through digital entertainment.

In order to emphasize the theme of the conference some special tracks and events were organized. One of them was the Art and Culture track, with papers, games and other forms of entertainment, and interactive works of art showcasing the diversity of art and culture found in today's digital artifacts. This diversity can also be found in the tracks on Creative Showcases and Demonstrations and the Poster and Late-Breaking Results tracks. All the presentations from the regular sessions and those of these tracks can be found in these proceedings. We received about 140 submissions in the various categories (papers, posters, demonstrations, workshops, panels). From the regular paper submissions, ten papers were accepted for long presentations (about 14%), and 20 for short presentations (about 27%). Many poster papers and papers accompanying demonstrations could be accepted. There are agreements with some journals to have special issues devoted to some subthemes of ACE 2012 and containing a selection of the best papers from ACE 2012.

ACE 2012 had several satellite workshops. There were regular workshops on entertainment research and technology, but new for ACE and particularly important for the theme of the conference were the Entertainment Kids Workshops. The underlying idea of these workshops is that entertainment can empower children and young people in developing countries and communities with creative thinking and new media technologies. We hope to nurture and inspire young children to create new value propositions that will benefit their individual selves, communities, and countries. We want to view young children in developing countries as creative innovators and ambassadors of new technologies, rather than passive end-user consumers. And this last point in particular was addressed successfully in many of the proposals for Kids Entertainment Workshops that the organizers received. Several of these workshops could be organized, aiming at children aged between 4 and 12 as participants. Among the issues that were explored individually or in small groups we can find participatory design, using gaming platforms for body movement design, tangible interfaces and storytelling.

During plenary sessions of the conference two panels were organized. One panel was devoted to the results of the Kids Entertainment Workshops. The other panel was titled: Where Buddhism Encounters Entertainment Computing.

At ACE 2012, as in all previous ACE conferences, prizes were awarded for the best papers and best demonstrations. The top three in each category were awarded Gold, Silver, and Bronze prizes. For the first time, in 2012, there was a special "Diamond Best Award" for the best academic work in any category. This was co-awarded together with Springer, with a book prize sponsored by Springer.

ACE attendees brought books for donation in the fields of digital media, computer science, electronics, and related areas. These books were presented to a high school in Nepal during ACE. It is hoped that this will be a positive push that will allow some smart Nepalese kids to have a jump start in creativity. Although it is a small contribution to Nepal, we hope it will inspire a few young people to become creative media designers or interest them to become computer scientists or engineers, and perhaps start a new game or Internet service. We hope to create a "geek" culture.

ACE 2012 was organized in Kathmandu, Nepal. We think that there is a perfect match between the theme of the conference ("Entertaining the Whole World") and the location ("The Roof of the World") with its political and economic problems. Nepal is a developing country. It is a rich country when you look at people, nature, and ambitions. It is a poor country when you look at characteristics that play a role in comparisons between countries when measuring the economic situation and economic developments. Obviously, ACE 2012 does not pretend to make immediate changes. But maybe the participants of ACE 2012 will learn from the theme, how it relates to a local situation, and how advanced research and advanced technology can be adapted to the affordable design and implementation of interesting entertainment applications. And, obviously, we hope the people that attended and experienced demonstrations learned that advanced research and technology can be used in creative and not necessarily expensive ways.

Part of the conference was organized in a Kathmandu hotel that hopefully, when necessary, will have utilities for generating its own electricity. For part of the conference there was no guarantee that electricity would be available owing to electricity rationing and power interruptions. Participants were asked to be prepared for situations in which they would have to present their paper, their poster, and their demonstration without having the guarantee that electricity is available. Workshop proposers and participants, including the Kids Entertainment Workshops, were asked to prepare their workshops and presentations in such a way that they could be successful without having access to electricity or when being forced to shift their activities to non-scheduled periods. We think that the creativity needed to deal with such situations is also helpful to designing and applying advanced entertainment technology in developing countries.

As can be expected, the organization of ACE 2012 was a team effort and a large number of people worked very hard to organize ACE 2012. A list of committees and committee members appears on the next pages. These committees were successful, because a record number of potential contributions were submitted and reviewed. However, particular thanks should go to Adrian Cheok who, together with our Nepalese research colleagues, took the daring initiative to have ACE 2012 in Nepal. And particular thanks should also go to the local organizers in Kathmandu for their pioneering efforts to make ACE 2012 a success, not only for the visitors from abroad, but also for the Nepalese community, from children to students, researchers, and policy makers interested in new and advanced technology and its use in creative applications that can bring joy.

August 2012   Anton Nijholt
                                                                        Teresa Romão
                                                                        Dennis Reidsma

Welcome Messages from the General Chairs

It gives me immense pleasure and utmost pride to welcome you all to the ACE 2012 conference proceedings. As we all know, the ACE conference is a multidisciplinary meeting attracting people of varied interests and disciplines across the globe. I feel honored and privileged to have such a mega conference held in the capital of the pristine Himalayan country, Nepal. Moreover, I am very happy to be one of the Organizing Chairs of the conference, hosted for the first time in Nepal.

All ACE participants were encouraged to present work they believe will shape the future, going beyond the established paradigms, and focusing on all areas related to interactive entertainment. I am very sure that the conference will make a tremendous contribution toward the development of new and compelling entertainment computing and interactive art concepts and applications.

I am also confident that the Kathmandu conference will be a vital guideline for future entertainment markets.

I hope you enjoy the proceedings of this event.

Aashmi Rajya Lakshmi Rana

Every nation has its own pop culture which can be developed and empowered by digital technology. This pop culture can bring about a stronger change and effect developing countries and children. I hope we have a happy convergence of culture and technology for everyone on earth!

Ichiya Nakamura

Organization

ACE Steering Committee

Chair

Adrian David Cheok — Keio University, Graduate School of Media Design, Japan

Members

Teresa Romão — CITI, FCT, Universidade Nova de Lisboa, Portugal

Masahiko Inami — Keio University, Graduate School of Media Design, Japan

General Chairs

Aashmi Rajya Lakshmi Rana — Kathmandu, Nepal

Ichiya Nakamura — Keio University, Japan

Program Chair

Anton Nijholt — University of Twente, The Netherlands

Program co-chair

Teresa Romão — CITI, FCT, Universidade Nova de Lisboa, Portugal

Social Media and Poster Chair

Andrés Lucero — Nokia Research Center, Tampere, Finland

Organizing Chairs

Aashmi Rajya Lakshmi Rana — Kathmandu, Nepal

Roshan Chamling Rai — Kathmandu, Nepal

Ajith Perakum Madurapperuma — Keio-NUS CUTE Center, Singapore

Creative Showcases Chairs

Dennis Reidsma — University of Twente, Enschede, The Netherlands

Shoichi Hasegawa — The University of Electro-Communications, Tokyo, Japan

Art and Culture Track Chair

Guenter Wallner   University of Applied Arts, Austria

Kids Workshops Chairs

Yoram Chisik   University of Madeira, Portugal
Janak Bhimani   Keio University, Japan

Workshops Chair

Fernando Birra   CITI, FCT, Universidade Nova de Lisboa,
                                 Portugal

Senior Program Committee

Elisabeth Andre   Augsburg University, Germany
Regina Bernhaupt   Ruwido, Toulouse, France
Nadia Berthouze   University College London, UK
Mark Billinghurst   HIT Lab NZ, University of Canterbury,
                                 New Zealand
Nick Bryan-Kinns   Queen Mary University of London, UK
Marc Cavazza   University of Teesside, UK
Luca Chittaro   HCI Lab, University of Udine, Italy
Kentaro Fukuchi   Meiji University, Tokyo, Japan
Mathew Gardiner   Ars Electronica, Linz, Austria
Chris Geiger   University of Applied Sciences, Düsseldorf,
                                 Germany
Florian Floyd Mueller   RMIT University, Melbourne, Australia
Beatriz Sousa Santos   Universidade de Aveiro/IEETA, Portugal
Masanori Sugimoto   University of Tokyo, Japan
Annika Waern   Mobile Life Center, Interactive Institute,
                                 Sweden

Program Committee

Clemens Arth   Fred Charles
Rogério Bandeira   Alan Chatham
Riccardo Berta   Foo Chek-Yang
Staffan Björk   Kai-Yin Cheng
Pedro Branco   Narisa Chu
Markus Broecker   Adrian Clark
Stefan Bruckner   Esteban Clua
Marian Carr   Antonio Coelho
David Carrol   Nuno Correia
Teresa Chambel   Paul Coulton

José Danado
Eduardo Dias
Paulo Dias
Frank Dignum
Carlos Duarte
Luis Duarte
Mirjam Palosaari Eladhari
Kjetil Falkenberg Hansen
Haakon Faste
Owen Noel Newton Fernando
Manuel J. Fonseca
Mark Gajewski
Eduardo Calvillo Gamez
Christos Gatzids
Roland Geraerts
Nicholas Gold
Lindsay Grace
Hayrettin Gürkok
Mads Haahr
Atsushi Hiyama
Christina Hochleitner
Jussi Holopainen
Wolfgang Huerst
Veikko Ikonen
Masataka Imura
Ido Aharon Iurgel
Rui Jesus
Arnav Jhala
Rui José
M. Carmen Juan
Ichiroh Kanaya
Hirokazu Kato
Norbert Kikuchi
Jongwon Kim
Ben Kirman
Florian Klompmaker
Jeffrey Koh
Itaru Kuramoto
Michael Lankes
Petri Lankoski
Iolanda Leite
Christopher Lindinger
Sheng Liu

Sandy Louchart
Joaquim Madeira
Angelika Mader
Aderito Marcos
Carlos Martinho
Maic Masuch
Kohei Matsumura
Oscar Mealha
Monica Mendes
Hongying Meng
Hiroyuki Mitsuhara
Ramon Molla Vaya
Leonel Morgado
Ann Morrison
Frank Nack
Jörg Niesenhaus
Ian Oakley
Philippe Palanque
Holger Reckter
Licinio Roque
Marco De Sa
Christian Sandor
Pedro Santos
Hartmut Seichter
Andrei Sherstyuk
Danqing Shi
Frutuoso Silva
A. Augusto Sousa
Maki Sugimoto
Kaoru Sumi
Cristina Sylla
Tsutomu Terada
Mariet Theune
Julian Togelius
Chad Toprak
Betsy van Dijk
Marco van Leeuwen
Herwin van Welbergen
Ana Isabel Veloso
Dhaval Vyas
James Young
Nelson Zagalo
Job Zwiers

Additional Reviewers

Dzmitry Aliakseyeu
Pedro Ângelo
Juha Arrasvuori
Cedric Bach
Katharina Emmerich
Cornelia Graf
Andreas Hartl
Wolfgang Hochleitner

Mark Lochrie
Michael Pirker
Mikko Rissanen
Johanna Schmidt
Samuel Silva
Andrej Varchola
Eduardo Veas
Kening Zhu

Keynote Talks

Keynote Talk: Spreading ICT in India: Connectivity, Content, Devices and Training for a Billion People

Kannan M. Moudgalya

This talk explains the Spoken Tutorial methodology that creates instructional material on ICT, suitable for self-learning. During the last year, about 100,000 students were provided free training on many open source software systems, in 1,000 colleges, through student and faculty volunteers. One may also access these tutorials from http://spoken-tutorial.org free of cost. Synchronous support can be provided through an ongoing teacher training program that allows up to 10,000 people to interact with experts with audio-video connectivity. We dub only the spoken part of these tutorials into the many languages of India to teach ICT to children weak in English, while keeping the employment potential intact. This method has the potential to also bridge the digital divide.

The Indian government is also establishing 1GBps connectivity in every one of the about 1,000 universities in India and their affiliated colleges. To realize the benefits of these ICT tools and techniques, one needs computers, which are unfortunately not affordable to most Indians. To provide this important link, this Mission has come up with the Aakash project. As a part of this project, for testing purposes, we have placed an order for 100,000 units of a 7" tablet, at a cost of INR 2,263 (about USD 40). We have been successful in porting to Aakash, C, C++, Python, PHP and Perl, and also Scilab, an open source alternative to Matlab. This device will also help access video content, e-books, and the Internet through wireless. Based on the feedback obtained through this pilot study, we will freeze the specifications and order several million units. Aakash will be demonstrated during this talk. A video that explains the current state of Aakash is available at http://media.sakshat.ac.in/Play/?ID=1. These projects are funded by the National Mission on Education through ICT.

The work reported in this talk has the potential to be of use to all children of the world in general, and to those in the developing world in particular.

Brief CV of Kannan M. Moudgalya

Kannan M. Moudgalya is a professor at IIT Bombay. He studied chemical engineering and electrical engineering at IIT Madras and at Rice University. He has been a visiting professor at the University of Alberta. He has written two textbooks: (1) *Digital Control*, published by John Wiley & Sons, Chichester and (2) *Optimization: Theory and Practice*, jointly with M. C. Joshi, published by Narosa, New Delhi.

He has published a large number of papers in refereed international conferences and journals in the areas of mathematical modelling, control, and simulation. Kannan is now devoting his time to spreading education on a massive scale, without quality dilution. He has been focusing on spoken tutorials, open source software systems, virtual labs and the low-cost tablet, Aakash. He has held the posts of Associate Dean (R&D), Head of Office Automation and Head of Distance Education, at IIT Bombay. He is a member of the Standing Committee of the National Mission on Education Through ICT, Government of India.

Keynote Talk: When Robots Do Wrong

David Levy

Before long, robots will be assisting us in many different aspects of our lives, becoming our partners in various practical and companionable ways and entertaining us. As robot and AI technologies advance, the proliferation of robots and their applications will take place in parallel with increases in their complexity. One of the disadvantages of those increases will be a burgeoning in the number of robot accidents and wrongdoings, resulting in enormous numbers of robot-based court cases throughout the developed world, many of them involving complex legal arguments based on technological evidence from expert witnesses.

Here we address the questions: What are the implications when something goes wrong? Who, or what, is responsible? Should responsibility be attributed to the robot itself, or to its manufacturer, designers or developers, or to its owner, or its operator . . .? And above all, how best should society deal with an ever-increasing number of robot accidents, their diverse causes and their negative consequences?

We discuss the concept of blaming the robots themselves for their accidents, based on three possible rationales for doing so: treating them as quasi-people, as quasi-animals, or simply as man-made products. And we examine how robots might be punished if society decides that they should take the blame for the accidents they cause.

We also consider the more likely approach of blaming homo sapiens, with the manifold complications that can affect the blame attribution process put forward as a powerful argument against society employing litigation as its primary response to robot accidents.

Robot vehicles are introduced as an example of a category of robot for which legal constraints already exist, namely, motoring laws, including the laws requiring cars and their drivers to be adequately insured. The idea of compulsory insurance, supported by a technologically driven system of enforcement, is extended from robot cars to robots in general as an alternative approach to litigation.

Brief CV of David Levy

David Levy graduated from St. Andrews University, Scotland, in 1967, and then taught practical classes in computer programming at Glasgow University for four years, before moving into the world of business and professional chess playing and writing. He wrote more than 30 books on chess, won the Scottish Championship, and he was awarded the International Master title by FIDE, the World Chess

Federation, in 1969. In 1968 David started a bet with four artificial intelligence professors that he would not lose a chess match against a computer program within ten years. He won that bet. Since 1977 David has been involved in the development of many chess playing and other programs for consumer electronic products. David's interest in artificial intelligence expanded beyond computer games into other areas of AI, including human–computer conversation, and in 1997 he led the team that won the Loebner Prize competition in New York. David won this prestigious prize again in 2009. His 50th book, *Love and Sex with Robots*, was published in November 2007, shortly after he was awarded a PhD by the University of Maastricht for his thesis entitled "Intimate Relationships with Artificial Partners." David is President of the International Computer Games Association, and CEO of the London-based company Intelligent Toys Ltd. His hobbies include classical music and playing poker.

Workshops and Panels at ACE 2012

Kids Workshops

- Dance It and Make My Sound with the Oriboo. Organizers: Elena Márquez Segura, Annika Waern, and Jin Moen
- Parapara Animation: Organizers: Daisuke Akatsuka, Brian Birtles, Hiroki Ito, Masami Ishiyama, and Satoko Takita Yamaguchi
- LuTrack: Bringing Tangible Interaction to Low-Computer-Literacy Children. Organizers: Javier Marco Rubio, Yoram Itzhak Chisik, Monchu Chen, Maria Clara Martins
- Playing with Blocks and Exploring Words and Sounds. Organizers: Cristina Sylla, Sérgio Gonçalves, Pedro Branco, Clara Coutinho, Valentina Nisi, and António Gomes
- Creative Design Workshop: Exploring Value Propositions with Urban Nepalese Children. Organizers: Alissa Antle and Allen Bevans

Regular Workshops

- Creating Pleasurable Interactive Brand Communications. Organizers: David Williams and Hiroaki Kawamura
- Mediated Yoga Experiences. Organizers: Monique Park, Mario Pinto, Monchu Chen, Valentina Nisi, and António Gomes

Panels

- Where Buddhism Encounters Entertainment Computing. Organizers: Daisuke Uriu, Naohito Okude, Masahiko Inami, Takafumi Taketomi, and Chihiro Sato
- Kids, Entertainment, Media Technologies and Developing Countries. Organizers: Yoram Chisik and Janak Bhimani

Partnership

ACE 2012 in Kathmandu, Nepal, was organized in partnership with EduPro:

Table of Contents

Long Presentations

Applaud Having Fun: A Mobile Game to Cheer Your Favourite Sports
Team.. 1
   Pedro Centieiro, Teresa Romão, and A. Eduardo Dias

Paranga: An Interactive Flipbook 17
   Kazuyuki Fujita, Hiroyuki Kidokoro, and Yuichi Itoh

Augmentation of Toothbrush by Modulating Sounds Resulting from
Brushing... 31
   Taku Hachisu and Hiroyuki Kajimoto

Bathcratch: Touch and Sound-Based DJ Controller Implemented on a
Bathtub 44
   Shigeyuki Hirai, Yoshinobu Sakakibara, and Seiho Hayakawa

Airstic Drum: A Drumstick for Integration of Real and Virtual
Drums... 57
   *Hiroyuki Kanke, Yoshinari Takegawa, Tsutomu Terada, and
Masahiko Tsukamoto*

Enhancing Level Difficulty and Additional Content in Platform
Videogames through Graph Analysis 70
   Fausto Mourato, Fernando Birra, and Manuel Próspero dos Santos

A System for Supporting Performers in Stuffed Suits 85
   Tatsuhiko Okazaki, Tsutomu Terada, and Masahiko Tsukamoto

Socially Present Board Game Opponents.......................... 101
   André Pereira, Rui Prada, and Ana Paiva

Localizing *Global Game Jam*: Designing Game Development for
Collaborative Learning in the Social Context 117
   *Kiyoshi Shin, Kosuke Kaneko, Yu Matsui, Koji Mikami,
Masaru Nagaku, Toshifumi Nakabayashi, Kenji Ono, and
Shinji R. Yamane*

Producing while Consuming: Social Interaction around Photos Shared
within Private Group... 133
   Dhaval Vyas, Yanqing Cui, Jarno Ojala, and Guido Grassel

Short Presentations

Extensible Sound Description in COLLADA: A Unique File for a Rich
Sound Design.. 151
  *Shih-Han Chan, Stéphane Natkin, Guillaume Tiger, and
  Alexandre Topol*

An Automatic Race Track Generating System 167
  Tai-Yun Chen, Hung-Wei Hsu, Wen-Kai Tai, and Chin-Chen Chang

Light Perfume: Designing a Wearable Lighting and Olfactory Accessory
for Empathic Interactions 182
  *Yongsoon Choi, Rahul Parsani, Xavier Roman,
  Anshul Vikram Pandey, and Adrian David Cheok*

A Survey of Players' Opinions on Interface Customization in World of
Warcraft 198
  Chris Deaker, Masood Masoodian, and Bill Rogers

53.090 Virtual Rusks = 510 Real Smiles Using a Fun Exergame
Installation for Advertising Traditional Food Products 214
  *Dimitris Grammenos, George Margetis,
  Panagiotis Koutlemanis, and Xenophon Zabulis*

Designing Playful Interactive Installations for Urban Environments –
The SwingScape Experience 230
  *Kaj Grønbæk, Karen Johanne Kortbek, Claus Møller,
  Jesper Nielsen, and Liselott Stenfeldt*

Flashback in Interactive Storytelling............................. 246
  Olivier Guy and Ronan Champagnat

SanjigenJiten: Computer Assisted Language Learning System within a
3D Game Environment 262
  Robert Howland, Sachi Urano, and Junichi Hoshino

A Caption Presentation System for the Hearing Impaired People
Attending Theatrical Performances................................ 274
  Yuko Konya and Itiro Siio

Emergent Gait Evolution of Quadruped Artificial Life 287
  Kinyo Kou and Yoichiro Kawaguchi

Enjoying Text Input with Image-Enabled IME 297
  Toshiyuki Masui

Train Window of Container: Visual and Auditory Representation of
Train Movement   309
  Kunihiro Nishimura, Yasuhiro Suzuki, Munehiko Sato,
  Oribe Hayashi, Yang LiWei, Kentaro Kimura, Shinya Nishizaka,
  Yusuke Onojima, Yuki Ban, Yuma Muroya, Shigeo Yoshida, and
  Michitaka Hirose

Pinch: An Interface That Relates Applications on Multiple
Touch-Screen by 'Pinching' Gesture   320
  Takashi Ohta and Jun Tanaka

Exploring Playability of Social Network Games   336
  Janne Paavilainen, Kati Alha, and Hannu Korhonen

A Gesture Interface Game for Energy Consumption Awareness   352
  Ricardo Salvador, Teresa Romão, and Pedro Centieiro

UBI, The Guardian Dragon: Your Virtual Sidekick   368
  Rossana Santos and Nuno Correia

Construction of a Prototyping Support System for Painted Musical
Instruments   384
  Yoshinari Takegawa, Kenichiro Fukushi, Tod Machover,
  Tsutomu Terada, and Masahiko Tsukamoto

Reflex-Based Navigation by Inducing Self-motion Perception with
Head-Mounted Vection Display   398
  Tomohiro Tanikawa, Yuma Muroya, Takuji Narumi, and
  Michitaka Hirose

POPAPY: Instant Paper Craft Made Up in a Microwave Oven   406
  Kentaro Yasu and Masahiko Inami

Art and Culture Track

Games Bridging Cultural Communications   421
  Adrian David Cheok, Narisa N.Y. Chu, Yongsoon Choi, and Jun Wei

Existential Waters: On Employing a Game Engine for Artistic
Expression within a Theater Play, and on the Implications of This
towards Existential Games   429
  Ido Aharon Iurgel and Mário Pinto

Reframing Haute Couture Handcraftship: How to Preserve Artisans'
Abilities with Gesture Recognition   437
  Gustavo Marfia, Marco Roccetti, Andrea Marcomini,
  Cristian Bertuccioli, and Giovanni Matteucci

PURE FLOW: Gallery Installation / Mobile Application 445
  Duncan Rowland and Katy Connor

Juke Cylinder: Sound Image Augmentation to Metamorphose Hands
into a Musical Instrument 453
  *Masamichi Ueta, Osamu Hoshuyama, Takuji Narumi, Sho Sakurai,
  Tomohiro Tanikawa, and Michitaka Hirose*

Extended Abstracts

Puppet Theater System for Normal-Hearing and Hearing-Impaired
People 461
  *Takayuki Adachi, Masafumi Goseki, Hiroshi Mizoguchi,
  Miki Namatame, Fusako Kusunoki, Ryohei Egusa, and
  Shigenori Inagaki*

Creative Design: Exploring Value Propositions with Urban Nepalese
Children 465
  Alissa N. Antle and Allen Bevans

DriveRS: An In-Car Persuasive System for Making Driving Safe
and Fun 469
  Anne Bergmans and Suleman Shahid

When Away Applaud Anyway 473
  Pedro Centieiro, Teresa Romão, and A. Eduardo Dias

Making a Toy Educative Using Electronics 477
  Edwin Dertien, Jelle Dijkstra, Angelika Mader, and Dennis Reidsma

Enhancing Tactile Imagination through Sound and Light 481
  Hideyuki Endo and Hideki Yoshioka

Streaming DirectX-Based Games on Windows 485
  *Alexander Franiak, Yohann Pitrey, Christoph Czepa, and
  Helmut Hlavacs*

Autonomously Acquiring a Video Game Agent's Behavior: Letting
Players Feel Like Playing with a Human Player 490
  *Nobuto Fujii, Yuichi Sato, Hironori Wakama, and
  Haruhiro Katayose*

Chop Chop: A Sound Augmented Kitchen Prototype 494
  Veronica Halupka, Ali Almahr, Yupeng Pan, and Adrian David Cheok

Time Telescopic Replay of Tactile Sensations 498
  Yuki Hashimoto

Compact Ultrasound Device for Noncontact Interaction 502
  Takayuki Hoshi

Pillow Fight 2.0: A Creative Use of Technology for Physical
Interaction 506
  Anne Sofie Juul Sørensen

Immobile Haptic Interface Using Tendon Electrical Stimulation 513
  Hiroyuki Kajimoto

STRAVIGATION: A Vibrotactile Mobile Navigation for Exploration-
Like Sightseeing 517
  Hiroki Kawaguchi and Takuya Nojima

Earth Girl: A Multi-cultural Game about Natural Disaster Prevention
and Resilience 521
  Isaac Kerlow, Muhammad Khadafi, Harry Zhuang, Henry Zhuang,
  Aida Azlin, and Aisyah Suhaimi

PowerFood: Turns Fruit Eating into Fun and Makes Snacks Not
Done 525
  Lies Kroes and Suleman Shahid

City Pulse: Supporting Going-Out Activities with a Context-Aware
Urban Display 529
  Mohammad Obaid, Ekaterina Kurdyukova, and Elisabeth Andre

Physiological Signals Based Fatigue Prediction Model for Motion
Sensing Games 533
  Ziyu Lu, Ling Chen, Changjun Fan, and Gencai Chen

JECCO: A Creature-Like Tentacle Robot 537
  Haipeng Mi and Yoichiro Kawaguchi

Yusabutter: A Messaging Tool That Generates Animated Texts 541
  Mitsuru Minakuchi, Shougo Kinoshita, and Yu Suzuki

HomeTree – An Art Inspired Mobile Eco-feedback Visualization 545
  Filipe Quintal, Valentina Nisi, Nuno Nunes, Mary Barreto, and
  Lucas Pereira

Augmenting Trading Card Game: Playing against Virtual Characters
Used in Fictional Stories 549
  Mizuki Sakamoto, Tatsuo Nakajima, and Todorka Alexandrova

Changing Environmental Behaviors through Smartphone-Based
Augmented Experiences 553
  Bruno Santos, Teresa Romão, A. Eduardo Dias,
  Pedro Centieiro, and Bárbara Teixeira

flona: Development of an Interface That Implements Lifelike Behaviors
to a Plant... 557
 Furi Sawaki, Kentaro Yasu, and Masahiko Inami

HOJI*HOJI: The Hole-Type Interactive Device for Entertainment...... 561
 Yuta Suzuki, Yusaku Okada, Hiroki Kawaguchi, Takashi Kimura,
 Yoichi Takahashi, Kodai Horita, Takuya Nojima, and Hideki Koike

t-words: Playing with Sounds and Creating Narratives................ 565
 Cristina Sylla, Sérgio Gonçalves, Pedro Branco, and Clara Coutinho

Semi-transparent Augmented Reality System 569
 Tomoya Tachikawa, Takenori Hara, Chiho Toyono,
 Goro Motai, Karin Iwazaki, Keisuke Shuto, Hiroko Uchiyama, and
 Sakuji Yoshimura

Awareness Support for Remote Music Performance 573
 Hiroyuki Tarumi, Keiichi Akazawa, Masaki Ono, Erina Kagawa,
 Toshihiro Hayashi, and Rihito Yaegashi

GENIE: Photo-Based Interface for Many Heterogeneous LED Lamps ... 577
 Jordan Tewell, Sunao Hashimoto, Masahiko Inami, and
 Takeo Igarashi

Disaster Experience Game in a Real World 581
 Sachi Urano, Peichao Yu, and Junichi Hoshino

Entertainment Displays Which Restore Negative Images of Shopping
Center... 585
 Sachi Urano, Tetsuya Saito, and Junichi Hoshino

Where Buddhism Encounters Entertainment Computing 589
 Daisuke Uriu, Naohito Okude, Masahiko Inami,
 Takafumi Taketomi, and Chihiro Sato

IUstream: Personal Live Streaming Support System with Automatic
Collection and Real-Time Recommendation of Topics................. 593
 Keiko Yamamoto, Soya Kirito, Itaru Kuramoto, and
 Yoshihiro Tsujino

Author Index.. 597

Applaud Having Fun: A Mobile Game to Cheer Your Favourite Sports Team

Pedro Centieiro[1], Teresa Romão[1], and A. Eduardo Dias[1,2]

[1] CITI, DI-Faculdade de Ciências e Tecnologia/Universidade Nova de Lisboa
2829-516 Caparica, Portugal
{pcentieiro,aed.fct}@gmail.com, tir@fct.unl.pt
[2] bViva International, B.V.
Romanovhof 9, 3329 BD, Dordrecht, Netherlands
edias@bviva.com

Abstract. This paper describes the design, implementation and evaluation of a multiplayer mobile game that enhances the remote fans experience during a live sports event broadcast. This prototype, called WeApplaud, encourages users to participate in the applause happening in the stadium, increasing their levels of fun and immersion in the live event. To achieve these goals, we explored the use of persuasive technology, together with the second screen concept, in order to create a motivating and innovative experience for the users. To test the WeApplaud concept, guide the system's design and evaluate users reactions, we conducted preliminary user tests. Results helped to validate our approach, but also identified some important refinements to be considered in future developments.

1 Introduction

The level of thrill and excitement felt during live events is a unique experience. Experiencing an event in first hand, instead of watching it on television, is very different: performance happens in front of our eyes, in real time, and we can cheer, chant and support the performers along with the other thousands of fans at the venue where the event is taking place. We can perform similar supporting actions at home; however, we do not have the same feeling of connection with the performers and the in-venue fans, and therefore we do not reach the same emotional level. Moreover, our home actions are not reflected in the live event, so the objective of supporting the performers is never really accomplished. Take for instance the world of sports, where a live match can evoke different types of emotions, either positive (like excitement and awe) or negative (as anger or disappointment). These emotions are amplified by the stadium atmosphere, which stands for all the emotional stimuli in a sports stadium, causing specific sensations and emotional reactions in individuals [1].

Since there are usually much more spectators watching a match at home than at the live venue (see [2], for example), we feel that there is room to introduce a new

A. Nijholt, T. Romão, and D. Reidsma (Eds.): ACE 2012, LNCS 7624, pp. 1–16, 2012.

paradigm to bring the venue atmosphere, its immersion and emotional level to the users' homes. To accomplish this, we plan to take into account the second screen concept that has become widely popular in recent years. Through this concept, we will study how persuasive technology concepts can encourage remote fans to cheer and interact with their favourite sports team. Players and fans at the venue will feel the encouragement coming from people watching the match worldwide (this is something that we will address in the future, due to the third parties involved) and they will all feel part of the same community.

Thus, it is our intention to create innovative forms of interaction between mobile devices and live sports, in order to enhance the users' experience during a sports event, increasing the connection between the fans watching the event live at the venue and the ones watching it on TV. It is important to note that many fans do not have the possibility to go to the venue, either due to the ticket price, distance, or the number of limited seats on the venue. This concept would increase remote fans' interest to watch sports events. To achieve the previous goals, we started by developing WeApplaud, a multiplayer mobile game that encourages users to participate in the applause happening in the stadium. Players can choose one of two teams, and they need to applaud during key moments taking place in the sports event. WeApplaud aims to study if this concept helps people remotely watching a sports event to have more fun and feel more engaged in the stadium experience and atmosphere, as mentioned before.

This paper is structured as follows. The next section presents some background related to the areas covered by this work. Section 3 describes our design concept, the interaction and entertainment provided by the prototype. Section 4 deals with the planning, execution and results of the user tests. Finally, Section 5 presents conclusions and directions for future work.

2   Related Research

According to Grudin [3], sports can be fundamentally enhanced with social experiences. Millions of fans like their favourite teams and athletes, so it is not surprising that the sports arenas and stadiums are the number two most checked-in places in the US (only after airports) [3]. The Sport Fan Motivation Scale created by Wann [4] is an instrument aimed to measure eight different motives of sport fans: eustress, self-esteem, escape, entertainment, economic, aesthetic, group affiliation and family. It is designed to illustrate the degrees of fan intensity and help sports decision makers determine how to increase fan involvement. WeApplaud focuses on eustress (positive stress that is created from taking part in a challenge), entertainment, and group affiliation (the desire to be with other people who share the same passion).

Persuasive technology purposefully applies psychological principles of persuasion to interactive media, aiming at changing users' attitudes and behaviours [5]. When it comes to changing attitudes and behaviours, timing and context are critical. Fogg [6] presents different principles applicable in persuasive computing: kairos, social facilitation, social comparison and competition. Furthermore, Torning and Oinas-Kukkonen [7] mention that social facilitation and competition are some of the least used design principles in persuasive technology conferences. Thus, in WeApplaud we decided to focus on those persuasive concepts to motivate users to support their team during specific key moments.

Ian Bogost [8] describes, in his theory on how videogames make arguments and influence players, that games may influence players to take action through gameplay. Games not only deliver messages, but also simulate experiences, and may become rhetorical tools for persuading players. Jesper Juul discusses the nature of games and refers to the shifting focus into players created by space games like Wii Sports and Guitar Hero [9]. WeApplaud was designed for users to mimic the clapping action, in order to further motivate users to support their team. Also, the concept of WeApplaud presented in this paper, makes use of the ideas supported by Juul, by creating a simple and clear game experience to players.

The use of a second screen provides functionalities to improve the viewer's experience. Usually this experience is made through mobile devices, like smartphones or tablets, and it can be completely passive (i.e. watch a backstage camera) or interactive (i.e. live chat with other viewers watching the same show). For example, during the Super Bowl 2012 edition, there were 13.7 million related tweets, and during the final three minutes of the game, fans sent an average of 10000 tweets per second [10]. This data shows that spectators are starting to be more open to comment, interact, and cheer through electronic devices during live events, than they used to. For example, in the Super Bowl 2008 edition the highest number of related tweets per second was only 27.

Many applications are using new methods to create a better second screen experience. One popular application is ConnecTV [11]. ConnecTV uses a fingerprinting process, similar to the one Shazam [12] uses for music. In this case, ConnecTV identifies in real time what it hears from the television. Recently, ConnecTV launched the possibility to identify a basketball match, and display real-time statistics and background information about the respective teams and players. ConnecTV further expands this concept by identifying when a timeout has been called on the court, and then it presents additional match highlights. This is similar to our concept, where users can remotely interact at specific key moments during sport events, in order to enhance their experience during the broadcasted match. Like in the stadium, it is necessary for remote fans to feel and experience something together, and the mere psychological act of being connected is a strong motivation factor for them. We want to go one step further and contribute to make fans, remotely watching a sports event, feel part of it, as much as if their they were at the venue. These fans should receive more immersive input and be also able to provide significant output to the sports event as if they were at the venue.

3   WeApplaud

Our main goal is to create innovative forms of interaction between mobile devices and live sports, in order to enhance the users' experience during a sports event, increasing the connection between the fans watching the event live at the venue and the ones watching it on TV. We aim at allowing remote users to feel and act as close as if they were at the event venue, and making their actions echo on the live event.

In this paper, we chose football as our case study (although the concept can be applied to other sports). Football (or soccer) is widely accepted as the world's most popular sport [13], it moves an incredible number of fans all over the world and generates strong emotions. Thus, we saw it as a natural fit to study and apply our concept. People watching a live event can interact and actually perform several actions. Applauding is one of the most common ones, so we started by focusing our study on this activity.

The goal of WeApplaud is to encourage remote users to participate in the applauses happening at the stadium. By doing that, we expect users to become more engaged in the broadcasted event, increasing their fun and immersion levels. Users will compete with their friends and other remote fans for the glory of becoming their team's top supporters. Furthermore, users will be able to gain achievements, badges and other digital rewards or even sponsored awards. This is the concept that we want to implement on the long term. The WeApplaud version presented in this paper aims at studying if the core concept of WeApplaud works (remotely clapping on key moments during live sports) and defining the application design.

Ideally, the interaction should be as intuitive and non-intrusive as possible, allowing users to just clap. Nevertheless, we need to identify and count the claps made by the users. By using a mobile phone while clapping, for example by holding a mobile device on one hand, and then moving the device as if we would hit the palm of the other hand (Figure 1), it is possible to detect claps by combining sound analysis and accelerometer data (more details about this on Section 3.1). This can be done by using either the front or back side of the device while clapping.

Fig. 1. Clapping action

As stated before, we strongly aim to create a fun and competitive experience. To achieve that, we explored two persuasive technology concepts: social facilitation and competition. Social facilitation suggests that allowing observation of the owner's performance by others increases the effectiveness of persuasion [6]. In other words, people perform better, when other people are present, participating or observing. Competition motivates users to adopt a target attitude or behavior by leveraging human beings' natural drive to compete [6]. When people engage in a competition, they want to win. Sometimes, they do not even care about rewards (either physical or digital), since the intrinsic motivations of being the best and seeing their rivals fail (*schadenfreude*) are sufficient [14].

Therefore, we created a multiplayer mobile game where players are challenged to applaud during key moments of a football match. To further enhance users' experience, two different kinds of challenges were included in our prototype, involving two kinds of applauses: free and synchronized applauses. During free applauses, players just need to keep clapping, like they would do in a normal applause action, to be rewarded with points. During synchronized applauses, like in rhythmic games, players need to be synchronized with the tempo to score points. Examples of synchronized applauses are the slow clap (which happens quite often on the triple jump, or before a free kick in football) and the claps that mark the rhythm of some football chants. These challenges should be triggered by the application at key moments of a match when fans at the corresponding event venue would start performing the same action. The underlying idea is that both of these actions make the remote fans synchronized with the fans at the stadium, creating the feeling of a unique community connected through the event that they are watching.

3.1   Prototype

The developed prototype simulates a football match broadcast, displayed on a TV screen, or projected on a wall, complemented with additional interface elements that point out the key moments, challenge users to applause, and reveal results (Figure 2a). The mobile devices are used for user interaction, allowing claps recognition and count. They are also used for input at the beginning of the game as well as for visual feedback at the end of the game, as explained below.

Although in the future this game can have several different possible configurations, this prototype, which was conceived to test the concept, guide the design, and evaluate users reactions, allows users supporting one same team (their National team) to compete for the best supporters. Before the WeApplaud game starts, each user must choose to play for one of the two teams of supporters (red team called "Reds" or the blue team called "Blues") that will compete head-to-head. To create a real time competition between the two teams of supporters, both are challenged to applaud during the same key moments, and supporting the same sports team, in order to promote group affiliation.

While watching the video content (simulating a football match live broadcast), both teams of supporters are presented with several challenges. Each time a team member performs a correct clap, the team is awarded 50 points and a consecutive streak count is started. In the free applause challenge every clap is a correct clap, while on the synchronized applause challenge a clap is only a correct one if it is synchronized with the tempo. Since it is very difficult to applaud at precise moments (we measure to millisecond accuracy), we have defined a threshold that allows users to get correct claps within a short interval (300 milliseconds). The consecutive streak count is associated with a score multiplier, and it is intended to reward the team that is synchronized with the tempo during a period of time. We defined four score multipliers: two, three, four and five. Each of these multipliers is achieved by doing two, four, six and eight consecutive correct claps, respectively. If a team member claps when he should not, that team's score multiplier is restarted. For example, if someone makes four consecutive correct claps, she will be rewarded with 150 points instead of 50, in the next correct clap. To visualize the team's performance we have added two bars to the display: one for the red team and other for the blue team. Each time users win points for their team the score bar increases accordingly. The team that fills the score bar quicker wins the challenge. To win the game, a team needs to have more points than the other team, at the end of the simulated broadcast. This is intended to motivate users not to give up, because there is always a chance to win, even after losing some of the challenges.

To make users aware of a current challenge (alert users when they need to applaud), we use three kinds of feedback mechanisms: a visual message on the top of the video (match displaying window) (Figure 2a), a hand inside a circle that keeps spinning on the mobile device display until the end of the challenge (Figure 2b) and we set the mobile device to vibrate, so it can get user's attention in a simple and seamless manner. This way, users do not need to keep aware of their mobile devices during the whole match. Furthermore, we have also synchronized the vibration with the rhythm that is necessary to follow. Therefore, in the beginning of a synchronized applause challenge, every time there is a vibration, users know that they need to applaud on that instant. It creates an action-reaction mechanism that helps users to recognize the rhythm and to keep following it after the vibration stops.

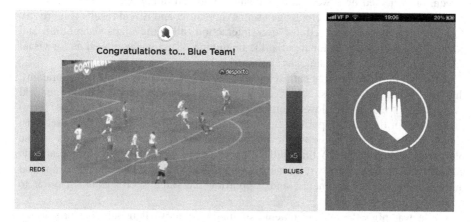

Fig. 2. Game screen on the (a) main display and on the (b) mobile device

To better explain how a game unfolds, we present the typical game flow:

1. Users are initially presented with the instructions on the main display (Figure 3(a)). During this phase, users can select one of the two teams of supporters on their mobile devices (Figure 3(b)).
2. After everyone has chosen theirs teams, the game starts.
3. The video (football match) is displayed on the main display. After a short time, the first challenge appears, where users are prompted to applaud after a dangerous

attacking play. We started with a simple challenge, since it would allow users to understand the concept of the game.

4. When the key moment ends, a message stating which team won that challenge appears on the main display, while on the mobile device a message shows how many points the user won in the challenge.
5. The video keeps playing, until another challenge appears (either a free applause challenge or a synchronized applause challenge).
6. The process repeats until the video (football match) ends.
7. A final screen appears showing the final results, both on the display and on the mobile device (Figure 4). The main display shows more detailed information regarding both teams of supporters, while on their mobile devices users can see how many points they won for their team.

Fig. 3. Start screen on the (a) main display and on the (b) mobile device

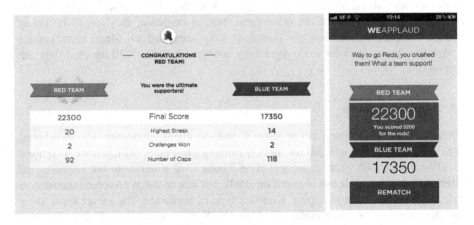

Fig. 4. Final screen on the (a) main display and on the (b) mobile device

3.2   Clap Detection

Besides the game experience, we also strongly focused on how to detect a clap. As mentioned before, users must hold a mobile device in one hand while clapping. We took three approaches to identify claps: by analyzing accelerometer data, by sound analysis and by merging both methods.

We started by following the approach implemented in [15]: to use the accelerometer to detect if there is a movement in a particular direction. While this approach works, users would be able to do a "clap" without the need to hit the other hand, just by wagging the mobile device. This issue is very common on Wii games, where a person stops mimicking the proposed action, and starts doing a simplified version of it (i.e. in Wii Sports, tennis can be played on the sofa just by moving the wrist, without the need to stand up and perform like a real tennis player).

Since a clap is only a clap if it hits something and generates a sound, we decided to analyze the sound to detect a clap. Every time there would be a volume peak, we would count as a clap. However, this approach has also its flaws, because a loud noise like talking aloud, blowing into the microphone or snapping the fingers, would also count as a clap.

Both of these approaches also have a common issue: it is necessary to find some good values as thresholds to tweak the algorithms, in order to have good rates of clap detection. This means that both of these approaches are very rigid, because they do not leave much room for error. If someone does a smooth clap, the algorithm might not detect it, because it was created only to detect claps above a certain threshold. On the other hand, if someone does a rough clap, it might count as several claps, due to the high variation of new reads. Therefore, we combined the two previous approaches so they could complement each other. In this new approach, when the mobile device detects a sound peak, it checks if there was a recent movement in a particular direction. If so, then it is counted as a clap, otherwise it is not. This way we have a more flexible system, where we do not resort so heavily on thresholds. Of course that users can also shout to the mobile device while they mimic the clapping action without hitting the palm of the other hand, but, in this case, they would be doing a more complex action than the one they were supposed to. Since users cannot exploit the system in order to do something simpler, then they will do what they are supposed to.

3.3   Implementation

WeApplaud was developed in Objective C and the client application was developed to be compatible with iOS 5.0 (or higher) running on iPhone 3GS, iPhone 4, iPhone 4S, iPod Touch (4th generation) and iPod Touch (3rd generation, but requiring an external microphone). It can also run on iPads, but due to the WeApplaud interaction style it makes no sense to deploy it on this type of hardware. The server application was developed to be compatible with Mac OS X 10.7 (or higher). During the user tests, we had a video projector connected to a computer running the server application and waiting for requests from the client mobile devices, but a TV could also be used.

WeApplaud is based on a client-server architecture. We used the Bonjour protocol to quickly identify the clients and the server. This means that this version of the prototype only works if both the server and the mobile devices are on the same wireless network. In order to not be dependent of third-party networks and to keep the process simple, the computer running the server application creates a wireless network for the clients to connect to. To handle the network communication between the mobile devices and the server, we used the UDP protocol through CocoaAsyncSocket (a TCP/IP socket networking library). This architecture will be very similar to the one that we will deploy on a real environment, where users are playing remotely from their homes. The only difference will be that instead of using Bonjour to identify the clients and the server, there will be a fixed IP associated to the server on the Internet, which the clients know in advance.

Finally, to keep the mobile devices synchronized with the server, we chose to start a clock at the beginning of the video (football match broadcast simulation). When the video is about to start, the server starts the clock and sends a message to all clients. This message is meant for all the devices to also start their clocks, in order to synchronize with the server. We chose to do this synchronization at the beginning, because it is the mobile device and not the server that verifies if a user clapped within the correct interval. The mobile device only needs to send a message stating that the user did a correct clap, and the server handles the rest (score, streak count and multipliers). If we designed the server to verify if a user did a correct clap, we would be heavily dependent on the network performance, and it could have a negative impact on the user experience. We are still dependent on the network performance, but only before the game starts, and not during it.

4   Evaluation

To test the WeApplaud concept, guide the system's design and evaluate users reactions, a first version of WeApplaud was implemented, and preliminary users tests were conducted. We mainly aimed to evaluate the entertainment concept created by WeApplaud, in order to ascertain if users would have fun with it. We were also interested in finding out if the interaction experienced by the users was immersive and appropriate to the proposed activity, and whether the application was easy to use, since these were also some of the goals that we had for the prototype (as mentioned in Section 3). All the gathered information allowed us to ascertain what worked and what did not, helping us to decide which topics should be refined in the future.

4.1   Participants and Methodology

The tests were conducted with sixteen voluntary participants, aged 23-43 with a mean age of 30.1. Twelve participants were male and four were female. All of them were familiarized with new technologies.

The user tests took place in a meeting room in our department at the University campus. Since it was important to simulate a real home environment, we used a projection screen and a set of speakers, so users could see and hear the broadcast like they would do at home (Figure 5). Of course that we are not expecting that most users have a projection screen at home, but the experience conveyed through this method is closer to a home setting, than the experienced through a computer screen. Moreover, video projections are already used in numerous occasions for displaying sport events' broadcasts for a large number of people (e.g. in bars, cafes, or other public spaces), where our concept can also be deployed.

Fig. 5. Participants interacting with WeApplaud

Before the tests, the mobile application was installed through ad-hoc deployment in the mobile devices handed by the users. The test sessions were conducted by two researchers, who played the roles of facilitator and observer. The first one had a more active role, giving an initial briefing and instructions to the participants and providing assistance for any problems that users might face. The second researcher focused on observing the way the tests unfolded, and how users reacted and interacted with the system.

We conducted eight test sessions, each with two participants. In each test session, only two participants were admitted in the room, in order to keep the experience unique to each pair of participants. Before starting to use the application, users were informed about the objectives of the test.

Users participated in a best-of-three session, where one participant played against the other until someone won two WeApplaud games. Thus, in each test session each participant played at least two games and at maximum three games.

The video content shown to the users during the tests focused on the Portuguese national football team. Since the user tests were conducted in Portugal, all participants were Portuguese and were supporting their national team competing for the best supporter. We chose an important match between Portugal and Bosnia on November 2011, where Portugal needed to win to qualify to Euro 2012. This video is 5 minutes long and was edited in order to create the challenges that we needed. We created four different challenges:

1. A free applause challenge after a dangerous attacking play.
2. A synchronized applause challenge, which consisted in a slow clap before a Cristiano Ronaldo freekick.
3. A free applause challenge after a goal.
4. A synchronized applause challenge, which was based on a Portuguese chant.

Lastly, at the end of each test session, users were asked to answer a questionnaire to evaluate WeApplaud's level of entertainment and usability. This questionnaire is detailed in the next sub-section.

4.2   Questionnaire

The first part of the questionnaire gathered users' personal data, such as age, gender, and their familiarity with new technologies. It also included questions related to the users' habits while watching sports events: how often do they watch live sports; how often do they watch sports on television; which additional devices do they use while watching live sports events on television and which activities do they perform while interacting with them. Then, the questionnaire focused on usability and user experience issues, including general feedback about the activity, application's usability and ease of use, users' entertainment and emotional involvement, and suggestions and comments.

The questions related with the general feedback, and usability issues were based on the USE questionnaire [16]. This questionnaire helps to assess whether an interface is well designed and to define which problems should be considered with higher priority. Users were asked to rate statements, using a five-point Likert-type scale, which ranged from strongly disagree (1) to strongly agree (5). These statements (presented in table 1) focused on the type of interaction and the different key moments that prompt users to applaud.

To evaluate the entertainment experienced by users, we also asked them to rate two statements using a five-point Likert-type scale. The statements were aimed to acknowledge if, by experiencing this activity, users felt more involved in the stadium atmosphere, and if the competition enhanced the level of entertainment during the broadcasted match.

To capture users' feelings and study their emotional involvement with the prototype, a question based on the Microsoft "Product Reaction Cards" [17], was included, since this method facilitates the measuring of intangible aspects of the user experience. Users were asked to select the words that best describe their experience while using WeApplaud. They could select as many words as they wanted from a list consisting of about 60% of words considered positive and 40% considered negative.

Finally, users could express any further suggestions and comments.

4.3   Results and Discussion

Regarding the users' habits while watching sports events, results show that the majority of the participants rarely watch live sports (56.25%). Some participants do not watch live sports (12.5%), but 31.25% watched live sports on a regular basis (25% weekly and 6.25% monthly). These results shifted when participants were asked how often they watch sports on television. Half of the participants watch sport events on TV on a weekly basis (50%), 12.5% on a monthly basis and 6.25% fortnightly. Still, 25% of the participants rarely watch sports events on TV, and 6.25% don't watch them at all. From those who watched it, 60% used additional technological devices during the broadcast.

Table 1. Statements, regarding general feedback and usability issues, rated by the users

Statements
General Feedback
S1. I liked to use WeApplaud.
S2. It is easy to learn how to use WeApplaud.
S3. It is easy to use WeApplaud.
Usability and Ease of Use
S4. The application correctly detects the clapping action.
S5. The way of applauding (how to hold the mobile device while clapping) is natural.
S6. The mobile device vibration helps to understand how and when to interact.
S7. I can use the application without exterior help.
S8. The feedback given by the application is useful.
S9. Free applauses, like the ones used after a dangerous play or a goal:
a) Are natural and suitable for the associated key moment of the match.
b) Are easy to perform.
S10. Synchronized applauses, like the ones used before a free kick:
a) Are natural and suitable for the associated key moment of the match.
b) Are easy to perform.
S11. Synchronized applauses, like the ones used during a chant:
a) Are natural and suitable for the associated key moment of the match.
b) Are easy to perform.

The most popular device used was the cellphone/smartphone (89%), then the computer (44%) and lastly the tablet (22%). From those who used additional devices, 89% performed activities related with the event and all of them performed other kinds of activities. Regarding the activities related with the event, browsing the web was the most common activity (67%), followed by sending SMS (56%), chatting (44%), accessing the social networks (33%) and making voice calls (22%). Regarding the activities not related with the event, browsing the web was again a popular choice (67%), but accessing the e-mail was the most popular activity (77%). Other activities performed were accessing the social networks (33%), chatting (22%) and playing videogames (22%).

These results showed us that the majority of participants were used to interact with technological devices while watching sports on television. Furthermore, almost all of the participants perform activities related with the event, and the cellphone/smartphone was the most popular device used to perform those activities. This reinforces our belief on creating a new paradigm for people to interact with mobile devices while watching live sports broadcasts.

As shown in Figure 6, most participants agreed with the statements concerning the general feedback (statements 1, 2 and 3). Participants liked to use WeApplaud and found it easy to learn and to use. The following statements were also positive. However, statement 6 showed that there was not a consensus with the fact that the vibrations help to understand how and when to interact. Taking this result into account, we aim to study different ways to provide users with clues on how and when to interact with the system. One possibility is to use sound instead of vibration to alert users when they need to interact and what they need to do. Moreover, the actions that need to be performed by the users while using WeApplaud are very similar to the ones they would do while watching a sports event live (they only need to use their phone as an accessory), so some users naturally knew what to do (e.g. follow a chant's rhythm) once they got the concept of the challenges.

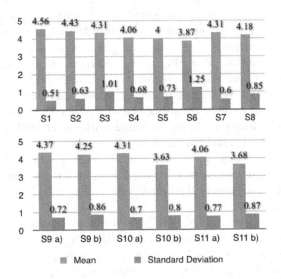

Fig. 6. Summary of results from general feedback and usability

Statements 4 and 5 also focused on key topics that we were eager to get feedback on, and although we did not have a strongly positive feedback, we are happy with the results. Most participants had the feeling that claps were correctly detected by the application and they naturally held their mobile phones while clapping. We observed that sometimes users felt initially hesitant on how to applaud, but after noticing that the score bar was filling in while they were clapping, they started to feel more confident and had no problems in using their mobile phones while clapping. It was also interesting to notice the different clapping styles of participants (different ways to hold the mobile device while clapping), with no interference on the clapping detection. Finally, regarding the different key moments that prompted users to applaud, the results were mixed. The majority of participants agreed that the free applauses were natural, suitable to the associated moments (a dangerous attacking play and a goal) and easy to perform. They also felt that synchronized applauses were natural and suitable to the associated moments (a slow clap and a chant), but they did not find them so easy to perform. According to our observations, this happened because the goal of the challenge was not very clear to the users for the first time they used the application. Once it got clear, the action itself was easy to perform. Also, as noted before, the use of vibrations to point out the clapping moments was not sufficient to help users to understand the way of interacting. Therefore, we feel that this is something that deserves our high priority in future developments.

Regarding the entertainment factor experienced by participants, we asked users to rate two statements: "competition promoted by WeApplaud contributes to increase the level of entertainment during the broadcasted match" and "WeApplaud contributes to make me feel more involved in the stadium atmosphere". On the first statement, showed that the competition promoted by WeApplaud clearly enhanced the level of entertainment during the broadcasted match (Mean = 4.375, SD = 0.81). This demonstrates that it is possible to create new ways of entertainment related with the event, so users can be more engaged with the broadcasted sport. According to our observation, most participants were really having fun, engaged in the game and eager to become the best supporter. Regarding the second statement, feedback was positive, although feelings were not very strong (Mean = 3.75, SD = 0.57). This reveals that WeApplaud represents a contribution to immerse remote users in the real environment of the sports event, but it can be complemented with additional forms of interaction or activities as we are already exploring for future work. Additionally, during the tests users were not watching a real broadcast, which contributes to reduce the immersion feeling, since they knew there was no real match happening at the that moment.

From the analysis of question based on the Microsoft "Product Reaction Cards" we concluded that all participants held positive feelings when classifying their experience using the WeApplaud.

The most selected word was fun (81%), followed by immersive (50%), pleasant and simple (44% each) and innovative and stimulating (37.5% each). We were already expecting the word "fun" to be one of the most popular ones, due to our observations during the tests. It was very frequent for participants to laugh, smile, get exalted and exchange comments about who was going to win. This also corroborates our goal of increasing users' fun while watching a sport event broadcast. While the word immersive was not as popular as the word fun, it was the second most selected, which we believe is something very positive even on the early stage of the prototype.

Lastly, we analyzed the comments and suggestions given by the participants. Ten of the sixteen participants expressed their opinion in three areas: scoring system, interaction and visual feedback. Regarding the scoring system, some users felt that those that are not clapping in the right tempo should be more penalized than they actually are, since it is easy to keep clapping from the beginning to the end of a synchronized applause key moment and still earn some points. However, we believe that it is better to reward players than to penalize them, and therefore, we plan to further reward those who are synchronized with the applauses. Some users also felt that the scoring system was not very clear, and we agree that it should be easier to understand. The interaction was also a popular topic amongst the comments, with some users stating that the rhythm of synchronized applauses was not very perceptible, and that they did not know when they should start and end clapping. As stated before, we intend to study the use of sound instead of (or to complement) the use of vibrations to overcome this problem. Finally, a minority of users expressed that it was not clear when a score bar was totally filled. This is something that we have already fixed, by adding a "Good Job!" message on the top of the bar, as soon as it is totally filled. This also informs users that they can stop applauding, since they have already reached the maximum score.

5   Conclusions and Future Work

This paper described a new concept of using mobile devices to interact with live sports. It presented WeApplaud, a multiplayer mobile game that takes users to participate in the applauses happening in the stadium during a live sports event. Through the use of persuasive technology concepts, WeApplaud encourages fans to applaud their favourite sports team during specific key moments of a match. This way, remote fans become more engaged in the live event being broadcasted, increasing their fun and immersion levels.

The conducted users tests were very positive. Users had a great time playing WeApplaud, a clear signal that the promoted competition encouraged them to have a more active role during the match and increased their fun. Although the results have showed us that the concept works, is easy to use and appropriate for the associated key moments, it still has some problems that need to be worked on. As stated in Section 4.3, we have identified those problems, and we have just started studying how to overcome them.

In the future, we aim to conduct remote user tests during a real live event TV broadcast, where users interact in real time from their homes, without being on the same shared place. This is something that will bring this concept closer to what happens in reality, and will provide unique feedback that we would not acquire otherwise. Although, we also plan to deploy WeApplaud on public places (e.g. bars or cafes), where small communities of people usually meet to watch sports events. Finally, we also intend to present WeApplaud's feedback on the stadium screen, so players and fans at the venue can feel the encouragement coming from people watching the match worldwide.

Acknowledgments. This work is funded by CITI/DI/FCT/UNL (PEst-OE/EEI/UI0527/2011). The authors thank Bárbara Teixeira for her contribution on the graphic design.

References

1. Uhrich, S., Benkenstein, M.: Sport Stadium Atmosphere: Formative and Reflective Indicators for Operationalizing the Construct. Sport Management 24(2) (2010)
2. Goal: 400 million viewers expected to watch Clasico between Real Madrid and Barcelona (2012), http://www.goal.com/en-my/news/3895/spain/2012/04/21/3050360/400-million-viewers-expected-to-watch-clasico-between-real (accessed May 10, 2012)
3. Grudin, N.: Social Sports: Facebook and the Fan-Centric Experience (2011), http://www.sloansportsconference.com/?p=669 (accessed May 11, 2012)
4. Wann, D.L.: Preliminary validation of the Sport Fan Motivation Scale. Sport & Social Issues 19(4) (1995)
5. Kort, Y., Ijsselsteijn, W., Millden, C., Eggen, B.: Preface. In: 2nd International Conference on Persuasive Technology, Palo Alto. Springer, Heidelberg (2007)
6. Fogg, B.J.: Persuasive Technology: Using Computers to Change What We Think and Do. Morgan Kaufmann, San Francisco (2003)
7. Torning, K., Oinas-Kukkonen, H.: Persuasive System Design: State of the Art and Future Directions. In: 4th International Conference on Persuasive Technology, California. ACM, New York (2009), article 30
8. Bogost, I.: Persuasive Games: The Expressive Power of Videogames. MIT Press, Cambridge (2007)
9. Juul, J.: A Casual Revolution: Reinventing Video Games and Their Players. MIT Press, Cambridge (2009)
10. Twitter: Post-Bowl Twitter analysis (2012), http://blog.twitter.com/2012/02/post-bowl-twitter-analysis.html (accessed May 10, 2012)
11. Connec TV (2012), http://www.connectv.com (accessed June 10, 2012)
12. Shazam (2012), http://www.shazam.com (accessed June 10, 2012)
13. FIFA, FIFA Research (2012), http://www.fifa.com/aboutfifa/organisation/marketing/research.html (accessed June 14, 2012)
14. Koster, R.: Theory of Fun for Game Design. Paraglyph Press, Phoenix (2006)
15. Sega Sports Japan: Mario & Sonic at the London 2012 Olympic Games (2012), http://www.olympicvideogames.com/mario-and-sonic-london-2012/ (accessed June 14, 2012)
16. Lund, A.: Measuring Usability with the USE Questionnaire. Usability Interface 8(2) (2001)
17. Benedek, J., Miner, T.: Product Reaction Cards (2002), http://www.microsoft.com/usability/UEPostings/ProductReactionCards.doc (accessed January 8, 2011)

Paranga: An Interactive Flipbook

Kazuyuki Fujita, Hiroyuki Kidokoro, and Yuichi Itoh

Graduate School of Information Science and Technology, Osaka University
2-1 Yamadaoka, Suita-shi, Osaka, 565-0871 Japan
{fujita.kazuyuki,kidokoro.hiroyuki,itoh}@ist.osaka-u.ac.jp

Abstract. E-books, which have become increasingly popular, potentially offer users attractive and entertaining interaction beyond paper-based books. However, they have lost physical features such as paper-like texture and page-flipping sensation. We focus on flipbooks and propose a novel book-shaped device for flipbooks called *Paranga* that embodies both these physical features and e-book interactivity. Paranga detects how quickly a user is turning pages and provides the tactile feedback of turning pages on his/her thumb by employing a rotatable roller mechanism with pieces of real paper. Using this device, we created several interactive flipbook applications in which the story changes depending on page-turning speed. This paper details the implementation of this device, describes the users' reactions at a conference exhibition, and discusses Paranga's possible applications.

Keywords: Virtual reality, book-shaped device, page-turning interface, e-books, tactile feedback.

1 Introduction

Have you ever been absorbed drawing on the end of textbook pages and creating a flipbook? Flipbooks are enjoyable because the characters in the picture come alive just by turning pages. In addition, flipping the pages creates tactile sensations that contribute to the flipbook's enjoyment.

Recently, e-books have grown in popularity. Most e-books only provide static documents, but some advanced approaches now exist that utilize e-book interactivity. *Alice for the iPad* [17], for example, enables us to interact with the characters and objects in the pictures by shaking or tilting the device. This implies that e-books potentially offer users attractive and entertaining interactions beyond paper-based books. However, e-books have lost physical features such as the shape of a book, paper-like textures, and page-flipping sensations. These features are quite important for effective navigation and reading [9], and they must also be important for enjoyable and comfortable reading.

Much research has focused on reproducing the physical features of paper, including proposals of page-flipping interaction methods on tablets [1, 2, 3, 4, 12] and development of a mechanism that detects the bending of pages, as with a paper-based book [14]. However, these methods only partially recreate paper features and most do not provide tactile feedback when turning pages. There are few studies that achieve a flick interaction through a large number of pages, which is essential for enjoying flipbooks.

A. Nijholt, T. Romão, and D. Reidsma (Eds.): ACE 2012, LNCS 7624, pp. 17–30, 2012.
© Springer-Verlag Berlin Heidelberg 2012

Thus, we focus on the flipbook as an example that emphasizes these physical features and propose a novel book-shaped device for flipbooks called *Paranga*. The name Paranga comes from an abbreviation of *parapara manga,* which is the Japanese word for flipbook. The main feature of Paranga is that it offers users the flipbook experience with both e-book interactivity and paper-book physical features. To achieve this, we first examined the mechanism that fully recreates the input and output of page-flipping interaction.

Figure 1 shows the overview of Paranga. Paranga has a rotatable roller with pieces of paper located at a user's thumb position. The user experiences tactile sensation from the rotation of the roller in conjunction with page-by-page animations on a liquid crystal display (LCD). Inside the device, there is a bend sensor and a rotary encoder to measure how fast the user intends to flip over the pages. Second, we also explored a new way of interactively enjoying e-books with Paranga: We created several installations in which the story changes depending on the page-turning speed and observed user reactions at a conference exhibition. In this paper, we discuss how real the page-flipping experience is with Paranga and how much it entertains people, and finally describe Paranga's possible applications.

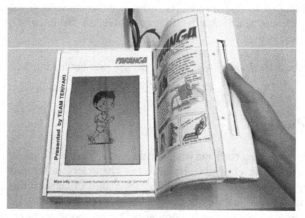

Fig. 1. Overview of Paranga Paranga is a book-shaped device that has a rotatable roller to provide a user with the tactile sensations of page turning.

2   Related Work

2.1   Recurrences of a Paper-Based Book

A lot of work has been done to reclaim the characteristics of paper-based books and documents since the early emergence of e-books. Today, most e-book readers on tablet devices employ page-flipping animations to navigate pages. Such

advancements indicate that page-turning interactions are natural and intuitive behaviors of reading books or documents.

There are several works that physically support page navigation. XLibris [12] is a
paper-like interface that has affordance of paper while reading on tablets. Instead of
scrolling, a page-turning interface using a pressure sensor is implemented on the tablet. Fishkin et al. [4] proposed embodied user interfaces that allow users to execute
physical gestures, including page turning, while interacting with documents. They
also introduced pressure sensors on the frame of the device to recognize these gestures. Chen et al. [3] proposed an e-book reader that has a two-facing dual-display
like a real book and designed such interactions as flipping, folding, and fanning for
the navigation of pages on the device. Tajika et al. [14] argued that the degree of
bending pages reflects how fast a user wants to turn pages and thus introduced a bend
sensor to input consequent page turning. TouchMark [15] introduced flexible physical
tabs on both sides of a tablet to enable such gestures as page thumbing and bookmarking. These works enable more natural and intuitive interactions of page navigation.
However, they only simulate partial factors of interactions with paper-based books;
that is, they only focus on the input of page turning and do not support the output of
paper's physical features, such as the feeling of paper-like textures and tactile sensations when papers hit a user's thumb.

Some research considers these physical features of paper-based books. The Listen
Reader [2] and SequenceBook [16] have actual paper-based pages with integrated
circuit chips and radio-frequency identification tags inside to recognize which page is
being turned. They have enabled computerizing e-books without losing paper's texture, but each page's content needs to be printed in advance or projected by a projector
from somewhere, which is not realistic for the practical uses of e-books or entertainment toys. Besides, they cannot, of course, support flipping over a large number of
pages as with a flipbook.

2.2   Extensions of E-Books

The increasing popularity of e-books has led to the emergence of new approaches that
utilize e-book interactivity. For example, some research aims to enhance users' content understanding. Sumi et al. [13] proposed an interactive system that automatically
converts electrical documents into illustrations and animates them with sounds for
children's comprehension.

For entertainment uses, the SIT Book [1] explores an interactive reading experience that combines multiple audio tracks with texts and images. The sound related
to texts and images is given to the user in every page, and its volume and amount of
reverberation can be controlled by the user. Many commercial products of interactive
content have recently become available for tablet devices. In Alice for the iPad [17],
for example, users can tilt and shake the device to interact with the characters and
objects that move along with physical simulations. SequenceBook [16] offers a new
experience in enjoying books: The users can vary the stories by changing the page
order. Thus, e-books no longer display only static documents and the ways of
enjoying e-books are becoming diversified.

2.3   Haptic Devices

There are many studies on reproducing physical sensations. Representative examples are PHANToM [8] and SPIDAR [11], which provide force feedback while inputting a three-dimensional position. Regarding tactile feedback to fingers, there are many works from various approaches, including using electrical stimuli to elicit sensations of texture [6] and using a special material of ionic conducting polymer gel film to allow users to feel the roughness of a surface [7].

On the other hand, some researchers have tried to recreate tactile sensations for entertainment uses. Ants in the Pants [10] presents sensations that resemble insects crawling on the user's skin with a glove having a matrix of motors and brushes inside. We also have proposed an umbrella-like device called Funbrella [5] that lets people experience rain with vibrations through the umbrella's handle. We implemented a mechanism using a voice coil motor and springs, which enables the recording and replaying of vibrations. These studies have confirmed that physical sensations are quite important for promoting familiarity and fun. However, there is little study on recreating page-turning sensations.

3   Paranga

3.1   Concepts

We propose a book-shaped device for flipbooks called Paranga. The concept of Paranga is to enable people to physically enjoy a flipbook. Unlike existing works, we aim to create a device that fully supports page-flipping interactions, including fine-tuning the page-turning speed and perceiving tactile feedback and the sounds of flipped pieces of paper. We believe this will bring back the fun, comfort, and intuitivity of the reading experience of paper-based books. Furthermore, we also explore a new way of enjoying e-books with interactive flipbook installations whose stories change depending on the user's page-turning speed.

3.2   Requirements for Implementation

To decide on the mechanism for creating a flipbook experience, we investigated what people do when flicking over a large number of pages in a book. We asked three participants to turn over the entire set of pages for several books of different size, thickness, and hardness of paper and observed their behavior. From this, we initially found that the degree of page bending determines the speed of page turning in all books: Sharper bending leads to faster page turning. We also found that the speed of page turning can be changed with tiny pressures and transitions of the user's thumb touching the sides of the pages. We then interviewed the participants as to what kinds of feedback they received while turning pages. This interview clarified that the participants not only obtained visual feedback (seeing the transition of pages), but also the tactile and auditory feedback of the edge of the pages hitting their thumbs. Thus, we established system requirements to allow people to experience the flipbook as follows:

The device should be book-shaped.

Back et al. states that books are most intuitive and natural as interfaces that navigate text documents [9]. In order to make the flipbook experience natural and intuitive, it is expected that the device should look like a paper-based book rather than a tablet.

The device should support the interaction of flicking over a large number of pages.

This is an essential factor in enjoying a flipbook, which existing e-books cannot do. From our observations of the users' page investigation, the interaction of flicking should be done by bending pages. Furthermore, a user should fine-tune the speed of turning pages by the pressure and transition of his/her thumb. For example, the user must be able to stop or slow page turning by increasing the pressure of his/her thumb on the edge of the pages.

The device should provide users with the visual, tactile, and auditory feedback of flipped pages.

With paper-based books, a user receives all of these types of feedback while he/she turns each page, so the device should also support them. Most existing e-books give us visual feedback by showing the animations of page turning, but there are very few works that consider tactile and auditory feedback.

Considering these requirements, we need to create a new mechanism. In order to support the interaction of bending pages, a flexible material, such as a sheaf of papers, rubber sheet, or sponge, should be used for the input part of the device. Additionally, a bend sensor located on the flexible material would be able to measure the bending degree as well as the work by Tajika et al [14]. The interaction with a user's thumb must implement both input and output; the input is to detect the thumb pressure that controls the speed of page turning and the output is to give the user tactile feedback while a piece of paper hits the user's thumb. Thus, we introduce a roller with pieces of actual paper. Rotation of the roller connected with a motor can infinitely give the user the tactile sensation of paper hitting his/her thumb and measuring the depression of the rotation by a rotary encoder can substantially detect thumb pressure.

3.3   Implementation

Overview

Figure 2 shows the system configuration of Paranga. Paranga includes two facing parts, like a real book. The right side is the page-turning part, while the left side is the display part. The page-turning part is easily bendable and contains a bend sensor, rotary encoder, and roller with pieces of paper equipped with a motor. The bend sensor detects the bending degree of the page-turning part and determines the rotating speed of the roller hitting a user's thumb. At the same time, the rotary encoder detects the depression of the rotation of the roller, which enables estimating the pressure with the user's thumb. As each page is flipped, the display part shows the next page's content after a paper-flip animation. By introducing this mechanism, users can fine-tune

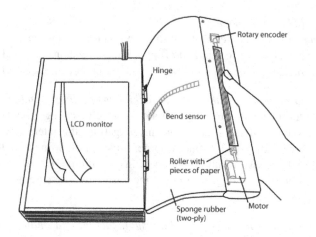

Fig. 2. System configuration

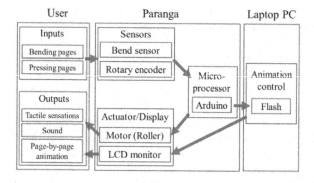

Fig. 3. System flow

the speed of page turning as they wish and receive the visual, tactile, and auditory feedback that is essential for enjoying a flipbook.

Hardware

Figure 3 shows the system flow of Paranga. The values of the bend sensor and rotary encoder are used as input, and they reflect the rotation rate of the motor and the content on an LCD monitor. We used Arduino (Duemilanove 328) as a micro-processor that is connected to a laptop through a USB. An 8-inch LCD monitor (plus one LCD-8000V, Century) is also connected to the laptop through RGB and acts as a secondary screen of the laptop. Flash software that is controlled by the Arduino runs on the secondary screen. The device has a 250 mm x 190 mm x 90 mm size—a little smaller than A4 size. The whole device weighs approximately 1400 grams. It is heavier than most dictionaries, but a user only has to hold the page-turning part, which is light (120 grams) enough to handle like an ordinary paper-based book.

The page-turning part is connected to the display part using two hinges. The page-turning part consists of two-ply flexible materials made of sponge rubber, a bend sensor, and a special roller mechanism with pieces of paper. We tested various types of materials as the main portion of this part, such as a sheaf of papers, plastic film, rubber plate, and sponge rubber, in preliminary studies. Through this experimentation, we found that the bending degrees of the inside and the outside page are totally different when we bend a book sharply because of thickness of the book. This is why we finally chose a 5-mm thick sponge rubber that is stretchable enough to endure a sharp bend. We used it stacked in pairs to behave like the inside and outside page, respectively.

There is a bend sensor (AS-BEND, AsakusaGiken) between the two sponge rubbers placed sideways on the center of the page-turning part. The sensor detects the bending degree by changing resistance value when the whole page-turning part is bent. The right edge of the sponge rubbers is equipped with a special roller mechanism. Figure 4 shows the details of this roller mechanism. In this mechanism, a cylindrical roller, motor, and rotary encoder share a shaft. On the surface of the cylindrical roller, 24 pieces of paper are radially attached and are inclined in one direction to imitate the side part of a paper-based book. A glossy and slightly hard paper was used by taking durability into account. The motor (and the roller) rotates depending on the value of the bend sensor, which sends tactile sensations to a user's thumb by touching the roller. In consideration of speed and torque, we decided to use a motor with a compact gearbox (Mini Motor Multi-Ratio Gearbox - 12-speed, Tamiya) at 89.9: 1 gear ratio. The rotation rate R is represented by $Eq.$ (1): B is the bending value extracted by the bend sensor, B_{th1} is the predefined threshold of bending degree

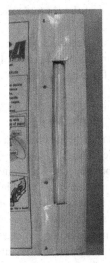 

(a) external appearance   (b) internal appearance

Fig. 4. Roller with pieces of paper

to start the motor's rotation, and B_{th2} is the predefined threshold of bending degree that gives the max rotation rate R_{max}.

$$R = \begin{cases} 0 & (B < B_{th1}) \\ \frac{R_{max}}{B_{th2} - B_{th1}}(B - B_{th1}) & (B_{th1} \leq B \leq B_{th2}) \\ R_{max} & (B > B_{th2}) \end{cases} \qquad (1)$$

This equation means that the rotation rate linearly gets high as the bending degree increases when the degree is between two specific thresholds. The thresholds, Bth1 and Bth2, and the max rate Rmax were determined through a number of preliminary studies so that behavior is as similar to a paper-based book as possible.

However, we found that the roller's rotating speed gets significantly slow when the user presses firmly on the roller with her/his thumb. Therefore, we installed a rotary encoder that enables obtaining 24 pulses per revolution on the shaft. We made the number of pieces of paper the same as that of the pulse so that it can generally sense the turning of each page. The rotary encoder detects the degree of rotating speed variation caused by the thumb's pressure and the system then calculates the rotation rate of the motor. Thus, fixed rotation rate Rfixed is represented as Eq. (2). Ractual is the actual rotation rate of the roller, which is calculated by the rotary encoder. a is a positive constant less than 1.

$$R_{fixed} = R + a(R - R_{actual}) \qquad (2)$$

This equation means that the rotation of the motor increases with depression of the motor's rotation caused by the thumb's pressure (which is equal to the difference between the rotation rate of motor R and the actual rotation rate R_{actual} extracted by the rotary encoder). The constant a determines the weight of the thumb's pressure effect, which was adjusted by another preliminary study.

We also considered supplying the users with auditory feedback. At first we thought that it was necessary to generate a paper-flipping sound using a speaker. However, we found that the sound of the roller mechanism during flipping was sufficient because it employs real pieces of paper.

The display part consists of an LCD monitor, a microprocessor, and an aluminum case for storage. The microprocessor is located under the LCD monitor. The display part also has four non-slip rubbers on the four corners of its back side so that a user can flip pages without holding that part with his/her left hand.

To enhance the reality and fun of the flipbook experience, we decorated the device like a comic magazine. We chose this design because the size and thickness of the device is originally similar to a comic magazine. We attached a front cover and inside cover (which doubles as instructions for the device's usage) with a cartoon-like design to the page-turning part. In order to avoid losing flexibility, pieces of cloth on which the design was printed were used instead of pieces of paper. We also decorated around the LCD monitor and the spine, and then attached a sheaf of pieces paper to the side of the device. These decorations create the appearance of a thick magazine containing several pages, even when the device is closed.

Software

The software for displaying the flipbook animations was developed in Adobe Flash. The software basically switches one image to another as each pulse (which generally corresponds with the timing of page turning) is received. At the same time, the software renders a flipped-page animation. In the preliminary investigation, we found that each page moves faster as page turning becomes more frequent, so we decided to linearly increase the speed of the animation as the rotation rate extracted by the rotary encoder Ractual increases. The animation is translucently shown because we found that the animation sometimes occluded the content and spoiled the experience.

Installations

We created three types of installations that highlight Paranga's characteristics of paper-book physical features and e-book interactivity. This interactivity we think is the ability to show not only sequential static images but also flexible contents according to the users' input: the speed of page turning (the page bending rate) in real time. The applications we created are as below:

E-book reader

This installation, with which users can read e-books, was made simply to test the intuitivity and comfort of flicking over many pages. Unlike most e-books, a user can recognize how many pages he/she turns from the tactile and auditory feedbacks.

Story-variable animation

This installation enhances the ordinary flipbook by showing interactive stories. The system has several animation loops that have respectively different stories and each animation loop can be switched to another one by changing page-turning speed in real time. In this implementation, we prepared four types of animation loops and switched them according to each of four staged page-turning speeds. For example, we made a simple animation titled A running boy (as shown in Figure 5). We created four animation loops in which a boy is walking, jogging, running, and sprinting, respectively. When a user is turning pages slowly, he/she can see the boy walking slowly (Figure 5 (a)). If he/she starts turning pages faster, the boy's speed increases (Figure 5 (b)) and, finally, he sprints wildly, swinging his arms and legs (Figure 5 (c)). In another installation entitled High bar (as shown in Figure 6), a stickman swings on a horizontal bar while slowly flipping (Figure 6 (a)), but he starts performing giant swings (Figure 6 (b)) and somersaults (Figure 6 (c)) during fast flipping. In this way, users can enjoy different stories with their own hands.

Scale-variable animation

This installation also augments the flipbook experience by changing the space-time scale depending on page-turning speed. When a user turns pages slowly, a page-by-page animation of a specific scene can be seen, like an ordinary flipbook. As the user turns the pages faster, the view gradually zooms in. When the page-turning speed exceeds a certain threshold, the view finally switches to another side of the scene that

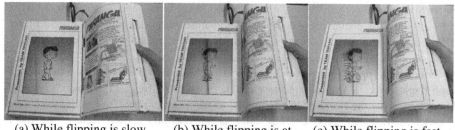

(a) While flipping is slow   (b) While flipping is at   (c) While flipping is fast
                                    medium speed

Fig. 5. A *running boy* (story-variable animation)

(a) While flipping is slow   (b) While flipping is at   (c) While flipping is fast
                                    medium speed

Fig. 6. High *bar* (story-variable animation)

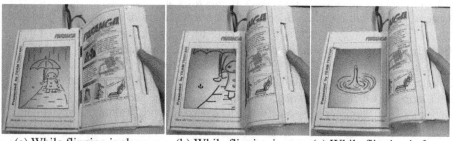

(a) While flipping is slow   (b) While flipping is at   (c) While flipping is fast
                                    medium speed

Fig. 7. A *girl in the rain* (scale-variable animation)

(a) While flipping is slow   (b) While flipping is at   (c) While flipping is
                                    medium speed   fast

Fig. 8. The *Matrix* (scale-variable animation)

has a different space-time scale. For example, we developed an animation entitled A girl in the rain (as shown in Figure 7). While turning pages slowly, there is a girl walking in the rain (Figure 7 (a)). When the page turning becomes faster, the view starts zooming in to one of the raindrops (Figure 7 (b)) and finally switches to slow-motion animation of the drop's descent, like a high-speed camera view (Figure 7 (c)). Another example is the one inspired by the film The Matrix (as shown in Figure 8). A stickman appears to be shot by another stickman while turning the pages slowly (Figure 8 (a)), but, when flipped fast, the view zooms in to the stickman being shot (Figure 8 (b)) and finally it is revealed that the stickman is actually twisting his body and dodging the bullets (Figure 8 (c)).

4   User Feedback and Discussion

We conducted a demonstration of Paranga at the SIGGRAPH Asia 2011 E-Tech exhibition over a period of three days. More than one thousand people from various countries experienced the Paranga interactive flipbook installations. During the demonstration, we received a lot of comments on the reality of the page-flipping experience, impressions of Paranga's interactivity, and its applications in the future. Figure 9 shows one scene of user reactions.

4.1   Interactive Flipbook Experiences

Most participants enjoyed the interactive flipbook experience with Paranga and provided positive comments. As expected, Paranga was especially preferred for its tactile feedback. We received such comments as "the sensation was quite close to that of paper-based books!" and "hitting the paper felt so comfortable." There were even some participants who became addicted to the feedback and kept turning pages for several minutes. We also received positive opinions beyond our expectation on the auditory feedback. Because of its reality, some participants even mistakenly perceived

Fig. 9. Users' reactions

that the sound was a recording of paper-based books broadcast from a speaker. On the other hand, some participants opined that the sound generated by the rotating motor was a little annoying.

Although we furnished only rough instructions about the usage of the device to the participants, almost all, including little children, figured it out at once and started bending the device and pushing the roller with their thumbs. This clearly shows that these interactions are quite familiar and intuitive to turning pages, and the mechanism we implemented efficiently supports these interactions. In addition, when we showed participants the e-book installation, many of them desired its mechanism to be installed in their usual e-readers. This further confirmed that these physical features are important for natural and comfortable interaction. On the other hand, some participants at first failed to use the device by changing the angle of the page-turning part or moving their thumbs from left to right when trying to turn pages. We need further investigation on page-turning interactions with paper-based books to fully recreate them.

We also observed that the participants enjoyed the interactivity of the installation. In particular, people found the story-variable animation significantly entertaining because it was easy for them to understand what was happening. Scale-variable animation might have been a little difficult to control since the participants were not familiar with altering scale with the page-turning speed. In addition, some participants did not intuitively sense that they could see a slow-motion-like animation by turning pages quickly. Nevertheless, both installations were generally accepted by most participants regardless of age, sex, or nationality.

4.2   Applications and Future Work

The user feedback establishes that Paranga adequately offers users flipbook experiences and already has the potential for various applications, such as a controller of e-book and children's toys. It is notable that the Paranga's page-flipping interface is effective for general use of viewers more than that of a flipbook viewer. In particular, this interface would demonstrate its ability when searching from hundreds of documents, photos, and videos: The user can easily find a certain page when he/she looks over the whole book, because every page can be seen through page turning as well as paper-based books. In current implementation, however, it was essentially difficult to turn a single page on the device and impossible to inversely turn pages. In the future, we plan to improve and support these interactions. Inverse page turning could be done by inverse bending if we put another bend sensor. Single page turning, for example, could be done by introducing a new roller mechanism in which each piece of paper on the roller has a physical touch sensor to detect when to flip each page accurately. After achieving these improvements, we also plan to conduct a usability test to confirm the practicality of the Paranga's page-turning interface in search tasks.

In addition, we have to reduce the weight and cost of the device for practical use. One of the solutions we think is to make it an attachment device for tablets like the iPad. To achieve this, the whole device must be the same size as the page-turning part of the current Paranga. One of our ideas is for the attachment to connect to a tablet through Bluetooth, which will make page-turning possible by wirelessly sending a rotary encoder pulse to the tablet. This mechanism would also reduce cost and be easily used as an additional function to ordinary e-book devices.

For use with toys, it is necessary to further add entertainment factors. For example, we developed several loop animations that were simple in story-variable animation. Longer and more complex stories with branches would be more interesting and enjoyable for repeated use. Another improvement we plan is to add a function for users to draw something on the display themselves. This would support the whole experience of a flipbook, including the phase of creating one.

5   Conclusions

We proposed a novel book-shaped device for flipbooks called Paranga that effectively recreates both the physical features of paper books and e-book interactivity. We investigated what happens when people turn pages and reproduced it by implementing a roller mechanism that detects how fast a user is turning pages and supplies him/her with the tactile feedback of turning pages on his/her thumb. Using this device, we made several applications of interactive flipbooks in which the story changes depending on the page-turning speed. User feedback confirmed that Paranga efficiently offers users a flipbook experience and its interactivity can be a new way of enjoying e-books. We plan to create a more precise mechanism to detect page turning and to simplify the device for entertainment applications, such as children's toys.

References

1. Back, M., Gold, R., Kirsch, D.: The SIT book: audio as affective imagery for interactive storybooks. In: Proc. of CHI 1999 Extended Abstracts, pp. 202–203 (1999)
2. Back, M., Cohen, J., Gold, R., Harrison, S., Minneman, S.: Listen reader: an electronically augmented paper-based book. In: Proc. CHI 2001, pp. 23–29 (2001)
3. Chen, N., Guimbretiere, F., Dixon, M., Lewis, C., Agrawala, M.: Navigation techniques for dual-display e-book readers. In: Proc. CHI 2008, pp. 1779–1788 (2008)
4. Fishkin, K.P., Gujar, A., Harrison, B.L., Moran, T.P., Want, R.: Embodied user interfaces for really direct manipulation. Commun. ACM 43(9), 74–80 (2000)
5. Fujita, K., Itoh, Y., Yoshida, A., Ozaki, M., Kikukawa, T., Fukazawa, R., Takashima, K., Kitamura, Y., Kishino, F.: Funbrella: recording and replaying vibrations through an umbrella axis. In: Proc. ACE 2009, pp. 66–71 (2009)
6. Kajimoto, H., Kawakami, N., Tachi, S., Inami, M.: SmartTouch: electric skin to touch the untouchable. IEEE Computer Graphics and Applications 24(1), 36–43 (2004)
7. Konyo, M., Tadokoro, S., Takamori, T.: Artificial tactile feel display using soft gel actuators. In: Proc. IEEE International Conference on Robotics and Automation (ICRA 2000), vol. 4, pp. 3416–3421 (2000)
8. Massie, T.H., Salisbury, J.K.: The phantom haptic interface: A device for probing virtual objects. In: Proc. of the ASME Winter Annual Meeting, Symposium on Haptic Interfaces for Virtual Environment and Teleoperator Systems, vol. 55-1, pp. 295–300 (1994)

9. O'Hara, K., Sellen, A.: A comparison of reading paper and on-line documents. In: Proc. CHI 1997, pp. 335–342 (1997)
10. Sato, K., Sato, Y., Sato, M., Fukushima, S., Okano, Y., Matsuo, K., Ooshima, S., Kojima, Y., Matsue, R., Nakata, S., Hashimoto, Y., Kajimoto, H.: Ants in the Pants. In: ACM SIGGRAPH 2008 New Tech Demos, vol. (3) (2008)
11. Sato, M.: Spidar and virtual reality. In: Proc. World Automation Congress, pp. 17–23 (2002)
12. Schilit, B.N., Golovchinsky, G., Price, M.N.: Beyond paper: supporting active reading with free form digital ink annotations. In: Proc. CHI 1998, pp. 249–256 (1998)
13. Sumi, K., Tanaka, K.: Transforming web contents into a storybook with dialogues and animations. In: Proc. WWW 2005, pp. 1076–1077 (2005)
14. Tajika, T., Yonezawa, T., Mitsunaga, N.: Intuitive page-turning interface of e-books on flexible e-paper based on user studies. In: Proc. MM 2008, pp. 793–796 (2008)
15. Wightman, D., Ginn, T., Vertegaal, R.: TouchMark: flexible document navigation and bookmarking techniques for e-book readers. In: Proc. GI 2010, pp. 241–244 (2010)
16. Yamada, H.: SequenceBook: interactive paper book capable of changing the storylines by shuffling pages. In: Proc. CHI 2010 Extended Abstract, pp. 4375–4380 (2010)
17. Alice for the iPad, http://www.atomicantelope.com/alice/

Augmentation of Toothbrush
by Modulating Sounds Resulting from Brushing

Taku Hachisu[1,2] and Hiroyuki Kajimoto[1,3]

[1] The University of Electro-Communications
1-5-1 Chofugaoka, Chofu, Tokyo 182-8585, Japan
[2] JSPS Research Fellow
[3] Japan Science and Technology Agency
{hachisu,kajimoto}@kaji-lab.jp

Abstract. Brushing teeth is a daily habit to maintain oral hygiene, including the maintenance of oral cleanliness and prevention of caries and periodontal disease. However, tooth brushing is often not carried out correctly or forgotten because the task is boring. Although several works have contributed to improving brushing performance and motivation, the feedback seems to be very remote from the brushing itself, i.e., not intuitive. In this study, we establish two objectives to deal with these issues. The first is not to present information on a visual display, but to augment the ordinary tooth brushing experience consisting of haptic and auditory sensations, while the other is to design the modulation so that users feel as if their teeth are gradually becoming cleaner, thereby providing the necessary motivation. To achieve these aims, we propose a novel approach to augment the tooth brushing experience by modulating the brushing sounds to make tooth brushing entertaining in an intuitive manner. A microphone embedded in the toothbrush records the brushing sounds, which are presented to users after being modified by a PC. In the experiment, we demonstrate that increasing the sound gain and manipulating the frequency can control the overall impression of brushing by giving a sense of comfort and accomplishment.

Keywords: Augmented reality, sound effect, tooth brushing.

1   Introduction

The purpose of personal oral hygiene, which is generally carried out using a toothbrush, is the maintenance of oral cleanliness and prevention of caries and periodontal disease. Ideally, brushing should be done frequently and correctly to achieve the desired effect. However, brushing is often not carried out correctly or simply forgotten because the task is boring. Thus, there are two main issues with current tooth brushing: one is the lack of motivation, while the other is using the incorrect technique for brushing. To deal with these issues, a wide variety of applications have been proposed in research and development studies on consumer goods.

A. Nijholt, T. Romão, and D. Reidsma (Eds.): ACE 2012, LNCS 7624, pp. 31–43, 2012.
© Springer-Verlag Berlin Heidelberg 2012

One of the reasons for the lack of motivation for tooth brushing is the negative reward; i.e., people brush their teeth so as NOT to get caries, which seldom motivates them. Therefore, if we can change this to a positive reward, they would be more highly motivated. Nakajima et al. proposed the virtual aquarium where tropical fish become active and produce eggs if the users brush their teeth [1]. Hasbro released Tooth Tunes, which consists of a small pressure sensor to detect contact between the bristles and teeth and a bone conduction speaker to play a music clip during contact [2]. These works contribute to motivating users by providing alternative rewards.

To guide the correct way to brush, the SmartGuide has been released by Oral-B. This divides the teeth into four sections and counts brushing actions on a liquid crystal display (LCD) showing how many times the users have brushed their teeth and still should brush them [3]. Chang et al. proposed the Playful Toothbrush, which encourages children to brush their teeth correctly by tracking the toothbrush and identifying where they are brushing [4]. In addition, the Playful Toothbrush feeds back a visual and auditory reward according to the correct brushing performance, thus motivating children to brush their teeth.

It is clear that these works succeed in improving the way we brush (i.e., correctness) and providing sufficient motivation (i.e., frequency). On the other hand, the quality of feedback is an issue for the following reason. Although the previous work presented cues with visual display or music to guide correct tooth brushing, the feedback seems very remote from the brushing itself. Thus, users are forced to understand what the cues mean. To deal with this issue, an approach that provides intuitive cues for correct tooth brushing, as well as motivating the users, is required.

In this study, we propose a novel feedback approach that makes tooth brushing entertaining in an intuitive way. To achieve this goal, we consider two objectives. The first is not to present information on a visual display, but to augment the ordinary tooth brushing experience consisting of haptic and auditory sensations. We believe that modulation of real sensations is the simplest, yet still a robust way of presenting information intuitively. The other is to design the modulation so that the user feels as if his/her teeth are gradually becoming cleaner, thereby providing motivation.

This paper begins with a review of prior work on sensory (haptic and auditory) presentation in the oral cavity. Then, we describe our proposed approach, which modulates the sounds resulting from brushing teeth to provide an increasingly comfortable sensation (i.e., intuitive cues) that motivates the users. Thereafter, we present a pilot study to demonstrate the efficacy of the proposed approach. Finally, the paper ends with a discussion of our future work based on the experimental results and our conclusions.

2   Related Work

A number of works studying sensory presentation in the oral cavity were carried out mainly to simulate or enhance the eating experience. Since the tooth brushing experience is mainly derived from haptic and auditory sensations, we focus on previous work related to these two sensory presentations in the oral cavity.

2.1   Presenting Haptic Sensation

Iwata et al. proposed the Food Simulator, which is a haptic interface that generates a force on the users' teeth simulating food texture by means of a one degree-of-freedom (DoF) mechanism [5]. They successfully presented food texture as well as chemical taste. However, applying a force feedback mechanism to a toothbrush is not practical because a multiple DoF force feedback device is required, thus leading to higher cost.

Hashimoto et al. proposed the Straw-like User Interface (SUI), which is an audio-tactile interface that presents the vibration and sound resulting from suction with a straw [6]. They demonstrated that the SUI can simulate the experience of drinking a wide variety of things. However, tooth brushing produces vibration and sound that would mask additional vibration. Thus, it is difficult to directly modulate the haptic experience of tooth brushing.

2.2   Presenting Auditory Sensation

Zampini and Spence found that the crisper and fresher potato chips were perceived as being, either the louder the overall sound level rose or the higher the amplified frequency of the biting sound became [7]. Koizumi et al. employed and developed this effect to augment the experience of biting and chewing foods by synchronizing the jaw action [8].

These techniques can be used to modulate the sensation in the oral cavity and can easily be realized using auditory interfaces, such as a microphone and headphones, without complicated mechanisms like haptic interfaces. Thus, employing these techniques is practical.

Furthermore, in the field of cross-modal research, it is well-known that the haptic perception of a variety of surface textures (including outside the oral cavity) can be changed by modulating the auditory cues resulting from exploration [7][9-11]. For example, Jousmäki and Hari demonstrated that sounds that are exactly synchronous with hand-rubbing modify the resulting tactile sensation (the parchment-skin illusion) [9]. The palm is perceived as being smoother and dryer, like the surface of paper, when the high-frequency component of the rubbing sound is amplified or the overall sound level is increased. We believe that this cross-modal phenomenon enhances the modulation effect.

3   Proposed Approach

From previous work on modulating sounds resulting from exploration, we believe that the technique can be applied to a toothbrush by simply embedding a microphone in the toothbrush and presenting modulated brushing sounds by applying audio filter (e.g., band pass filter).

By considering previous work, amplifying the low-frequency component evokes a moist (or sticky) and rough feeling on the teeth. This would make the users feel uncomfortable (Fig. 1-a). On the contrary, amplifying the high-frequency component.

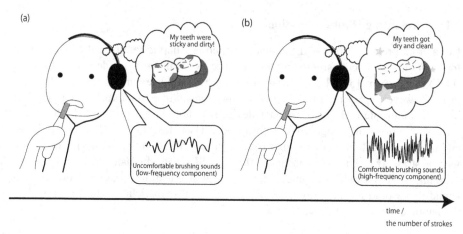

Fig. 1. The proposed approach: (a) the low-frequency component would evoke moisture (or sticky) and rough feeling on tooth (uncomfortable feeling). (b) the high-frequency component of brushing sounds would evoke dry and smooth feeling (comfortable feeling).

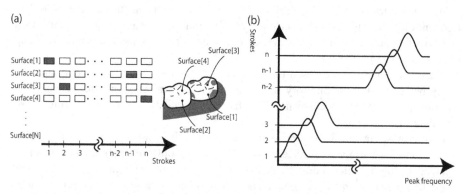

Fig. 2. Associating the proposed approach with a toothbrush tracking system, such as in [4]: (a) the system counts the number of strokes on each tooth, and (b) the peak frequency of the band pass filter is determined based on the count

of brushing sounds evokes a dry and smooth feeling on the teeth, thus making the users feel comfortable (Fig. 1-b).

We believe that it is possible to provide intuitive cues for users by controlling the level of comfort of sensations, allowing the users to be aware of the condition of their teeth; i.e., clear or dirty. Since the modulating sounds are derived from the original brushing sounds, this technique achieves our first objective; i.e., to augment the ordinary tooth brushing experience (intuitiveness). In addition, it would be possible to enhance the feeling of accomplishment by designing sound manipulation, since users would intuitively know the progress of cleaning, thereby addressing our second aim of motivating the users.

Furthermore, by associating the technique with a toothbrush tracking system, such as in [4], it is possible to present the condition of each tooth. The system counts the number of strokes on each tooth (Fig. 2-a) and modulates the sound to evoke either a comfortable or uncomfortable feeling based on the count (e.g., the peak frequency of the band pass filter is higher when the count increases, Fig. 2-b). For example, if a tooth has been brushed well, the system provides comfortable brushing (high-frequency) sounds (at Surface[2] and Surface[4] in Fig. 2); if not, it provides uncomfortable (low-frequency) sounds (at Surface[1] and Surface[3] in Fig. 2). This would enable users to know which teeth have been brushed enough and which have not. In other words, the user can intuitively know how many times and which teeth they should brush merely by brushing their teeth.

4   Experiment

To investigate whether our proposed approach can modulate the impression of tooth brushing, we conducted an experiment in which participants were asked to evaluate the feelings of comfort and accomplishment from brushing. The former feeling is mainly related to creating intuitive cues, while the latter is related to how the design motivates the users.

4.1   Setup

Toothbrush. We created a toothbrush with an interchangeable brush (ASIANETWORKS Co., Ltd.) to consider the sanitary issue, as shown in Fig. 3. The toothbrush has a length of 160 mm, with weight 20 g. Fig. 4 shows the internal configuration of the handle, which is made of acrylonitrile butadiene styrene (ABS) resin and contains a microphone (capacitor microphone, WM-61A, Panasonic Co.) to record brushing sounds, and a force sensor (miniature load cell, LMA-A-5N, Kyowa Electronic Instruments Co., Ltd.) to measure grip force. The microphone is attached to the central core, which connects to the brush, thus allowing brushing sounds to be recorded directly. The force sensor is fixed beneath the bump in the handle.

Recorded sound is sent to the microphone jack of a PC. The signal of the force sensor is also sent to the PC via a microcontroller (Arduino Duemilanove). These two signals are processed to provide auditory cues as described in the following section.

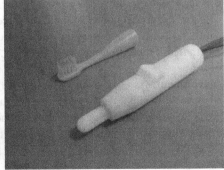

Fig. 3. Toothbrush used in the experiment

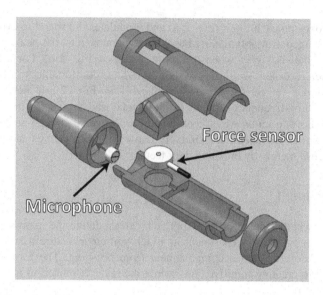

Fig. 4. Internal configuration of the handle of the toothbrush containing a microphone and a force sensor

Sound Processing. We used Max (version 6.0, Cycling '74) as the sound processer. For the brushing sound feedback, we used a band pass filter because this seemed to be the best filter to modulate sensation and express a wide variety of experiences in a preliminary investigation comparing a high pass, low pass, and band pass filter. We prepared five peak frequency conditions (500, 1000, 2000, 4000, and 8000 Hz) with a constant Q value (1.0). In addition, we prepared a non-filter condition as the control condition.

As indicated in previous work [7][9][10], the overall sound level affects the perception. Thus, we investigated three sound level conditions (-20, 0, and +20 dB). For the default sound level, i.e., the non-filter and 0 dB condition, the loudness of sounds was set at approximately 75 dB (A) using a sound level meter (digital sound level meter, TM-102, Sato Shouji Inc.). For the other conditions, the sound levels were set by Max.

In the experiment, the amount of force applied to the toothbrush affected the feelings of comfort and accomplishment from brushing. To avoid this, a beep sound was emitted if the grip force exceeded 20 N.

Environment. As shown in Fig. 5, the participants sat on a chair in front of a table and next to a sink, with headphones (sound-isolating earbud headphones, EX-29, Direct Sound Headphones Inc.) on their head. The toothbrush, an LCD, a ten-key keypad, a cup of water, and potato chips were placed on the table.

Fig. 5. Setup for the experiment

4.2   Procedure

The participants were instructed how to brush their teeth. They gripped the toothbrush in their right hands similar to holding a pen, with their thumbs on the bump of the handle (i.e., on the force sensor). They were instructed not to grip too tightly to avoid the beep sound (i.e., less than 20 N). They were asked to brush the buccal surface of the left upper second and third molars using five strokes and employing the Bass method [12].

In each trial, the participants first brushed their teeth under the standard condition (i.e., non-filter and 0 dB). Next, they brushed their teeth under a comparative condition. Then, they rated the subjective sensation of the comparative condition, such as feelings of comfort and accomplishment, using the ten-key keypad according to the analog scales on the LCD. The scales included 100 divisions with semantic anchors at either end of the scale bars. The left end (i.e., 0) of the comfort / accomplishment feeling bar represented "uncomfortable" / "not brushed at all", while the opposite side (i.e., 100) represented "comfortable" / "brushed well". The participants were asked to rate each of these two scales when the standard condition was rated 50. There was no limit on the time taken to respond.

Each participant performed this evaluation task 54 times; i.e., (five peak frequency conditions + one non-filter condition) × three sound gain conditions × three repetitions. Comparative conditions were randomly presented and the participants were unaware of the parameters.

Before the trials, the participants practiced this procedure a few times without the headphones. Every nine trials, they ate a piece of potato chip, chewing them on the left side to keep their teeth dirty. They were allowed to rinse their mouths freely during the experiment.

Seven participants—four men and three women—aged between 22 and 25 (mean = 22.9; SD = 1.2) took part in the experiment. All participants were right-handed.

4.3 Results

Comfort Feeling. The results of the feeling of comfort for the three sound gain conditions with respect to the six frequency manipulation conditions are shown in Fig. 6. A two-way within-participants repeated-measures analysis of variance (ANOVA) was performed on the data. The within-participants factors were Frequency Manipulation (i.e., peak frequency; 500, 1000, 2000, 4000, and 8000 Hz and the control condition) and Sound Gain (i.e., -20 dB, 0 dB, and 20dB).

The effect of Sound Gain was significant ($F(2, 12) = 4.51$, $p < 0.05$). The rating score for comfort was higher under the 0 dB condition (mean (M) = 52.4; standard deviation (SD) = 2.6) than either the -20 dB (M = 44.6; SD = 1.5) or 20 dB condition (M = 40.0; SD = 9.1).

The interaction effect between Frequency Manipulation and Sound Gain was significant ($F(10, 60) = 3.10$, $p < 0.01$). Simple main effects were found for Sound Gain under the 4000 Hz ($F(2, 12) = 4.69$, $p < 0.05$) and control conditions ($F(2, 12) = 7.68$, $p < 0.01$) and for Frequency Manipulation at the 20 dB level ($F(5, 30) = 4.69$, $p < 0.01$), which imply that the effect of Frequency Manipulation had a greater influence on comfort at 20 dB than at the other Sound Gain levels; i.e., -20 dB or 0 dB.

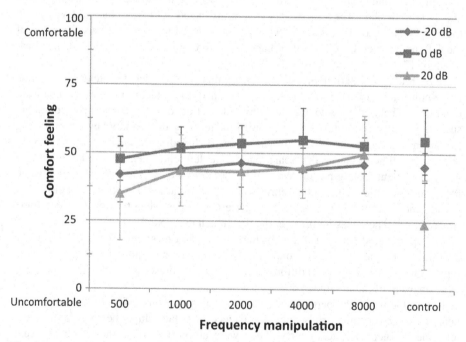

Fig. 6. Results of the experiment. Mean values of the comfort feeling for the three sound gain levels with respect to the six frequency manipulation conditions. Error bars denote standard deviation.

Accomplishment Feeling. The results for the accomplishment feeling for the three sound gain levels with respect to the six frequency manipulation conditions are shown in Fig. 7. An ANOVA was performed on this data similar to that for the comfort feeling data.

The effects of Frequency Manipulation ($F(5, 30) = 13.12$, $p < 0.01$) and Sound Gain ($F(2, 12) = 21.33$, $p < 0.01$) were significant. Furthermore, the interaction effect between Frequency Manipulation and Sound Gain was also significant ($F(10, 60) = 6.22$, $p < 0.01$). Simple main effects were found for Sound Gain under the 2000 Hz ($F(2, 12) = 5.12$, $p < 0.05$), the 4000 Hz ($F(2, 12) = 9.11$, $p < 0.01$), the 8000 Hz ($F(2, 12) = 18.33$, $p < 0.01$), and the control conditions ($F(2, 12) = 29.07$, $p < 0.01$) and for Frequency Manipulation under the 20 dB level ($F(5, 30) = 25.12$, $p < 0.01$), which implies that the effect of Frequency Manipulation had a greater influence on the accomplishment feeling than for the other Sound Gain levels; i.e., the -20 dB and 0 dB levels, as well as the comfort feeling.

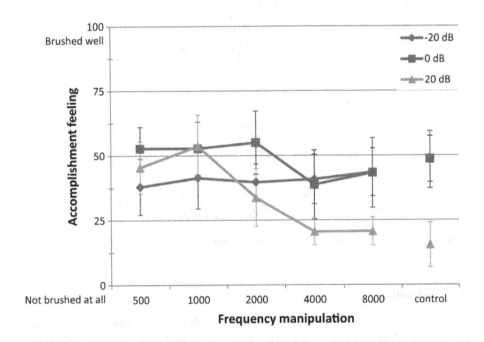

Fig. 7. Results of the experiment. Mean values of the accomplishment feeling for the three sound gain levels with respect to the six frequency manipulation conditions. Error bars denote standard deviation.

Correlation between Two Scales. We plotted all 378 pairs of scores on a two dimensional graph (with the x- and y-axes denoting the feelings of comfort and accomplishment, respectively) to investigate the coefficient of correlation between the two scales by applying linear approximation. As shown in Fig. 8, there was almost no correlation (R^2 = 0.2167), which implies that the participants distinguished two scales and a comfortable feeling did not always induce a feeling of accomplishment and vice versa.

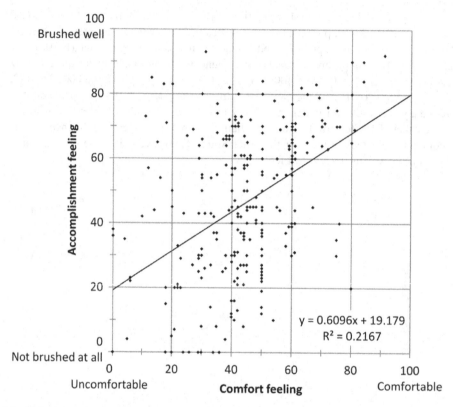

Fig. 8. Results of the experiment. The correlation between the two scales, that is, feelings of comfort and accomplishment.

4.4   Discussion

The results demonstrated that our proposed approach could modulate both comfort and accomplishment feelings by increasing the sound gain and manipulating frequency. Thus, it is possible to provide intuitive cues (i.e., comfortable versus uncomfortable) and to provide motivation by controlling the feeling of accomplishment.

After the experiment, four of the participants reported that the louder the sounds became, the higher the feeling of accomplishment was. On the other hand, another participant said that too loud a brushing sound evoked a feeling of insufficiency, because they felt as if they had not brushed their teeth by themselves, which probably explains the low rating of accomplishment feeling at 20 dB condition. Furthermore, two of the participants reported that some conditions were so loud that they felt uncomfortable, which probably explains the low rating of comfort feeling at 20 dB condition. Based on the comments that the 20 dB condition was felt to be too loud for some participants, we should consider an amplification level between 0 dB and 20 dB in future studies.

At the 20 dB level, on the other hand, frequency manipulation had a greater influence on both feelings as shown by the simple main effect. Regarding the comfort feeling, the participants felt comfortable when the higher band pass filter was applied. For the feeling of accomplishment, the participants felt an insufficiency feeling when the higher band pass filter was applied, which seemed to peak at around 1000 Hz.

At the -20 dB and 0 dB levels, on the contrary, frequency manipulation did not influence either feeling. One of the possible reasons for this at the -20 dB level is that the sound gain was so soft that the participants could not perceive the change in frequency. Even at the 0 dB level, the sound gain might not have been enough to perceive the change because applying the band pass filter decreases the overall sound level.

There was no correlation between the feelings of comfort and accomplishment. This tendency was especially notable at the 20 dB level as mentioned before. By taking into consideration the comments from the participants, the comfortable feeling seems to come from cues implying that the teeth have been cleaned and it is not necessary to brush them anymore. This feeling may be induced by presenting high-frequency components of the brushing sound that evoke a dry and smooth surface sensation as described in the parchment-skin illusion [9]. On the contrary, the score for the feeling of accomplishment decreased because the participants felt that they did not have to brush their teeth anymore; i.e., their teeth had already been cleaned. For the 1000 Hz condition, on the other hand, the participants felt something sticky like food debris on their teeth. Thus, they felt uncomfortable and dislodging this by brushing induced a sense of accomplishment. However, for the 500 Hz condition, the score for accomplishment shows a decreasing tendency. This could be because the participants perceived their teeth or the bristles as being something too soft to identify. Thus, they felt uncomfortable and no longer imagined that they were dislodging something. Furthermore, under the non-filter condition, both scores decreased significantly, confirming our previous discussion; i.e., too loud sounds induced an uncomfortable and insufficient feeling.

Two of the participants reported that the microphone picked up sound irrelevant to brushing, such as environmental sound and the sound produced by the electric cord touching the table. One solution is to employ a highly directional microphone or an accelerometer instead of the current omni directional microphone.

After the experiment, all participants reported that the experience of hearing their own brushing sounds was interesting and modulating the sounds somehow altered their tooth brushing experience.

5   Conclusion

This paper first addressed the current issue with tooth brushing, namely the quality of feedback. To deal with this issue, we established two objectives:

1. not to present information on a visual display, but to augment the ordinary tooth brushing experience; and
2. to design the modulation so that the user feels as if his/her teeth are gradually becoming cleaner.

Next, we proposed a novel approach to augment the tooth brushing experience by modulating the brushing sounds to make tooth brushing entertaining in an intuitive manner. A microphone embedded in the toothbrush records the brushing sounds, which are then modified by a PC and presented to users. In the experiment, we demonstrated that increasing the sound gain and manipulating frequency modulated the tooth brushing impression, in terms of feelings of comfort and accomplishment. However, it is still unclear what the optimal sound gain, frequency, and sound filter are. Thus, investigating these parameters is one of our future works.

In the future, we intend studying the efficacy of the presenting condition of each tooth (i.e., clean or dirty) through the proposed technique (as illustrated in Fig. 2) in conjunction with a toothbrush tracking system, such as that in [4]. Furthermore, we would like to conduct a long-term user study to verify whether our proposed approach can provide motivation and is compatible with daily life.

Acknowledgments. This work was supported by JSPS KAKENHI Grant Number 24004331.

References

1. Nakajima, T., Lehdonvirta, V., Tokunaga, E., Ayabe, M., Kimura, H., Okuda, Y.: Lifestyle Ubiquitous Gaming: Making Daily Lives more Plesurable. In: Proceedings of the 13th IEEE International Conference on Embedded and Real-Time Computing Systems and Applications, pp. 257–266 (2007)
2. Hasbro: TOOTH TUNES
3. Oral-B. Professional Care SmartSeries 5000 with SmartGuide Electric Toothbrush, http://www.oralb.com/products/professional-care-smart-series-5000/
4. Chang, Y.-C., Lo, J.-L., Huang, C.-J., Hsu, N.-Y., Chu, H.-H., Wang, H.-Y., Chi, P.-Y., Hsieh, Y.-L.: Playful Toothbrush: Ubicomp Technology for Teaching Tooth Brushing to Kindergarten Children. In: Proceedings of the SIGCHI Conference on Human Factors in Computing Systems, pp. 363–372 (2008)
5. Iwata, H., Yano, H., Uemura, T., Moriya, T.: Food Simulator: A Haptic Interface for Biting. In: Proceedings of the IEEE Virtual Reality, pp. 51–57 (2004)
6. Hashimoto, Y., Inami, M., Kajimoto, H.: Straw-Like User Interface (II): A New Method of Presenting Auditory Sensations for a more Natural Experience. In: Proceedings of the International Conference on Haptics, pp. 484–493 (2008)
7. Zampini, M., Spence, C.: The Role of Auditory Cues in Modulating the Perceived Crispness and Staleness of Potato Chips. Journal of Sensory Studies 19(5), 347–363 (2005)
8. Koizumi, N., Tanaka, H., Uema, Y., Inami, M.: Chewing Jockey: Augmented Food Texture by Using Sound Based on Cross-Modal Effect. In: Proceedings of the International Conference on Advances in Computer Entertainment Technology, vol. 21 (2011)

9. Jousmäki, V., Hari, R.: Parchment-Skin Illusion: Sound-Biased Touch. Current Biology 8(6), 190 (1998)
10. Guest, S., Catmur, C., Lloyd, D., Spence, C.: Audiotactile Interactions in Roughness Perception. Experimental Brain Research 146(2), 161–171 (2002)
11. Lederman, S.J., Morgan, T., Hamilton, C., Klatzky, R.L.: Integrating Multimodal Information about Surface Texture via a Probe: Relative Contributions of Haptic and Touch-Produced Sound Sources. In: Proceedings of the Symposium on Haptic Interfaces for Virtual Environment and Teleoperator Systems, pp. 97–104 (2002)
12. Bass, C.C.: An Effective Method of Personal Oral Hygiene; Part II. Journal of the Louisiana State Medical Society 106(3), 100–112 (1954)

Bathcratch: Touch and Sound-Based DJ Controller Implemented on a Bathtub

Shigeyuki Hirai[1], Yoshinobu Sakakibara[2], and Seiho Hayakawa[3]

[1] Faculty of Computer Science and Engineering, Kyoto Sangyo University, Japan
hirai@cse.kyoto-su.ac.jp
[2] Department of Frontier Informatics, Graduate School of Kyoto Sangyo University, Japan
sakura.colonnade@gmail.com
[3] Freelance, Osaka, Japan
irotori2@gmail.com

Abstract. Bathcratch is a music entertainment system that converts a bathtub into a DJ controller, allowing an average person in a bathtub to play scratching music. The system detects the squeaks made by rubbing the bathtub and associates them with several preset scratching phrases. In addition, capacitive touch sensors embedded in the tub allow the selection of scratching phrases and background rhythm tracks. Here, we provide a system overview and explain the design, user interface, music controller implementation of this system along with the feedback received for it during a public exhibition.

Keywords: Interactive Music System, DJ Scratching, Rubbing Interface, Acoustic Sensing, Squeaking Sound Detection, Capacitive Touch Sensor, Bathtub, Daily Life.

1   Introduction

The sounds that a bathtub makes when rubbed, brushed, or struck would be familiar to most anyone. We propose using the bathtub as an interface for creating music. To explore this concept, we developed Bathcatch, a system that detects squeaks made when rubbing a bathtub as well as sounds made by other such actions and converts them into musical sounds (see Figure 1). By embedding sensors that can detect touch and sounds, the bathtub is essentially converted into the user interface (UI) for a DJ controller. We intend for this to be a new way to make everyday activities more fun.

In this paper, we present a system overview and describe the method of interaction processing of scratching sounds with rhythm tracks. In addition, we describe the feedback received from the public at an exhibition where the Bathcratch system was installed.

2   Related Work

Considerable research has been conducted on music systems and UIs for DJ controllers, including inputs for scratching. For example of experimental turntables,

A. Nijholt, T. Romão, and D. Reidsma (Eds.): ACE 2012, LNCS 7624, pp. 44–56, 2012.

Fig. 1. Using Bathcratch in a Bathroom[1]

the DJammer [1], MusicGlove [2] and Wearable DJ System [3] are wearable UIs which allow users Air-DJ and scratching. Mixxx [4] uses ARToolKit to implement an augmented reality turntable that can play various sounds. D'Groove [5] has a turntable with force feedback as well as a DJ mixer that allows users to practice the fundamental techniques of DJing. Hansen uses the Reactable as an UI for DJ scratching [6][7]. Fukuchi's system uses a capacitive multi-touch surface and allows multi-track scratching [8]. The other turntable controller including commercial products for scratching is described in detail in Hansen's doctoral thesis [9].

Moreover, some research has been conducted on utilizing acoustic sensing in a UI. Scratch Input [10] detects scratching sounds and the associated finger motions using a piezo microphone attached to a wall, table, etc. Stane [11] attempted the detection of vibrations when the surface of a small device with built-in piezo sensors is scratched. This device also used various input patterns that depended on the vibration length. Skinput [12] uses sounds and machine learning to implement a UI. This system uses the human body itself as the UI by recognizing finger taps through vibrations transmitted along the skin surface using a piezo film rolled around the upeer arm. Lopes's system [13] uses sounds of finger, knuckle, fingernail and punch touches, in order to expand the input language of surface interaction.

3   System Overview

As shown in the overview in Figure 2, a contact microphone (a piezo sensor) is attached on the inside of the bathtub edge at the point where the right hand of the user would be placed. The microphone senses squeaks made when the bathtub is rubbed as the solid vibrations in the body of the tub. The sounds are processed by a software

---

[1] http://www.youtube.com/watch?v=kp_0rPx-RSY

called the Squeaking Sound Detector, which handles the rubbing input. For the left hand, capacitive touch sensors are provided, which allow various other inputs to be given to Bathcratch. These embedded sensors represent one novel feature of the system: they are invisible and do not impede everyday cleaning of the bathtub. A video projector installed above the tub projects virtual buttons over the touch sensors on the left side and marks the input area on the right for the contact microphone. Another novelty is the flexibility of the interactive display and its compatibility with an ordinary household environment. The Scratch Music Controller generates scratching phrases according to the detected squeaks and also changes the scratching effects and rhythm tracks in accordance with the touch inputs, as shown in Figure 3.

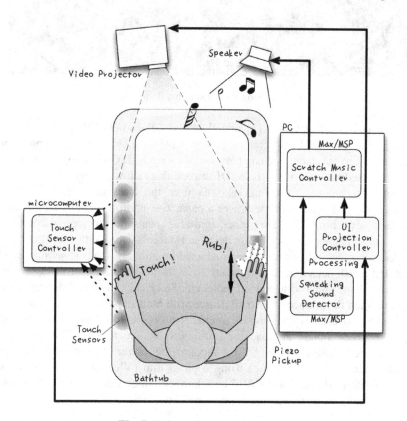

Fig. 2. Bathcratch system overview

4   Bathtub as Interaction Medium

4.1   Detecting Squeaks

This system must detect and differentiate between different squeaks and play associated scratch sounds. These squeaks have subtle differences depending on the

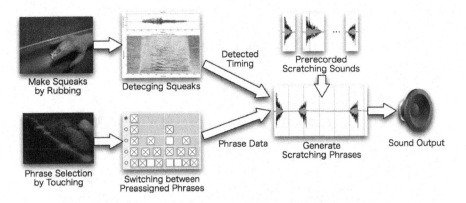

Fig. 3. Internal process of Bathcratch system

material of the bathtub and the way it is rubbed, for instance, with different finger angles, rubbing directions, and pressure values. However, these sounds have a fundamental frequency (F0) and specific harmonic structures, as shown in Figure 4. This spectrogram shows the harmonic structure and its continuous characteristic. We confirmed that the same characteristic exist for various bathtub squeaking sounds. The range of F0 is 100–600 Hz.

In addition to squeaks, taps and knocks on a bathtub also produce solid vibrations, although they do not have the same characteristics as squeaks; they have short durations and do not have a distinct harmonic component, as shown in Figure 5. The other sounds with harmonic components in a bathroom are human voices. However, we confirmed that a contact microphone attached to a bathtub filled with water will not detect a human voice. Thus, in order to isolate squeaks, the system must identify signals with a certain continuous harmonic structure and amplitude. However, the current system does not detect a continuous harmonic structure accurately. Hence, the external object sigmund~ in the Max/MSP software environment was used instead to estimate F0.

4.2   Detecting Touch Positions on Bathtub

The next input for this system is through touch positions on the edge of the bathtub, which allow switching between various functions while playing. We use capacitive touch sensors installed on the edge of the bathtub near where the user's left hand would be, as shown in Figure 6.

Usually, capacitive sensors respond to contact with water and are therefore used to measure water levels in tanks. Hence, recent multi-touch input devices tend to be incompatible with wet environments. However, the basic function of a capacitive sensor is to react to the presence of dielectric objects. Since water and the human

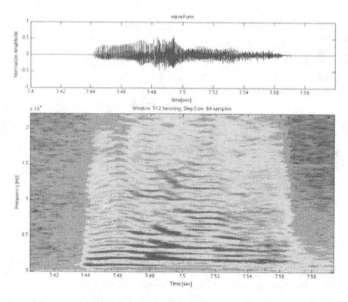

Fig. 4. Spectrogram of a bathtub squeak

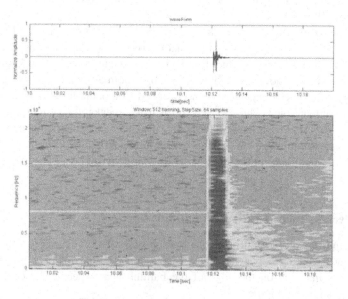

Fig. 5. Spectrogram of a bathtub knock

body have different relative permittivities, a capacitive sensor can indeed be used to detect human touch even when wet. Bathcratch uses the functionality to detct only human touches to change rhythm tracks and scratching sounds.

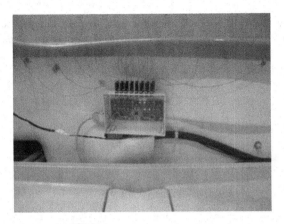

Fig. 6. Bathtub equipped with capacitive touch sensors

4.3   Projection Display

The embedded contact microphone and touch sensors are invisible and there no changes are made to the surface of the bathtub, as mentioned above. Instead, a video projector installed above the tub projects virtual interactive objects over the touch sensors and indicates a designated rubbing area near the microphone (see Figure 1). Note that the contact microphone (piezo sensor) can be installed anywhere on the bathtub edge as the solid vibrations are conducted quite well through the bathtub. The designated rubbing area is only intended as a visual aid to prompt the user to rub the bathtub.

5   Scratching Music Controller

5.1   Overview of Scratching Phrase Generation

The Squeaking Sound Detector and Scratching Music Controller were implemented as a Max/MSP patch, as shown in Figure 7. The checkboxes at the top are toggle switches to control the entire Bathcratch system in order to play specific rhythm tracks and to change the pitch of the scratching sounds. The faders control the volume of each scratching phrase and the master output. The checkboxes in the middle can be used to make scratching phrases, as described in the next section. To the right of these checkboxes is an option to set the tempo for the rhythm tracks and scratching phrases. The current Bathcratch system does not generate scratching sounds synchronized with the actual rubbing motion, but generates phrases synchronized with the tempo of the selected rhythm track. This is because of the latency in detecting squeaking sounds and the difficulty for users to rub and make squeaking sounds in synch with the rhythm track. Therefore, we designed the interaction of Bathcratch such that rubbing actions (making squeaking sounds) are first used to prearrange a set of scratching phrases, which can be switched by using the touch controls. Thus, any user can intuitively create DJ scratching sounds with relative ease. Note that we plan to implement synchronized, real-time scratching for experts in the next version of Bathcratch.

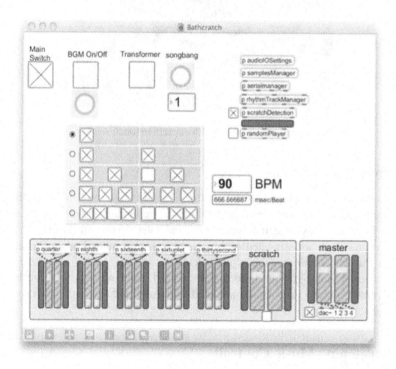

Fig. 7. Max/MSP patch for Bathcratch

5.2   Switching between Scratching Phrases

Five scratching phrases can be arranged freely based on half notes, quarter notes, eighth notes, sixteenth notes, and triplet notes. These phrases are prearranged with checkbox groups in the middle area of the patch shown in Figure 7, and icons representing each phrase are projected on the top of the touch sensors. Users can switch between the five scratching phrases by touching the projected objects. The five phrases are always played in the tempo of the current rhythm track, and Bathcratch outputs only the phrase selected by controlling faders for each phrase. Therefore, even if a user rubs vigorously and quickly, the output phrase is not changed. Furthermore, when a user selects another phrase before the current phrase has completed, a smooth transition is made using cross-fading effects.

5.3   Sound Sources and Effects for Scratching

Currently, this system plays prerecorded scratching sounds for each note in the scratching phrases. It is possible to assign a single sound source and slightly change each note in the phrase and to change the playback speed of the assigned source to create individual effects. By using these functions, the same sound source can be used in a phrase, although each note played is not the same. This reduces the number of sound files and materials necessary and makes it easy to create a phrase with a few sound sources. Even if only one sound file is assigned to all notes of all phrases, a wide repertoire of phrases can be realized by randomly changing playback speeds. Although individual assignments are performed before playing with this system, the randomizing mode can be controlled in real time using the touch inputs. This method of sound assignment and generating effects makes the phrases seem more natural and nonmechanical. In addition, actual DJs employ a variety of techniques on real turntables and faders, for instance, chirp scratch, forward/backward scratch, and transformer scratch. These functions of Bathcratch can be considered as simplified and modified functions that are carried out using actual turntables and faders.

5.4   Rhythm Tracks

We prepared a range of background rhythm tracks, for instance, OldSchool, Dubstep, JazzyHipHop, and Electronica, for the scratching performances. Users can select a rhythm track by sliding the track selection area over the touch sensors. However, the rhythm track manager always plays all tracks in parallel and only turns up the volume of the selected rhythm track while muting the others.

6   Demonstrations and Exhibit

The initial version of Bathcratch with a simple UI can seen on YouTube (Figure 1). The installation version of Bathcratch (Figure 8) with an improved UI (Figure 9) was exhibited at the 2010 Asia Digital Art Awards at the Fukuoka Asian Art Museum in Fukuoka, Japan, from March 17 to 29, 2011[2]. It was also been exhibited at the National Museum of Emerging Science and Innovation (Miraikan) in Tokyo on October 10, 2011. The UI was changed for this version since it was played on the sides of the bathtub (see Figures 10 and 11).

---

[2] http://www.youtube.com/watch?v=g-Z0visXQwo

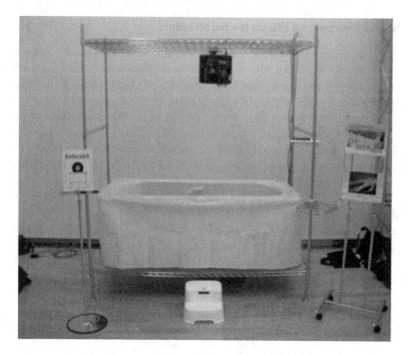

Fig. 8. Bathcratch installation

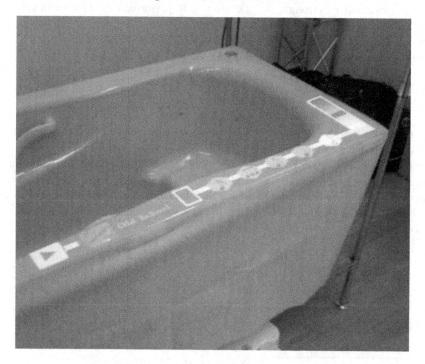

Fig. 9. User-interface of Bathcratch installation

Fig. 10. Exhibition at the Fukuoka Asian Art Museum in Fukuoka, Japan

Fig. 11. Demonstration at the National Museum of Emerging Science and Innovation (Miraikan) in Tokyo, Japan

The UI of the installation version presents a movable gradation square for rubbing on the right edge, as seen when standing to the side of the bathtub. The buttons used to select scratching phrases are along the left side of the square rubbing area. Each button represents a musical note, for instance, a quarter note, an eighth note, a sixteenth note, and Etcetera, which represents a fundamental note of a scratching phrase. Users can select and change phrases by touching these buttons. Moreover, on the left side, there are effect buttons to change the pitch of phrase notes as well as a sliding selector and a mute button for the rhythm tracks. Each icon of the sliding selector represents the characteristics of the associated rhythm tracks in terms of color and icon design[3].

We provided a wet sponge along with the setup to allow users to wet their fingertips and create squeaks when rubbing the bathtub. It was placed near the square area designated for rubbing.

A few drawbacks were noticed during this exhibition. One involves setting the input gain for the piezo sensor when there is no water in the bathtub. Turning a rhythm track up at high input gain causes misdetection of F0 because of interference with the notes from the rhythm track. This phenomenon does not occur when there is water in the bathtub. Therefore, we think that water acts as an attenuator that blocks surrounding sounds. Another problem is that some users could not understand the difference between the rubbing UI and the touch UI. Most of them did not rub but slid their fingertips lightly on the rubbing area despite the fact that they needed to make squeaks. Fortunately, the exhibition staff explained the operation of Bathcratch and showed users how to use it. This indicates that we need to improve the UI to more clearly indicate that a rubbing motion that produces squeaks is necessary.

7   Discussion

In Japan, there is a unique bathing culture. A lot of people feel bathrooms as amenity spaces with staying. The half-body bathing is typical of it. Hense, general bath modules in Japan have a feature to expand various functionalities with optional equipments. For instance, ceiling speakers for listening to music, ceiling illuminations with spotlights for room effects, a mist sauna apparatus for beauty and fine skins. People read books and listen to music while in half-body bathing or bathing with mist sauna.

The important point of Bathcratch is to make bathing in daily life more and/or inexperienced fun. This system needs audio equipment for output sounds, capacitive touch sensors, a contact microphone, a video projector and a PC for measurement and control of this system. Most bathtub in Japan mentioned above has a removable side panel. Optional equipments, for instance, whirlpool and heart rate monitor, can be installed inside a bathtub from the side. Figure 6 shows a bathtub removed a side panel, installed capacitive touch sensor unit and red lines as sensor electrodes. A contact microphone can be also installed in this space. The installation of these

---

[3] http://www.youtube.com/watch?v=5F5utOrVlcI

equipments are already available to existing bathtub. Only a video projector is not ease to install in above a ceiling. However, pico-projectors have a remarkable development at the present. We think a waterproofed type of pico-projector, which is ease to install beneath a ceiling, will be released sooner. Therefore, we also think Bathcratch will be released as a practical entertainment system.

8   Conclusion and Future Work

In this paper, we described Bathcratch, which allows anyone to create DJ scratching sounds by rubbing a bathtub. This system utilizes the squeaks produced by rubbing smooth surfaces—a bathtub in this case. The paper also describes the UIs used for rubbing and touch inputs, which were implemented with a projector, along with the systems for detecting squeaks and controlling the scratching music. Bathcratch was presented at several exhibitions, where it was awarded some prizes.

Squeaks produced by rubbing smooth surfaces are quite common in everyday life, for instance, when polishing mirrors, windows, bathtubs, and dishes. Therefore, this system can appropriate a casual action in daily life as a means of entertainment. People can control various devices via rubbing motions and squeaks. Moreover, the input functionalities of this system can be increased by including rubbing length and timing as additional parameters.

As a future work, we plan to simplify this system and analyze squeaking sounds accurately in terms of the timing. We will also analyze the feasibility of including various other aspects of rubbing motion as additional input parameters for a general UI, for instance, the number of rubbing fingers, rubbing direction, and the intensity. Finally, we would like to improve Bathcratch's entertainment functionality, including the music controller, and further explore the concept of entertainment with common objects found in a typical home.

Acknowledgments. This research was partially supported by a grant from Hayao Nakayama Foundation.

References

1. Slayden, A., Spasojevic, M., Hans, M., Smith, M.: The DJammer: "Air-Scratching" and Freeing the DJ to Join the Party. In: CHI 2005 Extended Abstracts, pp. 1789–1792 (2005)
2. Hayafuchi, K., Suzuki, K.: MusicGlove: A Wearable Musical Controller for Massive Media Library. In: Proc. of 8th Intl. Conf. on New Interfaces for Musical Expression, Genoa, Italy (2008)
3. Tomibayashi, Y., Takegawa, Y., Terada, T., Tsukamoto, M.: Wearable DJ system: a New Motion-Controlled DJ system. In: Proc. ACE 2009, pp. 132–139 (2009)
4. Andersen, T.H.: Mixxx: Towards Novel DJ Interfaces. In: Proc. NIME 2003, pp. 30–35 (2003)
5. Beamish, T., Maclean, K., Fels, S.: Manipulating Music: Multimodal Interaction for DJs. In: Proc. CHI 2003, pp. 327–334 (2003)

6. Hansen, K.F., Alonso, M., Dimitrov, S.: Combining DJ Scratching, Tangible Interfaces and a Physics-Based Model of Friction Sounds. In: Proc. of the International Computer Music Conference, San Francisco, pp. 45–48 (2007)
7. Hansen, K.F., Alonso, M.: More DJ techniques on the reactable. In: Proc. of 8th Intl. Conf. on New Interfaces for Musical Expression, Genova, Italy, pp. 207–210 (2008)
8. Fukuchi, K.: Multi-track Scratch Player on a Multi-touch Sensing Device. In: Ma, L., Rauterberg, M., Nakatsu, R. (eds.) ICEC 2007. LNCS, vol. 4740, pp. 211–218. Springer, Heidelberg (2007)
9. Hansen, K.F.: The acoustics and performance of DJ scratching, Analysis and modeling, Doctral Thesis, KTH (2010)
10. Harrison, C., Hudson, S.E.: Scratch Input: Creating Large, Inexpensive, Unpowered and Mobile finger Input Surfaces. In: Proc. UIST 2008, pp. 205–208 (2008)
11. Murray-Smith, R., Williamson, J., Hughes, S., Quaade, T.: Stane: Synthesized Surfaces for Tactile Input. In: Proc. CHI 2008, pp. 1299–1302 (2008)
12. Harrison, C., Tan, D., Morris, D.: Skinput: Appropriating the Body as an Input Surface. In: Proc. CHI 2010, pp. 453–462 (2010)
13. Lopes, P., Jota, R., Jorge, J.A.: Augmenting Touch Interaction Through Acoustic Sensing. In: Proc. ITS 2011, pp. 53–56 (2011)

Airstic Drum: A Drumstick for Integration of Real and Virtual Drums

Hiroyuki Kanke[1], Yoshinari Takegawa[2], Tsutomu Terada[1,3],
and Masahiko Tsukamoto[1]

[1] Graduate School of Engineering, Kobe University
[2] Faculty of System Information Science, Future University Hakodate
[3] PRESTO, Japan Science and Technology Agency
h-kanke@stu.kobe-u.ac.jp, tuka@kobe-u.ac.jp,
yoshi@fun.ac.jp, tsutomu@eedept.kobe-u.ac.jp

Abstract. Drum kits consist of various kinds of percussion instruments. As all percussion instruments are large and heavy, they are inconvenient for drummers to carry and set up. Virtual drums, which include motion sensors and enable drummers to imitate playing drums by stroking a virtual drum, are highly portable. However, drummers, who are used to playing real drums, have difficulty in demonstrating their drum skills with virtual drums because of the lack of feedback from stroking, low sound quality, and so on. Our proposed *Airstic Drum* achieves high portability and performance quality by integrating real and virtual drums. *Airstic Drum* can distinguish the stroking of virtual drums from the stroking of real drums, and it outputs digital sound only when the drummer strokes virtual drums. We have developed a prototype system and evaluated its effectiveness by actual use.

Keywords: Virtual drum, Real drum, Motion recognition.

1 Introduction

Drum kits are composed of various kinds of percussion instruments, such as snare drums, bass drums, and cymbals. Since each percussion instrument is large and heavy, it is inconvenient for drummers to carry and set up. This means that drummers usually use drum kits arranged at a venue beforehand such as club or ball room, and sometimes the kits lack some percussion instruments that the drummers want to use.

The electronic drum kit SPD-S [1], which has a flat surface divided into several electronic pads, has high portability, assigns various tones to each pad, and outputs sounds. However, it is difficult for drummers to apply conventional drumming techniques to it, because the layout of the electronic drums is completely different from that of real drums. Recently, virtual drums have been developed, such as Wii Music [2], WorldBeat [3], V-beat Air Drum [4], Virtual Xylophone [5], and Lightning [6], which enable drummers to output drum sounds by mimicking the motion of stroking a real drum. Virtual drums do not restrict space for

A. Nijholt, T. Romão, and D. Reidsma (Eds.): ACE 2012, LNCS 7624, pp. 57–69, 2012.
© Springer-Verlag Berlin Heidelberg 2012

playing because they do not require a real upper drumhead, and generate many percussion sounds using a sound generator. However, since drummers are not stroking a real drum, the drumming motion is harder to control. This prevents the drummers from keeping tempos and playing drum-rolls, rim-shots, and so on. Drummers, who are used to playing real drums, have difficulty in utilizing their drumming techniques with virtual drums. In this way, real and virtual drums have advantages and disadvantages. To solve this problem, we focus on the difference in frequency of using real drums. If we apply less frequently used drums to virtual drums, we achieve high portability and can keep the performance quality.

Therefore, the goal of our study is to construct *Airstic Drum* for integrating real and virtual drums. *Airstic Drum* can distinguish the stroking of virtual drums from the stroking of real drums on the basis of the data of an acceleration sensor and a gyro sensor that are embedded in the drum sticks, and it outputs digital sound only when drummers stroke virtual drums.

The remainder of this paper is organized as follows. Section 2 explains related work. Section 3 describes the design of *Airstic Drum*, and Section 4 explains the implementation of a prototype system. Section 5 describes evaluative experiment, and Section 6 explains the actual use. Finally, Section 7 gives conclusions and outlines future work.

2   Related Work

Some researchers have developed virtual drums, such as Wii Music, WorldBeat, V-beat Air Drum, Virtual Xylophone, and Lightning. For example, in Wii Music, a player uses a controller equipped with motion sensors. It outputs drum noises on the basis of stroking motion, which is recognized using acceleration data. Players can control drum sounds by changing the stroke of the controller. Users can enjoy playing the drum anytime and anywhere, but its performance quality is low because of the lack of feedback from stroking the virtual drum, and the low sound quality of virtual drums. While these electronic instruments are similar to the proposed system in controlling sounds by changing motion, they are not assumed to be used with existing instruments.

T. M. Patola evaluated the difference in performance quality between real drums and virtual drums, and described how virtual drums were difficult for keeping tempos accurately compared with real drums [7]. M. Collicutt et al. investigated the difference in motion between playing real drums and a virtual drum [8]. Trial users used four real percussion instruments and one virtual percussion instrument, and stroked each percussion in single and double strokes. The authors confirmed that when making a single stroke, players tended to raise their hand to a similar height with all the percussion instruments. On the other hand, the lack of tactile feedback made double stroking difficult, which resulted in low performance quality. The results of these experiments show that the performance with the virtual drums prevents drummers from fully displaying their

Usage of virtual drum

Fig. 1. An example of virtual drums

drum skills. In this research, we use the virtual drum in place of less frequently used real drums to improve the portability and keep the performance quality as much as possible.

3   Design

To solve the problems of the low portability of real drums and the low performance quality of virtual drums, we designed the *Airstic Drum* from the following policies:

(1) The support of real drums: We assume that *Airstic Drum* will be used in the performance in which a drummer uses real drums. It is difficult for the drummer to play the conventional virtual drums and the real drums at the same time, as drummers require high performance quality of the drums in concerts. They value the high performance quality of the real drums over the portability of the virtual drums. However, the frequency of usage of each drum is different. For example, standard drums such as hi-hats, snare drums, and bass drums are used frequently, but percussion instruments that are used as accents in music, such as the cymbal, the cowbell, and the mark tree, are used much less often when playing drums. We achieve high portability and performance quality by swapping less frequently used drums for virtual drums. Furthermore, we propose a recognition method that allows users to play both virtual and real drums at the same manner.

(2) Utilizing accumulated drum skills: Conventional electronic percussion instruments, such as SPD-S, which are composed of multiple drum pads, are extremely portable. When drummers, who is used to real drums, first use the electronic percussion instruments, they must practice using them due to the

Fig. 2. Control of outputs

difference in the layout and the size. On the other hand, our proposed system exploits the techniques that drummers have mastered with real drums. For example, as shown in Figure 1, when users play a drum set composed of real drums and a virtual cymbal, the proposed system distinguishes between stroking real drums and stroking virtual drums. When the system recognizes a virtual drum stroke, the system outputs an electronic cymbal sound as shown in Figure 2. If the system detects stroking of a real drum, it does not output any sound. In this way, drummers can use the proposed system without special training.

3.1   System Structure

Figure 3 shows a system structure of the *Airstic Drum*. This system consists of the drumsticks equipped with an acceleration sensor, a gyro sensor, a PC, and a MIDI sound generator. The sensor data are sent to the PC by wireless communication. The PC recognizes stroking motion on the basis of the sensor data and sends MIDI messages to the MIDI sound generator to output sounds when the PC recognizes the motion of the virtual drum.

3.2   Recognition Method for Stroking Motion

The proposed system recognizes the stroking motion of real and virtual drums. As it is a serious problem if sound is output with some delay after motion, we propose a motion recognition method that has high-speed recognition with

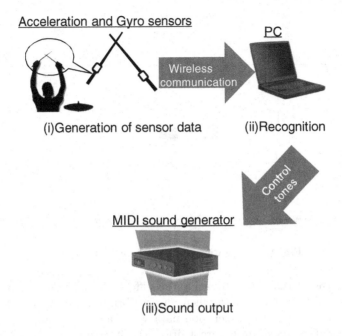

Fig. 3. System structure

enough accuracy. We investigated acceleration and gyro data in stroking a hi-hat, floor tom, and ride cymbal of real drums so as to prevent false recognition of virtual drums in the stroking of real drums. Figure 4 shows waves of acceleration and gyro data in the stroking of a real drum used as a typical part of a drum kit and a virtual drum.

Looking at the wave of the hi-hat, the acceleration data of the real drum are different from those of the virtual drum. Though the vibration (Figure 4 red square (i)) arising from stroking a hi-hat is a particular phenomenon, when the system uses this feature, sound delay arises. It is difficult to use this particular vibration to distinguish between the stroking of the hi-hat and the virtual drum. We should focus on the acceleration data of bringing the arm down when stroking the hi-hat. When the drummer brings his/her arm down to stroke the hi-hat and the stick hits the hi-hat, the acceleration drops rapidly and vibration occurs. On the other hand, when stroking the virtual drum, the drummer brings his/her arm down to stroke the hi-hat and the stick hits the hi-hat, the acceleration does not drop rapidly, since a drummer has to stop the stroking motion by himself/herself. Therefore, the hi-hat's duration (referred to as *Through Time* in this paper) from the time that it goes over a threshold (referred to as *Standard Strength* in this paper) to the time that the acceleration data go down the *Standard Strength* is different from that of the virtual drum, as shown by the blue circles in Figure 4. For example, if *Standard Strength* is 4000mG, *Through Time* is from 5ms to 15ms in stroking the hi-hat and is from 25ms to 40ms in stroking the virtual drum. The proposed system distinguishes the stroking of the hi-hat

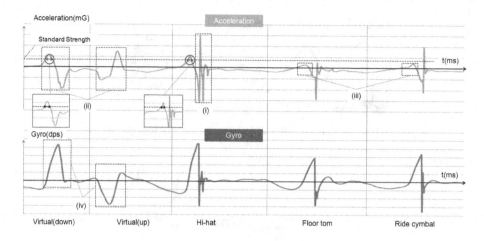

Fig. 4. Acceleration and gyro data of stroking

from that of the virtual drum by using the difference in *Through Time*. Additionally, acceleration sensor data when an user bring down the arm to stroke the virtual drum and the acceleration data when an user brings up the arm are symmetrical, as shown in Figure 4 (ii). If the system uses only the *Through Time*, the system recognizes bringing the arm up as a drum stroke as shown in Figure 4 (ii). To solve this problem, we use the data of the gyro sensor as well. The gyro sensor data of bringing the stick up are typically different from those of bringing the stick down, as shown in Figure 4 (iv).

For stroking the floor tom and the ride cymbal, the acceleration data before the stick hits the drums are fewer than those of stroking the virtual drums, as shown in Figure 4 (iii). This means that these strokes do not influence the recognition of stroking a virtual drum because the acceleration data do not exceed *Standard Strength* before the stick hits the drums. Also, while the vibration arises after the stick hits the drums, this feature does not influence the recognition because *Through Time* of stroking a real drum is shorter than that of virtual drums.

3.3   Deciding of Threshold Value

The proposed system requires high accuracy and high speed recognition for the stroking of virtual drums. The stroking motion is different for each drummer. The proposed system measures acceleration and gyro data of each player in advance and sets appropriate *Standard Strength* and *Through Time* for each player. For example, Table 1 shows recognition results from playing a phrase 10 times that involves stroking the virtual drum assigned to the crash cymbal used as part of a typical drum kit at the beginning of an 8-beat pattern, as shown in Figure 5. The recognition ratio shown in Table 1 is calculated on the basis of the true positive, which is the recognition ratio of playing a virtual drum (the left value on each cell in the table) and the true negative, which is the non-recognition

Table 1. Recognition ratio of each Standard Strength and Through Time

Standard Strength(mG)	Through Time(ms)						
	10	15	20	25	30	35	40
2000	90.0-54.3*	90.0-55.0	90.0-56.4	90.0-57.9	90.0-58.6	90.0-63.6	90.0-69.3
2500	95.0-60.0	95.0-61.4	95.0-64.3	95.0-69.3	95.0-75.0	95.0-81.4	95.0-87.1
3000	95.0-71.4	95.0-73.6	95.0-77.1	95.0-82.9	95.0-87.9	95.0-95.0	90.0-97.9
3500	100-80.0	100-87.1	100-91.4	100-95.0	100-97.1	95.0-100	65.0-100
4000	100-95.0	100-95.0	100-100	100-100	90.0-100	70.0-100	45.0-100
4500	100-98.6	100-100	100-100	95.0-100	75.0-100	60.0-100	15.0-100
5000	100-100	100-100	100-100	85.0-100	65.0-100	35.0-100	5.0-100
5500	100-100	100-100	90.0-100	75.0-100	55.0-100	20.0-100	0-100
6000	100-100	95.0-100	85.0-100	60.0-100	25.0-100	5.0-100	0-100
6500	90.0-100	80.0-100	65.0-100	45.0-100	15.0-100	0-100	0-100
7000	85.0-100	80.0-100	50.0-100	20.0-100	5.0-100	0-100	0-100

*True positive- True negative

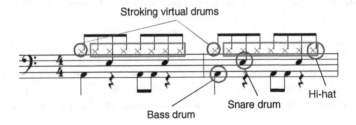

Fig. 5. 8-beat in stroking hi-hats

ratio of virtual drum in playing real drums (the right value on each cell in the table). The recognition ratio, of *Standard Strength* from 4000mG to 6000mG and *Through Time* from 10ms to 25ms, is 100%. We adopted values at the midpoint of a 100% recognition ratio area as the threshold value of *Standard Strength* and that of *Through Time*. In this case, the *Standard Strength* is 5000mG and the *Through Time* is 15ms.

3.4   Changing Sound by Stroking Direction

Our system allows users to control output sounds of virtual drums by orientation of stroking, as shown in Figure 6. The proposed system calculates the orientation by integrating gyro data. Furthermore, the orientation data help the system improve the recognition ratio the of stroking of real drums and virtual drums. For example, as shown in Figure 6, the proposed system prevents false recognition because the hi-hats of real drum are not set up in the area of the virtual china cymbal.

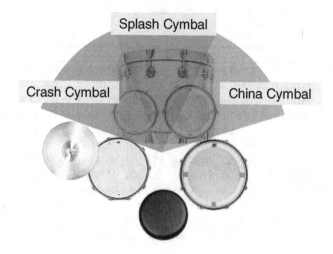

Fig. 6. An example of extension of sounds in detecting stroking position

3.5 Volume Control

The proposed system controls the sound volume of virtual drums to enable drummers to play virtual drums well. The sound volume is decided on the basis of the peak value of the acceleration data during the stroking of virtual drums.

3.6 Cut Off Sounds by Being Output Mistakenly

The system recognizes the output timing of sound by only using the motion of bringing the arm down when stroking. In this recognition, if the sound of virtual drums is output mistakenly when real drums are played, it interrupts the performance. Therefore, we propose a function that cuts off the sound that is output mistakenly at once when the player strokes a real drum. As described in Section 3.2, after the stroking of real drums, the vibration of acceleration data arises as a particular phenomenon. The proposed system uses this feature to cut the sound that is output mistakenly. To use this function, the proposed system will possibly minimize performance interruption.

4 Implementation

We implemented a prototype *Airstic drum,* as shown on the left in Figure 7. The inside of the prototype drumstick is shown on the right in Figure 7. The drumstick is the wooden type that is used in general drum performances and is attached with Wireless Technology WAA-010, equipped with a 3-dimensional

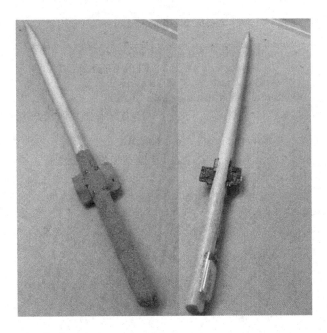

Fig. 7. A prototype of Airstic Drum

acceleration sensor and a 3-dimensional gyro sensor. The WAA-010 is attached to the middle of the drum stick so as not to touch fingers. Table 2 shows the specifications of WAA-010. We implemented a prototype system on Windows 7 using Microsoft Visual ++.NET 2008. Also, we used Roland SD-20 as a MIDI sound generator. Figure 8 shows a screenshot of the application for prototype. A user can set values of *Standard Strength* and *Through Time*, select the drum sounds, confirm the orientation of a drumstick and waves of acceleration and gyro data in stroking drums, and so on with the this application.

5   Evaluation

We conducted an evaluative experiment to investigate the recognition ratio to confirm the effectiveness of the proposed system.

In this evaluation, we used a phrase shown in Figure 5 as a trial phrase. The phrase uses the virtual drum as a crash cymbal, the hi-hat, the floor tom, and the ride cymbal. The virtual drum is only used at the beginning of each 8-beat pattern. The sound of the virtual drum is a digital sound produced by a MIDI sound generator and other percussion sounds are output from an acoustic drum kit. Testers repeated the phrase 10 times in this evaluation. Tempo is 100bpm (beats per minute). Two male university students took part in this evaluation. Both testers were experienced drummers and were able to play the trial phrase with the acoustic drum kit fully.

Table 2. Specification

Communications standards	Bluetooth Ver 2.0
	+ EDR Class 2
Baud rate	2.1Mbps
Communication distance	Up to 10m
Size	39(W)×44(H)×12(D)mm
Weight	20g
Power source	230mAh
	Lithium polymer battery

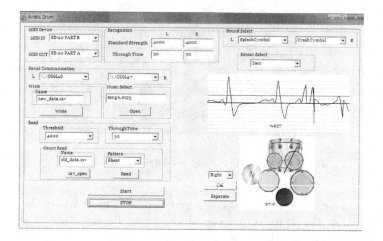

Fig. 8. Screenshot of the proposed application

Table 3 shows that the proper threshold values should be a 100% recognition rate when each tester strokes each percussion instrument. Also, Table 4 shows the recognition ratio of each tester stroking each percussion instrument using the threshold value adapted for each tester in Table 3. The recognition ratio shown in Table 4 is calculated on the basis of the true positive, which is the recognition ratio of playing a virtual drum (the left value on each cell in the table) and the true negative, which is the non-recognition ratio of virtual drum in playing real drums (the right value on each cell in the table).

As shown in Table 4, when Tester A played using the threshold value adapted for him, recognition ratio was 100% in all patterns and all percussion instruments. Also, when each tester played threshold values that were not adapted for themselves, for Tester A a false positive while playing real drums occurred, and for Tester B a false negative while playing virtual drums occurred. These results arose because the threshold value of Tester A's *Standard Strength* is higher than that of Tester B as a whole, and the threshold value of Tester B's *Through Time* is shorter than that of Tester A. Analyzing the performance data of Tester B, the

Table 3. The threshold value of each tester and each percussion instrument

	Tester A			Tester B		
	HH	FT	RD	HH	FT	RD
Standard Strength(mG)	5000	4500	4500	4500	3500	3500
Through Time(ms)	25	25	25	20	20	15

Table 4. The recognition ratio using the threshold value for each tester [%]

		Threshold of Tester A			Threshold of Tester B		
		HH	FT	RD	HH	FT	RD
	HH	100-100*	100-100	100-100	100-100	100-100	100-100
Tester A	FT	100-100	100-100	100-100	100-90.0	100-99.3	95.0-100
	RD	100-100	100-100	100-100	100-86.4	100-98.8	100-100
	HH	85.0-100	70.0-100	70.0-100	100-100	100-100	95.0-100
Tester B	FT	95.0-100	90.0-100	90.0-100	100-91.4	100-100	100-100
	RD	95.0-100	90.0-100	90.0-100	100-87.1	100-100	100-100

* True positive - True negative
HH:Hi-hat, FT:Floor tom, RD:Ride cymbal

motion of raising and lowering a drumstick was small when he stroked virtual drums. From the difference in the stroking motion among drummers, a different threshold value evidently exists for each drummer. Moreover, when both testers used the threshold value with which Tester B stroked hi-hats, false positives were seen in stroking real drums. Compared with stroking a floor tom or a ride cymbal, when drummers stroke the hi-hats several times in a row, such as an 8-beat pattern, an *up-down stroking* motion, in which drummers stroke both the edge and the top of the hi-hats in one stroke, is used frequently. With this playing style, when drummers perform a phrase in which stroking motion tends to change, the threshold value has a bias. Therefore, it is necessary to investigate the data in all kinds of phrases.

6   Actual Use

We used the prototype at the Illumine Kobe [9] event on December 12th, 2010, as shown in Figure 9. The drummer is the first author of this paper. At this event, he performed with an electric bass guitarist. He used two drumsticks equipped with sensors, and both sticks output different digital sounds. The performance quality with the proposed system was similar as that with a complete set of real drums. However, in stroking virtual drums, sometimes digital sound was not output due to non-recognition. The lack of sound is a serious problem that decreases performance quality. We need to investigate how to recognize the stroke of virtual drums with higher accuracy.

Fig. 9. Actual performance at Illumine Kobe in 2010

7   Conclusions

In this research, we constructed *Airstic Drum*, which integrates real and virtual drums. The proposed drumstick enables integration of virtual and real drums by recognizing the stroking motion using the acceleration and the gyro data unlike conventional virtual drums that must be used alone. Because in order not to output digital sounds of virtual drums when stroking real drums, drummers do not have to use particular motion that is different from usual drum playing, so drummers can use their conventional drumming technique. Moreover, the proposed system detects the orientation of stroking to change output sounds of the virtual drum. Also, drummers can control the sound volume of virtual drums by changing the stroking motion. Experimental results showed that the use of a proper threshold for each drummer enables effective integration of real and virtual drums.

For future work, we plan to reproduce the playing style of real drums in virtual drums and to increase the perception of the drummers and audience by visual feedback of stroking.

Acknowledgments. This research was supported in part by a Grant in aid for Precursory Research for Embryonic Science and Technology (PRESTO) from the Japan Science and Technology Agency and by a Grant-in-Aid for Scientific Research (A)(20240009) and Scientific Research for Young Scientists (B)(21700198) from the Japanese Ministry of Education, Culture, Sports, Science and Technology.

References

1. SPD-S, http://www.roland.com/products/en/SPD-S/
2. Wii Music, http://www.wiimusic.com/launch/
3. Borchers, J.O.: WorldBeat: Designing a Baton-Based Interface for an Interactive Music Exhibit. In: Proc. of the International Conference on Human Factors in Computing Systems (CHI 1997), pp. 131–138 (March 1997)
4. Silverlit V-beat AirDrum, http://www.silverlit.com/product_04.html
5. Patola, T.M., Kanerva, A., Laitinen, J., Takala, T.: Experiments with Virtual Reality Instruments. In: Proc. of the International Conference on New Interfaces for Musical Expression (NIME 2005), pp. 11–16 (May 2005)
6. Lightning, http://www.buchla.com/lightning3.html
7. Patola, T.M.: User Interface Comparison for Virtual Drums. In: Proc. of the International Conference on New Interfaces for Musical Expression (NIME 2005), pp. 144–147 (May 2005)
8. Collicutt, M., Casciato, C., Wanderley, M.M.: From Real to Virtual: A Comparison of Input Devices for Percussion Tasks. In: Proc. of the International Conference on New Interfaces for Musical Expression (NIME 2009), pp. 1–6 (June 2009)
9. Illumine KOBE 2010, http://cse.eedept.kobe-u.ac.jp/illumineKOBE2010/main.html

Enhancing Level Difficulty and Additional Content in Platform Videogames through Graph Analysis

Fausto Mourato[1], Fernando Birra[2], and Manuel Próspero dos Santos[2]

[1] Escola Superior de Tecnologia - Instituto Politécnico de Setúbal, Portugal
`fausto.mourato@estsetubal.ips.pt`
[2] Faculdade de Ciências e Tecnologia - Universidade Nova de Lisboa, Portugal
`{fpb,ps}@di.fct.unl.pt`

Abstract. In this article we present a system that enhances content in platform game levels. This is achieved by adding particular gaming entities and adjusting their arrangement, causing consequent changes in the inherent difficulty and in path related aspects. This idea follows our prior work for the automatic creation of level environments. Starting with a primal level structure and a corresponding graph that sketches the user path, the system detects mandatory and optional path sections and adapts them in order to create more elaborate challenges to the user, forcing detours to gather specific objects or trigger certain events. Alternatively, a designer can create that base level structure and use the algorithm to adapt it to a certain profile. Also, some adjustments can be made to enhance multiplayer cooperative gaming for uneven skilled players, where the path is adapted to force a difficult route to one player and an easier one for the other player. Our experiments showed interesting results on some popular games, where it is possible to observe the previous principles put into practise. The approach is generic and can be expanded to other similar games.

1 Introduction

This article presents an approach to improve Procedural Content Generation (PCG) techniques used in the context of automatic level generation for two-dimensional platform videogames. Typically, in a platform videogame, the user controls the movement of a character (or various users control their respective characters, for multiplayer games) in a scenario, performing jumps to avoid terrain gaps and traps and overcoming opponents in a simple manner, such as jumping over the enemy or shooting him with a certain weapon. In the context of PCG, this type of videogames has been interesting to study because its mechanics raises several non-trivial questions on the process of automatic level creation. At first, it is important to ensure that level elements are positioned to provide a valid level where the user can fulfill a goal. In addition, the element positioning must make sense as a whole, resulting in a visually plausible scenario. Also, the level has to represent an appropriate rhythmic set of actions that the user should complete in order to keep him/her engaged. Finally, it is also important to take into account that those actions represent a challenge with a certain difficulty that has to be perceived and estimated.

A. Nijholt, T. Romão, and D. Reidsma (Eds.): ACE 2012, LNCS 7624, pp. 70–84, 2012.
© Springer-Verlag Berlin Heidelberg 2012

In the scope of this work, the following platform videogames will be referred in order to support our tests and examples:

- *Infinite Mario Bros.*, an open-source *platformer* inspired by the classic videogame *Super Mario Bros.*, which has been used frequently in academia, namely in the development of intelligent agents to control the main character [14] and automatic level generation [9].
- The original version of the videogame *Prince of Persia*, which has unofficial level editors and technical details available online, as well as the recently released source code for the original *Apple* version of the game. This videogame has already been considered in research on the topic of computational complexity [15].
- *XRick*, an open-source remake of the original videogame *Rick Dangerous* which combines the free movement of *Infinite Mario Bros.* with closed environments similar to those in *Prince of Persia*.

The main motivation of this work is to provide content richness and personalization to platform levels that are created automatically in addition to simple linear gameplay. As we will see later in Section 2, where related work is unveiled, there are some interesting approaches on the subject of automatic level generation for platform games. Nevertheless, the main focus of the existing techniques typically goes to physical validity and definition of interesting sequences of challenges and actions without any particular meaning or context. This approach intends to be complementary as an additional step to any valid geometry generator, providing improvements in the content, such as:

- **Difficulty adjustment**, tuning the level to a certain player profile.
- **Challenge content improvement**, through the establishment of a non-linear path that consists of identifiable tasks such as, for instance, exiting the main path to grab a certain item and getting back to use it.
- **Inclusion of optional content**, as the system detects optional areas, which can be filled with bonus content defined by the game designer.
- **Multiplayer difficulty adjustments**, to adapt levels to be used simultaneously by players of distinct skills.

Our system starts with an imperfect level structure, which might be a basic geometry without additional gaming entities, and a corresponding graph. This graph is extracted from a list of rules that estimate the character's most relevant movements creating an approximate representation of the players' possible paths. Furthermore, the referred graph is analysed and every vertex is contextualized regarding its role on the objective of going from the starting point to the final position. After this graph analysis, a set of possible modifications is extracted. Some changes are iteratively selected from the referred set in order to reach a certain final value regarding level difficulty or length. Section 3 contains the details of this approach and explanations about how the system works. In Section 4 we will show some of the obtained results. An example case is provided and the generated changes are explained. Also, some performance questions are analysed and the usage in other games is considered. Finally, in Section 5 we will present the main conclusions and guidelines for future work.

2   Related Work

Platform videogames, in particular in the context of automatic content generation, started to be studied in academic context by Compton and Mateas [1] with an analysis of the main components and the definition of a conceptual model to define this type of games. Later, a more detailed analysis has been presented by Smith *et al.* [10]. In this work, authors suggest a conceptual hierarchy to define the entities that compose a platform game level. Those principles were used in the definition of a technique to automatically generate levels based on the rhythm associated to player's input and actions [11], which has been applied in the prototype *Launchpad* [13]. The main goal behind this idea is to keep the user in a mind state that Csikszentmihalyi's referred as Flow [2], representing the ideal feeling of control and immersion over a challenging task. It can be seen briefly as a state in-between boredom and frustration, meaning that the task is, respectively, too easy or too difficult. Smith *et al.* also studied the expressivity of this approach [12] regarding linearity and leniency, an approximation to the concept of difficulty. Finally, following the same line of work, the system *Polymorph* presented by Jennings-Teats *et al.* [3] is an effort to adapt difficulty directly in the generation process as the player is moving forward in the scenario. The presented ideas provide an interesting way to generate good challenges but they tend to be mainly directed to the creation of straightforward games in open scenarios or simple casual game environments. Still, it is possible to have an initial generation step based on those principles and a further step to complement the content as the one proposed on this article.

Another important work to refer with similar features was presented by Pedersen *et al.* [8], focusing the already referred game *Infinite Mario Bros.* Levels are generated according to certain parameters. In particular, parameterization was applied to the following aspects: existing gaps in the level, average gap size, gap distribution entropy and number of direction switches. The main study focused on the concept of difficulty and possible adjustments to fit the user skills but, again, the generation process is directed to the construction of a sequence of jumps without a particular semantic meaning, preventing this method to be directly applied to other games.

A different approach was proposed by Mawhorter and Mateas [4]. The main principle is the composition of a whole level based on small pre-authored chunks, which can be assembled together. This allows a more varied set of outputs, depending on the number, type and variety of chunks that are considered. Although the authors also focused the game *Infinite Mario Bros.* we believe that this is a valid principle for other videogames, in particular for the generation of scenarios that represent closed environments with rooms interconnected with tunnels. These structures are likely to be obtained using merely small-sized chunks. For instance, the videogame *Spelunky*, a platform like adventure game, uses very similar principles and consists on that type of environments.

Another example of automatic level generation was proposed by Mourato *et al.* [6], using evolutionary computation, in particular genetic algorithms, to search for good solutions according to design heuristics applied to a fitness function and mutation and crossover operators.

One exceptional case that is directed to complementary content rather than simple movement and jumps was presented by Nygren *et al.* [7]. The authors proposed a method to integrate puzzle based content that requires the player to explore the level. It involves a three step process which consists, namely, in: graph generation, graph to level structure transformation and content creation. In the first step, a graph of possible positions is randomly created using genetic algorithms. That graph is then transformed in a valid geometry that fits those movements, with a search-based process. Finally and again with a search-based process, possible modifications are identified for each level segment from which one is selected to meet certain criteria. Once again, the experiments were directed to the videogame *Infinite Mario Bros.*. In some of the results it is possible to notice the existence of multiple alternatives and paths that lead to a dead-end, thus creating an exploratory theme. In our approach, as we will further see, similar situations are identified but, in this case, the adjustment algorithm takes advantage of those features to compose additional challenges and force exploration.

3   Iterative Content Adaptation Algorithm

In this section we describe the details of our technique. As stated, it works as a complement to a previously created level structure, which has to be valid regarding possible paths but that can be incomplete regarding gaming entities such as enemies, traps or doors. Therefore, we will start by presenting the initial conditions and requirements. Afterwards, we will cover the graph processing principles and the main steps on the level enhancement based on that processing.

3.1   Initial Conditions and Content

As previously referred, our algorithm works on a graph based analysis. This means that, in addition to the basic level structure, it is required to have a graph representation of that structure or a method to obtain it. In this topic, our approach works in the inverse order of the technique proposed by Nygren *et al.* that was previously presented, as we extract the graph from the geometry instead of creating the geometry to a certain graph. As previously stated, the main advantage of our approach is that we not only identify alternative paths and detours but also use them to place additional gaming entities to encourage exploration.

It is important to clarify that we are working with directed graphs, as some transitions might be unidirectional, such as the character falling into a hole, which has no way back. To provide a clearer notation, we will avoid mixing representations. Therefore, all edges will be considered to be directed and the cases of undirected edges connecting vertices v_1 and v_2 will be represented as a directed edge from v_1 to v_2 and another directed edge from v_2 to v_1. Besides the notation issues, in some cases this distinction would be also mandatory because costs from v_1 to v_2 and from v_2 to v_1 might be different, as they may represent, for instance, a difficulty measure.

In our tests, we have been working with a grid based level representation where we have defined a set of pattern matching rules to extract the graph. In Figure 1, we present two examples of rules, composed by a pattern (on the left) and the corresponding graph entries (on the right) in the context of the game *Infinite Mario Bros.*. The complete set of rules is applied by going through the entire level grid searching for matches. Figure 2 shows a sample of the first level of the game *Prince of Persia* (on the left) and the corresponding graph (on the right) that will be considered on the analysis. That graph was obtained with the referred cell based pattern matching approach.

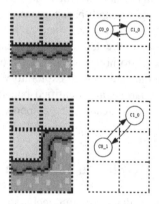

Fig. 1. Example of two rules for graph construction, consisting of a pattern (on the left) and the corresponding graph entry (on the right)

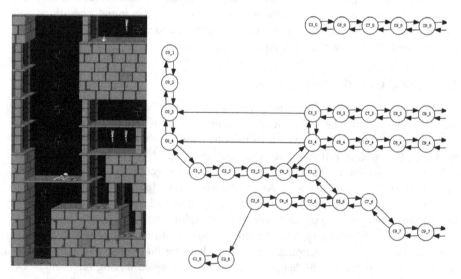

Fig. 2. A sample of the first level of the game *Prince of Persia* (on the left) and the corresponding extracted graph (on the right)

The usage of this approach allows fast calculations over the level structure without requiring modeling all the physical rules implemented on the game. Still, alternative techniques that provide a similar graph structure might be considered. For instance, Mawhorter and Mateas' chunk based approach, presented on the related work, uses anchor points in the construction process that work as possible character positions. It is plausible to consider that those anchors can be used to extract the graph in a similar way as the solution that we have explained before.

Another aspect that is important to take into account is that graph vertices represent only spatial information and do not contain any additional information about the character or game state. We have also done some experiments with that in mind, considering that a level cell may provide or require a certain item. For instance, one cell may provide the user a key and another cell may represent a door that requires that same key. However, this tends to increase significantly the graph structure. For every character's reference position, all combinations of items in the character's inventory must be considered, which means that, considering an original graph with n vertices corresponding to the reference positions, we will have a new graph with $n.2^i$ vertices, with i being the number of existing items in the level.

3.2   Graph Initial Processing

In order to reduce the computational effort of the algorithm, the first step is a graph compression that results on a reduced version with a smaller amount of vertices and edges. This compression involves removing vertices that are not significant to path computation processes and that can be seen as obvious intermediate steps in major transitions. In particular, the two following rules are applied:

- If a certain vertex v has exactly one incoming edge e_0 (from v_0) and one outgoing edge e_1 (to v_1), this means that, regarding path calculations, v is just a transitional step from v_0 to v_1. In this case, vertex v and edges e_0 and e_1 are removed from the graph structure. A new edge is created directly from v_0 to v_1 with a cost corresponding to the sum of the previous costs defined for e_0 and e_1.
- If a certain vertex v has exactly two outgoing edges e_{O1} and e_{O2} (to v_1 and v_2, respectively) and two incoming edges e_{I1} and e_{I2} from the same vertices, this means, in a similar way to the previous rule, that the vertex v is an intermediate step in the connection between v_1 and v_2 in both directions. Again, this vertex is removed and the previous edges are also replaced by one edge from v_1 to v_2 with a cost value summing the costs associated with e_{I1} and e_{O1} and another edge from v_2 to v_1 with a cost that sums those from e_{I2} and e_{O2}.

An example of the compression mechanism is provided in Figure 3, which contains a compressed version of the original graph represented in Figure 2.

Some restriction might apply in vertex removal. For instance, vertices corresponding to the start and end position should not be eliminated, as they have an active role on the level. This was implemented with the definition of a set of irremovable vertices.

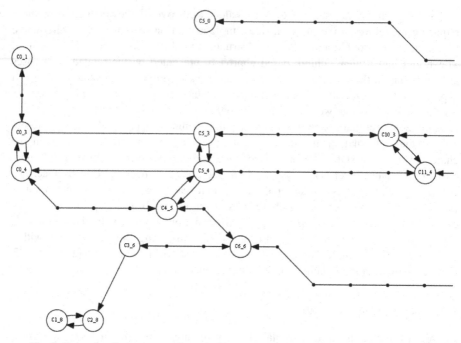

Fig. 3. Example of a compressed graph. The compressed nodes are marked with dots.

In addition, some particular compression schemes might be deliberated depending on the game that is being considered. For instance, in the videogame *Prince of Persia*, it is common to have the situation represented on the left part of Figure 4, which will be represented by the corresponding graph that can be seen on the right part of that same figure. The triangular shape represented on the graph image by the three interconnected nodes could be merged into a single node without compromising path calculations. As another example, with a simple rule set, hill platforms in the game *Infinite Mario Bros.* will tend to create excessive vertical movement alternatives and prevent vertex compression, such as the case in presented in Figure 5. Vertices corresponding to the middle cells of the hill platform could be removed without compromising path analysis.

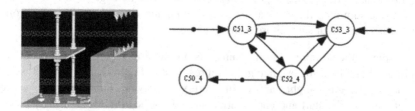

Fig. 4. An example of a potential additional graph compression in the game *Prince of Persia*

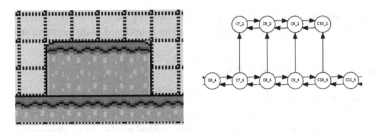

Fig. 5. An example of a potential graph compression case in the game *Infinite Mario Bros*

3.3   Path Extraction and Vertex Classification

Having a compressed graph representing the level, the next step consists on categorizing the meaning of each vertex considering all routes between the start and the end of the level. The algorithm searches every possible path from the level entry to the level exit, using a breadth first search and ignoring all alternatives that visit the same vertex multiple times.

Following this step, every vertex is labelled with one of the following values:

1. **Mandatory**, if the vertex exists on all calculated paths;
2. **Optional**, if the vertex is only on some of the calculated paths;
3. **Dead-end**, if the vertex is not part of any possible path and has only one outgoing edge to a certain vertex and one incoming edge from that same vertex, meaning that if the character reaches that position he/she has obligatorily to go back;
4. **Unreachable**, if the position that corresponds to the vertex cannot be reached by the game character;
5. **Vain**, if there is no way back from that vertex to the main path;
6. **Path to Dead-end**, to all remaining vertices that, by exclusion, have the only purpose of providing passage from mandatory or optional vertices to a dead-end.

In addition, a tree is created representing path segments and alternatives for each segment, recursively. Leaf nodes represent trivial graph transitions. In Figure 6 we present, on the left part, a simple graph and on the right part, the correspondent tree that was created.

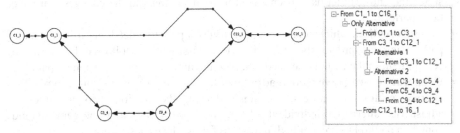

Fig. 6. Example of a graph (on the left) and the corresponding segment decomposition represented as a tree (on the right)

Also, difficulty is estimated for each established segment, allowing a direct shortest path calculation even if difficulty in some segments is updated to different values.

3.4   Level Completion Algorithm

The level completion algorithm adjusts the level focusing on difficulty and similar related aspects. For the definition of the algorithm itself, the exact concept of difficulty may remain undetailed and be implemented as the game designer considers best. The key idea that has to be present is that difficulty arises from base geometry such as jumps over gaps, from gaming entities, such as enemies and traps, and from path structure, which forces the user to accomplish additional jumps and to encounter additional gaming entities. By design, the algorithm will have little control over jumps, as it would require graph recalculations, but will have high focus on the control of additional gaming entities and the definition of a composed challenge.

Difficulty has been characterized and estimated in distinct ways. It can be seen as a success probability [5] or a sum of coefficients [13], among other alternatives.

For the purpose of this algorithm, the requisites are the following:

- A higher difficulty level means that the level is more difficult than another with a lower value.
- Every level segment can be analysed individually to produce a difficulty value.
- A succession of analysed sections with certain difficulty values produces a final difficulty value for that succession.

In the tests that we will present, we have considered a sum of coefficients approach, where every graph transition contain a certain value that can be estimated by the game designer or mapped to users' performance after some gaming sessions. Moreover, when the path section presents two or more alternatives, the difficulty value that is considered is the lowest, as we assume that the user would pick the easiest possible solution.

The algorithm is able to apply the following changes to the base level:

- **Change the difficulty of a segment**, which is done by adding or removing an enemy or a trap or making a gap larger or smaller. Again, this is achieved with a pattern matching rule set. The graph is kept the same but a parallel data structure stores the entities that have been added to each section and the changes that have been performed.
- **Detour creation**, which consists on identifying a path to a dead-end from the main path, using the previously referred vertex classification, followed by adding a certain item in the path to the dead-end and making it required on the main path.
- **Cooperative two player game adjustment**, consisting on identifying two parallel alternatives for one particular section and using the previous two principles to adjust each alternative individually for each player. In addition, the game should contain a method to prevent both players to follow the easiest alternative.
- **Bonus entity addition**, which consists on adding collectibles or minor power-ups on certain dead-ends, creating secondary goals for the player.

The previous changes occur based on probabilistic coefficients that are established by the system after analysing the following values:

- Total desired difficulty value (whole level);
- Mean desired difficulty value (per segment);
- Player state estimator for game state on each graph vertex, detecting periods of possible boredom, flow or frustration.

The algorithm works iteratively in multiple adjustment passages, with the level difficulty being analysed for each passage. The process stops when it reaches the desired value or a limit on the number of iterations. At the end of each step, the previous features are analysed and the probabilistic coefficients are defined for each path section. For instance, if the level is too short then the detour creation probability in each section is increased.

4   Results

The next example shows how a simple level can be tweaked by the system. We will consider the game *Prince of Persia* in particular because of the possibility of adding gates and step switches to open those gates, which is an interesting implementation of the referred detour creation concept.

We have manually created the level structure represented in the background of Figure 7, which is just a simple draft. The level does not contain enemies, gates, switches or any traps. The starting point is the door on the left side and the level ends when the character reaches the door on the right. The system extracted and compressed the level graph presented as on overlay on that same image. Nodes have been named according to their coordinates on the grid, also marked in the image for convenience.

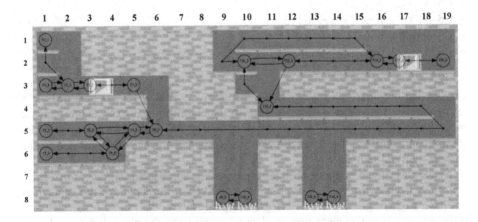

Fig. 7. The Graph generated from the example level

The system classified the vertices as follows:

- **Mandatory**: C3_3, C5_3, C6_5, C11_4, C10_2, C16_2, C17_2
- **Optional**: C12_2
- **Dead-end**: C1_1, C1_3, C1_5, C1_6, C19_2
- **Unreachable/ Vain**: C9_8, C10_8, C13_8, C14_8
- **Path to Dead-end**: C2_3, C3_5, C4_6, C5_5

In addition, the tree presented in Figure 8 was calculated.

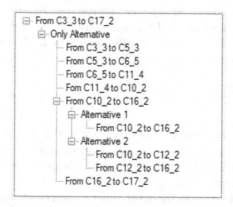

Fig. 8. Calculated tree with all possible paths from the beginning to the end of the level

The system also calculated routes to the existing dead ends. In this case, the system identified the possible routes:

- C2_3 → C1_3
- C2_3 → C1_1
- C5_5 → C3_5 → C1_5
- C5_5 → C4_6 → C3_5 → C1_5
- C5_5 → C4_6 →C1_6
- C5_5 → C3_5 → C4_6 →C1_6
- C17_2 → C19_2

Considering our approach for estimating difficulty, a value of 55 was obtained. As a test, we defined the desired value of 100, so the algorithm was expected to increase the existing difficulty. One example run presented the result (printed to console) showed on Figure 9. The changes were then applied to the level, generating the content showed in Figure 10.

As we have stated, we have been testing this same approach in *Infinite Mario Bros.* and *XRick*. In the first, the detour principle is unlikely to be applied as the game does not have triggering events or object gathering. However, the primal tests related to difficulty and bonus content presented good results and the algorithm was able to adapt level segments. Coins are willing to appear as bonus on dead-ends and the number of enemies vary to match desired difficulty. On Figure 11 we show an example of a randomly created level that has been perfected using our algorithm, matching a difficulty value defined by the user. As this game has a less restrictive set of movements, the entity placement is easier and less constrained. However, gap adjustments are hard to express because platforms can have different sizes and configurations.

```
Create Detour. Add button @ C1_1 and gate @ C5_3
Create Detour. Add button @ C1_5 and gate @ C8_5
Add guard @ C7_5
Add guard @ C17_5
Add spikes @ C18_5
Add guard @ C14_2
Add spikes @ C16_2
Final difficulty: 100
```

Fig. 9. Example of a set of computed modifications

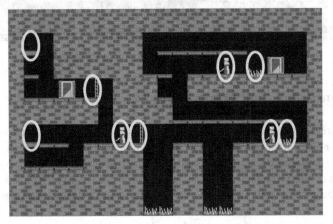

Fig. 10. Example of a tuned level for the game *Prince of Persia* (changes are marked with ellipses)

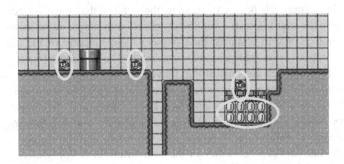

Fig. 11. Example of a tuned level for the game *Infinite Mario Bros.* (changes are marked with ellipses)

Regarding the game *XRick*, primal experiments have also been done with similar results. This is a game with strong emphasis on triggers, where the detour principle is applied. In Figure 12 it is possible to observe a level that was created with that in mind. The main structure was manually created with two obvious dead-ends accessible with the ladders. The system automatically added the two guards on the bottom, the bonus sphinx on the left dead-end and a trigger on the right dead-end, marked with a stick, which removes the spikes on the bottom allowing the character to go through in the path from the left entry to the right exit.

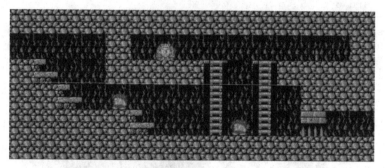

Fig. 12. Example of a tuned level for the game *XRick*

5   Conclusions and Future Work

We have presented a technique that, considering a roughly defined platform level and a corresponding graph, finalizes the level adding optional content and adjusting difficulty. The presented approach is mostly suitable for games that have somehow in its mechanics the principle of gathering certain objects or triggering some events to unlock passages. For this reason we focused with more emphasis the game *Prince of Persia*, where we could see how our algorithm included new content. In addition, primal experiments with other games showed promising results.

Filling a level structure with additional content and adapting paths to force some particular actions produces improvements in content richness to the topic of level generation. This approach brings context to the actions that must be performed in order to capture the user interest. Also, the proposed multiplayer adjustment algorithm allows cooperative play in a shared environment independently of the player skills, promoting gameplay as an interpersonal experience. The considered games and most of classic platform games are only single player, by which this particular concept is still theoretical. Some experiments were done assuming possible versions of *Prince of Persia* and *Infinite Mario Bros.* supporting two players and the output appeared coherent. For instance, in *Prince of Persia* a set of gates and triggers are placed to force one player to follow one passage and the other to follow another passage. Consequently, one aspect to consider in the near future is to apply effectively these principles to a multiplayer *platformer*. Currently, we are directing our attention to the game *Open Sonic*, an open-source game based on the popular videogame saga *Sonic – the Hedgehog* which allows this type of principle to be applied.

The approach for extracting a movement graph based on rules using patterns is an alternative to physical simulations as it provides a faster way to analyse level content.

Another goal that has been defined to a near future is to export the generated levels into the games to have users to play them. At the moment we have achieved that goal with *Infinite Mario Bros.* and *Prince of Persia*.

Acknowledgments. This work was partially funded by *Instituto Politécnico de Setúbal* under FCT/MCTES grant SFRH/PROTEC/67497/2010 and CITI under FCT/MCTES grant PEst-OE/EEI/UI0527/2011.

References

1. Compton, K., Mateas, M.: Procedural level design for platform games. In: Proceedings of the Artificial Intelligence and Interactive Digital Entertainment International Conference (AIIDE) (2006)
2. Csikszentmihaly, M.: Flow: The Psychology of Optimal Experience. Harper Collins, NY (1991)
3. Jennings-Teats, M., Smith, G., Wardrip-Fruin, N.: Polymorph: Dynamic Difficulty Adjustment through Level Generation. In: Proceedings of the Workshop on Procedural Content Generation in Games (2010)
4. Mawhorter, P., Mateas, M.: Procedural Level Generation Using Occupancy-Regulated Extension. In: CIG 2010 - IEEE Conference on Computational Intelligence and Games (2010)
5. Mourato, F., Próspero dos Santos, M.: Measuring Difficulty in Platform Games. In: Interacção 2010 – 4ª Conferência Nacional em Interacção Humano-Computador (2010)
6. Mourato, F., Próspero dos Santos, M., Birra, F.: Automatic level generation for platform videogames using Genetic Algorithms. In: ACE 2011, 8th International Conference on Advances in Computer Entertainment Technology (2011)
7. Nygren, N., Denzinger, J., Stephenson, B., Aycock, J.: User-preference-based automated level generation for platform games. In: IEEE Symposium on Computational Intelligence and Games (2011)
8. Pedersen, C., Togelius, J., Yannakakis, G.: Modeling player experience in Super Mario Bros. In: Proceedings of the 5th International Conference on Computational Intelligence and Games, CIG 2009 (2009)
9. Shaker, N., Togelius, J., Yannakakis, G., Weber, B., Shimizu, T., Hashiyama, T., Soreson, N., Pasquier, P., Mawhorter, P., Takahashi, G., Smith, G., Baumgarten, R.: The 2010 Mario AI Championship: Level Generation Track. Special Issue of IEEE Transactions on Procedural Content Generation (2010)
10. Smith, G., Cha, M., Whitehead, J.: A Framework for Analysis of 2D Platformer Levels. In: Proceedings of the 2008 ACM SIGGRAPH Symposium on Video Games, pp. 75–80 (2008)
11. Smith, G., Mateas, M., Whitehead, J., Treanor, M.: Rhythm-based level generation for 2D platformers. In: Proceedings of the 4th International Conference on Foundations of Digital Game (2009)
12. Smith, G., Whitehead, J.: Analyzing the Expressive Range of a Level Generator. In: Proceedings of the Workshop on PCG in Games, Monterey, CA (2010)

13. Smith, G., Whitehead, J., Mateas, M., Treanor, M., March, J., Cha, M.: Launchpad: A Rhythm-Based Level Generator for 2D Platformers. IEEE Transactions on Computational Intelligence and AI in Games (TCIAIG) 3(1) (2011)
14. Togelius, J., Karakovskiy, S., Baumgarten, R.: The 2009 Mario AI Competition. In: IEEE CEC - Congress on Evolutionary Computation (2010)
15. Viglietta, G.: Gaming Is a Hard Job, But Someone Has to Do It! In: Kranakis, E., Krizanc, D., Luccio, F. (eds.) FUN 2012. LNCS, vol. 7288, pp. 357–367. Springer, Heidelberg (2012)

A System for Supporting Performers in Stuffed Suits

Tatsuhiko Okazaki[1], Tsutomu Terada[1,2], and Masahiko Tsukamoto[1]

[1] Grad. Sch. of Engineering, Kobe University
[2] PRESTO, Japan Science and Technology Agency
tatsuhiko@stu.kobe-u.ac.jp, tsutomu@eedept.kobe-u.ac.jp
tuka@kobe-u.ac.jp

Abstract. Stuffed suits have been widely used at various events. However, performances with stuffed suits present two main difficulties in that performers are not aware of their postures because of the difference in the shape and size of the stuffed suits and the physical human body, and it is difficult for them to communicate smoothly with others because of limited visibility. These problems lead performers to train excessively to acquire a high degree of skill in performances. The main goal of our study was to construct a system to support performers in stuffed suits, which would enable them to act like the characters they represented. From the results we obtained from evaluating our prototype system, we confirmed that our method could effectively support performers in stuffed suits.

Keywords: Stuffed suits, HMD, Support.

1 Introduction

Stuffed suits are widely used at various theme parks and events because performances with them are popular with all ages, and it makes audiences smile and be happy. Performers in stuffed suits need to represent the characters they portray because they have to play the role of making characters in the virtual world appear in the real world. Posture and communication with others are the most important elements for them to portray characters credibly. However, performers in stuffed suits encounter two main difficulties: (1) they are unaware of their posture because of the difference in the shape and size of the stuffed suits and the physical human body, and (2) there is a difficulty in communicating smoothly with others because of limited visibility. In addition, since performers often gain visibility from parts other than the eyes of the character, they cannot look around by gazing when in stuffed suits. Therefore, they also cannot naturally communicate with others. To overcome these problems, performers have to train very hard to acquire high levels of skill in performances.

On the other hands, there has been many studies on user support with wearable computing technologies, such as Skinput [1] and A Haptic Wristwatch [2]. A user in wearable computing environments wears a computer, sensors, and actuators. Using this equipment, the computer knows the context of the user and provides various services in response to this context.

A. Nijholt, T. Romão, and D. Reidsma (Eds.): ACE 2012, LNCS 7624, pp. 85–100, 2012.

The goal of our study is to construct a system to support performers in stuffed suits, which will enable them to act like the characters the stuffed suits are meant to represent. The problems above occur because performers in stuffed suits cannot deal with them like they do with their own physical human bodies. Our system has two main functions to provide a sense of embodiment to the stuffed suits of performers, which support posing and enhance visibility. The results from evaluation indicated that our system could effectively support performers in stuffed suits. In addition, we actually used our proposed system at several events and confirmed that it was effective.

The remainder of this paper is organized as follows. Section 2 outlines related work. Section 3 describes the design of our system and Section 4 explains its implementation. Section 5 describes evaluation of the system and discusses the results. Section 6 describes actual use of the system, and Section 7 presents our conclusion and plans for future work.

2   Related Work

In the field of motion analysis, there have been researches on reconstructing the motion of an actor with a wearable system of outward-looking cameras [3], and on analyzing motions, such as the turns a snowboarder makes with GPS and a gyroscope attached to the snowboard [4]. In addition, Corinne et al. proposed a system that recognized upper body gestures by using strain sensors [5]. However, there have been no studies on supporting behaviors that have taken into consideration the difference in size between the actual body and stuffed suits.

In efforts to assist human visibility with cameras, there has been a system that displays images taken with a camera attached to the rear of a car [6]. Koeda et al. proposed a rescue assistance system to teleoperate an unmanned helicopter where the pilot could watch the images from cameras on the helicopter with a head mounted display (HMD) [7]. However, there have been no studies on assisting the human visibility that have taken into account the problems with wearing stuffed suits.

Some attempts with HMD have been made with research, to support users using wearable computing technologies. Stochasticks [8] is a practical application of wearable computing and augmented reality, which enhances billiards. The system in this research recognizes the position of the billiard table and the billiard balls, and displays an auxiliary line on HMD. Ikeda et al. evaluated the usefulness of providing information with HMD in interactive performances using a projector [9]. The Wearable MC System [10] enables a master of ceremonies (MC) to run events smoothly. An MC using this system can see scripts and instructions from the director with HMD. There have been many studies to support users using HMD with these systems and the usefulness of information presented with HMD was confirmed in each study. However, there have been no studies on supporting performers in stuffed suits with HMD.

· A boy playing with the keyboard   · A girl cling to the character

Fig. 1. Preliminary study

In research using wearable computing technologies in the field of entertainment, Tomibayashi *et al.* proposed Wearable DJ System [11]. This system enabled disk jockeys to perform DJ techniques by operating intuitive gestures using wearable acceleration sensors. A Wearable Musical Instrument by Dancing [12] could control performances by recognizing the steps of dancers in two phases on the basis of the characteristics obtained from an experiment on movement and sound.

3   System Design

3.1   Preliminary Study

We did a preliminary study to clarify problems when wearing stuffed suits, as shown in Figure 1. The first author of this paper wore the stuffed suit, which was designed for this study, and he made contact with people on the street for about two hours per day for five days. The details on the stuffed suit we used for this study are described in Section 5.

Even though the author could gain visibility from the nose of the stuffed suit, his field of view was restricted. This meant that he did not recognize children who came close to him and he had to turn the nose of stuffed suit toward them to see their faces. Moreover, he hit a wall in a narrow space and hit the face of stuffed suit against people while communicating with them since he could not clearly recognize his surroundings. In addition, there were problems in that he did not know what a pose to make and he did not know weather poses he assumed were a match for the character of stuffed suit.

Kind, Cute, Fun   **Strong, Angry**

Fig. 2. Difference in impression caused by posing

From the results of this preliminary study, we confirmed that support from performers wearing stuffed suits was important because it was difficult for them to perform like characters without having much experience.

3.2 Requirements

Our system helped performers wearing stuffed suits to perform like the characters they played, focusing on posing and communication. Figure 2 shows an example of the importance of posing. Different poses in the figure evoke different impressions of the character; the left of the figure creates a friendly impression while the right of the figure creates a powerful impression. If a performer in the stuffed suit of a cute character had posed like that at the right of the figure, people surrounding him would feel strange about the stuffed suit. In addition, communication between the performer and others is an important element that improves the impression of stuffed suits. If a performer in stuffed suit had acted unnaturally such as not looking at his/her respondent's face on shaking hands, it would have created a bad impression for others around them. From these considerations, we posed three problems from the constraints on conventional stuffed suits to be solved by our proposed system.

1. Performers cannot identify their postures because the shape and the size of stuffed suits differ from those of the physical human body.
2. It is difficult to smoothly communicate with others because of limited visibility.
3. Performers usually gain visibility from parts away from the eyes of stuffed suits, and it is difficult for them to communicate by eye contact.

Problem 1 causes difficulty in posing, and Problems 2 and 3 cause difficulty in communicating with others. To solve these problems, our system has two functions, i. e., support for poses support and enhanced visibility. The former

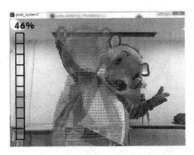 

Inaccurate pose   **Accurate pose**

Fig. 3. Snapshots on HMD with the proposed method

supports performers to recognize how close their poses are to the correct ones. The latter enable them to gain the visibility from the positions of cameras attached to the eyes and around the face of stuffed suits.

3.3 Support for Poses

The function to provide support for poses enables performers to watch themselves objectively and to know how close their poses are to the correct ones. Current images from a stuffed suit are taken by a camera placed outside and are displayed on the HMD the performer wore. In addition to current images, our system displayed target pose images that the performer should mimic. Our system calculates the difference between the images from actual poses and the target pose, and displays the parts that are different from the target pose. More concretely, it shows the images in red for incorrect parts and in green for correct parts, and a gauge on the left indicates the rate of agreement on how much the pose of the performer matches the target pose.

Performers recognize their poses objectively from these functions and can pose easily. The left of Figure 3 only indicates 46% accuracy because the actual pose is far from the target pose, and the right of the figure indicates 71% accuracy because the angle of the body and the position of the hands are correct. Even if performers have little experience, they can pose easily with this function.

The system calculates the differences in scores for hue, saturation, and brightness between each pixel of the current image and the target image, according to the following equation.

$$\text{Score} = \sqrt{10 \times (\text{hue})^2 + (\text{saturation})^2 + (\text{brightness})^2}$$

The hue value is 10 times due to its importance. Calculated scores are averaged in each area of 10×10 pixels and correct/incorrect are determined for each area according to a threshold set in advance.

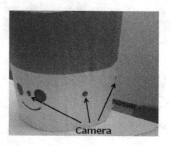

Fig. 4. An example of stuffed suit whose head is combined with the body

Fig. 5. Cameras around the head

3.4   Enhanced Visibility

It is difficult for performers with stuffed suits to smoothly communicate with others because of limited visibility. Especially when wearing stuffed suits where the head is attached to the body, as shown in Figure 4, performers must move their whole body to check the surroundings because they cannot only move the head. Moreover, performers often gain visibility from parts away from the eyes of stuffed suits, such as holes in the nose or mouth. This causes unnatural communication including mismatched gazing. To solve these problems, we propose a function that enhances visibility.

Performers can see the images from cameras attached to the eyes and multiple cameras around the face on the eye level of stuffed suits by wearing an HMD with this function, as shown in Figure 5. Two electromagnetic compasses are attached to the head of the performer and the body of the stuffed suit. The system recognizes the relative direction of the performer's head against that of the stuffed suit from the difference between the two compasses, and it changes the camera to be used to display images on the HMD according to the relative direction.

This function enables performers to check their surroundings easily and quickly react to the actions of people surrounding them. They can act naturally since performers can see the images from the eye level of stuffed suits. In addition, there is a possibility that a performer will gain the sensation that the size of his/her head is becoming similar to that of the stuffed suit by switching cameras according to the direction of the performer's face. We intend to evaluate this sensation in future work.

3.5   System Structure

Figure 6 shows the system structure, which consists of an HMD, a PC, cameras, and two electromagnetic compasses. An HMD and an electromagnetic compass are attached to the head of the performer and a PC is placed on his/her back. Multiple cameras and an electromagnetic compass for the function of enhanced

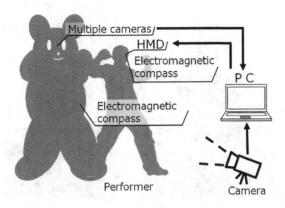

Fig. 6. System structure

visibility are attached to the head and the body of the stuffed suit. There is a camera outside for the function of supporting poses.

4 Implementation

We implemented the two prototypes shown in Figure 7. The head of the stuffed suit in Figure 7(a) is mainly made of foam polystyrene and the other parts are made of polyurethane. A helmet with an HMD is attached inside the head and a camera is attached inside the left eye of the suit. The width of the head, the body, the length of the leg, and the total height are 56, 71, 57, and 210 cm, respectively. Performers gain visibility from the nose of the stuffed suit, whose shape is elliptical and whose width/height are 15/8 cm, as shown in Figure 8(a). This means that visibility is restricted and dim because the nose is covered with mesh. The stuffed suit shown in Figure 7(b) is mainly made of containerboard. Multiple cameras are attached around the head. The width of the head, the body, the length of the arm, the leg, and the total height are 47, 64, 78, 54, and 190 cm, respectively. Performers gain the visibility from the mouth of stuffed suit, whose shape is arced and whose width/height is 10/0.7 cm, as shown in Figure 8(b). The performers' visibility is very restricted. The head is combined with the body.

The devices used for the function to enhance visibility are multiple cameras, two electromagnetic compasses, an A/D converter, and a microprocessor (Arduino nano). Arduino [13] is an open-source electronics prototyping platform based on flexible, easy-to-use hardware and software. The difference in the values of the two electromagnetic compasses attached to the head of the performer and the body of the stuffed suit is sent to Arduino. It control the relay according to the value and the signal from the camera connected to the relay is transmitted to the PC. The A/D converter then converts the analog signals from the camera into digital.

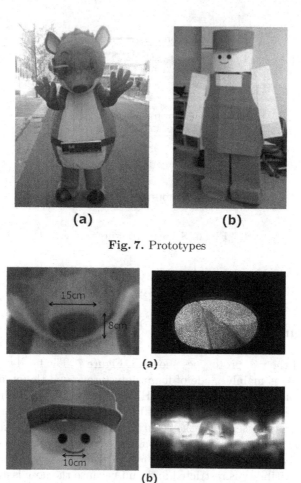

Fig. 7. Prototypes

Fig. 8. Visibility for each stuffed suit

We used a Fujitsu FMV-BIBLO MG/G73 computer, whose platform was Windows 7 for the PC, a Shimadzu DataGlass3/A for the HMD, and a Sparkfun electronics HMC6352 for the electromagnetic compass. We used a Logicool Qcam Orbit for the camera outside to provide the function to support posing and a back-up camera for the function to enhance visibility. We implemented the prototype system using Processing [14].

5   Evaluation

5.1   Evaluation of Support for Posing

To evaluate the function to support posing, 10 test subjects wore stuffed suits, as shown in Figure 7(a), and posed in three ways:

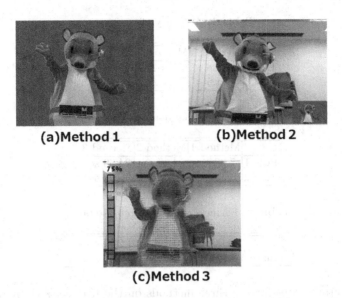

(a)Method 1   (b)Method 2

(c)Method 3

Fig. 9. Snapshots displayed on HMD

(a)Pose 1   (b)Pose 2

Fig. 10. Target poses

Method 1: Subjects pose looking at the target image shown in Figure 9(a).
Method 2: Subjects pose looking at the target image and the real image taken
by the outside camera show in Figure 9(b)
Method 3: Subjects pose using our method shown in Figure 9(c).

Subjects made two poses, as shown in Figure 10(a), where the direction of the
body faced the camera, and Figure 10(b), where the direction of the body faced
to the left obliquely to the camera. Participants practiced the procedure using
another pose before this evaluation. We subjectively evaluated the accuracy of
posing by using five levels (5: exactly the same as the target pose – 1: entirely
different from the target pose) for four elements: the right arm, the left arm, the
head, and the direction of the body and recorded the total score. In addition, we
evaluated smoothness when posing by measuring the time from when the pose
began to when it ended and subjects answered a questionnaire on the ease of

Table 1. Accuracy of posing

	Method 1	Method 2	Method 3
Pose1	12.8	15.4	17.2
Pose2	11.5	14.2	16.8

Table 2. Average time required to take pose

	Method 1	Method 2	Method 3
Pose 1	7.33 sec	14.36 sec	24.63 sec
Pose 2	10.03 sec	17.61 sec	30.09 sec

Table 3. Easiness of taking accurate pose

	Method 1	Method 2	Method 3
Average score	1.6	3.6	4.2

making accurate poses for the three methods on the five levels (5: it was very easy to pose accurately – 1: it was very difficult to pose accurately).

Table 1 summarizes the results for the accuracy of posing. Method 3 achieved the highest scores for both poses in accuracy. As a result of one-way ANOVA of the scores for accuracy, there were significant differences (Pose 1: f value=16.93, $p<0.01$, and Pose 2: f value=24.41, $p<0.01$). From multiple comparisons for each pose using Tukey's test, there were significant differences in Pose 1 between Methods 1 and 3 (t value=-5.80, $p<0.05$) and there were no significant differences between Methods 2 and 3 (t value=-2.43, $p>0.05$). For Pose 2, there were significant differences between Methods 3 and 1, 2 (Method 1, 3: t value=-6.70, $p<0.05$, Method 2, 3: t value=-3.43, $p<0.05$). We confirmed that our proposed function of providing support for posing was effective. Moreover, there is a possibility that our method will become more effective as the difficulty of posing increases from the results of two poses.

Table 2 lists the results for smoothness of posing. Method 1 took the shortest time and Method 2 took shorter than Method 3. We considered that it took a long time to make poses because subjects tried to match the details by checking their poses. Subjects also had to stand in predetermined positions because standing position of them was very important to match their poses to the target pose when using Method 3. We considered that it took them longer to make poses in Method 3 because they had to look for the predetermined position.

Table 3 summarizes the results for ease of making accurate poses. Method 3 achieved the highest score. As a result of one-way ANOVA for the score of smoothness, there were significant differences (f value=27.20, $p<0.01$). From multiple comparisons using Tukey's test, there were significant differences between Methods 1 and 3 (t value=-5.41, $p<0.05$), Methods 2 and 3 (t value=-7.04, $p<0.05$), and there were no significant differences between Methods 2 and 3 (t value=-1.63, $p>0.05$). We considered that the difference in scores between

Fig. 11. Action to move the gaze to the hand

Methods 2 and 3 was small because subjects had to look for the standing position to match their poses to the target pose in Method 3.

Throughout, We confirmed that performers tended to make the accurate poses more easily by watching themselves objectively and they posed more accurately by using the function to support posing. However, performers had to stand in predetermined positions when using the function to support posing. To solve this problem, we need to improve the function to be able to determine the accuracy of posing by using other approaches such as modifying the target image dynamically and using an accelerometer to acquire a user's posture.

5.2   Evaluation of Enhanced Visibility

Five test subjects made four actions that enabled the function of enhanced visibility to be evaluated.

Action 1: A subject turns his/her head in the direction that his/her communication partner in front of his/her is pointing. Then, he/she also point to the communication partner. The height of the hand position is the same as that of the height of the partner's eye. After three actions, he/she answers a questionnaire on the ease of understanding the action of his/her partner (5: he/she can understand it without unnatural actions such as looking for his/her partner's finger – 1: he/she cannot understand what was happening) and the ease of making actions (5: he/she can move his/her hand naturally – 1: he/she cannot move his/her hand to the appropriate position).

Action 2: As seen in Figure 11, the subject moves his/her gaze of the stuffed suit to the position of the hand of his/her partner. The partner moves three positions of his/her hand at random. The subject makes the above action once for each place and answers the questionnaire on the ease of moving his/her gaze of the stuffed suits to the exact position (5: he/she can move the gaze of the stuffed suits smoothly – 1: he/she cannot move it smoothly at all).

Action 3: A subject avoids an obstacle placed at the eye level of the stuffed suit. An aluminum can, whose height was 17 cm and width was 7 cm, as shown in

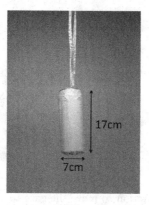

Fig. 12. The obstacle used for Action 2

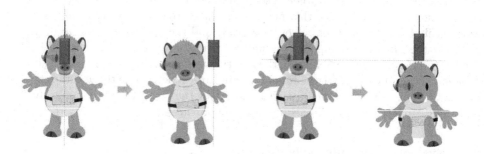

Fig. 13. Action to avoid sideways   **Fig. 14.** Action to avoid downward

Figure 12, is used as the obstacle in this evaluation. He/she makes two actions; the first is where he/she avoids the obstacle sideways, as shown in Figure 13, and the second is where he/she avoids it downward, as shown in Figure 14. He/she makes these two actions and answers the questionnaire on the ease of avoiding the obstacle (5: it is very easy to avoid it – 1: it is very hard to avoid it).

Action 4: A subject looks for five objects located around him/her within a radius of five meters at random. Then, he/she answers the questionnaire on the ease of recognizing his/her surroundings (5: it is very easy to find the objects – 1: it is very difficult to find them).

We used the stuffed suit shown in Figure 7(a) for Actions 1, 2, and 3 and used the stuffed suit shown in Figure 7(b) for Action 4. For Actions 1, 2, and 3, subjects can see the images taken by the camera attached to the eyes of the stuffed suit in our method. For Action 4, there is another proposed method in addition to the case of Actions 1, 2, and 3: there are five cameras around the face of stuffed suit. The conventional method means that subjects acted with the view from the hole made in the stuffed suits.

Results of Action 1. Table 4 summarizes the average score for Action 1. In its ease of understanding, the proposed method earned higher scores than the conventional method. In addition, from the t-test for the score for the ease of understanding, there were significant differences (t value=-5.10, p<0.01) and this confirmed that performers were able to react to the action taken at the position of the eye of stuffed suits smoothly with the function of enhanced visibility. In the ease of making actions, the proposed method also earned higher scores than the conventional method while there were no significant differences (t value=-2.45, p>0.05). There is a possibility that subjects were not able to recognize the position of the stuffed suit's arm even when using our method.

Results of Action 2. Table 5 lists the average score for Action 2. The proposed method achieved higher scores than the conventional method. In addition, from the t-test for the scores, there were significant differences (t value=-7.48, p<0.01) and this confirmed that the function of enhanced visibility was useful for moving the gaze of stuffed suits accurately.

Results of Action 3. Table 6 summarizes the average score for Action 3. The proposed method earned higher scores than the conventional method in both actions while there were no significant differences from the t-test for the scores (avoiding obstacle sideways: t value=-1.04, p>0.05, avoiding obstacles downward: t value=-1.51, p>0.05). The reason for this may have been that subjects could not recognize the exact distance between the stuffed suit and the obstacle because they were watching the images from the camera when using the function of enhanced visibility. To solve this problem, we need to devise a method where performers in stuffed suits can recognize the distance between stuffed suits and objects.

Results of Action 4. Table 7 lists the results for Action 4. From the results, the proposed method with five cameras achieved the highest score. There were significant differences (f value=34.67, p<0.01) from one-way ANOVA. As a result of multiple comparisons between each pair of methods using Tukey's test, there were significant differences between the scores when using five cameras and when using the conventional method (t value=-8.08, p<0.05) while there were no significant differences between the two proposed methods (t value=-2.31, p>0.05). One of the reasons for this is that subjects were able to move their bodies without caring about the surroundings because there were no obstacles around the stuffed suits in this experiment.

We confirmed throughout that performers could react to actions made at the position of the eye of stuffed suits more easily and they could move the gaze of stuffed suits accurately by using the camera attached to the eyes of the stuffed suits. In addition, we also confirmed that performers could recognize surroundings more easily with multiple cameras attached to the heads of stuffed suits. Therefore, performers can communicate with others smoothly and naturally by using the function of enhanced visibility.

Table 4. Result for Action 1

	Proposed	Conventional
Ease of understanding the action	4.4	1.8
Ease of making action	3.8	2.6

Table 5. Result for Action 2

	Proposed	Conventional
Ease of moving gaze	4.4	1.6

Table 6. Result for Action 3

	Proposed	Conventional
Easiness to avoid sideways	3.4	2.2
Easiness to avoid downward	3.6	2.2

Table 7. Result for Action 4

Proposed		Conventional
Five cameras	One camera	
4.4	3.6	1.6

Conversation with the MC

Fig. 15. Performance on the stage

6   Actual Use

We used the prototype system on the stage at Illumine Kobe 2010 [15] held at the
Hyogo Prefectural Museum of Art in Kobe City on December 12th, 2010. The
staffed suit with our proposed system communicated with the MC and danced
to music, as shown in Figure 15. It confirmed that the performer in the stuffed

suit could communicate with the MC by looking at him naturally and he/she could act by himself/herself because it was easier to recognize the surroundings. However, there was a problem in that it was hard to see the camera image when the light on the stage was not bright. In the future, we need to consider the use of infrared cameras to gain visibility even in the dark places.

7   Conclusion

This paper proposed a system of supporting performers in staffed suits and implemented functions to provide support in posing and enhance visibility. The results from evaluation confirmed the effectiveness of these two functions.

However, the function to support posing cannot be used in amusement parks even though it can be used on stage or for training because an external camera is required. We have to devise a way of using our method in actual amusement parks without any outside cameras. We plan to use wearable sensors to detect the posture of performers. By using this method, performers will be able to identify the accuracy of their poses regardless of their standing positions and make poses accurately. We need to devise a method for the function of enhanced visibility to present distance information between the staffed suits and surrounding objects because it is difficult to gain a sense of distance. We plan to implement a function that informs performers in staffed suits of the proximity of objects with proximity and vibration sensors.

An example of application of the system could be applied to support users, such as astronauts, since they always need to recognize their surroundings in states in which they cannot move freely. In addition, when giant humanoid robots are created in the future, the importance of the system to enhance visibility and to extend the sense of embodiment will increase.

Acknowledgement. This research was supported in part by a Grant in aid for Precursory Research for Embryonic Science and Technology (PRESTO) from the Japan Science and Technology Agency and by a Grant-in-Aid for Scientific Research(A)(20240009) from the Japanese Ministry of Education, Culture, Sports, Science and Technology.

References

1. Harrison, C., Tan, D., Morris, D.: Skinput: Appropriating the Body as an Input Surface. In: Proc. of the 28th Int. Conf. on Human Factors in Computing Systems (CHI 2010), pp. 453–462 (2010)
2. Pasquero, J., Stobbe, S.J., Stonehouse, N.: A Haptic Wristwatch for Eyes-Free Interactions. In: Proc. of the 29th Int. Conf. on Human Factors in Computing Systems (CHI 2011), pp. 3257–3266 (2011)
3. Shiratori, T., Park, H.S., Sigal, L., Sheikh, Y.: Motion capture from body-mounted cameras. In: Proc. of the 38th Int. Conf. on Computer Graphics and Interactive Techniques (SIGGRAPH 2011), vol. 30(4) (2011)

4. Holleczek, T., Scoch, J., Arnrich, B., Troster, G.: Recognizing Turns and Other Snowboarding Activities with a Gyroscope. In: Proc. of the 14th IEEE Int. Symposium on Wearable Computers (ISWC 2010), pp. 75–82 (2010)
5. Mattmann, C., Amft, O., Harms, H., Troster, G., Clemens, F.: Recognizing upper body postures using textile strain sensors. In: Proc. of 11th International Symposium on Wearable Computers (ISWC 2007), pp. 29–36 (2007)
6. Rear camera system, http://www.rearviewsafety.com/
7. Koeda, M., Matsumoto, Y., Ogasawara, T.: Annotation-Based Rescue Assistance System for Teleoperated Unmanned Helicopter with Wearable Augmented Reality Environment. In: Proc. of the IEEE International Workshop on Safety, Security and Rescue Robotics (SSRR 2005), pp. 120–124 (2005)
8. Jebara, T., Eyster, C., Weaver, J., Starner, T., Pentland, A.: Stochasticks: Augmenting the Billiards Experience with Probabilisteic Vision and Wearable Computers. In: Proc. of International Symposium on Wearable Computers (ISWC 1997), pp. 138–145 (1997)
9. Ikeda, J., Takegawa, Y., Terada, T., Tsukamoto, M.: Evaluation on Performer Support Methods for Interactive Performances Using Projector. iiWAS/MoMM 2009 Special Issue in Journal of Mobile Multimedia (JMM) 6(3), 207–226 (2010)
10. Okada, T., Yamamoto, T., Terada, T., Tsukamoto, M.: Wearable MC System: a System for Supporting MC Performances using Wearable Computing Technologies. In: Proc. of Augmented Human Conference 2011, AH 2011, pp. 25:1–25:7 (March 2011)
11. Tomibayashi, Y., Takegawa, Y., Terada, T., Tsukamoto, M.: Wearable DJ System: a New Motion-Controlled DJ System. In: Proc. of ACM SIGCHI International Conference on Advances in Computer Entertainment Technology (ACE 2009), pp. 132–139 (October 2009)
12. Fujimoto, M., Fujita, N., Takegawa, Y., Terada, T., Tsukamoto, M.: Musical B-boying: A Wearable Musical Instrument by Dancing. In: Stevens, S.M., Saldamarco, S.J. (eds.) ICEC 2008. LNCS, vol. 5309, pp. 155–160. Springer, Heidelberg (2008)
13. Arduino, http://www.arduino.cc/
14. Processing, http://processing.org/
15. Illumine KOBE 2010,
    http://cse.eedept.kobe-u.ac.jp/illumineKOBE2010/main.html

Socially Present Board Game Opponents

André Pereira, Rui Prada, and Ana Paiva

INESC-ID and Instituto Superior Técnico,
Technical University of Lisbon, Portugal
{andre.a.pereira,rui.prada}@ist.utl.pt, ana.paiva@inesc-id.pt

Abstract. The real challenge of creating believable and enjoyable board
game artificial opponents lies no longer in analysing millions of moves
per minute. Instead, it lies in creating opponents that are socially aware
of their surroundings and that can interact socially with other players.
In traditional board games, where face-to-face interactions, social actions
and strategic reasoning are important components of the game, artificial
opponents are still difficult to design. In this paper, we present an initial
effort towards the design of board game opponents that are perceived
as socially present and can socially interact with several human players.
To accomplish this, we begin by an overview of board game artificial opponents. Then we describe design guidelines for developing empirically
inspired social opponents for board games. These guidelines will be illustrated by concrete examples in a scenario where a digital table is used as
a user interface, and an intelligent social robot plays Risk against three
human opponents.

Keywords: Social Presence, Board Games, Artificial Opponents.

1 Introduction

Playing board games is generally a social event where family and friends get
together around a table and engage in face-to-face interactions, reading each
other's gestures and facial expressions. Examples of such rich social interactions
can be identified when we look at some recent examples of board games. Players
laugh with each other when someone makes an ugly drawing playing Pictionary,
yell at each other when someone makes a bad deal at Monopoly, use their facial
expressions to bluff while playing Poker, or can even mock somebody who does
not know the answer to a simple Trivial Pursuit question. In board games,
players are engaged with both the game and each other. Players are tightly
coupled in how they monitor the game surface and each other's actions [14]. The
rules and the game board are generally designed as gateways to stimulate social
interactions between players. Conversely, in computer games, players interact
mainly with the system rather than with other human players. Online multiplayer games and local multi-player games of new consoles such as the Nintendo
Wii or systems such as the Xbox Kinect try, in some ways, to fight the social
isolation of computer games. Nevertheless, all these examples still fall short when
compared to the social richness of traditional board games, where players engage

A. Nijholt, T. Romão, and D. Reidsma (Eds.): ACE 2012, LNCS 7624, pp. 101–116, 2012.

in face-to-face interactions in contrast to a "shoulder-to-shoulder" interaction where players face a TV screen. Recently, in the field of pervasive gaming [26], a sub area named computer augmented tabletop games have made efforts to gather the advantages of these two types of games. This area attempts to maintain the social aspects of traditional tabletop games while improving it with the unlimited possibilities offered by computerized technology. Our research is mainly focused in addressing one of the many advantages that augmented computation can bring to board games: the opportunity to create artificial opponents.

The first problem that artificial opponents face in highly social environments is related to their performance (playing strength). In games such as chess or checkers, where no social actions are required and an agent plays only against one human opponent, agents that play as well as the stronger players in the world already exist. However, in games where the mechanics involve social actions such as bluffing and diplomacy, or in games where an agent has to play against multiple human players, we still cannot create agents that can be compared to the human counterpart. The second problem that rises from the social inability of these kind of agents is the lack of social presence that humans attribute towards them. Social presence can be shortly described as the "sense of being together with another" [3]. If human players perceive artificial opponents as not socially present, their enjoyment while interacting with them will decrease [15]. Players have more fun when playing against friends or family because they share a history together, smile at each other, and some players can even have fun by looking at their opponent's defeated expression when they win. In some cases, when humans play against artificial opponents, they even choose to eliminate them from the game first, and play the game only with other human players [17].

In this paper, we start to address these problems by looking briefly into the current state of board game artificial opponents. Second, based on this research and on our previous work, we present five guidelines for designing socially present board game opponents. Following, we illustrate a scenario where a socially intelligent robot can play Risk against several human players. And finally we draw our conclusions and detail our future work directions.

2   Related Work

Social relationships are now being established with new forms of artificially intelligent beings, such as virtual agents [6] and robots [4]. Humans consider media devices as social beings [35] while knowing that these entities do not have real emotions, ideas or bodies. Artificial opponents can be examined as a potential instance of this effect. The first notion of an artificial opponent was "born" around 1769, when a chess automaton called "The Turk" had become famous before it was exposed as a fake. It was simply a mechanical illusion that allowed any person with high chess knowledge to hide inside and operate the machine. Nowadays, with the evolution of computers and computer programming, several artificial opponents for board games have been created, and evolved to the point where, giving chess as an example, the best chess program can beat the best human player in the world [5]. However, these opponents still have difficulties dealing with imperfect information and social behaviour. In games with these types of information, the tactical component is of secondary importance and the strategic intuition of players and their social skills are harder to simulate.

An example of a game where players have to deal with social and imperfect information is Risk, a popular board game for three to six players where each player tries to "conquer" the world. The Risk board game is constituted by several lands that are occupied by player's armies. By controlling these armies players can attack other players' territories and defend their own. This game suffers from imperfect information as its combats are defined by luck (using dice) and, most importantly, as a multi-player game it is difficult to predict other players' moves. Experienced Risk players use several kinds of social interactions to gain advantage in the game. Players can, for instance, try to influence other players to their own advantage or propose to form alliances against the strongest player. Human behaviour in this type of games is difficult to predict because players can decide their moves based on the social relationships that they have established with other players. A player can attack another player simply because of a grudge established in a previous game or merely to see an angry facial expression on his/her opponent.

Nevertheless, in research we can already find some interesting approaches to develop artificial opponents that deal with imperfect information. One approach [29] used Classifier Systems to classify a set of (state, action) pairs in a Risk game. These pairs represented game situations and actions that a sensible player should execute when faced with similar situations. However, results of this study showed that these agents still perform poorly when compared to humans, but could hold on their own against computer agents with fixed programmed strategies. Another interesting approach was developed by Johansson [17], where a multi-agent Risk system was defined. In this system each territory was an agent and these agents negotiated with each other which actions should be performed in the game. This system played a tournament against eleven other bots and ranked first by a large distance over their artificial opponents. In terms of efficiency, this multi-agent system also needed much less computation to win the games. While this work does show some success in dealing with imperfect information, it was designed specifically to compete against artificial opponents and discarded any kind of social information or interaction.

One of the few examples that uses a social agent as a board game opponent is a scenario where participants were able to play chess against a social robot [33]. In this scenario, users can take hints about the state of the game by looking at the robot's facial expressions. An experiment performed using this scenario studied user's enjoyment in two different embodiments. Half of the users played chess against a robot and the other half against an identical virtual embodiment displayed on an LCD screen. The robotic embodiment showed positive improvements in terms of user's enjoyment. However, another study [25] performed using this scenario showed that the social presence that participants attribute to such a robot decreases after several interactions. The longer players interact with nowadays artificially intelligent entities, the more this effect occurs, as social presence with these entities tends to decrease over time. It has been shown that if human players perceive artificial agents as not socially present their enjoyment and their intention to interact with these entities will decrease [15]. In the next section we will look into guidelines that aim to increase social presence in board game opponents.

3   Towards Socially Present Board Game Opponents

Social presence varies across individuals and across time for the same individual [3]. When we have been exposed for a long time to media artifacts, we have a higher knowledge of interacting with it, and it is possible to have an increased feeling of social presence. However, continued experiences generally cause the well-known habituation or novelty effect [19], this effect causes an initially higher sense of presence that fades away as users become more experienced with a novel technology. This novelty effect is present in almost all types of media, including artificial agents or robots [13]. Current artificial opponents lack social presence and when human players perceive artificial opponents as not socially present, their enjoyment while interacting with them decreases. Johansson [17] stated that "bots are blind and objective, while humans may decide to eliminate the bots first, just because they are bots". This sentence shows that, over repeated interactions, humans attribute very low sense of social presence to artificial opponents. To address this kind of degradation in interaction, in this section, we present five guidelines for designing more socially present board game opponents. These guidelines were based in research of the fields of social presence and board game artificial opponents, but also from our previous work where we extensively explored a scenario where a user plays chess against a social robot [24, 23, 25, 33, 32, 7]. In this section, we will argue that to improve social presence an artificial board game opponent should:

1. *Have a physical embodiment and be able to engage users in face-to-face interactions*
2. *Exhibit believable verbal and non-verbal behaviours*
3. *Comprise an emotion or an appraisal system*
4. *Be able to recognise, greet and remember users*
5. *Be able to simulate social roles common in board games*

3.1   Physical Embodiment and Face-to-Face Interaction

Interactivity is referred by most authors as the primary cause of presence. If users cannot interact with an artificial agent, they usually do not consider it as a social entity. There are different modes of interacting with a virtual agent, but in terms of social presence, face-to-face interaction is still considered the gold standard in communication, against which all platforms are compared [1]. As such, virtual agents or artificial opponentes that do not use the rich set of social behaviours and cues involved in face-to-face interaction are assumed to support less social presence. One reason why face-to-face interaction is preferred is that a lot of familiar information is encoded in the non-verbal cues that are being exchanged. When playing board games against digital opponents, the social possibilities are restricted. When someone plays against a human opponent, he/she can try to look for a hesitation or an expressed emotion that could indicate a bad move. In contrast when playing against a computer, in most cases, we can only see pieces moving on a graphical interface. Nevertheless, in both research and commercial applications we can already find some embodied artificial opponents. Embodied artificial opponents are in most part represented by simple avatars (static pictures) or by two or three dimensional animated virtual agents. It has been reported in virtual poker environments that the simple addition of a picture to personify players can be considered as more likable, engaging and comfortable [21]. More recently, we can also find examples where physically embodied agents (or robots) are used to simulate opponents. In our previous work, we have showed that by using a robotic embodiment, artificial opponents are reported to have an improved feedback, immersion and social interaction [33]. Kidd and Breazeal [20] also investigated people's differential responses between a robotic character, an animated character and a human. Interactions comparing the robot to the animated character, were rated as more enjoyable, more engaging, more credible and informative. Comparing to a human, the results of the robot were non significant and just slightly lower. In another study [18], participants felt a significantly stronger sense of social presence when they were interacting with a physically embodied Aibo robot than with a physically disembodied Aibo displayed on an LCD screen.

3.2   Believable Verbal and Non-verbal Behaviour

When we interact with virtual characters or robots, verbal communication offers the most attractive input and output alternative. We are familiarized with it, requires minimal physical effort from the user, and leaves users' hands and eyes free [43]. Voice is a potent social cue, it can even evoke perceptions that a machine has multiple distinct entities [28] or even personalities [9]. Non-verbal behaviour is used for communication, signaling and for social co-ordination. This kind of natural social behaviour can be interpreted by humans without the need to learn something new. As such, a human-like computer that can express patterned non-verbal behaviours can cause social facilitation in users. Believable non-verbal behaviours can also show autonomy and contribute to the feeling of social presence towards an agent [40]. An artificial opponent should be able to express its intentions and affective states, showing for example sad expressions when losing and happy expressions when winning. Believable non-verbal behaviours along with a believable vocalization system will increase an artificial opponent's realism and as such, users should be able to attribute mental states to it and perceive it as a social entity.

3.3 Emotion or Appraisal System

It is universally recognized that emotions have a powerful influence in our decision making [8]. The same holds true when players make decisions while playing
board games, they let their emotions take part in their decision process. Appraisal theories seem like the best alternative for influencing the decision process
with emotions and for generating emotional behaviour in an artificial opponent.
Appraisal is an evaluation of the personal significance of events as central an-
tecedents of emotional experience. Appraisal theories specify a set of criteria
or dimensions that are presumed to underlie the emotion constituent appraisal
process. These theories [22, 39] are built upon studying our brain processes.
While it is still difficult to simulate appraisal models in computers, given the
complexity of the mental structures that need to be simulated, some projects
[31] already successfully used an appraisal model, the OCC model [30], to simulate human cognitive processes in their applications. In our previous work [24],
a social robot provided feedback on the users's moves by employing facial expressions determined by the robot's appraisal system. This appraisal system was
composed by an anticipatory mechanism that created expectations on children's
upcoming moves, and then based on the evaluation of the actual move played by
children, an affective state was elicited, resulting in different facial expressions
for the robot. It was shown that the emotional behaviour expressed by this social robot increased the user's understanding of the game. In a small variation of
this scenario [32], we designed an artificial companion that commented a chess
match between two human players. Here, the robot showed empathic behaviors
towards one of the players and behaved neutrally towards the other. From this
study, we concluded that the simulation of simple empathic behaviours in a robot
can improve human-robot relationships.

3.4 Recognise, Greet and Remember Users

At the beginning of almost every social interaction, an initial introduction or a
greeting behaviour is appropriate and essential to take off most social interactions. We can obviously see this behaviour as constant in board game players. If
we want to create socially present artificial opponent's we should not skip this
important phase. Once that initial greeting behaviour has occurred, remember-
ing, deciding upon or mentioning our past history with others is one of our most
important social features and maybe the most essential way of establishing and
maintaining relationships. Sharing personal interests or preferences, as well as
showing some understanding of others' interests or preferences is a fundamental point in most relationships . Complex models of the human memory can
already be seen in human robot interaction research . The importance of such
mechanisms for fighting the habituation/novelty effect and for achieving longer
term interactions, have also been reported [2, 25]. In board games, we can assess
the importance of these mechanisms by some common game situations. Such
situations include when players' speech and in-game actions are influenced by
previous negative or positive relations established with others or by events that

took place earlier in the game, or in previous games. As such, in order to create believable agents that play more than one game with the same participants, they should remember each user individually and the past interactions with them.

3.5 Simulate Social Roles

Our final guideline is inspired by a rule of thumb described by Eriksson [12], that games should allow different modes of play based on social roles. Risk and most board games already support multiple social roles in their game-play. The challenge in our case is not to build games that can support various social roles. Instead, the challenge consists of endowing artificial opponents with the capability of simulating such roles. Examples of social roles in board games are: Helper – actively helping another player perform actions in the game; Dominator – trying to influence other players to perform specific actions for the player's own in-game benefits; Negotiator – negotiating between two other players; and Exhibitionist – performing actions in the game to gain the other players' attention. During the length of a single board game, players constantly change between social roles. A player that is displaying the social role of helper towards one player can later on adopt the social behaviour of dominator towards that same person. Concurrent social roles can also happen while playing board games. Players can, for example, exhibit both the social role of negotiator and dominator to try to influence players using external negotiation. Such social roles should be taken into consideration when developing artificial opponents for board games.

4 Scenario

In this section we describe a novel scenario (see Figure 1), where an artificial opponent plays the Risk board game against three human players. The goal of this artificial opponent is to be able to socially interact with multiple humans and still be socially perceived for extended periods of time. The human players use a digital table as the game's interface. Risk was chosen because it is a game where face-to-face interactions, social actions and strategic social reasoning are important components of the interaction. We will describe how we implemented this scenario relating to the guidelines defined above.

4.1 Physical Embodiment and Face-to-Face Interaction

In our scenario, over one side of a digital table stays a social robot that interacts with three other players on the three other sides of the table. With the use of such a setup, human players are still able to maintain face-to-face interactions between them and the robot, and still be aware of the game's interface as it happens in [11]. By using a digital table as compared to a vertical display, players can more easily be engaged with both the game and by each other [38]. For embodying the artificial opponent in our scenario, we used a social robot, the EMYS[1] (EMotive

---

[1] http://emys.lirec.ict.pwr.wroc.pl/

Fig. 1. EMYS, the social Risk player scenario

headY System) robotic head. For achieving believable face-to-face interactions we have developed a gaze system that equips this robot with the capacity of interacting with multiple players simultaneously in our gaming context.

Our artificial opponent gaze system uses speech direction detection, the context of the game and is based upon studying how humans behave in such context. After a brief analysis of how humans play the traditional Risk game, we established the patterns described in Figure 2. In Risk, players shift their focus between looking at different parts of the game board and looking at other players. Players look at the board when there is no activity in the game and they are thinking, or when other players make their moves on the board, which in our case is **touching the interface** by the use of a digital table. When inactive, players tend to look at the active player more than any other and we have also noticed that the factor that most influences the amount of time that participants tend to look at the board or at other players is their concentration in the game. We have modeled this behaviour by having a simple concentration appraisal variable (see subsection 4.3). When this variable is low, the robot is **unfocused** and tends to look more at other players and sometimes even discards looking at game events. When the variable is high, the robot is **focused** and looks more often at the game board simulating that it is thinking and looking at the game action attentively. The robot is able to look at different regions of the interface because when a user touches one area of the interface the robot is informed about the location of such touch. The values were fine tuned and previously parameterised with the robot in its predefined position in the table. The main limitation of our scenario is that the robot does not have any speech recognition capabilities. This was a design decision, since that with today's technology it would be almost impossible to recognize speech in a scenario where three different users may be talking concurrently. As such, for receiving user's input, our robot as in [7] only considers information provided by in-game actions. Users can only "communicate" with the agent by attacking it or by proposing an alliance using the interface on the digital table. The robot is able to perceive such events without using any kind of speech recognition. We believe that by making the proposal and acceptance of alliances occur in the virtual interface does not deteriorate the social experience and gives more contextual information about the task to the robot. However, in order to increase the robot's perceived social presence we found the need to implement a **speech direction detection** module in our robot in order to look at the direction of players when they are speaking. This module was implemented by using the Kinect and its SDK from Microsoft[2]. Using beamforming algorithms [42], the Kinect's microphone array gives us the position of the player, and we use that angle to look at that direction. Finally, when the agent decides to **speak to** a player (see 4.2), the gaze system also makes the robot look at the direction of the intended player.

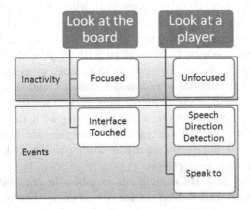

Fig. 2. EMYS, the social Risk player gaze patterns

4.2 Believable Verbal and Non-verbal Behaviour

In our scenario, the robot's non-verbal behaviour and gaze system is influenced not only by the agent's own appraisal system (see 4.3) but also by the other players' voice and game actions. The facial expressions and idle behaviours for EMYS were developed by Ribeiro et al. [37, 36]. These authors, took inspiration from principles and practices of animation from Disney and other animators, and applied them to the development of emotional expressions and idle behaviours for the EMYS robot. The idle behaviour was adapted to our scenario to work in conjunction with the gaze system presented above. Facial expressions are used in our scenario for establishing turn-taking and for revealing internal states like confusion, engagement, liking, etc. Finally, the robot's non verbal behaviour has a mood variable that can be either positive or negative. This variable is directly influenced by the power comparison with other players (see 4.3), and like we did with our previous scenario [24] it is mapped to a positive or negative posture.

---

[2] http://www.microsoft.com/en-us/kinectforwindows/develop/

Regarding the robot's verbal behaviour we took inspiration from the work of Taichi et al. [41] that examines the communication process of board game players. We have defined a typology of speeches adapted to the Risk game [34] by separating utterances that human players vocalize in their games in different categories. Categorizing the type of utterances and assessing the frequencies of each category helped us to determine where we wanted to focus our attention when creating artificial opponents for a particular scenario. Also, by doing this experiment we retrieved a database of possible utterances. This database contributed for the creation of a believable vocalization system, as the utterances in this system were retrieved from real human social behaviour. In our scenario, a high quality text to speech is used to vocalize these utterances.

4.3   Emotion or Appraisal System

In the section above, we cited our previous work where we categorized the type of utterances that human players vocalize in their games and asserted the frequencies of each of these categories. However, to model a socially intelligent opponent, such information still needs to be associated with players' decision processes in the social context of the game. To address this issue, we performed a protocol analysis [10] where participants were asked to think aloud while playing a Risk game. Players reported on their thought process both on their turn and on the other players turn, when they were still interacting with the other players. In this experiment, we were able to extract the most relevant variables that influence human's appraisal and decision process while playing Risk. These variables influence the moves that the artificial opponent chooses but also the selection of the utterances they say. By using such variables in our system we are now capable of generating social behaviour for our artificial board game opponent. Below we present the variables that influence the robot's appraisal.

Relevance. To appraise something, we first need to determine its relevance [39]. Assessing the relevance of a game event or even a spoken utterance is of extreme importance for board game players. During the other players' turns, commenting every move is not socially accepted as players would be perceived as annoying or bothering. Players usually comment only on relevant moves played by other players. For every event that occurs in the game we established a predefined value between zero and one. Examples of events valued as more relevant and therefore more likely regarded were, for instance, when someone chooses to attack the artificial opponent or when a player that it highly dislikes wins a continent. Events that were classified as having lower relevance were, for instance, attacks involving players that the agent had a neutral relationship with, or events with expected outcomes.

We use this variable to assess if the agent should comment on such event by generating a vocal utterance. The robot has more probability of speaking if the event is relevant, if time has passed since the last sentence that has been spoken and if the agent is familiar (consult Familiarity variable in this subsection) with the user responsible for the event. For that we generate a random number between zero and one and compare it with the formula below. If the number generated is below than the probability of speaking, the robot generates an utterance based on our database (see 4.2).

$$Relevance(event) \times Familiarity(E) \times TSinceLastSentence$$

Where time since last sentence increases slightly each second and becomes full (one) every minute. When the agent speaks this value is restarted.

Power. When playing board games, generally players are unfocused from their outside world and more focused on the game. For this reason, we can assume that outside power relationships do not majorly influence power relationships in the game, and players with most advantage in the game have clearly more power. As the Risk game is all about power, whoever controls more armies, lands and continents in the game is more powerful and can more effectively influence other players. For example, players with more power in the game can with higher success rates make another player loose interest in a target continent. We map this variable for each player (P) including the agent, and is determined by a predefined formula.

$$\frac{\sum Armies(P) + \sum Bonus(P) + \sum CardsValue(P)}{\sum Armies(allP) + \sum Bonus(allP) + \sum CardsValue(allP)}$$

This variable is used for shaping the robot's mood (as described in 4.2) but it is also one of the main variables in deciding the agent's moves in the game. For instance, when a player is becoming too powerful the robot may attack that player or generate a comment in order to influence the other players to attack him.

Concentration. This variable, as we mentioned before in subsection 4.1, directly influences the robot's gaze system. It is higher in the robot's turn in order to simulate that the robot is focused in deciding its move. This variable is lower on the other players' turn, when players take too long to play, or when all of the events that are occurring in the game are not related to the agent's game.

Familiarity. In both studies that we performed using the traditional Risk game, we had a pair of participants who already knew themselves and played games together. When players already know each other outside the game, or when they have played previous games before, it seems that players are more communicative and more willing to establish alliances between themselves. This variable is important for us twofold. The first reason is that the number of utterances that our artificial opponent can speak is limited. And it has been shown in long term studies that repetitive behaviours decrease social presence and believability. As such, it is advantageous for the artificial opponent to be shyer (less talkative) towards players that it interacted for limited time and only to become more familiar (talkative) with them over time. This appraisal variable never decreases and increases slightly every time the robot interacts with users, and considerably more every time a user proposes alliances with the robot.

Like/Dislike. Influenced by attacks and alliances in the current and in previous games we have a variable that can be positive (like) or negative (dislike) for each of the agent's opponents. This variable was also inspired by our experiments. When players were not attacking each other, they were nicer to each other, and the opposite occurred when they were attacking each other. As such, when a player attacks the agent, this appraisal variable towards him/her decreases. The variable increases slightly when players are not attacking the robot. Other situations where this variable changes is based on Heider's balance theory [16]. The Balance Theory hypothesis states that people avoid unstable cognitive configurations. For example, supposing that a person P1 is positively attracted to another person P2, if he believes that P2 is negatively attracted to P3. In order for the cognitive state to become "balanced" P1 must also become negatively attracted to P3. As such, when a player is attacking one of the robot's "most hated" opponents, the like variable increases. Conversely, if a player attacks one of the robot's "friends", this variable will decrease.

In Risk, players can propose alliances in any phase of the game. Our interface also enables players to propose alliances between themselves and the agent. When an alliance is formed, players belonging to the alliance cannot attack each other. However, this alliance can be broken at any time. We have noticed that some players take it quite personally when one player breaks the moral conduct by attacking and breaking the alliance without previous notice. It is although accepted to break alliances when doing so is inevitable for one's survival, or when the two players are the only remaining in the game. Establishment of alliances increases this variable, and breaking them can have a slightly negative effect or a really negative one. Some players attack other players simply because they are angry with them. This feeling can go to the extreme where the main objective of the player changes to eliminate the other player from the game.

Luck Perception. Dice rolls elicit players' strongest reactions in terms of emotional content [34]. When a player is having a lucky streak, the other players generally react to it. Moreover, when that streak breaks, strong reactions both in terms of verbal and non-verbal behaviour occur. For example, when one of our participants broke an opponent's lucky streak he yelled "bye bye" while waving his hand effusively. When asked about this behaviour, the participant told that the reasons behind his behaviour were that the other player was being too lucky and also that he was happy because he was not expecting to win the dice roll. As such, we can easily conclude that players are constantly "storing" in memory the luck that they attribute to other users. The opposite example, where players with constant bad luck ended up by winning dice rolls also happened several times in our study. In one of those cases one participant said to another while clapping his hands, "You won! At last". To our knowledge, no artificial opponent comments luck (being it dice throws or other events) in board games. We implemented this behaviour by monitoring participant's luck in the game and by using the Emotivector anticipatory mechanism [27] that we have used before in our chess scenario. By using this mechanism, when the artificial opponent is faced against someone lucky and wins, he gets happier because its expectations pointing towards victory were low. As such, the mismatch between expectations and actual result can make the artificial opponent display strong emotional reactions.

4.4   Recognise, Greet and Remember Users

In order to greet, recognise, gather a history or mention past events with users, an artificial opponent has to be able to recognize the user, or each user individually if playing against multiple opponents. Vision algorithms that deal with face detection and recognition are maybe the wisest option to consider for recognising users. In our case, we make each user login with their own private interface on the digital table, only then does the robot greet that particular user, and update the history with him/her. Some of the appraisal variables described in the section above evolve only during the game but some are stored in the agent's memory for future interactions. Familiarity is one of the variables stored in the agent's memory that will be remembered in future interactions. Luck perception is also stored in memory, so the agent can assess and comment if a player was lucky in previous games. Like/Dislike variables are also stored so the robot discloses, for instance, that it holds a "grudge" against a particular player, because of previous games. The last data that is stored in memory are the results and dates of previous matches. This kind of data is often mentioned in the beginning of the interaction, where the robot says for example: "One week ago I lost, today I am going to win!".

4.5   Simulate Social Roles

In our previous observations of users playing Risk, we have indeed noticed that users use these already identified social roles and change between them in the throughout of a game. Examples included players that in one phase of a game were exposing a Helper social role (actively helping another player without seeking any in-game benefit) and in later parts of the game a Violater role towards the same player (giving up in the game and trying to destroy a player just because of an argument). Risk is a highly social game that supports various social roles in its gameplay. Social roles are being taken into account in our appraisal system and our artificial opponent is capable of generating behaviour for each of these roles. For example, when the agent "likes" other players it can demonstrate the social role of Helper by saying encouraging comments such as "It went well this turn!". When the agent has a great advantage (high power) over the other players, it is also more likely to adopt the Dominator role by for example threatening other players.

5   Conclusions

In this paper, we addressed the problem of creating socially present board game opponents. Inspired by our previous design experience with board game opponents and by analysing the current limitations of artificial board game opponents, we delineate a set of guidelines for building scenarios that intend to have in its design socially intelligent board game opponents. These opponents present another direction in the design of intelligent user interfaces: rather than being focused on winning against human players by performing millions of operations per minute, these opponents are focused in displaying appropriate social behaviour and in being perceived as socially present by users.

By relating to these principles we have created a scenario where a social robot can play the Risk game against three human players that use a digital table as its interface. The digital table was built specifically for this scenario in order to accommodate the robot and the game's interface. The interface was implemented using the Unity3D engine[3] and the Risk artificial intelligence was built by analising open source risk games and taking into account how humans think while playing Risk. By following the proposed guidelines and by performing empirical studies on the target game, we believe that the next generation of board game opponents can be created.

Acknowledgments. The research leading to these results has received funding from European Community's Seventh Framework Program (FP7/2007-2013) under grant agreement no 215554, FCT (INESC-ID multiannual funding) through the PIDDAC Program funds, and a scholarship (SFRH/BD/41585/2007) granted by FCT.

References

[1] Adalgeirsson, S., Breazeal, C.: Mebot: a robotic platform for socially embodied presence. In: Proceeding of the 5th ACM/IEEE International Conference on Human-robot Interaction, pp. 15–22. ACM (2010)

[2] Bickmore, T., Picard, R.: Establishing and maintaining long-term human-computer relationships. TOCHI 12(2), 293–327 (2005)

[3] Biocca, F., Burgoon, J., Harms, C., Stoner, M.: Criteria and scope conditions for a theory and measure of social presence. Presence: Teleoperators and Virtual Environments (2001)

[4] Breazeal, C.: Designing sociable machines. In: Socially Intelligent Agents, pp. 149–156 (2002)

[5] Campbell, M., Hoane, A., et al.: Deep blue. Artificial Intelligence 134(1-2), 57–83 (2002)

[6] Cassell, J.: Embodied conversational interface agents. Communications of the ACM 43(4), 70–78 (2000)

[7] Castellano, G., Leite, I., Pereira, A., Martinho, C., Paiva, A., McOwan, P.: It's all in the game: Towards an affect sensitive and context aware game companion. In: ACII, pp. 1–8. IEEE (2009)

[8] Damasio, A.: Descartes' error: Emotion. In: Reason and the Human Brain. Grosset/Putnam, New York (1994)

---

[3] http://unity3d.com/

[9] De Ruyter, B., Saini, P., Markopoulos, P., Van Breemen, A.: Assessing the effects of building social intelligence in a robotic interface for the home. Interacting with Computers 17(5), 522–541 (2005)

[10] Ericsson, K.: Protocol analysis and expert thought: Concurrent verbalizations of thinking during experts' performance on representative tasks. In: The Cambridge Handbook of Expertise and Expert Performance, pp. 223–241 (2006)

[11] Eriksson, D., Peitz, J., Bjork, S.: Enhancing board games with electronics. In: Proceedings of the 2nd International Workshop on Pervasive Games-PerGames. Citeseer (2005)

[12] Eriksson, D., Peitz, J., Bjork, S.: Socially adaptable games. In: Proceedings of DiGRA 2005 Conference: Changing Views–Worlds in Play (2005)

[13] Gockley, R., Bruce, A., Forlizzi, J., Michalowski, M., Mundell, A., Rosenthal, S., Sellner, B., Simmons, R., Snipes, K., Schultz, A., et al.: Designing robots for long-term social interaction. In: IROS 2005, pp. 1338–1343. IEEE (2005)

[14] Gutwin, C., Greenberg, S.: The importance of awareness for team cognition in distributed collaboration. In: Team Cognition: Understanding the Factors that Drive Process and Performance, p. 201 (2004)

[15] Heerink, M., Ben, K., Evers, V., Wielinga, B.: The influence of social presence on acceptance of a companion robot by older people. Journal of Physical Agents 2(2), 33–40 (2008)

[16] Heider, F.: The Psychology of Interpersonal Relations. Lawrence Erlbaum Associates (1982)

[17] Johansson, S.: On using multi-agent systems in playing board games. In: Proceedings of the Fifth International Joint Conference on Autonomous Agents and Multiagent Systems, pp. 569–576. ACM (2006)

[18] Jung, Y., Lee, K.: Effects of physical embodiment on social presence of social robots. In: Proceedings of Presence, pp. 80–87 (2004)

[19] Karapanos, E., Zimmerman, J., Forlizzi, J., Martens, J.: User experience over time: an initial framework, pp. 729–738. ACM (2009)

[20] Kidd, C., Breazeal, C.: Effect of a robot on user perceptions. In: Proceedings of the Intelligent Robots and Systems (IROS 2004), vol. 4, pp. 3559–3564. IEEE (2004)

[21] Koda, T., Maes, P.: Agents with faces: The effect of personification. In: Robot and Human Communication, pp. 189–194. IEEE (1996)

[22] Lazarus, R., Folkman, S.: Stress, appraisal, and coping. Springer Publishing Company (1984)

[23] Leite, I., Castellano, G., Pereira, A., Martinho, C., Paiva, A., McOwan, P.: Designing a game companion for long-term social interaction. In: Proc. of Int. Workshop on Affective-Aware Virtual Agents and Social Robots, p. 10. ACM (2009)

[24] Leite, I., Martinho, C., Pereira, A., Paiva, A.: Icat: an affective game buddy based on anticipatory mechanisms. In: Proc. of the 7th AAMAS, vol. 3, pp. 1229–1232 (2008)

[25] Leite, I., Martinho, C., Pereira, A., Paiva, A.: As time goes by: Long-term evaluation of social presence in robotic companions. In: RO-MAN, pp. 669–674. IEEE (2009b)

[26] Magerkurth, C., Cheok, A., Mandryk, R., Nilsen, T.: Pervasive games: bringing computer entertainment back to the real world. Computers in Entertainment (CIE) 3(3), 4 (2005)

[27] Martinho, C., Paiva, A.: Using anticipation to create believable behavior. In: Proc. of the National Conference on Artificial Intelligence, vol. 21, p. 175. MIT Press (1999, 2006)

[28] Nass, C., Steuer, J.: Voices, boxes, and sources of messages. Human Communication Research 19(4), 504–527 (1993)

[29] Neves, A., Brasão, O., Rosa, A.: Learning the risk board game with classifier systems. In: Proceedings of the 2002 ACM Symposium on Applied Computing, pp. 585–589. ACM (2002)

[30] Ortony, A., Clore, G., Collins, A.: The cognitive structure of emotions. Cambridge Univ. Pr. (1990)

[31] Paiva, A., Dias, J., Sobral, D., Aylett, R., Sobreperez, P., Woods, S., Zoll, C., Hall, L.: Caring for agents and agents that care: Building empathic relations with synthetic agents. In: Proc. of 3rd AAMAS, vol. 1, pp. 194–201. IEEE (2004)

[32] Pereira, A., Leite, I., Mascarenhas, S., Martinho, C., Paiva, A.: Using Empathy to Improve Human-Robot Relationships. In: Lamers, M.H., Verbeek, F.J. (eds.) HRPR 2010. LNICST, vol. 59, pp. 130–138. Springer, Heidelberg (2011)

[33] Pereira, A., Martinho, C., Leite, I., Paiva, A.: icat, the chess player: the influence of embodiment in the enjoyment of a game. In: Proc. of the 7th AAMAS, vol. 3, pp. 1253–1256 (2008)

[34] Pereira, A., Prada, R., Paiva, A.: Towards the next generation of board game opponents. In: Proceedings of the 6th International Conference on Foundations of Digital Games, FDG 2011, pp. 274–276. ACM, New York (2011)

[35] Reeves, B.: The media equation: how people treat computers, television, and new media. Center for the Study of Language and Information, Cambridge, Stanford (1996)

[36] Ribeiro, T., Leite, I., Kedziersski, J., Oleksy, A., Paiva, A.: Expressing Emotions on Robotic Companions with Limited Facial Expression Capabilities. In: Vilhjálmsson, H.H., Kopp, S., Marsella, S., Thórisson, K.R. (eds.) IVA 2011. LNCS, vol. 6895, pp. 466–467. Springer, Heidelberg (2011)

[37] Ribeiro, T., Paiva, A.: The illusion of robotic life: principles and practices of animation for robots. In: HRI, pp. 383–390 (2012)

[38] Rogers, Y., Lindley, S.: Collaborating around vertical and horizontal large interactive displays: which way is best? Interacting with Computers 16(6), 1133–1152 (2004)

[39] Scherer, K.: Appraisal considered as a process of multilevel sequential checking. Appraisal Processes in Emotion: Theory, Methods, Research 92, 120 (2001)

[40] Slater, M.: Place illusion and plausibility can lead to realistic behaviour in immersive virtual environments. Philosophical Transactions of the Royal Society B: Biological Sciences 364(1535), 3549 (2009)

[41] Taichi, K., Sugiura, J., Makoto, I., Arakawa, C.: A typology of speeches within board game players for analyzing the process of games (2007)

[42] Van Veen, B., Buckley, K.: Beamforming: a versatile approach to spatial filtering. IEEE ASSP Magazine 5(2), 4–24 (1988)

[43] Yankelovich, N., Levow, G., Marx, M.: Designing speechacts: Issues in speech user interfaces. In: Proc. of the SIGCHI Conference on Human Factors in Computing Systems, pp. 369–376. ACM Press/Addison-Wesley Publishing Co. (1995)

Localizing *Global Game Jam*: Designing Game Development for Collaborative Learning in the Social Context

Kiyoshi Shin[1], Kosuke Kaneko[2], Yu Matsui[3], Koji Mikami[4], Masaru Nagaku[5], Toshifumi Nakabayashi[6], Kenji Ono[1], and Shinji R. Yamane[1,7]

[1] IGDA Japan, Japan
[2] Kyushu University, Japan
[3] Groovesync, Inc., Japan
[4] Tokyo University of Technology, Japan
[5] National Institute of Informatics, Japan
[6] Cyberz Inc., Japan
[7] Aoyama Gakuin University, Japan

Abstract. Making digital games can help people learn collaboratively. Recent advances in game education allow for experimental game development in a short time period with low cost. To examine the possibilities of game development and learning, we focus on the recent "game jam" approach in collaborative game development. The concept of game jam becomes well-known these days, however, its historical development, goals, and strategies have not yet been explored.

To bring game jam into the education and learning, we first look at its historical development and key concept referencing Global Game Jam, the biggest annual game jam in the world, and then we discuss the recent case of "localized" Global Game Jam–style events embedded in the social context of a specific region.

1 Introduction

The game development contingent comprises engineering teams from various disciplines including programming, interactive arts, and release engineering. Game developers also come from different genders, generations, or career backgrounds. They include the professional developers in the biggest software industry, amateur hobbyists, independent game developers, or graduate/undergraduate students.

In section 2, which follows, we describe the model of "Game Jam," the short-period game development workshop that emphasizes rapid team development. Since 2009, the annual event *Global Game Jam* has spread the game jam concept of all over the world. The success of Global Game Jam led to the next step, using Global Game Jam. In section 3, we propose the new typology of game jams besed on the historical development and design strategy. We discuss the new model of *localized* Global Game Jam (or, "mega–region" game jam) and provide the case study of the 2010 *Health Games Challenge* in the United States. In section 4, we

A. Nijholt, T. Romão, and D. Reidsma (Eds.): ACE 2012, LNCS 7624, pp. 117–132, 2012.

describe our trial, the 2011 *Fukushima Game Jam* in Japan. Both of these new syle of game jams succeeded to raise the public attention, but some issues such as reflection/review process are still remain. In the last section, we discuss our observations comparing other game jams.

2   Game Jam Approach

2.1   Historical Background and Core Concept

The game jam is an event in which game developers get together, develop a game, and release it in an extremely short period.

The game jam is a recent phenomenon— the earliest example of game jam is "0th Indie Game Jam" held from March 15th to 18th 2002[1]. Later it was demonstrated at the Experimental Gameplay Workshop session at the 2002 Game Developers' Conference. This kind of short-term experimental game development had been recognized among the game developer and programmer well and also to be included in a game design textbook[14]. At this point, the game jam had started as the experiment for game design professionals.

The origin of the major, organized game jam is the *Nordic Game Jam*[1], begun in January 2006 and arranged in cooperation among the Denmark chapter of IGDA (International Game Developers Association) , IT University of Copenhagen, and local game industries. *Nordic Game Jam* provided some popular characteristics for game jam: academic–industry collaboration and rapid development in two days over weekend. (The global wide-spreading process after *Nordic Game Jam* is to be described in section 2.2.)

The game jam is not well defined and its concept not well understood: in fact, it is often confused with a game programming contest[2]. Indeed, a game jam is closer to a musical "jam session" and not necessarily a contest. Moreover, the area of game jam is expanding beyond digital games and computer programming: 48–hour board game development became part of Global Game Jam since 2011.

In the earliest analysis of game jams, Musil and others [29] pointed out that the concept of game jam has not been formally discussed in spite of the public attention. They defined it as "a mix of design and development strategies" and broke it down into eight key concepts or strategies: (1) New Product Development, (2) Participatory Design, (3) Lightweight Construction, (4) Product Value-Focused, (5) Rapid Experience Prototyping, (6) Aesthetics and Technology, (7) Concurrent Development, and (8) Multidisciplinarity. As these key concepts or strategies are also found in other disciplines, they explained that these shared strategies make understandable "why game jams gain increasing popularity among the interaction design community and trend to be favored among other design approaches."

---

[1] http://nordicgamejam.org/

[2] It may be come from *Google Code Jam Contest*: http://code.google.com/codejam/

Additionally to this insight, we also point out other reasons why the game community would establish game jams globally and other communities[3] . Indeed, most of those key concepts had already been examined in computer science education through "DesignFest" or "CodeFest"[4], a short-term workshop in computer science education [4]. As with DesignFest/CodeFest, research in recent years has noted the benefits of game jams: (1) user innovation and game education, (2) the role models of the design challenge, and (3) the career development needed by the game industry. We expand on these elements in the following.

Toolkit for User Innovation: Von Hippel [15] had ever pointed out that the game industry experienced user innovations by "toolkit" approach over the decade. The various "game engines", toolkits for game development, provided a developer–friendly and cost–effective development environment. At the same time, game design or development courses became options for computer science education [7,35]. These modern game development environment provided students a way to learn through not only the "educational language" but also through the low–cost "professional toolkit"; it also prepared them for collaborative game development beyond the classroom.

Role models for the design challenge: Unlike other exercises, the game jam provides a strong role model for learners — *the game developers.* The importance of the role model can be found in the keynote talk at the first Global Game Jam in 2009 [13]. The keynote speaker Kyle Gabler, a co-developer of *World of Goo*, which won innovation and technical excellence awards at the 2008 Independent Game Festival[5], had ever reported on rapid prototyping experiments in his game development in graduate school. After the experiments from their experimental game development projects are published [31] [12], then their rapid prototyping became one of the topic of academic–industry collaboration [26].

Featuring Gabler and other game developers who explained the rapid short-term prototype development in their award-winning game, the first GGJ keynote succeeded encouraging the challenging game jam and in promoting the educational goal showing how the game jam can be applied.

Industry participation and professional development: Game jams attract not only interested students and independent developers: professional game developers (such as designers, developers, composers, or artists) in large game studios also take part as well. One developer said that participating not only in "external" game jams but also in "internal" game jams can keep studios agile. He also

---

[3] Not only the game developers community, ACM had ever also co-sponsored Global Game Jam 2011.

[4] http://DesignFest.acm.org/ OOPSLA community in computer science suggested that "DesignFest is about sharpening your design skills by rolling up your sleeves and working on a real problem with others in the field." Sometimes DesignFest included "CodeFest" or other technical challenges such as Extreme Programming (XP) practices. This XP shares some key elements of game jams.

[5] http://www.igf.com/

discussed that "internal" studio game jam as an opportunity not only for professional development, but also for organizational development, as he encourages role-switching in the game jam.

> Switching roles "can teach you a lot about the complexities [others] deal with on a daily basis," he said. "If you can understand what stresses people are under in their daily lives, you can better understand who they are as a human being and how to work with them." [30]

As this reflection explained, the game jam becomes popular among the game industry not just because it will help the team work, but because it can also help the business with the organizational development and learning.

As seen in past analysis and case reports in this section, the "mix of design and development strategies" nature of game jam provides unique experiences to each attendee. This highlights the importance of the selection of strategies and setting goals for each learner to get the maximum education befenits of the game jam.

2.2   From Nordic Game Jam to Global Game Jam

As we looked back, we found several reasons why the concept of the game jam expanded to the wider community. However, the game jam has never spread without the historical happenings in Global Game Jam.

Inspired by the success of original *Nordic Game Jam*, Global Game Jam was founded by IGDA education SIG in 2008; the first event was held in 2009 [22]. Today Global Game Jam recognized as the largest game jam in the world[6]. In Global Game Jam, game jam sites around the world are organized by volunteers. The participants are not allowed to come to the game jam with a team already formed; instead, they are expected to collaborate with other participants at the first time. There are no requirements of special skills needed — designers, developers, artists, students, and any other interested people are welcome. The major change since the Nordic Game Jam is the live streaming around the world — many of the game jam sites have live video feeds and all attendees and visitors are able to check in with each other. Year by year, Global Game Jam has grown; it annually gathers professionals, students and hobbyists. At Global Game Jam 2012, 10,684 individuals participated and 2,209 game projects were created. Jam sites were organized in 47 countries and announced to set Guinness World Record for the largest game jam in the world[7].

2.3   Learning from Global Game Jam

As the Global Game Jam became larger year by year, the learning during this unique event has been discussed. For example, Foaad Khosmood, one of the

---

[6] Nordic Game Jam has turned into the largest jam site among Global Game Jam sites.

[7] http://globalgamejam.org/

Global Game Jam 2012 directors, reported what game developers have learned from Global Game Jam [23]. He pointed out the six points:

1. Rapid prototyping experience
2. Opportunity for failure
3. Working in diverse teams
4. Tools assessment and selection
5. Research and user studies
6. Promotion

We can find not only the same elements as game jams described in Section 2.1, but also new elements like working in diverse teams, (global) user studies, and promotion. In other words, Global Game Jam brings these micro- and macro-challenges into the game jam. It provides both ad-hoc team development challenges through tele-presence experience at game developers' workplaces plus a sense of Internet user research. It offers experience in the collaborative or social aspects of game development and release engineering.

3   Localizing Global Game Jam

As we see above, the past analysis and case studies suggest the positive possibilities of the game jam approach in team development. Following the success of Global Game Jam, local game jams have been held at university or game studio in large cities. In the following, we examine the concept and framework *localized* Global Game Jam.

Global Game Jam itself is for general purposes, though it emphasizes "innovation, creativity, experimentation" on the top of its website. However, the style of Global Game Jam can be adapted to meet more specific purposes under the social context.

In this *localized* Global Game Jam(see table 1), we try to propose the game jam to emphasize the connections among game development workplaces. The game jam sites share specific social or regional contexts and work together on real-world problems.

Apps for Healthy Kids Game Jams: Nationwide Collaboration. From our viewpoint, the *Apps for Healthy Kids* game jams in 2010 are early cases of *localized* Global Game Jam — the nation-wide networked game jams embedded in a social context.

It is notable that the game jam approach is imported to the national campaign *later* (see table 2). In September 2009, President Obama launched the "Educate to Innovate" campaign [32]. The announcement included a statement on "National STEM Game Design Competitions," aimes at developing games to enhance students math and science skills. At the time, the U.S government focused on the "edutainment" approach rather than the game jam approach, the playing of educational games rather than the creating of innovative games.

Table 1. Proposed typology of Game Jams

	Global Game Jam (GGJ)	localized Global Game Jam	local Game Jams
Jam sites	distributed	distributed	standalone
Scale	global	mega–regional, or nationwide	city area, in house, or social event
Purpose	general	regional	local
Examples	GGJ	Apps for Healthy Kids game jams, Fukushima Game Jam	Indie Game Jam

However, social changes and expectations around game development were changing rapidly. In February 2010, the White House Office of Science & Technology Policy (OSTP) and the U.S. Department of Agriculture hosted the "Innovations for Healthy Kids Challenge Workshop." The workshop featuring leading experts in the fields of gaming and technology, considered the idea of a national movement to address childhood obesity. Then game jam approach appeared in this agenda. [3].

In March 2010, a message from the White House was delivered to the GDC (Game Developers Conference), held in San Francisco. The game developers who attended the conference received a communication from the U.S. chief technology officer with the letter from First Lady Michelle Obama [33]. It was about not the STEM education game, but the campaign to fight childhood obesity. It is no surprise that first lady is concerned about obesity among American children, but, her letter included a new challenge in game design and development: *Apps for Healthy Kids* competition announced by the White House, a move toward putting a call for game developers for national projects.

Finally, the game jam appeared to the national competition. IGDA, in partnership with the U.S. Department of Agriculture, announced *Health Games Challenge* [16], organizing game jams in major U.S. cities including Boston, Seattle, Orlando, Pittsburgh, Albany, Fairfax, Athens, and San Francisco, during the weekend of May 21, 2010, to "harness the creative and technical capabilities of video game developers" in support of the *Apps for Healthy Kids* competition.

The *Health Games Challenge* game jam was organized by IGDA, and while it was part of *Apps for Healthy Kids* competition, the IGDA established some new guidelines: for instance, while *Apps for Healthy Kids* competition was open only to U.S. residents, IGDA welcomed international participants.

Contribution from the Nationwide Challenge. From our viewpoint, the *Health Games Challenge* game jam had several unique contributions. Firstly it provided an early example of "a mega-region" game jam. Connecting nationwide large cities, it pulled together different actors, including academic communities, grass roots organizations, government agencies, and funding organizations. It is

Table 2. Timeline: Health Games Challenge 2010

Date	Event
2009.11	President Obama launch "Educate to Innovate" campaign
2010.01	Global Game Jam 2010
2010.02	Innovations for Healthy Kids Challenge Workshop held at White House
2010.03	First lady issues challenge to *Game Developers Conference*
2010.05	USDA announces the partnership with IGDA in *Apps for Healthy Kids* Game Design Competition
2010.05	*Health Games Challenge* game jam during May 21–23

also important that these large communities build the national campaign in the short period as seen in table 2.

Secondly it propose the model of participation and collaboration by different roles: As IGDA announced "All sites are encouraged to involve local youth, health experts and nutrition experts in their plans when possible."[16], the game development process is considered to be including users and not limited to game developers. Finally, these two contributions also brought the public awareness — the news media including *Washington Post* interviewed the developers and reported this new challenge on public health [27].

4   Fukushima Game Jam in Minamisoma

In this section, we focus on the *Fukushima Game Jam* [8], the recent localized Global Game Jam–style event designed in the social context of Japan.

4.1   Pre-history: Global Game Jam in Japan

IGDA Japan (the Japan chapter of the International Game Developers Association) has been promoting Global Game Jam with other related organizations in Japan. The impact of Global Game Jam in Japan has several aspects below.

Public awareness of game development: In the field of game development, the industry collaboration with universities and graduate schools in Japan is still at the beginning stage [28]. In this phase, hosting and promoting the Global Game Jam site at the university drew significant attention from game developers and a wider public audience.

---

[8] Called "FGJ" for short, the names of the co-sponsor and host city were added later to the full event name: *Tohoku IT Concept "Fukushima Game Jam in Minamisoma City" 2011.* http://fgj11.ecloud.nii.ac.jp/

For example, students and professional game developers at the GGJ2001 Tokyo site, the largest jam site in Japan, were featured on NHK (Japan Broadcasting Corporation) TV program aired nationwide. As another example, GGJ2011 Fukuoka site, Japan's second largest site, was publicized through a university press release and its promotion occurred a visit from the city mayor to the game jam workplace in local university.

Participatory design: As we described in section 2.1, it is pointed out that the participatory design is one of the key concept of game jam. The concept and practice of participatory design was developed in Scandinavia and introduced in the United States in the 1990s by a grass roots organization [25]. This participatory design movement, though, did not become widespread in some countries including Japan. As a result, the introducing of participatory design at the game jam was challenging topic in Japan.

Culture of prototyping: In spite of the creators and researchers' interest with the prototyping became more serious[6], Japanese game industry had less interested in prototyping in commercial game development than other countries. For example, rapid prototyping in game development had been featured at the SIGGRAPH symposium in 2007 [26], yet it took until 2010 for a major Japanese game developer to "discover" the power of prototyping [34]. Since Global Game Jam 2011, IGDA Japan re-emphasized the power of rapid prototyping in the real game development process.

4.2   Designing Fukushima Game Jam

The Fukushima Game Jam held by IGDA Japan is a nation-wide game development event similar to the *Apps for Healthy Kids* game jams. Its purpose, though, is not national welfare but disaster recovery after 3/11 and place-making for the future. Following the 2011 Tohoku earthquake and the nuclear disaster at Fukushima Dai-ichi in March, a worldwide support effort that included the game industries arose. Game designers and developers also streamlined the way to support disaster recovery by the power of the game development.

Differently from *Apps for Healthy Kids* game jams, it planed without governmental campaign and based on grass-rooted activities both online and offline. On July 9, Kiyoshi Shin, IGDA Japan president, posted a call for game developers to hold the game jam in Fukushima and broadcast it. At this time, neither sponsors nor workplaces lined up; however, the first sponsor raised the hand reply immediately via Twitter, and other IGDA/non-IGDA contributors from several locations followed, and we formed the Fukushima Game Jam steering committee. Finally, at the beginning of August, "Fukushima Game Jam" was scheduled to be held at the end of the month(see table 3).

4.3   Location and Goal Setting

The main site is located at Minamisoma, a city in Fukushima, located at the edge of the "preparation area" closed the evacuation area [24]. The people living

Table 3. Timeline: Fukushima Game Jam 2011

Date	Event
7/09	Twitter post calls for game developers to take part in undertaking a game jam in Fukushima
7/18	Discussion list open
8/03	Ustream program "Fukushima Game Jam special" airs
8/04	Ustream program "Toward Fukushima Game Jam" airs
8/05	First IGDA/Japan press release calls for participants, sponsors, and remote jam sites
8/24	Ustream program "Pre-Fukushima Game Jam" airs
8/26	Tour bus depart from Tokyo to Minamisoma
8/27	**Fukushima Game Jam**: Day 1 morning shor visit to the tsunami disaster area 10:45 Team building 11:00 Theme and achievements announced 13:30 Early presentation (Scanning drawings by the invited children) 22:00 Alpha version release
8/28	**Fukushima Game Jam**: Day 2 08:00 Beta version release 10:00 Playable version release (public demo play for online/offline visitors) 17:00 Completed version release
8/31	Ustream program "Post-Fukushima Game Jam" airs

in Minamisoma had become well known through uploaded video massage after the disease [9] and its stories in TIME 100 [2].

Generally, the game jam sites are held often at universities which have the best access to broadband Internet; however, there are no universities in Minamisoma City so we arranged the broadband access to the main game jam site. It was held at Minamisoma City Culture Hall, a concert hall located about 25 km north of the Fukushima Daiichi nuclear power plant.

Some game developers join the main site(a group from Tokyo arrived by bus), and others joined the five satellite sites including Tokyo and Fukuoka. Each jam sites provide an Internet broadcast of the workplace and the panel sessions at each stage of development.

4.4 Designing Game Jam with Purpose

The basic rules of Fukushima Game Jam are similar to those of the Global Game Jam [9]. Designers, developers, artists and *anyone* are welcome, but no one allowed

---

[9] There is some time compression as compared to the Global Game Jam. The development period is not 48 hours but 30 hours because of the bus tour schedule, which includes viewing the Minamisoma disaster area.

to come to the game jam with a team already formed. All games must adhere to a general theme and other constraints announced at the start of the jam. All the games are uploaded and the developers' presentations are provided.

Furthermore, a number of optional challenges are available. This kind of limitation is usually for experimental design trials. Using these constraints, we try to provide a goal to formalize the game jam's "mix of design and development strategies" and motivate teams to take on the challenges.

Guideline in the Social Context. In the theme and challenges for the Fukushima Game Jam, we embedded the social context into the game development. The theme of FGJ was "Tsunagari," meaning "relation" or "connection". In addition to the theme, there were eight additional "achievements," the sub-themes that developers can include for the extra challenge:

(1) Collaboration At the main site, we invited local children and scanned their drawings (See Figure 1). We strongly recommended that each team incorporate the images into their games.

(2) Tohoku Include the specialties from the Tohoku area (the north-eastern region of the Japan mainland) in the game, such as famous locations or local products.

(3) First contact The game can be enjoyed even by someone who has never played games before.

(4) No instruction Set up the game in such a way that the player can play without consulting instructions.

(5) Five minutes limit The game is less than five minutes long.

(6) Language Free The game contains no words or text at all.

(7) Interface The game is played using a device other than a mouse, keyboard or gamepad.

(8) Link The game makes use of data from an online web service such as Facebook, Twitter or Google Maps.

The general theme, which consider relations or connections reflects the collaboration after 2011 Tohoku earthquake and the difficulty of post-Fukushima divisions [5]. As the post-Fukushima serious situation requires the collaboration under diverse risks, we emphasized the sense of collaborative development in diverse team and society.

Each design challenge achievements also come from our social context. Achievement number (1): we invited the children and parents with the cooperation of Minamisoma City to participate and tried to include them in the collaborative development, not only using the their images but also providing them with demo games and collecting their feedback. (2) This embeds cultural research on local topic. Numbers (3), (4), (5),and (6) are to emphasize the user-focus rapid prototyping that makes collecting feedbacks easier. Numbers (7) and (8) offer technical challenges.

Fig. 1. Children's Drawings at Fukushima Game Jam: Some are by freehand, and some try "bit-map" version by hand

4.5 Results and Considerations

In this 30 hours game jam session in the weekend, we have

Nationwide Jammers. More than 100 developers took part in Fukushima Game Jam, and 25 game titles (including uncompleted projects) are released. Detailed numbers of game developers are below:

- Main site: 44 (25 from Tokyo, 19 from Tohoku region)
- Tokyo: about 40 (2 sites including part-time attendee)
- Fukuoka: about 30
- Sapporo: 7

International Output. To both emphasize the feeling of collaboration and raise public attention, we tried to broadcast the report from the workplace in both Japanese and English. Before the kickoff, IGDA's global developer community and international game development media including *Gamasutra* and *EDGE Online* distributed articles on Fukushima Game Jam.

During the Fukushima Game Jam, we offered some materials in English:

1. Official Guide in English:
   http://fgj11.ecloud.nii.ac.jp/?page_id=808
2. Live streaming short programs in English from Fukushima Game Jam [18,19,17] It includes not demonstration but panel sessions and video report from the short tour in Minamisoma area.
3. Public chat logs: Mainly in Japanese and partly in English
4. Video message from satellite sites. In addition to real-time streaming, the NII Tokyo satellite jam site added English captions later [8].

These materials in English helps international publicity. Several month later, IGDA Japan representative received 2011 MVP award from IGDA. About the same time in March, Fukushima Game Jam also reported in English[10].

Connecting Subcultures. Each jam site organizer try to form the teams from the attendee list. We arranged to form diverse teams at the main site: students, senior professionals, and amateur/non-commercial experts gathered. Not all the team included the professional game developer and some team are led by non-commercial game developer (There are large communities of non-commercial games in Japan focusing on genres such as RPG [20], shooting games, action games, novel games, and others [21].) The game jam connect these different generations and subcultures.

Another site focused not on the diverse teams but on small teams. One of the Tokyo sites, co-operated with the game programming contest, formed four teams consisting of two to four members so that the programmers can demonstrate their programming.

Connecting with Games. The design challenge to collaborate with the local children— via their drawings on the first day and their test play on the second day—was issued to all the game development teams. Some design change occurred after the test play. Moreover, the children's drawings created active communications and rich variations between jam sites and public audiences.

Compared with Global Game Jam, the social interactions around the game projects/titles were less frequent. That could be because Global Game Jam website provided a learning portfolio features including the game developers' profiles to support social interactions and review comments.

Reflection and Review Activities. Though the completed games can be download from the website, we have some opportunities for the review and reflective learning process. Compared with Global Game Jam, this reflection occurred fewer. Since 2011, IGDA has picked up the featured games from the Global Game Jam in its monthly newsletter[10]. As this monthly information encourages self-reflection by reviewing and motivation for the next development, the same kind of continuous learning activities also will be required in other game jam.

4.6   What Succeeded and Failed

As described in this section, we tried to combine the social concerns with the mixture of game development ideas in Fukushima Game Jam. Compared with *Apps for Healthy Kids* game jams, Fukushima Game Jam demonstrated that the mega-region game jam can be organized without the connection with national campaign.

In the short period of weekend, the jammers formed the diverse teams (or homogeneous small teams at some site) and have some unique collabotarive opportunities that cannot occur in the usual life at classroom or professional studio.

---

[10] http://www.igda.org/newsletter/

There are local events during the weekend(see table 3): a short visit to the tsunami disaster area in the morning day 1, inviting local kids to the jam site in the afternoon day 1, and inviting local kids to the test play in the day 2. Combining with the first achievement on "Collaboration", all the teams at main site import or arrange some of the drawing by children. Moreover, some teams accept the feedback from children to the game design during the test play. These amazing collaboration experiences have the greater impact than we expected and reported in some media articles.

Reflection process after the uploading the game titles were not so frequent nor strong. Designing the social review event is the future issue. Though we provided the talk session program in English, the description and introduction of game titles are almost in Japanese. To encourage the social review not only with Japanese, the development shedule more than 30 hours limitation may be required.

5   Conclusion

In this overview of collaborative game development, we look back at the historical development and conceptual framework of the game jam, especially Global Game Jam style. And we propose the *localized* Global Game Jam approach for connecting the Global Game Jam experience with real problems in the social context.

We illustrate with two cases of *localized* Global Game Jam: *Health Games Challenge* in the U.S., 2010, and *Fukushima Game Jam* in Japan, 2011. *Health Games Challenge* connects jam sites, which are mainly in large cities, as part of national problem-solving campaign. *Fukushima Game Jam* is a grass roots event designed not only to connect sites but also to focus on a specific place–making at outside of large cities.

By localizing Global Game Jam experience, each game jam organizers designed the game jam with purpose to solve real social problems. In this process, they collaborated with different actors — from U.S. government to grass root communities — and tried to maximize the benefits of the game jam. *Localized* Global Game Jam provided the new approach on the situated learning and wide range of public awareness. After the early stage of the public awareness, the long stage of disaster recovery and development will be continued. In the next stage, the possibility of *localized* Global Game Jam approach is not yet evaluated. As Florida and others pointed out, the creative industry can form a "mega-region" economic or population development [11]. The relationship between *localized* Global Game Jam approach and mega-region activities should be examined in the future.

Acknowledgments. Thanks to all the sponsors and supporters.   After submitting this paper, we have held Fukushima Game Jam in Minamisoma again during August 3–5, 2012[11]. In this second Fukushima Game Jam, more satellite jam sites joined not only in Japan but also in Taiwan. Also thanks to the new parners in 2012.

---

[11] http://fgj12.ecloud.nii.ac.jp/

Author Contributions

Design of the release schedule and the team arrangement: KM. Design of the participatory workshop: MN. Coordination and management: TN and YM. Jam sites operation: MN, KK, and TN. Analysis: KS, KO, and SY.

References

1. Adams, E.: Technology inspires creativity: Indie Game Jam inverts Dogma 2001! Gamasutra (May 31, 2002), Online article available at http://www.gamasutra.com/view/feature/2989/technology_inspires_creativity_.php
2. Beech, H.: Katsunobu Sakurai: Boat rocker. Time (2011), http://www.time.com/time/specials/packages/article/0,28804,2066367_2066369_206646100.html; 2011 TIME 100, April 21, Online article available at http://ti.me/sAxjAE
3. Chopra, A.: Seeking game-changing solutions to childhood obesity. Office of Science and Technology Policy Blog (February 4, 2010), http://www.whitehouse.gov/blog/2010/02/04/seeking-game-changing-solutions-childhood-obesity-0
4. Clyde, S.W., Crane, A.E.: 'Design-n-Code fests' as capstone projects for an Object-Oriented software development course. Computer Science Education 13(4), 289–303 (2003)
5. Dickie, M., Cookson, C.: Nuclear energy: A hotter topic than ever. Financial Times (November 11, 2011), Online article available at http://www.ft.com/intl/cms/s/0/aa0a40ec-0aea-11e1-b62f-00144feabdc0.html
6. Dow, S.P., Heddleston, K., Klemmer, S.R.: The efficacy of prototyping under time constraints. In: Proceedings of the Seventh ACM Conference on Creativity and Cognition, pp. 165–174. ACM (2009)
7. El-Nasr, M.S., Smith, B.K.: Learning through game modding. Computers in Entertainment 4(1) (2006)
8. ericuei: Fukushima Game Jam, Tokyo NII satellite campus (2011), video available online at http://www.youtube.com/watch?v=duanoZ7Sq5A
9. Fackler, M.: Minamisoma mayor's YouTube plea gets big response. New York Times (2011), http://www.nytimes.com/2011/04/07/world/asia/07plea.html, April 6. Online article available at http://nyti.ms/p10bsj
10. Fermi, O.: Tsunami-struck Fukushima community inspires creative recovery. Online article in On the Neutron Trail (March 6, 2012), http://neutrontrail.com/2012/03/tsunami-struck-fukushima-community-inspires-creative-recovery/
11. Florida, R., Gulden, T., Mellander, C.: The rise of the mega-region. Cambridge Journal of Regions, Economy and Society 1(3), 459–476 (2008)
12. Gabler, K., Gray, K.: Build a game in seven days. Game Developer Conference 2006 Presentation (2006), GDC Radio podcast available at http://cmpmedia.vo.llnwd.net/o1/gdcradio-net/GDCR/gdcr_018.mp3
13. Global Game Jam: 2009 Global Game Jam keynote (January 2009), Video available online at http://www.youtube.com/watch?v=aW6vgW8wc6c
14. Hall, J.: Indie Game Jam: An outlet for innovation and experimental game design. In: Fullerton, T., et al. (eds.) Game Design Workshop, 2nd edn., pp. 403–406. Morgan Kaufman Publishers (2008)
15. von Hippel, E.: Democratizing Innovation, ch. 11. MIT Press (2005)

16. IGDA: International Game Developers Association and U.S. Department of Agriculture host Apps for Healthy Kids game jams. Press Release (May 11, 2010), http://www.healthgameschallenge.org/igda-release.php
17. IGDA Japan: FGJ special report in English. Recorded live streaming (2011), http://www.ustream.tv/recorded/16925331 (Recorded at 2011/08/28 14:29 JST. Length: 56:58)
18. IGDA Japan: FGJ2011 in English #1. Live streaming recorded at 2011/08/27 (2011), http://www.ustream.tv/recorded/16899567 Length: 27:40
19. IGDA Japan: FGJ2011 in English #2. Live streaming recorded at 2011/08/28 (2011), http://www.ustream.tv/recorded/16911587 Length: 66:02
20. Ito, K.: Possibilities of non-commercial games: The case of amateur role playing game designers in Japan. In: Proceedings of DiGRA 2005 Conference: Changing Views—Worlds in Play. Digital Games Research Association (2005), http://www.digra.org/dl/db/06278.00101.pdf
21. Ito, M., Okabe, D., Tsuji, I. (eds.): Fandom Unbound: Otaku Culture in a Connected World. Yale University Press (2012)
22. Jacobs, S.: Global Game Jam 2009: A worldwide report. Gamasutra (February 25, 2009), Online article available at http://www.gamasutra.com/view/feature/3943/global_game_jam_2009_a_worldwide_.php
23. Khosmood, F.: Representing Global Game Jam. IGDA Perspecrives Newsletter, p. 23 (August issue 2010), Online version available at http://www.igda.org/newsletter/wp-content/uploads/2010/08/IGDAPerspectivesNewsletter08-2010.pdf or http://www.igda.org/newsletter/2010/08/18/representing-the-global-game-jam/
24. King, R.S.: Post-Fukushima world. IEEE Spectrum 48(11), 44–45 (2011), graphic by Carl DeTorres, Online version available at http://spectrum.ieee.org/static/the-postfukushima-world
25. Kuhn, S., Winograd, T.: Participatory design. In: Winograd, T. (ed.) Bringing Design to Software. Addison-Wesley Professional, ACM Press (1996), profile 14
26. LaBounta, H., Gingold, C., Townsend, J., Gray, K., Buchanan, J., Caballero, V.: Rapid prototyping: Visualizing new ideas. In: Sandbox 2007: Proceedings of the 2007 ACM SIGGRAPH Symposium on Video Games, pp. 157–158 (2007)
27. Laris, M.: Designers create video games to teach kids about healthy diets. Washington Post (May 23, 2010), Online article available at http://www.washingtonpost.com/wp-dyn/content/article/2010/05/22/AR2010052203342.html
28. Mikami, K., Watanabe, T., Yamaji, K., Ozawa, K., Ito, A., Kawashima, M., Takeuchi, R., Kondo, K., Kaneko, M.: Construction trial of a practical education curriculum for game development by industry-university collaboration in Japan. Computers & Graphics 34(6), 791–799 (2010)
29. Musil, J., Schweda, A., Winkler, D., Biffl, S.: Synthesized essence: what game jams teach about prototyping of new software products. In: Proceedings of the 32nd ACM/IEEE International Conference on Software Engineering, ICSE 2010, vol. 2, pp. 183–186. ACM (2010)
30. Nutt, C.: MIGS 2010: Game Jam Your Studio! Gamasutra (November 10, 2010), Online article available at http://www.gamasutra.com/view/news/31476/
31. Shodhan, S., Kucic, M., Gray, K., Gabler, K.: How to prototype a game in under 7 days: Tips and tricks from 4 grad students who made over 50 games in 1 semester. Gamasutra (2005), online feature article available at http://www.gamasutra.com/features/20051026/gabler_01.shtml

32. The White House Office of the Press Secretary: Remarks by the president on the "education to innovate" campaign (November 23, 2009), Online article available at http://www.whitehouse.gov/the-press-office/remarks-president-education-innovate-campaign
33. The White House OSTP Pressroom: U.S. CTO Aneesh Chopra delivers First Lady's challenge to Game Developers Conference. Press release (March 11, 2010), Online version available at http://www.whitehouse.gov/administration/eop/ostp/pressroom/03112010
34. Toriyama, M., Maeda, A.: Postmortem: Square Enix's Final Fantasy XIII. Game Developer 17(9), 24–29 (2010), another exclusive version available online at http://www.gamesetwatch.com/2010/10/exclusive_behind_the_scenes_of_3.php
35. Zyda, M.: Creating a science of games. Communications of ACM 50(7), 26–29 (2007)

Producing while Consuming:
Social Interaction around Photos Shared within Private Group

Dhaval Vyas[1], Yanqing Cui[2], Jarno Ojala[3], and Guido Grassel[2]

[1] University of Twente, The Netherlands. & ABB Corporate Research, Bangalore, India
dhaval_vyas@yahoo.com
[2] Nokia Research Center, Helsinki, Finland
{yanqing.cui,guido.grassel}@nokia.com
[3] Tampere University of Technology, Finland
jarno.ojala@tut.fi

Abstract. User-generated content plays a pivotal role in the current social media. The main focus, however, has been on the explicitly generated user content such as photos, videos and status updates on different social networking sites. In this paper, we explore the potential of implicitly generated user content, based on users' online consumption behaviors. It is technically feasible to record users' consumption behaviors on mobile devices and share that with relevant people. Mobile devices with such capabilities could enrich social interactions around the consumed content, but it may also threaten users' privacy. To understand the potentials of this design direction we created and evaluated a low-fidelity prototype intended for photo sharing within private groups. Our prototype incorporates two design concepts, namely, FingerPrint and MoodPhotos that leverage users' consumption history and emotional responses. In this paper, we report user values and user acceptance of this prototype from three participatory design workshops.

Keywords: Social networks, Photo Sharing, Consumption, Personal content.

1 Introduction

The amount of personal content in the online world is growing exponentially. People can easily capture and share personal content such as photos, videos, audio tracks and textual data on social media platforms such as Facebook, Google+ and MySpace. The meaningfulness and emotional attachments to such user-generated content make it important, rather than its ownership [21]. The main focus, however, has been on the explicitly created content. In this paper, we are interested in exploring the use of implicitly created personal content, in particular, users' browsing history, usage, log data and access patterns that are not made visible and explicit, in the current research. The way people consume others' and their own content can provide some useful insights about this invisible social interactions. By capturing people's consumption-related information inferences about very simple social interaction such as "who has seen my profile" to more complex social interactions such as "what type of connections (family, friends or colleagues) are interested in my activity X" can be

A. Nijholt, T. Romão, and D. Reidsma (Eds.): ACE 2012, LNCS 7624, pp. 133–150, 2012.
© Springer-Verlag Berlin Heidelberg 2012

made. Additionally, we believe that users' consumption patterns can be used to design new social features and better recommendation mechanisms.

In fact, studies have shown that consumption activities, such as browsing a friend's profile page, status updates or photos, account for the majority of all user activities on Social Networking Services (SNS) such as Facebook, MySpace, Hi5 and Orkut [11, 25]. Recent research has shown that consuming or browsing, accounts for 92% of all user activities [11]. Clearly, people spend much more time in consuming content as compared to explicitly reacting to it (e.g. by commenting) or actively publishing. Such studies drew our attention to an unexplored design space where we as designers and developers of social media services can leverage consumption related information for supporting new social interactions. We term this particular design direction as *producing while consuming*. The phenomenon itself is explored in a few projects [25, 12, 29, 30]. It is, however, largely overlooked in the user study literature. Some of the popular SNS, such as Orkut and Friendster have used features such as "Recent Visitors" to provide a history of profile views. Flickr also includes statistics that show the interaction and viewing history on users' photos. Facebook recently also introduced the "seen by" feature which informs a user that his or her post or message has been read by the recipient. Moreover, advanced approaches are used [28] to collect a broader set of "interaction metadata" that can convey information about who saw it, who said what when they saw it, what was pointed at when they said it, who did they see it with and for how long, how many times and so on.

In this paper, we explore 'producing while consuming' as a new research topic for always-connected smart mobile devices. The current generation of smartphones, equipped with the state-of-the-art sensing technologies and their ever so present nature in people's everyday lives make them a potential source for capturing users' consumption-related behaviors. For the purpose of exploring the design direction of 'producing while consuming', we studied the use of a low-fidelity prototype - PhotoBook that focused on photo sharing within private groups, such as close friends and families. In addition to basic photo browsing features, we incorporate two design concepts in PhotoBook: FingerPrint and MoodPhotos. The FingerPrint concept allows users to view *consumption patterns* (frequency, and recentness of visitors) related to their photos and represents this by a set of layered fingerprints on the top of the photo. The MoodPhotos concept reveals how the visitors reacted to an owner's photos by capturing visitor's facial expressions associated with photos. On a photo sharing gallery, these two concepts enable relevant people to view how visitors have been consuming photos with a representation of fingerprints and emotional responses.

Revealing people's consumption-related activities has strong privacy concerns. For example, people may not want others to know their current activities or their high interest in certain shared content. Realizing this, we first decided to apply a participatory design approach to verify general user value of the 'producing while consuming' research theme and evaluate privacy risks at an early stage of design. We organized three participatory design workshops involving three different situations and user groups. Our results provided reflections on the design direction of 'producing while consuming'. Our participants viewed the two design concepts as a means for lightweight feedback, which provided reassurance and a sense of connectedness. We also observed that our participants found that revealing their consumption patterns did not greatly compromise their privacy, as the photo sharing was within their private group. Overall, we lay stepping stones for further development in the 'producing while consuming' design direction.

2   Related Work

From the literature, we will discuss some related work on photo sharing activities and current studies that leverage users' consumption patterns.

2.1   Photo Sharing

There is a rich body of literature on personal photos and practices related to photo sharing. We will limit the scope of our literature review to only photo sharing using technology. For a much broader review on photo sharing, we refer you to Sarvas and Frohlich's [24] recent text book.

Social networking services are by definition computer-mediated services that allow users to share their own content, integrate content and interact with others [9]. Olsson [20] emphasizes that when people share photos online with relatives and close friends the main motivator is also to strengthen the existing relationships, as an addition to reminiscing and reliving certain events and storytelling [26, 27]. Self-presentation and expressional needs also play a big role in photo sharing regardless of the size of the target audience [22]. Putting ones' photos visible for others online seems to include a motivational aspect of collecting others' comments and also to follow the interaction, discussion and history around the photos and even archiving it [18, 19]. Photos that are commented by other users seem to found a new content object that is valuable for the owner as an entity including all the interaction history from other viewers.

The storytelling aspect of digital photos is well emphasized in Balabanovic et al. [2], where in a study the authors explored two categories of methods people used in telling stories from digital photos: photo-driven and story-driven. Using semi-structured interviews, Miller and Edwards [16] studied digital photo sharing practices of 10 participants on Flickr. They explored two categories of users: people who were still following the Kodak Culture and 'Snaprs'. Snaprs are the ones who shared their photos even outside of their social network with fewer concerns for privacy. Their immediate focus was on taking photos then sharing them to relevant people. Ahern et al. [1] identified four factors that could affect people's privacy while sharing digital photos: security, identity, social disclosure, convenience. Bentley et al. [4] compared personally captured photos to commercially purchased music and found several similarities. From this comparative study, they found out that 1) users search with fuzzy concepts and settle for an "okay" option, and 2) users change their mind during the search process and end up with something completely different.

Photo sharing via camera phones is also a well-researched area. Kindelberg et al.'s [14] study of camera phone users led to a taxonomy of six affective and functional reasons for image capture on a camera phone: individual personal reflection, individual personal task, social mutual experience, social absent friend or family, social mutual task, and social remote task. Van House et al. [26, 27] studied kinds of images taken and patterns of sharing with cameraphones and the MMM upload software among a graduate student cohort at UC Berkeley, and among more general cameraphone and Flickr users. Olsson et al. [22] studied users' needs for sharing the digital representations of their life memories. They identified three main motivations: personal growth and identity (no sharing), strengthening social ties (sharing with family and friends) and expressing/getting attention (sharing with anyone). In a field study, Jacucci et al. [10] explored how people actively construct experiences using mobile devices capable of sharing multimedia content. In particular, the authors suggest that continuity, reflexivity with regard to the self and the group, maintaining and re-creating group identity, protagonism and active spectatorship were important social aspects of the experience. Another such event sharing study that comes close to our research interests was done by Esbjörnsson et al. [7]. From an ethnographic study at car racing venues in the UK and Sweden, the authors describe three interesting findings that can be useful for supporting event sharing at car racing venues: viewing paradox of spectating, active spectating and role of sociability.

2.2   Leveraging Consumption

In [11], authors explore user activities in four popular social networks: Orkut, MySpace, Hi5, and LinkedIn. In a 12-day period, an average user interacted with 3.2 contacts in total, but these users interacted visibly (e.g. using comments) with only 0.2 friends. The study shows that the amount of all interaction is 16 times greater than the amount of visible interaction. In [5], the authors explore user activities on Facebook, Twitter, and Flickr with their mobile devices. Their result reveals that the users only attend to a small proportion of a full content set, such as content recently published and content from selected contacts. Both studies indicate to the potential of users' consumption behaviors.

The following studies attempt to leverage users' consumption data by revealing visitors. A study [3] shows that feedback mechanisms (on consumption activities) made people feel comfortable to share their location information with friends and strangers. It also reduced their privacy concerns. In this study, a mobile location-based application was deployed in Facebook. One group of users received feedback, i.e. they could check who viewed their locations. The other group of users did not receive this feedback information. As a result, the study found the first user group was more positive about sharing their locations than the second group. Orkut and Friendster have added a "Recent Visitors" feature, with an assumption that this will increase the level of interactions among users. However, existing studies do not agree with the value of such designs. One study [25] suggests that the design did not typically lead to reciprocity. The authors investigated the impact of the "who've viewed you" feature in China's RenRen, one of the biggest regional social networks. From more than 93% of users, less than 10% of latent relationships are reciprocal.

Some early systems explored the feasibility of 'producing while consuming'. For example, the PhotoLoop [29] is a system that automatically captures users' activities while watching slideshows. It uses video/audio recordings and integrates this data (slideshows and video narrations) to create attractive content. The concept provides functions similar to our MoodPhotos feature, where they allow recording videos of users who look at photos. PhotoLoop is aimed for a stationary context, which differs from the present study about mobile scenarios. Mobile devices tend to be used pervasively in different time, locations, and social contexts. A combination of such information can lead to more sensitive situations.

The concepts addressed in this paper all deal with automated content capturing and sharing. There are many earlier studies in this general direction. The WillCam [30] proposed a digital camera that helps users to add visual annotation while taking pictures. The annotation includes facial expressions of the photographers that are taken by another camera attached at the back. CenceMe [17] is a system that infers the presence of individuals using sensor-enabled commercial mobile phones and shares this information through Facebook, MySpace and other online SNS. As for image sharing, CenceMe supports a feature to automatically take and share random photos without any control from users. All of these concepts promote automation in terms of content sharing. However, these systems are seldom systematically verified from a user experience perspective.

3   Exploring Consumption with Photos

We are exploring mobile services for users to share their photos within their inner circles, i.e., closest friends and family. In our current setup, users can directly upload photos to a shared album which is accessible to relevant users. Additionally, we are using face recognition tools to identify people in photos and provide them access rights. The private group setting is the key differentiator here, compared to the existing photo sharing tools such as Facebook or Flickr.

To explore the 'producing while consuming' design direction, we introduce two features to this photo sharing setup: FingerPrint and MoodPhotos. Both the features are meant to capture user' consumption behaviors and utilize this information to enrich social interactions around the consumed content.

3.1   FingerPrint

The FingerPrint concept uses the metaphor of physical photo sharing where viewers unintentionally leave their fingerprints on photos. The concept allows users to view consumption patterns about their photos and represents this by a set of layered fingerprints on the top of the photo. Figure 1 shows two screens of the FingerPrint concept, where Figure 2A depicts a normal photo gallery visible to everyone and Figure 2B shows a view where all visitors' consumption patterns are represented with different fingerprints laid on the top of the photos. This view is visible to only specific people. These fingerprints are shown in different colors, sizes and intensity to represent type of friends (e.g. colleague, family), frequency and recency; respectively.

On the technical side, the concept uses the front camera of mobile phones to detect the face of the viewer (to verify that somebody is looking at a photo). It calculates the amount of time spent on photos and also takes into account the number of finger gestures (e.g. zoom-in with two fingers). Additionally, it records the eye-gaze using front camera, to place a fingerprint in a particular portion of the photo.

Fig. 1. The FingerPrint concept. (A) the default view, and (B) consumption patterns with fingerprints.

3.2 MoodPhotos

MoodPhotos gathers a user's facial expressions when he/she browses a shared photo album and shares these facial expressions to other users when they browse the same photo. This design feature relies on the front camera of mobile phones to capture users' mood photos.

Figure 2 illustrates how the design concept MoodPhotos works in a shared photo album. When a user browses a photo from a shared album for a prolonged time, an emoticon appears in the corner of the photo. The emoticon is equipped with a counter that indicates how many mood photos other people have left on the image (in Figure 2A). The user can check out the mood photos in detail by pressing the emoticon button (in Figure 2B), and add his/her mood photo from a sequence of photos that the device has automatically captured while he/she was viewing the image (in Figure 2C). These photos are meant to reflect natural responses of the user. Consequently, user can choose an appropriate mood reaction from these photos or pose for new ones.

Fig. 2. The MoodPhotos Concept. (A) the default view to browse photo; (B) the view to check mood photos in detail. (C) the view to add own mood photos.

As a general UI concept, MoodPhotos embodies many alternatives. The above-mentioned example details the use case where users exchange concrete portrait photos as emotional response to a photo. Alternatively, these impressions can be abstracted into emoticons on the basis of the facial expressions of the viewers. As Figure 2 shows, a user must initiate the operation to share a mood photo. Alternatively, the system can be more proactive when it detects "dramatic" expressions from the viewers. Given the privacy risks, the system needs to ensure users immediately awareness of mood photos to be shared.

4   User Studies

Given the stringent privacy concerns with both of our design concepts, we took the first step by exploring users' reactions using a paper-based low-fidelity prototype. In this study, we intended to explore users' 'realistic' behaviors hence it was important to use real photos in our prototype [8]. We recruited two student groups and one elderly women's group for our user studies. Each group consisted of 4 close friends. Our user studies consisted of two stages:

1. Each participating group was asked to organize a common social event, where individuals were asked to capture at least 20 photos at the event. In order to gain real emotional responses, the participants were instructed not to reveal or share the photos before the participatory design workshop. After the event, all these photos were sent to us so that we could use them in our PhotoBook prototype (Figure 3A).
2. Each group was invited to a participatory design workshop. They were asked to individually browse through the PhotoBook and leave fingerprints and mood reactions. In the PhotoBook, all the photos had a layer of transparency (Figure 3B) for the participants to annotate their consumption-related data. A real-time, photo sharing simulation was created where participants were provided with an opportunity to capture their own photos to leave facial reactions (Figure 3C).

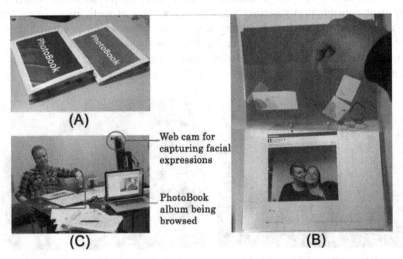

Fig. 3. The PhotoBook prototype (A), photos with a layer of transparency (B), and the setup of our photo browsing sessions (C)

4.1   Participants

Three group of users participated in this study. Group A consisted of students (2 males, 2 females, ages 27-30), who organized a bowling event and had a dinner together. Group B consisted of younger students (3 males, 1 female, ages 22-26), who went to a music concert called "Lost in Music 2011" – an indoor festival in Tampere. Group C was a photography club that consisted of four pensioners (all females, ages 67-72). They arranged a party together at one of the group members' home in Tampere. The first group captured 223 photos, the second group had 378 photos and the third group captured 181 photos, hence the total of 782 photos.

4.2   Participatory Design Workshops and Photo sharing Simulation

From the photos we collected from our participants, we created a physical album out of them. Since all participants were familiar with web-based photo sharing, our PhotoBook layout had similarities with existing photo sharing tools. In addition to making the photo album, we added a transparency on the top of each photos. This transparency was meant to store all the consumption related information. We made three version of the PhotoBook album with different photos in each version.

To simulate photo sharing act, we positioned our participants in three separate rooms of a large user experience facility in our company. One room had two participants and; the other two rooms had one participant each. Each room had a version of PhotoBook album, a web camera for taking pictures, a set of fingerprint stickers in different colors and sizes and relevant stationary. A researcher was responsible to explain the procedure of the workshop and acted as a helper to the participants (Figure 4A). The researcher began with explaining the two design features of the PhotoBook (FingerPrint and MoodPhotos). The participants were asked to browse through the PhotoBook album and use the available material to convey their consumption patterns. The researchers helped participants in capturing their facial expressions while browsing through the photos and prompted them to stick the appropriate ones on the transparencies. We also arranged a color printer, from which we gave them prints of their photos during ongoing sessions. In each room, a user was given 30 minutes to browse through the photos.

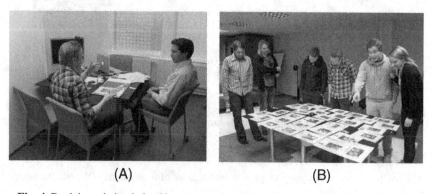

(A)   **(B)**

Fig. 4. Participant being helped by a researcher (A) and a group interview session (B)

At the end of the browsing, researchers would carry the PhotoBook album and to the next room. All the three versions of PhotoBook were circulated to different rooms along with the researchers. During the individual sessions they added comments and communicated with each other through the photo book. This way the PhotoBook versions brought information related to consumption data to the next participants and allowing sharing of photos and the information about the way they are consumed. During the procedure, each researcher talked to all participants in turn. In a way, researchers pretended to be the "technology" that shares photos between all participants, adding the functionality of the service and supporting the interaction.

At the end of the whole simulation, we collected all photos annotated with different consumption behavior and invited our participants to a group interview (Figure 4B). In the interview, we discussed their experience of using such a prototype in their real life, especially focusing on the FingerPrint and MoodPhotos concepts. The most commented photos were scattered around the table so the users were able to see the collection they had created together in the events, by additional content and comments from the simulation sessions.

We transcribed both the individual and group sessions and analyzed our results using an affinity diagram technique. We also used the photo collections from PhotoBook to associate their comments with their photos.

5   Results

Our PhotoBook prototype and the participatory setup were intended to explore how people's consumption related behaviors can be utilized such that they could bring value to people's interaction with personal content (in this case, photos). As an overall finding, the users were positive about leaving fingerprints and mood reactions to photos so others could see them. Nearly all the photos received fingerprint marks. About one quarter of photos received mood photos during our study. In the following, we provide details of some important findings from our study.

5.1   Consumption as Content

As our participants viewed photos in the PhotoBook prototype, they indirectly contributed to the original content, by leaving fingerprints, mood reactions and in some cases comments. Figure 5 shows two examples where photos are annotated by sticking 'named' fingerprints and mood reactions to express that these photos have been 'seen' by specific participants and what kind of facial reactions the photos evoked, respectively. The prototype was designed in a way that this consumption data is shown as an overlay of the original photos such that original photos remain as they are. However, it was observed during our participatory design workshops that participants viewed photos in terms of how they were consumed. For example, commenting on a mood reaction on her photo, a participant said: *"Mood photos could raise social interactions. When you see the reactions of others, it gives you reactions. It also works when you don't have a comment to add but want to share the feeling.*

If you put a smiley, it is just a smiley." With the consumption data added on the top of photos, participants not only shared experiences from the actual event where a photo was taken but they could continue their interaction after the event was over. Similarly, our participants were also very careful about how they represented their consumption patterns. Participants intentionally left cues on photos to add meaningfulness to those photos. In cases where they found less interesting photos in the PhotoBook, they decided not to leave any cues about their consumption behaviors. Here is a comment from one of the participants: *"I think it is not that special. Maybe it is because I have seen many pictures of me like that! It doesn't give me any special memories of that night. It is not special for me, it is not even funny for me."*

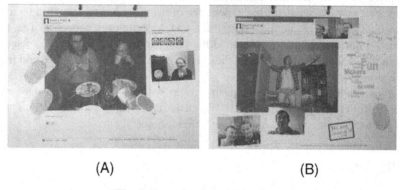

(A)   (B)

Fig. 5. Example of annotated photos

As the consumption data were added by others the photos became collectively owned by the people who viewed them. On several occasions, the consumption patterns even became more important than the actual photos. As shown in Figure 5b, when participants saw a very provocative photo of a fellow member of their group (Group B), they reacted by adding their mood expressions. Here the mood photos were used as a means for poking fun at the person in the photo. Figure 5b is an example where different mood photo reactions led to an extended social interaction over the consumption data. A participant who left his mood reaction said: *"I'd like to add my mood here because Heikki and Päivi have given thumbs up to Matti's photo. It's like "oh, not again". There are always pictures like this from Matti (laughing). It's typical Matti!"* In this example, the mood photos were not only a response to the shared photos, but a response to mood photos left by other group members.

This way, on several occasions participants' fingerprints and their mood reactions became an important source of social interactions. As we showed, participants poked fun at each other and extended their social interaction by adding their reactions on the original photos.

5.2   Lightweight Communication and Sense of Connectedness

FingerPrint and MoodPhotos supported lightweight interaction, which convinced the users to produce more content over shared photos. Referring to FingerPrint, a participant commented: *"Usually, I don't leave comments on my friends' photos. Since, my fingerprints are automatically taken; it seems useful to leave a mark on photos in this way."* Referring to the MoodPhotos, a participant commented, *"Sometimes it is hard to tell about your feelings with words. This is a much better way to tell the author of the photo how you feel."*

The idea of collecting all the event photos from every photo taker into a same album was highly appreciated. Users wanted to see photos from all the members put together. They appreciated seeing the different viewpoints, to get pictures of themselves in the process and to an get idea how others experienced the event.

Enhanced social connectedness was the key user value of FingerPrint and MoodPhotos. These features made photo sharing more "personal" than conventional feedback mechanisms such as "like" button or comments. For example, Figure 6 shows a photo of Group B, where all the four participants have reacted either via a fingerprint or a mood photo. Referring to this example, one participant commented: *"This is a nice group photo I took it when we first started drinking. When I see the mood reactions of my friends, it makes me believe that this photo gave the same kind of pleasure and feeling to them as it did for me."* Several participants also suggested that with a fingerprint on a photo they are reassured that specific people have seen the photo. One participant commented: *"I like when my parents for example pay attention to my photos. Fingerprints would be a feature for paying that attention."*

Fig. 6. A group photo with added consumption patterns

The participants also agreed with utilizing the information from translucent consumption to develop new features for filtering, prioritizing and categorizing photos. For example, the number of fingerprints on a photo can be seen as a factor for making certain interpretations about the photo. One participant suggested that *"there could be statistics to tell which photos are popular and how many viewers there are, and that could even be shown without giving out viewers' information"*. Referring to the MoodPhotos, a participant commented, *"It is fun to see the pictures of others, but more value would be if we could categorize the photos by the viewer's mood. We could see the photos that have raised anger, happiness, disgust or such."*

These experiences are already possible with the lightweight mechanisms of liking a photo and leaving text comments. Features such as MoodPhotos further contributed to this possibility as it could cover photos that do not trigger any user comments or likes.

5.3   Feedback Disclosure Practice and Policies

When users left MoodPhotos or FingerPrint to shared photos, their behaviors were regulated by two types of policies. They restricted the kind of feedback they left on photos and they needed to carefully select the photos they disclosed their feedback over. This was particularly the case for MoodPhotos as the mood photos can reveal un-intended information.

The users appeared to have good consensus in selecting the photos that they choose to leave feedback on. In this study setup, all the users in each group were aware of the photographed events, therefore, they were able to quickly pick up the photos that deserved their attention. Here are some examples of photos that received intensive feedback. In Group A, one photo featured one member made a funny face when undressing himself. In the same group, another photo featured a group member hugging a girl. The featured girl was not known to the other members of the group; therefore, the photo itself stimulated intensive feedback in the user interviews. In Group C, one photo featured a collection of handcrafted artifacts in the place where the group held their event. All the handicrafts were made by the event host, who was a part of this study group. Based on our interviews, the lady was well known in her friend circles for this hobby of hers. In Group B, one photo featured a blurring figure of a member of the study group who was about to go out of a door. In the participatory design workshop, all the group members left their feedback to this photo because of the accidental special effects of the photo.

In the user interviews, we also noticed that people skillfully avoided some kinds of photos when leaving feedback. One of the most common examples was when they intentionally avoided paying attention to photos where they appeared. While acknowledging that they would closely watch these photos, they avoided leaving their finger prints. After all, nobody wanted to project a "self-centered" public image. In another case, the users avoided photos that may carry some sensitive information. In Group B, rumors went that two of the group members were secretly dating each other. So other participants avoided paying too much attention to the photos featuring the couple to avoid the potentially awkward moments.

The users explained their concerns about the kinds of feedback they gave when browsing shared content. The most common user concern was that the system could give away "inappropriate information". For FingerPrint, the users could accidently stop on a page for prolonged time, which did not necessarily communicate their interest in the photo. For MoodPhotos, one participant pointed that she did not want to share her natural mood with her friends. She commented that she usually checked photos when she was bored. Therefore, she doubted that people would share strong emotional responses when encountering with some significant photos. Another participant said that she would not always be at her best moments when she browsed a shared album, for example, in the early morning before wearing a makeup. She did not want to share any part of her face in her mood photos.

Overall, privacy did not emerge as a major concern as far as the system did not give the information away without users' consent. One main user concern was to whom the information was accessible. Since the information was shared within close groups, mainly the people who participated in the event, the users were open to sharing their consumption patterns via finger prints and mood photos.

The users suggested different disclosure policies for FingerPrints and MoodPhotos. FingerPrint should follow "opt-out" strategy. The system shares finger prints automatically and supports quick removal. All users applied FingerPrint to most photos. Some participants even suggested to add FingerPrint to all the photos they browsed by default. Opt-out policy probably serves this frequent usage best. MoodPhotos should follow "opt-in" strategy. The system takes mood images automatically but only shares them when initiated by a user . Participants mainly used MoodPhotos for the significant photos that triggered "big feelings", not for the photos that plainly documented what was going on. They did so to make mood photos more valuable. It is of note that most study participants agreed with the value of automation on the condition they could intervene. For example, some users suggest the system to proactively prompt them to share mood photos when detecting some big feelings from the users.

There were differences between the groups especially regarding to the openness of sharing and commenting. Some of these concerns seem to be related to the age and experience of SNS use, but most habits of commenting and collaborating seemed to repeat regardless of the group all of them commented and created collaborative content to the book in a similar fashion.

6   Discussion

Digital services reflect the way people are connected to each other. For example, Facebook often reflects our offline social network. The current literature suggests that people are more often connected to their real-life connections rather than searching for new contacts [15]. What people do on these services often reflects what people do or want to do in real life. When designing social software applications, we believe in the importance of mimicking real-life events. In such events, people presented are typically engaged in rich social encounters. Some conversations occur about the photos, but more often the conversations occur with the photos. Photos are just contextual cues for the social encounters behind them. As a story listener, we always display our subtle expressions and gestures; as a storyteller, we constantly monitor how other people respond and guide our conversations accordingly. We constantly switch roles in these social encounters when together we construct shared experiences.

'Producing while consuming' is one meaningful attempt to mimic real-life situations in the context of social sharing services aimed at private groups. By allowing people to easily share their consumption activities, we essentially allow people to engage in a social encounter where people can all equally contribute to an ongoing conversation. Everybody in a private group can signal to each other and follow others' signals. This differs from existing services that emphasize the role of content producers at the expense of other group participants.

From our participatory design workshops we learned several important aspects of the 'producing while consuming' design direction. We will discuss these aspects in the following.

6.1   Blurring Boundaries: *Publisher* and *Consumer*

Current approaches to leverage users' consumption patterns [25] focus on providing feedback to content producers to improve their comfort levels and allay privacy concerns. With the 'producing by consuming' design direction, we go a step further by utilizing users' consumption behaviors to design creative ways of communicating via such behaviors, not only to the owners of the content but to others who are allowed to view such details. In FingerPrint and MoodPhoto concepts, we experiment with representing consumption behaviors of people such that they invoke possibilities for social interactions.

In 'producing by consuming', participants move between being a consumer and a publisher. As they consume content of others, they indirectly produce content (in our case, their fingerprints and facial reactions) which become associated with the original content. Interestingly, with such an arrangement, the resulting content become collectively owned.

As we saw in the participatory design workshops, the fingerprints and mood reactions encouraged further social interaction among our participants. Examples discussed in figures 4B and 5 show that such consumption behaviors motivated participants to playfully interact with others only via the consumed content. In these examples, our participants also reacted to the mood reactions by leaving fingerprints. Hence, as the consumption increases the creation of new content also go up. In some cases, reactions such as *"why did Jarno not leave a fingerprint on this photo, did he even look at this one!"* showed that by making consumption visible, our participants' expectations were raised. Hence the value and meaningfulness of the content is shared by the original content as well as the visible consumption data.

'Publishing while consuming leverage "invisible" user activities thus convert all people into active content publisher. In early studies about online communities, "lurking", or the activities of "reading posts but never posting", is typically perceived as a negative activity [23]. These people free ride the content produced by others, but they do not generate content for others. With 'publishing while consuming' designs, we can change the "lurking" phenomena. On the one hand, parts of the lurker's activities become visible for others, so it is rare to be a lurker. On the other hand, with easy mechanisms to participate, many lurkers will start to explicitly publish more often.

6.2   Increasing Social Presence

'Publishing while consuming' can make people share more content and engage in social connections. People may also end up becoming more socially aware of each other. They can effortlessly notice cues left by others even when they do not intentionally look for such content. We believe that all these factors contribute to the positive experience over social networking services because all of these factors are essential motivations for people to use these services [6].

MoodPhotos has a direct way of presenting emotional responses and feeling of people when they view photos. Whereas, FingerPrint served as a subtle, reassuring feature that informs a user that 'a close one has seen my photos'. With these different types of communication channels, a feeling of connectedness is generated. We believe that in a private group sharing (close friends or family members) such openness in sharing photos and consumption patterns of people may generate a more open atmosphere in the group and may even lead to more photos shared. The long-term impacts of these features deserve more attention in the future studies.

We foresee that with a fully functional system, 'publishing while consuming' may persuade people to give away relevant contextual information. As research has shown, when convinced by the potential values, people are willing to make some compromise [23]. In this study, we find that people gain sufficient social interaction benefits when giving away some level of private information. Purely from a technologist's perspective, this is a good direction to expand people's comfort zone in sharing their contextual information. It is of note that we do not intend to start an argument that it is beneficial to persuade people to make privacy compromises. This argumentation certainly deserves attention in a separate discussion.

6.3   Limitations: Location and Context

From the beginning of this research, we were sensitive about the issues related to people's privacy. Our participatory design approach was carefully placed to simulate realistic situations, involving natural data from our participants. As PhotoBook is not a full-fledged system, we could not explore the opportunities and hurdles added by the locational and contextual aspects. The way people consume content in the real-world may differ from what we observed in these simulated design workshops. As this was clearly an early design phase, where we wanted to collect early feedback from users and inform our future design.

In this study we gathered user stories about how they regulate their feedback sharing behavior. For example, we learn that the privacy concerns are tied directly to the type of content that is shared between users, for example, the photos revealing potentially sensitive information. The privacy issues may start to arise when a user is viewing a photo that he/she should not be viewing or is not expected to be viewing. In a short user study sessions as ours, we did not record any examples of such photos being taken and/or viewed. Without these types of critical cases, it is hard to accurately evaluate privacy concerns in these design concepts. As a general limitation of this study, users must imagine scenarios where their privacy might be at risk. What participants say and what they actually do in a realistic scenario may also differ. Therefore, we interpret the result as an early sign for future study. The final privacy evaluation needs a further field study with implemented systems in our future work.

7   Summary and Future Work

Our PhotoBook prototype and the participatory setup were intended to explore the values of leveraging people's consumption related behaviors to enrich social interaction with shared personal content (in this case, photos). As a general finding, we found that 'producing while consuming' was beneficial for enriching social interactions in agreement with [25], and that it invited reciprocity. Close groups appear to be a good setting for the 'producing while consuming' designs. An early study with the "Who've Seen You" feature shows that the feature did not often lead to reciprocity in an open social network [11].

The value of FingerPrint and MoodPhotos was obvious to users as the publishers of photos. People are generally positive about obtaining the possibility to access information from others, although they do not necessarily want to publish their own information for others in return [25]. In our study, we found that this unwillingness to publish may not be an issue for close groups. We understand that people are interested in building their relationships with each other within a close group. Concepts such as FingerPrint and MoodPhotos are good channels to bond these relationships.

In summary, this user study implies that 'publishing while consuming' could be a promising design theme. In the next step, we are developing functional systems based on these concepts and deploying them in field studies to verify if the design theme of 'publishing while consuming' is as much promising as we have seen in these participatory design workshops. In an ongoing research, we are implementing and deploying a system that supports FingerPrint and MoodPhotos, and comparing the system with a baseline photo sharing system without such functions. The baseline system support lightweight feedback mechanisms, similar to 'like' or +1 buttons in Facebook and Google+. The major difference is that users currently explicitly share their consumption patterns (through likes and text comments) as opposed to the implicit sharing of fingerprint marks.

Acknowledgments. We would like to thank our participants for their valuable feedback. We thank Arto Lehtiniemi and Sanna Mallinen for helping in the study. This study was hosted by Nokia Research Center and was partly funded by the Finnish Funding Agency for Technology and Innovation TEKES. Financial support for writing this paper also came from the European Commission, within the framework of the ARTEMIS JU SP8 SMARCOS project 100249 - (www.smarcos-project.eu).

References

1. Ahern, et al.: Over-exposed?: privacy patterns and considerations in online and mobile photo sharing. In: Proceedings of the SIGCHI Conference on Human Factors in Computing Systems (CHI 2007), pp. 357–366. ACM, New York (2007)
2. Balabanoviç, M., Chu, L.L., Wolff, G.J.: Storytelling with digital photographs. In: Proceedings of the SIGCHI Conference on Human Factors in Computing Systems, pp. 564–571. ACM, New York (2000)

3. Benevenuto, F., Rodrigues, T., Cha, M., Almeida, V.: Characterizing user behavior in online social networks. In: Proc. IMC 2009, pp. 49–62. ACM (2009)
4. Bentley, F., Metcalf, C., Harboe, G.: Personal vs. commercial content: the similarities between consumer use of photos and music. In: Proceedings of the SIGCHI Conference on Human Factors in Computing Systems, Montreal, pp. 667–676. ACM, New York (2006)
5. Cui, Y., Honkala, M.: The Consumption of Integrated Social Networking Services on Mobile Devices. In: Proc. MUM 2011, pp. 53–62. ACM (2011)
6. Cui, Y., Wang, L.: Motivations for accessing social networking services on mobile devices. In: Proc. AVI 2012, pp. 636–639. ACM (2012)
7. Esbjörnsson, M., Brown, B., Juhlin, O., Normark, D., Östergren, M., Laurier, E.: Watching the cars go round and round: designing for active spectating. In: Proceedings of the SIGCHI Conference on Human Factors in Computing Systems (CHI 2006), pp. 1221–1224. ACM, New York (2006)
8. Hagen, P., Robertson, T., Kan, M., Sadler, K.: Emerging research methods for understanding mobile technology use. In: Proc. OZCHI 2005. Computer-Human Interaction Special Interest Group (CHISIG) of Australia, Narrabundah, Australia, pp. 1–10 (2005)
9. Iriberri, A., Leroy, G.: A life-cycle perspective on online community success. ACM Computing Surveys 41(2), 11:1–11:29 (2009)
10. Jacucci, G., Oulasvirta, A., Salovaara, A.: Active construction of experience through mobile media: a field study with implications for recording and sharing. Pers. and Ubi. Compu. 11(4), 215–234 (2007)
11. Jiang, J., Wilson, C., Wang, X., Huang, P., Sha, W., Dai, Y., Zhao, B.: Understanding latent interactions in online social networks. In: Proc. IMC 2010, pp. 369–382. ACM (2010)
12. Jedrzejczyk, et al.: On the impact of real-time feedback on users' behaviour in mobile location-sharing applications. In: Proceedings of the Sixth Symposium on Usable Privacy and Security (SOUPS 2010), Article 14, 12 pages. ACM, New York (2010)
13. Kairam, S., Brzozowski, M.J., Huffaker, D., Chi, E.H.: Talking in circles: selective sharing in Google+. In: Proc. CHI 2012, pp. 1065–1074. ACM Press (2012)
14. Kindberg, T., Spasojevic, M., Fleck, R., Sellen, A.: The Ubiquitous Camera: an In-Depth Study of Camera Phone Use. IEEE Pervasive Computing 4(2), 42–50 (2005)
15. Lampe, C., Ellison, N., Steinfield, C.: A face(book) in the crowd: social Searching vs. social browsing. In: Proc. CSCW 2006, pp. 167–170. ACM (2006)
16. Miller, A.D., Edwards, W.K.: Give and take: a study of consumer photo-sharing culture and practice. In: Proceedings of the SIGCHI Conference on Human Factors in Computing Systems, pp. 347–356. ACM, New York (2007)
17. Miluzzo, et al.: Sensing meets mobile social networks: the design, implementation and evaluation of the CenceMe application. In: Proceedings of the 6th ACM Conference on Embedded Network Sensor Systems (SenSys 2008), pp. 337–350. ACM, New York (2008)
18. Odom, W., Zimmerman, J., Forlizzi, J., Choi, H., Meier, S., Park, A.: Investigating the presence, form and behavior of virtual possessions in the context of a teen bedroom. In: Proc. CHI, pp. 327–336. ACM Press (2012)
19. Odom, W., Sellen, A., Harper, R., Thereska, E.: Lost in translation: understanding the posession of digital things in the cloud. In: Proc. CHI, pp. 781–790. ACM Press (2012)
20. Olsson, T.: Understanding Collective Content: Purposes, Characteristics and Collaborative Practices. In: Proceedings of the Fourth International Conference on Communities and Technologies (C&T 2009), pp. 21–30. ACM, New York (2009)

21. Olsson, T., Toivola, H., Väänänen-Vainio-Mattila, K.: Exploring characteristics of collective content: a field study with four user communities. In: CHI 2008 Extended Abstracts on Human Factors in Computing Systems, pp. 2967–2972. ACM, NY (2008)
22. Olsson, T., Soronen, H., Väänänen-Vainio-Mattila, K.: User needs and design guidelines for mobile services for sharing digital life memories. In: Proceedings of the 10th International Conference on Human Computer Interaction with Mobile Devices and Services, pp. 273–282. ACM, New York (2008)
23. Preece, J.: Sociability and usability in online communities: determining and measuring success. Behaviour & Information Technology 20(5), 347–356
24. Sarvas, R., Frohlich, D.M.: From snapshot to social media: the changing picture of domestic photography. Springer, London (2011)
25. Tsai, J.Y., Kelley, P., Drielsma, P., Cranor, L.F., Hong, J., Sadeh, N.: Who's viewed you?: the impact of feedback in a mobile location-sharing application. In: Proc. CHI 2009, pp. 2003–2012. ACM, New York (2009)
26. Van House, N.A.: Collocated photo sharing, story-telling, and the performance of self. Int. J. Hum.-Comput. Stud. 67(12), 1073–1086 (2009)
27. Van House, N.A.: Personal photography, digital technologies and the uses of the visual. Visual Studies 26(2) (2011)
28. Vennelakanti, R., Dey, P., Shekhawat, A., Pisupati, P.: The picture says it all!: multimodal interactions and interaction metadata. In: Proc. ICMI 2011, pp. 89–96. ACM Press (2011)
29. Watanabe, K., Sugawara, K., Matsuda, S., Yasumura, M.: Time-Oriented Interface Design: Picking the Right Time and Method for Information Presentation. In: Jacko, J.A. (ed.) HCII 2009, Part I. LNCS, vol. 5610, pp. 752–759. Springer, Heidelberg (2009)
30. Watanabe, K., Tsukada, K., Yasumrua, M.: WillCam: a digital camera visualizing users' interest. In: Extended Abstracts of CHI 2007, pp. 2747–2752 (2007)

Extensible Sound Description in COLLADA:
A Unique File for a Rich Sound Design

Shih-Han Chan, Stéphane Natkin, Guillaume Tiger, and Alexandre Topol

CEDRIC, CNAM, 292 Rue Saint-Martin
75003 Paris, France
{shihhan.chan,tiger.guillaume}@gmail.com,
{stephane.natkin,alexandre.topol}@cnam.fr

Abstract. Most standard scene description languages include a sound description and factorize common elements needed by the description of visual and auditory information. Both aspects are described with the same coordinate system for example. However, as soon as a dynamic description or external data are required, this benefit is lost and all the glue must be done by a programming solution that does not fit designers or authors usual skills. In this paper we address this problem and propose a solution to give back to designers the bigger role even when the scene is dynamic or based on procedural synthesizers. This solution is based on the COLLADA file format in which we have added sound support, scripting capabilities and external extensions. The use of this augmented COLLADA language is illustrated through the creation of a dynamic urban soundscape.

Keywords: sound design, scene description language, COLLADA.

1   Introduction

Nowadays, almost all applications exploit visual and audio senses of the user in order to notify tasks execution and achievement. Such a traditional application will initialize and render both media independently. Rendering each at a time is mandatory since they don't use the same pipeline and the same rendering device. For the initialization process, an application will load or generate the correct parameters for each media, will most likely have to make some coordinate system changes and/or duplicate some structures in memory. Hence, linking auditory and visual information together in the same resource file would ease the audio-visual overall description of an application.

Moreover, visuals and sounds can be generated in different ways, by several methods, which might be used within the same application. For example, in a video game, graphics can be made by 3D models textured with still (2D bitmap) or moving (2D videos) images and be animated either by keyframed (animation files) or physics (set of parameters). For the auditory part, a game can play a stereo music or a synthetized ambiance mixed with spatialized sound sources with different effects. The usual way to link all these different resources is to code inside the application both the

A. Nijholt, T. Romão, and D. Reidsma (Eds.): ACE 2012, LNCS 7624, pp. 151–166, 2012.

initialization of individual resources and the link between them. This can be done either in a roots way by hard-coding it or by using a scene designer like those implemented in Unity, UDK or CryENGINE.

This last way to build a scene by spatializing audio-visual objects (or assets or prefabs) is indeed very powerful as it simplifies greatly the work of programmers and the interactions needed with level designers. However this solution is proprietary and exploits generated files in an unknown binary syntax and tightly linked to the underlying game engine. It is absolutely not a general description that can be shared between different software solutions and thus easing the sharing of resources. For this reason, some authors prefer to use open standards to describe their 3D environments. The most well-known and used standards for describing multimedia scenes and contents will be presented in the next section.

These are partial solutions to our problem which is to describe a rich interactive audiovisual scene in which sounds (or any other media) could be rendered by reading resource files or by a procedural way which requires connecting to a script or an external program. Our main target applications are developed within the Terra Dynamica project. The purpose of this French government funded project is to build a 10000+ agents city simulation core and propose tools to drive and render such simulation. The CNAM is in charge of the design and development of the audio engine.

After the state of the art on sound capabilities in scene description languages (section 2), we present the descriptive solution our sound engine relies on (section 3). The choice was made to add sound support to the well-known COLLADA file format and to enhance it with scripting capabilities. In section 4, we compare how our proposal can ease the work of sound designers. Finally, in section 5, we conclude and present our future work.

2   Sound in Scene Description Languages

Interactive rich multimedia presentations are making their entrance into the world and are being increasingly used for newscasts, education material, entertainment, etc [1]. In this context, a scene description language that enables complex synchronization and authoring interactivity for content production is demanded.

A scene description language refers to any description language to describe an audio-visual presentation composited from several medial components. The language can be interpreted by a rendering program that will generate, either in real time or in batch, a perceptive (animated image and sound) representation of the scene.

Among an assortment of scene description languages formats for sounds, there are SMIL, VRML/X3D and MPEG-4 BIFS containing descriptions of both visuals and audios, and others like SDIF, SpatDIF, ASDF and XML3DAUDIO composing pure-aural scenes.

From the audio aspect, MPEG-4 AudioBIFS provides probably the most advanced among the existing scene description languages. The BInary Format for Scenes (BIFS) is comprised of both 3D and 2D objects interlinked to form the scene graph of a MPEG-4 world. It has a great portion of the structure inherited from VRML. AudioBIFS describes the audio scene in MPEG-4 BIFS. More than twenty audio nodes, each of which has its own functionality and semantic, has been specified over three versions of AudioBIFS.

However, due to its complex structure and it requiring massive amounts of data processed, the interpretation of the whole capability of MPEG-4 scene description has never been implemented. Secondly, formats that are the most widely used are usually intended for web contents delivery (e.g., SMIL, X3D) or computer music technology (e.g., SDIF, SpatDIF). A scene description that meets our expectation of bringing sound into virtual cities has not yet been made. In the following sections, we consequently propose a novel approach of adding an audio scene into COLLADA format that is easy to use, exchangeable and transportable among various applications, and allowing advanced interactions. Referred languages like SMIL, X3D and MPEG-4 AudioBIFS, have provided basic and useful information of sound functionalities that can be applied to our new audio scene description standard.

3   A Rich and Extensible Sound Description in COLLADA

A COLLADA [8, 9] defines an open standard XML schema from which digital contents of assets can be easily retrieved. It is an intermediate language for transporting data among various interactive 3D applications. It is also a neutral interchange format between several authoring tools, such as geographic information system applications (e.g., Google Earth, ArcGIS), asset repository systems (e.g., 3DVIA, Google Warehouse), web 3D engines (e.g., Papervision3D, Google O3D, Bitmanagement), and game engines (e.g., Unity, Ogre, Torque 3D). COLLADA is not only widely used in desktop applications, but it's also well suited for working with 3D contents on the web for its inherent use of web technologies (i.e., XML syntax and URI resource identifiers).

The present COLLADA scene consists of "visual" objects and "physics" and "kinematics" simulations. The three descriptions are independent but there is a mapping between the corresponding components.

Among the existing scene description languages, MPEG-4 BIFS gives a most well-established auditory scene structure. Inspired by the notion of AudioBIFS, we propose an object-based audio subgraph to the COLLADA scene. In contrast with the visual scene graph that represents the geometric relationship between graphical objects and the background space, an audio scene represents a signal-flow graph describing digital-signal-processing manipulations [3]. The chain of processing goes from bottom to top in the audio subgraph. Each child element outputs the data to one or more parent nodes above. The leaves and intermediate nodes do not play sounds themselves; only the result in an audio object, in which an audio subtree is rooted, is presented to the listener. Audio objects can also be associated with visual nodes for further geometry control.

In addition, we suggest the integration of the soundscape conception into the hierarchical scene with the intention of adding a sense of aural depth. Due to that the basic soundscape categories are significantly related to human perceptual habits, they are easily applicable for the synthesis and analysis of all such electroacoustical soundscapes, usually referring to virtual acoustic environments [10].

More complex dynamic behaviors is now required for interactive applications. The content needs to evolve not only for the interaction with the user but also for the interactivity between the different elements of the content [8]. Accordingly, we introduce to COLLADA a description language that is able to script the dynamic phenomena of the virtual city. This solution is expected to be able to apply on not only the audio but also the visual and physics capabilities in the COLLADA scene.

3.1   Static Scene

Audio Nodes

The COLLADA auditory scene is constructed by two genres of audio elements. The first is made up by *Audio Stream* that contains sound stream data throughout the signal processing chain. Among these are *<audio_source>*, *<audio_buffer>*, *<audio_delay>*, *<audio_mix>*, and *<audio_switch>*, whose functionalities and semantics are inherited from MPEG-4 AudioBIFS. These elements are intermediate nodes that do not directly send streams to the presenter. The *<sound>* and *<sound_2d>* nodes can also be mapped to those of AudioBIFS, although they are not the roots in the COLLADA audio subtree. What takes place is a node named *<audio_object>* that finishes sound result at the top of each audio subgraph. A novel element, *<sound_ext>* that is particularly designed for external programmed sounds with an extended control of self-defined parameters, is introduced to the sound nodes level.

The second type of audio nodes is *Audio Effect*. Unlike *Audio Stream* elements carrying sound data, the *Audio Effect* elements provide only the control of sound effects that can be applied on *Audio Stream* elements for delivering DSP effects.

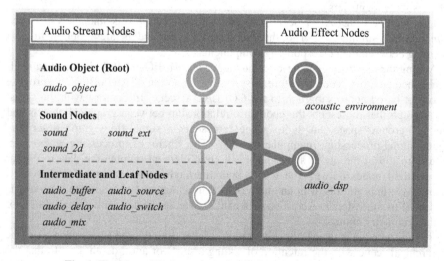

Fig. 1. The hierarchical structure of the audio nodes in COLLADA

The hierarchical structure of COLLADA audio nodes is illustrated in Fig. 1. The elements in the left are the *Audio Stream* nodes layered in three stages. Auditory data are routed from bottom to top. In the lowest level, there are intermediate nodes and leaves performing mathematical operations on the audio signals they carry; then in the middle, sound nodes served as junctions organizing and passing along the streams and parameters to the root audio object that will present the result to virtual listeners. On the other hand, the *Audio Effect* nodes, including *<audio_dsp>* that applies DSP effects on individual audio stream nodes and *<acoustic_environment>* that adds perceptual value to the entire audio scene, are designed for "painting" acoustic colors to enhance a sense of persuasive acoustic space.

In the following content, we present further details about the functionality of each node and give examples of the implementations.

Audio Stream Nodes

- *<audio_source>*

The *<audio_source>* element adds a sound source into the scene. The current <audio_source> element not only supports the import of common audio PCM file formats, such as WAV, MP3, or OGG, but other extensive designer-generated sounds, like Fmod EVents (FEV) or Pure Data (PD) patches, can also be processed over the usage of the *<audio_source>* elements. Existing COLLADA typed data elements *<newparam>* and *<setparam>* are taken to self-define parameters for the extensive sound types. One can use *<newparam>* to create a new, named parameter of an audio source and assign it a type and an initial value, which can later be modified by the *<setparam>* during the instantiation process, or can even be reassigned inside the dynamic script in real-time

- *<audio_buffer>*

The *<audio_buffer>* element records a segment of sound to be used in interactive playback. It is similar in concept to the VRML node *AudioClip*, but can be used in broadcast and other one-way streaming media applications.

- *<audio_delay>*

The *<audio_delay>* element allows child sounds to be temporally delayed or advanced for synchronization.

- *<audio_mix>*

The *<audio_mix>* element is used to mix M channels of sounds into N channels through a simple matrix calculation. One is able to control the proportions of the input sounds that are mixed to the output by manipulating the entries specified in the mixing matrix.

- *<audio_switch>*

The *<audio_switch>* element selects a subset of the input channels to pass through. In addition to the existing functionalities, a new *random* feature is provided to make it possible to select randomly from a number of child nodes (not channels explicitly) to pass through. This is useful, especially when there is an abundance of a certain type of sound, and one doesn't want to choose one source in particular.

- *<sound>*

The *<sound>* element defines sound in a 3D scene. It may also, but not necessarily, be linked with visual nodes in the visual subgraph of the COLLADA scene. The sound is emitted in an elliptical pattern formed by two nested ellipsoids, which are oriented by extending the *direction* vector through the sound emitter's *location*. Within the inner ellipsoid, the sound loudness is scaled by the value of the *intensity* field and there is no attenuation; between the inner and outer ellipsoids, the sound level is decreased linearly from 0 dB (minimum) to -20 dB (maximum); outside the outer ellipsoid, no sound is played. The field *spatialize* specifies if the audio object is perceived as being directionally positioned relative to the virtual listener. The value of the *priority* decides which sounds to be played when there are too many active sound nodes to be played at once because of the limits of the system load.

- *<sound_2d>*

The *<sound_2d>* element defines sound in a 2D scene. The semantics are identical to those in *<sound>*, except that *<sound_2d>* is unavailable in 3D context.

- *<sound_ext>*

The *<sound_ext>* element is an innovation designed to bring programmed sound into the scope of COLLADA sound schema. In the entertainment production, interactive sounds are typically reproduced via middleware audio toolkits (e.g., Fmod, Wwise, XACT) or visual programming languages (e.g., Max/MSP, Pure Data). For this reason, we are dedicated to standardize the description of the design process in order to facilitate the communication among content designers.

Given that the nature of the programmed sound is often complicated beyond the comprehension of the *<sound>* element, also that the properties of the *<sound>* element are not always necessarily in use in this case, we coin an element, *<sound_ext>*, along with an extended control of self-defined parameters.

- *<audio_object>*

The *<audio_object>* element is the root node in the audio subtree of COLLADA scene. It is the result that will be presented to the listener. Thanks to the notion of the *<sound_ext>*, COLLADA ought to be able to import designer-generated sound formats. However, this capability is limited to specific platforms to which the technique conforms. Therefore, the information of associated profile must be specified. The COLLADA *<profile_COMMON>* is designed to ensure that the content embraced can be interpreted by all the COLLADA-compatible applications. As opposed to the common profile, other profiles encapsulate data types specifically conforming to particular platforms. Extensive sound objects are accordingly declared in this scope.

The *<audio_object>* element for the audio scene is mostly equivalent to the *<physics_model>* in the physics scene. So the approaches of connecting the audio scene with the visual scene in COLLADA are very similar. First, an *<audio_object>* can be instantiated under a specific transform node (i.e., to dictate the initial position and orientation) by pointing the *parent* attribute in *<instance_audio_object>* to the *id* of a *<node>* in the visual scene. Alternatively, the child sound element corresponding to the *<rigid_body>* node is allowed to overwrite the transforms of the visual node element defined by the *target* attribute in its instance.

Furthermore, we intend to integrate the urban soundscape system into the COLLADA audio scene in order to enrich a sense of aural depth of the field. Our first attempt is to add a *layer* property to instantiated audio objects in the audio scene. The *layer* is a list of names indicating which soundscape layer that the instantiated audio objects belongs to. Each instance of audio object can be added to multiple layers by setting a list of whitespace separated layer names, or assigned to the default (non-specific) layer by leaving its layer unspecified.

Audio Effect Nodes

- *<audio_dsp>*

The functionality of *<audio_dsp>* element is similar to that of AudioFXProto in MPEG-4 AudioBIFS. In contrast to AudioFXProto which are relay nodes in the stream processing flow, *<audio_dsp>* contains no sound data but a set of DSP effects together with parameters. The *<audio_dsp>* node can be appended to any COLLADA audio node defined in above. Then the DSP effects will be applied to the output channels of its parent node. The DSP settings contained in *<audio_dsp>* include *<audio_dsp_compressor>*, *<audio_dsp_delay>*, *<audio_dsp_equalizer>*, *<audio_dsp_filter>*, and *<audio_dsp_reverb>*.

- *<acoustic_environment>*

The *<acoustic_environment>* element is represented by perceptual parameters. One can use the *<preset>* child element to select from preset generic, outdoor-city (e.g., inside_car, small_street, wide_open_space, outdoor_stone_walls) or indoor-room (e.g., bathroom, hallway, small_room) environments. Another option is to instantiate an *<audio_dsp_reverb>* element which has already been stored in the library. Both methods enable individual DSP reverb parameters (e.g., decay_time, late_dealy, diffusion, master_level) to be overridden to customize the reverb.

Audio Scene

The design of the COLLADA audio scene follows the same philosophy of visual, physics and kinematics scene graphs to maintain the consistency of the overall structure. In accordance with our proposition, COLLADA is divided into four parallel scenes. Each sub-scene is independent but the nodes, from one scene to another, can be associated with each other and share properties. Fig. 2 demonstrates the subgraphs of COLLADA scene and how they can be connected with each other.

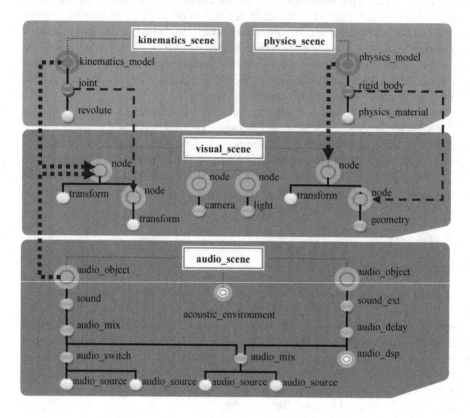

Fig. 2. An Example of the scene graphs in COLLADA

The *<audio_scene>* element specifies an environment in which sonic objects are instantiated and simulated. The active *<audio_scene>* is indicated by instantiating them under the main *<scene>*.

The *<technique>*s can also be helpful under multiple applications or game statuses. They generally act as a "switch", selected by a platform or program specified with the *profile* attribute. Each audio scene can contain various techniques, each of which describes a customized scenario comprising one or many audio objects and acoustic environment settings. With this feature, an audio scene is capable of describing a wide variety of circumstances. This shall, as well, provide a semantic choice for different applications in different principles to arrange the priority of the layer represented.

In order to enrich a sense of aural depth of the field, we integrate the soundscape system into the audio scene. The way we implement it for the audio scene is based on the layering design and evaluation procedure in the COLLADA visual scene.

Like how it is defined in the *<node>* element, the *layer* attribute of *<instance_audio_object>* or *<instance_acoustic_environment>* contains not a single value but a list of names. Matching it with the *layer* name for each rendering pass in the *<evaluate_scene>* can determine the soundscape layer to be evaluated. An audio scene may instantiate multiple audio objects, but only those that have their *layer* attribute names matched against the *layer* names of the evaluation scene that will be processed during the rendering pass. Likewise, a room effect setting for acoustic environment only affects the same-layer objects. The control of which layer to playback can also be adjusted by dynamic scripts in keeping with the game status. Sounds in different layers may be rendered with different channel setups in accordingly. For example, mono for the foreground and stereo for the midground. By default when no layer is specified, we elect to have all auditory contents be stereo.

3.2   Dynamic Script

Cued by time or movements, adaptive audio in virtual cities is able to travel among different perspectives from background via midground to foreground and vice versa. Sound like motion objects can be transferred from one state into another by an event trigger [11]. Given that the scene graph technology is reaching its limit to manage all the relationships between objects, a script language for describing more complex dynamic behavior for interactive applications is demanded. Consequently, we suggest a high-level JavaScript-like language (embedded or external) that enables scripting of auditory behaviors from sound designers' perspective yet in a programming solution. This script can be considered as an interface glue code between COLLADA and the audio API.

The sound engine architecture diagram depicted in Fig. 3 explains how enriched COLLADA can integrate sound resources by embodying extensive sounds in the COLLADA scheme, and further simplify the procedure and communication by specifying interactions in script manipulation.

Unlike delivery formats that are intended to contain the information for interactive applications, COLLADA provides a standard language to describe 3D assets but not their runtime semantic [12]. As such, definition and implementation of how the content will be used is left to the application writer. It is not our intention to change its position in the production pipeline. So even though all the intelligence is described and comprehended within COLLADA script, the effort of realization shall be made by the importing application.

In the following, we introduce several properties and methods to COLLADA acoustic components for the first implementation, and give examples of how they run in our script.

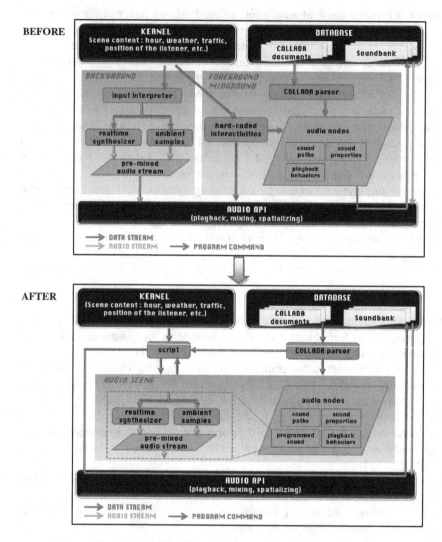

Fig. 3. COLLADA Integration in Sound Engine Architecture

Audio Object

An *audio_object* can be played back automatically or triggered by an event, such as a mouse-click or collision. Playback methods simply plays, stops or pauses the selected *audio_object*.

The *param* property is an array mapped to the parameters of a sound. This is not a property of the *audio_object* itself but its child sound node. Depending on the type of the child sound node, it may refer to a different semantic and functionality. For instance, *param[0]* of *sound* is its *direction*, whereas it indicates *intensity* for *sound_2d*, or the first self-defined parameter for *sound_ext*.

In the following example, we play the rpmAO object; then get the rpm parameter value (rpmVal) from a game component (car1) frame-by-frame and update the *param[0]* of the child sound node (<*sound_ext*> in this case) of rpmAO with this value.

Example:

```
var car = app.getComponentByName("car1");
var rpmAO = scene.audioScene.getAudioObjectById("rpm");
rpmAO.play();
function update()
{
    var rpmVal = car.getParamByName("rpm");
    rpmAO.sound.param[0] = rpmVal;
}
```

Audio Scene

By default, <*audio_scene*> picks up the <*audio_object*>s laying in the <*technique_common*>. Modifying the value of *profile* attribute for <*technique*> by scripting can dynamically switch the <*audio_scene*> from one game state to another.

The *audio_scene* object has another property named *acoustic_environment* that is linked to the <*acoustic_environment*> element. The next example demonstrates how to fetch the value of "outdoor" parameter from the application and assigns it to the environment's *preset*. For instance, if the application world is currently in a "large_street", the environment's *preset* will be fed an integer "2" correspondingly.

Example:

```
function Enum(){}
Enum.OutEnv = {small_street:1, large_street:2}
var env = app.getParamByName("outdoor" );
// var env = Enum.OutEnv.large_street = 2
scene.audio_scene.acoustic_environment.preset = env;
// scene.audio_scene.acoustic_environment.preset = 2
```

4   Sound Design

In this section a sound design pipeline is proposed based on the COLLADA sound description exposed above. This pipeline relies on the close dialogue between Pure Data patches and COLLADA files and allows sound design for an interactive project to be developed closely to the graphic assets. We will first discuss the actual evolution of sound design techniques for interactive environments, then the linking of

COLLADA files with Pure Data and finally the architecture of the basic Pure Data patch dedicated to the COLLADA *<sound_ext>/<audio_source>* element.

4.1   Interactive Sound Moving to Procedural Production

The classic way of designing sounds for interactive and/or virtual objects [11] is to create the appropriate audio material aside from the virtual environment. These sounds are created from genuine recordings or based on soundbanks or synthesized. Sometimes the ending result is a mix of all of these techniques. Tools used to design the sound (e.g., filters, samplers) are frequently included in a Digital Audio Workstation (DAW) environment (e.g., ProTools, Logic). These production environments were originally conceived for musical or audio documentary production as well as for linear audiovisual production.

The designed sounds are then included into the virtual environment. This can be done by the mean of either a generic sound engine (e.g., Fmod, Wwise) or a specifically developed solution. Within the sound engine, the sound designer defines the rules and behaviors applied to the playback and synthesis of sounds. These rules are based on the description of interactive events which unique ids are linked between the sound engine and the virtual environment with a dedicated API.

The sound is then tested within the virtual environment. If the result does not fit the expectations, the whole creation pipeline may be started over from DAW to integration. Another downside regarding this pipeline is inherent to the creation of the environment itself: as the graphic objects are developed, their needs in terms of sound might change. Hence sound production is separated from the visual production in time: sound design is often one of the last steps in the production process.

However, recent studies about sound design tend to focus on different strategies interlinking visual and audio. The improvements are reaching towards procedural ways of generating interactive soundscapes. Multiple goals are pursued with these strategies. One of the first intends is to create a non-repetitive design so that the listener does not have the feeling of hearing twice the same soundscape; using procedural audio is also a way to reduce memory consumption by switching from sample playback to sound synthesis [21] or to use refined strategies of audio playback such as granular [13] and concatenative synthesis [14, 15].

Fields of application range from interactive installation to video games. On this matter, video games are completing a full circle as sound was originally synthesized within chips [16]. Tools dedicated to real time synthesis are showing up in major video game sound engines such as Fmod and Wwise. Furthermore, dedicated procedural plugins for environmental sound design such as AudioGaming's "Audio Weather" are released. Research in the field of interactive procedural audio is also leading to synthesis solutions [22] and sound description languages [17].

4.2   Proposal for Interactive Sound Design

Our proposal is to simplify the sound design pipeline described in 4.1 using the COLLADA sound description of the virtual environment. We intend to link this description to the sound design tools. We also want this sound design architecture to communicate with any sound API and visual rendering engine so that it is possible to use to produce audio in a wide range of applications and environments. Hence our proposed architecture remains independent from the choice of sound APIs and rendering engines (e.g., Unity, UDK, Ogre).

As a sound design tool, we propose to use Pure Data. Pure Data is an open source graphical programming environment. It has been used in variety of artistic installations and interactive media creations. Pure Data is a rich tool for audio design [18] allowing many different treatments and techniques of synthesis [19]. Many other solutions for graphical programming exist such as Reaktor, Max/Msp, or Bidule. Pure Data appeared easier to integrate in our project and provides a large amount of libraries allowing us to program the main features we need.

Linking between Pure Data and COLLADA is done through the *<sound_ext>* node described above. The node points at the file path of the attached Pure Data patch and describes the essential characteristics of the sound, just like the *<audio_source>* node.

The *<audio_source>* being at the lowest level of the audio COLLADA description, a sound of *<audio_object>* may be composed of several *<audio_source>* nodes. From a sound design point of view, this architecture makes layering easier regarding Audio Object sonification. Furthermore, the editing of a complex audio object does not lead to the destruction of the sound attached to it but to the edition of the joint audio layers.

4.3   Pure Data Design

As Pure Data patches are attached to the *<audio_source>* nodes, their design is intimately linked to its functionalities. They also receive data from the dynamic script. The following paradigm shows the connections coming in and out of the standard Pure Data patch attached to an *<audio_source>* and a dynamic script.

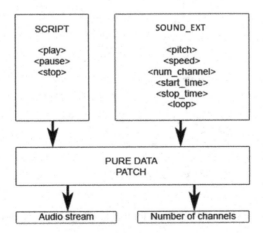

Fig. 4. Flows Coming In and Out of the Standard Pure Data Patch

The COLLADA *<audio_source>* element describes the following functions:

- *<loop>* defines the looping behavior of the sound a value of 0 sets the sound to loop forever and any other value sets the number of time the sound is played.
- *<pitch>* controls the payback pitch shifting of the sound, it is specified as a ratio where 1 indicates the original bitstream pitch.
- *<speed>* controls the playback speed of the sound, values other than 1 indicate multiplicative time-scaling by the given ratio.
- *<start_time>* specifies, in seconds, the starting point of playback.
- *<stop_time>* specifies, in seconds, the stopping position of playback.
- *<num_chan>* describes how many channels of audio are there in the decoded stream.

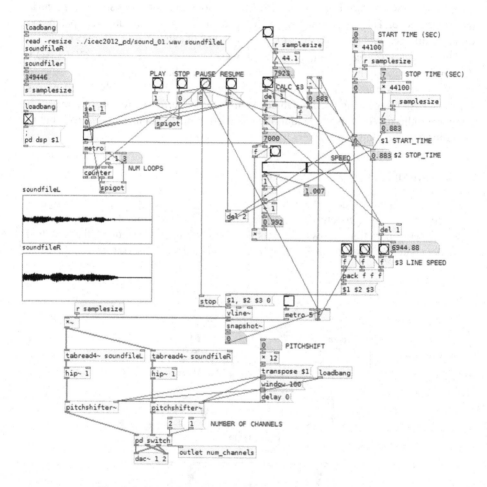

Fig. 5. Basic Pure Data Patch for the *<audio_source>* Nodes

Plus, dynamic scripting in COLLADA allows for a patch to receive Play, Stop, Pause and Resume information so that the sounds are triggered accordingly to the dynamic events of the scene.

Pure Data patches output two streams: the audio stream of the patch and the number of channels used within it. The number of channels information is used by the nodes *<audio_mix>* and *<audio_switch>* for processing purpose.

We implement these functionalities inside the basic Pure Data patch (Fig. 5) initiated in the *<audio_source>* node. Ratio and time values are rescaled to match their description inside the Pure Data patch. It gets then possible to playback the complete sound attached to one `<sound_ext>` or a part of it, at a selected pitch and speed. These functionalities are close to granular synthesis requirements [20] so further possibilities should be considered besides simple audio playback.

5   Conclusion and Future Work

Merging Pure Data sound production and COLLADA sound description is an efficient way of quickly building interactive audio scenes. Scripting and external linking capabilities added in our proposal will permit to describe even richer functionalities like those listed below.

Regarding the sound design aspects, further developments should be conducted in terms of sound granulation. Random values of pitch shifting, grain amplitude, densities and envelopes would increase the sensation of non-repetitive soundscape.

So far, the sound description properties apply for sample playback functions. Adding descriptive parameters applicable to pure synthesis, such as additive synthesis, would allow extended design functionalities. These parameters could consist in high level description of spectral characteristics.

Also, semantic descriptors could be sonified with corpus based concatenative synthesis. The aim is to create generic Pure Data concatenative patches dedicated to classes of *<audio_source>* nodes, for example, footsteps and engines.

References

1. Shao, B., Velazquez, L.M., Scaringella, N., Singh, N., Mattavelli, M.: SMIL to MPEG-4 BIFS Conversion. In: Proceedings of the 2nd International Conference on Automated Production of Cross Media Content for Multi-Channel Distribution (AXMEDIS), pp. 77–84 (2006)
2. Pihkala, K., Lokki, T.: Extending SMIL with 3D audio. In: Proceedings of the International Conference on Auditory Display (ICAD), pp. 95–98 (2003)
3. Scheirer, E.D., Väänänen, R., Houpaniemi, V.: AudioBIFS: Describing audio scenes with the MPEG-4 multimedia standard. IEEE Transactions on Multimedia 1(3), 237–250 (1999)
4. Main SDIF site, http://sdif.sourceforge.net/
5. SpatDIF Project: SpatDIF specification V 0.2 (2011)
6. Geier, M., Ahrens, J., Spors, S.: Object-based audio reproduction and the audio scene description format. Journal Organised Sound 15(3), 219–227 (2010)

7. Potard, G., Burnett, I.: Using XML Schemas to Create and Encode Interactive 3-D Audio Scenes for Multimedia and Virtual Reality Applications. In: Plaice, J., Kropf, P.G., Schulthess, P., Slonim, J. (eds.) DCW 2002. LNCS, vol. 2468, pp. 193–203. Springer, Heidelberg (2002)

8. Arnaud, R., Barnes, M.: COLLADA: Sailing the Gulf of 3D Digital Content Creation. A K Peters Ed. (2006)

9. Barnes, M., Finch, E.L.: COLLADA – Digital Asset Schema Release 1.5.0 Specification. Sony Computer Entertainment Inc. (2008)

10. Truax, B.: Soundscape Composition as Global Music: Electroacoustic Music as Soundscape. Organised Sound 13(2), 103–109 (2008)

11. Collins, K.: Game Sound: An Introduction to the History, Theory, and Practice of Video Game Music and Sound Design. MIT Press (2008)

12. Arnaud, A., Parisi, T.: Developing Web Applications with COLLADA and X3D (2007)

13. Paul, L.J.: Granulation of sound in video games. In: Proceedings of the AES 41st International Conference (2011)

14. Brent, W.: A timbre analysis and classification toolkit for Pure Data. In: Proceedings of the International Computer Music Conference, ICMC (2010)

15. Schwarz, D., Beller, G., Verbrugghe, B., Britton, S.: Real-time corpus-based concatenative synthesis with CataRT. In: Proceedings of the 9th International Conference on Digital Audio Effects, DAFx 2006 (2006)

16. Farnell, A.: An introduction to procedural audio and its application in computer games. In: Audio Mostly Conference (2007)

17. Veneri, O.: Architecture d'un intergiciel pour la création sonore dans les jeux vidéo. PhD thesis, Conservatoire National des Arts et Métiers (2009)

18. Farnell, A.: Designing sound. MIT Press (2010)

19. Puckette, M.: The theory and technique of electronic music. World Scientific Publishing (2007)

20. Truax, B.: Real-time granular synthesis with a digital signal processor. Computer Music Journal 12(2) (1988)

21. Misra, A., Cook, P.R., Wang, G.: A new paradigm for sound design. In: Proceedings of the 9th International Conference on Digital Audio Effects, DAFx 2006 (2006)

22. Verron, C., Aramaki, M., Kronland-Martinet, R., Pallone, G.: A 3D immersive synthesizer for environmental sounds. IEEE Transactions on Audio, Speech, and Language Processing 18(6), 1550–1561 (2010)

An Automatic Race Track Generating System

Tai-Yun Chen, Hung-Wei Hsu, Wen-Kai Tai, and Chin-Chen Chang

1 National Dong Hwa University, Taiwan
2 Nation United University, Taiwan
{m9821003,d9821008}@ems.ndhu.edu.tw
wktai@mail.ndhu.edu.tw, ccchang@nuu.edu.tw

Abstract. In this paper, we propose an automatic race track generating system based on difficulty evaluation and feature turns detection for providing users skill-matched contents. Given a start point, a goal point, and a difficulty expectation chart, our system ranks all candidate race tracks according to the similarity with respect to the given difficulty curve. Then, user can choose a satisfied track and export it into a racing car simulator to play.

The system automatically creates the racing line for the input race track. Then, the line is used to segment turns in the race track, and the corresponding ideal maximum speed variation is exploited to evaluate the difficulty by our proposed Turnscore formula. Also, the corresponding curvature chart of the racing line is encoded as a string and the characterized regular expression for feature turns is being matched in the string for identifying feature turns.

As the experimental results show, the feature turns detection is of high accuracy and the difficulty evaluation is reliable so that our system is effective to provide skill-matched race tracks for users.

Keywords: Difficulty Evaluation, Race Track Generation, Racing Line, String Searching, Procedural Content Generation, Feature Detection.

1 Introduction

Automatic race track generation is essential to car racing games for appealing players with keeping update contents. Also, most players who are playing racing games would like to drive cars at race tracks with different levels of difficulty according to their skill of driving. Therefore, an automatic race track generating system demands the ability of difficulty evaluation for race tracks. The research goal of this paper is to develop such an automatic race track generating system on street maps.

We use the street map of real world from Open Street Map [1]. The network information of the street map is transformed as a graph. Then, all simple paths from the given start point to the goal is what users need. Our system calculates the racing line for a given race track. And, based on it, we can obtain the variations of the ideal maximum speed of the ideal car on the race track. The variation of the maximum speed is exploited to segment turns and evaluates

A. Nijholt, T. Romão, and D. Reidsma (Eds.): ACE 2012, LNCS 7624, pp. 167–181, 2012.

their difficulty in the race track. In addition, some well-known feature turns, namely hairpin turn, the S-turn, etc., are identified to highlight the prominent characteristics of the race track by using string matching. Each sample point at the racing line is encoded into a three-character string to represent the curvature, the trend of the curvature, and the slope of the curvature. Every feature turn can be characterized as a regular expression consisting of the three characters and this expression is used to match substrings in the string representation of the race track.

By the system, all feasible race tracks are ranked according their difficulty matching to a difficulty expectation chart given by users. The referential information such as the length of the race track, the ideal fastest time to finish the race track, all detectable feature turns and the number of turns in the race is displayed in the system for assisting the race track selection. Users can export a suitable race track into a racing car simulator to play with.

Many experiments have done to verify the correctness of the proposed difficulty evaluation algorithm and the feature detection algorithm. The racing statistics of 2010, 2011, and 2012 Formula One and comment of professional commentators were used to verify the proposed difficulty evaluation method. Moreover, we have conducted a user study to show the correctness of our evaluation method. As experimental results show, our difficulty evaluation method is with 62% accuracy with respect to the professional commentator's comments. However, our evaluation is highly related to the timing of professional driver's performance. As the verification for the feature turns detection, we compared our results with the listed three feature turns from the comments of the professional commentators. As experimental results show, the feature turns we found is very close to those commentators indicated.

Our contributions are listed as follows. First of all, the difficulty of the race tracks could be quantified by our evaluation method. And, the race track of car racing games can be automatically generated to adapt to the level of player's skill. Secondly, the feature turns where will be critical points in the racing game in the race track can be identified to enhance the gameplay. Finally, our system automatically generates various race tracks for players to choose such that automatic content generation of car racing games is feasible.

The organization of this paper is as follows. In the next section, we briefly describe some background information and related work. Section 3 presents the system we proposed in detail, while Section 4 shows the experimental results. The conclusions and the future work are drawn in the final Section.

2   Related Work

The racing line used to be manually created using an editing tool by a professional[7]. Another way to create a racing line manually is to drive in a given race track, and the driving path is recorded as the racing line. Both are empirical approaches so that they are time-consuming. Recently Colin McRae Rally[6] calculates the racing line by an artificial neural network which is trained by professionals. It uses the Feedforward multilayer perceptron with correct input variables. The RPROP Learning algorithm[8] he suggested is more efficient compared to other algorithms[9][10]. Unfortunately, the AI driver based on the algorithm is still beaten by a skilled human-player because the racing line is not precise enough.

Forza Motorsport powered by Microsoft uses a reinforcement learning technique, Q-learning, to train the AI driver in game for finding the racing line[11]. First, all possible racing lines are determined from the table of data. The second step is to change the racing line based on the situation in game. The learning technique lets the AI be trained by players and makes the game more playable. However, the key problem of machine learning is unpredictable. The Open Car Racing Simulator[12] uses the K1999 algorithm[13] to calculate an approximate racing line quickly. The racing line is composed of many sample points by minimize their curvature without taking physics into account.

Braghin et al.[14] tried to take the shape of the race track, aerodynamics, and traction of cars into account to calculate the racing line. They address that the racing line of a race track is located between the shortest path (SP) and the minimum curvature path (MCP) of the race track. This is an important definition for racing line generation. Cardamone et al.[15] employ a generic algorithm to find the racing line according to the above observation. The linear combination of SP and MCP computes the best racing line. The fitness function it used is to simulate a lap time by the racing line in The Open Car Racing Game. The algorithm is general in that it could be applied to any racing games, but the simulation time is too long to be real-time.

In 2010, Gran Turismo 5[17] provide a tool to let players choose a style of background, a number of sectors, the difficulty, curvature, and width of each sector to automatically create a race track. Although the parameters players can specify are not enough at all, the idea makes the game more playable and creative. Chen et al.[18] present an idea to produce a large street network based on tensor field. The tensor field guides the users to generate a street network intuitively, and it allows the users to combine various global and local modeling operations. The disadvantage is that the street network they produced is regular, so the main application is in urban layout. Then, Galin et al.[19] present another algorithm to generate roads on a given scene with terrains and natural obstacles. Given an initial and a final point on the scene, the system automatically creates a path connecting both points based on some constraints. The path can even cross a river by building a bridge, or cut across a mountain by constructing a tunnel. The disadvantage is that users cannot control the detail of generating except modifying the parameters they used.

3   Automatic Race Track Generating System

The goal of the automatic race track generating system is to effectively and efficiently find candidate race tracks which satisfy the expectation of users such as difficulty from the street map of real world. Figure 1 shows the framework of our system. First, users are required to specify parameters: a start point, a goal point, and a difficulty curve. Then, our system find out all simple paths (tracks) from the start point to the goal in a constrained region, and all found paths are ranking by the difficulty. Third, the proposed feature detection algorithm detects all features for each track. Finally, users can choose a track and export it into a racing car simulator to play with.

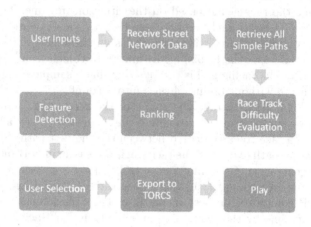

Fig. 1. The framework of our automatic racing track generating system

3.1   Difficulty Evaluation

Overview. The difficulty evaluation of the race track has been regarded as an art because race track designers design tracks according to their own experience so far. However, formulating the design is essential for automatic race track generation. The steps of difficulty evaluation are as follows as shown in Figure 2. First, we calculate an approximate racing line for a given track. Then, we obtain a maximum speed chart based on the curvature of the racing line. Based on the maximum speed chart, the race track is segmented into turns and straight lines. Finally, each turn is scored high if it is more difficult to drive through.

Turn Detection. All methods to get the racing line are digging into decreasing the curvature of driving path. In fact, driving along a path with less curvature may keep the higher speed [14]. The geometry of the race track is not the only parameter we should consider, so the physics of the car, the environment, and the interactive with other cars are elements to affect the racing ling. The reason of that an AI driver without cheating cannot beat a skilled human-player reminds us that to get a best racing line is still a difficult challenge.

Two key points we considered simply to get the best lap are that shortening the driving path and keeping the highest driving speed. Therefore, we increase

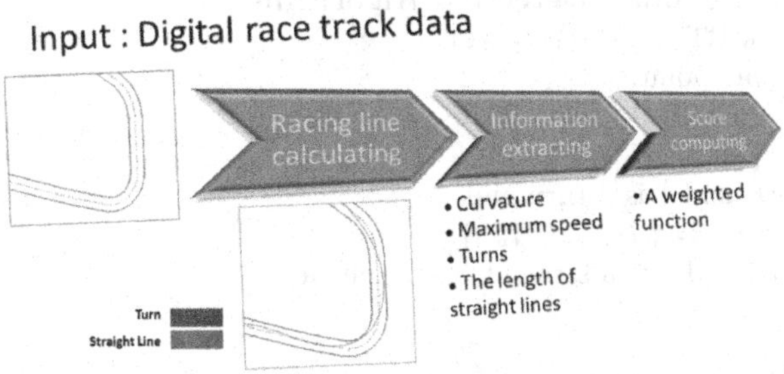

Input : Digital race track data

Fig. 2. The framework of our difficulty evaluation algorithm

the radius of curvature to get higher maximum speed. The racing line we implemented is approximate minimum curvature path [13]. We get the curvature chart according to the racing line. By the chart, we calculate the maximum speed chart using equation 1 [14]. All cars' physical parameters we used are formula one racing car data of TORCS [12].

$$v_{max} = \sqrt{\mu\rho(g + \tfrac{F_a}{m})}$$

(1)

The basic elements of the race track are turns and straight lines. Straight lines are located between turns. All turns and straight lines in a race track can be segmented according to the maximum speed chart. The algorithm is shown below. The input data of the algorithm is sample points of the race track. The critical point between turns and straight lines is one which has significant changes of the maximum speed. We traverse all sample points to get all start and end points of turns and straight lines by the algorithm.

Rating. The curvature, the maximum speed, turns, and straight lines in a race track are the key parameters of the proposed evaluation. The turn evaluation, $TurnScore(v_{min}, v_{diff})$, relates to the minimum speed of the maximum speeds in a turn and the braking distance the racer should take before a turn. The speeding term ($v_{max} - v_{min}$) of the evaluation means that the racer is hard to achieve a high speed in a turn with high curvature. The braking term represents the braking distance. The braking distance relates to the timing and the degree of braking for the racer. The longer braking distance the more difficult is. Intuitively, when v_{diff} approaches to zero, the racer can pass the turn without braking at all. The higher score the more difficult a turn is. The formula is defined as follow:

$$TurnScore = \begin{cases} \omega_1 (v_{max} - v_{min}) + \omega_2 v_{diff} & \text{if } \delta_{min} < v_{min} < \delta_{max} \\ \omega_1 v_{min} + \omega_2 v_{diff} & \text{, otherwise} \end{cases}$$

(2)

Turns and Straight Lines Detection Algorithm
Input:a race track RT = $\{s_0, s_1, K, s_n\}$
where s_i is a sample point.
Output:
a turn list TL = $\{ t_0, t_1, K., t_m \}$
where t_i = { start, end } is a turn and
a straight line list SL = $\{ l_0, l_1, K, l_m \}$
where l_i = { start, end } is a straight line segment.
begin
   turn T;
   straightLine L;
   L.start = s_0;
   foreach s_i ∈RT **do**
     if s_{i-1}.maxspeed = ∞ **and** s_i.maxspeed != ∞;
       T.start = s_i;
       L.end = s_i;
       SL.insert(L);
     if s_i.maxspeed = ∞ **and** s_{i-1}.maxspeed != ∞;
       T.end = s_i;
       TL.insert(L);
       L.strat = s_i;
   end
end

Fig. 3. Turns and Straight Lines Detection

, where v_{min} is the minimum speed of the maximum speeds in a turn, v_{max} is the maximum speed of an ideal car according to equation 1. v_{diff} is the difference between the maximum speed of a car entering the turn, v_{in}, and the minimum speed of the maximum speeds in the turn, v_{min}. ω_1 and ω_2 are weights for weighting speeding term and braking term respectively. Notice that a turn with v_{min} below a given threshold δ_{min} is hard to tell the difficulty. Similarly, v_{min} higher than a given δ_{max} is hard to tell either. There are two reasons to make the high speed turn more difficult: the time of determining the turning point is very short, and the gravity the driver sustained is quite large.

3.2　Feature Detection

Some specific combinations of turns increase the difficulty of the race track such as a combination of S-turn and double-apex turn. Besides, some special single turns increase the difficulty as well such as hairpin turn. These special turns and specific combinations feature a race track and must inform racers.

    To find out the feature of a race track, the entire race track is encoded into a string according to the race track's corresponding curvature chart, and a string searching algorithm is used to match feature turns. Figure 4 shows an example substring for the first turn. Each sample point at the racing line is encoded into a three-character string, $N_C C_T N_S$ where N_C, C_T, and N_S represent the curvature, the trend of the curvature, and the slope of the curvature respectively.

The range of the curvature, N_C, is large, i.e., from zero to infinite. Hence we quantize the curvature into ten degrees, represented as 0 to 9 from low to high. The trend of the curvature, C_T, has four possible types by taking the previous sample point and next one into account. They are "M" which means the local maximum of the curvature, "m" which means the local minimum, "U" which the curvature is increasing, and "D" which represents the decreasing curvature. The slope of the curvature, N_S, is the curvature variation of two adjacent sample points and is quantized into ten levels, from 0 to 9.

Every feature turn can be characterized as a regular expression consisting of the three characters, $N_C C_T N_S$. And the syntax used in our proposed regular expression is as follows. A plus sign, $+$, or a minus sign, $-$, located behind the N_C or N_S means that the curvature or its trend can be more than or less than a given curvature. The numeral of a superscript of the character shows the times of multiplicity. We may add a plus or minus sign behind the superscript. We list all feature searching details at Table 1.

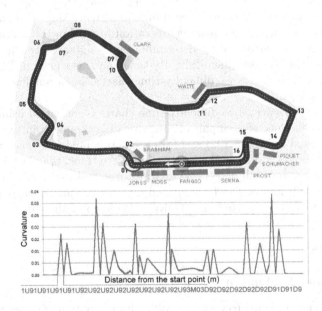

Fig. 4. (top) The layout of the Melbourne Grand Prix Circuit of the 2010 Formula 1 Australian Grand Prix where the black thick line represents the race track, the white arrow is the start direction, and the dotted line is the middle line of the race track. (bottom) The curvature chart of the racing line for race track in (top). The red string below the chart is the encoded string for the first turn of the race track by the proposed encoding algorithm.

Table 1. All feature turns information

Name	Searching expression	Example
Hairpin Turn	$\gamma_h + M0$	The 11th Turn of the Suzuka Circuit
Double-apex Turn	$?UX?U(X+\gamma_d)+, ?UX?U(X-\gamma_d)-$	The 7th and 8th turns of the Bahrain Inter. Circuit
S Turn	$\gamma_s+M?(?D?)^{\gamma^k}-(\gamma_i-$ $m?)(?U?)^{\gamma^k}-(\gamma_s+M?)$	The 9th and 10th turns of the Albert Part Circuit

3.3   User Interface

The user interface and the framework of the system are shown in Figure 5. Users have to specify the start point and end point, and optional checkpoints on the area of interested of a street map for enumerating all feasible race tracks. Notice that in our system the street map of real world from Google Map[5] is used. The number of feasible race tracks can be further reduced by given a distance constraint and a bounding area which constrains the extent of race tracks as shown in Figure 5. Then, all feasible race tracks are ranked according their difficulty matching to a given difficulty expectation chart.

To search a feasible path in a given extent of the street map, the network information of the street map obtained from Open Street Map [1] is transformed as a graph G and the simple path enumeration algorithm[16] is applied. The difficulty ranking is performed by determining how similar between a searched race track and the user specified difficulty-time chart as shown in Figure 5(B). Users are allowed to sketch the difficulty-time chart using a polyline as a shown example in Figure 5.

The similarity between two difficulty-time charts is measured using the sum of the squared distance of each pair of corresponding sample points. The ranked race track is listed in Figure 5(C) and for each highlighted race track we display referential information such as the length of the race track, the ideal fastest time to finish the race track, all detectable feature turns and the number of turns in the race track to help user select a preferred race track. Finally, the selected race track (streets) can be exported into TORCS [12] for play the game.

4   Results

4.1   Difficulty Evaluation

There are two experiments to verify the difficulty evaluation of a race track. The first experiment compares the difficulty of a race track our system evaluated with the difficulty measured by using real timing data of formula one races and comments of the professional commentators. The second experiment is to conduct a user study. All collected data from testers were analyzed to see if our evaluation matches tester's performance.

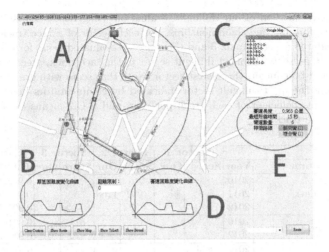

Fig. 5. The user interface of the proposed automatic race track generating system: (A) the map browser, (B) the expected difficulty-time chart sketched by the user, (C) a list of the ranked race tracks, (D) the difficulty-time chart of the selected race track , and (E) the referential information of the selected race track

Verification. The statistics of all racers' timing records of many races from the official formula one website [20] were analyzed and derived a formula for scoring the difficulty for sections of race tracks as follow:

$$SectorScore = 10 * (Avg_L - Avg_H)^2 / Avg \qquad (3)$$

where Avg is the average time of all records of each sector, and the Avg_H is the average time of top quarter records at a sector, and Avg_L means the average time of the last one quarter records. The formula 3 is designed for distinguishing the racers' skill at a sector. Notice that the score is normalized by the average time of all records, Avg.

In addition, we collect many comments of the professional commentators[2] to verify our evaluation. Commentators always tag some critical points at their comments for some race tracks which will affect the result of racing significantly. That means the difficulty of sections including critical points should be higher than those not.

The racing statistics of 2010, 2011, and 2012 formula one championships have been used to verify the proposed difficulty evaluation. All experimental results are shown in Table 2. The score with red color represents the most difficult sector in its race track, green is less difficult sector, and blue means the easiest section relatively. Also, a score with gray background color represents the most difficult sector commented by commentators. The C.C. we used to verify the degree of correlation is the Pearson product-moment correlation coefficient[22].

Table 2. The verification of our difficulty evaluation using racing statistics of 2010, 2011, and 2012 formula one championships. For each sector of a race track, we show the score calculated using formula 3 and the score we evaluated using formula 2. Score with red color represents the most difficult sector in the race track, green color means less difficult, and blue means the easiest sector. Note that score with gray background color represents the most difficult sector indicated by commentators believed. C.C.1 is the correlation coefficient of each track per year, and C.C.2 means the correlation coefficient of each track.

Track Name	Year	Sector 1 Score	Our	Sector 2 Score	Our	Sector 3 Score	Our	C.C.1	C.C.2
Albert Park	2010	1015		646		1890		0.97952	
	2011	1492	1409	1092	1268	2321	1564	0.98526	0.92108
	2012	1291		837		1920		0.99784	
Bahrain Inter. Circuit	2010	999	987	2675	1559	811	817	0.99169	0.75760
	2012	598		1117		472		0.99076	
Sepang Intel. Circuit	2010	844		4641		280?		0.81182	
	2011	316	564	1397	1290	1132	1397	0.93760	0.51718
	2012	351		1065		1050		0.99076	
Shanghai Intel. Circuit	2010	614		1270		76?		0.75386	
	2011	490	552	851	1170	931	1093	0.95964	0.65769
	2012	443		651		76?		0.96821	
Circuit de Gilles Villeneuve	2010	1218	1409	1317	1185	924	854	0.79236	0.82074
	2011	1174		1135		778		0.94794	
Circuit de Catalunya	2010	809	778	1530	1376	812	1295	0.60756	0.57826
	2011	1199		1822		1466		0.88663	
Istanbul Speed Park Circuit	2010	1038	1609	1205	1349	218	1004	0.82471	0.81957
	2011	1155		11?		580		0.90924	

We calculate a C.C. for each track per year and all years, and the average correlation coefficient for all records is 0.902 which means that the higher score we evlauated the more distinguishing a sector is. Furthermore, 94% of C.C.1 is greater than 0.7 which indicates highly linear dependence between the two scores. 57% of C.C.2 is larger than 0.7, and 100% of C.C.2 is larger than 0.4 which means that the two scores are significantly linear correlative. The lowest C.C.2 is calculated from the race record of the Malaysia Grand Prix at Sepang Intel. Circuit because the timing record of racer No. 25 in 2010 is the outlier which causes the difference much larger.

As you can see in Table 2, there are 13 sectors marked as the most difficult sectors by commentators and 61.5% of them matched our evaluations. In our evaluation algorithm, we don't consider the influence of a race track's height because we don't have the height information of all tracks. Therefore, it would cause some estimation error.

User Study. To evaluate the accuracy and reliability of the proposed difficulty evaluation, we invited ten male testers aged from 18 to 30 years old to join our user study. Among testers, 5 testers who seldom play any kind of racing games are totally newbies in racing games, 4 testers who play some racing games are not expert, and one tester who has played racing games for more than ten years is good at racing games. The experimental environment is the professional racing suit, AP1 [21]. The testers were given a racing task to get the best lap in specific race track, the Istanbul Speed Park Circuit. Before starting the task, they were asked to drive in two simple race tracks for a period of time to practice the physics of the racing car.

In total, we recorded 332 records from the user study. According to the rules of the formula one, the timing record of the lap is set as an invalid record if the four wheels of the racing car are out of the track at the same time. Therefore, about 21% of all records are valid. We compute the v_{diff} in each turn of each valid data for further comparison.

The average value of v_{diff} of each turn is shown in Figure 6. The turn ID is listed in difficulty we evaluated order descendingly. From Figure 6, each averaged v_{diff} is correlated to each turn score. The trend of the v_{diff} is descending as similar as the difficulty we evaluated. This means that our evaluation algorithm is effective and reliable. Moreover, the ranking chart in Figure 7 visualizes the high correlation between the score we evaluated from user study and from formula 2.

We also calculate the Normalized Discount Cumulative Gain[23] which measure the degree of relativity between the rank of the score form user study and the rank of our evaluation. We get a quite high score, 0.9077, ranged from 0 to 1. We also calculate the extracted tester's NDCG between the rank of standard deviation and the score we evaluated, and the result is 0.8803. In summary, the statistics of the user study shows highly correlation to the score we evaluated.

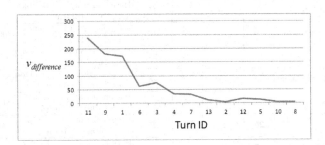

Fig. 6. The average v_{diff} of each turn in our user study. The number at horizontal axis represents the turn id listed in difficulty order descendingly. The vertical axis shows the v_{diff} (km/h).

4.2   Turn, Straight Line, and Feature Detection

To verify the correctness of turns, straight lines, and feature turns detection, we collected eleven digital race tracks of formula one to test. Instead of using the racing line we determined, we use the racing line shown at the official website for the detection. The experimental results are shown in Table 3. As you can see, the accuracy of turns and straight lines detection is high; 8/11 of tracks

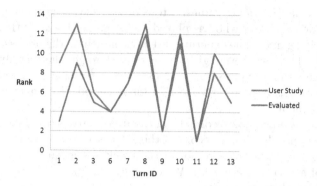

Fig. 7. The ranking chart for the user study's score and the evaluated score. The horizontal axis indicates the turn id, and the vertical axis shows the rank of each turn's score.

Table 3. The result of the turns, straight lines, and feature detection according to the midline

Track Name	official website		We detected			Accuracy(%)	
	Turns	S. Lines	Turns	S. Lines	Feature Turns	Turns	S. Lines
Bahrain Inter. Circuit	15	15	16	16	Haripin-Turn(2) Double-apex Turn(2) S-turn(2)	94%	94%
Albert Park	16	16	16	16	Haripin-Turn(0) Double-apex Turn(0) S-turn(7)	100%	100%
Sepang Intel. Circuit	15	15	15	15	Haripin-Turn(1) Double-apex Turn(3) S-turn(3)	100%	100%
Shanghai Intel. Circuit	16	16	11	11	Haripin-Turn(2) Double-apex Turn(4) S-turn(3)	69%	69%
Circuit de Catalunya	16	16	16	16	Haripin-Turn(1) Double-apex Turn(4) S-turn(4)	100%	100%
Circuit de Monte Carlo	19	19	24	24	Haripin-Turn(5) Double-apex Turn(2) S-turn(7)	79%	79%
Istanbul Speed Park Circuit	14	14	18	18	Haripin-Turn(0) Double-apex Turn(1) S-turn(7)	78%	78%
Circuit de Gilles Villeneuve	12	12	15	15	Haripin-Turn(1) Double-apex Turn(0) S-turn(5)	80%	80%
Valencia	25	25	25	25	Haripin-Turn(3) Double-apex Turn(1) S-turn(9)	100%	100%
Silverstone Circuit	17	17	19	19	Haripin-Turn(0) Double-apex Turn(3) S-turn(7)	89%	89%
Nurburgring	15	15	14	14	Haripin-Turn(1) Double-apex Turn(3) S-turn(5)	93%	93%
Average Accuracy						89%	89%

is higher than accuracy 80%. One detected sample testing race track , Sepang Intel. Circuit, is shown in Figure 8 corresponding to the feature of rack track illustrated at the official website in Figure 9. Due to the fact that our detection is on the basis of racing line, turns which is recognized visually from official website may not be detected by our method. During the third turn of the Sepang Intel. Circuit, the racers don't need to brake at all. That turn is regarded as a straight line. Thus, by the point of view of drivers, our detection is of 100% accuracy.

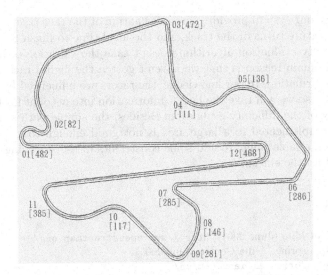

Fig. 8. The digital race track of the Sepang Intel. Circuit. The line segment with green color shows the straight line of the racing line, and the red line segment is the turn we detected. The red numeral represents the turn id, and the numeral in square brackets is the score we evaluated.

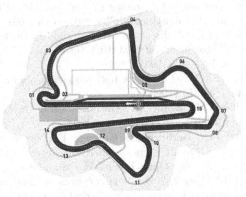

Fig. 9. The Sepang Intel. Circuit of formula one from the official website [20] illustrates the racing line (dotted line), sectors using different color, and turns (numeral). Note that the green circle in the middle of the race track represents the start point.

5   Conclusions

We propose an automatic race track generating system based on real streets with difficulty evaluation and feature detection. By our system, users can create a satisfied race track intuitively and export it into a racing car simulator to play. Besides, our system provide more information of the race track such as the length, the feature turns of the track, and the ideal time to finish the track.

Our difficulty evaluation algorithm doesn't take the variation of height into account. The main reason is that we haven't gotten the digital race track with the height information. In our knowledge, the racers are influenced by the variation of height, so we will take the height information into account for improving the accuracy of the difficulty evaluation. Besides, the simple path searching algorithm we implemented in a large area is not good enough to get all simple paths in a reasonable time. To add some constraints in the searching algorithm might speed up the efficiency.

References

1. Open Street Map (June 2001), http://www.openstreetmap.org/
2. Allianz Sponsoring Media Center (June 2005),
   http://sponsoring.allianz.com/en/
3. Wymann, B.: TORCS Robot Tutorial (February 24, 2005),
   http://www.berniw.org/
4. F1 Tracks for TORCS (June 2011), http://apr-free.info/joomla/
5. Google Map (June 2011), http://maps.google.com.tw/
6. Hannan, J.: Interview to jeff hannan (2001),
   http://www.generation5.org/content/2001/hannan.asp
7. Lecchi, S.: Artificial intelligence in racing games. In: 2009 IEEE Symposium on Computational Intelligence and Games, CIG 2009, p.1 (2009)
8. Riedmiller, M., Braun, H.: A direct adaptive method for faster backpropagation learning: the RPROP algorithm. In: 1993 IEEE International Conference on Neural Networks, vol. 1, pp. 586–591 (1993)
9. Tollenaere, T.: SuperSAB: fast adaptive bacl propagation with good scaling properties. Neural Networks 3(5) (1990)
10. Schiffmann, W., Joost, M., Werner, R.: Optimization of the Backpropagation Algorithm for Training Multilayer Perceptrons (1994)
11. Stern, D., Candela, J.Q., Herbrich, R., Graepel, T.: Playing machines: Machine learning applications in computer games. Microsoft Research Cambridge (2008)
12. TORCS Team. TORCS (The Open Racing Car Simulator) Official Site. Latest Version: TORCS 1.3.1 (May 2, 2010), http://torcs.sourceforge.net/
13. Coulom, R.: Reinforcement Learning Using Neural Networks, with Applications to Motor Control. PhD thesis, Institut National Polytechnique de Grenoble (2002)
14. Braghin, F., Cheli, F., Melzi, S., Sabbioni, E.: Race driver model. Computers and Structures 86(13-14), 1503–1516 (2008)
15. Cardamone, L., Loiacono, D., Lanzi, P.L., Bardelli, A.P.: Searching for the Optimal Racing Line Using Genetic Algorithms. In: 2010 IEEE Symposium on Computational Intelligence and Games (CIG), pp. 388–394 (August 2010)
16. Rubin, F.: Enumerating all simple paths in a graph. IEEE Transactions on Circuits and Systems 25, 641–642 (1978)
17. Gran Turismo 5 (2010), http://en.wikipedia.org/wiki/Gran_Turismo_5
18. Chen, G., Esch, G., Wonka, P., Muller, P., Zhang, E.: Interactive Procedural Street Modeling. ACM Transactions on Graphics 27(3), 103:1–103:10 (2008)

19. Galin, E., Peytavie, A., Marechal, N., Guerin, E.: Procedural Generation of Roads. Proceedings of Eurographics 29(2), 429–438 (2010)
20. The Official Formula One Website, http://www.formula1.com/
21. The Official APIGA Website, http://www.apiga.com.tw/
22. Soper, H.E., Young, A.W., Cave, B.M., Lee, A., Pearson, K.: On the distribution of the correlation coefficient in small samples. Appendix II to the papers of "Student" and R. A. Fisher. Biometrika 11(4), 328–413 (1917)
23. Jarvelin, K., Kekalainen, J.: Cumulated gain-based evaluation of IR techniques. ACM Transactions on Information Systems (TOIS) 20, 422–446 (2002)

Light Perfume: Designing a Wearable Lighting and Olfactory Accessory for Empathic Interactions

Yongsoon Choi[1,2], Rahul Parsani[2], Xavier Roman[2],
Anshul Vikram Pandey[2], and Adrian David Cheok[1]

[1] Graduate School of Media Design, Keio University, Japan
[2] Keio-NUS CUTE Center, Interactive Digital Media Institute, National University of Singapore
`{goodsoon96,rahul.parsani,xavier.roman,`
`anshul.bits,adriancheok}@gmail.com`

Abstract. In this paper we present *Light Perfume*, a wearable system that helps the users and their communication partner to mirror their nonverbal communication cues together using factors such as speed of blinking and color in lights and subtle perfume emission from a wearable accessory during a face-to-face conversation. This is based on the concept of mirroring, whereby each user is stimulated with the same visual and olfactory outputs to strengthen a user's psychological bond with the partner using the accessory. We initially explain the motivation and design of the prototype for the *Light Perfume* system. We evaluate the system using a semantic differential method and show how the system can be used to affect the impression formed of the user by others and explore the potential usage of the entertainment accessory.

Keywords: Empathy, mirroring, wearable media, lights, perfume, light perfume, synchronization, communication.

1 Introduction

According to the social psychologist, Konrath (2011), college students in the U.S. are 40% less empathic today than they were in 1979, with the steepest decline recorded in the last ten years [1]. Young people lack empathy despite being constantly connected to others via social-networking sites and mobile devices [2]. In our contemporary digitized world, we now live in an increasingly diverse, globalized, and complex society. We think, ironically, people come in contact with vast numbers of their counterparts each day leading to more superficial relationships [3].

There is no doubt that the influence of the Internet and digital media is ever-growing and that as time goes by, more and more people get connected to it. However, it is also true that there is a growing debate about whether or not it actually helps to bring people closer together [4].

Today's digitalized communication technologies engage the visual and auditory senses through the use of video, sound or text. These devices leave out other senses and produce interactions that lack certain important characteristics that are unable to substitute real face-to-face communication [5].

A. Nijholt, T. Romão, and D. Reidsma (Eds.): ACE 2012, LNCS 7624, pp. 182–197, 2012.
© Springer-Verlag Berlin Heidelberg 2012

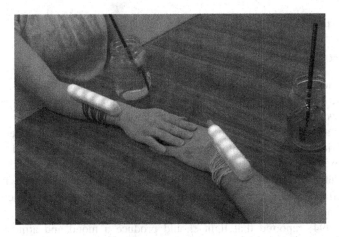

Fig. 1. An application of Light Perfume: A couple holding hands during a face-to-face conversation

The quality of interactions we experience with someone through a social networking site will never be of the same standard as if you were having a face-to-face conversation while maintaining eye-contact and holding hands, although people are now better able to get in touch with others than ever before.

In human relationships, mirroring someone's body language makes them feel accepted and creates a bond with the other person. It is a phenomenon that occurs naturally between friends and people of equal status [6]. The mimicry can act as a kind of "social glue" and foster rapport in subtle ways. This kind of "emotional link" affects people's psychological regulation of our impression on the other party [7].

We address this problem in current relationships with our project, *Light Perfume*, which is a wearable fashion accessory that helps people mirror their nonverbal cues during social interactions through visual and olfactory stimulations. Each wearer's system measures these cues through movement and sound sensors that are mapped to output values that are stimulated simultaneously from either system. The output expressions are combinations of the frequency and color of light and a perfume scent. Our goal is to help people strengthen their emotional bond with others during social interactions through these mirrored expressions.

In this paper, we explore the effect of lights and fragrance, and review the relationship of mirroring with empathy for social interactions. We describe the design of *Light Perfume* and the mirroring interaction based on eye-contact with others. Then we show that *Light Perfume* has a similar effect to that of mirroring behavior in psychology. We demonstrate that it is possible to use *Light Perfume* to affect a person's impression positively on their partner during their interpersonal social interaction based on a user study we conducted using a semantic differential (SD), interviews and video observations. We conclude by discussing the results and limitations of the study followed by our plans for the future.

2   Related Works

2.1   Effects of Lighting and Smell

Various studies have shown that particular lights and smells can unconsciously help people create emotional moods and feelings [8-11]. It also affects people's perceptions, judgments, work performance, and help develop their relationships [10-12].

There are a number of publications that report research conducted to determine the effect of various lights and color conditions on peoples' feelings [8-11]. Research conducted by Frasca (1999) on interior design for ambulatory care facilities reports some important design factors. The research reports that color and lights have a profound influence on patients and consumers, such as consumer satisfaction, stress level, health and well being [9].

Flagge (1994) reported that light should produce a mood and atmosphere in a room, which corresponds to people's demand and expectation [10]. Kaufman and Christensen (1981) noted that light can play an important role in reinforcing special perception, activity and mood setting [11].

Smells can also evoke strong emotional reactions. In surveys on reactions to odors, responses show that many of our olfactory likes and dislikes are based purely on emotional associations [13]. According to Kate (2007), the positive emotional effects of pleasant fragrances also affect our perceptions of other people. Unpleasant smells can also affect our perceptions and evaluations [12]. One study in her report, the presence of an unpleasant odor led subjects not only to give lower ratings to photographed individuals, but also to judge paintings as less professional [12].

2.2   Mirroring and Empathy

Mirroring is the behavior in which one person copies another person usually while in social interaction with them. It may include miming gestures, movements, body language, muscle tensions, expressions, tones, eye movements, breathing, tempo, accent, attitude, choice of words/metaphors and other aspects of communication [14]. It is often observed among couples or close friends. For example, person A and B are engaged in a conversation. A might mirror some of B's mannerisms, leading B to like A more, trust them, and think of A as more similar, even though both are unaware that any mimicry took place. All this has been confirmed by psychological research [15, 16], leading to a popular perception that imitation is the best form of flattery.

Mirroring in social psychology is closely linked with empathic communication in Neuron Science. Rizzolatti and Arbib (2004) discovered from the frontal lobes of monkeys that when a monkey performs a single, highly specific action like pulling, pushing, tugging, grasping, or putting a peanut in the mouth, different neurons fire in response to different actions [17]. But what is astonishing is that any given mirror neuron will also fire when the monkey in question observes another monkey performing the same action [17].

Discovery of mirror neurons has helped understand to a great extent a number of human features, from imitation to empathy, mind reading and language learning.

Whenever we watch someone else doing something (or even starting to do something), the corresponding mirror neuron might fire in our brain, as a result of which we can read and understand the other person's intentions [18]. Damages in these cerebral structures can be responsible for mental deficits such as autism. Without these neurons, an autistic child can no longer understand or empathize with other people emotionally and therefore, completely withdraws from the world, socially [18].

The lack of proper empathic and emotional connection with another party may lead to a disconnecting in the important abilities in human interpersonal communication and socialization [19]. Maia Szalavitz (2010) also states this, *"Without empathy, we would have no cohesive society, no trust and no reason not to murder, cheat, steal or lie. At best, we would act only out of self-interest; at worst, we would be a collection of sociopaths [20]."*

A consistent finding in the literature is that empathy improves people's attitudes and behaviors towards other individuals or groups, while a lack of empathy is associated with more negative attitudes and behaviors including their social communications [21, 22].

3   Light Perfume

3.1   Design Concept

Light Perfume is designed as a wearable accessory to help people feel bonded towards each other using lighting and olfactory outputs by mirroring the expressions between the user and his or her partner.

When a user meets with his or her conversation partner, *Light Perfume* mirrors a user's nonverbal cues such as wearer's gesture, movement, voice and environmental sounds around him through a wearable *Light Perfume* accessory. The shared cues are actuated with same blinking frequency and lighting color while simultaneously emitting the same fragrance during face-to-face communication.

Fig. 2. The interaction process of the Light Perfume system: people get synchronized through eye-contact

The concept of *Light Perfume* can be explained as an accessory, which helps people feel synchronized during a conversation and the seamless actuation of mirrored expressions between the user and his or her partner, can make them feel more connected and comfortable during a conversation.

For the first prototype, the actuator was designed in a bangle in order to directly stimulate a user's eyes and unobtrusively stimulate a user's nose from the wrist. The aroma is created by heating solid perfume and emitted by the movement of the wearer's conscious and subconscious body gestures during a face-to-face meeting. To mirror the non-verbal cues in interpersonal communication, we reused the Sound Perfume glasses [23] that we designed in the previous project. The information between users and their partner was exchanged through eye-contact interaction using the embedded IrDA transceiver of the glasses.

3.2   Interaction

There are three components in the *Light Perfume* system:

• **IrDA Glasses (Sound Perfume Glasses):** It help the users share their nonverbal communication cues data naturally through eye contact interaction during face-to-face conversation through an Infrared Data Association (IrDA) transceiver.

• **Mobile Phone Application:** It helps users set the MAC address of the IrDA glasses and *Light Perfume* accessory, and also make the setting of the connection between the users' and their partners' bangles.

• **Light Perfume Accessory (Bangle Type):** It has sensors to measure the wearer's nonverbal communication cues and actuators for the lighting and fragrance expressions.

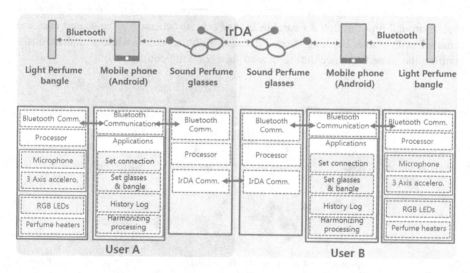

Fig. 3. System configuration: *Light Perfume* system

As shown in Fig. 2 and 3, when a user starts a face-to-face conversation with another person; his or her nonverbal communication cues such as body posture, gestures, voice and environmental sounds are sensed by the *Light Perfume* bangle and shared between each system through an IrDA module located in the bridge of the Sound Perfume glasses [23]. The partner's nonverbal communication cues are synchronized with the user's cues in the mobile phone application and forwarded to the *Light Perfume* bangle to actuate. This is done by blinking LEDs at the same frequency and color and actuating the same perfume aroma from the *Light Perfume* bangle on their wrists. This direct lighting expression and indirect stimulation of the same aroma makes the user feel that there's something about the partner he or she likes, and creates a stronger bond between each other during a face-to-face conversation.

3.3   Prototype of Light Perfume

The aim of the first model of the *Light Perfume* system was to design a proof-of-concept prototype. We conducted two brainstorming sessions to find a suitable accessory that can sense the wearer's gesture, movement, voice and environmental sounds around him or her. This data is then used to express lighting changes and perfume emission simultaneously. We selected the bangle form factor for *Light Perfume* as a fashion accessory since we were convinced that accessories worn on the forearm or wrists were suitable for sensing the user's gestures and movements. It was also easier for the user to notice the lighting expression changes and fragrance emissions. In addition, it gave us more space to work with for the actuators and sensor circuitry, required to realize this.

The original idea of interpersonal interaction for the synchronization was based on the distance between the users and their partner. As it is considerably difficult to stably find the target partner based on proximity using Bluetooth communication in the mobile phones, we decided to reuse the IrDA glasses that we designed in previous project [20] for the first prototype.

The *Light Perfume* bangle communicates with the user's smartphone via Bluetooth and uses the IrDA sensor in the Sound Perfume glasses to exchange the sensed nonverbal communication cues data with the partner. In response, the partner's phone communicates with his or her bangle, which controls the mirroring data between the user and his or her partner and expresses the same color and blinking frequency on the LEDs while emitting the same aroma during face-to-face encounters. Fig. 5 shows the combined usage of the Sound Perfume glasses with the IrDA transceiver [23] and the *Light Perfume* bangle.

3.4   Mobile Control Application

The application was developed for the Android 2.3.3 Platform based on the Sound Perfume mobile application [23]. We added functions to: 1) Set the user's bangle

MAC address in the settings menu and 2) A button that configures the Sound Perfume glasses to switch to *Light Perfume* mode. This mode could only use IrDA transceiver for interpersonal communication.

3.5   Light Perfume Bangle

The *Light Perfume* bangle was designed using the Arduino Pro Mini and consists of two sensing and two actuation modules as shown in Fig. 4. We embedded a triple axis accelerometer to sense the user's body gestures and movement and a microphone to sense voice and environmental sounds during the face-to-face encounter with the partner. Moreover we used five RGB LEDs to actuate the color and blinking expressions and eight channels of heaters to actuate the different kinds of smell expressions in the bangle.

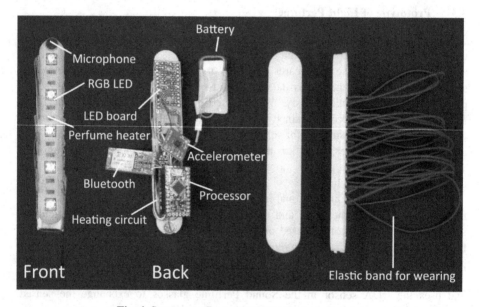

Fig. 4. System configuration: *Light Perfume* Bangle

The processor controls the sensing, actuation and communication with the mobile phone application through Bluetooth from the bangle. Fig. 4 shows the configuration of the *Light Perfume* bangle and an elastic band is added to the bottom of the cover to facilitate easy wearing.

• **Processor:** We used the Arduino Pro Mini that is connected to eight digital channels for the perfume heaters, receive and transmit lines for Bluetooth and four analog channels for control of the microphone and accelerometer.

• **Battery:** An attachable and rechargeable battery (Lithium-ion polymer battery, 3.7 V / 400 mAH) was used. The average current consumption was 40 mA, but it could reach approximately 300 mA for a few seconds when the perfume heater is switched on.

• **Bluetooth:** It provides the wireless communication between the mobile phone application and the *Light Perfume* bangle.

• **Heating circuit:** We make heat by passing amplified electric current through a 12 Ω resistor based on lab tests [23].

• **Sensors:** a triple axis accelerometer was used to sense the context of the user's movements and a microphone was used to sense the user's background sounds that can explain the user's environment.

• **LED circuit:** This was designed to control the five RGB LEDs.

• **Lighting and perfume actuator module:** The structure of the actuator module was designed to heat solid perfume using a resistor. The actuator construction has a string of five RGB LEDs and eight channels of perfume.To make a small bangle actuator, we used LEDs with a bulb size of 5 mm and designed the eight different perfume containers, each containing a 12 Ω resistor for heating the solid perfume as shown in Fig 4.

• **Mapping the relationship between sensing and actuation:** According to Choi's (2008) study, LED, Electroluminescence (EL) materials such as EL-wire, EL-sheet, and EL-tape are used for the expression of color, brightness, blinking speed and rhythm change of lights in fashion media. Color expressions are easily recognized by the wearer and others compared to other visual elements. Additionally the dot-form using LEDs, the line-form using EL-Wire, and the surface-form using EL-Sheet are all possibilities that are expressed in fashion [24]. Although there are many different types of visual expressions used in lights, in this study we focused on the basic expressions; color and blinking frequency. Initially for this research, we selected five colors; white, yellow, green, blue, and purple, and five different speeds; faster, fast, normal, slow, and slower. For smell samples, we reused the eight perfume samples we selected in previous project [23]. We defined five levels of input data from the accelerometer and microphone as shown in Table 1.

Table 1. Input levels for Light Perfume

Group	Movement (any axis) / Level	Noise / Level / Example
1	Under ± 1 m/s2 / Slower	Under 20 dB / Very Calm / A recording room
2	± 2 ~ 4 m/s2 / Slow	21 ~ 40 dB / Calm / A quiet room
3	± 5 ~ 7 m/s2 / Normal	41 ~ 60 dB / Normal / Conversation
4	± 8 ~ 10 m/s2 / Fast	61 ~ 80 dB / Loud / Cars in a big city
5	Over ± 11 m/s2 / Faster	Over 81 dB / Very Loud / Honking or shouting

These values are shared with the partners system and the output is selected based on the maximum of their respective values from the findings from the pilot study, For example, if the user has a "1 – Slower" movement and "1 – Very calm" noise data, meets his partner who has "3 – Normal" movement and "5 – Very loud" noise data, their mirroring noise data is "3 – Normal" and movement data is "5 – Very loud". The movement data controls the frequency of the LEDs, perfume heating channel and heating time, while the sound data controls the color of the LEDs. The corresponding stimulation for each output value is given in Table 2.

Table 2. Output levels in Light Perfume

Average value	Movement Data (Blinking frequency / Perfume channels & time)	Sound data (Color (RGB))
1	0.3 Hz / 1ch. & 5 sec.	purple (112, 0, 146)
2	0.6 Hz / 2ch. & 8 sec.	blue (27, 141,237)
3	1.2 Hz / 3ch. & 10 sec.	green (108, 255, 43)
4	2.4 Hz / 4ch. & 15 sec.	yellow (255,255, 0)
5	3.6 Hz / 5ch. & 20 sec.	white (255, 1255, 255)

3.6   System Evaluation

We recruited four volunteers from our laboratory, who were not involved in the design of this project, to help us evaluate the current system and interaction process. All of them noted the appearance of the bangle was not appealing and using the elastic band was inconvenient. However, we believed that these issues were not serious enough to interfere with the user study for our system, described more in the next section.

4   User Study

The psychologist, Nicolas' (2009) research examined the effect of mirroring; when a stranger mimics someone's verbal and nonverbal expressions, higher positive judgment of the mimicker was found [25]. The mirroring also produced various positive social behaviors such as spontaneity to help, and compliance to a request by the mimicker [25].

The user study was executed with 18 participants to know whether the effect of the *Light Perfume* experience can make the user feel similar feelings such as gesture and tonal mimicry, as well as the formation of positive impressions towards their partner.

4.1   Pilot study

The pilot study was executed with four volunteers (2 couples) who work in the laboratory. We gave them three minutes to converse while using the system and didn't give any guidance and restrictions. During the observation, two couples noticed that their *Light Perfume* systems were actuated by their gestures and voices. And one couple noticed the synchronized actuation between them. They seemed to enjoy the mirrored expressions. They were moving their arms, and tapping the bangle with their fingers to see the changes in the expression.

However, in the case of the other couple, they didn't recognize the mirrored expression. During the interview, they pointed out the expressions from the bangle, especially the lighting, were rapidly changed and they could not understand the reason. This happened because the bangles showed lights corresponding to the average values obtained from both bangles. Moreover this qualitative analysis of *Light Perfume* provided no insight into the changes the participants felt while using the system.

We decided to use a semantic differential (SD) method to measure the changes in the impression through the *Light Perfume* system and to use a fixed expression in to order to reduce the noise in the data and help us analyze the results.

4.2   Main Study

4.2.1   Participants

Eighteen volunteers were recruited for the study (67% female; average age 24 years) from our laboratory. A set partner was chosen for this experiment, who was a female who has just joined our lab as an intern student. Based on the findings of our previous project, we assumed that the formation of impression will be different based on their previous relationship[23]. We made two groups: Group A had previously met the female partner and Group B had no previous encounter with the set partner.

4.2.2   Apparatus

The study was conducted in the meeting room of the laboratory where we setup two chairs facing each other. The *Light Perfume* bangle and IrDA glasses were laid on the table between the chairs. We recorded each participant's interactions using a video camera placed beside the desk at an angle facing the participant to later analyze the changes in their subconscious facial expressions, gestures, and any verbal feedback provided during the test. Participants always sat on the same chair facing the fixed partner. They were allowed to wear the *Light Perfume* bangle and IrDA glasses in a way that was comfortable to them. The doors were opened so that we could ventilate the room between experiments.

4.2.3   Stimuli

To know the relationships of stimuli types and forming impression, we chose two stimuli sample sets for each of the divisions that received stimuli. The expressions from A set had positive impressions and the expressions from B set had comparatively negative impressions.

Table 3. Choosing the stimuli sets: Bolded words were the representative impressions

Stimuli sets	Sample code/ description	Extracted impressions
A set (positive)	LC4 / blue color LED	sorrow, **soft**, majesty, coldness, water, eternity, heaven, **peaceful**,
	LB3 / normal speed of blinking	relaxing, slow, **comfortable, soft**
	F1 / floral	sweet, romantic, girly, **smooth**, delicate, **soft**, warm, happy, pleased, sweet
B set (negative)	LC1/ red color LED	**hot, dangerous**, Love, liveliness, activeness,
	LB1/ fastest speed of blinking	fast, **dangerous**, excited, uncomfortable, nervous, **hot**, hard, powerful, angry, dull, bad, exciting,
	F2/ green	fresh leaves, familiar, grass, natural, energetic,

4.2.4   Response Format

After the encounter, each participant was asked to rate their impression about the set partner through an online survey immediately. Huma's SD (2010) was used to study the impression comparison between genders and her categorization of measuring impression was adapted and pretested for impression formation assessment [26]. We used a seven point rating scale with four dimensions: Sociability, Ethics, Power and Activity. The items contained in each dimensions are shown in Table 4. The online SD form was presented to the participant by randomizing the order of the items. The form also gathered the participant's demographic information, age, gender and race.

Table 4. The structure of the semantic differential: based on Huma's impression formation assessment

Dimensions	Impression assessments
Sociability	cold – warm friendly – unfriendly pleasant – unpleasant close – distant optimistic - pessimistic
Ethics	fair – unfair sincere – insincere honest – dishonest correct – incorrect
Power	obedient – independent cowardly – courageous weak – powerful bold – shy determined - undetermined
Activity	passive – active apathetic – energetic static – dynamic

4.2.5   Procedure

Each participant was provided an overview of experiment and an explanation of the procedure and response format. They were then given three minutes to converse the partner as shown in Fig. 5. Depending on the division, the participant would not be stimulated, played the Set A stimuli or Set B stimuli. The participants were then asked to fill out an online survey form immediately. After that we had an interview to ask their impression the fixed partner.

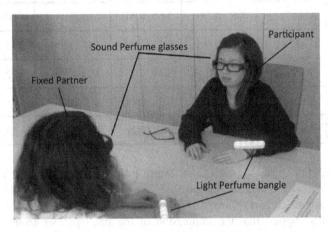

Fig. 5. Light *Perfume* bangle actuates the synchronized lighting expressions and emit the same perfume odor during the face-to-face encounter

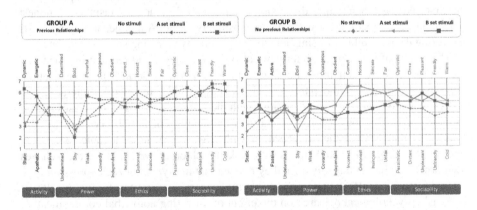

Fig. 6. Visual comparison of participants' impressions of their communication partner

4.2.6   Result

The analysis of the results was done based on the graph of mean values shown in Fig. 6. The results overall showed that all participants had enhanced impression values

Table 5. The mean scores of the four dimensions across the different groups: the yellow cells mark the meaningfully increased mean scores and blue cell marks the meaningfully decreased mean score based on corresponding no stimuli scores. And the values in ( ) is the standard deviation values (bold values show the meaningful values).

Groups	Stimuli	Sociability	Ethics	Power	Activity
A	None	**4.20**	**5.08**	**3.87**	**3.78**
	A set	**5.47 (0.74)**	5.67 **(0.44)**	4.07 (1.49)	4.00 (1.5)
	B set	**6.27 (0.49)**	4.75 (1.17)	4.47 (3.55)	5.33 (3)
B	None	**4.40**	**5.33**	**3.73**	**3.22**
	A set	**5.67 (0.82)**	6.08 **(0.44)**	4.00 (1.28)	4.11 (1.36)
	B set	5.20 (1.06)	4.25 **(0.2)**	4.13 **(0.69)**	3.89 **(0.86)**

in their sociability dimension, such as 'warm', 'friendly', 'pleasant', 'close', and 'optimistic'. We also could see the positive impression on the ethics dimension of impression, such as 'correct', 'honest', 'sincerer', 'fair' in Group B .

These results suggest that the impression of the fixed partner from participants enhances his or her sociability dimension, similar to much psychological research on mirroring nonverbal communication cues in a face-to-face conversation. Another interesting finding was that for Group B, participants who were meeting the partner for the first time, had their Ethics dimension ('fair – unfair', 'sincere – insincere', 'honest – dishonest', 'correct – incorrect') change positively by Set A and negatively by Set B indicating the possibility of being able to control this by changing stimuli samples.

The results of participants' interviews also showed they could feel the link between the expressions and felt more familiar with their partners during the conversation. Participants often used the phrases such as 'easy with', 'fun with', 'interact', and 'affect' that are related to the interactions with the partner as opposed to phrases related to their internal feelings. Moreover, through the analysis of the observation, we also found that they started the conversation with *Light Perfume* as a topic, once they realized their *Light Perfume* bangles were linked each other, we could see them shakes their arms together animatedly once they noticed that the synchronized expression.

Light Perfume affects people's mirroring experience similar to the results of Nicolas's psychological research on the effect of mirroring nonverbal communication cues in a social conversation.

4.2.7 Limitation

The method by which we form an impression about someone is very subjective, complex and context-based during a face-to-face interpersonal encounter. We could see the following limitations in the user study:

1) The need to investigate the biases that effect user's impressions during face-to-face interpersonal interactions. The user study might also be affected by the user's age, gender and race.

2) The number of participants per each condition is very small (N=3), hence there are a variation between their rating making the results. Therefore, the interpretation of the results needs to be further empirically tested after more data has been gathered.

3) Previous relationships formed about someone are very subjective. In our study, we assumed that we could group together participants who had met the set partner into a single Group A, though this may introduce bias into the data.

4) The selection of stimuli samples; A set and B set was subjective and which cannot map all possible emotions or impressions.

5   Discussion

The current version of *Light Perfume* system is a proof of concept design and it is not aesthetically appealing as a fashion accessory. We need to aesthetically design new *Light Perfume* accessory to adapt this idea to our real world.

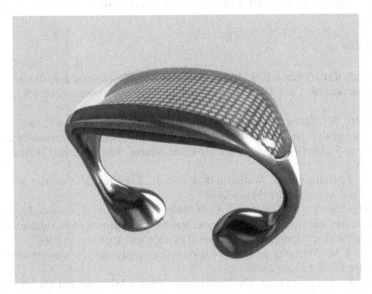

Fig. 7. New aesthetic design of Light Perfume (rendered image)

We found the synchronize expression with their partner based on movement and voice from *Light Perfume* can help people mirror together. It can also help people feel socially connected or enjoy with their partner while mirroring their expression during recreational activities and interaction. Some of the promising usage scenarios include sports spectators as they share their zeal and enjoy the game, people singing or dancing together in a karaoke or disco. The mirroring nonverbal cues between *Light*

Perfume accessories can also help people enhance their bonding, unity, and social interaction in any scenario which involves face to face communication.

6   Conclusion

This paper shows our design process of the *Light Perfume* system and also provides some evidence that the system could help the user make a more sociable impression towards their partner through mirrored blinking and color of light while smelling the same perfume fragrance. It could also help users express the ethical impression to others if they were meeting their partner for the first time.

Our next step in this project would be to improve our design by making it more aesthetically pleasing and to explore the different fashion accessory that can help people to feel bonding through the *Light Perfume* system.

We hope that this research and mirroring concept with lighting and perfume stimulation could positively help people bring closer, develop emotional connection and impression, and make them enjoyable together. As a result, *Light Perfume* will help people build meaningful and emotionally involving relationships and communication, such as empathic interactions with each other.

References

[1] Konrath, S.H., O'Brien, E.H., Hsing, C.: Changes in Dispositional Empathy in American College Students Over Time: A Meta-Analysis. Pers. Soc. Psychol. Rev. 15(2), 180–198 (2011)

[2] O'Brien, K.: The empathy deficit, http://www.boston.com/bostonglobe/ideas/articles/2010/10/17/the_empathy_deficit/ (accessed June 11)

[3] Milgram, S.: The Experience of Living in Cities. Science, New Series 167(3924), 1461–1468 (1970)

[4] Boase, J., Horrigan, J.B., Wellman, B., Rainie, L.: The strength of internet ties. Pew Internet and American Life Project (2006)

[5] Doherty-Sneddon, G., Anderson, A., O'Malley, C., Langton, S., Garrod, S., Bruce, V.: Face-to-face and video-mediated communication: A comparison of dialogue structure and task performance. Journal of Experimental Psychology: Applied 3(2) (1997)

[6] Iacoboni, M.: Mirroring people: The science of empathy and how we connect with others2009: Picador USA (2009)

[7] Iacoboni, M.: Face to Face: The Neural Basis of Social Mirroring and Empathy. Psychiatric Annals (2007)

[8] Valdez, P., Mehrabian, A.: Effects of color on emotion, vol. 123(4). Department of Psychology, University of California, Los Angeles (1994)

[9] Frasca-Beaulieu, K.: Interior Design for Ambulatory Care Facilities: How To Reduce Stress and Anxiety in Patients and Family. The Journal of Ambulatory Care Management 22(1), 67–73 (1999)

[10] Flagge, I.: of Light and Architecture. Ernst & Sohn, Berlin (1994)

[11] Kaufman, J.E., Illuminating Engineering Society of North America: IES lights handbook. Application volume. Illuminating Engineering Society of North America, New York (1981)

[12] Fox, K.: The Smell Report – An overview of facts and findings. Social Issues Research Centre (2007)

[13] Brewster, S., McGookin, D., Miller, C.: Olfoto: designing a smell-based interaction. In: CHI 2006, pp. 653–662 (2006)

[14] Mirroring (psychology), http://en.wikipedia.org/wiki/Mirroring_(psychology) (accessed May 14)

[15] Romano, D.M.C.: A Self-Psychology Approach to Narcissistic Personality Disorder: A Nursing Reflection. Perspectives in Psychiatric Care 40 (2004)

[16] Fay, W.H., Coleman, R.O.: A human sound transducer/reproducer: temporal capabilities of a profoundly echolalic child. Brain and Language 4, 396–402 (1977)

[17] Rizzolatti, G., Craighero, L.: The mirror-Neuron system. Annu. Rev. Neurosci. 27, 169–192 (2004)

[18] Szalavitz, M., Perry, B.D.: Born for love: why empathy is essential–and endangered. William Morrow, New York (2011)

[19] Rifkin, J.: The empathic civilization: the race to global consciousness in a world in crisis, 674 p. J.P. Tarcher/Penguin, New York (2009)

[20] Szalavitz, M.: How Not to Raise a Bully: The Early Roots of Empathy (2010), http://www.time.com/time/health/article/0,8599,1982190,00.html (accessed May 25)

[21] Baron-Cohen, S.: Mindblindness: As essay on autism and theory of mind. Recherche, p. 67 (1995)

[22] Khilawala, R.: Lack of Empathy in Relationships, http://www.buzzle.com/articles/lack-of-empathy-in-relationships.html (accessed June 5)

[23] Yongsoon, C., et al.: Sound Perfeum: Designing a Wearable Sound and Fragrance Media for Face-to-Face Interpersonal Interaction. In: Advances in Computer Entertainment Technology (2011)

[24] Yongsoon, C., Younghwan, P., Jihong, J.: A study on the emotion expression using lights in apparel types. In: Proceedings of the 9th International Conference on Human Computer Interaction with Mobile Devices and Services, pp. 478–482 (2007)

[25] Gueguen, N., Jacob, C., Martin, A.: Mimicry in Social Interaction: Its Effect on Human Judgment and Behavior. European Journal of Social Sciences 8(2) (2009)

[26] Huma, B.: Gender Differences in Impression Formation. Comparative Research in Anthropology and Sociology 1(1), 57–72 (2010)

A Survey of Players' Opinions on Interface Customization in World of Warcraft

Chris Deaker, Masood Masoodian, and Bill Rogers

Department of Computer Science, The University of Waikato, Hamilton, New Zealand
{cjd27,masood,coms0108}@cs.waikato.ac.nz

Abstract. Massively multiplayer online role-playing games, such as World of Warcraft, have become very popular in recent years. These types of games often provide the player with a wide range of game abilities, weapons, tools, options, stats, etc. which grow in number as the player progresses through the game. This in turn makes the user interface of the game more complex and difficult to interact with. Games such as World of Warcraft attempt to combat this by providing mechanisms (e.g. add-ons) for interface customization by the player. However, it is unclear which aspects of the game interface players prefer to customize, or what effects those customizations have on their gameplay experience. In this paper we present a survey of World of Warcraft players to identify their opinions on game interface customization preferences. The results of this survey are likely to apply to other massively multiplayer online role-playing games.

Keywords: Computer games, game interface customization, survey, player experience, massively multiplayer online games.

1   Introduction

The popularity of massively multiplayer online role-playing games (MMORPGs) has steadily increased over the past decade, to become a multi-billion dollar industry [1], servicing tens of millions of subscribers [2]. World of Warcraft[1] (WoW) alone boasted over 10 million active subscribers at the end of 2011 [3]. MMORPGs allow players to inhabit a character inside of the game world, and compete with non-player and player characters with the goal of improving their own character. For instance, in WoW low-level characters have few abilities to use, with players unlocking more and more abilities as their character progresses, increasing the number of potential approaches to in-game situations. However, as character level increases, so does the complexity of the game interface.

One method of addressing this complexity is using interface customization packages or add-ons which alter the interface of the game in some way, in order to assist the player (see Fig. 1). A number of popular MMORPGs provide support for such

---

[1] http://us.battle.net/wow/en/

A. Nijholt, T. Romão, and D. Reidsma (Eds.): ACE 2012, LNCS 7624, pp. 198–213, 2012.

add-ons, including WoW, RIFT[2], Warhammer Online: Age of Reckoning[3] and Age of Conan[4]. These add-ons allow players to customize their game interface by modifying its visual aspects (e.g. adjusting the colour, texture, shape and position of the player health bar, etc.), onscreen information (e.g. providing detailed statistics of player damage output, etc.), gameplay assistance (e.g. hints and alerts for upcoming events in specific scripted encounters, etc.), and a variety of other aspects of the interface.

Fig. 1. The default WoW interface (left) and a highly customized WoW interface (right)

Despite the existence and use of a large number of these types of add-ons for a range of MMORPGs, their effectiveness in providing assistance to the users by reducing the complexity of the game interface has not been investigated. It is also unclear which aspects of the interface players prefer to customize, or what impact such customizations have on their gameplay experience.

Furthermore, while previous studies have investigated player behavior, for instance within MMORPGs [4-6], and some potential benefits of interface improvements [7, 8], there is a lack of research exploring the relationship between player characteristics and the ways in which they choose to modify their in-game interfaces.

In this paper we aim to address some of these questions by reporting on a survey of WoW players, which we have conducted to investigate the motivational factors relating to interface customization by the players, and the effects of these types of customizations on their gameplay experience.

2   MMORPG Player Motivation

Understanding players' experience of computer games, and factors such as motivation which enhance that experience, is important for designing more engaging games [9].

In an effort to establish an empirical model of player motivation in online games, Yee [10] conducted a study of MMORPG players that revealed 10 motivational subcomponents, which could be grouped into 3 overarching components of *achievement*,

---

[2] http://www.riftgame.com/en/
[3] http://warhammeronline.com/
[4] http://www.ageofconan.com/

social, and *immersion*. The validity of this 3-component taxonomy was later investigated and ratified by undertaking similar experiments using participants from a non-Western culture, as opposed to Yee's original study where the participants were predominantly from a Western culture. These experiments confirmed self-reported statistics through comparison against collected in-game behavioral metrics [11].

A later survey by Yee [4] of over 30,000 MMORPG players extended this model by further dividing subcomponents to include two additional super-components of motivation: *escapism* and *manipulation*. This survey also provided valuable insight into typical MMORPG player demographics, finding the average age of participants to be 26.57 years, with an average weekly play time of 22 hours. Further, Yee found that "play motivations in MMORPG's do not suppress each other" [10], as previously suggested by Bartle's taxonomy of Multi-User-Dungeon players [12], indicating that players may be simultaneously engaged by a variety of motivational factors.

User interfaces play an important role in facilitating users' interaction with any software, and computer games are no exception. Recent studies have shown that user interfaces can contribute to game players' motivation. For instance, Adinolf & Turkay [13] conducted an online mixed method survey of 871 players of several different MMORPGs (including 500 WoW players), finding that interface quality and interface customizability are important and desirable features when establishing and maintaining player *engagement* and *motivation*. Specifically, 90% of the participants that played WoW indicated that they use custom interface modifications or add-ons when playing the game [13].

Interface customization may be one of the ways in which players attempt to reduce the complexity of MMORPG interfaces, which tends to increase as the game progresses, thus increasing players' cognitive load. For instance, Ang *et al.* [14] have identified 'user interface overload' as one of a variety of cognitive loads experienced by a typical MMORPG player, where players "failed to attend to important information as the game screen contained a lot of other irrelevant information" [14]. In response to this, it was observed that players "learn to prioritise tasks and information". The players also "learn not to attend to irrelevant information" and "become more aware of important information that requires constant attendance such as health status" [14].

Complexity of user interfaces can also have an impact on the game *flow*, as identified by Jones [15] in a discussion of the application of Csikszentmihalyi's theory of Flow [16] to electronic learning environments. Jones discusses the eight required elements of flow, and their manifestations in video game environments, which include factors related to control and familiarity with the user interface; or more specifically "mastering the controls of the game, such as mouse movement or keyboard combinations" [15].

Despite the empirical evidence supporting the importance of reducing complexity in user interfaces of games, there is very little research on the role customization methods could play in reducing this type of interface complexity, particularly in MMORPGs.

3   Survey of WoW Players

Our long-term research objective is to develop and evaluate methods of providing adaptive user interfaces to MMORPG players, as a form of customization, in order to reduce game interface complexity, and therefore potentially improve gameplay experience. Before this can be achieved, however, it is important to better understand how interface customization affects gameplay experience, particularly in terms of player motivation.

As a first step contributing towards this, we have carried out an online survey of WoW players ratings of a set of motivational factors, relating to interface customization in WoW. We have chosen WoW due to its popularity amongst MMORPG players, and the fact that, as mentioned earlier, add-ons are commonly used by WoW players.

3.1   The Survey

For this study, we developed an online survey consisting of three parts[5]. The first part obtained basic demographic information about the gender and age of survey participants. The second part of the survey asked participants to answer a set of questions relating to their general gameplay habits, preferences and motivations when playing WoW. This included the number of years they had played the game (answer: between 0-8 years), the average number of hours they play each week (answer: open-ended), whether they currently had any characters that had achieved the maximum in-game level (answer: yes/no), and a rating of their perceived level of knowledge of in-game mechanics (answer: on a 5-point Likert scale ranging from *very low* to *very high*).

Participants were asked to rate the importance of a number of motivational factors for playing WoW. The ratings were collected using a 5-point Likert scale, with anchors 1 (*not important*) and 5 (*very important*). The factors used were those identified by Yee's taxonomy of motivational factors in online games [10]. These factors and their overarching components, as identified by Yee [10], are listed in Table 1. Participants were also asked to comment on any other aspects of WoW which they felt were important, but had not been mentioned in this part of the survey.

The third part of the survey asked the participants to answer a set of questions pertaining to interface customization within WoW. This included whether the participants used third-party interface modifications or add-ons (answer: yes/no), and whether they felt that some add-ons gave players an unfair game advantage (answer: yes/no). Participants were asked to describe any functionality which they felt was not provided by existing add-ons, and to list any add-ons which improved their gameplay experience (answer: open-ended).

A 5-point Likert scale was then used to rate the importance of a number of effects of interface customization when playing WoW. These effects were:

---

1. Removing unnecessary information from the default interface.
2. Providing additional information not available in the default interface.
3. Improving the look and feel of the default interface.
4. Providing easier access to important game functions or features.

Finally, the participants were asked to rate the importance of interface customization in relation to the motivational factors rated in the previous section of the questionnaire (see Table 1) using a similar 5-point Likert scale, with anchors 1 (*not important*) and 5 (*very important*). These ratings were subsequently compared during the analysis with previously collected importance ratings for those factors (see Section 3.3)

Table 1. List of motivational factors used in the survey

Motivational factor	Overarching component
Advancement	Achievement
Mechanics	
Competition	
Socializing	Social
Relationships	
Teamwork	
Discovery	Immersion
Role-playing	
Character customization	
Escapism	

3.2 Survey Participants

Requests for participation in our survey were posted on a number of WoW-related internet forums[6]. In total 158 participants completed the survey, of whom 78% were male and 20% female (2 participants did not provide their gender).

The average age of the participants was 24.7 years old ($SD = 8.1$). Participants reported an average weekly play-time of 19.7 hours per week ($SD = 15.7$). The average participant age and play-time were similar to those of participants in a survey of 30,000 WoW players by Yee, where the average participant age was 26.57 years, with an average weekly play-time of 22 hours [4]. Fig. 2 shows the distribution of age and weekly play-time of our study participants.

Active participation in the forums from which the participants were recruited indicates a strong level of interest in the game. Therefore, it was expected that in general, respondents would be knowledgeable about game mechanics and available add-ons. This was confirmed by the survey results which indicated that most of the survey participants could be considered as being above average in their expertise in WoW. On average they had played the game for 4.6 years ($SD = 2.0$), and 95% of them had

---

[6] Including the official WoW game forum at:
http://us.battle.net/wow/en/forum/

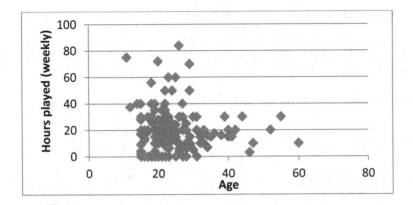

Fig. 2. Participant age and average weekly play-time

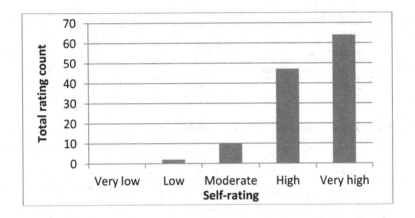

Fig. 3. Knowledge of in-game mechanics

achieved the maximum game level with at least one character. Over 90% of the participants reported a high level of knowledge of in-game mechanics (either 4 or 5 on a 5-point scale), as shown in Fig. 3.

In terms of interface customization, 92% of the participants reported that they currently modify their interface using third-party interface add-ons – confirming results of a previous survey by Adinolf & Turkay where 90% of the participants that played WoW reported using add-ons [13]. While the WoW terms of service prevents add-ons from providing significant 'game-breaking' competitive advantages, 23% of the participants indicated that they believe that some add-ons give players an unfair advantage in-game. However, 22% of the participants claimed that they use add-ons that they believe can provide an unfair in-game advantage. This indicates that the perception of potential issues with fairness does not discourage add-on usage by at least some of the players.

3.3   Ratings of Motivational Factors

Table 2 shows the participants' ratings for the importance of motivational factors in general, while Table 3 shows their ratings for the importance of customization for those motivational factors.

Table 2. Ratings for the importance of motivational factors in general

Factor	Importance (1: not important, 5: very important)				
	1	2	3	4	5
Advancement	2	2	28	68	58
Mechanics	1	6	28	64	59
Competition	12	21	47	45	33
Socializing	3	15	45	55	40
Relationships	14	26	56	33	29
Teamwork	1	6	24	64	63
Discovery	5	14	47	44	48
Role-playing	76	43	23	6	10
Character customization	5	14	34	56	49
Escapism	11	17	51	36	43

Table 3. Ratings for the importance of customization for motivational factors

Factors	Importance (1: not important, 5: very important)				
	1	2	3	4	5
Advancement	19	5	34	51	49
Mechanics	9	4	29	45	71
Competition	20	13	34	32	59
Socializing	64	46	32	13	3
Relationships	91	32	26	8	1
Teamwork	19	13	43	51	32
Discovery	59	29	40	22	8
Role-playing	88	27	31	9	3
Character customization	55	32	35	22	14
Escapism	66	22	39	18	13

Table 4 shows the average ratings for the importance of motivational factors in general along with average ratings for the importance of customization in terms of those factors. With the exception of *competition*, all motivational factors were rated higher in general than in terms of customization specifically. However, the difference between means of *competition* ratings was not statistically significant (paired T-Test, $T_{157} = 1.69$, p = 0.09).

Table 4. Average ratings for the importance of motivational factors in general and for customization

Factor	Average rating (S.D.)	
	General	Customization
Advancement	4.1 (0.8)	3.7 (1.3)
Mechanics	4.1 (0.9)	4.0 (1.1)
Competition	3.4 (1.2)	3.6 (1.4)
Socializing	3.7 (1.0)	2.0 (1.1)
Relationships	3.2 (1.2)	1.7 (0.9)
Teamwork	4.2 (0.9)	3.4 (1.2)
Discovery	3.7 (1.1)	2.3 (1.2)
Role-playing	1.9 (1.2)	1.8 (1.1)
Character customization	3.8 (1.1)	2.4 (1.3)
Escapism	3.5 (1.2)	2.3 (1.3)

The ratings for individual motivational factors were grouped into the over-arching factors of *achievement*, *social*, and *immersion*, as shown in Table 1. Sub-component factors were given equal weightings. Table 5 shows the average ratings and standard deviations for combined sub-factor ratings.

Table 5. Average ratings for over-arching motivational factors

Factor	Average rating (S.D.)	
	General	Customization
Achievement	3.9 (1.0)	3.8 (1.3)
Social	3.7 (1.1)	2.4 (1.3)
Immersion	3.3 (1.4)	2.2 (1.3)

We carried out a two-way analysis of variance on participant ratings against motivational factors and area of importance (general or customization-specific). Statistically significant main effects were observed for motivational factor, $F(9, 1413) = 110.19$, $p < 0.001$, and area of importance, $F(1, 157) = 247.90$, $p < 0.001$. More interestingly, there was a statistically significant interaction between motivation and area of importance, $F(9, 1413) = 46.81$, $p < 0.001$. Fig. 4 shows average ratings for all motivational factors, both for general importance and the importance of customization.

A second two-way analysis of variance was carried out using participants' ratings against the area of importance and over-arching motivational factors (see Table 1 and Table 5). Again, statistically significant main effects were observed for motivational factor, $F(2, 314) = 138.93$, $p < 0.001$, and area of importancem, $F(1, 157) = 232.72$, $p < 0.001$. Finally, there was a statistically significant interaction between motivation and area of importance, $F(2, 314) = 75.11$, $p < 0.001$.

The effect of this interaction can be seen in Fig. 4, showing a notable difference between the importance of customization for *achievement* factors when compared to *relationship* and *immersion* factors. The difference between the three factor groups for general importance is more subdued.

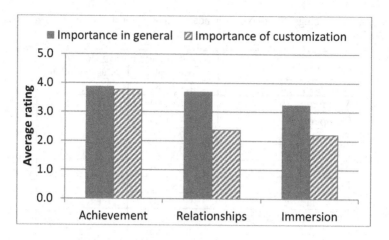

Fig. 4. Average ratings of the importance of motivational factors (by grouping)

To view this in more detail, Fig. 6, Fig. 7 and Fig. 8 show plots of ratings for general importance, and for the importance of customization, for *achievement*, *relationship*, and *immersion* factors respectively.

One interesting observation is that there is a strong positive correlation between the importance rating of *achievement* for both general importance and interface customization ($r = 0.89$). In contrast, correlations between general and customization-specific rating are negative for both *relationship* and *immersion* factors ($r = -0.77$ and $r = -0.53$ respectively), as well as being weaker for *immersion* specifically.

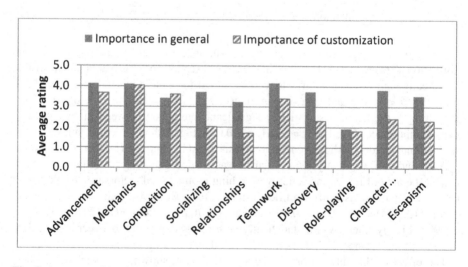

Fig. 5. Average ratings for the importance of motivational factors in general, and for customization

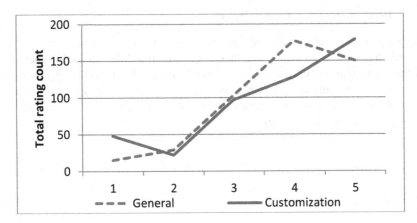

Fig. 6. Importance of achievement related factors

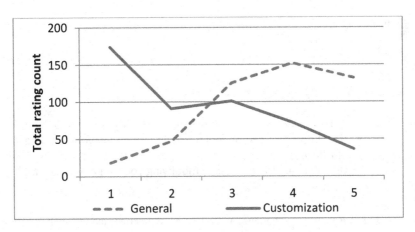

Fig. 7. Importance of relationship related factors

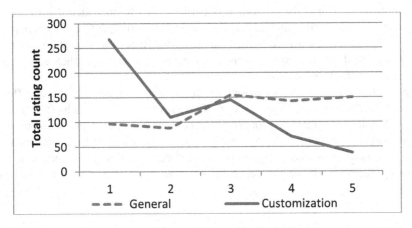

Fig. 8. Importance of immersion related factors

3.4   Effects of Interface Customization

Participants were asked to rate the importance of interface customization in WoW. 132 participants (83%) indicated that they considered the ability to modify their interface important (ratings of either 4 or 5 on a 5-point scale), with 109 participants (69%) selecting a rating of very important (see Fig. 9). This result was not surprising, given the potential benefits and advantages to be gained from interface modification (discussed in sections 3.5 and 3.6).

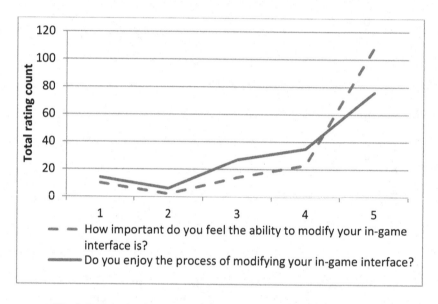

Fig. 9. Ratings for importance and enjoyment of interface modification

More unexpected was the proportion of participants who indicated that they enjoy the process of modifying their game interface. 111 participants (70%) reported a positive experience when modifying their game interface (see Fig. 9). Section 3.5 discusses more detailed feedback from participants detailing what they enjoy about the interface customization process.

Fig. 10 shows a plot of the participants' ratings for the importance of four different effects of interface customization. Over 60% of respondents gave each effect a rating of 4 or 5, indicating that all proposed effects were considered important to some degree. Furthermore, this indicates that players may modify their interfaces for a range of reasons simultaneously, rather than focusing heavily on one area (e.g. improving accessibility) at the detriment of other areas (e.g. improving interface aesthetics).

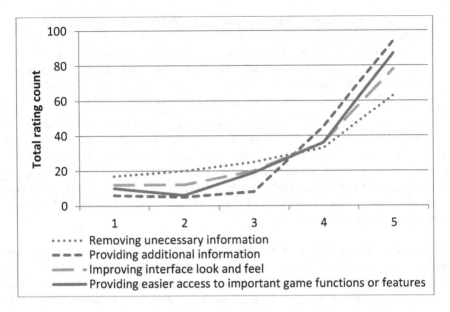

Fig. 10. Ratings for the importance of the effects of interface customization

3.5   Reasons for Interface Customization

The survey also sought participants' feedback, through several open-ended questions, on the main reasons for using the interface customization add-ons they use, or would like to use if they were available. In general, the responses to these questions can be classified into a number of categories: simplification and consolidation of information, performance advantages and functionality, aesthetics, and enjoyment of the customization process. These are discussed in more detail below.

Simplification and Consolidation of Information. The most prevalent theme within participant feedback was the need to maximise the availability of relevant and important information, while removing or decreasing the focus given to less important information[7]:

> *"I try to take a minimalist approach to my customization, displaying the highest amount of relevant information in the smallest, most unobtrusive space as possible."*

Participants frequently cited the need for critical information to be shown in the centre of the screen, where the player character is shown:

> *"One of the primary things that is extremely lacking in the default interface is clustering and localization of important information. Ideally, and this is how I design my interfaces, all the most important information should be near where you are most often looking: your character.*

---

[7]   Participants' comments are given in quotes to illustrate points made.

"Because the focus of our play experience happens at the center of the screen, where our toon [character] is, the most important information should be relatively close to that area. From there, the information should radiate out from the center as it becomes of less immediate importance. Ultimately, if the information is not necessary during the majority of gameplay, it should be hidden from the screen and accessed through keybind or mouseover."

Comments on consolidation generally mentioned the need to improve the visibility of *"important"* information, without discussing what determines the relevance or importance of a particular feature at any given time. As WoW supports character classes of various roles and archetypes, as well as a number of different in-game goals, we suggest that distinguishing important information from extraneous data may be dependant upon individual player character attributes and goals. This subject may benefit from further study in future.

Performance Advantages and Functionality. A number of performance-focused interface add-ons exist, providing functionality such as the ability to track detailed character damage statistics, monitor effects that assist and harm characters, and provide players with alerts for scripted events during dungeon encounters. These add-ons can provide players with a competitive advantage, either over other players (if those players choose not to utilize similar add-ons), or over non-player characters within the game:

"I optimize my interface like I optimize my gear or my talents, because it has a measurable impact on how well I'm capable of playing."
"It's much easier to have an add-on ready to go, instead of having to alt-tab before every flight [to obtain information from outside of the game], or figuring out the best route to take when farming herbs."

While most participants remarked that add-ons made their role *"easier to perform"*, feedback from participants that played healers (i.e. characters that focus on aiding and supporting allies in battle) indicated that they felt that add-ons were necessary in order to perform their role effectively:

"I'm a healer and must be observing to help find important information which can either save or [fail] the attempt."
"I play healers almost exclusively and I need to know Buffs, HOTs, dispellables, and health in full without other distractions."

Aesthetics. Aesthetic preferences were often informed or related to other considerations, such as immersion, and practical aspects such as efficiency:

"Allowing the player to personalize their gameplay experience based on their needs (i.e. the type of content they do, the level of play they are at and how much information they require to function, and personal preference regarding look and feel)."

Minimalism and *"cleanliness"* was repeatedly discussed – *"Minimalist UI's result in greater screen real estate which is important for immersion and spacial awareness."*

– as was the removal or modification of default interface elements or textures, which participants described as *"ugly"* or *"unessential clutter"*.

Finally, participants expressed a degree of satisfaction with the ability to tailor their interface to their personal preferences:

"I just want to make it pretty and intuitive."
"Making my screen look the way that I want it specifically."
"Making the game experience 'my own'."

Enjoyment of the Customization Process. While including some overlap with feedback on aesthetics, enjoyment of the act of customization was an unexpectedly popular effect discussed by the participants. This supports the ratings collected and discussed in Section 3.4. It should be noted that the survey did not differentiate between customization in the form of players writing their own add-ons or in-game scripts, and a higher-level approach, such as players simply installing and using add-on packages created by other players. The relevant comments received tended to focus on the satisfaction of creating or building a personalized interface:

> *"The customization for its own sake is a big deal to me. That is, I am quite certain that I could find pre-built interfaces that do what I want better than what I have, but what I have is MINE."*

Beyond self-expression, feedback indicated that participants enjoyed frequently updating and redesigning their interfaces. Presumably, as there are realistic limits on the practical benefits between custom interface configurations, reconfiguring an interface may not always improve its functionality, and may in some cases result in equivalent, or even inferior functionality. Besides cases where players are replacing deprecated add-ons with improved or updated versions, this indicates the strong appeal of novelty (relative to the appeal of improved functionality) when players are considering modifications to their interface.

3.6   Interface Customization and Gameplay

The survey also aimed to find out if interface customization gave the players any clear gameplay advantages. As mentioned earlier, a considerable number of the participants (22%) reported that they use add-ons which they believe can provide them with an unfair in-game advantage. Only 2 participants (1% of all participants) reported that they believe add-ons can provide an unfair advantage to players, and that they did not personally use interface add-ons. These results indicate that the perception of potential issues with fairness does not discourage interface customization by using add-ons.

One possible explanation for this is the feeling that in order to remain competitive, any available in-game advantage must be utilized. Participants saw add-on usage as another factor influencing success, similar to character itemization or ability usage:

> *"Everyone has the same access to the same addons, so a player who chooses to use default raid frames or not run a raid/PVP addon is only giving themselves a disadvantage. No different than choosing not to use the best gear available to you."*

"Most mods give people an advantage over people who prefer the default interface. I wouldn't call it unfair though, since these mods are readily available for everyone."

Several participants identified a previously available add-on, which they felt provided an unreasonable advantage to players. This add-on, AVR (Augmented Virtual Reality)[8], allowed players to draw lines, circles and other markings onto objects within the game world. This was typically used to identify and communicate locations of interest or importance to other players, in order to aid players with positioning in dungeon encounters. In some of these encounters, correct player positioning was integral to success, and usage of this add-on allowed players to greatly simplify the encounter by reducing the need to communicate directly with other players. The WoW interface API was eventually modified in such a way that AVR was effectively disabled. The participant response to this (which was largely critical of the existence of AVR) indicates that there are limitations to the degree of simplification of gameplay which players are willing to accept as reasonable.

4   Conclusions

In this paper we have presented a survey of WoW players to identify their opinions on game interface customization through the use of add-ons. The results of this survey show that there are several motivational factors for playing WoW – supporting findings of previous studies on MMORPGs – and that the importance of interface customization varies for these different factors.

Our study also shows that the players surveyed have different motivations for customizing the game interface of WoW. These are to: simplify and consolidate information, gain performance advantage and functionality, alter aesthetics, or simply enjoy the customization process. Although these motivations are not mutually exclusive, they have varying levels of importance to different players.

In addition the study shows that there are interface customizations that some players would not consider undertaking because this would give them an unfair gameplay advantage, despite the fact that these modifications are permitted under the games terms of service. However, the boundaries distinguishing what modifications are acceptable or not are rather subtle.

We believe that although our study has specifically targeted WoW players, its findings are likely to apply to other MMORPGs. In particular, the results highlight the importance of providing players with the means to significantly modify their interface, especially in relation to achievement-focused gameplay elements.

Based on the findings of the survey reported here, we are currently in the process of developing adaptive user interface techniques for WoW which would provide some of the benefits of interface customization add-ons, by automatically presenting players with options that aim to reduce the complexity of the WoW interface for intermediate to advanced players. In response to the feedback received regarding the goals and

---

[8] http://www.wowace.com/addons/avr/

motivations of interface customization, this development is focused primarily on providing players with information necessary to improve performance in achievement-focused gameplay.

Acknowledgements. We would like to gratefully acknowledge the contributions of our survey participants for their time and valued feedbacks.

References

1. Future Publishing Limited, http://www.edge-online.com/news/mmo-industry-report-shows-mixed-fortunes
2. MMOData.net, http://www.mmodata.net
3. AOL Inc., http://wow.joystiq.com/2012/02/09/world-of-warcraft-subscriber-numbers/
4. Yee, N.: The Demographics, Motivations, and Derived Experiences of Users of Massively Multi-User Online Graphical Environments. PRESENCE: Teleoperators and Virtual Environments 15, 309–329 (2006)
5. Suznjevic, M., Stupar, I., Matijasevic, M.: MMORPG player behavior model based on player action categories. In: Proceedings of the 10th Annual Workshop on Network and Systems Support for Games, pp. 1–6. IEEE Press, Ottawa (2011)
6. Son, S., Kang, A.R., Kim, H.-C., Kwon, T.T., Park, J., Kim, H.K.: Multi-relational social networks in a large-scale MMORPG. In: Proceedings of the ACM SIGCOMM 2011 Conference, pp. 414–415. ACM, Toronto (2011)
7. Achterbosch, L., Pierce, R., Simmons, G.: Massively multiplayer online role-playing games: the past, present, and future. Comput. Entertain. 5, 1–33 (2008)
8. Cornett, S.: The usability of massively multiplayer online roleplaying games: designing for new users. In: Proceedings of the SIGCHI Conference on Human Factors in Computing Systems, pp. 703–710. ACM, Vienna (2004)
9. Maruyama, Y., Masoodian, M., Rogers, B.: A Survey of Japanes Gamers' Ratigns of Experience Elements for Different Game Genres. In: ACE 2011. ACM Press (2011)
10. Yee, N.: Motivations of Play in Online Games. Journal of CyberPsychology and Behavior 9, 772–775 (2007)
11. Yee, N., Ducheneaut, N., Nelson, L.: Online gaming motivations scale: development and validation. In: ACM Conference on Human Factors in Computing Systems, CHI 2012 (2012)
12. Bartle, R.: Hearts, Clubs, Diamonds, Spades: Players Who Suit MUDs. The Journal of Virtual Environments 1 (1996)
13. Adinolf, S., Turkay, S.: Controlling Your Game Controls: Interface and Customization. In: 7th Annual Games+Learning+Society (GLS) Conference, pp. 13–22. ETC Press (2011)
14. Ang, C.S., Zaphiris, P., Mahmood, S.: A model of cognitive loads in massively multiplayer online role playing games. Interacting with Computers 19, 167–179 (2007)
15. Jones, M.G.: Creating Electronic Learning Envnironments: Games, Flow, and the User Interface. In: Selected Research and Development Presentations at the National Convention of the Association for Educational Communications and Technology (AECT), pp. 2803–2806 (1998)
16. Csikszentmihalyi, M.: Flow: The Psychology of Optimal Experience. Harper Perennial, New York (1991)

53.090 Virtual Rusks = 510 Real Smiles Using a Fun Exergame Installation for Advertising Traditional Food Products

Dimitris Grammenos, George Margetis,
Panagiotis Koutlemanis, and Xenophon Zabulis

Foundation for Research and Technology - Hellas (FORTH), Institute of Computer Science
{gramenos,gmarget,koutle,zabulis}@ics.forth.gr

Abstract. This paper presents an innovative advergame installation for promoting the brand and products of a company producing Cretan rusks. The paper first presents some background and related work. Then, the requirements set towards creating the game are outlined, followed by concept creation and design decisions taken to meet these requirements, as well as a description of the user interface, gameplay and technical characteristics of the resulting game. The game has been installed with remarkable success in two different food exhibitions in key locations in Athens, Greece, where it has been played by more than 500 people of ages ranging from 2 to 76 years old. A large variety of qualitative and quantitative data were collected. The paper presents several findings stemming from these data. Additionally, changes made to the game as a result of the findings are presented, along with lessons learnt from the acquired experience.

Keywords: Advergames, marketing, game design, public interactive installation, experience design, casual games, serious games.

1 Introduction

Typically, the promotion of products in food exhibitions and points of sale is performed through the dissemination of paper material such as posters and leaflets, as well as through tasting and dispensing of free samples. Sometimes, simple audiovisual means like videos, and / or rolling presentations are additionally used. Admittedly, this approach has several drawbacks:

1. It is passive. Potential clients are mere recipients of information. Thus, it is left to their personal initiative to get (further) interested in the advertised products.
2. Everybody does it. Especially in large exhibitions, there is little differentiation among exhibitors, making it very difficult to stand out from the crowd.
3. The time that each visitor is 'exposed' to a brand and its products is minimal.
4. Recollecting which product was made by which company may be particularly hard after one has seen or tasted several products of the same type.
5. It can quickly become tiring and boring.

A. Nijholt, T. Romão, and D. Reidsma (Eds.): ACE 2012, LNCS 7624, pp. 214–229, 2012.

In the past few years, a trend towards more active, user-involving marketing of products has surfaced, through the use of interactive games purposefully designed for a specific brand. This trend is commonly referred to as advergaming [19] (from "advertising" and "gaming"). Most existing advergames are targeted to personal computers (e.g., downloadable or Web-based programs [3]), game consoles [19] and mobile devices. Still, large multinational brands such as BMW [11], Goodyear [6], Coca Cola [21], etc., often employ advergames as a means of enhancing their "outdoor advertising" campaigns, i.e., advertising that reaches consumers while they are outside their homes. In this context, this paper presents the concept creation, experience design, software development and user-based assessment of an advergame installation that was developed by the Institute of Computer Science of the Foundation for Research & Technology – Hellas (ICS-FORTH). The game is targeted to promoting, in exhibition spaces and key points of sale, the brand and products of "Kriton Artos"[1], a company producing traditional Cretan rusks.

2   Background and Related Work

Product placement or, in-game advertisement (IGA), in video games started since the early 1980s [19]. At about the same time, advergames also appeared [19] representing a more dynamic marketing approach, eventually blurring the lines between entertainment and persuasion [3]. Up to now, advergame research has mainly focused on online / web-based games, primarily targeting children and young(er) adults [3; 25]. According to eMarketer [5] display ads, advergames and advertising on web-based game portals are the leading game-related ad segments in the US. By 2013, the worldwide social game ad market is expected to reach $641 million. In the past few years there has been an increasing interest in analyzing and testing several aspects of advergames. In this context, related findings [e.g., 9; 25] support that congruity between the brand and the content of the game impacts brand memory and attitudes towards the game. Congruity can be assessed across a number of dimensions, including [14] function, lifestyle, image and advertising. Evidently, there is a fine balance in the level of game-product congruity, since too little congruity may result is inferior memory effects, while, according to the Persuasion Knowledge Model [7], too much may raise mental barriers against the communicated message.

Several papers [e.g., 2; 10; 20; 22] reference, analyze or contribute towards attaining the "holy grail" of (adver)games - the feeling of flow (or optimal experience). The term was originally introduced by Csikszentmihalyi [1] regarding rewarding everyday life and work activities in which people are highly involved. A key element for achieving flow is a perfect balance between one's skills and a task's challenge. Experiments by Waiguny et al [23] and Gurau [10] confirmed that an optimal challenge flow state can positively influence brand evaluations in advergames and the buying behavior of players. Based on flow theory, there have been several attempts [2; 10; 22] to develop theoretical frameworks for inducing flow within games, also mapping

---

[1] www.kritonartos.gr

the 8 original flow elements specified by Csikszentmihalyi to respective gameplay elements. Overall, research findings converge towards the fact that advergames are an effective tool for achieving brand awareness [9; 10; 12; 23; 25] and that they have a clear advantage over past approaches [24]. Furthermore, there is evidence that if a game is entertaining, it has a positive influence on brand marketing due to emotional conditioning [10; 23], where the enjoyable gaming experience is combined with a specific brand, and subconsciously recollected in future situations. An interesting fact is that prior game-playing experience does not seem to relate to advergame brand memory [9; 18; 24]. Additionally, there is some indication that players who perform well within the game environment tend to retain in-game advertising messages better than players who perform badly [8]. Another important fact is that players who are aware of the presence of in-game advertising are statistically more likely to be happy with its use [12]. A discussion of the vast literature regarding the design of successful games is beyond the scope of this paper. There has been some work specifically targeted to advergames, such as a list of characteristics of a successful advergame defined by companies specialized in this genre [10], and O'Green's [17] "Top things NOT to do in advergaming".

A key differentiating factor of the presented work over previous efforts is that, up to now, although a number of public advergame installations have been developed, neither related design information, nor qualitative or quantitative assessment data have been published.

3   Game Design

After conducting several meetings with representatives of the food company, a set of goals that the target game should meet were agreed. More specifically, it should:

1. Allow the broader public to learn about, recognize and remember the brand's name and products and establish a positive image about them.
2. Link the brand and its products with the island of Crete, reinforcing the fact that they are locally-made and traditional.
3. Inform about potential uses of the products.
4. Establish a mental connection between the products and notions such as exercise, healthy living, positive energy, having fun.
5. Provide an opportunity for rewarding active visitor participation (e.g., through complimentary samples).
6. Accommodate players of all ages, with or without previous exposure to games. Multiple player (cooperative / competitive) games should also be supported.
7. Facilitate the collection of contact information.
8. Provide the means for word-of-mouth advertising (e.g., through social networks).
9. Allow for a high-profile, dynamic presence of the company in exhibition spaces and points of sale.
10. Last less than 2 minutes, so that players do not get tired, those waiting in line do not get bored, and a high throughput of players can be achieved.

In response to these requirements, and also building upon related work, it was decided to create a Kinect-based PC exergame [16], involving physical activity as a means of interacting with the game. The game would be projected against a large surface, making it highly visible to exhibition visitors. The main reasons for selecting Kinect were that it allows for non-instrumented game control through natural movements, which also afford higher levels of engagement and social behavior [15], performs well under various environmental conditions, and comes at a very low cost. In this respect, it was decided to just use the depth camera's image in order to render a virtual shadow of the players, instead of tracking body skeletons. The rationale was two-fold. On the one hand, it was assumed that it would be easier for people, especially "non game-players", to identify with their shadow rather than with an avatar, thus achieving a higher level of control and immersion [22]. On the other hand, this approach allowed for maximum flexibility regarding the number, posture and size of players, as well instantly joining and leaving the game, thus maximizing the opportunities for social interaction [22]. The downside was that people with larger body sizes had a clear advantage, and there was the possibility of accidental "intrusions" in the play area.

Fig. 1. Screenshot of indicative gameplay

The envisioned gameplay[2] is simple, straightforward, and has very clear goals [22]. Players perceive their bodies as shadows projected on a brick wall (Figs 1 & 2). Depending on the players' number, there may be one or two baskets at the two bottom sides of the wall (Fig. 2). A 'rainfall' of rusks starts. Players must use their shadows to put the rusks into their basket. Rusks that fall on the floor are broken into pieces. The game ends when a certain number of rusks have fallen. In order to cater for the aforementioned design goals, the following features were originally included in the game:

1. The company's logo appears on a prominent position on the brick wall and on the player's baskets. Also, its motto (as Cretan as it can get) appears as graffiti on the wall. All in-game graphics are actual photos of the company's products.

---

[2] Videos of indicative play sessions can be found at:
http://www.youtube.com/user/icsforthami

2. When the game starts, a card appears for 5 seconds presenting products and facts about the company.

3. Two musical scores are used combining traditional Cretan music with a modern beat. Additionally, the moves required by the game implicitly refer to traditional Cretan dances. Level selection buttons are Cretan versions of "smilies". The "game over" sign appears as a road sign, which is eventually shot (an infamous practice occasionally performed in the Cretan mainland) and destroyed.

4. If players manage to put together a round rusk and a tomato, a dakos, a popular rusk-based Cretan dish, is created, which provides bonus points if put in a basket.

5. Players receive appropriate, immediate, contextualized feedback [4; 22] for all their actions. For example, when an object falls in their basket, a text object pops-up illustrating the points won or lost.

Fig. 2. Playing a two-player competitive game

6. The game requires considerable body movement that increases as time passes. A lot of playtesting has taken place regarding gameplay pace, so that it applies pressure but does not frustrate players [4]. To better match player's skills to game challenge [22], three alternative levels of difficulty have been designed: (a) easy, targeted to small children and older players, (b) hard, for hardcore and returning players and (c) normal, for everyone else.

7. In order to deliberately create a "memorable moment" [13], when the end of the game approaches, a huge amount of rusks suddenly start to fall. To notify players about this event, a bleating goat appears, providing a humorous note, but also another link to Cretan tradition. Additionally, the music shifts to a faster tune.

8. For rewarding players, when a specific score level is reached, a bag of rusks jumps out of the basket, which can then be redeemed with an actual product.

9. During gameplay, at moments that are likely to provoke interesting players' poses the game automatically takes photos of them. Additionally, when the game ends, a photo countdown ("smile moment") appears allowing players to pose. Game graphics, including the company logo, are overlaid to the photos, which are presented on screen when the game finishes and can be sent to the players via e-mail.

10. Distinct high scores are kept per difficulty level and number of players. If the last game played resulted in a high score, the last photo taken is presented on the game's main screen.
11. As a means to ensure that the total gameplay period will not exceed a maximum time limit, all falling objects come with a lifespan which may vary depending on the level of difficulty, type of object and time of appearance. When an object reaches the last 9 seconds of its "life", it gets a reddish hue (i.e., becomes hot) and a countdown number appears on it.

More than 50 hours of playtesting along with the employment of observational usability assessment methods took place in order to fine-tune the gameplay and also debug the game, in a realistic installation at the premises of ICS-FORTH, with more than 30 players of both genders, with ages ranging from 4 to 52 years old.

4   Installation 1: Syntagma

The game was installed in an exhibition of traditional Greek food products from the 29th till the 31st of March 2012, in a space located in the central metro station of Athens, at Syntagma Square. The overall setup (Fig. 3) included a 1280x800 short-throw projector, adjusted on a custom floor stand, capable of producing an image 2.8m wide x 1.75m tall from a distance of 1.8m. As a means of "hiding" the projector and keeping players from accidentally bumping on it, a small banner was adjusted to an extendable arm, which was fixed upon the projector's stand. A Kinect was mounted on a stand at about 0.5m above the floor surface. A red line was stuck on the floor, designating the limits of the play area.

Fig. 3. Game installation at the Syntagma Metro station

In the course of three days, the game ran for a total of 30 hours. It was played 203 times (resulting in the fall of 20.010 virtual rusks) by 173 distinct players (Fig. 4 - left), 127 of which were female (73%) and 46 male (27%). Their age ranged from 3 (four players) to 76 years (Fig. 4 - right). The exact number of players per age range is presented in Table 1. Seventy-one (41 %) players stated that they had never played any type of video game before. 136 single-player and 67 two-player sessions took place. In five cases the game was concurrently played by 3 players. The average duration of a game session was 89 seconds.

When asked to provide an e-mail address in order to receive photos that were automatically taken by the game, all 86 people who had one, agreed. Five (elderly) persons said that they did not have an e-mail but said that one of their relatives would contact us in order to receive the photos. No one ever did. Also, it was observed that 9 out of 10 people, without this being a prerequisite in any way (implicitly or explicitly), prior of after playing the game, themselves (or their parents), bought one or more products from the booth.

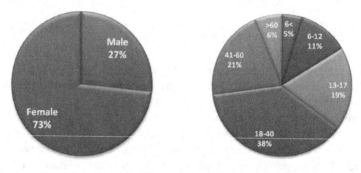

Fig. 4. Installation 1: Player gender (left) and ages (right)

As a means of collecting detailed qualitative data about the game and its impact, a 20-item questionnaire was created. The first 6 items regarded the players' profile. The 11 next items were statements rated using a Likert scale from 1 to 5 (see Table 2) measuring on the one hand the success of the game and the user experience; while on the other hand the potential impact and usefulness of the game as a marketing tool. Finally, there were 3 open-ended questions. After the first ten failed attempts of interviewing players who were discouraged by the length of the questionnaire, the use of the questionnaire was discontinued. Instead, players were asked to verbalize their opinion about the game, and their answers were recorded. All players stated that they liked the game and that they enjoyed playing it. More than 100 people used words like "fantastic", "great", "very good", or another synonym. Most of the players also thanked us for offering them so much fun and for having a very good time.

After the event, the evaluation questionnaire was posted on-line and a link to it was included to the e-mails with the photos that were sent back to the players. Out of the 86 e-mails sent, 25 recipients answered the questionnaire. 18 of them (72%) were female and 7 (18%) male (Fig. 5 - left). 13 respondents (52%) were 18 to 40 years old and 12 (48%) were 41 to 60. Also, 13 (52%) were familiar with the food company before playing the game, while 12 (48%) were not. The frequency at which respondents play video games is illustrated in Fig. 5 (right). The aggregate results of the Likert-scale statements are shown in Table 2. Among the things that respondents mentioned in the open-ended questions were that they liked: the responsiveness of the game; the (easy) way it was controlled; its high quality; its originality; the fun they got out of it; the fact that their whole family could play it; the music. On the negative side, two respondents wrote that they would like to play more times, or for a longer period, one said that towards the end the game became too difficult for him and another one did not like the music. The "other comments" section mainly included congratulations, statements about the originality of the idea and questions about where and when they could play it again.

Table 1. Installation 1: Number of players per age range

Age	6<	6-12	13-17	18-40	41-60	>60
Players	8	20	33	65	36	11
%	5%	11%	19%	38%	21%	6%

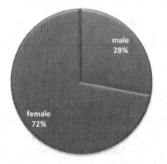 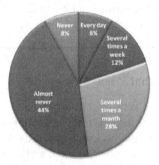

Fig. 5. On-line questionnaire: Player gender (left) and frequency of playing video games (right)

4.1   What Went Right

The reaction of all people to the game, including those who played it, their parents and friends, but also bystanders, other exhibitors and people just passing by was 100% positive. Everyone had a lot of fun and considered it as a very good means for product promotion. The company advertised by the game definitely benefited both in terms of publicity and of highly increased on-the-spot sales. Players of all ages were able to tell the name of the brand and the type of products it makes.

Regardless of the totally uncontrolled installation environment, the game ran astonishingly robustly. There was not a single technical problem (bug, crash, game reaching an undesirable state, loss of recorded data, etc.) during any of the game sessions.

On the first day of the exhibition the game was presented on MEGA (TV) Channel, on the morning show with the highest ratings in Greek television[3]. This day, more than 85% of the people visiting the booth mentioned viewing the game on TV. The next two days this percentage has fallen to about 60-65%. On the second day, the game also appeared on national television[4].

---

[3] http://youtu.be/ZkVrtXuotjM
[4] http://youtu.be/4vjLYM-3CgU

Table 2. On-line evaluation questionnaire results

Question (1=strongly disagree, 5=strongly agree)	AVG	STD
1. I liked it.	4.7	0.5
2. It was easy to learn how to play.	4.6	0.6
3. It responded correctly and timely to my actions.	4.2	0.9
4. The difficulty level was appropriate for me.	4.3	1.0
5. It was fun.	4.9	0.3
6. The graphics used were of high quality.	4.3	0.7
7. I liked the music.	4.2	1.0
8. It helped me familiarize with the brand "Kriton Artos" and its products.	4.2	0.8
9. It helped me realize that the products of "Kriton Artos" are traditional Cretan products.	4.0	0.9
10. It contributed towards creating a positive image about "Kriton Artos" and its products.	4.4	0.6
11. It positively affected me towards purchasing products of "Kriton Artos".	4.0	0.9

4.2   What Went Wrong

For several reasons, almost no one would read the advertising card at the beginning of the game. First, playing instructions game were not included, the time that the card was shown on the screen was usually dedicated to explaining how to play. Additionally, most texts were too long, and also it was too obvious that this part was just a bold advertisement that did not have something to do with the gameplay [7]. The fact that the projector was just a few centimeters in front of the playing area had two disadvantages: (a) there were times where someone had to hold the player back to avoid bumping on it and (b) it prevented shorter children from moving closer to the Kinect and enlarging their "shadow". Also, the idea of hanging the banner from the projector base was (obviously) bad, since whenever someone hit the banner, or there was a sudden breeze, the projector would shiver. Additionally, nobody would read the banner. Thus, it was placed against the booth's wall. Most of the players would try to leave the play area immediately after the "Game Over" sign appeared. Since the last photo was taken after that, we had to orally instruct players to wait for it. The decision to place the photo of the last high scorer on the game's title screen was not very good, since: (a) due to the short life of the event, there were very few returning players; and (b) those who had just played the game were deprived the opportunity to have a last peek at their photo before leaving the play area.

5   Installation 2: Zappeion

The game was installed (Fig. 6) at the "Tastes & Life" exhibition at the Zappeion Exhibition Hall, in Athens, from the 20th till the 22nd of April 2012. Based on previous experience, but also on new requirements of the food company, a number of changes were made to the game setup and software.

Fig. 6. Game v.2 installation at Zappeion Exhibition Hall

First of all, an ultra-short throw projector was used, which produced the same image size as in the previous installation, with additional brightness, from less than 1m distance, thus freeing up valuable space in front of the play area. Also, no projector stand was required, thus simplifying the whole installation. The red tape was replaced by a red ribbon loosely tied on two short free-standing poles, so that if someone stepped on it, it would move along, thus avoiding potential accidents. Additionally, this approach allowed to easily shift the play area closer to the screen whenever needed, e.g., to better accommodate (younger) players. A custom projection screen was fixed against the booth's back side. The banner moved to a much more prominent (and stable) place, underneath the projection screen.

Based on the observations collected during the first installation (see Section 5.3) the following adjustments were made to the game:

- Cards with brief instructions about the game appear at the beginning. The last card is an advertisement that contains just a photo and the name of a product. Since this is the last in a series of cards that the player reads to learn about the game, it is always read before even realizing its purpose.
- The "smile moment" appears prior to the "Game Over" sign.
- When a game finishes, the last photo taken appears on the title screen until a new game starts.

Additionally, the food company wanted to promote a new series of "small bites" rusks coming in nine variations. In order to make players aware of the different flavors, a "small bites bar" was added near each basket. The bar contains grayed out icons symbolizing the 9 flavors. Every time a player collects one of them, the corresponding symbol lights up and a sound effect is heard. Each "small bite" scores 2 points. Additionally, if all 9 flavors are collected a bonus of 25 extra points is gained.

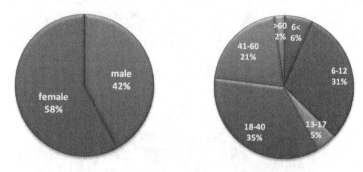

Fig. 7. Installation 2: Player gender (left) and ages (right)

In three days, the game ran for a total of 24 hours. It was played 343 times (resulting in the fall of 23.700 rusks) by 337 distinct players (Fig. 7 - left), 195 of which were female (58%) and 142 male (42%). Their age (Fig. 7 - right) ranged from 2 (five players) to 75 years (played against his 70-year old mate). The youngest player was so short, that she had to stand on a box of rusks in order to appear on the screen. The number of players per age range is presented in Table 3.

Table 3. Installation 2: Number of players per age range

Age	6<	6-12	13-17	18-40	41-60	>60
Players	22	103	16	118	70	8
%	7%	31%	5%	35%	21%	2%

Table 4. On-the-spot questionnaire results

Question (1=strongly disagree, 5=strongly agree)	AVG	STD
1. I liked it.	4,63	0,54
2. It was easy to learn how to play.	4,68	0,56
3. It was fun.	4,82	0,43
4. It helped me familiarize with the brand "Kriton Artos" and its products.	4,08	0,93
5. It contributed towards creating a positive image about "Kriton Artos" and its products.	4,41	0,83
6. It positively affected me towards purchasing products of "Kriton Artos".	4,1	0,87

216 single-player and 127 2-player sessions took place. 39 people won a bag of rusks and 65 achieved to fill in the "small bites bar". The aggregate score of all players was 23.700. In 20 cases the game was concurrently played by 3 or more players. The maximum number of concurrent players was 6. In 55 cases children played along with their (grand)parents – sometimes both of them were adults. The average duration of a game session was 101 seconds (due to the newly-introduced game instructions). 165 persons provided their e-mail address to receive the game photos. This time, a much shorter questionnaire was employed. It was briefly presented to the respondents

who were then left to fill it in by themselves. When the questionnaire was returned, a short informal discussion was often held, aiming to clarify or even verify the selected scores (especially if they were all very high). Of all the people asked to fill it in, only one refused, explaining that she was in a hurry. A total of 100 people responded, 61 female and 39 male (Fig. 8 - left). 66 respondents were 18 to 40 years old, 28 were 41 to 60 and 6 over sixty. 39 were familiar with the company "Kriton Artos" before playing the game while 61 were not. The frequency at which respondents play video games is illustrated in Fig. 8 (right). The aggregate results of the Likert-scale questions are shown in Table 4, while the detailed scores are illustrated in Fig. 9. There were 28 respondents who scored 5/5 all six Likert-scale statements.

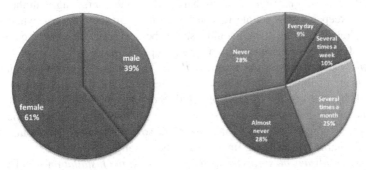

Fig. 8. On-the-spot questionnaire: Player gender (left) and frequency of playing games (right)

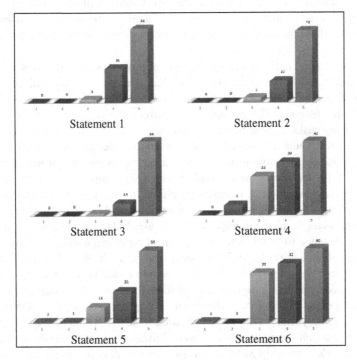

Fig. 9. On-the-spot evaluation questionnaire scores

6   Lessons Learnt

This section summarizes the empirical knowledge gained through the two public installations, analyzing the evaluation questionnaires, as well as observing and discussing with hundreds of players of various ages.

1. *Fun rules!* People of all ages want to have fun. If you achieve this, they will instantly like you. They will smile at you, thank you, and shake your hand. They will also listen to you, give you their contact data, answer your questions, taste, and most probably, buy whatever you sell.
2. *Live bait catches more fish.* When there was no one interacting with the game, we had to keep inviting people to come and play. On the contrary, when someone was already playing there would usually be several "volunteers" queuing up - very often ones from "unexpected" age groups.
3. *Details matter, but not the ones you think.* There were several times and reasons that made us thinking about not running the installation at all, because we considered that the quality of the presentation or the overall experience was deteriorated. After asking the players we found out that they did not notice or care about anything of the things that we were so much concerned about. They had fun, the game was working fine, it made them feel good.
4. *There will always be surprises waiting for you at the installation site.* Even if you think that you have taken every detail into account, be prepared to face last-minute challenges. A bag of tools and a ball of string will come in handy. Design your installation so that it can accommodate dynamically changing environmental variables. Allow for quick and easy adjustment of software parameters that might be affected.
5. *Vanity sells (i.e., make it personal).* Find a way to put the player's face in the game world. Allow players' to keep and share this image. They will love it. They will give you their contact data without a second thought.
6. *Keep it simple, but...* The gameplay was extremely simple: "use your shadow to put as many rusks in your basket as you can". Even 2-year old Maria, after playing the game, being all excited about it, would wander around explaining to anyone standing nearby how to play: "Big basket, rusks put in – many many rusks, yeaah!" Still, for people more familiar with video games and returning players, there was another layer of complexity, aiming to provide additional interest and thrill; different types of rusks and combinations would result in higher scores.
7. *If the rules can bend, the gameplay will not break.* The design decision to use the players' distance from the wall as the game's input mechanism, instead of tracking their bodies, proved to be very successful, since it offered high control flexibility. There were times were 3 or more people would play cooperatively using a single basket, parents carrying their children in their arms, couples hugging or fighting, people holding bags, food, employing various items to augment their reach, extremely short / tall players, children sneaking in a hand, etc.
8. *Realism and fun often do not mix well.* Initially, a quite realistic and accurate physics model was adopted (e.g., collision among all rusks, bouncing behavior of

objects). As playtesting revealed, when some of the model's parameters were tweaked (or even totally removed, as in the case of rusk collision) the game was much more fun and "fluid".

9. *Boost player success.* We knew that most people would play the game just once. Also, a lot of them would not be familiar with video games and we did not want anyone to end the game with very low or no score. Thus, a small number of rusks fall directly in the player's basket. Additionally, in the latest version, in order to increase the possibility of filling in the "small bites bar", only flavors that have not already been collected by the player appear in the game.

10. *A thing about adults 18 to 40.* Players in this age-range were the ones with the most inhibitions towards playing the game, mainly being afraid of becoming embarrassed in public. Still, there was not a single person who abandoned the game prior to finishing it, or mentioning of having regretted playing it.

11. *Full body control (?)* Although players were given the hint that the best play posture was keeping both hands spread in the air, the majority used just one hand, probably due to the fact that there are not many real life tasks requiring bimanual interaction. Additionally, about 25% of the players would place their hands in front of their torso, trying to reach and grab the rusks on the (distant) wall.

12. *It ain't over 'til it's over.* As explained in more detail in Section 5.3, you should not present anything to the players after the "game over" message.

13. *Playtest, playtest and then, playtest some more.* The endless hours of playtesting really paid off. To this end, the continuous renewal of our pool of playtesters was crucial, since every person would play the game in a slightly different way, doing, discovering, or saying something new.

14. *If you want to collect data, you should do it on the spot.* In both installations, 99% of the people who had an e-mail address instantly gave it away without a second thought in order to receive their photos. In the first installation, only 25 out of the 86 people who received this e-mail responded to the accompanying on-line questionnaire. In the second installation, all people – except just one – who were asked to fill in the questionnaire on-the-spot agreed.

15. *Less data is better than no data (i.e., keep it short).* People should not spend more time filling in data than actually playing the game.

7   Conclusions

The game was indisputably very fun. The related statement in both questionnaires was the one with the highest average rating and the least standard deviation. Additionally, one can safely conclude that the game achieved all its design goals. On the one hand, it offers a highly entertaining experience; on the other hand, it positively contributes to the marketing of "Kriton Artos" company and its products, reinforcing previous research findings [9; 10; 12; 23; 24; 25]. To this end, from the questionnaires and interviews with respondents, it emerges that the game's marketing impact was greater towards people not familiar with the brand, since those already familiar would rather base future purchase decisions on known product quality. Another potential benefit is that since the game made a lot of people happy, due to emotional conditioning [10; 23] this feeling will subconsciously be associated with the company's products.

A very interesting observation was a significant shift in player behavior and mood. Most people, prior to playing, would speak formally, keeping a distance from the persons running the booth. Afterwards, the majority of them would adopt a much friendlier attitude, being open to discussion, as well as to learning about and tasting the advertised products.

Having conducted several user-based evaluations in the past, one of the concerns regarded the validity of the questionnaires' results which seemed to be considerably (positively) biased. One of the possible explanations for this fact may be the euphoric state in which these players were observed to be after playing the game. Still, the on-line questionnaires which were completed within a time distance from the event reinforce the good results. One may claim that this fact justifies the success of the game as a marketing tool. Also, for the real skeptics (like ourselves) there is a collection of more than 2.000 photos recorded by the game showing people of all ages widely smiling and genuinely having fun.

In conclusion, the overall result proved to be more than just a game. It became a memorable experience for its players, but also for all of us who shared their happiness and excitement. In this respect, probably the best remark was made by a 64-year old chubby woman working as a cleaning lady, who enthusiastically exclaimed when the game finished: "This is fantastic! It totally makes you forget where you are!"

Acknowledgments. This work has been supported by the FORTH-ICS RTD Programme "Ambient Intelligence and Smart Environments". The authors express their gratitude to Anthony Katzourakis for creating the game graphics and to Haris Kenourgiakis who composed the original musical score. We would also like to thank Mr. Manolis Damianakis and Mr. Giannis Manidakis of "Kriton Artos" for their support towards realizing the public installations.

References

1. Csikszentmihalyi, M.: Flow: The psychology of optimal experience. Harper Collins, New York (1990)
2. Cowley, B., Charles, D., Black, M., Hickey, R.: Toward an understanding of flow in video games. Comput. Entertain. 6(2), Article 20 (2008)
3. Dahl, S., Eagle, L., Baez, C.: Analyzing advergames: active diversions or actually deception. An exploratory study of online advergames content. Young Consumers 10(1), 46 (2009)
4. Desurvire, H., Caplan, M., Toth, J.A.: Using heuristics to evaluate the playability of games. In: CHI 2004 Extended Abstracts, pp. 1509–1512 (2004)
5. eMarketer With Rise of Social, There's a Game for Any Marketer (2011), http://www.emarketer.com/Article.aspx?R=1008652 (retrieved November 21, 2011)
6. eventology Goodyear Virtual Pits 3D (2008), http://www.eventologyglobal.com/proyectos_eng.php (retrieved October 22, 2011)

7. Friestad, M., Wright, P.: The persuasion knowledge model: How people cope with persuasion attempts. Journal of Consumer Research 21(1), 1–31 (1994)
8. Grace, L.D., Coyle, J.: Player performance and in game advertising retention. In: Proc. of ACE 2011, Article 55 (2011)
9. Gross, M.L.: Advergames and the effects of game-product congruity. Comput. Hum. Behav. 26(6), 1259–1265 (2010)
10. Gurau, C.: The Influence of Advergames on Players' Behaviour: An Experimental Study. Electronic Markets 18(2), 106–116 (2008)
11. iLogic: BMW 1 Series: Projection Mapping Racing Game (2012), http://www.ilogic.co.za/interactive-projection-campaign-case-study (retrieved February 10, 2012)
12. Ip, B.: Product placement in interactive games. In: Proc. of ACE 2009, pp. 89–97 (2009)
13. Jenkins, H.: Game Design as Narrative Architecture. In: Harrington, P., Frup-Waldrop, N. (eds.) First Person, pp. 118–130. MIT Press, Cambridge (2002)
14. Lee, M., Faber, R.J.: Effects of product placement in on-line games on brand memory. Journal of Advertising 36(4), 75–90 (2007)
15. Lindley, S.E., Le Couteur, J., Berthouze, N.L.: Stirring up experience through movement in game play: effects on engagement and social behaviour. In: Proc. of CHI 2008, pp. 511–514 (2008)
16. Mueller, F., Agamanolis, S., Picard, R.: Exertion Interfaces: Sports over a Distance for Social Bonding. In: Proc. of CHI 2003, pp. 561–568 (2003)
17. O'Green, J.: Top things NOT to do in advergaming (2008), http://www.imediaconnection.com/content/18067.asp (retrieved December 6, 2011)
18. Peters, S., Leshner, G., Bolls, P., Wise, K.: Get in the Game: The effects of advergames on game players' processing of embedded brands. In: Proc. of International Communication Association (2009), http://citation.allacademic.com//meta/p_mla_apa_research_citation/3/0/1/1/2/pages301128/p301128-1.php (retrieved November 21, 2011)
19. Rohrl, D. (ed.): 2008-2009 Casual Games White Paper (2009), http://wiki.igda.org/Casual_Games_SIG#White_Papers (retrieved December 6, 2011)
20. Sherry, J.L.: Flow and media enjoyment. Communication Theory 14(4), 328–347 (2004)
21. SiA Interactive: Coca-Cola Virtual Penalty Kicks (2007), http://www.siasistemas.com/sitio2/eng-050753.html (retrieved October 22, 2011)
22. Sweetser, P., Wyeth, P.: GameFlow: a model for evaluating player enjoyment in games. Computers in Entertainment 3(3), 1–24 (2005)
23. Waiguny, M.K.J., Nelson, M.R., Terlutter, R.: Entertainment matters! The relationship between challenge and persuasiveness of an advergame for children. Journal of Marketing Communications 18(1), 69–89 (2012)
24. Winkler, T., Buckner, K.: Receptiveness of gamers to embedded brand messages in advergames: Attitude toward product placement. Journal of Interactive Advertising 7(1), 37–46 (2006)
25. Wise, K., Bolls, P.D., Kim, H., Venkataraman, A., Meyer, R.: Enjoyment of advergames and brand attitudes: The impact of thematic relevance. Journal of Interactive Advertising 9(1), 14 (Fall 2008)

Designing Playful Interactive Installations for Urban Environments – The SwingScape Experience

Kaj Grønbæk[1], Karen Johanne Kortbek[2], Claus Møller[2],
Jesper Nielsen[2], and Liselott Stenfeldt[2]

[1] Center for Interactive Spaces, Department of Computer Science, Aarhus University,
Aabogade 34, DK-8200, Aarhus N, Denmark
kgronbak@cs.au.dk
[2] Alexandra Institute, Aabogade 34, DK-8200, Aarhus N, Denmark
{kortbek,claus.moller,jesper.nielsen,
liselott.stenfeldt}@alexandra.dk

Abstract. This paper discusses design issues in the development of playful outdoor interactive installations featuring kinesthetic interaction and immersive music experiences. The research is based on the development and evaluation of the novel SwingScape installation, which is a permanent installation at an urban playground. The objectives of SwingScape are to encourage physical activity as well as creating a playful and social experience in an urban space. The interaction techniques include movement sensors built into swings, LED lights, and an ambient loudspeaker system covering approx. 180 square meters. The design issues include: creating playful and collective interaction, making a familiar swing interaction simulate the experience of a music mixing board, providing gentle integration of multimedia (light and sound) in the atmosphere of an urban space, and finally making installations robust and safe for an urban outdoor setting. The SwingScape installation has been developed in three phases for quite different urban settings, and the experiences from these are generalised to contribute to a foundation for design of interactive urban installations.

Keywords: Interactive light and sound installation, urban environments, outdoors settings, collective and playful activities, familiarity, user experience.

1   Introduction

The research behind this paper has taken place within the context of long-term activities in the city of Roskilde, Denmark, where the goal has been to develop and explore interactive playful installations in urban environments.

Physical space in urban environments can be seen as two extremes of a spectrum: those consisting of large distances, which induce feelings of coldness and grandeur and those of small distances, which call for intimacy and privacy. However, most contacts often take place in the in-betweens, the semi-private, and the half public. Therefore, SwingScape is an interesting example of an interactive urban installation, challenging the traditional urban space by creating opportunities for collective interaction in the zones in-between.

A. Nijholt, T. Romão, and D. Reidsma (Eds.): ACE 2012, LNCS 7624, pp. 230–245, 2012.
© Springer-Verlag Berlin Heidelberg 2012

During this process, the SwingScape installation has been developed and evaluated in various urban contexts; Roskilde city (at the Winter Festival) (see Figure 1), Roskilde Festival, and at PIXLpark – a raw industrial area in Roskilde. These experiences have lead to a number of generalisable findings that will be valuable for future designers of interactive multimedia installations for urban environments.

The final SwingScape installation consists of a large 180 sqm scaffolding setup with eight traditional swings equipped with movement sensors, and an ambient light and sound scape controlled by the swings' movement. The installation consists of two zones that illuminate in different colours when people swing.

Fig. 1. The SwingScape installation

The authors of the paper have been responsible for the development of the installation as well as the following evaluations among users. The development has taken place in close collaboration with the organisations in Roskilde, who are responsible for the future operation of the installation in the context of PIXLpark together with a number other installations and mobile games.

In [10], the notion of "interactive spatial multimedia" is introduced to denote multimedia integrated in the physical architectural environment, i.e. modern instantiations of Krueger's classical Responsive Environments [12]. In [10] there is a proposal for specific techniques aiming at developing such installations for art museums. This paper extends these ideas to an urban context, and proposes concepts and design parameters to address interactive multimedia installations in urban contexts.

The paper is structured as follows: Section 2 briefly reviews related work. Section 3 introduces design principles and interaction techniques. Section 4 describes how we implemented these principles technically in the final SwingScape installation. Section 5 discusses lessons learned based on qualitative evaluations of the various setups of SwingScape. Section 6 discusses challenges to consider when designing interactive installations for urban environments. Finally, section 7 concludes the paper.

2   Related Work

The focus of this paper is the synergy between: urban environments, familiar playful interaction, and aesthetic and kinesthetic interaction. While numerous installations exist for urban environments [4],[16],[5] only a few of these focus on large-scale physical installation based on interaction through familiar artefacts. In the following, we will highlight a few works of particular interest due to affording plain interaction.

Inspiration from urban domain was, e.g. Pianotrappan [15], which enhances stairs in a subway with analogue graphics defining each step of the stairs as piano keys. When walking on the steps a referring note is played, thus users play the stairs as a piano. The concept of adding sound and visual identity to familiar stairs, encouraging people to use stairs rather than escalators, was a great source of inspiration to us. Another project from the domain is "PLAYorchestra" [16], which inspires collective use and thus transforms the aesthetics of the urban space. By sitting on different cubes, individual instruments are played as part of a common classical music piece. As being a part of the urban space these installations facilitates collective interaction and hereby supports the behaviour and the atmosphere of this space. The earlier work on aesthetic interaction [14] has in the project been used as a way of stimulating multiple users to create a collective music experience beyond what is possible for an individual.

With regards to a movement-based perspective, kinesthetic interaction [5][9], concerns the bodily user experience. In projects such as Run Motherfucker, Run [18], Explosion Village [5] and Rope in Space [17] where all inspiring. Run Motherfucker, Run utilises a treadmill as means of interaction demanding high physical activity from the users. Rope in Space utilises a physical/virtual tug rope, which congregates competitors, still maintaining the high physical level of activity. The concept of Explosion Village is to interact collectively by hammering on barrels, and thus be rewarded by the appearance of a huge flame. In these three projects, the kinesthetic interaction establishes engagement and the activity becomes a motivating factor per se.

Regarding familiar interaction, e.g. PingPongPlus [23] has been of interest. It utilises ordinary ping-pong paddles and balls, where the table is digitally enhanced into a reactive table that senses the ball and supplies auditory and visual feedback. SMS Slingshot [20] draws likewise on the familiarity aspect by utilising a slingshot. An SMS is being sent to a wall by using the known actions of shooting a slingshot. In both projects the users find no difficulties in interacting due to the familiarity and direct simple ease of use.

In the SwingScape project, we were inspired by the manner in which the above projects worked with the urban space and directly addressing play and joyfulness as a means of motivating to interact. Furthermore, the deliberate use of familiar artefacts as the primary point of interaction and enhancing the experience with sound and light was the fundamentals of SwingScape.

3   Design Principles and Interaction Techniques

SwingScape is an interactive installation with the aim to revitalise urban spaces by: 1) motivating people to outdoor activity even in cold seasons. A main source of inspiration for this was the ice skating rink, which is a traditional popular outdoor activity in winter time; 2) creating familiar interaction similar to skating and swinging; 3) creating a collective installation, which invites people to join in and let go of their usual behavioural patterns; 4) creating a landmark to draw attention among users.

This focused the design on simplicity and playful interaction embracing social and collaborative atmospheres. The idea was to investigate how these objectives could be obtained by utilising light and sound as the main forms of expression in order to affect the manner in which we act in public environments.

The installation was originally developed for a specific city plaza in the city of Roskilde, Denmark. The plaza is placed in between routes of movement and can therefore be seen as a dynamic meeting point for both people passing by on a bike, by car or by foot. Thus, physical movement and dynamics around and within the installation has been the starting point of the design.

During the transformation from event to permanent installation, we undertook various experiments, e.g. numbers of swings, physical space around them, and adding and subtracting soundtracks to swings. The original version of SwingScape consisted of ten swings - each with different soundtracks as part of a sonic universe. Five of the swings control tracks with beats, and the remaining five control tones of the music. In the following, we discuss design objectives in detail.

3.1   Familiar Playful Interaction

With the above objectives as a starting point, we focused on developing a concept with base in a known and familiar interaction – rocking a swing. The swing is a familiar artefact for most people from their childhood. Using intuitive interaction, SwingScape was supposed to appeal to a wide range of users: children using it as traditional swings, teenagers pushing the swings and using them as a jukebox, adults experimenting with the different tracks, and elderly resting their feet whilst slowly rocking the swing.

When interacting with SwingScape, the user is able to affect the visual and auditory universe by utilising the different swings. The sound from the swing on which the user finds herself, is predominant in the users sonic feedback, making the audio experience in each swing area unique depending on which has been chosen. Together with other people, the user can consciously create a remix of a song by planning which swings to use. Furthermore, the simplicity of the changing lights has clear references to the dynamics of computer games, where the user is familiar to visual feedback when making a move.

3.2   Aesthetic Forms of Expressions

In [14] the notion of aesthetic interaction has been introduced to focus on the forms of expressions that add emotional values to the use experience. When developing installations for urban spaces, new opportunities and challenges for aesthetic expression are revealed compared to indoor use, for example, in museums.

One of the aims of SwingScape was to draw attention and invite citizens to take part in a collective experience and use the urban space in new manners. The intention was to make SwingScape work whether it is experienced within the installation (immersed experience), just outside, or far away from the installation (see Figure 2).

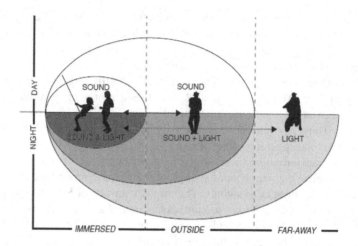

Fig. 2. Aesthetic forms of expressions in SwingScape and their zones of effect

Sound Expressions

A major parameter in relation to creating an aesthetic experience in the urban space has been the soundscape. Primarily due the fact that sound is audible all times a day in contrast to light, which only is an efficient form of expression at night.

The ambition was to develop a music installation in harmony with the kinesthetic experience, i.e. not compromising with the sonic experience. A cooperation with a musician from the electronic music genre was therefore made early in the process.

Fig. 3. A) SwingScape seen from far away. B) SwingScape seen just outside.

One of the primary design objectives was to experiment with how to create a meaningful interaction between the kinesthetic of the body and music - the movement of the swing acts like a metronome in music setting the pace, which influenced the development of soundscapes. Further investigations of the intrinsic rhythm of the swings revealed different tempi that worked really well and this was incorporated to the development of the soundscapes. As a means of motivation, the sound was designed such that the volume increased concurrently with the height of the swings.

Going from being a temporary to a permanent installation, new expectations to the soundscape have emerged. Now, the soundscape is much more varied and the users of the installation have the possibility to make their own custom soundtracks.

Light Expressions
Using light as a form of expression was in this context powerful due to the long dark hours during the Scandinavian winters. To make a successful installation, motivating people to take a detour past the centre of the city, it was important to work with lightning, which could be seen from far away.

The installation works as a landmark through use of light (see Figure 3.A). By being a visual landmark one's attention is attracted from a distance, and you are guided to the installation as by a lighthouse. The experience already from the longer distance builds up your expectations. (Figure 2 – "far away", Figure 3.A). Getting closer to SwingScape, you are invited into an experience space where you can be a part of the sonic universe from a spectators view (Figure 2 – "outside", and Figure 3.B).

Fig. 4. The immersed experience

As you enter the installation you experience how the light creates a fictive demarcated room giving you the conception of being "inside" a smaller room (Figure 4).

The light tubes are connected to the frames of the structure and hereby highlighting the borders of the installation. By highlighting the borders, the physical boundaries are emphasised which states the clear demarcations of being inside or outside the installation – and more importantly creating a space toned with unnatural light (blue and green colours). Light also brings another aspect to the installation. During At night, a challenge in urban space is often that the darker areas create a feeling of insecurity. The intentional use of lightning may bring safety to the urban space and hereby enhance the motivation for using the installation.

3.3   Collective Use of the Installation

The installation is made to bring people together, motivating them to move, and to interact with sound and light in the urban space. The installation works well if a group of 3-4 people, who know each other, wish to experience it. They can activate a small number of swings and collectively move between different swings to experience various combinations of beats and melody tracks.

Single users get a limited experience of being able to activate swings by hand and move between zones within the short timeframe that an unmanned swing use to fade to silence. Thus, the installation invites users to communicate and interact collectively, ideally making single or dual users call for by-passers, to extend the experience.

3.4   From Temporary to Permanent Use

SwingScape was created for the Winter Festival 2010 in Roskilde, which was on for two nights. Five months later, the installation was re-established at the music event, the Roskilde Festival, where it was exposed to 90.000 visitors for four days and nights, and finally, SwingScape was recently made into a permanent outdoors installation as part of a digital playground in Roskilde.

Winter Festival 2010

As mentioned above, SwingScape was developed for the Winter Festival (also called the "Ånd- og Videnfestival" - translation: "Spirit- and Knowledge Festival") in the centre of Roskilde in February 2010. The context was Roskilde city and it was supposed to reach a wide target group – all citizens of the city.

There were ten physical swings and the floor was covered with a green turf, which together with the wooden swings was supposed to refer to and bring warm associations to summertime, and was at the same time meant to be a contrast to the otherwise cold and rough urban surroundings. The choice of materials was together with the sound- and light design important for creating the aesthetic experience of the installation in order to attract citizens. The Winter Festival only lasted two nights, and the installation was supervised by two guards 24/7.

Roskilde Festival 2010

The installation was in summer 2010, re-established at the Roskilde Festival, which is an interesting context for testing new urban concepts. During the festival event, it is one of the largest temporary cities in Denmark; approximately 40.000 visitors intensively used the SwingScape installation day and night.

Compared to the first context, where it was only supposed to run during the nights, we were now challenged to make a new setup, which could work during the day as well. It is almost impossible to compete with the sunshine when coming to light, and therefore we found it important to unfold the audio experience even more. Another audio setup was created, being more "dreamy" and acoustic than the first one made for the Winter Festival. After one day, we realised that mixing the two setups gave the best result – giving variation to the soundscape 24/7. Furthermore, modifications to the floor were made, to obey to safety regulations a heavy rubber floor was laid out.

PIXLpark 2012

Recently, SwingScape was setup permanently in PIXLpark – a digital playground in Roskilde. This context is an old concrete factory and the surroundings are grey, industrial and raw. SwingScape was chosen for the digital playground, because of the duality of being a raw stabile, industrial construction during the day and being a strong, atmospheric landmark during the night-time. The centre of the swing area is set to always be lit, and gives a feeling of security to the area. For the permanent installation, a third sound scape setup was developed. This one being more a kind of a "sound puzzle", with animal sounds and realistic sounds inspired by nature. In PIXLpark, there are also offices where people work and it has therefore been important to work with a soundscape being interleaved in the natural surroundings. Finally, the Danish playground legislation required some adjustments of the physical construction.

4   Swingscape Technical Implementation

This section describes the SwingScape implementation in terms of infrastructure, sensors, light and sound control tools. Figure 5 shows SwingScape infrastructure and components. One swing cell is shown, while all indoor parts are shown in a grey box.

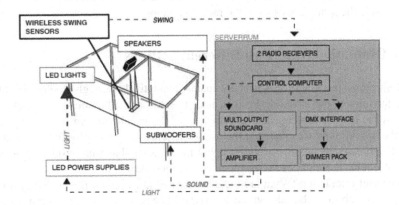

Fig. 5. The SwingScape technical infrastructure

4.1   Swing Seat Sensors

Battery operated wireless accelerometer sensors are placed in a cavity inside each (polyethylene) swing seat, protecting the electronics and making the swings appear ordinary to the public. Action starts when one or more of the swings are moved – accelerometers detect motion, a microcontroller will perform signal analysis and transmit MIDI note commands over 2.4 GHz radio to one of the two receivers. The corresponding radio receiver passes received MIDI commands to the control computer.

4.2   Light and Sound Control

The control computer will according to pre-programmed schemas activate the lights and sounds that correspond to the activated swing(s) in the current soundscape. The overview shows two signal chains – one for sound (red) and one for light (blue). The multi-output soundcard is connected to the amplifiers and speakers for each swing plus the subwoofer. The DMX interface is followed by a DMX dimmer pack and low voltage LED power supplies for the LED light strips that surround each swing cell. This system architecture allows all content (sound and light) to be defined in software at any time and also provides easy access to various computer generated usage data.

4.3   Radio System Issues

Initially, the seats were made of wood, which during dry weather worked fine. However, rain caused problems in terms of poor radio performance - caused by water turning the swing seats and the surrounding surfaces into radio absorbers. In turn, the dual AA alkaline batteries inside the swing seats started running out of power too quickly due to automatic increase in radio communication. Thus we had to replace the wooden seats with new polyethylene seats, as well as the two AA batteries in the seats with a single lithium 3.6V AA cell, and finally mount the sensors in IP67 sealed boxes inside the seats. This solved the radio problems.

5   Evaluation from Two Different Settings

The SwingScape installation has been evaluated qualitatively through video observations and interviews at the Roskilde Festival and in PIXLpark. The aim of the evaluations was to examine the use case and experiences of the installation. In the following, we describe in brief how we evaluated the user experiences from the Roskilde Festival and provide more details on how we did it in PIXLpark, as well as what results we got from the evaluations. Presentations of results focus on four focal points:

1) Playful Interaction (What are the users doing? I.e. what do they say they do, and what can we observe they do on the videos?); 2) Experience (What did the users experience? And how did they like the installation and the atmosphere in it?); 3) Collective communication (Did the users communicate with others when using the swings, and if so, how? Did they communicate with strangers? And did they see it as a social or individual experience?); 4) Understanding & Familiarity (Did the users understand the concept of the installation? For example, did they understand that what happened depended on what they did? And did they ascribe a familiarity to the installation?).

5.1   Evaluations from the Roskilde Festival

During the four festival days, twelve explorative interviews were conducted. Each interview had 1-3 interviewees, whom were addressed immediately after having tried the installation. The users were video recorded while swinging and the following interviews were recorded on a dictaphone. The evaluation was carried out at different times of the day to see how that would inflict upon the users' overall experience.

We strived to interview users in different age segments and group sizes. The age span was from 17-53 years; however, most of the interviewees were in their twenties (the average was 26 years of age). In order to practically manage the interview, which was at a noisy location close to the installation, we found it important that the groups were not too big. The duration of the twelve interviews was 9 minutes in average (5:10 minutes to 13:18 minutes), and the users were rewarded with a ticket for a beverage. The interviews were semi-structured. First, the users were asked factual questions, such as how long they had tried SwingScape, and if they had tried it more than once. Following this, the interviewees were asked about their usage and impression, as well as questions regarding their communication and understanding.

Playful Interaction
Observations and interviews revealed that users spent 3-10 minutes in the swings after being in queue. In turn, they often ran up on the platform and grabbed the nearest swing. If they where there with others, they would choose swings opposite one another if possible, facing each other. Video observations showed that the swings at times were used by more than one person, thus making them social and playful artefacts. Most people would only try one swing, as all of the swings were in use constantly. Thus, the users did not experiment with several swings and many did not notice that they were creating the sound. When users were asked what they did, most of them said that they tried to swing as high as possible. Furthermore, those who were there with others said that they were looking at each other, and a few said that they tried to swing in time with each other.

Experience
When asked for immediate reactions, eight of the interviewees said they felt like a child again. Two groups said, that they "lost track of time". In addition, most of the interviewees found the installation relaxing, and four mentioned that they liked the breeze then swinging. Those who had tried the installation both at night and in daylight said that they liked it better at night due to the lights, which were much more predominant in the dark. Furthermore, the swings were less crowed at night, which the users liked. At day, many were turned off by the long queue, and thus, most of the interviewees had only tried the installation once.

Collective Communication
The users did not talk much when using SwingScape. However, if others they knew were present, they were conscious of what they did; e.g., whether they would initiate a competition for the highest swing. Furthermore, the users were asked if they perceived it as an individual or a social experience. In four of the interviews, the answer was 'individual'; in three it was 'social', and in the remaining five it was both. Even some of the users who were there with someone they knew would say that the experience was individual, because "You fall into your own world". None of the interviewees talked to strangers when swinging. Some said they liked relaxing and

swinging by them selves. Others thought it was a social experience because they were there with others. "It wouldn't have been as fun without my friend", said a 21-year-old girl, and two 29-year-old guys said they wouldn't have used the swings if they were alone.

Understanding and Familiarity

With regards to the users' understanding of the installation and concept, it was clear that no one knew that they themselves created the music. Due to the fact that all seats were continuously occupied and that the users swapped seats a few at a time (instead of all at once), the installation was mostly regarded as "the cool swings with the music". Thus, the swings themselves were a familiar concept; however, mixing music when using them, was not easily comprehended in the given context. Many paid compliments to the music, however, a few did not even notice the music due to a concert nearby, and none of them experienced that the volume increased concurrently with the height of the swings. The lights were only noticed at night and not that they followed the movement of the swings. At night, the lights were predominant, and at day, the music was what people noticed (except when there were concerts close by). Most of the interviewees were surprised when they learned about the concept and logic after the interviews. However, in spite of the lack of understanding, the swings were very popular at the festival. They were mainly seen as a place for relaxation and fun.

5.2   Evaluations from PIXLpark

Since the opening of PIXLpark, we have conducted an evaluation with video observations and four explorative interviews in daylight. Each of the interviews had 1-4 interviewees aged between ten and 39 years. Group 1 consisted of four people between 16 and 24, who had visited the installation 5-6 times before. Group 2 was a couple in their late thirties with a 10-year-old daughter, who was there for the first time. Group 3 consisted of four 13-year-old boys, who had tried SwingScape on several occasions, and the fourth interview was with a 21-year-old man, who visited the installation with two others for the first time. The duration of the video recorded interviews, were 8:30 to 10 minutes. The interviews were semi-structured. To compare the answers with those given in the interviews at the Roskilde Festival, we took the same interview guide as a starting point and only made smaller adjustments to fit the new context.

Playful Interaction

Both the video observations and the interviews revealed that what the users did after sitting down and starting to swing was to experiment with the installation. Most of them tried out other swings and communicated with other users verbally or non-verbally about which ones to try. Group 1 said that they "...started to use signs with the body to communicate and plan which types of music they wanted to make by selecting the right swings". The interviewee in the fourth interview said "Just moving from one swing to another is quite an experience in itself". The family (group 2) also experimented with other swings; however, not until they had the whole installation for themselves, because they were afraid of disturbing other users. Further, group 2 said that they competed on who could swing highest; though this objective was less general than in the Roskilde Festival interviews. On average, the users spent approx. 25 minutes in the installation at PIXLpark.

Experience

All of the interviewees were excited and found that SwingScape was great fun. The young ones in group 1 were initially surprised that the swings were accompanied by sounds, but they quickly discovered how to collaborate on creating music. Group 2 said: "There is a nice atmosphere in the installation. It feels a lot like walking into some kind of space". Initially, group 2 did not think of the swings as being "active" as they called it, and were positively surprised when they discovered the sounds when they commenced swinging. The teens in group 3 thought SwingScape was "awesome", they particularly liked the sound changes, making it exciting for them to return "wondering which sounds are on today". Furthermore, they liked the direct response from the swings. However, sometimes they were unable to distinguish the sound from their own swing. The father in group 2 also thought the auditory variation between swings was fairly subtle. The young man in the fourth interview also enjoyed the experience very much and thought it was "different". Even though it was his first visit, he had a good grasp of the concept: "It seems like it plays louder and louder, the more you swing. And it plays different sounds... it kind of makes a tune. Then perhaps, one plays a bit more drums and one more the guitar. I think it's super cool".

Collective Communication

The interviewees were asked, if they thought of it as a social experience or as an individual experience. All of the groups except the family (group 2) thought of it as mainly a social experience or that it was more fun when they were more than one. The father in group 2 thought it was both, and that it would have been easier to explore the installation on his own. He thought he would have discovered the variations in the sounds had he not been obliged to push his daughter on the swing. However, he also liked to be more people "to find a sense of oneness with others". Group 2 did not talk much during use, as they preferred to listen to the sounds. The young people in group 1 mostly communicated through body language, because they found it hard to make themselves heard above the music. But when they spoke, it was about composing a great tune. In addition, they would not just enter SwingScape without asking, if others used it. One of the teens in group 3 had tried SwingScape on his own, but enjoyed it much more when trying it with others: "It is more fun when you can play tunes". As was the case with group 1 and 2, the teens did not talk much, except about the music composition: "You would say 'wow that sounds cool. Try that swing over there!'". In addition, they thought it was quite cosy despite the fact that they did not talk much. The 21-year-old man in the fourth interview also thought of it as a great social experience, and that he would bring his family there for future birthday parties and the like.

Understanding and Familiarity

The understanding of the SwingScape concept was visible both via body language in the videos, and in the utterances of the users' when talking about their actions and experiences. Firstly, no one had doubts that they were intended to be swings, but that they were not ordinary swings. We asked them explicitly if they experienced something different depending on what they did; and what they thought the logic was behind the technical part of the installation. Contrary to most of the interviewees at the Roskilde Festival, all of the interviewees at PIXLpark understood that they were initiating and collaboratively controlling the sounds. In addition, groups 1, 3 and 4 also discovered the soundscape change. Group 2 and 3 even had a quite accurate explanation of the technical construction. However, in broad daylight (as in all of the interviews), it was difficult to see the lights of the installation and that it would follow the movements of each swing. Only the teenagers who had been there on numerous occasions (one could see the installation from his bedroom window) knew that, and especially liked it in the evening, "because then it is really cool - because there are lights".

Finally, each group was asked about their opinion of the main concept. All groups interpreted the installation as either a musical instrument, a playground or as a combination of the two. Further, despite the swings, they did not consider it as a children's installation, but that it embraces a broader target group due to the musical experience and atmosphere. To conclude, the evaluations have pointed to the fact that there have been challenges in making such a large-scale interactive urban installation, and that these challenges have differed from one setup to the other. Thus, the next section will deal with these challenges and discharge into generalisable do's and don'ts.

6   Challenges for Interactive Urban Installations

Based on the development experiences and the evaluations, we discuss important challenges that we dealt with and that are applicable in general for urban installations.

Challenge 1: Immersive Sound may Disturb City Life. The purpose of the installation is to give users a playful and immersive music experience. This requires fairly loud music; however, for urban spaces with quiet living and office areas this may lead to unwanted noise and disturbance. Thus, it is necessary to calibrate music and sound levels to the given context.

At the Winter Festival, where the installation was placed at a fairly quiet square, the sound was calibrated to create attention about the installation at the square, such that by-passers not able to see the installation would be dragged by curiosity from the sound to get to the installation. Here it is a challenge to create such attention without being too noisy and also to create attention when nobody was activating the swings.

On the contrary, at the Roskilde Festival, the surroundings were very noisy by music coming from several competing scenes in the neighbourhood. Also, all the swings were in almost continuous use, making it hard to experience the activation of different tracks. In this context, the volume has to be loud and the subwoofer turned up, and much of the interactive experience comes from the light feedback, making the sunny daylight experience become hard to interpret as an interactive experience at all. Several interviewed users reported that they felt they were swinging to the music and not in fact creating the music and light experience.

Finally, PIXLpark, is an open space, and the sound can affect living areas in the neighbourhood relatively far away. Thus, the sound volume has to be adjusted to not make noise for the living areas. Running the same few tracks will create a too monotonic sound experience for neighbours. Thus, several different soundscapes were made to choose among, where some are more melody oriented and less beat oriented. The sound should gently invite people from the living areas to come down and use their bodies to experience and change the music experience. A lot of young people pass by the installation everyday – a motivation for them to stop and try the swings out, is to offer a change of soundscapes from time to time.

Challenge 2: Light Expressions Degrade During Daytime. Light is a great tool for creating atmosphere in an interactive installation. But working with light in an urban installation will always be a challenge, thus it is next to impossible to compete with the sun. This gives the installation two expressions; one at day, and another at night. Therefore, it is important to work with another effect to draw attention to the installation during daytime.

Challenge 3: Obtaining Outdoor Robustness and Safety 24/7. Making an interactive installation robust and reliable enough to withstand all kinds of weather and vandalism is an immense challenge. Numerous physical adjustments of the first design were made along the way. For instance, to obtain an approval in relation to formal playground rules for a permanent installation, a lot of safety measures in terms of foam and falling surfaces have been added. Lighting devices have been made stronger and more sealed to be able to last in all sorts of weather, the scaffold welded together to manage the potential rough use of it and secured flooring to carry weight from returning jumping around. Finally, the seats that contain the radio to communicate sensor data to the controlling computer had to be replaced from wood to a plastic material. This was due to the fact the wooden seats absorbed too much water hindering the radio communication making the energy consumption of the senders going up and in turn require frequent battery exchange.

Challenge 4: Too Many and Too Few Concurrent Users. Being too many users, i.e. all swings being occupied, limits the experience - the variations in the mix of tracks are hard to hear even though swings are used in varying manners. It is therefore a challenge to create a balance where the interaction technique actually makes people go off swings after having used them for some period of time and at the same time provide the feeling of freedom and control to the use. The size of the installation may influence the collective use patterns. It remains to be analysed whether people are reluctant to approach the installation and disturb others even though there are vacant swings. With a relative short distance between swings, some people may think they disturb the comfort zone of others by sitting on a swing. More evaluations are needed to analyse such use patterns and provide knowledge for future designs.

Challenge 5: User Contributions versus Aesthetic Control. A general challenge for interactive works of art, narratives and designs is how much freedom should the user have when it comes to the level of contributions and options of action? This question is contradicted with the question of how to make an aesthetic coherence in the installation, which is pleasurable for the user to engage with? The more control the designers have over the installation, the more coherent and exciting the experience may become. On the other hand, the higher level of interactivity the users experience, the less controlled and coherent the experience may become [11]. For future versions of SwingScape, we consider opening up for users to submit soundscape compositions via a moderator, who assesses the submission similar to App store verification, and if it meets requirements, it may become an option in the installation. Such features have so far been omitted, because they require extra interaction for users to choose among compositions and recordings, and mechanisms to avoid intrusive playback or invocation of user compositions overruling the choices of others.

7   Conclusion

This paper has described and discussed design issues for the development of outdoor interactive multimedia installations combining playful kinesthetic interaction with light and sound feedback as the aesthetic forms of expression. The research is based on the development of the novel SwingScape installation, which is now a permanent installation at an urban playground. The objectives of SwingScape were to encourage people to become physically active in a playful and social atmosphere in the urban space. The design issues discussed include: creating playful and collective interaction, gentle integration of light and sound in the atmosphere of an urban space, and making installations robust and safe for an urban outdoor setting. Evaluations of the SwingScape experiences discussed stemming from two quite different urban settings show that the design objectives have been largely fulfilled, and the principles and challenges may be generalised to future design of interactive urban installations.

Acknowledgments. Thanks to colleagues at Centre for Interactive Spaces, The Alexandra Institute and Dept. of Computer Science, Aarhus University, Denmark. Furthermore, we thank Roskilde Festival, Roskilde Municipality and composer/musician, Rune Wehner.

References

1. Blythe, M.A., Overbeeke, K., Monk, A.F., Wright, P.C. (eds.): Funology: From Usability to Enjoyment. Human-Computer Interaction Series, vol. 3. Kluwer Academic Publishers (2004)
2. Bowman, M., Debray, S.K., Peterson, L.L.: Reasoning about naming systems. ACM Trans. Program. Lang. Syst. 15(5), 795–825 (1993)
3. Brown, L.D., Hua, H., Gao, C.: A widget framework for augmented interaction in SCAPE. In: Proc. of the 16th Annual ACM Symposium on User Interface Software and Technology, UIST 2003, pp. 1–10. ACM, New York (2003)
4. Dalsgaard, P., Halskov, K.: Designing Urban Media Façades – Cases and Challenges. In: Proceedings of CHI 2010, Atlanta, USA (2010)
5. Explosion Village (2008), http://www.illutron.dk/posts/183

6. Fogtmann, M.H., Fritsch, J., Kortbek, K.J.: Kinesthetic Interaction – Revealing the Bodily Potential in Interaction Design. In: OZCHI 2008. ACM, Cairns (2008)
7. Forman, G.: An extensive empirical study of feature selection metrics for text classification. J. Mach. Learn. Res. 3, 1289–1305 (2003)
8. Fröhlich, B., Plate, J.: The cubic mouse: a new device for three-dimensional input. In: Proceedings of the SIGCHI Conference on Human Factors in Computing Systems, CHI 2000, pp. 526–531. ACM, New York (2000)
9. Grønbæk, K., Iversen, O.S., Kortbek, K.J., Nielsen, K.R., Aagaard, L.: Interactive Floor Support for Kinesthetic Interaction in Children Learning Environments. In: Baranauskas, C., Abascal, J., Barbosa, S.D.J. (eds.) INTERACT 2007. LNCS, vol. 4663, pp. 361–375. Springer, Heidelberg (2007)
10. Kortbek, K.J., Grønbæk, K.: Interactive spatial multimedia for communication of art in the physical museum space. In: Proc. of the 16th ACM International Conference on Multimedia, MM 2008, Vancouver, Canada, pp. 609–618. ACM, New York (2008)
11. Kortbek, K.J.: Staging as a Holistic Perspective on Interaction Design for Public Environments. PhD Dissertation. Dept. of Computer Science, Aarhus University (2011)
12. Krueger, M.W.: Responsive Environments. In: Wardrip-Fruin, N., Montfort, N. (eds.) The New Media Reader, pp. 379–389. The MIT Press, Cambridge (2003)
13. Lorenzo-Hemmer (April 2012), http://www.digitalshadows.de/?cat=4
14. Petersen, M.G., Iversen, O., Krogh, P., Ludvigsen, M.: Aesthetic Interaction - A pragmatic aesthetics of interactive systems. In: Proc. of the 5th Conference on Designing Interactive Systems (DIS 2004), pp. 269–276. ACM, New York (2004)
15. PianoTrappan (2009), http://www.rolighetsteorin.se/pianotrappan
16. PLAYorchestra, http://www.philharmonia.co.uk/thesoundexchange/live_projects/play_orchestra/
17. Rope in Space (2009), http://www.aec.at/center/en/2012/02/28/rope-in-space/
18. Run Motherfucker, Run (2001), http://www.marnixdenijs.nl/run-motherfucker-run.html
19. Sannella, M.J.: Constraint Satisfaction and Debugging for Interactive User Interfaces. Doctoral Thesis. UMI Order No. GAX95-09398. University of Washington (1994)
20. SMS Slingshot, http://www.vrurban.org/smslingshot.html
21. Spector, A.Z.: Achieving application requirements. In: Mullender, S. (ed.) Distributed Systems. ACM Press Frontier Series, pp. 19–33. ACM, New York (1989)
22. Tavel, P.: Modeling and Simulation Design. AK Peters Ltd., Natick (2007)
23. Xiao, X., Bernstein, M.S., Yao, L., Lakatos, D., Gust, L., Acquah, K., Ishii, H.: Ping-Pong++: community customization in games and entertainment. In: Proceedings of the 8th International Conference on Advances in Computer Entertainment Technolog (ACE 2011), Article 24, 6 pages. ACM, New York (2011)
24. Yu, Y.T., Lau, M.F.: A comparison of MC/DC, MUMCUT and several other coverage criteria for logical decisions. J. Syst. Softw. 79(5), 577–590 (2006)

Flashback in Interactive Storytelling

Olivier Guy and Ronan Champagnat

Université La Rochelle/L3i, La Rochelle, France
{olivier.guy,ronan.champagnat}@univ-lr.fr

Abstract. We have a lot of literature on the static media but few on interactive ones. Many doubt [Costikyan, Juul...] that it is possible to use stylistic
devices such as the ones that have pervaded the history of the 'one- way' storytelling. We have tried to imagine what it would be to have a flashback in IS.
Stylistic devices, in classic media are not as immersive. They are immediately
filtered by language – especially books- while IS has the major flaw of being
sometimes incapable of telling a story by itself as it relies so much on intuition.
The existence of the flashback in IS is possible to the condition of the narrative device called Uchronia, which leaves a chance of occurrence to potential
futures that might have happened.The last part is made for designers who want
to try to build Flashback IS application while taking back up on this paper. We
have taken a lot of inspiration from movies, classics as well as modern and we
have tried to set up a blueprint for an outline of a stylistic grammar in IS, starting
with the device of flashback.

On the one hand we have decided to use the theory of language as it is the
material of imagination – the one that makes stories- to try to find out if flashback was compatible with emergence and game engineering. On the other hand,
we wanted to provide the basis for experimentation of interactive flashbacks – as
we have tried to demonstrate exists under certain conditions- and we hope for
other multimedia and stylistic devices in IS.

Keywords: Serious games, interactive storytelling, design narration pilot,
stylistic devices, language theory, intelligent agents, video game aesthetics,
communication between artists & engineers, game design, playability.

1   Introduction

Flashback in IS has not been studied as far as we know on a formal scientific basis,
and we have not heard of any serious commercial game that would have made a serious experiment of a playable flashback. Therefore, we barely know the grammar of
this stylistic interactive device, as an aesthetic device or a psychological device to an
audience.

INTERACTIVE FLASHBACK NEEDS TO BE DEFINED and FRAMED

Marc Vernet (Vernet, 1975) wrote that ' whether it is a testimony or a simple memory,
the part that is given as a flashback seems more true, more essential, as the part that is
shown as the present'. We know that interactive storytelling would like to become more
and more expressive. We would like to provide what we know from other means of
expression to support designers who would like to create analepsis in their systems.

A. Nijholt, T. Romão, and D. Reidsma (Eds.): ACE 2012, LNCS 7624, pp. 246–261, 2012.
© Springer-Verlag Berlin Heidelberg 2012

Homer used analepsi in the first verses of the Iliad and do we have to remind how much moviemakers love to use those sorts of things? In this text, we will mostly use the words analepsis and flashback indifferently to speak of the same thing.

Then why does IS should do without the possibility of experimenting with such an emotionally powerful, a beautiful, styl istic device?

It is a powerful tool. In every fiction, it involves a wonderful array of affects – nostalgia, relief, tension, surprise, curiosity...- to tell stories that involve the user more and more. Moreover in non-interactive fiction, we know that this involvement is not as immersive as it is within the realm of interactivity.

Interactive storytelling (IS) has evolved so much that there is a question of an identity relation between video games and other media. The scientific community seems to be arguing on what can be considered a story in a video game. Can we be certain that it is even possible? We will try to define what is a flashback in IS, as there are no convincing examples as far as we know and what shape it could have within a video game. Henry Jenkins reported that Jesper Juul using Quake as an example argued that flashbacks were impossible within games, because the gameplay always occurred in real time. (Juul, 1998)

Most of the games that we wil l mention in this paper will either be Quake-likes or 'action-adventure' games. We will follow the typology described by Stephane Natkin mostly because they tend to be one of the richest genres in terms of narrativity. We will only consider playable flashbacks as there are no specific differences between a cut scene flashback from a video game and one from a movie.

In the second part of this paper we have thoroughly described templates of stories that might be transposed from cinema to IS to help any designer who'd like to create such a story. The idea is to provide template stories systems with models of ready-made stylistic devices of analepsis (Nakasone, 2006).

2   Definition

We bring a few necessary notions to the non-specialist.

'A flashback is fundamentally a movement on the axis of the diegetic time. A first sequence used as reference sets us at ti me O while the next sequence sends us back at time A, in the past. Obviously the distance in ti me between the events in the movement back to the past (A) and the first storytelling varies greatly from movie to movie.[...] The only cases which can cause problems are the ones that start with a sequence chronologically located before the rest of the movie.' (Mouren, 2005)

'As soon as we understand the sum of limits that a gameplay takes as a constrained form of storytelling, we see the advantages of stereotypy and serialization. They offer a preexisting story – a latent one- to the player without having to develop the narrative, and save the elements of a movie-like directed fiction.' (Letourneux, 2006)

Some authors have different definitions of the flashback 'A flashback is not only a movement back in time. This stylistic device expresses equal ly dream, digression, parentheses, and even theatrical asides.' (Guerin, 2003) By definition, it seems that this author is confusing embedded storytelling with flashback sequence storytelling.

Fig. 1. The respective domains of flashback, dream, digression, parentheses, and theatrical asides

Matthieu Letourneux reminds us the old quarrel between the ludologists and narratologists, where Greg Costikyan made an interesting distinction seeing stories as inherently linear and games as nonlinear, making them ontologically incompatible. However if we trust this point of view, it would be useless to allow a gameplay within a flashback. Either we should keep our flashback a static nonplayable part of the game, or discard any classic flashback narrative to keep a real time game. (Costikyan G., 1994)

Games may use all the grammar of movies in non-interactive cut scenes. The question is about where it fits in interactive storytelling.

Another difference appears as Mouren reminds us that, in film 'there's no present time of enunciation, the past in movies relates only to the 'first story' which is the time of reference', whereas a game occurs in real time following the actions of the player.

In silent movies, once it was written cardboards that were indications of analepsi. The more the audience became 1 iterate and the least the use of explanations was inevitable. In soundtrack movies, the story has a dual storyline, the story order often has a complex result which mingles what is played visually by the actors and what is said by the narrator. On a regular basis the voice over can give hints on the period of time or to measure the analepsis.

3   Is a Flashback Possible In a Video Game?

Language semiotics could help our understanding of that matter.

We will try to make an argument about whether an interactive storytelling could hold a flashback, as Jasper Juul stating the real time nature of games made a point that it was impossible. If language is a system, a structure of signs in an order of signs, every semantic field is already structured. We have to reconsider certain critics addressed to language, among them those addressing the behavior of language regarding the real and the truth. The French language dialectician Henri Bergson mentions (Bergson H. , L'évolution créatrice, 1907) 'the general condition of the sign [...] is to note, under a fixed form, a static aspect of reality [p328] [...] Language itself [...] is made to designate things and just things [p161]'. In the end Bergson, has an instrumental conception of language and would have agreed with Leroi-Gourhan

(Leroi-Gourhan, 1964) whose opinion was that language and tools were inseparable: both of them allow us to have reality at our disposal. Meanwhile, language is after all just a collection of juxtaposed signs which prevents us from accessing the deep understanding of reality, as he calls it 'a veil' (Bergson H.). In other words, we would be in the domain of imagination defined by Jacques Lacan (Lacan, 1962) when we watch *Reservoir dogs* by Quentin Tarentino. While we would be in the domain of the real when we play Quake without any way to make an analysis first hand of it, or reach the deep meaning of what we see.

- Interactive storytelling is by definition not fixed, and it is deeply inscribed into reality whereas classic media analepsis is static and inscribed in language.
- This is why language happens to give the impression that it fixes a flash of a moving heterogeneous, qualitative, continuum, in the outside world as well as within ourselves.
- In this context Jasper Juul could be right; we have left the realm of language for the one of the real.

3.1   Images and Immediacy: The Strength and Weakness of Interactivity

While reasoning produces stylistic devices, images and immediacy are mostly intuitive.

In *La Pensée et le Mouvant* (Bergson H. , La pensée et le mouvant, 1923) (p. 99) Bergson admits:' what is the primary goal of language? It is to establish a communication towards cooperation. Language conveys orders or warnings, it prescribes or describes.' To him it is a signal, this conception relates the nostalgia of the author of immediacy, and that he would like language to be as truthful and as rich as possible to reality. He adds:' Intuition is the direct vision of mind by mind. Nothing else stands in-between: the point of refraction through a face of the prism of which facet is space and the other is language.' [p. 35]

- Do we have to remind the main difference between non-interactive medium and interactive ones is identification for the 1st and immersion for the 2nd? In the second the affect of belonging to the space of the medium is the characteristic of the relationship with the player.

Language is just a collection of labels that speech juxtaposes; it is powerless to convey the 'indivisible continuity' of the real, intuition can reveal the being in its purity. Far from having to have a conceptual language of logical or operational classification, intuition has recourse to a language full of imagery, such as poetry in a noninteractive medium. If it is below language it also means that it is below algorithm language. Bergson, as well as Lacan (Lacan, 1962) acknowledged that it was impossible to pass on intuition, which is bound to 'overlap ideas'. Finally, he said, in *La pensée et le mouvant:* 'at least it may be done for the most concrete of ideas that surround the threshold of images. As soon as we tackle the spiritual world, the image, if it can only suggest, can give us a direct vision.'

- In other words, showing moving images, devoid of intentionality, of a story does not al low us a wide and complex array of abstract ideas. We may agree that it might be impossible to show a flashback in a realtime IS but, maybe for a slightly different reason; we do not have enough words for abstraction and conceptualization. Words spatialize the initial intensity by 'dissipating' the simple state that it produces in humans. Truth may be perceived only below, or beyond words, by intuition for example.
- The more we develop the 'grammar' and 'vocabulary' of our medium the more we will be able the use complicated stylistic devices. Images cannot be conceptualized and manipulated as easily as words. Images and realtime on their part have the advantage to convey a feeling of truth & even poetry.

3.2   If Imagery and Intuition Are So Wonderful Why Not Make All IS as a FPS-Like?

IN THE END THE MORE A STORY IS FILLED WITH LANGUAGE, THE MORE A STORY IS TOLD, THE LESS IT IS WITHIN INTUITION. WE COULD THINK THAT IMAGERY IS ALL POWERFUL, BUT WE NEED CONCEPTS.

Language has a symbolic value; Leibniz (Leibniz) warned about it long ago: only god may think without a sign. Indeed, language threads a veil between things and us; but 'spoken words', and not 'speaking words' as Merleau-Ponty said (Merleau-Ponty, 1945). In other words, poetry may convey things that are out of the reach of conceptual language. It is true that it has the right to a special existence as imagery, but humans cannot think imagery by itself. We need the word, even when they want to report about limit experiences such as those of watching IS and having to put it into words afterwards, to conceptualize the experience of pure imagery.

3.3   Uchronia

Then there is a short conclusion of our hypothesis on the existence of interactive flashback in IS.

Michel Foucault explains this as causality is one of the principles of the coherence of the world. The cause of all phenomena is a phenomenon without which this phenomenon would not happen. This principle regulates so much our occidental world that we get sometimes confused between the causes and the consequences. A story is not only a chain of events but also a chain of causes and consequences. As says the linguist Tzvetan Todorov (Todorov, Les genres du discours, 1978) on the principle of transformation, not only an event follows to a previous one, but it is the consequence of it.

- We have to admit that the primary time of narration might be changed by what has happened by gameplay in the past. Because if there is no possibility of changing the present by a playable flashback there's no point to make a flashback, playable. This is a stylistic device called Uchronia-Utopia in history.

4   Melodrama vs. Flashback

THE QUESTION OF MELODRAMA IS VERY SPECIFIC TO AN ARTICLE WROTE BY HENRY JENKINS, AND IT IS ADDRESSED HERE BECAUSE WE WANT TO AVOID ANY KIND OF COGNITIVE CONFUSION WITH THE FLASHBACK.

As Henry Jenkins (Jenkins, 2004) defines melodrama in several terms that we want to differentiate from the actual flashback, because the difference does not seem so obvious when we read his paper.

A differential analysis of flashback and melodrama.

Flashback	Melodrama
Switchover from the diegetic chronology	Spaces and artifacts bear witness of past narrative information
Stylistic process	External projection of internal states
Intervention of some kind of director	Research of an affective potential through the use of costumes, art direction, lightning choices...
Explicit story element	Conclusions drawn implicitly by the gamer, present time is never left
The whole range of stylistic flashback, we're in a hypertext process	Powerful feelings of loss or nostalgia, especially in those instances where the space has been transformed by narrative events

   If the flashback only exists as a reference from the past, it is in no way like a flashback. What the previous statement offers is to show an evolution in the gameplay in real time according to past events as taken into account by the system whereas a flashback is more a reenactment of something that occurred as if it was in real time. In Jenkins case the enunciation time –real time- remains at all times. It would be at the best, melodrama. Anyway, on an aesthetic level, if melodrama can turn out to be sublime under brilliant hands it is most of the time, simplistic and extravagant (Souriau, 1990).

5   A Vocabulary of Flashback

Linking can easily lose the audience as Truffaut (1988) said 'a flashback is not authenticated as such as its starting point but as its arrival point'. Old movies were not made to be understood to have non-linking flashbacks; they even might have had some of them, or be built to have one by their makers and go unnoticed. We are not even speaking of flashbacks in IS where it should be as difficult to be understood by the user.

THE MAGNITUDE is the size of the story –not of the diegesis- that's covered by the flashback. EXTERNAL means that the events of the analepsis happened outside of the timeline covered by the diegesis of the primary story. INTERNAL means that it happened after the point 0 of the storyline of the primary storytelling. It may be DUAL, meaning that it is external in the beginning and internal in the ending point li ke in the movie '*La mariée était en noir* 'by François Truffaut, by this case does not occur very often.

Another consideration is whether it is <u>CONTINUOUS;</u> does the flashback relate the events in one piece or do we have links to the primary story i n-between sequences?

5.1   An Aesthetic Consideration on Continuity

Most of the time discontinuous stories provide a feeling a conflict between the present and the past: in psychoanalytic movie such as those of Hitchcock, the montage of flashbacks gives a feeling of repressed memories which keep coming back into conscience. In *Once upon a time in the West* the motive of vengeance is being clarified and becomes stronger as the criminal past of Harmonica man's target – Henry Fonda's character- reappears.

To this purpose we may use the example of *The Thin red line* by Terrence Malick (1998) that uses the contrast of a dozen scenes of happiness of soldiers in times of peace cut by scenes of war. The primary story is about war; the flashback is external, discontinuous, multiple and happens in their lives before the war.

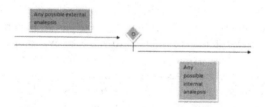

Fig. 2. A Distinction Internal/External Analepsis

5.2   A Note on a False Interactive Flashback

In *Duke Nukem 3D* (3D Realms, 1996) the gamer could be taken from a time to another by crossing through a 'time machine door'. Obviously, this cannot be considered as a real flashback as it uses props to give the illusion of a gameplay in the past, however we never leave the real time.

Non-interactive medium	Interactive storytelling
Analepsis has been used since the Iliad by Homer	Analepsis has no known real known example; we have examples of mistakes made by inexperienced gamemasters in roleplaying games which usually turn quite bad.
Analepsis is used on a regular basis	Some people believe that analepsis does not even exist in IS
Analepsis is clearly defined	Confusions happen often between analepsis and other aesthetical forms
The only problem is the one of mise-en-scene	In addition to mise-en-scene, it has to be actionable (in the past)
It is static	It poses the problem of temporal paradox
The past is supposed to be true	The past may be false, and can be modified
Nobody in the audience feels weird about seeing or reading about an analepsis in itself.	The user is referred to the enunciation: a very strong feeling of Deus ex-machina feeling comes out of the process.
If the analepsis requires the intervention of a narrative device, then it is not an analepsis (time machine, superpower...)	If the analepsis requires the intervention of a narrative device, then it is not an analepsis (time machine, superpower...)

Fig. 3. Comparison of Interactive/Non-interactive analepsis

6   The Form of the Flashback: A Toolbox for Designers

In classical western rhetoric, this chapter would concern what Quintilian called *dispositio,* or the syntax of analepsis.

6.1   The Crux of the Plot Is at the End of the Story

The purpose of this kind of flashback is explanatory. Usually on a movie screen it lasts from a few seconds to several minutes. If its magnitude covers only the crux of the plot, then we have to admit that it is not very broad, in proportion to the storyline.

6.2   The Past of a Character Has to Be Explained

In this case the flashback is situated in the first half of a movie, most of the time. It does not give clues about crucial elements of the plot, but usually puts into light a mysterious part of the personality of an important character. Roland Barthes would say that this analepsis is less a *function* than a *hint*. Examples of this method are numerous li ke in the character impersonated by Bogart in *Casablanca* (Curtiz, 1943) or in *Gattaca* (Niccol, 1997) when a 20 minutes sequence tells us how the main character has not been genetically engineered but has tried to overcome illegally this problem in a futuristic and repressive society.

6.3   The Brutal Start Has to Be Clarified

The sequence from the start is very agitated and brutal. The diegesis has to be made clearer in the following sequences by an external analepsis of limited magnitude. It is the case in the movie Fight club by David Fincher (1999), where the hero starts with a gun barrel between his teeth and initiates through a voice over a mandatory flashback to explain his situation.

6.4   The Flashback Takes Most of the Story

Some stories like Lolita (Stanley Kubrick, 1962) have most of their length taken by an analepsis. In the case of Lolita it is continuous but, it may be different, multiple, discontinuous, non- linking etc. The movie starts with James Mason who comes to kill the character of Peter Sellars the story then, goes 4 years earlier to tell more about the events that occurred at time 0.

6.5   The Flashback Is Internal

The Law of non-repetition — as hard as it is to believe that we could imagine such an aesthetic law- : in an authentic text, there are no repetitions. (Tzvetan Todorov (1980), Poétique de la prose, suivi de Nouvelles recherches sur le récit. Seuil, Paris.) According to this law, which is usually accepted most of the time, with a few exceptions, internal flashbacks happen seldom as they always have some kind of potential of breaking the agreement with the audience. For instance, reenactments of a scene that already occurred is better accepted than an analepsis out the blank, or a change in the point of view, or in the perceptions in the same scene, which can be played in this manner several times like in *Incident at the corner* (Alfred Hitchcock, 1960). In other cases we have several examples of well tolerated uses:

- The director wants to emphasize an object, a fact, a memory, or stress, or juxtapose in the present somethi ng that happened before;
- She wants to fill the gap in an ellipsis;
- He wants to recapitulate, or sum facts that happened during the story, as in America, America (Elia Kazan, 1963).

7   Towards a Grammar of the Flashback: Indepth

7.1   The Flashback in a Whodunnit or Psychoanalytic Story

These themes are dear to Hitchcock and Truffaut who spoke of it in their famous recorded conversations (1983). These stories, although quite different in their themes, work in the manner in which they use their denouement flashback in a very similar manner. Thus *Marnie* (1964), by Alfred Hitchcock or almost every novel by Agatha Christie - or any of its movie adaptation such as Murder on the orient express by Sydney Lumet (1974) -makes the same use of the final flashback in regards to the plot. In one way or another the flashback is used in cathartic way to find out what happened, and in the first case who has perpetrated the crime and in the second case to discover, in a rather silly parody of the Freudian theory, which trauma is making the patient sick – who by the way is treated by the effects of the resurgence of the trauma to her conscience. In both cases, justice has been made or a patient was treated, the hero is the detective or the patient — or the doctor who treats the patient-: the flashback gives the feeling of a euphoric denouement (Vernet, 1975).

7.2   Eclectic Flashbacks or Trying to Show Various Things

A naturalistic tendency would be to show things as they are in real life — i.e. based on a contemporary urban life, people talking, most of the time (Woody Allen, 1993, Woody Allen on Woody Allen); or based on some action movies on an uninterrupted firework (Jullier, 1997). A flashback could then introduce some variety in the story.

7.3   Introducing Contrast

As we have mentioned before flashbacks can introduce contrast in a story such as in *Johnny got his gun* with the memories of Johnny, or in *Le crabe tambour* by Pierre Schoendoerffer with the main story happening in a cold stormy sea while memories happen in Indochina or Africa, movies have numerous examples of interesting contrasts through flashbacks.

7.4   Freudian Psychology and Time-Saving of a Character's Past

As we have noticed a flashback is very useful as it provides the means to avoid verbosity in dramatization of some sequences. One of much used 'time-saving', is whenever a behavior of a character has to be justified through its past. This process is so common – there was even a fad that seems over since the years 1940-50 of the psychoanalytical movie- that it is barely noticeable now. First a pathological , or at least a noticeable, behavior catches the attention of the audience, and second a flashback conveniently comes to explain this behavior within the past of the character -or even more supposedly Freudian, the childhood. Dario Argento has elected to explain the murderous behavior of some of his main characters by their pasts. Hitchcock has also done so in *Psycho*. Another good example of this narrative system is *Belle de jour* by Luis Bunuel with Catherine Deneuve where the prostitute has internalized a very complex system of fantasies in which sexual abuse, remembrances, religion, and debauchery are supported by flashbacks. Although, this last example speaks more about Luis Bunuel Himself than about the character he designed for Deneuve. A designer shows sometimes, and in many cases she is expected to do so, more than she is willing to expose of herself. We have to acknowledge that a closed, done, finite, character, has something of predictable and disappointing.

7.5   The Tragic Dimension of Completing a Short Story with a Long Analepsis

Usually those stories start 'from the end', which means that the, often tragic, ending of the story is the opening of the mise-en scene, while the rest of the movie is a huge flashback that gives away the reasons of such a beginning. This structure contains such powerful emotions – that are mostly used in tragic stories, we have no unarguable explanation so far for this, but other genres do not go along as well as tragedy-that it has been used by the best for the most prestigious works of fiction: *Une femme douce* (Robert Bresson, 1968), *Othello* (Orson Welles, 1952), *The man who shot Liberty Valance* (John Ford, 1975), *La femme d'à côté* (François Truffaut, 1981), *La signora di tutti* (Max Ophüls, 1934)... We are just naming a few of the most prestigious ones, and the list could be amazingly long just for those. The story does not have to start with death; it may start with decay or decline as in Amok (Joel Farges, 1992) or Lola Montès (Max Ophüls, 1955).

In a classic Greek sense, a tragic piece did not rely on any suspense, whenever the audience went to watch the Oresteia, there was no question whether it was going to end well. This kind of flashback allows some leeway to the designer to play with the genre and give a true feeling of tragedy to the user. It is the case with the *Othello* of Orson Welles, or *Le rouge et le noir* by Claude Autant-Lara – which starts with the execution of Julien Sorel. Speaking of Greek tragedy about this form flashback is not an hyperbole, knowing the fate of the characters, while following, loving, identifying, being immersed with them is probably as deep as it was to do so with any Greek hero. For instance Truffaut started *La femme d'à côté* with an idea that obsessed him, and was at the root of his work and probably his mind: a man and a woman are not made to live together although they can't live apart. From the very beginning the audience knows that this is not going to end well, the dramatic tension is contained elsewhere.

7.6   Filling the Gaps in the Story or How to Avoid Losses of diegetic Time with Internal Flashbacks

Suppose that an event E has to last on a screen for 20 minutes, and we have to cut it to 5 while maintaining a quality standard to the story as nobody would notice the cut in the diegetic time... How about an internal flashback of some event that is filtered through some character who tells about it without it actually happening in real time? Abstraction, in linguistic code is inherently time saving and very efficient for anyone who is concerned about story quality. This is why showing a multimedia memory of what happened in E through what is saying the character is probably a good compromise.

This process is also used very often in the genre of the Whodunnit as a reenactment allows the detective to find out what happened in the past and way to a flashback where the audience sees the truth.

7.7   Can a Flashback Show a Lie?

Whereas it is accepted that any character may lie in a multimedia context, can a designer show it? When discussing the question with Truffaut, Hitchcock (Hitchcock/Truffaut, 1983) said something close to: I said something that I should never have done... A flashback that was a lie... In movies, we tolerate very well that some man might tell a lie. Moreover we accept the fact that whenever a story of the past is told by a voice over it could be illustrated by flashback images, as if it was happening in present time. In this case, why could not we tell a lie inside of a flashback?

(*in Stagefright*, 1950)As we have mentioned, a character can lie through his voice because this sequence is purely subjective, while a visual sequence is never absolutely subjective it is a fictional reference (Vernet, 1975). Images are always contaminated by the idea of objectivity, by convention; they never can be purely subjective. Therefore we might say, maybe sadly, that the audience is so accustomed to watch images that tell the truth, that lying with them would create a cognitive dissonance that would make them uncomfortable. We have to mention several experiments which prove that memories can lie to their very owner (Loftus, E. F.; Pickrell, J. E., 1995), indicating that apart from conventions, no reasons whatsoever could prevent designers from writing untrue flashbacks.

Then if a flashback is ontologically objective, while words can lie, designers may use analepsi to prove wrong a character while he says something opposite, or in any way different than what is shown. The effect may be sometimes comically pathetic when a character wants to avoid disclosing something, or making an event look better than it was. Again if the convention we mentioned was ineffective, the comical effects would be as well. Most of the time when a movie breaks this convention, the whole plot revolves around this rule-breaking such as in Fight club (David Fincher, 1999), Usual suspects (Bryan Singer, 1995), or Snake eyes (Brian DePalma, 1998). Whereas Hitchcock makes a deliberate lie, the case is not as difficult with contradictory versions, such as with Kurosawa who believes that the truth is not within the reach of the human mind...

7.8   Can It Tell Contradictory Versions?

In *Rashomon* (1950) for example, flashbacks show different versions which do not lie in a narrow sense of the word but tell a subjective truth, in an individual value sense of the word. The rapist, the raped, the victim, are all questioning the – an all Japanese- value of honor. None of them is lying, they all see the world in the predicate of their beliefs, which they do not see as obviously as the audience does. This movie has inspired many other 'multi-versions of the same event' movies such as *Girls* by Georges Cukor (1957), *Basic* by John McTiernan (2003), *The woman in question* by Anthony Asquith (1950). Some are more like reenactments – there are numerous examples of these stories- multiple flashbacks shows different versions, they are not showing memories but reconstructions as in Manhattan murder mystery by Woody Allen (1992).In a different way, we may have the same flashback with different interpretations (such as in playing of a voice over).

7.9   The Truth, The Images, and the WORDS.

We have seen above that a flashback was construed as more true than the main story, as a consequence many multimedia stories get their support from a flashback which relieves the dramatic tension as it is supposed to tell the truth –at least more than the rest of the present of the storytelling. Those genres are Whodunnits – where it tells the truth about the crime, a first step towards justice-, psychoanalycal stories – where the flashback treats the neurosis etc. If we consider again the *episteme* as it is in

Foucault, the past is the cause of the present, the memory is the main road to the preservation of our true selves, our identities. Thus many movies show protagonists who have lived through a painful past – such as a love story, in *Casablanca* by Michael Curtiz- whom she does not want to speak about anymore, but which she remembers perfectly well and which comes to her consciousness every now and then to hurt her. In that sense, the huge flashback of *The man who shot Liberty Valance* by John Ford, is only there to tell – which will never be known in the diegesis- the truth.

Using this presupposed objectivity of the images of the analespsi some directors have used it as a testimony from the past that would again tell the truth. In Fury (1936) by Fritz Lang, a 1st flashback, purely voiced, happens during the trial while Joe is in the street, and walks in front of a shop window, inside which a double bed is exposed; he then hears a sentence said by the voice of his fiancée, Katherine, coming back from the time when then walked in front of the same store. He turns back as he was subject to a sound hallucination, a little farther, after his fiancée came to ask him to tell that he was actually alive, to try to stop the trial of the lynching; he makes moves like he wants to push away these hallucinations – feelings of guilt. In a 3rd flashback Katherine remembers, Joe's brothers comes to visit her; one of them lights a cigarette; the face of her fiancé in jail comes to her memory; again as a hallucination. She accepts to testify that Joe is dead, burnt alive. The audience knows it is false. Why? Lang uses two sorts of flashback devices; on the one hand, images from the past -the lynching- recorded by a neutral device – or supposedly so- , and on the other hand, mental images –hallucinatory- that have no value of truth for a third party, but have some kind of influence on the character.

Truffaut used a similar process in a slightly different way; *in Une belle fille comme moi (1972)* Camille is in Jai l for a murder that she did not commit, the truth is on a recording in 8 mm. In the end this film, is the diegetic device that will prove that she is innocent.

7.10   The Implicit Flashback

A definition is required probably before continuing under this category; intertextuality is the relationship between the meanings that are put by the subject of the enunciation between the texts that are by this process entering a dialog within one another, reconstructing one another through the culture of the subject. Intertextuality means that there is no immutable meaning, but that semantics of a text is a dynamic. (Multiple authors, 2007, Grand dictionnaire de linguistique & des sciences du langage, Larousse, Paris)

Some stories have made the choice of putting inserts that are not inside the diegesis. They are interesting because of their extradiegetic existence and their powerful evocative in the audience memory and culture. For instance, October by S.M Eisenstein juxtaposed small figurines of Napoleon with scenes of Kerensky to produce meaning by effects of montage. If we refer to Genette's (1975) notion of intertextuality in the specific context of Soviet Russia, we know that Napoleon is an invader, brutal, and dictatorial. In another context, the movie was made at a time when the Koulechov effect was discovered by the very same Soviet school of moviemaking.

There's not much doubt to the sense we can give to the montage of SM E; Kerensky is a dictator with a Napoleonic complex. (Октябрь, USSR, S.M Eisenstein, 1927).

7.11   An Offer of a Structure of Interactive Storytelling Based on the *RESER VOIR DOGS*

Reservoir dogs is a Heist movie. A very – too much - well explored genre. Tarentino had noticed that every heist movie so far was focused on the preparation and the actual heist. The originality of this movie is that no image of the actual heist is shown. The numerous in this film flashbacks introduce the characters that are round and well defined, and also the days and hours preceding the attack. Two gangsters M. White and M. Orange, who is badly wounded, arrive in the place that was supposed to be the haven after everything was over. After a short while M. Pink comes in. Lots of conversations go on where the three characters try to figure out why the plan has failed.

They could be PCs. Their goals might be:

- M. Pink could try to run away safe with the money;
- M. White could try to figure out who M. Orange really is;
- M. Orange could try to blur everything and not be discovered – avoid dying and avoid the killing of innocent people.

Their dialogs are illustrated with scenes of flashbacks of what followed the heist, mostly violent scenes that might be playable as a shoot them up – in a quite subtle way as there are a lot of civilians, and everyone wants to remain clean of crimes (especially Orange).

Then Flashbacks go a little farther back in time to introduce the characters and the way they were recruited by the kingpins, they bear the names of each character and still cut the dialogs, from ti me to time. Everything has started to fail much earlier before the arrival at the warehouse, they could easily be made playable, improving – or not- the present situation in the primary story.

The last and longest of the flashbacks is probably the one that will bring the most and interesting opportunities for creativity as at first M. Orange has to learn a dealer story to be credible as a cop, to be able to infiltrate the gang. This flashback is not linear, it is embedded – and nested- in the main story's flashback, while Orange is trying to be convincing to the other gangsters, the – made up- story is illustrated by a false flashback. Moreover this nested flashback is complicated by the fact that the police chief who is training Orange teaches him to mix lies with real life memories so that he is more convincing.

I might have had given ideas to make a gamedesign for this last piece but it is tricky enough to leave gamedesigners a full range of imagination.

8   General Conclusion

We have seen the definition of a flashback and that it inherits most of its properties from movies. It is easier to have a cut scene than to offer a gameplay inside of it, but the only real technical challenge would be to do so. Movies have a very complete set of expressive tools that video games still lack and the solving of linearity against interactivity is still pending.

The only accomplished way to resolve at that point the will of a storyteller -who tailors a flashback as a way to improve the style of his story- and the perpetual present of the game is to use actual technologies of hypertext.

- We believe that an IS flashback may exist under the following conditions only:
- If there are no devices that allow the player to go back in the past;
- The IS has an ambition to tell a story, not one that wi ll be told by players after the end of the play session;
- We have to admit that the game needs the risk of failing, the risk of a 'game over'; therefore it implies the problem of changing the present as we al low the player of changing the past. The notion of Foucault an Uchronia are therefore indispensable in this case;
- It has to have a structure that relies to a certain extent on the word, or on a central route of cognition as experimental psychologist say. It is too difficult to tell a story only by – peripheral- intuitive processing.
- If it is not confused with the device called ' interactive melodrama';

The flashback has to fit the enunciative strategies of the designer, and has to fit the present time of the story.

There's also a major problem of finding the right proportion of intervention of the artists and gamedesigners as it seems impossible so far, to find a game that would fit the characteristics that we mentioned, and on another hand that would have a complex system engine from which would emerge a narrative flashback. Stéphane Donikian is also probably right when he states: 'The main problem to solve relates to the fusion of narration and interactivity, understood, the immersion in the gaming universe and identification to the characters of the story.' (Donikian, 2004)In the end, this field has a lot to experiment; we hope that the outline of grammar will lead to fascinating experiments in the design of IS.

References

[1] Duke Nukem 3D (1996) [Motion Picture]
[2] Allen, W.: Woody Allen on Woody Allen trad. Gallimard, Paris (1993)
[3] Bazin, A.: Le cinéma de la libération à la nouvelle vague. Paris: Les éditions des cahiers du cinéma (1983)
[4] Bergson, H.: L'évolution créatrice. PUF, Paris (1907)
[5] Bergson, H.: La pensée et le mouvant. PUF, Paris (1923)
[6] Bergson, H. (n.d.): Le rire. PUF, Paris
[7] Cavazza, Pizzi: International conference on technologies for interactive digital storytelling and entertainment, TIDSE 2006 (2006)
[8] Ciment, M.: Passeport pour Hollywood. Seuil, Paris (1987)

[9] Costikyan, G.: I have no words and I must design. In: Salen, K., Zimmer-man, E. (eds.). MIT Press, Cambridge (1994)

[10] Donikian, S.: Modélisation, contrôle et animation d'agents virtuels autonomes évoluant dans des environnements informés et structurés. HDR IFSIC, Rennes (2004)

[11] Gardiès, A.: Le récit filmique. Hachette, Paris (1983)

[12] Genette, G.: Palimpsestes. Le seuil, Paris (1982)

[13] Guerin: Le récit de cinéma. Cahiers du cinéma/Scérén-Cndp, Paris (2003)

[14] Hitchcock, A., Truffaut, F.: Dialogues. Ramsay (édition définitive), Paris (1983)

[15] Jenkins, H.: The game design reader. In: Salen, K., Zimmerman, E. (eds.). MIT Press, Cambridge (2004)

[16] Jost, F.: Un monde à notre image/énonciation, cinéma, télévision. Méridiens-Klincksieck, Paris (1992)

[17] Juul, J.: A clash between games and narratives. Presented at Digital Arts and Culture Conference, Bergen, Finland (1998)

[18] Lacan: Ecrits. Seuil, Paris (1966)

[19] Lacan, J.: Le séminaire sur l'Identification IX. le seuil, Paris (1962)

[20] LeBlanc, M.: Tools for creating dramatic game dynamics. In: The Game Design Reader. MIT Press, Cambridge (2004)

[21] Lefebvre: Une philosophie et une pratique de l'expression et de la reflexion. Gallimard, Paris (1949)

[22] Leibniz. (n.d.): Nouveaux essais sur l'entendement humain. Retrieved from Leibniz, Nouveaux essais sur, http://fr.wikisource.org/wiki/Nouveaux_Essais_sur_l%E2%80%99entendement_humain

[23] Leroi-Gourhan, A.: Le geste et la parole. Albin Michel, Paris (1964)

[24] Letourneux, M.: Genvo, S., In: Le game design de jeu vidéo. L'Harmattan, Paris (2006)

SanjigenJiten: Computer Assisted Language Learning System within a 3D Game Environment

Robert Howland, Sachi Urano, and Junichi Hoshino

University of Tsukuba, Tsukuba, Ibaraki, Japan
rob@robhowland.net, me@sachiurano.jp,
jhoshino@esys.tsukuba.ac.jp

Abstract. Imagine being able to approach any object in the real world and instantly learn how to read and pronounce the name of the object in any other language. This paper proposes the use of a system that simulates this idea by utilizing the video game medium in a way that makes learning a new language simple and fun. The system was designed specifically for the new technologically-inclined generation that might benefit greatly from learning within a game environment. The process of learning a new language with this system strays from previous and conventional methods in that it employs a more visual-spatial approach to learning. Additionally, this system engages the player through the use of industry-standard video game elements such as a 3D environment, controllable main character, item collection system, scoring system, and complex rewards system. By keeping in line with what people expect from standard video games, this game is capable of holding the player's attention for longer periods of time than when compared classes, textbooks, or tutors.

Keywords: Language Learning, Educational Games, Serious Games, Edutainment, Visual-Spatial, Auditory-Sequential, Immersion.

1 Introduction

Learning a new language is not an easy task. When one even considers the idea, they are met with many challenges and fears that can potentially deter them from believing that gaining fluency is within their grasp. Even with all the tools that technology offers us today in regard to Language Learning, the endeavor still demands a considerable amount of time. Generally speaking, gaining fluency in a foreign language is reserved for those with a true passion for both the language and the culture, as the effort involved in the process has been calculated at around the 10,000-hour mark [1]. But thanks to advancements in transportation and peace between nations, our world is growing more and more diverse as people are now able to spread out and explore it. Languages themselves are the all-important keys to the world and we must always try to find new ways to help spread this knowledge in an effort to bring people closer together.

We propose a game system that provides language learners and students alike with the means to increase their vocabulary in their desired language. This is accomplished through the exploration of 3D environments modeled after a variety of everyday

A. Nijholt, T. Romão, and D. Reidsma (Eds.): ACE 2012, LNCS 7624, pp. 262–273, 2012.

environments from real life. Since the process of learning a language is such a long-term endeavor, a game system was selected for this project based on how effective video games are at capturing the attention of players for extended periods of time. This effectiveness can be seen by examining the amount of time people spend playing video games, which has been studied quite thoroughly in recent years.

A global study conducted in 2009 by The Nielsen Company on both men and women between the ages of 13-24 concluded that on average, gamers play between 14-19 hours per week, with females playing between 10-17 hours per week, and males playing between 17-24 hours per week [2]. In regard to this game system, great care was taken to ensure that it would capture and hold the attention of the player in very much the same way that mainstream video games can. Furthermore, in regard to using a game system as a means to teach, video games inherently promote active learning by shifting players into the participant role, which is particularly ideal when learning a new language [3] .

This system has been designed specifically with the language student in mind in that it allows players easy access to all the information they need. We strongly believe that by using this system, language learners will be capable of gaining fluency in their target language faster than with traditional methods such as textbooks or classes [4]. The game was designed with a primary focus on entertainment value, and a secondary focus on language learning. This serves to motivate players to continue playing the game, thus keeping them on track with their goal. This is also to ensure that players are able to enjoy the gameplay experience in a way that differs from the normal educational gameplay experience. This "Entertainment First" philosophy is seen in both the learning environment and the gameplay.

In recent years, the title of "Serious Game" has been used to describe games designed for a primary purpose other than entertainment [5]. Many such games have been gaining a great deal of attention in that they have a more noble cause. While this system may have objectives apart from just entertainment, the core focus of the game is still entertainment itself. The underlying intention of helping to facilitate the learning of a new language, while noble, is still only secondary. A long time was spent on conceptualizing the game through the creation of various designs for the learning environment and the main character (Fig. 1).

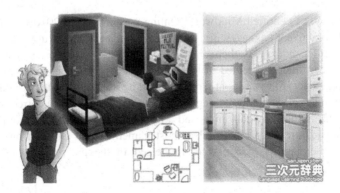

Fig. 1. Concepts depicting the character and environment

2   Related Works

There has been a great deal of research into the development of new software and other methods utilizing technology as a means to facilitate better language learning. Many of these also employ a more visual approach to learning. Popular language learning software programs such as Rosetta Stone provide users with images rather than text, which are representative of what they are learning. However, a study conducted in 2008 regarding their "Dynamic Immersion Method" concluded that the research principles regarding the shortcomings of traditional language instruction were not successfully implemented in the software [6].

Nevertheless, Rosetta Stone's visual learning style still allows users to anchor newly acquired vocab words directly to the images on the screen, which has been proven to be more effective than simply learning the word based on its direct textual translation [7]. SanjigenJiten achieves this same result by using 3D objects in the very same way that Rosetta Stone uses 2D images.

There have been a few notable language learning projects also situated in 3D environments. One of these projects, known as SGLL ProjectX, was developed in 2008 by students at the Dublin Institute of Technology's School of Computing. The ProjectX system places users in a 3D environment with a static camera and gives users the ability to move around by selecting objects in the scene, which the camera changes to focus on. The system is essentially a collection of mini-games linked by a common theme [8]. The user carries out certain tasks such as gathering ingredients to make a recipe in a 3D kitchen environment or completing a grocery list in a 3D marketplace environment.

A related system that was designed for practical use in the real world called Google Goggles makes use of smart phone cameras. Although this project is not a game system, it still has practical language learning applications. The camera converts images of objects or words into text, which can then be translated via Google Translate. However, this system is still in development and as stated by Shailesh Nalawadi, one of the system's developers, Google Goggles "doesn't work well yet on things like food, cars, plants, or animals" [9]. Nevertheless, this system has great potential for language learning applications.

An online system entitled Middworld Online was created in 2010 for Middlebury College's Interactive Languages division. This system connects users to an online interactive world and guides them through coursework, activities, and mini-games designed to keep them immersed in the language [10]. One such mini-game places users in charge of waiting tables at a restaurant. The users must interact with customers and keep them all happy by taking their orders and making the correct responses. Mistakes result in unhappy customers and a lower overall score. Middworld Online's in-game graphics are on par with what most gamers would expect from an online game world, helping to keep players immersed in the game while still actively learning.

3   Game Design

3.1   System Overview

System Concept. This system was conceptualized with the intent to increase the rate of overall language acquisition by players by providing them with quick and easy access to the information they need. One of the major goals of the project was to allow players the freedom to select absolutely anything in their environment and get the object's name and pronunciation in their target language instantly.

The idea originated from the author's method of studying Japanese by taping flash cards to various appliances in his own home. The author describes himself as a visual-spatial learner and attributes the effectiveness of this method to the way his brain stores information in an image format as opposed to auditory-sequential learners, who tend to store information based more on what they hear [11].

This system's use of a visual-spatial learning style provides the new technological-ly-inclined generation with a new way to study a second language and could be considered by many people as significantly more appealing than traditional methods, such as textbooks, classes, or tutors [12].

By playing this game, the user has proven to be at least somewhat interested in learning a new language, but whether or not they continue to use this system relies on two main factors:

— The overall effectiveness of the game.
— The overall entertainment value of the game.

Attention, Interest, and Motivation. Assuming that the game is indeed an effective means of learning a new language, the dependence shifts to the question of entertainment: is this game enjoyable? There is no questioning whether or not the user would like to learn a new language, but how motivated and focused the user is could range anywhere from mildly interested to extremely passionate. Keeping the user's attention, regardless of how interested they are in actually learning the language was a major goal of this project. In regard to any subject, even if the subject material is incredibly dull and uninteresting, providing the user with enough stimulation could essentially trick them into learning the information anyway, simply because they enjoy the process more than the material itself, in this case, simply playing the game [13].

In regard to the user's attention span, even passionate users will have a limit. There is always going to be a point where any human being decides they have played enough for the day. But whether they will pick up the game where they left off is another issue. Once the player has stopped playing the game, they need to have enjoyed the experience enough to decide to come back for more. Whether or not the user found it to be both effective and enjoyable is the real test in overall appreciation of the game itself. If it is both of these things, then it has proven the game to be worth the user's time [14].

Through the use of various industry-standard game elements, players can be motivated to continue playing in a number of ways. Item and object collection with an on-screen tracking system showing their progress gives the player goals to strive for. The addition of a good rewards system that triggers a new reward every 10 or so objects further motivates the player to keep collecting in order to earn more rewards. Moreover, dangling an "Ultimate Reward" in front of the player for finding all the objects or items in each level or even the entire game drives the player even further toward playing to completion [15].

Aside from actual gameplay elements, storytelling is the one aspect of video games, and most media entertainment, that really takes hold of the player's interest. The success of most good video games can be attributed to a good storyline and the same is true for a good movie and even a good book for that matter. Malone suggests that if you have just read all but the last chapter of a murder mystery, you have a strong cognitive motivation to bring completeness to your knowledge structure by finding out who the murderer was [16]. Weaving a well-told story will most certainly keep people's attention until the very end. By providing the player with an enticing storyline, they will feel obligated to play through to completion, just to see how it all turns out for everyone in the end.

3.2   User Experience

First Impression. When the player begins the game, they are prompted to select their native language and then the language they wish to learn. Once these options have been set, they arrive at the main menu where there are a few other useful settings such as camera and audio options. The game will begin once the "Play" button is selected. Once the game has finished loading, a tutorial window is displayed, allowing the player to get a feel for how to control the character and interact with objects in their environment (Fig. 2). From the beginning of the game, the player has complete control over the character and is free to wander around and thoroughly explore, as well as interact with their environment. This free roam exploration part of the game is referred to as "Explore Mode."

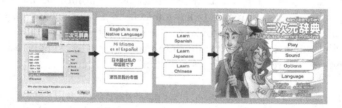

Fig. 2. Screens of First Impression

Explore Mode. While in Explore Mode, the player is able to select any object on the screen with the mouse, which causes the name of the selected object (noun) to be displayed in the box on the bottom of the screen (Fig. 3). Double-clicking an object displays the "Info Menu" screen, providing more details about the object, such as the word's part of speech, pronunciation description, translation into the player's native language, and a synonym (if applicable). A speaker button beside each word plays oral pronunciations when selected (Fig. 4). Additionally, a "+ Vocab" button is located in the bottom right of this window. Clicking this button stores the word in the player's Vocab List, which keeps track of all added words and whether the player has learned them or not (Fig. 3).

Fig. 3. Screenshot depicting the learning environment

Fig. 4. In-game windows shown in various language modes

Time Attack Mode. During Explore Mode, the player will eventually accumulate 10 words in their Vocab List. At this point, they will be given the option to enter Time Attack Mode in order to test themselves on the words they have added to their Vocab List. The game creates separate lists of 10 words based on the order in which the words have been added by the player. Upon entering Time Attack Mode, the player will be prompted to select the list they wish to play. This List Select Menu shows all the lists the player has created, along with the previous score, if applicable. Once a list has been selected, the player will be prompted to find each word in the environment as they appear on the screen in under the time limit. Players can also check the results for each word individually in their Vocab List (Fig. 4).

Parts of Speech. Regarding adjectives and verbs within the game, some words will have additional tabs located at the top of the Vocab Word window, which provide a description of the selected object (adjective), or an action associated with that object (verb). Based on the structuring of the game, however, these tabs are initially locked and cannot be accessed until after the word itself (noun) has been learned. Once a tab has been unlocked, the player will then be able to view and add the containing adjective or verb to their Vocab List. The reason for this is that the adjectives and verbs used in the game are directly related to the nouns themselves and an understanding of the noun is required in order to know what the trait or action is describing. By allowing the player to learn the parts of speech in this order, they will have a better grasp of how to use the words they've learned in complete sentences.

3.3   Practical Applications

Intended Audience. SanjigenJiten is designed for personal use amongst people who wish to learn a new language on their own and for those who might have some difficulty staying on task and keeping focused when using conventional methods of language learning. The task of learning a new language can be discouraging for many people, which adversely affects even the best learners' motivation to keep at it. This game aims to assist these learners and visual-spatial learners alike by making the learning process a bit more interesting and fun [17].

The intended user base is primarily young students between the ages of 10 and 20, especially among those who have an interest in video games. Today's current technologically inclined generation of students, especially those in developed countries such as the United States and Japan, are for the most part already comfortable playing games and interacting with 3D environments, making them prime candidates for success with using games such as SanjigenJiten to facilitate effective learning.

Educational Institutions. Although the game is designed for use in the home by individuals, the game is easily adapted for use in educational curricula. An example of this would be for teachers to provide students with take-home copies of the game and give daily homework assignments to find and study specific words in the environment. With the assistance of a few creative language instructors, this game system could easily find its way into educational institutions worldwide.

The idea of bringing video games into the classroom could drastically change the way we look at education as a society and allow educators to reevaluate what keeps students motivated when it comes to retaining new information. Students everywhere, especially young students, often struggle with keeping focused both in class and at home in regard to the course material unless they have a strong interest in what they are learning. By bringing games to the classroom, educators may see a surprising boost in overall classroom participation as well as an increase in class grade averages.

4   Assessment Experiment

4.1   Initial Trials

Based on data gathered from two trials that were conducted, the general consensus about the game has been overwhelmingly positive. In our initial trial, conducted on August 21, 2011, we presented an early build of the game system to eight Japanese test subjects, all with no prior orientation or knowledge of the game system. We asked them to try and learn the system on their own using three PCs running on Windows 7. In this early trial, half of the test subjects required some assistance in understanding the game and its various functions, while the other half managed to understand how the game worked on their own without any intervention. We have since included a short tutorial in the game.

Once comfortable with the system, test subjects were instructed to add 10 new words to their vocabulary list within the game. They were then instructed to enter Time Attack mode and test themselves on these 10 new words. The game provided each test subject with 120 seconds to locate the 10 words in their environment, one at a time. Once they completed this task, or the time ran out, the test subjects were given a written test made from the words they had just studied within the game. The test results reflected that the test subjects were indeed learning through the use of this system and surveys showed that all test subjects enjoyed the game and actually preferred it over traditional methods.

Table 1. Test results from the early trials for SanjigenJiten

◊	Test Group A	Test Group B
Time Attack	86%	74%
Written Test	90%	70%

4.2   Survey Responses

A second trial was conducted from November 10, 2011 to December 10, 2011 in which twenty Japanese and English language students at varying levels of understanding in their respective target languages were provided with a copy of the game system on a website "Survey Monkey". They were asked to play in their free time and to please complete a short survey about their experience (Fig. 4). Nineteen of the twenty students completed the survey and their responses were overwhelmingly positive as well [18]. These results have provided some very helpful insight into what aspects of the system are working effectively (Fig. 5-7).

The responses in Q1, while 90% positive, indicate that the game could be improved upon in many ways. The data in Q2 was indicated that 95% of users had little to no difficulty understanding the game, showing the effectiveness of the tutorial we added. In Q3, 42% of users responded that they definitely learned something while 37% were confident that they gained some new knowledge by playing. The results for Q4 indicate that the video game medium is indeed an effective means of generating interest in the subject material (Fig.6). Q5 served as a means for us to measure our user base's current understanding of the target language, which helps us to better assess their experience with Time Attack mode. Q6 was presented because we wanted to get a feel for how people might compare this game with other currently available learning tools (Fig. 7). Additionally, the game has been available online since March 16, 2012 and has been downloaded over 3,900 times. Based on the response, we are excited to see how SanjigenJiten will do once it is out on the market.

Survey Questions

Q1) How much did you enjoy your overall game-play experience?

Q2) How difficult was it for you to learn how to play?

Q3) Do you feel you learned something by playing the game?

Q4) Do you feel this game helped in keeping you focused?

Q5) What was your level of understanding of the language prior to playing the game?

Q6) How do you feel this game compares to other Language Learning software?

Q7) In regards to Language Learning, which method do you prefer?

Fig. 5. Questions from the survey we conducted

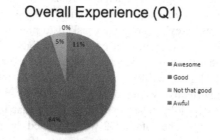

Fig. 6. Chart depicting results from the survey

Help with Focus (Q4)

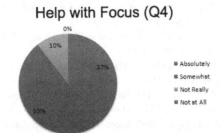

- ■ Absolutely
- ■ Somewhat
- ■ Not Really
- ■ Not at All

Fig. 7. Chart depicting results from the survey

Software Preference (Q6)

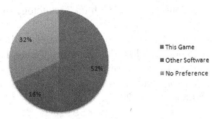

- ■ This Game
- ■ Other Software
- ■ No Preference

Fig. 8. Chart depicting results from the survey

5 Conclusion

We proposed a new game system that provides language learners and students with the means to increase vocabulary in a desired target language. This is accomplished through exploration of 3D environments modeled after everyday environments from real life. An assessment of the game helped show the game is both enjoyable and successful in motivating users to continue learning.

References

1. Eaton, S.E.: How Long Does it Take to Learn a Second Language?: Applying the "10,000-Hour Rule" as a Model for Fluency. Onate Press, Calgary (2011)
2. Flamberg, M.: The Value Gamer: Play and Purchase Behavior in a Recession. Nielsen Video Game Tracking Survey (2009)
3. Bowman, R.F.: A Pac-Man theory of motivation. Tactical implications for classroom instruction. Educational Technology 22(9), 14–17 (1982)
4. Rüschoff, B., Ritter, M.: Technology-enhanced Language Learning. Computer Assisted Language Learning 14(4), 219–232 (2001)
5. Michael, D.R., Chen, S.L.: Serious Games: Games That Educate, Train, and Inform. Course Technology PTR. Muska & Lipman/Premier-Trade. Cincinnati, OH (2005)
6. Nielson, K., Doughty, C., et al.: Final Technical Report E.3.2 Rosetta Stone™ Findings. Center for Advanced Study of Language, University of Maryland (2008)

7. Webber, N.E.: Pictures and Words as Stimuli in Learning Foreign Language Responses. The Journal of Psychology 98(1), 57–63 (1978)
8. Dunne, M.: SGLL Project X. Dublin Institute of Technology, Dublin (2008)
9. Neven, H., Nalawadi, S.: Google Goggles (2009), http://www.google.com/mobile/goggles/#text
10. Vogel, T., Cook, S.: MiddWorld Online. Middlebury College, Middle-bury (2010)
11. Mathewson, J.H.: Visual-Spatial Thinking: An Aspect of Science Often Looked Over by Educators. Science Education 83, 33–54 (1998)
12. Silverman, L.K.: Upside-Down Brilliance: The Visual-Spatial Learner. The Institute for the Study of Advanced Development, Denver (2005)
13. Elliott, J., Adams, L., et al.: No Magic Bullet: 3D Video Games in Education. Georgia Tech College of Computing, Atlanta (2002)
14. Prensky, M.: Digital Game-Based Learning. McGraw-Hill, NY (2001)
15. Pillay, H.K., Brownlee, J.M.: Cognition and recreational computer games: implications for educational technology. Journal of Research on Technology in Education 32(1), 203–216 (1999)
16. Malone, T.W.: What makes things fun to learn? A study of intrinsically motivating computer games. Report CIS-7. Xerox Palo Alto Research Center, Palo Alto, CA (1980)
17. Regian, J.W., Shebilske, W.L., et al.: Virtual Reality: An Instructional Medium for Visual-Spatial Tasks. Journal of Communication 42(4), 136–149 (1992)
18. Howland, R.: SanjigenJiten Survey (2011), http://www.surveymonkey.com/s/K5SYYGZ

Appendix

1. You can download SanjigenJiten from the official website:
   http://sanjiten.com/
2. Two more in-game screenshots:

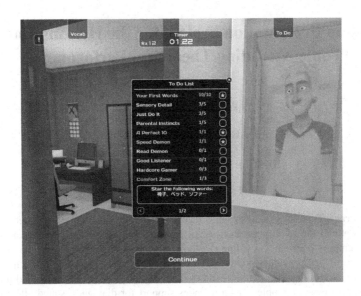

A Caption Presentation System for the Hearing Impaired People Attending Theatrical Performances

Yuko Konya and Itiro Siio

Ochanomizu University 2-1-1 Otsuka, Bunkyo-ku
Tokyo, Japan
{yuko.konya,siio}@is.ocha.ac.jp

Abstract. This study addresses information support for hearing impaired people who attend theatrical performances. In present Japan, there are a few theaters that employ programs providing captions for hearing impaired people. The few programs that provide captions only show dialogues and sounds (musical note icons). We propose, implement, and evaluate a caption presentation method for hearing impaired people, which includes support for dialogues, sound effects, and audience responses.

1 Introduction

According to government research conducted in 2006, there were 270,000 hearing impaired people in Japan, which was 0.22% of the population. However, hearing often deteriorates with age [5], and the Japanese population is aging faster than any country in the world [1]. In future, the demand for subtitled videos, movies, and theater performances will increase. The Ministry of Internal Affairs and Communications (MIC) in Japan has promoted barrier-free broadcasting. From 30% to 60% of terrestrial broadcasts provide subtitles for hearing impaired persons [10]. In contrast, very few movies or theater performances have subtitles or any form of captioning. Only three of 2,719 titles listed on an internet portal site provide barrier-free subtitles, a mere 0.1% of the theater performances in Tokyo in 2011. It is difficult to produce subtitles in Japanese because it takes four times longer to correct subtitles using the kanjis (Japanese characters) than European or American languages [2].

In this study, we report a subtitle display system that includes audience reaction and discuss the results of an evaluation.

2 Enjoyment of Visiting Theaters

When non-hearing impaired people visit theaters, they enjoy many aspects of the play: the acting, music, sound effects, and stage sets. They also gain enjoyment from participating in a shared experience. Audience reactions, such as laughing, smiling and clapping, are contagious. Individuals respond to the reactions of other members of the audience. These shared reactions are one of the enjoyable elements of the

A. Nijholt, T. Romão, and D. Reidsma (Eds.): ACE 2012, LNCS 7624, pp. 274–286, 2012.
© Springer-Verlag Berlin Heidelberg 2012

experience. Tatsumoto et al. [13] showed that while watching videos in a shared environment, the reason for laughing is changed from "something funny makes you laugh" to "laughter makes something funny." They found that "watching together" increases enjoyment.

An interview to find whether the situation is similar for a theatrical event was conducted with 11 people (3 men, 8 women) in the age range of 20–50. All the people interviewed had attended a play in a theatre. All of them indicated that being part of an audience is an important part of the experience. They gained a sense of reality from the atmosphere in the theater that amplified their enjoyment. We drilled down and explored the initial answers in greater depth to determine what constitutes a sense of reality for people watching a play. The findings are presented in Table 1.

Table 1. Sense of reality during a theatrical performance

What enhances a sense of reality for audience members in a theater	Types of sensation
Air movement when actors move or the audience reacts physically	tactile
Audience reactions such as laughter, crying, or other vocal responses	auditory
Perceived suspense or tension when the audience is suddenly still or silent	auditory and tactile

The interviews revealed that audience reaction influences the enjoyment of a theatrical performance. All the interviewees confirmed that tactile and auditory information is important and contributes to the sense of reality.

For the most part, the stage is positioned directly in front of the audience and their attention is focused on the stage in a dark theater. Consequently, it is difficult for an individual to visually sense the audience's reaction. Vocalizations and the auditory perception of movement from other audience members are thus helpful to enhance the sense of reality. Previous captioning systems only present subtitles for the actors' spoken words and explain sound effects, but do not include indicators for the audience's reaction. We believe that presentation of the audiences' reactions will transform the theater-going experience for hearing impaired persons.

3   Related Works and Previous Technology

In this section, we review related work and describe a proposed captioning system for a theater performance.

3.1   Captioning System for Theater Performances

There are some existing systems for displaying subtitles in theaters. These are not always exclusive for the deaf and hard-of-hearing. A few programs that provide captions for hearing impaired persons only show dialogues and sound effects.

There are two types of systems: open and closed. In the open system, visual aids are displayed or projected onto a screen on the stage. In a closed system, such as the "G-mark portal subtitle system" [7][11], a tablet PC or a personal monitor near the user's seat displays the subtitles.

An advantage of the open system is that the subtitles appear on the stage. People who would benefit from the assistance do not have to divert their attention to a secondary device. The open system does not require special individual equipment. A disadvantage is that people who do not need the assistance provided by the subtitles may find them distracting. In a closed system, audience members can choose to use or not use the device and can select the type of subtitles presented; for example, English subtitles for foreigners, Japanese subtitles for hearing impaired persons, and no subtitles for people who do not require any assistance. However, audience members who must refer to a tablet or monitor will occasionally miss either a part of the performance or a subtitle because they must alternatively look at the stage and the device.

Recently, some systems using a head-mounted display (HMD) instead of personal monitors have been developed [4][12]. However, similar to 3D glasses, HMDs are difficult to wear for an extended period of time. HMDs also require a constant change in focal length. The users have to adjust their focus between the stage and the subtitles on the HMD. This is particularly distracting and tiring in a play where the actors move frequently. However, HMDs have potential and continue to be developed. They have advantages and disadvantages. Perhaps the biggest disadvantage is that they are tiring and consequently distract the users enjoyment of the performance.

3.2   Subtitle Display Method in a Related Field

There is a similar study to our proposed system in another field. Fujii et al. [3] demonstrated subtitles in a balloon field as a support system for the deaf and hard-of-hearing participating in a video conference. They compared two types of subtitle displays: balloon and linear. The balloon display was determined to be preferable to the linear display in terms of enjoyment, user-friendliness, and affording realistic sensations. Because many people in Japan are familiar with Manga, most are aware that a balloon tail indicates the position of the speaker.

However, in its present state, this system would be difficult to use for a play because it was developed for video conferencing where the attendees, unlike actors in a play, do not move very much.

4   Problems

There are various problems associated with the existing subtitle systems for theatrical performances: missing a subtitle or an action on stage, difficulty locating a particular speaker, and difficultly sensing the audience's reaction. Each of these problems is discussed in the following sections.

4.1   Problems Associated with Subtitles

To understand the plot of a play, an audience member needs to know who is speaking as well as what is being said. Subtitles should provide both pieces of information. When non-hearing impaired persons watch a play, they recognize who is speaking by the movement of a speaker's lips, the direction of the voice, and the quality of the voice, e.g., they can immediately determine if the speaker is male or female. By contrast, when hearing impaired persons watch a play with subtitles, they recognize who is speaking because the subtitles identify the role (e.g., Hamlet, Macbeth) and provide the text of the speech. In an open subtitle system, which allows the audience to keep their attention on the stage, they may also rely on the movement of the speakers' lips. A proficient lip reader could understand the story without subtitles. However, if there are many actors on stage, it would still be difficult to locate the speaker. This difficulty would be compounded if the actors are constantly moving on the stage. In addition, it may not always be possible to identify the speaker by role because the electronic display of an open system is limited to one or two lines of text. A closed system is more confusing than an open system because the user must constantly move between the personal monitor and the stage.

4.2   Problems Associated with Perceiving Audience Reactions

As mentioned in Section 2, awareness of audience reaction is important to a person's enjoyment of a play. However, the subtitles presented in the existing systems (dialogue and sound effects) do not indicate the audience's reactions, for example smiling, laughing, and clapping. In a well-attended small theater where the spectators are seated close together, it is possible to sense the audience reactions. However, in larger venues, where an individual may be seated at some distance from other audience members, this becomes more difficult. Moreover, audience reactions may be very subtle because Japanese people tend to not express strong feelings in public. This is a distinct disadvantage for hearing impaired people in terms of their ability to perceive audience reactions.

5   Our Approach and Implementation

To solve the problems described in Section 4, we propose a new open subtitle system. Because an open system is not entirely suitable for non-impaired people, we attempted to integrate the subtitle screen in such a way that it has minimal distraction.

We divided a screen area into two parts. One part displays dialog and sound effects, and the other displays the audience's reactions. Fig. 1 and Fig. 2 illustrate how subtitles would be displayed. Fig. 3 shows the layout of the stage.

A projector is positioned in the center of the stage. Subtitles are projected on the screen. An operator responsible for providing information about subtitles and the audience reaction is seated near the boundary between the stage and the auditorium.

Balloon subtitle on a screen

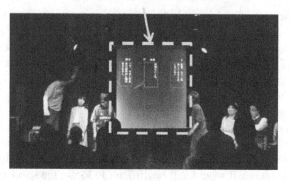

Fig. 1. The entire stage

Acting near the screen balloon tail direction toward the actor.

Fig. 2. Actors in front of the subtitle screen

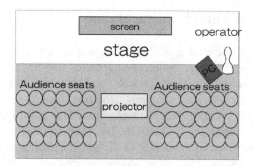

Fig. 3. Layout of the stage

5.1   Subtitle Display Area

Our system uses 80% of the total screen area to display subtitles and audience reaction, as shown in Fig. 1 and Fig. 2. From this total subtitle display area, 80% displays subtitles and the remaining 20% of the displays audience reaction icons, as shown in Fig. 4. The system has five display functions: dialog balloons, dialog balloon border colors, hand signs, music, and stage properties.

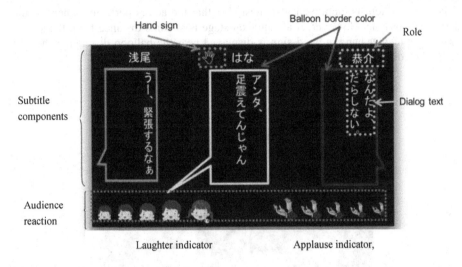

Fig. 4. Overview of the system interface

Balloon-Shaped Dialog Area

As shown in Fig. 4, the system displays dialogue text in a balloon and identifies the actor's role above the balloon. There can be a maximum of three lines in one balloon; each line can contain nine characters.

Line breaks can be inserted for readability. Hearing impaired audience members would be able to follow complicated, fast-moving dialogue. The direction of the balloon tail indicates the actor who is speaking. When actors perform in front of the screen, the balloon tails are shortened and positioned on the outside edges of the screen, as shown in Fig. 5.

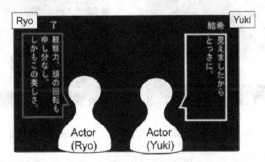

Fig. 5. Action in front of the screen. Balloon tail direction indicates the actor.

Border Color of Balloons

The balloon border color can be set to coincide with the color of the actor's costume. Because it is difficult to differentiate between some colors, such as red and orange, and because colors can be altered by stage lighting, additional help is provided by identifying the role above the dialogue balloon.

Hand Signs

When this system is employed, it is desirable that the actors perform as near to the screen as possible. However, if an actor on stage is at some distance from the screen and raises his/her hand, a hand sign is displayed near the balloon displaying the text for his/her dialogue, as shown in Fig. 6.

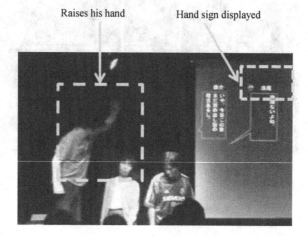

Fig. 6. Case of a distance between the screen and an actor; an actor raises his hand

Displaying Indicators for Background Music and Stage Properties

Background music and staging are important aspects of a theatrical production. As shown in Fig. 7 (left), a musical note icon could be used to indicate music. This icon is often used in the subtitles that accompany television program. Including notations

Musical notes indicate background sounds   Screen used to indicate set decoration

Fig. 7. Optional use case of the interface. Musical notes indicate background sounds. Text describes the sound (left). Screen used to indicate the set decoration (right).

to explain onomatopoeia has also been considered. Moreover, as shown in Fig. 7 (right), the screen can be used to clarify the importance of particular stage settings that relate to the action of the dialogue. In recent years, techniques for projecting background images to enhance the stage settings have improved [9] and in many cases it is not necessary to install a screen for a subtitle

5.2   Audience Reaction Displaying

An audience's reaction is displayed on the lower 1/5th of the area for a subtitle display. This is a better position of sight when reading subtitles, under the restriction of the screen. From the interviews, we learned that auditory information, particularly laughter and applause, are important aspects of the audience response. Icons for these two elements have been created. The size of the icon can be controlled to indicate intensity. Five different sizes are available. The intensity of the laughter or applause is determined by a human operator who controls the display. Although there are costs associated with a human operator, the operator's response may be more representative of the entire audience's response than that of an automated sensor. An example is shown in Fig. 8.

Displaying audience reaction: laughter and applause

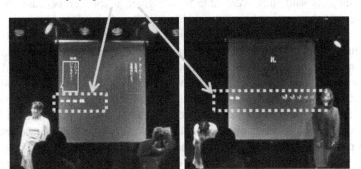

Fig. 8. Pictures of audience reaction indicators

6   Evaluation

We evaluated the system in two situations. The first was at a dress rehearsal and the second was at an actual theatrical performance that held two performances a day and a total of eight performances . The system was placed on the stage, as shown in Fig. 3. A projector was positioned in the center of the stage. Subtitles were projected onto the screen. The evaluation experiment was conducted over four days for performances on November 10–13, 2011. The theater had a capacity of approximately 50 people. The barrier-free performance, which was a comedy with eight actors, lasted approximately 85 min.

6.1   Interview and Result

Two hearing impaired students were interviewed after the dress rehearsal. The interviewee asked questions about four items, as shown in Table 2.

Table 2. Evaluation questionnaire

No	Confirmation item		Questionnaire
1	Enjoyment of a play		Did you enjoy the play with subtitles?
2	Matching speaker	Effect of color	Did the balloons' colored borders help you find the speaker?
3		Effect of balloon shape	Did the balloon tails help you find speaker?
4	Audience reaction display		Did the audience reaction icons enhance your enjoyment of the play?

Two hearing impaired students and three non-hearing impaired students attended a dress rehearsal, which was virtually the same as the public performance, and all five participants were able to enjoy themselves. In response to question 2, the hearing impaired subjects said they were able to recognize a speaker because the actor's clothes were of the same color as the dialogue balloon's border. Although they said that it was hard to distinguish red from orange, having the actor's role positioned near the dialogue balloon helped them to determine which actor was speaking. In response to question 3, they felt that the direction of the balloon tails was helpful and made it easier to connect "the movement of lips with the direction of the tail" and thus to "identify the speaker." The hearing impaired participants indicated that the hand sign, which appears when the actors making a gesture are positioned at a distance from the screen, was also helpful. For question 4, opinions were divided because there were only five people in the audience during the rehearsal. One hearing impaired participant said that it was an important feature even though there was not a great deal of noticeable audience response at this particular performance. The other said that it was unnecessary information because he was absorbed in the play.

6.2   A Questionnaire about the Theater Experience

A questionnaire was administered to 97 audience members after watching a public performance. The audience included two hearing impaired and four visually impaired participants. Ninety-one audience members had neither visual nor hearing impairments. Before the performance, the captioning systems was explained to ensure that the participants understood that the subtitles would be displayed on the screen placed in the center of the stage center and that laughter and applause icons would be displayed in the lower 1/5th of the display area. The questionnaire was comprised of the questions listed in Table 2. The participants could select from four options (agree, somewhat agree, somewhat disagree, Disagree). A free entry column for written responses was included.

6.3   Survey Result

The responses of all 97 participants were similar. The overall results are shown in Fig. 9. With regard to enjoyment of the play, 89% of the subjects choose "Agree" or "Somewhat agree." For the questions about the balloon tail indicating the position of the speaker and the coordination of the color of the balloon border with the actor's costume, approximately 80% of subjects selected positive options. For the enhancement of the sense of reality from displaying the audience reaction, 64% of the subjects had a positive response. The responses from the hearing impaired participants are presented in Table 3.

The two hearing impaired persons selected "Agree" for the first three questions and "Somewhat agree" for the question about whether the sense of reality was enhanced by the audience reaction icons.

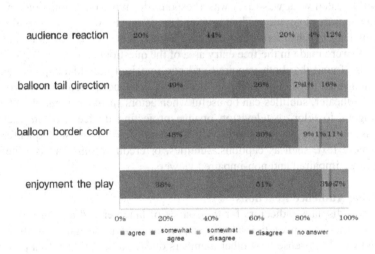

Fig. 9. Results of audience questionnaires (n = 97)

Table 3. Hearing impaired participants' questionnaire responses

	Q1	Q2	Q3	Q4	Free Written Responses
No 1	Agree	Agree	Agree	Somewhat agree	A larger subtitle is better because of presbyopia
No 2	Agree	Agree	Agree	Somewhat agree	Showing the conversation tone is better.

6.4   Discussion

We were able to draw some conclusions from the results of the interviews and questionnaires. The participants' responses to our questions about the ability to find a speaker and displaying audience reactions were noteworthy and are discussed in the following sections.

Finding the Speaker

Various aspects of the system were designed to help hearing impaired individuals identify a speaker. These included matching the speaker with the subtitle, indicating the position of the speaker by the direction of the balloon's tail, coordinating the color of the balloon's border with the actor's costume, and providing a hand icon to indicate gestures when an actor was at some distance from the screen. The hearing impaired participants indicated that such additional information were helpful. Moreover, the questionnaire results show that the system is not a distraction for non-impaired audience members and does not interfere with their enjoyment of the performance and in fact, in some cases, it was helpful. For example, "it was convenient when it was hard to catch what was said" was a response from both non-impaired and hearing impaired members of the audience. Another comment was that "subtitles on TV programs may be obstructive, but this has a good feel, like a manga comic." These comments were made in the free entry area of the questionnaire.

We also found that both impaired and non-impaired individuals potentially found our system beneficial. For example, because it may be difficult to control volume levels in a theater, subtitles can be useful when actors speak very quietly. Our system is analogous to telop, a television opaque projecting device used in television to broadcast an image without the use of a camera. Telop is most frequently used to superimpose text, such as captions, subtitles, or credit scrolls, and is beneficial for both hearing impaired and non-impaired viewers.

Displaying Audience Reactions

Our system displays indicators for the sounds of laughter and applause from the audience on the bottom of the subtitle display area. It is designed to allow hearing impaired people to sense how other members of the audience react to a performance. Because of the limited number of participants, we could not draw firm conclusions from the post-dress-rehearsal interview. In this evaluation, we did not have sufficient responses from hearing impaired individuals. Majority of the questionnaire responses came from non-impaired individuals. However, the comments in the free entry area of the questionnaire were helpful. Some participants suggested that audience response icons created a sense of community or unity with other audience members. Others felt that the audience response icons caused them to exaggerate their reaction in order to contribute to the prevailing atmosphere. We found that there is a tendency for an impaired person and a non-impaired person to collaborate when watching a theatrical performance. Although the effectiveness of displaying audience reactions was recognized by the audience, the presentation needs to be refined and elaborated.

7   Summary and Future Work

We proposed a caption presentation method that uses dialogue balloons and audience reaction indicators to enhance the experience of hearing impaired individuals attending theatrical performances. The design features includes a directional balloon tail and color coordinated balloon borders to help the hearing impaired persons locate the speaker more easily. The system also displays indicators for the sound of laughter and applause from the audience at the bottom of the subtitle display area. This feature is designed to help the hearing impaired people sense the audience's reaction. Evaluation experiments were conducted and good results were obtained from a small number of hearing impaired individuals. Although the audience reaction display did not heighten the enjoyment as much as expected, the subtitles enhanced the audience's enjoyment of the play and enabled them to find the speaker. Opinions about displaying audience reactions were divided. In general, our results showed a tendency of impaired and non-impaired individuals to collaborate in the effort to enjoy a play.

In future, we will implement a sensor to automatically register the audience reaction. We need to acknowledge that the screen, which is installed in the center of the stage, limits the actual performance area. We will investigate methods to display captions that allow the performance area to be increased. Because our results indicate that all people can benefit from the captioning system, we will consider improvements that take into account both hearing impaired and non-impaired individuals.

References

1. Annual Report on the Aging Society: 2010, Cabinet Office Japan,
   http://www8.cao.go.jp/kourei/english/annualreport/2010/pdf/
   p2-3.pdf
2. Association of Cochlear Implant Transmitted Audition (ACITA),
   http://www2u.biglobe.ne.jp/~momo1/sub1/new_sub/akemi100619.html
3. Ayako, F., Hiroaki, N., Takehiko, Y.: Speech Balloon Captioning System for Meetings based on Automatic Speech Recognition. In: Proc. 13th International Conference on Human-Computer Interaction (HCII 2009), pp. 313–317 (2009)
4. BBC, http://www.bbc.co.uk/news/technology-14654339
5. Mizuno, E.: Investigation of Hearing Compensation Needs and Issues in Elderly People. LifeDesign REPORT (January-February 2009)
6. Engeki Life, http://engekilife.com/
7. G-mark, Earphoneguide Co., Ltd., http://www.eg-gm.jp/g_mark/index.html
8. Ministry of Health, Labour and Welfare. Investigation of actual conditions disability children and persons (2008), http://www.mhlw.go.jp/toukei/saikin/hw/
   shintai/06/index.html
9. Seiko epson corp. Support to performance with a projector (2009),
   http://www.epson.jp/osirase/2009/091104_2.html
10. The Ministry of Internal Affairs and Communications (MIC), Actual Results of Subtitled Broadcasting, http://www.soumu.go.jp/main_sosiki/joho_tsusin/eng/
    Releases/Telecommunications/100913_b.html

11. Theatres of Japan Arts Council,
    http://www.ntj.jac.go.jp/nou/caption_system.html
12. Web-shake Air, Media Access Support Center (NPO),
    http://npo-masc.org/cn15/pg242.html
13. Tatsumoto, Y., Shimizu, A.: Does amount of "laughter of pleasure" increase by the presence of other persons?: An electromyographic study. The Bulletin of Kansai University of Welfare Science, 97–107 (2007)

Emergent Gait Evolution
of Quadruped Artificial Life

Kinyo Kou[1] and Yoichiro Kawaguchi[2]

[1] Graduate School of Interdisciplinary Information Studies,
The University of Tokyo, 7-3-1 Hongo, Bunkyo-ku, Tokyo, Japan
kou.kinyo@gmail.com
[2] Interfaculty Initiative in Information Studies, The University of Tokyo

Abstract. We developed a simulation model and generated a gait pattern for quadruped artificial life. The model is based on three dimensional physical simulation using a physics engine. Neural networks are used to control each leg, and the genetic algorithm is used to evolve the gait. The generated gait pattern is similar to the gait called "walk" in real-world animals. An analysis is conducted of the developing gait pattern, in addition to the final result. The emergent walk-like gait is similar to a newborn baby crawling on the floor, and it would appear that the artificial life struggles to go straight ahead on the midway of evolution.

Keywords: Quadruped artificial life, emergent movement, genetic algorithm, neural networks.

1 Introduction

Artificial life, which is a field of study based on the features of actual creatures, has a great potential in entertainment such as video games and interactive arts. Evolution is a frequently used concept in artificial life. Creatures evolve, trying to behave in a better way. However, less attention have been paid to the developing behavior in artificial lives, compared to the final results of a series of simulation experiments.

In this paper, we focus on the gait of the quadruped artificial life, which is an artificial creature with four legs. Compared to artificial lives having six or more legs, it is difficult to simulate four legs creatures' movement in a three-dimensional environment. This is because four legs artificial lives tend to fall over, since there is a moment when less than three legs touch the ground during walking. In this work, we use neural networks to control each leg, and a genetic algorithm to evolve the gait.

Four-legged animal is familiar to us. Not only horses, dogs or other mammals, human babies also crawl on four legs. Some irregular movements of walking may be observed, especially in the earliest stages of the animals' lifetimes. Since the artificial creatures also gradually become able to walk well, the irregular movements of gait would exist in artificial creatures. The purpose of this paper is not only to generate a stable gait autonomously, but also to study the midway behavior of evolution.

A. Nijholt, T. Romão, and D. Reidsma (Eds.): ACE 2012, LNCS 7624, pp. 287–296, 2012.

2 Related Work

A number of evolutionary experiments of artificial life have been performed. Turk [1] proposed a competition model in two dimensional environments, and a wide variety of movements could be seen among the evolved creatures. Experiments in three-dimensional environments are also performed [2] [3] [4]. In these works, both the movements and the morphology of the artificial lives evolve simultaneously. The role of each part of the body is often undecided. Every part in the whole body can perform as legs or arms, and other body parts need to behave as a creature. Though this approach is effective in generating interesting and unpredictable behaviors, it is usually difficult and of no utility to make a close analysis of the creatures' movement strategies.

A different approach is performed in this paper. Every leg of the quadruped artificial life has to fulfill the role as an actual leg. This approach makes it easy to conduct a detailed analysis of the gait pattern, gives meaning to track the movement of each leg through the entire evolution.

Beer et al [5] used neural networks with a pacemaker neuron to control a six-legged insect. However, we believe that the simulation model without pacemaker neurons is more similar to real-world animals. The operation of each neuron is inspired by "sensor-actuator networks" by van de Panne [6]. Input neurons, inner neurons, and output neurons are adopted into each leg to control it, while the neural network in our work only has one-way connections.

3 Method

3.1 Mechanical Configuration

The quadruped artificial life in this work is shown in Fig.1. It consists of one torso and four legs. Each leg has three degrees of freedom (DOF) in total: two DOFs in the shoulder joint and one DOF in the knee joint.

Fig. 1. Quadruped artificial life

Each leg has four sensors and three actuators on it. There are three angle sensors, which read the angle of each joint. There is also one force sensor on the toe of each leg, which reads the force applied to each toe. Three actuators are all angular actuators, which generate joint torques by the PD controller. A PD controller is a feedback control system using proportional values and derivative values to calculate the final output. The proportional gain and the derivative gain are determined through a trial and error process in this work.

The placement of actuators and sensors is shown in Fig.2, and the details of the sensors and actuators on the artificial life are shown in Table.1 and Table.2.

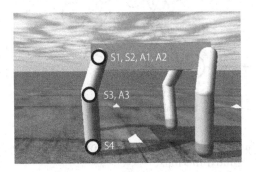

Fig. 2. The placement of actuators and sensors

Table 1. Sensors on each leg

Name	Kind	Place	Output Range
S1	Angle	Shoulder	$[0, 0.8\pi]$
S2	Angle	Shoulder	$[-0.5\pi, 0.7\pi]$
S3	Angle	Knee	$[0, 0.8\pi]$
S4	Force	Toe	$[0, \infty)$

Table 2. Actuators on each leg

Name	Kind	Place	Input Range
S1	Anglular	Shoulder	$[0, 0.8\pi]$
S2	Anglular	Shoulder	$[-0.5\pi, 0.7\pi]$
S3	Anglular	Knee	$[0, 0.8\pi]$

3.2 Neural Network

The neural network adopted in this work is shown in Fig.3. Four input neurons, four inner neurons and three output neurons are used here. Input neurons read real-time parameters from sensors, and output neurons set real numbers to actuators. Four legs have the same network each, but they work separately. Integer values in the range [-3, 3] are used as weights of the connections.

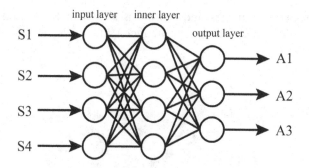

Fig. 3. Neural network on each leg

The activation functions of input neurons corresponding to the angle sensors (S1 – S3) are rectangular functions:

$$f(u) = \begin{cases} 1 \ (t_{min} \leq u \leq t_{max}) \\ 0 \ (u < t_{min}, t_{max} < u) \end{cases} \tag{1}$$

where u is the input value and $f(u)$ is the output value of the input neurons. t_{min} is the low threshold and t_{max} is the high threshold. These threshold values will be determined by the genetic algorithm.

The activation function of input neurons corresponding to the force sensor (S4) is a step function:

$$f(u) = \begin{cases} 1 \ (u \geq t_{min}) \\ 0 \ (u < t_{min}) \end{cases} \tag{2}$$

where t_{min} is the low threshold of the force sensor.

The activation functions of inner neurons are also step functions:

$$f(u) = \begin{cases} 1 \ (u > 0) \\ 0 \ (u \leq 0) \end{cases} \tag{3}$$

where u is the input value from the input layer and $f(u)$ is the output value.

The activation functions of output neurons are sigmoid functions:

$$f(u) = \frac{1}{1 + \exp(-\frac{u}{c})} \tag{4}$$

where u is the input value from the inner layer and $f(u)$ is the output value to the actuators (A1 – A3). Parameter c will be determined by the genetic algorithm.

3.3   Genetic Algorithm

We regarded some parameters in neural network as genes, and implement the genetic algorithm. Roulette wheel selection and uniform crossover are used in our implementations. The genes we used are shown in Table.3. The total gene length is 204 bits.

Table 3. Actuators on each leg

Gene	Bit length of one gene	Total gene number	Total bit length
Weight of the connections	3	28	84
Angle sensor threshold	6	6	36
Force sensor threshold	3	1	3
Parameter of sigmoid function	3	3	9
Initial direction	6	12	72

There are five kinds of genes: the weight of the connections, the angle sensor threshold, the force sensor threshold, the parameter of sigmoid function and the initial direction of each leg. The first three kinds are explained above. The parameter of sigmoid function is the parameter c in equation 4. In the case of these four kinds of genes (weights, angle thresholds, force thresholds and parameters of sigmoid function), same values are used in four legs. In order to make four legs move separately, different initial directions are set to each leg. In the initial period of the simulation, the neural network of each leg does not work and all actuators generate torques according to these initial direction genes.

4   Creature Evolution

4.1   Implementations

Genes in the first generation are generated at random. The motion of each leg is determined by the neural network. A three-dimensional physical simulation is performed using the Open Dynamics Engine [7], and the fitness value is calculated for each individual creature. A genetic algorithm is used to earn new genes of the next generation when all individual creatures in the current generation have been simulated. The total population in one generation is 100, and the simulation ends when the generation number reaches 300.

4.2   Fitness Value

The fitness value for the genetic algorithm in this work is not simply the distance which the creature travelled. Quadruped artificial lives especially tend to fall over in the first generation, because all genes are generated at random. If we use the travelled distance as fitness value, the genes of the creatures which dived forward will spread in the population. The motion we are expecting is not diving but walking, therefore the diving motion should be eliminated.

The way to count up the fitness value in this work is as shown below.

(1) Define two variables: l_{past} and l_{now}. Set fitness value $F = 0$.
(2) Update l_{past} with current x position.
(3) After a simulation time Δt, update l_{now} with current x position.
(4) (a) If $l_{now} - l_{past} > \Delta x$, then $F = F + 1$, $l_{past} = l_{now}$.
　　(b) If $l_{now} - l_{past} < -\Delta x$, then $F = F - 1$, $l_{past} = l_{now}$.
(5) Repeat operation (3)–(4) until the whole simulation time ends.

Using this algorithm, it is able to give a low fitness value to a diving motion and a high fitness value to a walking motion, because this algorithm is closely related to "how long the creature proceeded" instead of "how far the creature proceeded." When the creature falls over, the duration of movement is short. On the other hand, when it walks, the duration of movement is long. Therefore walking motions can be sorted out from diving motions. In this work, Δt is set as exactly one percent of the whole simulation time. Accordingly, the maximum of the fitness value will be 100. However, there is not yet a decisive method to determine the value of Δx. Through some preliminary experiments, Δx in this work is set as approximately two percent of the body length. This means the creature will travel more than twice the length of the body during the simulation time if the fitness value reaches the maximum.

We also put two additional force sensors on the creature: one is on the belly and the other is on the back. If these two force sensors touch the ground during the simulation, the fitness value will be set to zero. This means the creature has to use not its torso but its legs to proceed.

5   Results and Analyses

A walking pattern similar to the gait called "walk" in real-world animals has been generated. We named this movement "walk-like gait." The movement of one cycle in the last 300th generation is shown in Fig.4. The gait pattern shown in the figure is the best individual, who scored the highest fitness value among the 100 individuals. This emergent movement is similar to a newborn baby crawling on the floor, desperately trying to keep on going. The relative x position of each leg to the center of gravity of the torso in 300th generation is shown in Fig.5. The artificial life steps its four legs forward in a certain order: right front leg, left back leg, left front leg and then right back leg in a cycle. The creature walks in a straight line at constant speed. The two front legs and the two back legs each have similar wave shape. Note that this walk-like gait pattern was automatically generated, and each leg is moving independently. There is no pacemaker to control the phase of each leg. Generally, the conditions of the legs in each moment during the walking process are more significant than a determinate speed,

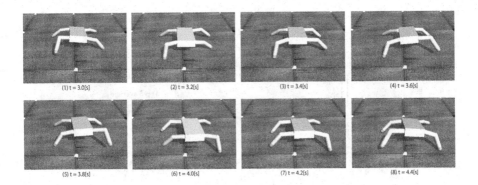

Fig. 4. Movement of one cycle in 300th generation

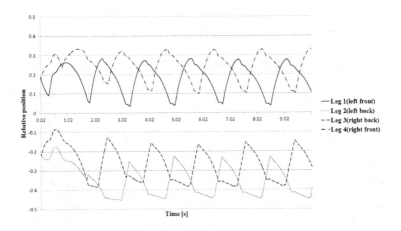

Fig. 5. Relative x position of each leg in 300th generation

therefore we believe the absence of a pacemaker is more similar to real-world animals.

The fitness value transmission is shown in Fig.6. In the early generations, the artificial life could not walk forward well at all. The fitness value sharply increased around 60th generation in Fig.6. Accordingly, an unsteady gait first emerged in 50th generation.

The relative x position of each leg in 50th generation is shown in Fig.7, and that in 250th generation is shown in Fig.7. In these developing generations, the gait cycles are unsteadier. Nevertheless, it would appear that the artificial life struggles to go straight ahead on the midway of evolution. The efforts of the quadruped artificial life to walk well can be observed by comparison between Fig.7 and Fig.8.

In 50th generation, though the artificial life could proceed constantly, the gait pattern was quite unsteady, and the path of the artificial life was out of line to

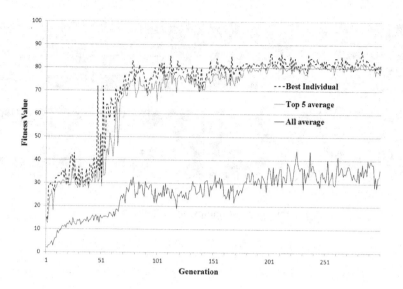

Fig. 6. Fitness value transmission

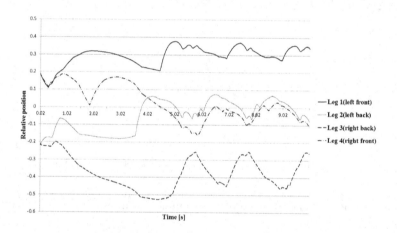

Fig. 7. Relative x position of each leg in 50th generation

the right. This is why the left back leg stepped forward and the right front leg stepped back in the Fig.7. This pattern is far from walk gait. Firstly, the left back leg and the right front leg move in the same phase, while each of the four legs moves non-simultaneously in walk gait. Furthermore, the legs occasionally kicked the ground more than once in one cycle. This can be regarded as the disorder of the gait. Finally, each leg has a quite different moving pattern. For example, the length of stride of the left back leg is obviously shorter than that of the right back leg. The well-organized walk gait should express the same wave shape.

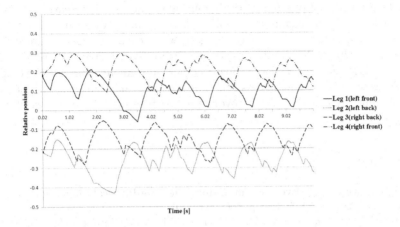

Fig. 8. Relative x position of each leg in 250th generation

The creature became better at walking in 250th generation. It became able to head in a straight line, and each leg expressed a more similar wave shape. This moving pattern is much closer to a well-organized walk gait. On the other hand, the jaggy part in the graph shows that the disorder of the gait still exists. There is a period when leg repeats kicking the ground and swinging down in a short time.

Despite this disorder of the gait, the artificial life continued to move ahead along the way of evolution. This emergent movement was mechanically born from four sensors on each leg. The sensing data having passed through the neural networks seems to give the creature a will to move ahead.

6   Conclusion and Future Work

We succeeded in creating a walk-like gait for quadruped artificial life. This gait is a cyclic walking movement and the quadruped artificial life walks in a straight line at constant speed. The emergent walk-like gait is similar to a newborn baby crawling on the floor. We also analyzed the moving cycle of each leg in developing generations, in addition to the final generation. Though some disorder of the gait was observed in the midway behavior of evolution, each of the creatures seems to have a strong will to move ahead.

There are some avenues for future works. In this paper, we focused on straight-ahead movement. Other movements, such as changing direction and jumping, would also create emergent behavior. The behavior of walking towards a target could be expected by combining the movement of changing direction and walking straight, i.e., applying the changing direction behavior until the creature heads the target, and subsequently applying the walking straight behavior. Only three movements are required in this chasing target behavior: walking straight, turning right and turning left. However, the discontinuous connection of each movement would be an essential problem which determines whether the creature can walk well or not. Another avenue is to link each leg by a network and adopt a parameter, which determine phase of the gait, while each leg moves separately in this work. By doing this, we can expect to generate a wider variety of gait, and analyze the organizing process of the developing movements. Finally, it would be interesting to apply a new fitness function to the creature after it once learned to walk. This application could provoke the creature to walk in a new, efficient manner.

References

1. Turk, G.: Sticky feet: Evolution in a Multi-Creature Physical Simulation. In: Proceedings of Artificial Life 12, pp. 496–503 (2010)
2. Miconi, T.: Evosphere: evolutionary dynamics in a population of fighting virtual creatures. In: IEEE Congress on Evolutionary Computation 2008, pp. 3066–3073 (2008)
3. Sims, K.: Evolving 3D morphology and behavior by competition. In: Proceedings of Artificial Life 4, pp. 59–69 (1994)
4. Sims, K.: Evolving virtual creatures. In: Proceedings of SIGGRAPH 1994, pp. 15–22 (1994)
5. Beer, R.D., Chiel, H.J., Sterling, L.S.: Heterogeneous neural networks for adaptive behavior in dynamic environments. In: Advances in Neural Information Processing Systems 1, pp. 577–585 (1989)
6. van de Panne, M.: Sensor-actuator networks. In: Proceedings of SIGGRAPH 1993, pp. 335–342 (1993)
7. Open dynamics engine, http://www.ode.org/

Enjoying Text Input with Image-Enabled IME

Toshiyuki Masui

Faculty of Environment and Information Studies
Keio University
5322 Endo, Fujisawa, Kanagawa 252-8520, Japan
masui@pitecan.com
http://pitecan.com/

Abstract. Tremendous amount of images are used on modern Web pages, but images are rarely used in everyday communication via e-mail, SMS, SNS, etc., although many communication systems allow the use of images in the message. We believe that images can greatly enhance the quality of communication if they are appropriately used with alphabetical texts, and we created a text input system with which users can handle images on HTML editors and word processors just like they can handle words in East-Asian languages. In this paper, we show how images are useful in everyday communication, and show how we can handle images with existing popular dictionary-based text input systems for East-Asian languages. Images are not only useful for rich communication, but they are fun to use and useful for conveying emotions.

Keywords: Text Input Systems, Image Input, Input Method Editor, IME, Dictionary-based Text Input.

1   Introduction

Tremendous number of images are used on modern Web pages for various purposes. Images are not only used for showing pictures, but they are used for showing background patterns, punctuation replacements, graphs, etc. Images are now even used in the main part of a paper like [3] for better understandings. (Fig. 1)

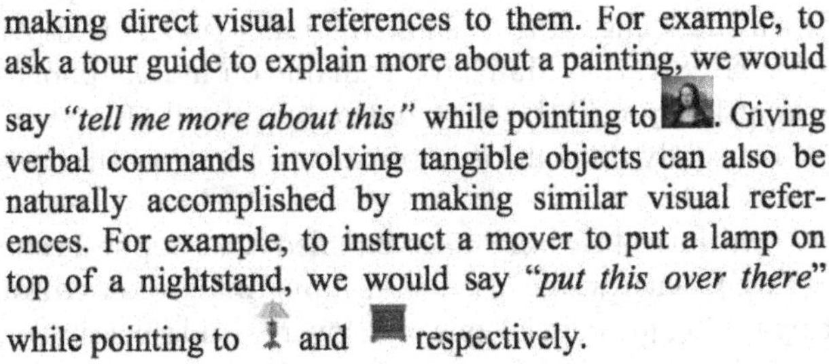

making direct visual references to them. For example, to ask a tour guide to explain more about a painting, we would say *"tell me more about this"* while pointing to ![]. Giving verbal commands involving tangible objects can also be naturally accomplished by making similar visual references. For example, to instruct a mover to put a lamp on top of a nightstand, we would say *"put this over there"* while pointing to ![] and ![] respectively.

Fig. 1. Portion of the Sikuli paper

A. Nijholt, T. Romão, and D. Reidsma (Eds.): ACE 2012, LNCS 7624, pp. 297–308, 2012.
© Springer-Verlag Berlin Heidelberg 2012

Edward Tufte is proposing the use of small graphs called Sparklines, which can be mixed in the text part of documents[2].

Use   [edit]

Sparklines are frequently used in line with text. For example: The Dow Jones index for February 7, 2006 ⸺⁀⁔⁔⁕⁕ Where this occurs, the sparkline is typically about the same height as the text around it.

Fig. 2. Example usage of a Sparkline

Young people are getting used to using images in their e-mail messages. More than half of the Japanese Android users are exchanging HTML messages using the "Decoration Mail" feature of e-mail applications[1], with which users can use fancy images in HTML-based e-mail messages.

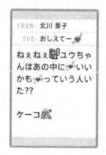

Fig. 3. Examples of "Decoration Mail" messages

On the other hand, elder people are still exchanging text-only messages, since composing an image-mixed text is not an easy task for them. If a user wants to put an image in his text on a word processor, he has to locate the image, copy the image to the paste buffer, and paste the image to the document. If he is using HTML, he has to save the image somewhere with an appropriate URL, and enclose it with the <img> tag to show the image in the text. Various kinds of applications for "Decoration Mail" are available on mobile phones to support easy composition of fancy HTML texts, but only a small number of images are provided, and it is usually difficult or impossible to use custom images given by users.

In this paper, we introduce an image-enabled text input system, or *input method editor* (IME), with which users can input images on editors and word processors just by typing pronunciations or keywords and selecting one candidate from the candidate list generated from the input, in the same way that Japanese

---

[1] http://podcast-j.net/archives/2012/04/mmd-android-ios-decome.php

mobile phone users are entering Japanese Kanji characters. Using our IME, users can compose a text mixed with images and words in Japanese, English, Chinese and any other language, with the same input method popular on Japanese mobile phones.

2 Dictionary-Based IME

Composing Japanese and Chinese texts on PCs and mobile phones has been thought to be a formidable task, and various text input methods have been proposed and used for composing texts in those languages. Almost all the Japanese PC users are currently using variations of "Kana-Kanji conversion method" for entering Japanese texts, where a user enters the complete pronunciation of a Japanese sentence using a standard QWERTY keyboard, and the IME converts it into a corresponding Japanese text. For example, when a user wants to enter "東京駅に行きます" (I'll go to Tokyo Station), he enters "toukyouekiniikimasu" and types the conversion key to get "東京駅に行きます".

Typing characters like "toukyouekiniikimasu" without an error is not very difficult using a standard QWERTY keyboard, but it is not easy when using a small keyboard on a mobile phone. So, Japanese mobile phone users are using simpler dictionary-based predictive text input systems with which only a small number of keystrokes are required for entering words. When a mobile phone user types "touk", words like "東京"(Tokyo) and "東京駅"(Tokyo Station) are listed as candidate words, and the user can select one from the list. With this method, users have to select a word in a sentence one by one, but using a good prediction algorithm, the number of keystrokes required for the user is reduced dramatically.

Fig. 4 shows how a sentence is composed using the POBox text input system[1] on an Japanese mobile phone introduced in 2003. When a user types a character "お"(o), candidate words are listed at the bottom of the display so that the user can select one of them if he finds the word he wanted to enter. After selecting a word, next input word is predicted from the selected word and listed as new candidates.

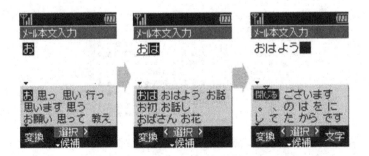

Fig. 4. POBox on a 2003 mobile phone

Dictionary-based IMEs are widely used for composing East-Asian languages, but the same technique is useful for Europian and other languages, and even for programming languages. The Emacs editor has the "abbreviation" feature, where users can explicitly define short abbreviaion strings for long words. For example, if the user defines an abbreviaion "ab" for "abbreviation", he can type the Ctrl-X key and single quatation(') key after typing "ab" to generate "abbreviation". Using an abbreviation dictionary, he can type "ma" to get "Massachusetts", type "mo" to get "Missouri", etc. Emacs also has the "dynamic abbreviation" feature, where users can enter a long word just by typing the Meta-/ key after typing the first several characters of a word which appear somewhere in the text. For example, when a user edits this text and type "ab" and type Meta-/, "ab" will be expanded to "abbreviation", because this text contains the word "abbreviation" which begins with "ab". In this case, the text under composition is used as the dictionary for expanding a prefix of a long word.

The idea behind these features are almost the same as Japanese IMEs on mobile phones. The difference is that IMEs for Asian languages are heavily used for entering various texts, while static and dynamic abbreviation feature is invoked by the user only once in a while.

We have created an IME which supports entering images in the same interface as entering words in Japanese and other languages. When a user enters the first part of the pronunciation of a word or a image, candidate words and images are displayed in the IME's candidate list, and the user can select one from the list and paste it into the text.

3   Image-Enabled IME

3.1   Using UTF Image Characters

Punctuations, exclamation mark, question mark, and other symbols are used in English texts, and face marks (e.g. ":-)") are used everywhere these days. In addition, various symbolic characters are defined in UTF, and we can use UTF characters like ☺, ☹, ♕, ♆ for fun. If we define a pronunciation to each

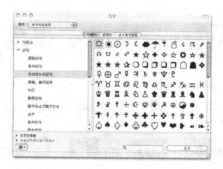

Fig. 5. UTF symbol characters available on Mac

character, we can use it in dictionary-based IMEs. For example, if we define a pronunciation "rain" to ☂, we can enter the character just by typing "rain", as shown in Fig. 6.

Using an IME with appropriate dictionary, we can enter a UTF character like ☂ just by typing "rain".

Fig. 6. Typing "rain" to get " ☂ "

Fig. 7. Selecting " ☂ " by typing the space key, and continue entering texts

3.2   Entering Images

Fig. 8 shows how we can enter an image of a fish on a word processor (TextEdit on Mac). When we type "sakana"(fish) in our IME, we can see the Kanji character "魚"(fish) and other fish images displayed as candidate words, since the pronunciation "sakana" is defined for the fish images.

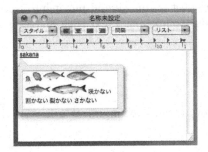

Fig. 8. Entering "sakana" to get a list of fish images

When we type the space key, the first candidate ("魚") is selected and put into the text editing area.

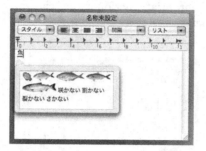

Fig. 9. Selecting "魚" by typing the space key

We can select the candidate by typing the space key and the backspace key. When we type the space key n times, we can select the n-th candidate and show it in the text area. When we type the return key, the selection is fixed and the candidate list disappears.

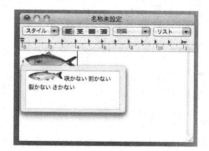

Fig. 10. Selecting tuna by typing the space key several times

In this IME, we can select an image and put it into word processors just like we enter Japanese words. Composing a text with images is as easy as composing a Japanese text.

4   Examples

In this section, we show various examples of using our IME for fun and for practical purposes.

4.1   Using Enhanced Punctuations

Question mark("?"), exclamation mark("!"), and other punctuation symbols
have long been used for adding extra meanings and emotions to sentences. Using
our IME, we can use various images for expressing feelings.

If we define a pronunciation "surprised" to images of surprised faces and
put them into the IME dictionary, we can get a list of surprised faces by
typing "surp" (Fig. 11), and select one of the surprised faces and paste
it in the text (Fig. 12), just like we can enter Japanese words into the text
area.

Fig. 11. Showing surprised faces by typing "surp"

Fig. 12. Selecting one of the surprised faces and pasting it into the text

4.2   Intuitive Expression

Sometimes images are easier to understand than text symbols. When you want
to have a meeting between 14:00 and 16:00, you can write a messsage like "Let's
have a meeting at 14:00 today". However, if the recipient didn't read the message
carefully, he might come to the meeting at 4:00pm instead of 14:00. If we use
clock symbols instead of numbers like Fig. 13, nobody can make a mistake of
this sort.

Fig. 13. Using clock images for specifying time

4.3 Using Faces Instead of Using Names

Instead of saying "Lena is coming today", we can use her face, if "Lena" and her image are defined in the dictionary. This is another example where using an image is more intuitive than using a text.

Fig. 14. Lena is coming today

4.4 Using Internet Search

Basically, all the images and words should be stored in a local dictionary, but we can also use a service like Google Image Search[2] for finding images of celebrities and famous places. Since it is almost sure that we can find President Obama's face from the Internet, we don't have to register it in the dictionary beforehand. (Fig. 15)

4.5 Dynamic Image Creation

We can also use images dynamically generated from the parameters given by the user. In the example shown in Fig. 16, the user is trying to enter an image which represents the RGB parameter. When the user enters "0000ff#", a blue rectangle image corresponding to the parameter is dynamicaly generated and listed as a candidate. (Fig. 16)

---

[2] http://www.google.com/imghp

Fig. 15. Entering "obama!" to get images of President Obama

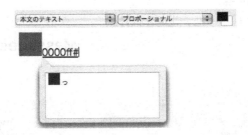

Fig. 16. Generating an image from RGB value

In the same way, it is possible to generate a Sparkline image or an analog clock image from the parameters given by the user.

4.6   Composing Attractive E-Mail Messages

Using our IME, we can easily select beautiful images and paste them to e-mail message (Fig. 17). A message with beautiful images are much more attractive than a text-only message. People don't use images in e-mail communications just because they cannot enter images as easily as entering texts. Just like Web pages became popular to the public after the introduction of the Mosaic browser which could display images on Web pages, we expect that people use more images in their everyday communication if input systems like ours become popular.

5   Implementation

5.1   Handling Images in IME

Our IME is implemented in MacRuby, using the IMKit text input library on MacOS. Since IMKit does not support image handling, image data is copied to

Fig. 17. Composing an e-mail message with beautiful images

the paste buffer and then pasted to editors and word processors every time it is selected by the user.

5.2 Registering Images in the Dictionary

We are using the data on Gyazo image upload service[3] for the images handled in the IME. All the image data on Gyazo have unique MD5 IDs calculated from the image data, and the images used in our IME are cached in an image folder. If a user wants to enter an image from its pronunciation, he should register the pair of the pronunciation and the ID in the dictionary.

We also provide a way to upload a clipped image on the desktop and register it with the pronunciation. If we are browsing the ACE2012 Web page and we want to use the image in the IME, we can invoke the clipping/registering application (Gyazo), specify the clipping area, and enter the pronunciation for the image (Fig. 18).

---

[3] http://Gyazo.com/

Fig. 18. Registering the ACE2012 icon with pronunciation "ace"

After the image is registered in the dictionary, we can type "ace" to find the image and paste it to the application.

Fig. 19. Using the icon of ACE2012 in TextEdit

6   Conclusions

Receiving a message with beautiful images is pleasant, but composing a message with images has been a pain. Composing a message in Japanese and Chinese used to be a big pain more than 10 years ago, but it was alleviated after the introduction of dictionary-based IME, and now everyone is exchanging Japanese and Chinese messages between mobile phones without pain. Using a dictionary-based IME for entering images, we hope we can enjoy exchanging messages full of images.

The Japanese word "楽" has two meanings: "easy" and "to enjoy". People have been trying to develop easy-to-use IMEs for many years, but we think we are now able to create IMEs with which we can enjoy text and image input tasks.

References

1. Masui, T.: An efficient text input method for pen-based computers. In: Proceedings of the SIGCHI Conference on Human Factors in Computing Systems, CHI 1998, pp. 328–335. ACM Press/Addison-Wesley Publishing Co, New York (1998), http://dx.doi.org/10.1145/274644.274690
2. Tufte, E.: Beautiful Evidence. Graphics Press (2006)
3. Yeh, T., Chang, T.H., Miller, R.C.: Sikuli: using gui screenshots for search and automation. In: Proceedings of the 22nd Annual ACM Symposium on User Interface Software and Technology, UIST 2009, pp. 183–192. ACM, New York (2009), http://doi.acm.org/10.1145/1622176.1622213

Train Window of Container:
Visual and Auditory Representation
of Train Movement

Kunihiro Nishimura, Yasuhiro Suzuki, Munehiko Sato, Oribe Hayashi,
Yang LiWei, Kentaro Kimura, Shinya Nishizaka, Yusuke Onojima,
Yuki Ban, Yuma Muroya, Shigeo Yoshida, and Michitaka Hirose

The University of Tokyo,
7-3-1, Hongo, Bunkyo-ku, Tokyo, 113-8904, Japan
{kuni,sato,olive,kimuken,nshinya,onojima,ban,
yuma,shigeodayo,hirose}@cyber.t.u-tokyo.ac.jp,
yasusay@rcast.u-tokyo.ac.jp
http://www.cyber.t.u-tokyo.ac.jp/~kuni/

Abstract. A container for cargo use travels various countries with a
lot of kinds of goods. It arrives at a place with some goods, and then
it leaves to a different place with different goods. A container itself is
a kind of transportation in the viewpoint from goods. We imagined if
the goods were we, a container would be a train. We have proposed a
new experience-based artwork using a container to resemble to a train,
named Train Window of Container. In this paper, we discuss the system
implemented in a container that provides us to feel a sense as if we were in
a train. When you enter the container, you can see various kinds of scenes
through train windows and can also hear a sound of train movement.
You can see scenes of Japan, Korea, France, and so on. Inside of the
container is dark which provides you a new sense of moving with visual
and auditory information. For the implementation of the artwork, we
used 10 displays as windows of train and 10 speakers for the sound, and
showed video of landscapes. We exhibited the artwork for five days and
had about 13,000 audiences.

Keywords: Virtual Reality, User Interface, Simulation, Visualization,
Media Art, Entertainment, Video.

1   Introduction

A container is an object used for or capable of holding especially for transport or
storage. A container for cargo use travels various countries with a lot of kinds of
goods. We imagined that when we can feel a container is moving, we could find
the new viewpoint of container. A container itself is a static and heavy object.
When we add visual and auditory information, we assumed that we could feel
a container as a different object. It was our original concept of an artwork. In
the view point of goods or cargo, a container is a kind of transportation system.

A. Nijholt, T. Romão, and D. Reidsma (Eds.): ACE 2012, LNCS 7624, pp. 309–319, 2012.
© Springer-Verlag Berlin Heidelberg 2012

Thus, we wanted to make a transportation system using a container for us. We selected a motif of transportation system as a train. Then we proposed an artwork named "Train Window of Container" that makes a container as a train. The concept image of "Train Window of Container" is shown in Figure1.

The concept of "Train Window of Container" is to make a train using a container with focusing on windows of train. In a train, there are windows that provide landscapes. From windows and landscapes, we can know a train is moving or stopping. Thus our direction is to extract windows as essence of a train. We have implemented windows of train in a container that makes us to feel as if we were in a train.

When you are in the train, sometimes you will be confused when the opposite train begins to move. It is difficult to get which train begins to move from the scene of train windows. This is a hint for the artwork that stimulates audiences visually in order to let them to feel movement of the train.

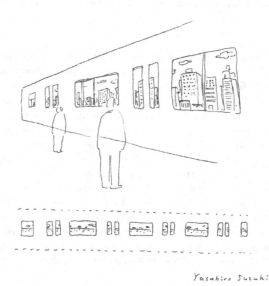

Yasuhiro Suzuki

Fig. 1. Concept of Train Window of Container

2   Train Simulator

There are a lot of train simulators in the world. For example, the Railway Museum in Japan[2], they have train simulators by Ongakukan Co. Ltd.[1]. In the museum, we can enjoy driving of steam locomotive that requires us to put coal on a fire to drive it. It designed to drive it in order to feel real.

They pursue to develop train simulators as real as possible. It can use as training of drivers of train. It can also use as games. Some companies are focusing on software of train simulators, and others are focusing on both hardware and software.

In this paper, we dont focus on developing a train simulator. We propose to develop a system that is extracted an essence of train that provides us to feel as if we were in a train. We focused on visual and auditory representation of train movement.

3   Design of a Container

To develop a container as a train, we focused on windows of train. Our assumption is that there is an essence of train in the relationship with windows and landscapes go by. When the landscapes go by, we can feel the movement and speed of train. The train should have several windows and the movement of landscapes should be synchronized. We also think the sound is important to enhance reality. Thus we designed Train Window of Container to put multiple windows on a wall of a container. We also designed to set up speakers as an auditory stimulation. We remove other stimulation except visual and auditory information. Thus inside of a container is black color and there is no lamp in order to be dark.

We designed a train window figures based on a real train car of Yamanote-line that is the most famous line in Tokyo, Japan. We traced the ratio of the window ratio from the Yamanote-line train car.

A container is a about 12 meters long, about 2.3 meters width, and 2.38 meters height. A real train car has about 20 meters length. Thus, we cannot make a train of container as the same size. Thus we selected two doors with two windows and four windows for one side. Total number of windows is eight for one side, six-teen for both sides.

We also wanted to feel a container longer than a reality. Thus we introduced a perspective design to interior of the container. That is, the width and height of entrance is bigger than that of backside. The perspective design is shown in Figure 2.

Based on this design, we have developed a prototype model (about one meter length) in order to check our design (Figure 3). In the prototype model, we changed the parameter of the ratio of perspective design. Then we set the ratio of perspective design as 15%. The backside is 15 % smaller than that of entrance. We aimed that audiences cannot feel the perspective design, but they can feel longer than a real size, especially when they see the inside of the container from the entrance.

We also put plasma displays and LCD displays as windows on a wall of the container. There are eight windows, based on the size of the windows, we determined to use 5 displays for each side, 10 for total as shown in Figure 2.

Then we implemented a container as Figure 4.

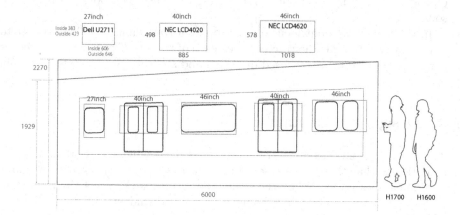

Fig. 2. Perspective Design of Train Window of Container

4   Design of a Software

We designed software of Train Window of Container with visual and auditory representations. As shown in Figure 2, there were 10 displays and 10 speakers in a container. We prepared 10 PCs to generate images for each displays and also prepared sound controller for 10 speakers. We made one host PC for control everything as a server and all other PCs were connected via a network (TCP/IP) as clients

When a train starts to move, a landscape will go by. We propose to make this effect by a very simple way.

For the contents of landscapes, we use videos that are taken from a real train window. The videos should be played with time delay among displays in order to show a landscape goes by. The first display plays a video at first then the second display plays the same video a little later. And other displays play the same video in turns. Then we can see a landscape is connecting each other and a container is going forward and moving. We also put a time delay for playing sound of video in synchronization with displays.

5   Exhibition of the Artwork

We have exhibited Train Window of Container at the Tokyo Designers Week 2010 that was held at Meiji-Jingu-Gaien, Tokyo, Japan. The event was opened from October 29 to November 3, 2010. On October 30th, the exhibition was canceled on the day because of a big typhoon in Tokyo. Thus it was five days exhibition. Each day, it was opened from 11am to 10pm except the last day. In the last day, it was opened from 11am to 6pm. The exhibition was told that there were 80,000 to 100,000 audiences.

Fig. 3. Prototype Model of Train Window of Container

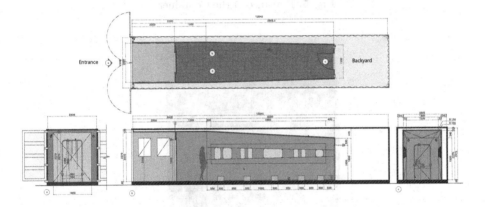

Fig. 4. Whole Design of Train Window of Container

The container from outside is shown in Figure 5.

During the five days exhibition, there were about 13,000 audiences to the Train Window of Container. Each hour, there were from 120 to 490 audiences. Sometimes, it was very crowded, but audiences are used to use crowded trains in Tokyo. Thus, it did not a matter.

The image of entrance of the exhibition of Train Window of Container are shown in Figure 6.

We prepared several contents. Contents were taken by a normal video camera not only from a window of a train but also a window of a steam locomotive, a ferry, an escalator, and an elevator. We took contents in several countries, including Japan, Korea, France, and Hong Kong. We edited all contents that

Fig. 5. Entrance of the Container

Fig. 6. Entrance Picture of the Container

have one to two minutes' length. We prepared 15 to 20 contents. Audiences can enjoy several landscapes, especially, foreign countries.

There were two sides in a container. A normal way is to play one video for both sides. Another way is to play two videos that have the similar train speed for each side.

Figure 7 shows inside of the container. It was dark and audiences could see windows and landscapes well. We put long chairs each sides. Audiences can sit down the chairs like a commute train. Figure 8 shows a contents of ferry taken in Hong Kong. Figure 9 shows a contents which is shown a video with an upside-down scene. It makes us weird feeling.

6   Evaluations

Based on the number of audiences, more than 10% of audiences of the event comes to our exhibition. We can say it was a popular exhibition.

We also asked audiences to answer several questionnaires. We prepared eight questionnaires as a following Table1.

Table 1. Questionnaires

Q1	Could you feel as if you were on a Train?
Q2	Could you feel that the container is moving?
Q3	Was the container longer than expected?
Q4	Could you enjoy the landscapes go by from the train window?
Q5	Could you see the landscapes from the windows were in series?
Q6	Could you feel as if you were moving?
Q7	Could you feel sick in the container?
Q8	Could you find that the size is smaller in the back than that of the entrance?

We prepared 5 levels evaluation choices. The results are shown in Figure 12.

There were 94 respondents. Based on Figure 10, number of male and female are almost the same. From Figure 11, 20s were the main population among respondents.

Q1 indicated that many people could feel as if they were riding a train. Of course, the container was not move at all. So, it is hard to feel the movement physically. However, the answer indicates they could fell riding a train. It shows that we could extract an essence of a train. Q2 indicates that it is a little hard to make a physical movement by only using windows of train. Thus the result is not so obvious.

Q3 is a question related to the perspective design. The perspective design works audiences to feel a little longer. When we look up Q8, audiences could not find changing of the size between entrance and back. We put 15% reduction of the size, we can say the effect is a small but it did not bother audiences because they could not notice it.

Fig. 7. Inside of Train Window of Container

Fig. 8. Contents of Ferry in Hong Kong

Q4 and Q5 are questions related to the method of playing videos with time delay among displays. The result was good scores. It could show the landscapes go by from the train windows in series. Audiences could enjoy the landscapes. We asked audiences to put some comments other than the eight questions. Many people mentioned that they could enjoy the landscapes, especially, foreign scenes.

Fig. 9. Contents of Train with an upside-down scene

In the container, it is dark and only displays and speakers worked. Visual and auditory information were directly showed to audiences. We were worried about sickness of virtual reality. We asked the sickness in Q7. The result was very good that audiences were not sick in the container. We put multiple displays in the container but we could avoid audiences sick.

We could get some comments from audiences. They could enjoy the artworks as if they travel somewhere. Several audiences comments that contents were good because they could enjoy the landscapes of foreign countries and could feel extraordinary experiences. Others said that they could enjoy the sound as if the container is vibrating like a real train. Several audiences commented it was interesting experience because they could feel visual and auditory information but they can feel vibrations or moving scene. These comments indicate it was success to archive our concept of the artwork.

An audience mentioned that when he took photos in the container, the photos were as if they took the photos from a real train. It is true that when we took pictures for archiving, we felt the same impression.

Some audiences indicated that they could not feel oppression when they entered the container. I think there were many containers at the exhibition, thus audiences know the size of containers. However they did not feel pressure so much. We think it is because the perspective design and landscapes.

Many audiences commented that "interesting" or "enjoyed". These were good feedbacks for us.

We can say that we could archive our purpose to make a feeling of a train in the container using visual and auditory information.

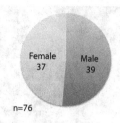

Fig. 10. Respondent: Distribution of Sex (n=76)

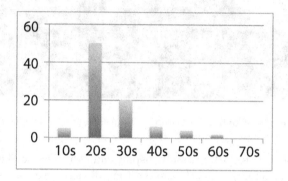

Fig. 11. Respondents: Distribution of Age (n=87)

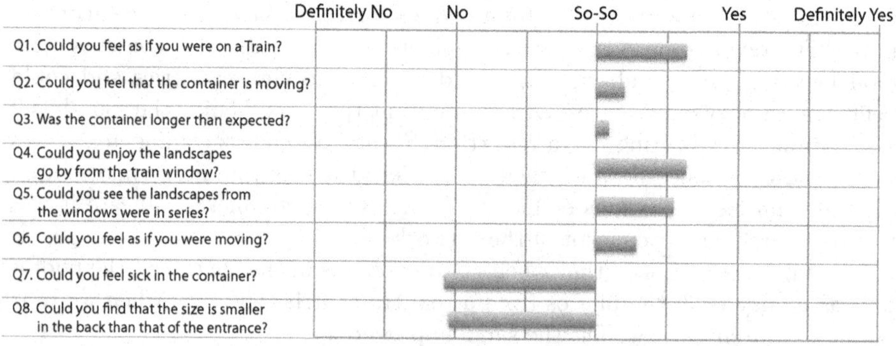

	Definitely No	No	So-So	Yes	Definitely Yes
Q1. Could you feel as if you were on a Train?					
Q2. Could you feel that the container is moving?					
Q3. Was the container longer than expected?					
Q4. Could you enjoy the landscapes go by from the train window?					
Q5. Could you see the landscapes from the windows were in series?					
Q6. Could you feel as if you were moving?					
Q7. Could you feel sick in the container?					
Q8. Could you find that the size is smaller in the back than that of the entrance?					

Fig. 12. Answers of the Questionnaires (n=94)

7   Conclusions

We proposed an artwork "Train Window of Container" which aims to extract an essence of train. We introduced visual and auditory stimulation into a container in order that audiences can feel as if they were on a train. In addition, we proposed a simple video playing method with a time delay using multiple displays to show landscapes from a train window in a container.

We implemented the artworks and exhibited the artworks for five days. We had about 13,000 audiences. They could enjoy the exhibition from our observation and subjective investigation.

In terms of a design of a container, audiences could feel that the container is a simulator of train. We designed the train window based on a real train, used LCD and plasma displays as windows, and shows videos in windows at the exhibition. Many audiences indicated that they could enjoy the landscape of foreign countries as if they were in a train. Thus we can say that the first concept of our artwork worked well.

We also introduced the perspective design which ratio is 15 % for the inside of the container in order to show the container longer than real. The ratio of perspective worked well in the viewpoint that almost audiences could not notice the perspective. However, the effect is small from the questionnaire.

From questionnaires, the result weakly indicates that our visual and auditory stimulation worked well. The simple video playing method also worked well that audiences could see the landscapes from the windows in series. We think it was because the videos were synchronized in terms of movement. The sound was also effective to feel presence, especially feeling of vibration.

The contents itself were received well. Audiences tried to figure out where the contents were taken. Video of a steam train was also good, especially the sound. It is easy to understand the content is a steam train that it is hard to ride recently. A ferry contents was interesting. We could feel rocking movement of a ferry. Audiences also enjoyed the upside down scene because it was the first experience to ride an upside down train.

The hardware setup itself was a simple virtual reality system, however the effect was more than expected. We are thinking to apply this simple method to a real museum that doesn't have enough budgets to introduce realistic train simulators. We succeed to extract an essence of a train ride, thus we can use this proposal to an experienced based exhibits.

For the future work, we want to have a further survey of essence of a train or other things. It is a kind of deformation of simulator. When we can make an effective simulator, it will be useful in various fields.

Acknowledgments. A part of this work was supported by JST CREST JST CREST Technology to Create Digital Public Art project.

References

1. Ongakukan, co. ltd., http://www.ongakukan.info/
2. Railway museum, http://www.railway-museum.jp/

Pinch: An Interface That Relates Applications on Multiple Touch-Screen by 'Pinching' Gesture

Takashi Ohta and Jun Tanaka

Tokyo University of Technology, School of Media Science
takashi@stf.teu.ac.jp, j.tanaka@eje-c.com
http://www2.teu.ac.jp/media/~takashi/cmdeng/CmdEng/

Abstract. We devised a new user interface that relates applications running on multiple mobile devices when the surfaces of juxtaposed screens are merely pinched. The multiple-screen layout can be changed dynamically and instantly even while applications are running in each device. This interface can introduce a new kind of interaction: rearrangement of devices triggers a certain reaction of contents. We expect this interface to show great potential to inspire various application designs, and we expect to enrich the contents by offering interaction that a single display or a static multi-display environment cannot provide. To prove and demonstrate that the interface is functional, we implemented a framework for using the interface and developed several applications using it. Although these applications are simple prototypes, they received favorable responses from audiences at several exhibitions.

Keywords: User Interface, Multi-Display, Interaction, Mobile Device, Touch Screen, Dynamic Reconfiguration, Face-to-Face.

1 Introduction

Through our experience of creating interactive applications on multi-display environment, we felt it would be possible to create more interesting representations using multiple displays if we were able to add more dynamical features to them. Multi-display systems are generally static in their composition, and are mainly used for offering a very large screen or high-resolution display [1][2]. If interactive applications such as media-art works run on a multi-display system, then multiple displays can be expected to give more impact to an audience than when running on a single display. However, if the usage of multi-display stays in forming a larger but single virtual screen, then the designs and the interactions of applications are not expected to be too much different from those designed for a single display. Although that is suitable for scientific visualization purposes, we believe that using multiple displays has greater potential as a platform for interactive applications.

In pursuing the potential of multi-displays, we decided to ascertain the ways that the displays' layout can be changed interactively even when applications are running. We sought an interaction as such that changing of displays' layout causes an application's reaction. First, we created applications that achieve

A. Nijholt, T. Romão, and D. Reidsma (Eds.): ACE 2012, LNCS 7624, pp. 320–335, 2012.

such interaction with notebook PCs [3], by attaching sensors to them. However, because notebook PCs are still large and heavy to carry around casually, we were not able to find appropriate application scenarios. Because mobile devices such as smartphones and tablet PCs have become popular, we decided to import the idea and mechanism to these platforms, which are ideal candidates for our purposes because of their mobility and popularity.

We do not want to attach sensors to mobile devices, and it would not be tolerable if it were done by opening a configuration panel on a screen and registering the devices manually one by one. We want to create a more interactive interface to achieve the action. We propose a simple and intuitive interface to do so, using a "pinching" gesture accomplished by putting the forefinger and thumb on juxtaposed screens and swiping them as if to stitch them together. This linking of displays is possible by choosing mobile devices with a touch screen for our platform. We also use "shaking" of a device to break the connection. We prepared the framework using the interface's functions and created three prototype applications to demonstrate that this interface can be a foundation of various representations.

As described in this paper, we present the concept and the mechanism of our interface, its implementation, and the applications developed using the interface.

2   Related Work

Several reports in the literature have described research using dynamically reconfigurable multiple display devices. "Data Tiles" consists of a flat display and tiny transparent tiles [4]. Each tile has an RFID tag, and reading sensors are mounted on the panel, so that the system can recognize when a tile is placed on the panel. When a tile is placed, contents associated with each tile's category are displayed automatically on the panel in that area. This research demonstrates a kind of interface in that multiple displaying units are used, and making physical interaction as placing a unit onto a panel to trigger content to react. Other studies have investigated the use of physically independent displaying devices. "ConnecTables [5]" is a work that develops a system that dynamically connects two displays and makes them a single virtual screen to produce a collaborative workplace. A display unit, called ConnecTable, is built using a graphic tablet and built-in-sensor. They detect each other when they are moved close. Then their screens are connected to form a single display area. On the connected screen, users can share information by moving displayed objects between devices. Hinckley proposed the use of a bumping of displays to trigger a connection [6]. An acceleration sensor can detect a vibration by the bumping motion. Then display regions are connected to form a single workplace. "Stitching [7]" is a similar method that has been examined for building a collaborative workplace by multiple displays. This method uses a stylus pen for connecting displays. The system recognizes the pen's continuous movement that spans over multiple displays, and forms a temporary single screen by deducing relative positions of displays by making the pen's trail be drawn as continuous line. These studies show variants of the approach, some use sensors to detect the physical contact of displays, some use a gesture to know it occurs, and other approaches use a pen's trail to ascertain positions more precisely.

Some works uses mobile devices. "Junkyard Jumbotron [8] is an application that combines devices including smartphones or/and PC displays, and binds them into single large virtual screen. It configures the relative positioning of each device by detecting specific graphical markers displayed on each display using a camera. "Shiftables [9] designs a specific tiny block device with a display, equipped with a built-in-sensor on its four sides to detect the others. That approach can be characterized as similar to ConnecTables and Hinckley's work.

Differences of the research objective explain the differences between these projects and our work. Our approach is similar to "Stitching" at taking a relative display's position by the drawn trail on screens, but we weighed more on the aspect of changing the display layout dynamically. We use the gesture not only for prompting connection of the displays, but making it as an interface to invoke a reaction of applications. Additionally, we chose the gesture of "pinching" as a physical analogy of gluing two things together, so that a user can have a feeling of actually connecting devices manually. Junkyard Jumbotron was designed to create a single large screen with temporarily assembled devices, whereas ours work is intended to produce an application platform that uses the change of display layout as a means of interaction. Therefore, Junkyard Jumbotron detects and configures the display positioning as a whole at one time, whereas ours does not use such a configuration approach.

An important difference from Shiftables is that our system uses ubiquitous devices such as smartphones. Shiftables are designed for one player possessing specifically tailored devices, whereas we expect a person to call friends to bring their devices to play together. Using temporarily assembled devices is our approach's major feature.

3   "Pinch" Interface

We would like to use multiple displays not for building a static large virtual screen, but for creating fascinating interactions of contents triggered by rearrangement of the display layout. For that purpose, we need an interactive and instant means to reconfigure the display layout. We also want to change the layout repetitively, and to be able to add or remove devices at any time. We do not seek a configuration tool to do that. We want a certain interaction that prompts connecting of displays and which also triggers the reaction in contents simultaneously. When we choose smartphones (iPhone) and tablet PCs (iPad and iPod Touch) as our platform, we came up with the idea of using a "pinching" gesture because these devices are typically equipped with touch screens, which we think we can use.

What we call "pinching" is an action of putting a forefinger and thumb on each display surface of two juxtaposed devices, and making a swiping gesture of them until they meet. The salient advantage of the pinching gesture is that it is extremely simple and intuitive. One can be reminded easily that this is an action to stitch something together. It is also extremely easy to deduce the physical position of screens by the gesture if we assume that it is applied by the forefinger and thumb of the same hand: we can safely expect that these fingers move along the same straight line, in opposite directions, applied at the very same time, on screens facing the same direction. Such information is obtainable by detecting a touch on the screen. A pinched pair can be determined by sharing this information among devices and finding a pair of information that meets the conditions explained above. Consequently, a pinching action on the touch screen enables the connection of displays without extra sensors.

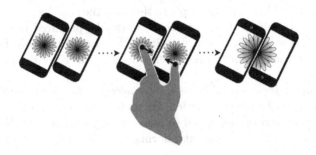

Fig. 1. Connect displays using a pinching gesture

The gesture is not useful only for making a connection of displays. We want an interface that relates the displayed contents, rather than that for connecting the devices. For example, as shown in Fig. 1, when two displays are pinched, these displays are connected. At the very same time, the image appears throughout the screens. In other words, we want to achieve interaction of contents, which will occur by moving displays around. Designing a reconfigurable multi-display system itself is not the direct objective of this research.

To realize such an interaction, it is necessary that an application to react to an event of connection or disconnection of displays with the pinching action. We design these two events to occur spontaneously without requiring an extra step to relate the application's content. We expect that this approach can produce fascinating applications that make users feel as though they control digital contents by physically handling objects.

4   System Design

In this section, we explain the design and implementation of the interface system. Our intention is to have a dynamic interaction of a gesture and content. Therefore, one can apply a pinching gesture while the application is running. The entire procedure for connecting displays and letting applications react to the event can largely be done in three steps: find the pinched pair, determine the screen positions, and call an appropriate reaction in an application. We explain here how these steps are implemented and what tasks are done in each step.

4.1 Determine a Connected Pair

When an application starts, it seeks others on a network. Once finding the other devices on which a compatible application is running, the application registers their network addresses and establishes a connection with them. Finding others on a network is done automatically using Apple's Bonjour protocol. This protocol is useful for publicizing a network service to other devices. The bonjour protocol deals with the identifier designating a kind of service and the type of transport protocol, in a format like "_pinch._tcp". In this way, the application can find other fellow "Pinch"-able applications on the network. We prepared the function for network connection so that it can use either Wi-Fi or Bluetooth. Each has its merits and shortcomings in terms of performance, which we discuss in a later section.

Once a group of devices establishes the connection, they are ready to send and receive information of a pinching action. On each device, the application observes whether a swiping motion is applied to its screen. When the application notices that a swiping occurs, it sends out information related to that motion to all other devices (Fig. 2).

Fig. 2. Broadcasting of motion data

Information on the motion consists of data listed as shown in Table 1. If a swiping motion results from a "Pinch" action, then the swiping motion can be expected to occur at two devices simultaneously. Therefore, if an application receives swiping information and also has its own at that duration, it can deduce whether it results from a pinching action by comparing the time stamps in the respective devices' information. A pair of swiping motions is identified as a pinching gesture when data or these motions satisfy the following conditions.

- if motions occur simultaneously
- if a screen's surface is directed to the same orientation
- if swipes move in opposite directions

As might be apparent from the explanation above, no central architecture exists for managing the information entirely. Network communications are done by peer-to-peer among devices, with no server delivering application contents. The processes are running on each device independently, only exchanging necessary information on necessary occasions with corresponding devices. Additionally, it does not need any extra devices such as sensors attached to the display device. Detecting a motion applied onto the touch screen can provide sufficient information to configure the connection. These features of having no centric server and no extra attachment provide greater advantages in realizing the use of multiple displays by temporarily gathered commodity devices.

Table 1. Broadcasting of motion data

attribute	explanation	value
Timestamp	time of swipe motion	*t*
Screen Size	screen size (in pixel)	*{width, height}*
Location	swipe terminal position	*{x, y}*
Direction	swipe direction in screen	*right, left, up, down*
Orientation	screen orientation	*portrait, landscape, ...*
Roll	roll of device position	*roty*
Pitch	pitch of device position	*rotx*
Yaw	yaw of device position	*rotz*

4.2   Connection of Screens

After a pinched pair is discovered, because we allow an arbitrary screen layout, the need exists to determine each device's screen coordination relative to the others. The pair has the information of the swipe motion of the other device of the pair. Therefore, each can deduce the relative position by analyzing that data.

To explain the process, we assume the swipe motions shown in Fig. 3. The procedure to determine the relative screen coordination is conducted as depicted in Fig. 4. The following are what are performed in each step.

1. position screens A and B as overlapping completely
2. move screen B by the distance between swipe A's location and screen A's center position
3. rotate screen B by the difference of the two devices' directions
4. move screen B further by the distance between swipe B's location and screen B's center position

Using these procedures, an application run on each device can know the other connected screen's relative location and can convert the position of the objects on the other screen to its own coordination, and vice versa. This process is also applicable to screens of different sizes. Therefore, the mechanism works with the combination of smartphones and tablet PCs.

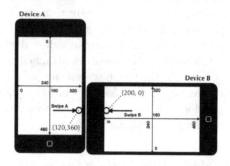

Fig. 3. Swipe motion and screen coordinates

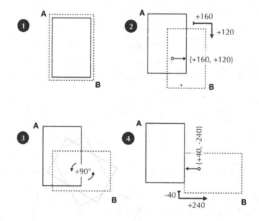

Fig. 4. Process to determine relative screen coordinates

4.3   Application Programming Framework

We designed a programming framework for the benefit of developing the applications compatible with the interface. It handles the procedures of networking, detection of pinching action, conversion of screen's coordinates, relaying messages among multiple devices, and disconnection by a shaking gesture, and so forth. It covers most of the system work and saves a developer from coding these parts. Fig. 5 shows that the framework's layer is constructed. With the framework, developers can concentrate only on the coding of graphics and reactions.

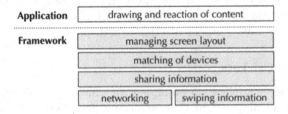

Fig. 5. Framework layers

The class structure of the framework is shown in Fig. 6. The framework is currently implemented in Objective-C for iOS 5 and after, for the use on iPhone, iPod Touch, and iPad. Most of the functions are gathered under the *PinchController* class. Therefore, a developer can appreciate the Pinch interface's functions only by using the class and designating one's own View object in it.

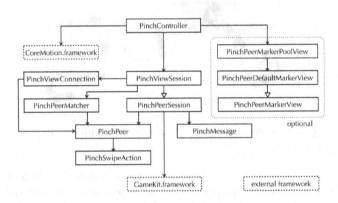

Fig. 6. Class structure of the framework

Other important classes in the framework are *PinchControllerDelegate* and *PinchControllerMessage*. The former is the class that receives a message when a device is connected with others. Using this class and set reaction in the methods it provides, an application can react when displays are connected. Each application's specific reaction should be called by here. *PinchMessage* is for a container of a message and is used for sending and receiving it between devices. It also supports the relay of a message through multiple devices.

5   Applications

We developed applications that employ the "Pinch" interface to examine whether the system is actually as functional as we expected. In addition, we designed three applications to demonstrate that the interface can afford to create the variety of interaction. In this section, we also explain what should be prepared in each application side to have a proper reaction to a display's layout change.

5.1 Traveling Crickets

This is a very simple application example with which a graphic object can move among multiple displays when they are connected. When the application is started on one display, a cricket appears in a grass field that appears on the screen. When tapping just behind the cricket, it jumps and moves forward. The movement is, however, restricted by the screen's boundary. When the insect reaches an edge, it bounces and retreats. Connecting a new display provides an additional field onto which the cricket can move beyond the edge of one screen. When the cricket goes beyond a boundary to a different screen (Fig. 7), the chirping sound of the cricket moves together with it and is heard from the next device as well.

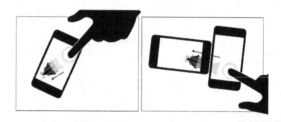

Fig. 7. Cricket moves beyond the edge to a different display

Making a graphic object move between devices is done in the following way (as shown in Fig. 8). Here, we proceed to an explanation by assuming that an object is originally located on the screen of device A.

1. set positions of the cricket's original location and destination in device A's screen coordination
2. deduce these positions in device B's screen coordination
3. create a copy of the cricket object in device B, at the cricket's original position converted to device B's screen coordination
4. move cricket objects on both screens simultaneously
5. remove the cricket object from device A after the animation is completed

As explained above, motion of an object between the displays is done by copying the object instance to a new device when the object moves over to a different screen. This differs from the approach by which a central device does all the calculation on the graphical object's movements, and broadcasts them to other devices. This benefits our choice of platform because none of the devices becomes indispensable, which means that any device can be removed from the connection. This application design therefore lends flexibility to the system and the interface.

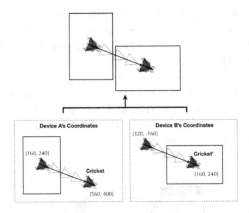

Fig. 8. Convert coordination between screens

5.2 Dynamic Canvas

This is an application that creates a single virtual screen by multiple displays, as is generally done with an ordinary multi-display approach. The difference is that the virtual screen is formed and reformed dynamically by attaching or retracting displays. The size of an image or a movie shown there is also adjusted dynamically to appear as large as it can be within the virtual screen's larger allowed direction size (Fig. 9). The size of the entire virtual screen is recalculated repeatedly and the shown image or movie's size is adjusted at the instant whenever a display is added or removed from the entire formation. When the connection is broken, the image appears on every screen so as to fit into a single display size.

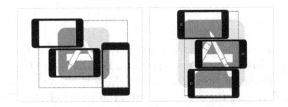

Fig. 9. Image displayed throughout multiple displays

To realize this effect, we let all devices retain information related to the virtual screen's size, and the local screen's origin point in that virtual screen's coordination. When an additional device is joined to form the virtual screen, the device to which the new device is attached directly renews its information related to the virtual screen. Then it sends out the renewed information to its direct neighbors and makes them update their information. Subsequently, they also send information again to their own neighbors. The updated information related to the virtual screen's size is therefore relayed to all devices by repeating this. To prevent the information circulated endlessly, the framework prepared the function to relay the information among many devices. That function prevents sending of the same information repeatedly to the same device by adding a unique identifier to the information. A device stops sending the information forward when it receives a message that arrived earlier. The routing of messages is depicted in Fig. 10. Sending messages stops at the devices where a message has already been sent via another device.

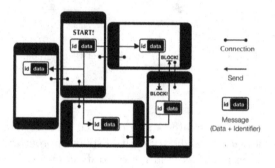

Fig. 10. Relaying message to entire devices

For displaying an image or a movie, determine which device holds the virtual screen's central position. Then decide the size of the image from the virtual screen's size. Then each device draw its own part, which is possible because each device knows its own position in the virtual screen coordinates.

5.3 Tuneblock

The third application is for composing and playing music. At the start, a rectangular space with a tiny dot appears on screen. Fig. 11 shows that the player can place a tiny silver circle on these dots by touching the screen. A sound is played when a scan line traverses the screen and hits these tiny circles. The sound pitch is determined according to each circle's position.

Fig. 11. Screen image of Tuneblock

Although the single device's screen affords only a very short melody, it can be elongated by adding another display later. When the scan line reaches the end of one device, it sends a message to the next device to begin its turn. When the scan line reaches the end of the last device, scanning begins again from the first device. Relaying of a message is necessary to realize this looping of playing sound. Connecting the devices works not only to elongate a musical note: tunes set in each screen are played in chorus if another display is connected in parallel in relation to the scanning line's direction of movement (Fig. 12). Although the same setting of circles remains on each device, we can play a different melody or sound by altering the display layout.

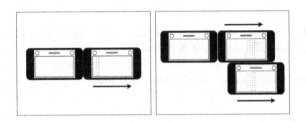

Fig. 12. Relaying message to entire devices

5.4   Variation of Application Design

These three applications (Fig. 13) represent different aspects of the feature of dynamically changeable multiple display. One allows graphical objects to move beyond screen boundaries to the other device. The other one uses multiple displays to form a single virtual screen, whereas the last one uses an event of connecting displays for prompting the applications to run cooperatively. The applications are simple and straightforward in representing each aspect, but we think we were able to show different usages of the function the interface can offer, and demonstrate the potential of such system as a platform for interactive applications. However, we would like to develop applications of more sophisticated idea and design in the future.

All of these applications are designed not only for multiple displays. In principle, the applications are designed so that they are playable on a single screen, and so that they have extra interaction when connected with others. This design principle can enable people to play the application both alone or with friends. In addition, interaction of more different types can be expected with the interface. For example, the connection is done only on the same plane currently. However, with a slight tweak, we think a three-dimensional display construction is possible. This would enlarge the possibility further.

When considering the situation of how people play applications using this interface, a group of friends or colleagues gather to play because one person might not afford so many mobile devices. In such a situation, we would be able to

Fig. 13. Image of applications employing Pinch interface actually running on iPod touch: left, Tuneblock; right top, Traveling Cricket; right bottom, Big Canvas

develop social type applications of a new kind. The applications require face-to-face communication. Therefore, it is useful for encouraging viral advertisement. Pursuing such an aspect for using this interface and applications for encouraging people to have communication with physical contact is a future objective.

6   Evaluation

In this section, this report describes the system performance including a test of elapsed time in connecting the devices. We also report feedback from the audiences at conferences where we exhibited the applications.

6.1   Device Response

First, we examine whether the connection is actually established and whether the system can deduce a correct direction for the connection. Many combinations exist in the orientation of devices for a connection like that shown in Fig. 14, and more when one considers four sides to put other devices. We examine by observation if a virtual screen's coordinates are built consistently with the displays' physical placement. We use the application of a moving cricket to verify that the combinations of two or three devices are handled properly. We confirmed that all of these are processed correctly.

We observe that a little discrepancy of finger size exists in the matching of screen coordination from physical placement. This cannot be avoided when trying to ascertain a position by touching the screen with a finger. About 2.5 mm of slip is observed, on average, with a maximum value of 5 mm, although this number is expected to differ among people and the mode of moving fingers; especially a touch by a thumb induces greater slippage. However, we need no such high accuracy for our purposes. A small slip between the juxtaposed screens does not deter us from regarding the two displays as connected.

As a pinching action not only for connecting displays but also for prompting applications to react, the response time to the action is critical for realizing the sufficient interaction. We measured the elapsed time for connection and

Fig. 14. Variation of the display layout

disconnection of different protocols. Response is almost instant with UDP and Bluetooth, while it takes about a second with TCP via Wi-Fi.

Lastly, we examined how many devices can join the connection simultaneously. With the Wi-Fi protocol, we observe that the connection is successful for up to six devices, but Bluetooth fails with more than four devices. This is perhaps attributable to the restriction of the hardware or the system framework. The number of communications increases drastically because the system currently uses all-to-all communication to find a pair where a "pinch" action is applied. Although the mechanism itself allows any number to join simultaneously, it takes longer to find a pair. Therefore, it takes longer to react. The connection sometimes becomes unstable according to network conditions. We must establish a networking algorithm that provides a faster and more stable connection, and which makes the system more robust for allowing the connection of a larger number of devices.

6.2   Audience Feedback

We have presented the applications at several conferences and exhibitions. Responses from the audience members when they actually try the application by themselves are favorable and show their great enjoyment. The applications even received an award at a certain conference as the most impressive demonstration by attendees' votes. At such occasions, we administered questionnaire surveys and interviewed some audience members about how they evaluated the contents and the interface.

We wanted to ascertain by the questionnaire if the interface is accepted as natural for the purpose, and if users felt that it inspired various new application ideas. Table 2 shows results of the questionnaire survey. We asked if they felt that the interface is natural for connecting displays (Q1), and if it inspires new ideas of applications (Q2). Additionally, we asked respondents if they want to develop applications individually (Q3) when the audience develops applications individually (which is expected because many researchers and students were in the audience at that conference). We obtained extremely positive answers to all of these questions. We were especially gratified to learn that a majority of people answered that the interface inspires new ideas and that they want to develop their own applications themselves.

Table 2. Questionnaire about the "Pinch" interface

	Question	Yes	No
Q1	do you feel the interface intuitive and natural?	30	2
Q2	can you come up with any application ideas with the interface?	27	5
Q3	do you want to develop an application by yourself?	20	1

7 Conclusions

We devised a new interface that connects displays of mobile devices dynamically, and have applications to react automatically to the change of display arrangement. The objective of our approach is the creation of a dynamically reconfigurable multi-display environment as a new platform for interactive media contents. Using "Pinching" action to prompt connection of the displays provides an intuitive interface because the gesture is an analogy of stitching things. Additionally, we created applications to react to the change of display arrangement, which means that the pinching action is useful not only as the interface for connecting displays. Simultaneously it is a trigger the causes an application's response. The fun with our approach derives mostly from the fact that no extra step is necessary to have a reaction of applications other than connecting displays.

Along with that interface concept, applications should be designed so that the action of connecting and disconnecting of displays triggers responses in them, which will bring a possibility of creating various new ideas in application design. In theory, no limitation exists for the number of displays; an application will have benefit if it is designed to run either on single display or with any number of multiple displays.

We produced three prototype applications of different types to demonstrate that the interface and applications are actually functional. By creating three applications, we also sought to show that the interface can become a platform that can produce various applications. We presented these applications at some conferences and exhibitions, and received favorable feedback and comments from the audience. Although applications are simple in terms of their contents, the idea of the interface and actions is apparently as appreciated as we had expected. Although it only accommodates display arrangements in-plane, the interface is applicable to three-dimensional placement with minor alterations.

Other merits of our approach are the selection of the application platform. Because mobile devices such as smartphones and tablet-PCs are now sold and owned as commodity gadgets of which many people own one or two, there are plenty of occasions during which several devices can be gathered at the same spot, without the need to purchase a set of devices. This aspect engenders another possibility of the applications. One might call friends or colleagues to try the application using this interface even if one person is unlikely to own several smartphones. Consequently, the application will encourage face-to-face communication, unlike SNS or chat applications offering a communication over network. We are considering applying this interface to offer face-to-face social networking applications or advertisement purpose. We are planning to pursue that aspect and to design applications encouraging such communication as subject of future work.

Acknowledgement. This research was supported by a Grant-in-Aid for Scientific Research (c), 24500154, 2012, funded by MEXT (the Ministry of Education, Culture, Sports, Science and Technology, Japan).

References

1. Ni, T., Schmidt, G.S., Staadt, O.G., Livingston, M.A., Ball, R., May, R.: A Survey of Large High-Resolution Display Technologies, Techniques, and Applications. In: Proceedings of the IEEE Conference on Virtual Reality (VR 2006), pp. 223–236. IEEE Computer Society, Washington, DC (2006)
2. Li, K., Chen, H., Chen, Y., Clark, D.W., Cook, P., Damianakis, S., Essl, G., Finkelstein, A., Funkhouser, T., Housel, T., Klein, A., Liu, Z., Praun, E., Samanta, R., Shedd, B., Singh, J.P., Tzanetakis, G., Zheng: Building and Using A Scalable Display Wall System. IEEE Comput. Graph. Appl. 20(4), 29–37 (2000)
3. Ohta, T.: Dynamically reconfigurable multi-display environment for CG contents. In: Proceedings of the 2008 International Conference on Advances in Computer Entertainment Technology (ACE 2008), p. 416. ACM, New York (2008)
4. Rekimoto, J., Ullmer, B., Oba, H.: DataTiles: a modular platform for mixed physical and graphical interactions. In: Proceedings of the SIGCHI Conference on Human Factors in Computing Systems (CHI 2001), pp. 269–276. ACM, New York (2001)
5. Tandoor, P., Prante, T., Müller-Tomfelde, C., Streitz, N., Steinmetz, R.: Connectables: dynamic coupling of displays for the flexible creation of shared workspaces. In: Proceedings of the 14th Annual ACM Symposium on User Interface Software and Technology (UIST 2001), pp. 11–20. ACM, New York (2001)
6. Hinckley, K.: Synchronous gestures for multiple persons and computers. In: Proceedings of the 16th Annual ACM Symposium on User Interface Software and Technology (UIST 2003), pp. 149–158. ACM, New York (2003)
7. Hinckley, K., Ramos, G., Guimbretiere, F., Baudisch, P., Smith, M.: Stitching: pen gestures that span multiple displays. In: Proceedings of the Working Conference on Advanced Visual Interfaces (AVI 2004), pp. 23–31. ACM, New York (2004)
8. Junkyard Jumbotron, http://civic.mit.edu/blog/csik/junkyard-jumbotron
9. Merrill, D., Kalanithi, J., Maes, P.: Siftables: towards sensor network user interfaces. In: Proceedings of the 1st International Conference on Tangible and Embedded Interaction (TEI 2007), pp. 75–78. ACM, New York (2007)

Exploring Playability of Social Network Games

Janne Paavilainen, Kati Alha, and Hannu Korhonen

University of Tampere
Kanslerinrinne 1
FI-33014, University of Tampere, Finland
{janne.paavilainen,kati.alha,hannu.juhani.korhonen}@uta.fi

Abstract. Social network games in Facebook are played by millions of players on daily basis. Due to their design characteristics, new challenges for game design and playability evaluations arise. We present a study where 18 novice inspectors evaluated a social game using playability heuristics. The objective is to explore possible domain-specific playability problems and to examine how the established heuristics suit for evaluating social games. The results from this study show that some implementations of the social games design characteristics can cause playability problems and that the established heuristics are suitable for evaluating social games. The study also revealed that inspectors had problems in interpreting cause and effect of the found problems.

Keywords: Social Games, Free-to-Play, Playability, Heuristics, Evaluation, Facebook.

1   Introduction

Social games, i.e. games played on social network services such as Facebook, attract millions of players [25]. These games are mainly based on the free-to-play revenue model where the game can be acquired and played free of charge. Monetization is realized through micropayments, which allow access to exclusive content and offer faster progression in the game [25]. The term "social game" was coined by the game industry and, rather than highlighting the social nature of these games, it emphasizes in the gaming platform, the social network service [6].

The heuristic evaluation method together with playability heuristics have been used successfully in evaluating games on different platforms [11, 12, 17]. In heuristic evaluation, the inspectors evaluate the game design and search for problems according to heuristics, which are rule of thumb statements or guidelines [22]. If the game design violates these heuristics, it can lead to playability problems and diminished enjoyment. Playability heuristics are used to support the evaluation and to help pay attention to certain aspects that are known to have influence on playability [10]. The heuristic evaluation method has been acknowledged to be a successful method for finding playability problems [3, 9].

This paper presents results from a study where 18 novice inspectors did a heuristic evaluation on the social game *Island God* (Digital Chocolate, 2010) using existing playability heuristics [11, 12]. The primary objective was to study social games from

A. Nijholt, T. Romão, and D. Reidsma (Eds.): ACE 2012, LNCS 7624, pp. 336–351, 2012.

the perspective of playability, and to explore possible domain-specific problems. The secondary objective was to evaluate how well the established playability heuristics are suited for evaluating design characteristics of the social games. The results from this study reveal that some implementations of social game design characteristics can cause playability problems and they should be acknowledged. The established playability heuristics are suitable for evaluating social games as they are able to describe also domain-specific problems of the social games.

2   Social Game Design Characteristics

To evaluate the playability of social games, we must take an in-depth look on social games design characteristics in theory and practice. By understanding these characteristics, we are able to study their inherent effect on the playability and player enjoyment.

The social games design values resemble those found in casual games. Kultima has defined casual games design values as Accessibility, Acceptability, Simplicity and Flexibility [14]. Like casual games, social games are easy to access, featuring acceptable themes and simple gameplay while offering flexibility in regard to different motivations for spontaneous play.

Järvinen [6] has defined five design drivers for social games: Spontaneity, Symbolic physicality, Inherent sociability, Narrativity, and Asynchronicity. Spontaneity, for example, means that in social games complicated sets of actions are simplified into a single mouse click. Similarly, Inherent sociability opens up possibilities for team formation through the social network [6]. Ventrice [27] has defined three objectives for social games: 1) build a persistent society, 2) maintain a consistent sense of discovery, and 3) spread the game virally. Sense of discovery, in this context, means that there is always something new for a player to acquire and experience [27].

Paavilainen [18] has analyzed Järvinen's and Ventrice's models and proposed ten initial high-level heuristics for the design and evaluation of social games: Spontaneity, Interruptability, Continuity, Discovery, Virality, Narrativity, Expression, Sharing, Sociability and Ranking. Social games are easy to access and they support sporadic, spontaneous gameplay. They progress continuously, updated with new content as the game advances. Viral messages are used for acquisition and retention purposes through narratives which are posted on the social network feeds. Social games support player expression in various ways and provide means for reciprocity in the network. The game mechanics are tied into the players' social network, thereby fostering collaboration and competition between friends.

In practice, social games are continuously updated services rather than stand-alone products [6] and they can be acquired and played free of charge. The developers are continuously monitoring players' interaction through metrics and the gameplay is adjusted accordingly, aiming to monetize the players via micropayments and sustain a viral growth in the social network. Through micropayments, the players can progress faster in the game and acquire exclusive content. In regard to the social network utilization and viral growth, the game design tries to attract people who are not currently playing the game. This happens by incorporating players' friends from their social network into the game to play together. Successful games rely on a large player bases as only five to ten percent of the players will make in-game purchases. [16]

An example of a common monetizing method is the offline progress mechanic, which comes in two different types; appointment and energy. The appointment mechanic dictates that a player must wait for certain game tasks to be completed, e.g. crops take time to grow before they can be harvested. The player can speed up the growth through micropayments. The energy mechanic works similarly. The player has a certain amount of energy and game actions consume that energy. When all energy is depleted, the player must wait until the energy is replenished or the player can fill in energy resources through micropayments. Both mechanics funnel the player into in-game purchase decision situations, which are usually prompted with pop-up windows.

Developers also need to pay attention to how the game is played and how the game design encourages players to continue playing the game. Luban [16] presents a sequence of events that propel the player in a game:

1. The player understands what he or she needs to do in the game
2. The actions can be performed easily
3. The player succeeds in performing the actions
4. The player receives a reward
5. The player discovers short term objectives and knows how to reach them

In addition to this, the game design often creates a continuous loop of tasks which will attract players to return to the game. If a player does not return and complete the tasks, they may be discarded and the player is not rewarded for her efforts. This will create a need to return to the game regularly and complete the tasks. [16]

The aforementioned design characteristics of social games influence the user interface design, and the interface should be easy to understand by different player groups. Main controls usually stand out and are centralized. Navigation is simplified and usually contain less than three navigation layers. Game objectives and progress indicators are also clearly visible on the screen. The challenge of user interface design is that all controls, indicators and game content should be fitted into a small window on the screen as social games run in windowed mode by default. [16]

Tyni et al. [25] present a detailed gameplay analysis from the social game *FrontierVille* (Zynga, 2010) and their findings on the effects of free-to-play revenue model, sociability and rhythmic design reflect well the aforementioned design characteristics. *FrontierVille* represents the simulation genre of social games, where a player completes simple quests by building houses, raising livestock, helping friends and doing other tasks which are tied into the game's theme.

3   Playability Heuristics

For the heuristic evaluation we needed a playability heuristic set that would cover the design characteristics of social games. First, we reviewed the social game heuristics from Paavilainen [18] but they were not concrete enough to be used by novice inspectors effectively. Then, we reviewed some of the well-known playability heuristic sets [3, 4], [11, 12], [20, 21] that have been published in this research domain. After a review, the playability heuristics from Korhonen and Koivisto [11, 12] were selected for the study as they cover usability, gameplay and multiplayer aspects exclusively (Table 1). It was interesting to note that even though these heuristics have not been designed for social games, most of the design characteristics can be found in these heuristics and their descriptions. In addition, the selected heuristics have been used, validated and reviewed in several other studies [9, 10, 11, 12, 17, 18].

The selected heuristics are organized into three modules: Game Usability, Gameplay and Multiplayer. The Mobility module from the original heuristic set was left out as these heuristics were not applicable in this study.

Table 1. Playability heuristics organized in Game Usability (GUx), Gameplay (GPx) and Multiplayer (MPx) modules

GU1	Audiovisual representation supports the game.	GU7	Control keys are consistent and follow standard conventions
GU2	Screen layout is efficient and visually pleasing.	GU8	Game controls are convenient and flexible.
GU3	Device UI and game UI are used for their own purpose.	GU9	The game gives feedback to the player's actions.
GU4	Indicators are visible.	GU10	The player cannot make irreversible errors.
GU5	The player understands the terminology.	GU11	The player does not have to memorize things unnecessarily.
GU6	Navigation is consistent, logical and minimalist.	GU12	The game contains help.
GP1	The game provides clear goals or supports player-created goals.	GP8	There are no repetitive or boring tasks.
GP2	The player sees the progress in the game and can compare the results.	GP9	The players can express themselves.
GP3	The players are rewarded and rewards are meaningful.	GP10	The game supports different playing styles.
GP4	The player is in control.	GP11	The game does not stagnate.
GP5	Challenge, strategy, and pace are in balance.	GP12	The game is consistent.
GP6	The first time experience is encouraging.	GP13	The game uses orthogonal unit differentiation.
GP7	The game-story supports the gameplay and is meaningful.	GP14	The player does not lose any hard-won possessions.
MP1	The game supports communication.	MP5	The game provides information about other players.
MP2	There are reasons to communicate.	MP6	The design overcomes a lack of players and enables soloing.
MP3	The game supports groups and communities.	MP7	The design minimizes deviant behavior.
MP4	The game helps the player to find other players and game instances.	MP8	The design hides the effects of the network.

4   Method

4.1   Inspectors

The inspector group consisted of 18 novice inspectors (9 male, 9 female) and they were between 20 and 58 years old with an average age of 28.3 years. Ten inspectors had some experience on usability evaluations, mainly from prior university courses. Two inspectors stated having work-related experience as well, while none of the inspectors had evaluated video games before the experiment. We decided to use novice inspectors as they were readily available and the lack of their expertise was countered with the sheer number of inspectors and additional training.

The gaming preferences and time spent on gaming varied among the inspectors, and the inspectors represented various different gamer mentalities in casual, social and committed categories [7]. Almost all had some gaming experience, as 16 inspectors had played video games at least sometimes. The reported gaming preferences covered all of the most popular platforms and all major game genres, the most popular ones being adventure games, followed by sports games. As social games target a wide audience of people with different gaming backgrounds (or no prior experience in games at all), the variability among inspectors is seen to be beneficial.

The inspectors' experience with social games was much scarcer than in video games in general. Eleven inspectors had never played social games before the experiment, and one inspector had only tried them out once. Among the six inspectors who played social games, the most popular games were *FarmVille* (Zynga, 2009) and *FrontierVille*. The inspectors had no previous experience with the game evaluated in the study.

4.2   The Social Game Evaluated

The game evaluated, *Island God* (Figure 1), is a free-to-play tribe simulation game on Facebook. The game was selected because at the time of the study, it was one of the newest social games, the inspectors had no experience on it, and the initial examination by the authors suggested that there would be discoverable playability problems. *Island God's* gameplay and design characteristics also resemble *FrontierVille* and other highly popular social games, like *FarmVille*, *CityVille* (Zynga, 2010) and *CastleVille* (Zynga, 2011). *Island God* uses offline progress mechanics similarly to these games. The primary mechanic is energy-based and the appointment mechanic is used as a secondary mechanic for completing time-consuming tasks like chopping woods, cutting rocks and worshipping the god.

In *Island God* the player acts as a god on an island with the purpose of expanding the island, increasing the number of worshippers, and perfecting the island with buildings, totems and other decorations. The player can play as a good or evil god, depending on whether she blesses or smites her minions. Thematically the game borrows these conventions from the classic god game *Populous* (Bullfrog, 1989) and like the aforementioned social games, *Island God* is played on an internet browser and uses Flash technology.

Fig. 1. *Island God* in full screen mode

The player has an axonometric perspective into the game world and the game is controlled with a mouse. Being free-to-play game, it features micropayments for exclusive content and gameplay accelerators for progressing faster in the game. The game is designed to funnel the player into situations in which the player is encouraged to pay micropayments or virally spread the game inside of her social network.

The versatile functions of the social network platform are used extensively in the game design. Players can visit their friends' islands and do various chores to help them out. The players are also able to send gifts to both playing and non-playing friends. The game emphasizes reciprocity by suggesting the player to "send gift back" when the player receives a gift. Sending gifts to non-playing friends works as viral marketing, as the non-playing friends can become playing friends by clicking the gift link. Player's achievement narratives such as gaining new levels can be posted on the Facebook wall, which aims to elicit curiosity among non-playing friends, thus luring them to install the game on their account.

4.3   Procedure

Before the inspection of the game, the inspectors participated in two 90 minute lectures on the heuristic evaluation method and two four hour workshops where they acquired hands-on experience of conducting heuristic evaluation for website interfaces and video games. In the second workshop the inspectors evaluated a city management game *EnerCities* (Paladin Studios, 2010). This exercise evaluation was done with the same heuristics as used in the study, alongside with the white paper that describes the heuristics in more detail [8].

EnerCities resembles *Island God* in some extent as both games run in a browser, use a similar axonometric perspective and focus on management tasks with a similar control scheme. *EnerCities* is not purely a social game, though it can be played on Facebook and it features minimal viral aspects (e.g. posting score to the player's wall). *EnerCities* is completely free and does not feature micropayments or offline progress mechanics. The heuristic evaluation of *EnerCities* was considered a success as the inspectors found and discussed 54 unique playability problems, but the results of this training workshop are not in the scope of this paper.

The inspection of *Island God* was given as a home assignment to the inspectors and they were instructed to play the game for approximately two hours during one week. Due to offline progress mechanics and other design characteristics of social games [6, 25, 26], it was crucial that the inspection consisted of several play sessions during an extended period of time. On average, the inspectors reached levels 7 or 8 by the end of the study. There were no specific scenarios given, instead the inspectors were instructed to play the game according to the in-game tutorial and later on freely as they wished. The inspectors were instructed to write down all encountered playability problems and assign violated heuristics to these problems.

After the evaluation reports were returned, three meta-evaluators analyzed the findings together. The meta-evaluator group consisted of one method expert, one domain expert and one double expert. The analysis of the playability problems was based on the descriptions that the inspectors provided. Problems were verified by playing and studying the game, and mutually agreeing upon violated heuristics. The meta-evaluators studied the descriptions of the heuristics [8] and used their own expertise on similar types of problems. The meta-evaluators categorized 169 reported issues, and identified 50 unique playability problems and all of them were assigned with one violated heuristic. The ability of finding descriptive heuristics is an indication that the heuristic set covers the design characteristics of social games.

As this is the first evaluation study on social games using playability heuristics, only one game was evaluated. We wanted to ensure that the established playability heuristics are applicable for the evaluation. This study also gives insights if the procedure should be modified for the future studies on social games' playability.

5   Results

In this section, we focus on the seven most common playability problems found in *Island God* (Table 2) in detail to see what kinds of problems the inspectors found and what playability heuristics were used to describe them. We also present the meta-evaluators' analysis of the problems and the violated heuristics as assigned by them. The seven problems were reported by at least 27% of the inspectors (5 out of 18) and the two most common problems were reported by 10 out of 18 inspectors (55%).

Table 2. A list of most common playability problems found from *Island God.*

No.	Problem Title	Found by	Assigned Heuristics by the Inspectors (number of inspectors in parenthesis)		Meta-evaluator Heuristic
#1	Boring Tasks, Quests and Gameplay	10	GP8 (10)	GP5 (1)	GP8
#2	Pop-ups Interrupt the Gameplay	10	GU1 (1) GU2 (2) GU8 (1)	GU12 (1) GP4 (1) Unassigned (4)	GU6
#3	No Difference between Good and Evil	8	GU5 (1) GU9 (1) GP2 (1) GP7 (1)	GP9 (2) GP10 (2) GP13 (1)	GP10
#4	Selecting Overlapping Objects is Difficult	7	GU1 (1) GU2 (2)	GU8 (3) Unassigned (1)	GU1
#5	Help is Not Available	7	GU12 (7)		GU12
#6	Awkward Cursor Interaction Mode	6	GU6 (1) GU8 (4)	GU10 (1)	GU6
#7	Friend Requirements for Progress	5	GP4 (1) GP5 (1) GP8 (1) GP8 (1)	GP10 (1) GP11 (3) GP12 (1) MP6 (1)	MP6

5.1 Boring Tasks, Quests and Gameplay

Ten inspectors considered that the game features boring tasks and quests, which in turn leads to boring gameplay. Similar tasks repeated over and over again like lighting up torches and gathering massive amounts of resources for no apparent reason. The violated heuristic was assigned consistently and both the inspectors and the meta-evaluators concluded that it is GP8 "There are no repetitive or boring tasks".

One inspector additionally assigned GP5 "Challenge, strategy, and pace are in balance" to describe the problem but the lack of balance in challenge, strategy or pace is actually the consequence of repetitive and boring gameplay, and the analysis of the heuristic descriptions support the selection of heuristic GP8.

5.2 Pop-Ups Interrupt the Gameplay

Ten inspectors felt that the constant pop-ups, which act as a funnel to monetize or distribute the game virally, are disturbing gameplay. The pop-ups appear frequently and caused frustration as they must be addressed before continuing gameplay. The meta-evaluators agreed with the inspectors that the pop-ups are problematic and they require an unnecessary navigation step. Therefore, the violated heuristic was assigned to be GU6 "Navigation is consistent, logical and minimalist".

Assigning the violated heuristic to describe the problem was a tricky task. Four inspectors left the violated heuristic unassigned and six inspectors assigned a different heuristic than the meta-evaluators. The assigned heuristics were related to both Game Usability and Gameplay categories. One inspector assigned two violated heuristics; GU2 "Screen layout is efficient and visually pleasing" and GP4 "The player is in control". Other inspectors suggested heuristics GU2, GU1 "Audio-visual representation supports the game", GU8 "Game controls are convenient and flexible", GU12 "The game contains help" and GP12 "The game is consistent".

None of these heuristics address the problem according to the heuristic descriptions. GU1 and GU2 describe problems related to audiovisual aspects in the game world and in the user interface. GP4 and GP12 are gameplay heuristics related to player control and consistency of the game and therefore do not describe this game usability problem accurately. Assigning GU12 to describe the problem was probably an unintentional mistake because the problem and the heuristic have no resemblance.

5.3   No Difference between Good and Evil

Eight inspectors reported that although the player can choose to do good or evil deeds, it has no meaning in the game. These acts effect on morality points, but the inspectors did not experience any influence beyond that in the gameplay. The inspectors were left unsure if there is a real difference between the two paths. Based on the heuristic descriptions, the meta-evaluators assigned the violated heuristic GP10 "The game supports different playing styles" for the problem.

Two inspectors assigned the violated heuristic congruently with the meta-evaluators. Other suggested heuristics were GU5 "The player understands the terminology", GU9 "The game gives feedback on the player's actions", GP2 "The player sees the progress in the game and can compare the results", GP7 "The game story supports the gameplay and is meaningful", GP9 "The players can express themselves" and GP13 "The game uses orthogonal unit differentiation".

As the problem descriptions revealed that the inspectors felt unsure of whether good or evil deeds had any influence in the game or what they actually mean in the game, they assigned heuristics GU5 or GU9 to describe the problem. However, as this is primarily a gameplay problem, heuristics addressing game usability issues should not be used to describe it.

The rest of the suggested heuristics are related to gameplay, but they do not describe the problem accurately either. GP2 refers to an issue that the game should show the player's progress and present it either explicitly or implicitly. In this sense, constant behavior as a good or an evil god should be visible to the players. This is actually manifested through the morality point indicator, but it has no clear influence on the gameplay. The heuristic GP7 could be justified as the game world indicates the possibility of being good or evil in the game, but there is no narrative story to support such behavior. GP9 is a somewhat reasonable choice, but it describes what happens after the problem occurs, i.e. the players cannot express themselves by being good or evil. GP13 refers to the game entities that a player can manipulate in the game and not the thematic role of the player.

5.4   Selecting Overlapping Objects Is Difficult

Seven inspectors reported difficulties in selecting graphical objects in the game world as they overlap or are close to each other. Items and minions tend to get behind trees and sometimes the inspectors had to remove trees out of the way, which was considered tedious and a waste of the energy resource. The meta-evaluators concluded that the violated heuristic GU1 "Audio-visual representation supports the game" describes the problem accurately.

One inspector assigned the same violated heuristic as the meta-evaluators. Three inspectors assigned heuristic GU8 "Game controls are convenient and flexible" to describe the problem. Two inspectors selected GU2 "Screen layout is efficient and visually pleasing" and one inspector left the violated heuristic unassigned.

Heuristic GU2 refers to the layout of user interface components on the screen and not to the game world objects. Assigning the heuristic GU8 to the problem is an example of mixing up the cause and the effect of the problem as although the overlapping game objects are hard to select, it is not because of inconvenient game controls, but because of the game's visual representation.

5.5   Help Is Not Available

Another playability problem that was consistently reported by seven inspectors was the absence of in-game help. For example, the inspectors were not able to find help to explain how to acquire certain resources or how using the good or evil god power affects the gameplay. All the inspectors and the meta-evaluators agreed congruently that the violated heuristic is GU12 "The game contains help".

The developers added the in-game help later after our experiment and there was a dedicated user interface component to access the help directly.

5.6   Awkward Cursor Interaction Mode

Six inspectors considered the cursor interaction mode in the game problematic. The default mode selects and activates objects in the game world. When building new constructions in the game world, the cursor changes to a silhouette of a building and the mode is active until a player has finished the task. However, there was no obvious way to revert back to selection mode. During the study, the inspectors found a loophole where setting up the building into an illegal building area, e.g. on the ocean, would change the cursor interaction mode back to the default mode, thus canceling the construction. The meta-evaluators concluded that the violated heuristic was GU6 "Navigation is consistent, logical and minimalist", because the user interface requires illogical steps to change the mode.

One inspector assigned the violated congruently with the meta-evaluators. Four inspectors assigned GU8 "Game controls are convenient and flexible" and one inspector assigned GU10 "The player cannot make irreversible errors". GU8 does not describe the problem well, because the problem does not stem from the game controls, but from the navigation interaction. The heuristic GU10 is related to consequences of the cursor mode, as the player might accidentally set up unwanted buildings.

Later on this problem was addressed by the developers by adding a user interface component for changing the cursor interaction mode.

5.7   Friend Requirements for Progress

Five inspectors felt that the game stagnates if the player does not have enough friends in the game. For example, finishing certain buildings becomes difficult and the game stagnates if the player does not have friends who can send the required items to complete the construction. The meta-evaluators agreed that the heuristic MP6 "The design overcomes lack of players and enables soloing." describes the problem accurately.

One inspector assigned the heuristic congruently with the meta-evaluators. Two inspectors suggested GP11 "The game does not stagnate", one suggested GP4 "The player is in control" and the last one suggested multiple heuristics; GP5 "Challenge, strategy, and pace are in balance", GP8 "There are no repetitive or boring tasks", GP10 "The game supports different playing styles", the aforementioned GP11 and GP12 "The game is consistent". Again, GP11 represents the effect, not the cause, of the problem. The design prevents progress without friends, thus resulting in a stagnated game as progress is halted. GP10 could be considered as the violated heuristic, if playing without friends was considered to be a playing style per se. The rest of the suggested heuristics do not reflect the problem accurately.

6   Discussion

Based on our findings we argue that social games design characteristics can cause playability problems when implemented in their current form. In *Island God*, these design characteristics were implemented in such way that they disturbed the game play, thus causing playability problems to appear. The problems presented in the previous section reveal that three of them emerge from the design characteristics of social games, making these problems domain-specific. These three playability problems, namely "Pop-ups Interrupt the Gameplay", "Boring Tasks, Quests and Gameplay", and "Friend Requirements for Progress", cover all the evaluated heuristic categories: Game Usability, Gameplay, and Multiplayer.

The four Game Usability problems were related to pop-up dialogs, overlapping graphical objects, missing help and cursor interaction modes. The pop-up dialogs are used in many social games to induce the player to pay micropayments or to execute viral actions such as sharing points or inviting friends to play. If the game relies heavily on using pop-up dialogs, this may become a playability problem as these dialogs constantly interrupt the player's interaction flow with the game. In *Island God*, the pop-up dialogs were used in key gameplay events (e.g. when leveling up) and they also appeared at regular intervals on their own. From a broader design perspective, pop-up dialogs are generally frowned upon as they interrupt the user and demand additional interaction [19]. As these pop-up dialogs stem from the free-to-play model due the need for monetization and virality [25], it can be stated that this is a domain-specific problem in social games.

The problem with overlapping graphical objects is common among social games. For example, all of the popular simulation games (*FarmVille, FrontierVille, CityVille, CastleVille*) suffer from the problem as they feature a similar axonometric perspective as *Island God*. As these types of games have a lot of clickable content fitted into a small space, it is inevitable that graphical objects get hidden behind each other. As the games have evolved, developers have added more content as well as more impressive graphics and animations, which have made this problem even more evident. The problem lies in the axonometric perspective, which represents a 3D world on a 2D plane. In a true 3D world, the problem could be overcome with a change of the viewing angle, but none of the aforementioned games feature such an option as they are not true 3D worlds. Many social games allow the player to rotate or move objects, but this does not fix the problem. As the problem originates in the perspective type and how the game world is represented, it cannot be stated that it is domain-specific per se. However, it is notably common among social games as the axonometric perspective is more casual and smoothly running alternative to a true 3D world with possibly even more complex interaction scheme.

It was a bit surprising that so many inspectors saw the missing help as a playability problem. Social games often follow the design value of Simplicity [14], which means that the gameplay mechanics are easy enough to be understood by playing the tutorial. It is possible that some of the inspectors looked for the help section because there is a heuristic referring to it, not because they needed help themselves. However, some of the inspectors did mention not finding specific information that they were seeking, suggesting that there was a lack of information in the game. After the study, the developers included a separate help section to the game. The missing help is not a domain-specific problem and many social games have separate help sections.

The cursor interaction mode problem has its roots in the development technology. *Island God*, like many other social games, is based on Flash which allows for a very simple control scheme, usually restricted to moving the cursor on the screen and left mouse click for selecting objects and executing tasks. If the gameplay features more complicated tasks, there is a need for a toolbar where the appropriate cursor mode can be (de)selected. This feature was also implemented later into the game. Solving this problem with additional user-interface element brings up a tradeoff situation as the more complex interaction possibilities will reduce the accessibility of the game. Another option would be the use of right click to cancel actions but this is not possible with Flash as by default it will open up the Flash menu. As this problem stems from the features of Flash, it cannot be seen as a domain-specific problem.

The two Gameplay problems were related to boring gameplay and indifference of being good or evil in the game. Social games tend to be simple and repetitive, which leads to loss of interest in the gameplay. This can be examined from two perspectives. First, social games' development cycle to initial launch is very short when compared to traditional video games [1]. This means that there is less content and complexity in these games. Second, there is the tradeoff between accessibility and depth. As social games try to appeal to a very broad and heterogeneous audience with different skill levels, the learning curve and the threshold to play must be low. The free-to-play model forces the developers to aim their game to mass audiences to create viable revenue streams [16]. Thus, the game cannot be too complex or it loses its casual nature, the design value of Simplicity [14]. The overall simplicity and boring gameplay can be seen as a domain-specific problem for social games as it is interlinked closely with the design characteristics [6, 18] and this has been acknowledged by others as well [2, 13, 23, 24]. However, simplicity does not automatically mean boring gameplay, as games like *Chess*, *Mahjong*, *Solitaire* and *Tetris* (Pajitnov, 1984) can prove. These classic games offer simple game mechanics but they also offer variable challenge levels and emergence, which results in good replay value.

The lack of difference between good and evil arises from *Island God's* narrative and gameplay features which imply that there are two sides to choose from. Although this is not a domain-specific problem, it does stem from the simplicity and shallow content of social games [24]. Furthermore, as social games are typically published quickly and evolved while online, it is possible that this feature of the game was meant to be developed further later on, or the players were not able to reach high enough level to see the differences.

The one Multiplayer problem related to playing without friends is a domain-specific problem. Social games aim for viral growth and they include features that encourage recruiting friends to play the game (e.g. [16, 25]). If a player does not have enough playing friends, the game progresses slowly or requires money to advance. It may also mean that the player has to send requests to friends in order to advance. This feature in social games has received critique in more recently published social games as well [13].

Our results provide interesting findings regarding the use of established playability heuristics for finding playability problems in social games. The 18 inspectors found total of 50 unique problems from *Island God* and the coverage of the playability heuristics to describe the problems was good as the meta-evaluators were able to assign a single violated heuristic to all unique problems. Although the inspectors sometimes had difficulties in analyzing the problems, the meta-evaluators were able to either confirm or correct the inspectors' analysis and the playability heuristics clarified the reasons for the problems.

For some problems, assigning a violated heuristic was straightforward as the identified problem and a playability heuristic description were similar. This was seen in problems #1 and #5 (Table 2) in which the inspectors and the meta-evaluators assigned the violated heuristic consistently.

The difficulties in describing the problems using playability heuristics can be seen in two different cases. In the first case, considering problems #2 and #6, the problems were more difficult for the inspectors as the assigned heuristics varied and usually they did not correspond to heuristics that the meta-evaluators finally assigned. Both of these problems required an in-depth analysis of the problem and knowledge of the heuristics. Especially difficult was problem #2 about constant pop-ups, which caused additional navigation steps for a player.

In the second case, the inspectors had difficulties in differentiating between the cause and effect of the playability problem. This was especially visible with the problems #3, #4 and #7 where the inspectors assigned heuristics which addressed the consequence of the problem and not the actual problem itself. For example, in problem #4, some inspectors focused on the difficulty to click the right object. However, the problem originated from the game's visual representation as the objects overlap each other due the axonometric perspective.

It was surprising to find out that the inspectors had difficulties in interpretation of the playability problems and analyzing the root cause of the problem. This is a known challenge for analytical inspection methods and it has been referred as an evaluator effect in the literature [5]. The evaluator effect might originate from multiple reasons such as evaluation expertise of the inspectors, but it might also be related to inspectors' cognitive styles [15]. It is also possible that in game evaluations such interpretation problems are more common than in other products because both gameplay and user interface influence how a problem appears and make it more difficult for inspectors to judge what is the cause and the effect of the found problem. Addressing a problem with violated heuristics from both Game Usability and Gameplay categories is a clear indication of this because playability problems usually originate either from the user interface or gameplay, but not both. In previous studies playability experts typically assign only one violated heuristics to describe the problem [10, 17] and the meta-evaluators in this study were able to do the same.

Although our inspectors had difficulties analyzing the problems, they were able to find substantial amount of playability problems by playing the game. This indicates that novice inspectors are able to find problems, but experts are needed to understand the problems thoroughly as the novice inspectors lack the analytical expertise.

The social games domain sets new design challenges as the players can pick up and discard games easily and free-of-charge. In this kind of environment, ensuring good playability is important from the perspectives of acquisition, retention and monetization of players. Our study has shown that heuristic evaluation with the established playability heuristics has potential for finding and analyzing playability problems in the social games domain. Being agile and cost-effective [17] qualitative method, we believe it is well suited for the fast development cycle of social games.

7   Conclusion and Future Work

In this paper we have presented a study to explore playability of social network games. The objective was to find out possible domain-specific problems and to test the applicability of using established heuristics when evaluating social games. In the study 18 novice inspectors conducted a heuristic evaluation on playability for the *Island God* social game. The inspectors found 50 unique problems and the seven most common problems were presented and discussed in detail.

Three out of the seven most common problems were domain-specific for social games and they were related to gameplay, user interface and multiplayer aspects of the game. These domain specific problems are derived from design characteristics of the social games. The results also indicate that the established playability heuristic set was capable of describing these domain-specific problems.

In the future, we will continue exploring the playability problems of social games in larger scale studies. As these games are constantly updated after the initial launch [25], the inspection time should be extended to get a more holistic view from the game. This would require additional longitudinal inspection methods, such as experience diaries to be used during the evaluation.

References

1. Baraf, E.: From Two Years to Two Months: Transforming a Studio. Gamasutra Online Magazine (2010), http://www.gamasutra.com/view/feature/4324/from_two_years_to_two_months_.php
2. Bogost, I.: Cow Clicker: The Making of Obsession (2010), http://www.bogost.com/blog/cow_clicker_1.shtml
3. Desurvire, H., Caplan, M., Toth, J.: Using Heuristics to Improve the Playability of Games. In: CHI Conference, Vienna, Austria (April 2004)
4. Desurvire, H., Wiberg, C.: Game Usability Heuristics (PLAY) for Evaluating and Designing Better Games: The Next Iteration. In: Ozok, A.A., Zaphiris, P. (eds.) OCSC 2009. LNCS, vol. 5621, pp. 557–566. Springer, Heidelberg (2009)
5. Hertzum, M., Jacobsen, N.E.: The Evaluator Effect: A Chilling Fact About Usability Evaluation Methods. International Journal of Human Computer Interaction 13(4), 421–443 (2001)
6. Järvinen, A.: Game Design for Social Networks: Interaction Design for Playful Dispositions. In: Sandbox 2009, pp. 95–102. ACM Press (2009)
7. Kallio, K.P., Mäyrä, F., Kaipainen, K.: At Least Nine Ways to Play: Approaching Gamer Mentalities. Games and Culture 6(4), 327–353 (2011)
8. Koivisto, E.M.I., Korhonen, H.: Mobile Game Playability Heuristics (2006), http://www.forum.nokia.com
9. Korhonen, H.: Comparison of Playtesting and Expert Review Methods in Mobile Game Evaluation. In: Fun and Games 2010 Conference, pp. 18–27. ACM Press (2010)
10. Korhonen, H.: The Explanatory Power of Playability Heuristics. In: ACE 2011. ACM Press (2011), article no. 40
11. Korhonen, H., Koivisto, E.M.I.: Playability Heuristics for Mobile Game. In: MobileHCI, pp. 9–16. ACM Press (2006)
12. Korhonen, H., Koivisto, E.M.I.: Playability Heuristics for Mobile Multi-player Games. In: DIMEA, pp. 28–35. ACM Press (2007)
13. Kuchera, B.: SimCity Social is a collection of dirty tricks pretending to be game play. The Penny Arcade Report (2012), http://penny-arcade.com/report/editorial-article/simcity-social-is-a-collection-of-dirty-tricks-pretending-to-be-game-play.php
14. Kultima, A.: Casual Game Design Values. In: Proceedings of the 13th International MindTrek Conference: Everyday Life in the Ubiquitous Era. ACM, Tampere (2009), http://doi.acm.org/10.1145/1621841.1621854
15. Ling, C., Salvendy, G.: Effect of Evaluators' Cognitive Style on Heuristic Evaluation: Field Dependent and Field Independent Evaluators. International Journal of Human-Computer Studies 67(4), 382–393 (2009)

16. Luban, P.: The Design of Free-To-Play Games: Part 1. Gamasutra Online Magazine (2010), http://www.gamasutra.com/view/feature/6552/the_design_of_freetoplay_games_.php?print=1
17. Paavilainen, J., Korhonen, H., Saarenpää, H.: Comparing Two Playability Heuristic Sets with Expert Review Method: A Case Study of Mobile Game Evaluation. In: Lugmayr, A., et al. (eds.) Media in the Ubiquitous Era: Ambient, Social and Gaming Media, pp. 29–52. IGI Global (2011)
18. Paavilainen, J.: Critical Review on Video Game Evaluation Heuristics: Social Games Perspective. In: FuturePlay 2010, pp. 56–65. ACM (2010)
19. Palmer, D.E.: Pop-Ups, Cookies, and Spam: Toward a Deeper Analysis of the Ethical Significance of Internet Marketing Practices. Journal of Business Ethics 58, 271–280 (2005)
20. Pinelle, D., Wong, N., Stach, T.: Heuristic Evaluation for Games: Usability Principles for Video Game Design. In: CHI 2008, pp. 1453–1462 (2008)
21. Pinelle, D., Wong, N., Stach, T., Gutwin, C.: Usability Heuristics for Networked Multiplayer Games. In: GROUP 2009, pp. 169–178 (2009)
22. Schaffer, N.: Heuristic Evaluation of Games. In: Isbister, K., Schaffer, N. (eds.) Game Usability: Advice from the Experts for Advancing the Player Experience, pp. 79–89. Morgan Kaufmann (2008)
23. Sheffield, B.: Gamelab 2011: MUD Creator Bartle: 'Current Social Games Are Not Fun'. Gamasutra Online Magazine (2011), http://www.gamasutra.com/view/news/35551/Gamelab_2011_MUD_Creator_Bartle_Current_Social_Games_Are_Not_Fun.php
24. Steinberg, S.: Social Games: 5 Growing Threats to Watch, Industry Gamers Exclusive (2011), http://www.industrygamers.com/news/social-games-5-growing-threats-to-watch
25. Tyni, H., Sotamaa, O., Toivonen, S.: Howdy Pardner!: On Free-to-play, Sociability and Rhythm Design in FrontierVille. In: MindTrek 2011. ACM Press (2011)
26. van Meurs, R.L.M.: And Then You Wait: The Issue of Dead Time in Social Network Games. In: DIGRA 2011 (2011)
27. Ventrice, T.: Building the Foundation of a Social Future (2009), http://www.gamasutra.com/view/feature/4210/building_the_foundation_of_a_.php

A Gesture Interface Game
for Energy Consumption Awareness

Ricardo Salvador, Teresa Romão, and Pedro Centieiro

CITI, DI-Faculdade de Ciências e Tecnologia/UNL
Quinta da Torre
2829-516 Caparica, Portugal
{rmssalvador,pcentieiro}@gmail.com, tir@fct.unl.pt

Abstract. Decreasing the energy consumption is an important goal for environmental sustainability. This paper describes MAID (Motion-based Ambient Interactive Display), an interactive public ambient display system, driven to motivate behavior changes regarding domestic energy consumption, through a persuasive game interface based on gesture recognition technology. The developed prototype guides players through the different rooms of a house, where they have to find out what is wrong and practice the correct actions to save energy, using similar gestures to the ones they would use in the real world to achieve the same goals. The system provides feedback regarding the consequences of each action. The paper also describes and presents the results of a user evaluation study performed during an open day event, attended by 6000 high school students, at our University Campus.

Keywords: Persuasion, Behavior change, Public Ambient Displays, Kinect, gesture interfaces.

1 Introduction

Many environmental problems occur due to our erroneous and exaggerated use of Earth resources. Recent studies suggests that, within USA, 22% of domestic energy consumption could be eliminated, if people engage in more appropriate behaviors, such as replacing traditional light bulbs with low-energy or adjusting thermostats and turning off lights when leaving rooms [13]. Each one of us can contribute to reduce domestic energy consumptions and consequently CO_2 emissions. Small individual actions may seem insignificant, but together everyone's efforts can have a great impact on the environment. Persuasive technologies [5] can be used to make people aware of the consequences of their actions and teach them how to proceed, helping them to change their attitudes and behaviors. MAID is a game deployed on an interactive public ambient display (PAD) system, which explores the use of natural hand gestures. The system delivers a persuasive interface, using gesture recognition and presence detection. The main objective of MAID is to instruct (or remind) users about simple procedures to save energy, showing them how easy it is to have a huge impact on the environment by taking simple actions in their daily lives. MAID

A. Nijholt, T. Romão, and D. Reidsma (Eds.): ACE 2012, LNCS 7624, pp. 352–367, 2012.

provides users with an interactive scenario, which can be manipulated simply by hand gestures. Users need to browse the scenario, trying to find out what is wrong and applying the corresponding changes. The impact of those changes is explained by audio feedback and it can also be visualized by the corresponding saved amount of money and reduction in CO_2 emissions. MAID is intended to be deployed in public areas, persuading users that walk by, to learn and adopt pro-environmental behaviors in their everyday lives.

This paper follows the previous publication related to MAID [25], offering further and updated details on the inner workings of the prototype and presenting the results of user tests.

MAID has been developed in the scope of Project DEAP, which aims to introduce new paradigms for environmental awareness, helping to motivate citizens to become more environmentally responsible in their everyday lives and engaging them in environmental preservation activities.

This paper is structured as follows: section 2 describes the state of the art related to the main areas covered by the presented work; section 3 presents MAID prototype; section 4 deals with the planning, realization and results of the user tests, and finally, section 5 presents conclusions and directions for future work.

2   Related Work

Persuasive technology is the general class of technologies that purposefully applies psychological principles of persuasion to interactive media, aiming at changing users' attitudes and behavior [11]. The term captology was coined by BJ Fogg, and is derived from computers as persuasive technology [5]. It focuses on the design, research, and analysis of interactive computing products created to change people's attitudes and behaviors.

Persuasion technologies can and have been applied within several contexts, such as commerce, health care [3], education [17] and environment [4, 7, 16, 21, 15]. Several approaches explore the use of games as persuasive tools to influence players to change certain behaviors. Regarding domestic energy consumption, some applications have been developed. Power Agent [1] is a mobile pervasive game for teenagers, designed to influence their everyday activities and electricity usage patterns in the household. Power Agent is played on standard Java-enabled mobile phones and uses real power consumption data collected via existing metering equipment used by the energy company. The underlying design idea is to let players (one for each house) compete in teams (cooperate with their families) and learn hands-on how to save energy in their homes. Power Explorer [8] builds on the previous research on Power Agent and uses a similar technological set-up, but focuses on real-time feedback. The game design teaches the players about the consumption of their devices and encourages them to adopt good habits. Some other applications focus on providing feedback based on real-time domestic energy consumptions measurements [10, 14, 18].

Although these approaches seem to produce positive results, they rely on the use of mobile devices and the deployment of specific energy consumption devices (connected to the home central electric power meter or appliances), which involves additional costs and set-up. We aim at using players' free time in public spaces, such as shopping centers or waiting rooms, to both motivate and educate them towards home energy saving behaviors. Our approach is based on the assumption that a change in behavior requires both motivation to act as well as knowledge of what to do. According to Fogg [6], behavior changes can be achieved through the conciliation of three main factors: Motivation, ability and trigger. Thus, our design exposes several common inappropriate behaviors that must be noticed and corrected by the players through a public display. Actions that can be taken to reduce energy consumption include turning lights off, unplugging standby equipment, as well as replacing traditional light bulbs with low-energy ones. The interaction with the public display is performed by hand gestures similar to the ones required to perform the appropriate action in real life, so players can learn and rehearsal these actions and may easily recall them later. Additionally, to make players aware of the consequences of their actions, the system provides feedback regarding the costs saved and the quantity of CO_2 emissions avoided. To have a more impressive effect and emphasize how individual actions can have a significant contribution to the global achievements, feedback is based on what would be saved or avoided if everyone in the country would take a certain action.

Hand gestures were chosen to avoid the need for any additional device, as well as to allow players to perform actions as similar as possible to the real ones. According to [9] gestures are a viable method of interaction with public digital. Their work contributes to the understanding of how people perceive, respond to and interact with interactive gesture based public displays outside the controlled environment of a research lab. Their findings support both the observe-and-learn model [19] and the Honeypot effect [2] and we followed some of their recommendations that were appropriate for our case study. A public display allows for a broader dissemination of a message, since besides the user directly interacting with it, all members of the audience can receive the output from the public display.

We also considered the four-phase framework" proposed by Vogel and Balakrishnan [23] which covers a range of activities from distant implicit public interaction to personal interaction, motivating users to get close enough to interact directly with the public display.

Diverse technologies have been explored to recognize gestures for interacting with public displays. Vogel and Balakrishnan [24] explored the use of free-hand interaction by employing a sensor data glove. Shoemaker et al. [20] introduced the shadow reaching technique that uses a perspective projection of the user's shadow on the display surface, controlled directly by the user through body positioning, to allows him to adjust the effective range of interaction over the a large area. However, Kinect sensor of the Microsoft Xbox console [11] represent a non-invasive technique for acquiring hand gestures which allows the creation of a natural interface that do not require user manipulation of additional devices.

Implementing a successful gesture-based interface also requires the challenging task of designing a set of effective gesture commands that allows users to interact in a natural, familiar and effortless manner. This is particularly important in the context of sporadic interaction with public displays when users have limited time to learn and explore the application [22]. As we mentioned before, our gesture set was designed to resemble the corresponding real world actions, so the gestures would be easier to understand and recall.

3   System Description

MAID (Motion-based Ambient Interactive Display) is a game deployed on an interactive public ambient display (PAD) system, which explores the use of natural hand gestures. It is driven to motivate behavior changes regarding domestic energy consumption, through a persuasive interface based on gesture recognition technology. The main objective of MAID is to instruct (or remind) users about simple procedures to save energy, showing them how easy it is to have a huge impact on the environment by taking simple actions in their daily lives.

The developed prototype guides players through the different rooms of a house, where they have to find out what is wrong and perform the correct actions to save energy, using similar gestures to the ones they would use in the real world to achieve the same goals. The impact of those actions is explained by audio feedback and can also be visualized by the corresponding saved amount of money and reduction in CO_2 emissions. MAID is intended to be deployed in public areas, capturing the attention and persuading passing-by users to learn and adopt pro-environmental behaviors in their everyday lives.

It would be expected from a Public Ambient Display System that the main component would be the display itself. In most common implementations of a PAD, in order to add interactive components to the interface, the interaction method used is integrated in the display itself (touch-screen), or attached to it, in the form of button panels or controllers. To the common user, the main component will still be the display, but the center piece of the MAID's architecture is a motion-detection 3D sensor device - "Kinect for Xbox 360" by Microsoft - that is used to obtain the ambient contextual data. MAID is implemented in C++, using OpenGL technology for graphics processing, following a highly modular and configurable development strategy and allowing gameplay scripting. It can also be connected to a Facebook application, which allows users to share their experiences and increase the exposure of the project.

3.1   Architecture

The MAID development was done on a Linux based operating system, since early on most of the software development involving the Kinect was only available for this platform. So most of the technological options for the development process were based on what the Linux platform had to offer. The application is built over the NITE middleware, using the FreeGlut implementation of the OpenGL framework for graphics processing, being one of the most widely supported 3D graphic platform available for Linux. The textures applied in the application are loaded from png files, allowing transparency support. For configuration file management, the development was supported by the libconfig Linux library, following a modular and configurable development strategy in order to allow gameplay scripting. Most of the interface components, like all the textures used for the graphic rendering, the size and type of the fonts applied, the sound tracks used, the interaction parameters, the textual content, among many other options of the interface are configurable. The gameplay itself can be modified, by adding or removing rooms from the scenario, as well as by adding or removing interactive elements from each room.

Another component of the MAID is a sound engine that serves as a complementary mean of communication, speaking out loud most of the textual information presented in the interface, via Festival text-to-speech engine. It also manages the playback of soundtracks using the FMod framework, supporting multichannel direct playback of multiple audio formats, like wav and mp3. Figure 1 shows MAID's architecture.

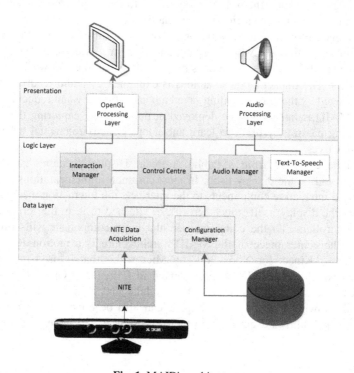

Fig. 1. MAID's architecture

3.2   Gameplay

To play the game, users need to approach the public display and interact with the system by hand gestures. Several rooms of a house can be explored. Users should select one room at a time and take the appropriate actions to reduce energy consumption and CO_2 emissions. The objective of the game is to save as much energy as possible, solving all the situations presented by the different game scenarios. Each situation is associated with a different electronic equipment that, when misused, can decrease the home energy efficiency.

Players receive visual and audio feedback while performing the different actions to save energy, as explained later in the paper, to make them aware of the consequences of their actions and how their small contribution can produce a significant impact in the global reduction of CO_2 emissions.

3.3   Interface

To motivate users to get close enough to interact directly with the system's information and according to [23], a four stage interface was created:

- Stage 1: An idle state, in a context where no user was identified in the surroundings. The interface presents minimal content.
- Stage 2: A user was detected, and the interface tries to captivate his attention through a greeting message.
- Stage 3: A user is still standing in front of the display and the application invites him to further interact with the system. The user is invited to produce an activation gesture, with his hand, in order to calibrate the gesture recognition system.
- Stage 4: An interactive scenario is presented to the user. He can now explore it, through hand gestures.

To exit the game, the user just has to walk away from the PAD.

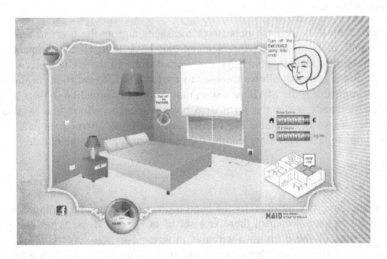

Fig. 2. The MAID's main interface

The first three stages are articulated in order to build momentum and anticipate the final stage. In this final stage a typical video game interface format is presented, composed of a game terrain, a head-up display (HUD) and a pointer (Figure 2). As explained below, it also features a direct interaction mode, which allows users to perform actions, like changing a lamp, by using hand gestures.

Game Terrain

The game terrain is a 2D representation of a home scenario. The user will start in a room of the house, and at any given time, he can select another room from the house plan in the lower right corner of the display. Each room has a set of interactive areas/objects, in a gameplay model similar to what could be found in a point-and-click adventure game. These areas correspond to situations that should be corrected, representing desirable user behavior changes. The players should scan the scenario and search for these situations, controlling the pointer (see 3.3.3) through hand-gestures. Some clues are provided by the system: pop-up balloons point out each situation and an assistant speaks out a description of the situation when the corresponding area in the game terrain is appointed by the user.

HUD

The HUD is composed by a configurable set of gages translating the current game status into a graphical representation that the player can easily assess (figure 2):

- A classic needle gage showing the current consumption of the home in Kw/h.
- A counter gage presenting the daily CO^2 emissions that would be avoided if the actions were taken in every home in the country, in t/m^2.
- A counter gage showing the home annual costs saved when taking the current actions, in euros.

These gages help to deliver the persuasive messages, urging the users to realize that together small individual behavior changes can have a significant impact in the environment and to change their behaviors in real life. In the HUD there is also an interactive house plan that allows the user to move to a different room in the house. The final component is the MAID assistant that delivers information to the user when the context demands so, in the form of a pop-up speech balloon that is also read through a text-to-speech system. The MAID assistant gives instructions that help the users to complete tasks and hints leading the users to accomplish the objectives of the game.

Pointer

The pointer is directly controlled by the hand of the user during the exploration of the 2D scenarios. In each scenario, there is a set of hoverable areas. When the pointer hovers over one of these areas, a circular progress bar pops up, representing the hovering elapsed time. While hovering, a tooltip pops up with information related to the actions that could be taken to optimize that particular situation (figure 2). The MAID assistant, in the HUD, also delivers a speech regarding the hovered area. If the hovering lasts for the full load time, the user then enters the direct interaction mode.

Fig. 3. Direct Interaction Mode: Turning off a Thermostat

Direct Interaction Mode

When entering the direct interaction mode, the interface changes: the HUD disappears, and the center stage is cleared to house an enlarged version of the chosen situation/object (Figure 3). Here the user is asked to perform a specific hand gesture, which triggers a reaction on the object. For example, the user could enter the direct interaction mode by selecting a Thermostat in the game scenario (Figure 2), he would then be asked to perform a circular gesture to turn off the thermostat (Figure 3). The correct gesture is illustrated by the ever present MAID assistant (an animation depicts the correct gesture) and it is intended to match the gesture that should be done to perform the corresponding action in the real world. Upon the completion of the challenge, a congratulatory message is displayed along with complementary information, like fun facts, related to the action performed. Finally the interface returns to its previous state, allowing the user to explore another situation/object. At this point the counter gauges are updated to reveal how much would be saved in costs and CO_2 emissions if this action was performed in every house in the country. To make these changes in the counter gauges noticeable, the sound of changing gauges is played to match the gauge animation resembling a classic split-flap display.

Gesture Commands

There are four distinct gesture types that are implemented in MAID and can be used to create new interactive objects. The gesture recognition is based on single hand position detection. The length of the hand movements is configurable, but generally it should not go beyond an arm's reach, so the user doesn't have to move around to produce the target gestures. This is done to reduce the complexity of the gestures, to reduce the clutter free area needed for the detection and also to increase the reliability of the hand position recognition.

The following gesture types were implemented (figure 4):

- Pushing or pulling hand motion, used for objects' manipulation such as pulling a power adapter from a wall socket or tapping a light switch.
- Vertical sweeping hand motion, used for objects' manipulation, such as opening window shutters.
- Horizontal sweeping hand motion, used for objects' manipulation, such as opening sliding windows.
- Circular hand motion, used for objects' manipulation, such as unscrewing a light bulb and screwing in a new one or adjusting a thermostat.

The gesture commands were designed to resemble the corresponding real world actions, so they could provide a more natural interface and be easier to understand and to recall later.

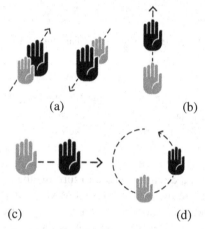

(a)   (b)

(c)   (d)

Fig. 4. Gesture commands: (a) Pushing and pulling; (b) Vertical Sweeping; (c) Horizontal Sweeping; (d) Circular motion

Facebook Interaction

At any given time, while exploring the game terrain, the user can publish a picture with the current game status to the Facebook social network, sharing them with the world. The interface that guides the user through the process is based on the direct interaction mode, where a hoverable Facebook icon is integrated in the interface (figure 2), outside the frame that contains the game terrain. After hovering over the icon the interface moves to a mode similar to the direct interaction mode, where a mirror image of the Kinect RGB camera feed is presented, with a circular progress bar painted over. While the circle fills in the user has time to strike a pose and get ready for the shot. As soon as the circle is fulfilled (Figure 5), a picture is taken and the user is informed that the picture was published in the project DEAP's Facebook wall. In order to send the information to the social network, a Facebook Application was created, and together with the association of the application with the DEAP project Facebook page, access tokens were generated to allow us to publish the pictures directly from the MAID to the DEAP Facebook page photo gallery. This mechanism is implemented using a cURL command that sends the pictures and the corresponding descriptions to the photo gallery, using the generated access token for authentication. The picture is published in the MAID gallery of the DEAP project Facebook page, with a description that reflects the player's current progress in the game, for example (Figure 5):

"Action-shot taken by the MAID: At the time of this picture, the user had optimized the power consumption of the MAID home, in order to save up to 64Kw per month."

Fig. 5. Facebook picture capturing interface

Fig. 6. MAID photo gallery picture

In this case the user had optimized the MAID home in order to save 64Kw per month. After this data is published, the result isn't presented to the user, in order to persuade him to visit the project's Facebook page (figure 6), where he can "like" or even "tag" any picture, exploring the social network graph structure to spread the information and divulge the message behind the MAID.

4   Evaluation

A user study was conducted to evaluate MAID usability, gameplay and effects on users. Twenty six users aged 15-28 (average of 17.5) participated in the evaluation procedures (21 male and 5 female). All of them were familiarized with new technologies.

MAID was deployed on a large event for teenagers, an open day at our University Campus attended by 6000 high-school students. They were free to participate in the MAID evaluation as well as to experiment other activities in the event.

The MAID has three basic factors to take into account for the setup process: space, lighting and audience. Regarding space, the Kinect needs the player to be at least 1.8m away from the sensor and a 1.8m wide area around the player that is clutter free [11]. Concerning the audience, the display system used has to take into account the size of the potential audience, so for a large audience we use a projector, but for a small audience we can use a large wide-screen display. Regarding lighting, regular projectors need low lighting to deliver an acceptable definition and also the Kinect sensor should not be exposed to direct sunlight. For this evaluation study we had enough space and control over lighting conditions, which allowed us to use a projector and get a projection area large enough so that the audience does not need to crowd the user interacting with the MAID. The projector was overhead mounted to maximize the unobstructed area needed for the projection. The Kinect was mounted below the projection screen, and the users were positioned at a minimum distance of 2 meters from the sensor, with about 1.8m radius with no obstruction, allowing freedom of movements. Due to space constraints (other activities were occurring in the same room), audience was kept on the right side of the MAID deploying area.

The test sessions were conducted by two researchers, who played the roles of facilitator and observer. The first one had a more active role, giving an initial briefing and instructions to the participants and providing assistance for any problems that users might face. The second researcher focused on observing the way the tests unfolded, and how users reacted and interacted with the system.

Before starting to use the application, users were informed about the objectives of the test. After a short description of the application and an explanation of the goals to be achieved, users were encouraged to explore MAID. They could do it for as long as they liked, as in a real setting. During the tests the observer took notes of the users' behavior and verbalizations, providing a record of any issues explicitly mentioned by users.

At the end of each test, participants were asked to answer a questionnaire to assert their reactions, gather some personal information and collect their feedback and comments.

4.1   Questionnaire

The questionnaire captured users' personal data, experimental feedback and comments. The first part covered basic personal information like the participant's age, gender, familiarity with new technologies and frequency of use of Microsoft Kinect.

The second group of questions was related with general feedback and usability issues, as well as with the appropriateness of the gestures (figure 8 e 9). Users were asked to rate statements, using a five-point Likert-type scale, which ranged from strong disagreement (1) to strong agreement (5).

The third part of the questionnaire included questions about the users' energy consumption attitudes and how the experience motivated them to change their behavior. The fouth part of the questionnaire was based on the Microsoft "Product Reaction Cards", in order to capture the user's feelings towards the MAID. Users were asked to choose the words that best described their experience while using the application from a list of 20 words, a set that included about 60% of words considered positive and 40% considered negative. The participants could choose any number of words that they deemed adequate to describe their reaction. Finally, the questionnaire also included an open question, in order to gather comments and recommendations regarding future developments of additional features and to obtain a more general evaluation of the system.

4.2 Results and Discussion

Many participants had never used the MS Kinect before (54%), as shown in figure 7, and MAID had took on the rule of introducing them to gesture based interfaces.

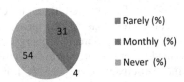

Fig. 7. Kinect usage

Regarding the second group of questions, the results are very positive, as it can be observed in figure 8 and 9. The majority of participants liked to use MAID and found it easy to learn and to use. They considered the feedback and the information provided by the application useful and they were willing to use MAID in public spaces. Observations revealed that users had fun while using MAID and their friends, in the audience, were commenting and giving suggestions.

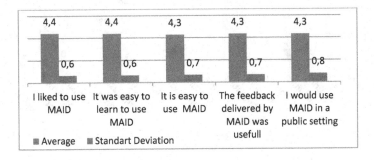

Fig. 8. Summary of results from general feedback and usability

Results regarding the gesture commands were also very positive (figure 9). Participants considered the gestures natural and appropriate to mimic the real action, as well as easy to perform. Horizontal sweep was the gesture that marginally achieved the most positive results.

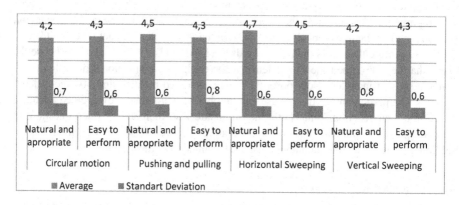

Fig. 9. Summary of results regarding gestures commands

The questionnaire also included questions about the users' energy consumption attitudes and how the experience motivated them to change their behavior. All participants except two, considered that MAID provided them with new useful information and knowledge regarding domestic energy consumption and that their experience using MAID made them aware of the consequences of their appliance usage patterns. Half of the participants were already following some of the MAID suggestions in their everyday lives before the user tests. But most importantly, 50% of the participants reported that they were motivated by MAID to implement the given suggestions, and 46% answered "maybe". So, MAID seems to have a persuasive effect and may potentially influence people to change.

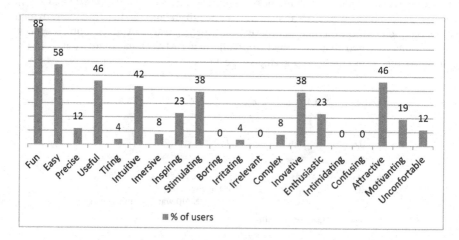

Fig. 10. User experience feedback

From the analysis of question based on the Microsoft "Product Reaction Cards" we concluded that all participants held positive feelings when classifying their experience using the MAID (figure 10), 85% of the users selected the word "Fun", which is an important quality of an application of this kind to be deployed in public spaces. Other positive top selected words were: Easy (58%), Attractive (46%) and Useful (46%). All positive words included in the set were selected by the users, and given the word choice, the users valued the overall look and usability aspects of the application. Even though most of the feedback was positive, some negative words were also selected by only one or two participants: Complex (8%), Tiring (4%) and Irritating (4%).

A few users reported that the hand gesture interface became tiring after a few minutes of interaction. Applications like MAID should not be used for a long time and users must be able to accomplish the game objectives in a few minutes.

The Facebook interface was also well received by the users, but only two participants took individual pictures. Most participants took group pictures with their friends. Fourteen photos were published, but most participants seem to forget to later visit the project Facebook page to check their pictures. A different mechanism must be explored to connect MAID with Facebook, preferentially without requiring users to login to their Facebook account when using MAID.

5   Conclusion and Future Work

This paper presents MAID, an interactive public ambient display system, driven to motivate behavior changes regarding domestic energy consumption, through a persuasive game interface based on gesture recognition technology.

The system was evaluated during a large event for teenagers, an open day at our University Campus attended by 6000 high-school students. Results were very positive. Most participants in the user tests liked to use MAID, found it fun and easy to use and considered that MAID provided them with new useful information regarding domestic energy consumption and that they were motivated to implement the suggestions provided by MAID in their everyday lives. Therefore, MAID seems to have the potential to influence people to change. However, we are aware that further tests need to be conducted in order to measure the persuasive effect of the game in the long term.

According to the evaluation results, the designed gesture commands seem to be appropriate for the purpose and easy to perform.

The Facebook interaction component of MAID would also benefit from some improvements, like giving the user the possibility to confirm or retake a shot, before it is sent to Facebook, or even cancel the whole process without taking any shot. This would increase the usability of this functionality. It also needs a mechanism that would allow the user to link the photograph taken directly to his account. This could be done with a QR code, were the MAID after taking the shot and sending it to Facebook, would generate a unique QR CODE that would link to the picture, so that the user could use a handheld device, such as his mobile phone to open the link and see the picture through his Facebook account.

Acknowledgments. This work is funded by Fundação para a Ciência e Tecnologia (FCT/MEC), Portugal, in the scope of project DEAP (PTDC/AAC-AMB/104834/2008) and by CITI/DI/FCT/UNL (PEst-OE/EEI/UI0527/2011). The authors thank Bárbara Teixeira for her contribution on the graphic design.

References

1. Bang, M., Gustafsson, A., Katzeff, C.: Promoting New Patterns in Household Energy Consumption with Pervasive Learning Games. In: de Kort, Y.A.W., IJsselsteijn, W.A., Midden, C., Eggen, B., Fogg, B.J. (eds.) PERSUASIVE 2007. LNCS, vol. 4744, pp. 55–63. Springer, Heidelberg (2007)
2. Brignull, H., Rogers, Y.: Enticing People to Interact with Large Public Displays in Public Spaces. In: Proc. of INTERACT 2003, Zurich, Switzerland, September 1-5, pp. 17–24 (2003)
3. de Oliveira, R., Cherubini, M., Oliver, N.: MoviPill: Improving Medication Compliance for Elders Using a Mobile Persuasive Social Game. In: Proc. of UbiComp 2010, Copenhagen, Denmark, September 26-29, pp. 251–260. ACM (2010)
4. Dillahunt, T., Becker, G., Mankoff, J., Kraut, R.: Motivating environmentally sustainable behavior changes with a virtual polar bear. In: Proc. of Pervasive 2008 Workshop on Pervasive Technology and Environment Sustainability, Sydney, Australia, May 19-22, pp. 58–62 (2008)
5. Fogg, B.J.: Persuasive Technology: Using Computers to Change What We Think and Do. Morgan Kaufmann Publishers, San Francisco (2003)
6. Fogg, B.J.: A behavior model for persuasive design. In: Proc. of the 4th International Conference on Persuasive Technology, Claremont, USA, April 26-29, pp. 40:1–40:7 (2009)
7. Froehlich, J., Dillahunt, T., Klasnja, P., Mankoff, J., Consolvo, S., Harrison, B., Landay, J.: UbiGreen: Investigating a Mobile Tool for Tracking and Supporting Green Transportation Habits. In: Proc. of CHI 2009, Boston, USA, April 4-9, pp. 1043–1052. ACM Press, New York (2009)
8. Gustafsson, A., Bang, M., Svahn, M.: Power Explorer: a casual game style for encouraging long term behavior change among teenagers. In: Proc. of ACE 2009, Athens, Greece, October 29-31, pp. 182–189. ACM, New York (2009)
9. Hardy, J., Rukzio, E., Davies, N.: Real world responses to interactive gesture based public displays. In: Proc. of the 10th International Conference on Mobile and Ubiquitous Multimedia (MUM 2011), Beijing, China, December 7-9, pp. 33–39 (2011)
10. Jahn, M., Jentsch, M., Prause, C.R., Pramudianto, F., Al-Akkad, A., Reiners, R.: The Energy Aware Smart Home. In: Proc. of FutureTech 2010. IEEE Press, NY (2010)
11. Kinect for XBox 360 (2011), http://www.xbox.com/kinect
12. de Kort, Y.A.W., IJsselsteijn, W.A., Midden, C., Eggen, B., Fogg, B.J. (eds.): PERSUASIVE 2007. LNCS, vol. 4744. Springer, Heidelberg (2007)
13. Laitner, J.A., Ehrhardt-Martinez, K., McKinney, V.: Examining the Scale of the Behaviour Energy Efficiency Continuum. In: European Council for an Energy Efficient Economy Conference, Cote d'Azur, France, June 1-6, pp. 217–223 (2009)
14. Mattern, F., Staake, T., Weiss, M.: ICT for green: how computers can help us to conserve energy. In: Proc. of e-Energy 2010 (2010)
15. Miller, T.M., Rich, P., Davis, J.: ADAPT: audience design of ambient persuasive technology. In: Proc. of CHI EA 2009, pp. 4165–4170. ACM, New York (2009)

16. Reitberger, W., Ploderer, B., Obermair, C., Tscheligi, M.: The PerCues Framework and Its Application for Sustainable Mobility. In: de Kort, Y.A.W., IJsselsteijn, W.A., Midden, C., Eggen, B., Fogg, B.J. (eds.) PERSUASIVE 2007. LNCS, vol. 4744, pp. 92–95. Springer, Heidelberg (2007)

17. Revelle, G., Reardon, E., Mays Green, M., Betancourt, J., Kotler, J.: The Use of Mobile Phones to Support Children's Literacy Learning. In: de Kort, Y.A.W., IJsselsteijn, W.A., Midden, C., Eggen, B., Fogg, B.J. (eds.) PERSUASIVE 2007. LNCS, vol. 4744, pp. 253–258. Springer, Heidelberg (2007)

18. Reeves, B., Cummings, J.J., Anderson, D.: Leveraging the engagement of games to change energy behavior. In: Gamification Workshop at CHI 2011 (2001)

19. Rubegni, E., Memarovic, N., Langheinrich, M.: Talking to Strangers: Using Large Public Displays to Facilitate Social Interaction. In: Marcus, A. (ed.) Design, User Experience, and Usability, Pt II, HCII 2011. LNCS, vol. 6770, pp. 195–204. Springer, Heidelberg (2011)

20. Shoemaker, G., Tang, A., Booth, K.S.: Shadow reaching: a new perspective on interaction for large displays. In: Proc. of UIST 2007, pp. 53–56. ACM, New York (2007)

21. Takayama, C., Lehdonvirta, V., Shiraishi, M., Washio, Y., Kimura, H., Nakajima, T.: ECOISLAND: A System for Persuading Users to Reduce CO2 Emissions. In: Proc. of the 2009 Software Technologies for Future Dependable Distributed Systems (STFSSD 2009), pp. 59–63. IEEE Press, Washington (2009)

22. Vatavu, R.D.: Nomadic Gestures: A Technique for Reusing Gesture Commands for Frequent Ambient Interactions. Journal of Ambient Intelligence and Smart Environments 4(2), 79–93 (2012)

23. Vogel, D., Balakrishnan, R.: Interactive public ambient displays: transitioning from implicit to explicit, public to personal, interaction with multiple users. In: Proc. of the 17th Annual ACM Symposium on User Interface Software and Technology (UIST 2004), pp. 137–146. ACM, New York (2004)

24. Vogel, D., Balakrishnan, R.: Distant freehand pointing and clicking on very large, high resolution displays. In: Proc. of the 18th Annual ACM Symposium on User Interface Software and Technology (UIST 2005), pp. 33–42. ACM, New York (2005)

25. Salvador, R., Romão, T.: Let's move and save some energy. In: Proc. of the 8th International Conference on Advances in Computer Entertainment Technology (ACE 2011), Article 86. ACM, New York (2011)

UBI, The Guardian Dragon:
Your Virtual Sidekick

Rossana Santos[1] and Nuno Correia[2]

[1] CITI, Departamento de Informática
Faculdade de Ciências e Tecnologia, FCT
Universidade Nova de Lisboa
2829-516 Caparica, Portugal
and Escola Superior de Tecnologia de Setúbal
Instituto Politécnico de Setúbal
[2] CITI, Departamento de Informática
Faculdade de Ciências e Tecnologia, FCT
Universidade Nova de Lisboa
2829-516 Caparica, Portugal
rossana.santos@videocitta.com.pt, nmc@fct.unl.pt
http://img.di.fct.unl.pt

Abstract. This paper presents a form of interaction with virtual characters. A virtual character can play the role of a user's sidekick. Sidekicks interact with real and fictional characters helping them to overcome challenges. UBI, the Guardian Dragon, is a virtual sidekick that can help a user explore a space. UBI is part of vuSpot. With vuSpot we aim to design and develop an infrastructure, adaptable to a space that uses existing video cameras networks to provide means for augmenting spaces and supporting interactive experiences. vuSpot has several components, being the interaction with virtual characters one of the most important. With this component we intend to explore new forms of interaction using Augmented Reality and mobile devices. The interaction consists of performing physical actions that are captured on video and are recognized. The reaction of the characters to those actions is superimposed on the video stream that the user will visualize on the mobile device. This action-reaction environment allows a more interesting space exploration and provides means for gaming.

Keywords: Mobile Applications, Augmented Reality, Interaction, Virtual Characters.

1 Introduction

Many real and fictional characters have sidekicks. Doctor Watson is Sherlock Holmes's sidekick since late 1800 but there is also Don Quixote's Sancho Panza, Batman and Robin and Conan O'Brien and Andy Richter among many. Who hasn't dreamt of having a sidekick like these? Sidekicks help the characters develop the plot of a fictional story and contribute to making it more interesting.

A. Nijholt, T. Romão, and D. Reidsma (Eds.): ACE 2012, LNCS 7624, pp. 368–383, 2012.
© Springer-Verlag Berlin Heidelberg 2012

People are more technologically aware than ever. As such we can take advantage of users enjoying to explore new technologies to develop new forms of visiting places. When exploring a space, technology can aid in the quest for finding more information or in making the exploration more fun. Nowadays, new forms of user interaction are emerging that can lead to alternative ways of exploring spaces.

vuSpot provides a virtual sidekick to help the user explore a space. Space exploration can be done by following a certain route or by playing games. The use of wireless networks make it possible for the information captured by a video camera network to be transmitted to mobile devices. This information can be augmented with information related to the space and users, providing means for the user to explore the space and obtain more information about it, which can be filtered by areas of interest.

The virtual sidekick UBI is superimposed on the video stream of the area where the user is located and this stream is sent to the user's mobile device so she can see UBI and where he is virtually at the space. The user interacts with UBI by performing actions around his surroundings. Augmented Reality provides additional information and means to create a virtual environment that meets the user's interests and encourages exploring a space and interacting with it. Users can interact with virtual characters, other users and with virtual and real objects of the space, creating a collaborative environment.

The remainder of this paper is structured as follows. We review related work in Section 2. In Section 3 we discuss the desired characteristics of the sidekick character. In section 4 we describe how interaction with the sidekick can take place. The architecture of the system is explained in Section 5 and a scenario of use is outlined in Section 6. We conduct a user test, based on the "Wizard of Oz" approach, to evaluate interaction with the sidekick in Section 7. Finally, we draw our conclusions and describe future work in Section 8.

2   Related Work

Video streams can be enriched with information relevant to the user or the context, which is chosen according to location, profile and activities. In [2] is presented a survey of technologies used in Augmented Reality and its applications. A video-conferencing system is proposed in [11]. The virtual viewpoint system for the video-conferencing is also used to generate live 3D avatars for collaborative work in virtual environments, for example, a guide in a virtual art gallery.

The virtual characters have to be carefully designed. In the same way as avatars need the user to be able to identify with them [17], the design of a virtual character can obey the same guidelines.

The use of video equipment is becoming increasingly more accessible, often at the expense of purchasing low-resolution video capture equipment which poses difficulties for the recognition of objects and the space. A major challenge faced in this type of systems is the recognition of the space. The use of Microsoft Kinect cameras [8] facilitates the space recognition but the video camera networks we find present at the spaces are traditionally part of the surveillance system and do not use Kinect. In some cases additional cameras have to be installed in specific locations to make sure details are captured and some of these cameras can be Kinect cameras.

The UMass Smart Space [10] combined virtual reality with real video information that is handled locally by the smart-camera, which then communicates the necessary information to the system of virtual reality to mirror the real world. Speed is gained as the bandwidth used is much smaller and the transition between cameras is facilitated.

For virtual and augmented environments, it is essential that the equipment is the least intrusive possible and wireless [12]. In the pioneer project NaviCam [13] the use of PDA with a small built-in camera allows the user to receive more information about the environment, through the recognition of colorful markers placed in the environment. The use of markers for the recognition of the location of the user and points of interest is common [15], but there are situations where it is not desirable to alter the environment and the detection and location is made by using the natural elements present in the space [9].

The use of mobile devices for viewing and manipulating video requires an increased computational capability that most mobile devices do not have. A solution to this problem is to search, in the vicinity of the device, for other suitable machines and use them, opportunistically, to perform the computation instead of the mobile device [3,18].

The POLYMNIA project [1,4] goal is to develop a platform for entertainment in leisure parks. Users visiting the park, register themselves and provide a face and full body photograph. With the use of cameras scattered throughout the park visitors are tracked using cloth and facial recognition techniques. At the end of the visit it is possible to produce a video of the visit by combining the video footage where the visitor was recognized. This techniques can be used to locate a user in a space without the use of a GPS.

The use of the information acquired is a controversial issue even when used by law enforcement agencies and other entities for crime control and it is often alleged to breach the privacy of citizens [7]. This is an issue that may limit the use of the information and has to be carefully thought.

In [5], a study on how to design avatars was conducted, the values for 2D and 3D characters on the "Time to perform a task" and the "Average number of correct answers" have no significative differences. In [14] it is stated that a 3D model is not much more appealing than a 2D model but 2D models should only be used when there is little interaction of the avatar with the environment.

3   The Sidekick Character

A sidekick is a character that is attractive, charismatic and reliable. The user needs to feel comfortable with the sidekick and it should induce a feeling of trust. We created UBI, the Guardian Dragon (Figure 1).

Fig. 1. UBI, the Guardian Dragon

The dragon was chosen because of the image of strength and wisdom it possesses. In the interviews conducted, 69% all of the interviewees responded positively to the use of a dragon (see Figure 13). The interviewees that responded negatively preferred an animal image and none preferred a humanoid character. In the interviews, the qualities most frequently chosen for the sidekick were: happy, nice, colorful and discrete. In fiction writing [6] there are several types of dragons. A Guardian Dragon is considered a playful and curious dragon that likes to observe humans and enjoys their company. They are faithful protectors and have powers that grow as they interact with humans. They are invisible and quiet, except for some moments in which they can be very exuberant making noises and becoming visible to some people. They have a good sense of humor and love pranks. Because of these characteristics the guardian dragon was chosen for the sidekick character.

Dragon characters tend to show some aggressiveness, which is not a good characteristic when we want the user to interact with the character. We chose to make it look childish since it is supposed to inspire happiness and not fear and yet maintain the dragon personality. Dragons come in all kind of colors. The color green was chosen because it is a color associated with calmness and nature (and hope).

The sidekick is not a user avatar so it does not have to follow avatars' design guidelines although some of them can be used as hints to what facilitates interaction [5,14]. As a first approach for the animation we chose a 2D graphics of the dragon. It simplifies the computation and is able to provide the user the necessary information for the tasks. In the future, experiments with 3D dragons will be performed.

4   Interaction

When visiting a space some objects or locations might turn the attention of the visitor, that wishes to find more information about them. A fast way to provide this information is using the visitor personal mobile devices to ask for information and visualize it. Mobile devices can be used to guide a visit, just provide extra information or be a tool to interact with the space and other visitors.

Augmented Reality can be used to give additional high detailed information about the environment. With the creation of virtual objects and virtual characters, the space can be augmented to contain information that might be available in other spaces and that complements it (for example, in other exhibitions). This information has to be superimposed on video so the video cameras network used for surveillance along with other cameras strategically placed can be used to capture the user action and superimpose the reactions. This enlarged video stream is sent to the user mobile device providing the additional information the user is searching. The information given can be adapted to the user age and interests, which must be supplied to the system. The visitor can see her sidekick by visualizing the augmented video stream (see Figure 2 (a)) displayed by the mobile device. These characters might introduce historical or science fiction elements and exist to add extra context to the visit. By performing actions in the surroundings of the sidekick or with the use of the mobile device input capabilities, a visitor can interact with it. The system recognizes those actions, by processing the video stream, and produces a reaction of the sidekick that is superimposed on the video stream and can be visualized on the mobile device (see Figure 2 (b)). A guided tour can be taken by following the instructions of the sidekick and receiving from it additional information about the space and points of interest. Taking such a guided tour has advantages like avoiding crowded points of interest.

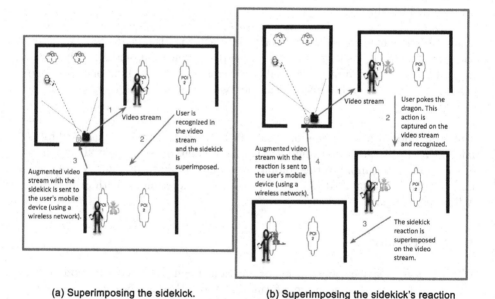

(a) Superimposing the sidekick.   (b) Superimposing the sidekick's reaction to the user's action.

Fig. 2. Interaction

Other information can be superimposed onto the video stream. Additional virtual characters can be found along the tour to give emphasis to the context, for example, how people dressed or how an handcraft was done. A more interactive way of visiting the space is playing a game. The sidekick plays an important role while playing a game. Beside the virtual information available for all visitors, the user can get more information through the sidekick that can give hints that help the visitor to discover hidden details of the space and guide the visitor through the space in the quest for answers to enigmas.

5   vuSpot Architecture

The system is structured as a client-server architecture (see Figure 3). The client is responsible for receiving from the server the augmented video stream and displaying it. It is also responsible for sending to the server the user input and any information from sensors present in the device. Besides communicating with the clients, the server is responsible for the communication with the video cameras surveillance system and the database, that stores all the information needed for the system and contains several modules.

The Information Manager is responsible for gathering, and storing in the database, all information to visualize and information about user requests. The Communications Manager exchanges with the clients all information needed by the system. When a user selects a location to explore, the Positioning Manager finds the cameras with views relevant for the coordinates given and the Video Capture Manager returns references to the video streams of those cameras. The Video Stream Composer composes a video (using the relevant video stream of the location) with additional and relevant information about the space and other users. This information is received from the Detection Module, Overlay Module and Application Logic Manager.

The Detection Module is used to detect other people in the location and their actions, objects of the space and virtual objects and characters. When in the outdoors the information from the user mobile device's GPS can be used along with blob detection and tracking. When no GPS information is available tracking of the user is made by inferring the user position from the video steams using face recognition algorithms and detection and tracking of blobs. This approach is prone to errors. These errors can be overcome with the use of Microsoft Kinect [8] cameras in order to get a notion of depth. The Detection Module also detects user movements. This is necessary for the superimposing of reactions to those movements. The detection of the movements is achieved by calculating optical flow averages at specific locations (for example, in the area where the surroundings of the sidekick intersect the user blob)[1].

The Overlay Module overlays on the video the information relevant for the user visit, like information about sidekicks, points of interest in the space, virtual characters and virtual objects. The Application Logic Manager generates

---

[1] Using openFrameworks with OpenCV and the addon ofxCvOpticalFlowLK from Flightphase.

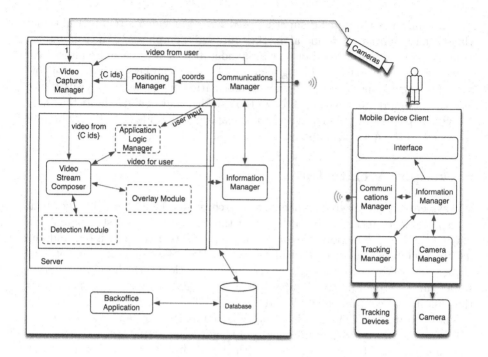

Fig. 3. vuSpot architecture

information about the context, user actions and interaction results. The resulting video is sent to the Communications Manager to be delivered to the client. The client receives the video stream so that the user can visualize her sidekick and other virtual elements present near her location. Interaction can be done by using the input capabilities of the mobile device or by performing actions near the sidekick. This will trigger a reaction to be superimposed on the video stream.

Delivering video streams to mobile devices depends on the speed of the wireless networks and computational power of the mobile device. The video stream adapts to the mobile device capabilities dropping frames if needed. This strategy will lower the performance of the application but will make it possible to use with slower wi-fi networks and mobile devices.

6   Scenario of Use

It is possible to interact with a virtual character, called UBI (Figure 1). UBI is the Guardian Dragon of one of the authors (Rossana). When Rossana is recognized in the video stream, UBI is superimposed (see first image of Figure 4) and very basic forms of interaction are being recognized making UBI react. In the future more complex actions will be possible and UBI can act as a helper, tour guide, mystery solver. To use the system, a visitor, has to be identified through a

Fig. 4. User recognition and superimposing the sidekick. Example of interaction: poking.

pre-registered username. The information about the user interests has to be also provided. When looking at the display of the mobile device, a video stream of the location where the user is will be visualized. This video stream is captured by the video camera network present at the space and augmented with information relevant to the user. In this video stream the user will also visualize her sidekick (see second image of Figure 4).

Interaction can be done by performing movements within the location where the (invisible) sidekick is in the space. Using algorithms to recognize user actions (for example, tapping or waving hello in the surroundings of the sidekick) in the video stream [16], a reaction to those actions can take place (see Figure 5). If the user looks at the display of the mobile device and sees UBI to her left, she can wave at UBI, and he will say "Hello!" and flap his wings. If the user starts moving, UBI can suggest the best route to avoid crowded places. When a user stops near a point of interest, UBI gives more information about it. UBI doesn't like to be poked (or bumped into) (see third image of Figure 4). When this happens he gets anfry and breaths fire. The UBI's reactions can be seen

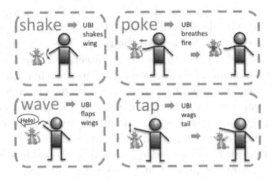

Fig. 5. Examples of interaction with the virtual character UBI, the Guardian Dragon

in the mobile device display also superimposed onto the video stream. Other virtual elements can exist and enhance the visiting experience providing extra information to the visitor. They can give information about themselves or about the space.

7   Evaluation

The goal of this user test is to evaluate how users interact with the virtual character in the proposed video based environment. Participants were asked to visit the simulation of an art gallery and play a word guessing/quiz game. Afterwards they were asked to answer a paper questionnaire regarding the experience of interacting with a virtual character "UBI, The Guardian Dragon" present in the game.

The word to guess was "lollipop". Each POI had an enigma related to that POI for the participant to solve (see Figure 7). If the participant answered the enigma correctly (using the touch functionality of the mobile device to choose her answer from a multiple answer list) she would earn a letter. The goal of the game was to guess or earn all the letters of the word. UBI's role in the game is to show the enigmas, tell the participant if she got the answer right, give hints if she requests it and guide her through the exhibition.

7.1   Participants

The test was conducted with thirteen participants. The participants were three females and ten males with ages ranging from 24 to 42 years old, being the average age 32,2 years. All the participants are used to use mobile phones and eight own smart phones.

7.2   Test Description

The setup of the test simulates a gallery showing an exhibition about famous people. In this gallery there are five Points Of Interest (POIs) scattered throughout the space for the participant to visit: Joan Miró, Don Quixote, Pythagoras, Steve Jobs and Luís Vaz de Camões. Each POI is physically represented by images and text on a wall or object (see Figure 6). The test was conducted following a "Wizard of Oz" approach. Some architecture modules were not used to ensure a stable behavior of the dragon. This means that the actions of the participant are not automatically recognized from the video stream and that the superimposed reaction of the dragon is not done by the system. Instead the reactions of the dragon are triggered by one of the authors while observing the participant. With this test we intended to evaluate if the gestures the participant has to make (see Figure 5) are adequate and comfortable and if interacting with an "invisible" character present at the space would be a good experience.

Fig. 6. Test setup

The participants were also questioned about the characteristics of the virtual character.

We created an iPhone application called "UBI, the Guardian Dragon". This mobile application allows the user to play a puzzle game called "Guess the Word". In the game, the participant has to guess the eight-letter word "lollipop". Each of the four distinct letters is a reward or is guessed by solving enigmas that are provided while visiting the space. In this game there is a virtual character called UBI, which is a guardian dragon. UBI is visualized using the display of the iPhone. When the participant approaches a POI, UBI shows an enigma, which consists of text written on the display of the iPhone (see Figure 7). POIs can be visited in any order. All POIs except Luís Vaz de Camões POI have a puzzle each, one for each distinct letter of the word. The Luís Vaz de Camões POI is the location of the end of the game, so it doesn't have an enigma. When you solve a puzzle, UBI shows a letter. If you do not know the answer and you need a hint you can ask the dragon (see Table 1) by waving at the location he appears to be at the space. The participant has to estimate that location by visualizing UBI in the video stream, being shown in the mobile device, and imagine the virtual character at that location in order to be able to wave correctly. Multiple choice values for the answer are shown at the display of the mobile device and one has to be selected using the touch screen. When the participant discovers the four letters she heads to the final location (POI Luís Vaz de Camões) to get a prize. UBI helps the participant to go to the end (see Table 1) by wagging his tail if she is going on the right direction or breathing fire if not. When UBI wants the

Fig. 7. Visualization of an enigma and reaction to the correct answer

Table 1. Participant's actions and correspondent UBI's reactions

Participant's action	UBI's reaction
wave	shows clue
poke/slap	breaths fire
wrong way/wrong action	breaths fire
correct way/correct action	wags tail

attention of the participant he flaps a wing. If at any point the participant does something that UBI doesn't like he breaths fire and if the user does something he likes (like pet him) he wags his tail.

The equipment used in the test was an iPhone, a 13" MacBook Pro, a Microsoft Kinect camera and a firewire video camera. An ad-hoc wireless network was created for the iPhone and MacBook to communicate with each other.

7.3 Results

In this section we will discuss the results of the user test.

Hints were obtained from UBI by waving at him. Since waving is a common human gesture we wanted to assess if waving would be an adequate gesture for obtaining information from the virtual character. Only 8% of the participants considered that waving for hints was difficult (see Figure 8). 69% considered it easy or very easy and 23% had an average difficulty. We considered that waving can be used for interaction although participants aren't comfortable being seen waving at an invisible being. Not all participants (31%) tried to make UBI angry (see Figure 9). The ones that tried did it by poking or slapping him. We noticed that one of the first reactions of some participants was to try to make him angry. We concluded that a reaction to violence has to be always implemented to indicate to the participants that they are not being nice to the sidekick. 23% considered easy to make UBI angry, 31% had an average difficulty and 15% considered it difficult. 61% of the participants had fun interacting with UBI (see Figure 10). 31% considered it average. Some of these participants did not use all means of interaction with UBI available (see Figure 9) and considered that it

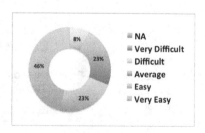

Fig. 8. Question: Is it easy to obtain a hint from UBI?

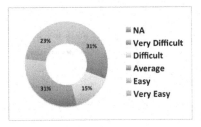

Fig. 9. Question: Is is easy to make UBI angry?

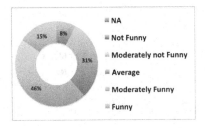

Fig. 10. Question: Is is fun to interact with UBI?

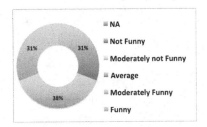

Fig. 11. Question: Is it fun UBI interacting with the user?

would have been funnier if they did. UBI also interacts with the participant. He accomplishes this by breathing fire if the participant is doing something wrong or wagging his tail if the participant is performing a task correctly. 31% of the participants considered it funny, 38% moderately funny and 31% average (see Figure 11). With these results we concluded that interaction with the participant is very important and a big part of the attractiveness of interacting with a virtual character comes from the expectation of it interacting unexpectedly at some point in time. The results show that the large majority of the participants prefer to play the game while interacting with a virtual character (see Figure 12).

Another question asked was "Would you recommend an application with interaction with virtual characters to your friends?". 77% of the participants would recommend it and 23% might recommend. Interaction with virtual characters can be an added value to a game played in a space and participants had a positive reaction towards the concept. We wanted to know if the participants would

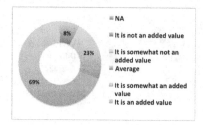

Fig. 12. Question: Is the interaction with UBI an added value to the game?

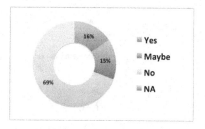

Fig. 13. Question: The virtual Character of the game is a dragon, an imaginary creature. Would you prefer another kind of image?

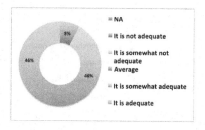

Fig. 14. Question: Is the communication of the enigmas and hints (using text) adequate to the context of the game?

prefer that the character were a different image than a dragon. 69% of the participants consider that a dragon image works well for the purpose (see Figure 13). 15% might prefer a different image and 16% prefer another image. These last participants prefer the image to be of an animal. The communication of the enigmas and hints was done using text that could be read from the display of the mobile device (see Figure 7). Other possibilities like audio could be used. The great majority of the participants consider it adequate or somewhat adequate (see Figure 14). The comments they gave were that if audio was used it would be difficult to memorize the enigmas and hints but it would be helpful to hear them. Another disadvantage would be that the hints could not be images. A mix of both forms of communication appears to be the best solution. Participants were asked if they were willing to carry more devices with different sensors if it would give more functionalities to the application. In this question, opinions

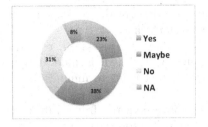

Fig. 15. Question: Are you willing to carry more devices with different sensors if it would give more functionalities to the application?

divide, 31% of the participants are not willing to carry more devices and 23% would (see Figure 15). 28% answered maybe. The most common reason for the rejection or doubt was the size and weigh. If the extra devices could be small and light more users would be willing to use them.

92% of the users considered that the vibration functionality would be a major added value to the interaction and 8% are in doubt. When visiting a space the attention should be focused on the space and points of interest of the space and not on the mobile device. Without a way of getting the attention of the user to the virtual character, participants tend to keep on looking at the display to check if the character is interacting. This action is distracting and has to be avoided.

8   Conclusions and Future Work

The work proposed aims at exploring and developing alternative solutions for interacting with virtual characters.

The computational capacity of the network of computers linked to a video camera network system is used to support the computations needed for the information augmentation that cannot be done by mobile devices.

Augmented information allows the creation of virtual characters providing additional information and means to create a virtual environment that meets the user interests and encourages exploring the space.

Studying how visitors are able to interact with the space, virtual elements and with each other, is one of the main goals of vuSpot. This information will be used to design better interfaces and new forms of interaction.

To make a visit of a space more interactive, games can be played and virtual characters and objects can give hints to guide the visitor to another location in the space and point out interesting details of the space that could not be noticed easily. If playing a game or taking a guided tour, the information given can also depend on the stage the visitor is in.

We evaluated how users perceive interacting with virtual characters. The results showed that the participants are fond of interacting with virtual characters. The words: innovative, fun, easy to use, pleasant and simple were used to describe the experience of using the application to play a game and interact with a virtual character. They also thought that a dragon is an adequate image for a virtual character such as a sidekick.

Although the 2D dragon character meets our requisites, we consider that a 3D model is more appealing. A 3D dragon is under design. We also need to work on the Microsoft Kinect video streams to minimize errors on determining the user location.

There are some issues concerning the frame rate of video streaming to the mobile device. We used the TCP protocol to stream the video frames. In a near future a faster video streamer will be needed.

The applications for this system include gaming, virtual tours, entertainment and education.

Acknowledgments. This work is partly funded by the Fundação para a Ciência e a Tecnologia, Ministério da Educação e da Ciência, Portugal, grant SFRH/BD/46980/2008 of the UT Austin Portugal Program and by the Center for Informatics and Information Technology (CITI), Departamento de Informática (DI), Faculdade de Ciências e Tecnologia (FCT), Universidade Nova de Lisboa. Escola Superior de Tecnologia de Setúbal do Instituto Politécnico de Setúbal.

References

1. Anagnostopoulos, V., Chatzis, S., Lalos, C., Doulamis, A., Kosmopoulos, D., Varvarigou, T., Neuschmied, H., Thallinger, G., Middleton, S.E., Addis, M., Bustos, E., Giorgini, F.: A cross media platform for personalized leisure & entertainment: The polymnia approach. In: AXMEDIS 2006: Proceedings of the Second International Conference on Automated Production of Cross Media Content for Multi-Channel Distribution, pp. 283–290. IEEE Computer Society, Washington, DC (2006)
2. Azuma, R., Baillot, Y., Behringer, R., Feiner, S., Julier, S., MacIntyre, B.: Recent advances in augmented reality. IEEE Computer Graphics and Applications 21(6), 34–47 (2001)
3. Balan, R.K., Gergle, D., Satyanarayanan, M., Herbsleb, J.: Simplifying cyber foraging for mobile devices. In: MobiSys 2007: Proceedings of the 5th International Conference on Mobile Systems, Applications and Services, pp. 272–285. ACM, New York (2007)
4. Beales, R., Middleton, S., Addis, M.: Ambient multi-camera personal documentaries. In: Visual Media Production, IETCVMP (2007)
5. Boberg, M., Piippo, P., Ollila, E.: Designing avatars. In: Proceedings of the 3rd International Conference on Digital Interactive Media in Entertainment and Arts, DIMEA 2008, pp. 232–239. ACM, New York (2008)
6. Conway, D.J.: Dancing with Dragons. Llewellyn Publications (2003)
7. Hempel, L., Topfer, E.: Cctv europe, final report. Centre for Technology and Society, Technical University Berlin, Germany (August 2004)
8. Microsoft (online May 2012) microsoft kinect (2010)
9. Ong, S.K., Yuan, M.L., Nee, A.Y.: Tracking points using projective reconstruction for augmented reality. In: Proceedings of the 3rd International Conference on Computer Graphics and Interactive Techniques in Australasia and South East Asia, GRAPHITE 2005, November 29-December 02, pp. 421–424 (2005)

10. Ou, S., Karuppiah, D., Fagg, A., Riseman, E.: An augmented virtual reality interface for assistive monitoring of smart spaces. In: Proceedings of the Second IEEE Annual Conference on Pervasive Computing and Communications, PerCom 2004, March 14-17, pp. 33–42 (2004)
11. Prince, S., Cheok, A.D., Farbiz, F., Williamson, T., Johnson, N., Billinghurst, M., Kato, H.: 3-d live: real time interaction for mixed reality. In: Proceedings of the 2002 ACM Conference on Computer Supported Cooperative Work, pp. 364–371 (2002)
12. Rasmussen, N., Storring, M., Moeslund, T., Granum, E.: Real-time tracking for virtual environments using scaat kalman filtering and unsynchronized cameras. In: International Conference on Computer Vision Theory and Applications (VISAPP) (February 2006)
13. Rekimoto, J., Nagao, K.: The world through the computer: computer augmented interaction with real world environments. In: Proceedings of ACM UIST 1995, November 15-17, pp. 29–36 (1995)
14. Wagner, D., Billinghurst, M., Schmalstieg, D.: How real should virtual characters be? In: Proceedings of the 2006 ACM SIGCHI International Conference on Advances in Computer Entertainment Technology, ACE 2006. ACM, New York (2006)
15. Wagner, D., Schmalstieg, D.: First steps towards handheld augmented reality. In: Proceedings of the Seventh IEEE International Symposium on Wearable Computers, October 18-21, pp. 127–135 (2003)
16. Wren, C., Azarbayejani, A., Darrell, T., Pentland, A.: Pfinder: real-time tracking of the human body. Transactions on Pattern Analysis and Machine Intelligence 19(7), 780–785 (1997)
17. Yang, J.: e-race: Avatars, anonymity and the virtualization of identity (March 2011) (online May 2012)
18. Yang, K., Ou, S., Chen, H.-H.: On effective offloading services for resource-constrained mobile devices running heavier mobile internet applications. IEEE Communications Magazine 46(1), 56–63 (2008)

Construction of a Prototyping Support System for Painted Musical Instruments

Yoshinari Takegawa[1], Kenichiro Fukushi[2], Tod Machover[3], Tsutomu Terada[4], and Masahiko Tsukamoto[5]

[1] Future University Hakodate, Japan
`yoshi@fun.ac.jp`
[2] Tokyo Institute of Technology, Japan
`fukushi@media.mit.edu`
[3] MIT Media Lab, USA
`tod@media.mit.edu`
[4] Kobe University /Japan PRESTO, Japan Science and Technology Agency
`tsutomu@eedept.kobe-u.ac.jp`
[5] Kobe University
`tuka@kobe-u.ac.jp`

Abstract. Recently there have been many works of research and products which make use of electronic and information technology to equip a piece of paper with interactive functions. Examples include picture books which output animal noises, and the use of electric circuits drawn on paper, in conductive ink, to facilitate the output of light and sound. However, these technologies do not have a function that enables customization of the output that is linked to an input interface. The instrument's sound is composed of various kinds of tone and pitch and the effect of a single note is different from that of chords and melody. When users are designing a painted musical instrument they find out problems with the instrument and then discuss and test the design using the customize function, which selects and outputs the sound of the instrument. Therefore, the goal of our study is to construct a prototyping support system for painted musical instruments. By drawing shapes on the paper with conductive ink users create input interfaces to which they can then assign different sounds flexibly and intuitively.

1 Introduction

Recently there have been many works of research and products which make use of electronic and information technology to equip a piece of paper with interactive functions. Examples include picture books which output animal noises, and the use of electric circuits drawn on paper[1,2], in conductive ink, to facilitate the output of light and sound. Integrating interactive functions and the physical environment, such as a piece of paper, some fabric or a wall, enhances our capacity for self-expression. It enables us to comment on our experience of life, our situation and even our dreams. However, these technologies do not provide the option to customize the output which is linked to an input interface, referred to as a switch in this paper.

A. Nijholt, T. Romão, and D. Reidsma (Eds.): ACE 2012, LNCS 7624, pp. 384–397, 2012.

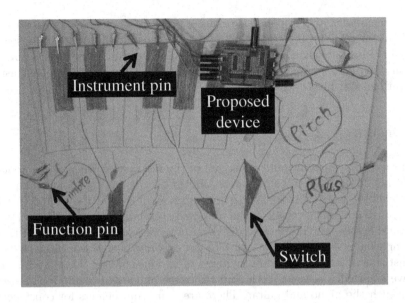

Fig. 1. A snapshot of the proposed system

Users design a musical instrument by drawing their own design on a piece of paper which is wired to a device that will produce the sound of the instrument. The user can refine the sound of the instrument through a process of trial and error. The instrument's sound is composed of various kinds of tone and pitch and the effect of a single note is different from that of chords and melody. When users are designing a painted musical instrument they locate problems with the instrument and then discuss and test the design using the customize function, which allows them to alter configurations of the instrument such as pitch and tone.

There are some general-purpose devices used in physical computing which have a sensor board that connects sensors, switches and sliders. These devices are good tools for enabling customization of painted musical instruments. However, users are required to design an electric circuit, program the action of the microcomputer and prepare switches of various different shapes. Conventional general-purpose devices have difficulty meeting these requirements and responding flexibly to change.

Therefore, the goal of our study is to construct a prototyping support system for painted musical instruments.

Users can create various kinds of musical instrument with the proposed system, as shown in Figure 1. When the user touches the piano and leaf that are drawn on the paper, the sound is output. Tone and pitch can be altered by touching different fruits. By drawing shapes on the paper with conductive ink, users create input interfaces to which they can then assign different sounds flexibly and intuitively.

The remainder of this paper is organized as follows: section 2 describes the design of the prototyping system, section 3 explains its implementation, section 4 explains our evaluation and discusses the results, section 5 describes actual use, section 6 explains related work, and finally section 7 describes our conclusions and outlines our future work.

2 Design

The proposed system outputs the sound of the instrument when a user touches the design drawn on a piece of paper. Additionally, it has a customize function, which enables users to alter the instrument's sound, so that they can create the kind of instrument they desire. The proposed system is intended for use by one or several people who design and discuss a musical instrument as part of home-work or as a personal work of art. The process involves drawing the shape of the instrument and then adding switches of various shapes. Users are assumed to have knowledge of tone, pitch, and the usage of conventional musical instruments such the piano and guitar. There are four requirements for constructing a prototyping system which are listed below:

(i) Diversity: To make switches of varying shapes and sizes
There are not only rectilinear switches but also artistic curvilinear switches on a painted musical instrument. Users draw various kinds of switches in the beginning stage of creating a painted musical instrument. Therefore, the system must enable the switches to function as input interfaces on the painted musical instrument. Additionally, the system must be able to work with various kinds of switch.

(ii) Adaptability: To add, remove, or adjust switches and alter the sound assigned to the switches quickly and intuitively
As many creative ideas arise in the prototyping stage, the shape of the switches and the mapping between a switch and its sound will be altered several times. Additionally, to allow creative freedom, it is important that users are able to edit the switches quickly and intuitively. In this way, users can create higher quality and more refined painted musical instruments through a continuing process of trial and error.

(iii) Seamless change: To alternate between the allocation of switches and drawing of the musical instrument seamlessly
As the design of the switches is important to the appearance of the painted musical instrument, it is most practical to design the switches and the main body of the instrument simultaneously. Therefore, it is vital that users are able to switch easily between allocating switches and drawing the musical instrument.

(iv) Situation independence: Being able to use the system in any situation
Ideas arise in various situations, not only when users are working on the design of a painted musical instrument at home or in the office, but also when doing

everyday activities such as commuting, cooking or cleaning. In order that users can test out ideas as they arise, the system must be able to be used anytime and anywhere, regardless of situation.

2.1 Consideration of the Input Interface

Conventional input interfaces such as buttons and sensors have difficulty responding to design alterations flexibly. Therefore, to satisfy the need for diversity (i), our system utilizes conductive ink to make input interfaces. Parts painted with conductive ink act as the antenna of a capacitive sensor, and they are activated like digital buttons. Pencil, black paint, LessEMF CuPro-Cote[3] and Y-SHIELD HSF54[4] can all be used like conductive ink.

Pencil is a highly flexible medium. An object drawn lightly with a pencil has high resistance, and it does not work as an antenna, but an object drawn thickly with a pencil has low resistance, and it works as an antenna. Additionally, when using pencil, users are able to change the design of switches flexibly, as it is easy to alter or remove them with an eraser. These features satisfy the requirements relating to adaptability and seamless change which were mentioned earlier. CuPro-Cote and HSF54 have superior conductivity. Users are able to paint over switches that have been painted with CuPro-Cote or HSF54 in advance, with all-purpose paint, which is useful when it comes to finalizing the design of a painted musical instrument.

2.2 The Creation Process of a Painted Musical Instrument

The creation process of a painted musical instrument is as follows:

1. Drawing the desired design
2. Painting the switches of the musical instrument with conductive ink
3. Using connecting pins, which the proposed device provides, to create a bridge between the drawn switches and an electric circuit, which is part of the device and which calculates capacitance as shown in Figure 1.
4. Mapping the sound of the instrument to the pins
5. Touching a switch to output sound

The proposed system is very simple to use. The system is able to output sound from a switch of any shape or size and because users create switches simply by drawing shapes onto paper no knowledge of electronics is needed. Furthermore the only materials required, besides the proposed device, are paper and conductive ink.

However, users cannot control the volume of sound from a painted musical instrument dynamically because of limitation of a capacitance sensor. Painted musical instruments cannot give tactile feedback to users in the same way that pressing a piano key or twanging a string can.

Table 1. List of the function pins

Name	Explanation
Plus Pin	Incrementation of the pitch by a value of one
Minus Pin	Decrementation of the pitch by a value of one
Pitch Pin	To set pitch
Octave Pin	To set octave
Tone Pin	To set tone
Volume Pin	To set volume
Group Pin	To create a group
Keyboard Pin	To create a keyboard
String Pin	To create a stringed instrument
Percussion Pin	To create a percussion instrument
Copy&Paste Pin	To copy and paste the assigned sound of a pin to a different pin
Recording Pin	To record the sound of several pins and assign it to one pin

2.3 Mapping Method

The proposed system has a wide range of instrumental sounds, which is composed of a lot of tones and pitches, allowing users to create various painted musical instruments. Mapping between the instrument's sound and the switches must be completed with only the proposed device to satisfy the requirements for situation independence (iv). However, the number of pins which is equipped with the proposed device is limited and the sole output interface is a speaker to output audio. Therefore, to satisfy the adaptability requirements (ii) despite the limitations of the system, we propose flexible and intuitive methods of mapping between the switches and sounds of the instrument.

The proposed device has two types of pin: an instrument pin connected to a switch for outputting sound, and a function pin for the mapping of an instrument pin as shown in Table 1). A user can draw switches for not only an instrument pin but also a function pin as shown in Figure 1. Additionally, the proposed system has a unique sound effect for each function pin to enable the user to recognize the activation of the function. The default setting of all the instrument pins is that the instrument setting is piano and the pitch is Middle C, which has a MIDI note value of 60.

Adjustment Method

To alter the pitch of a switch, a user connects the *Pitch Pin* to the switch. When the user taps the *Plus/Minus Pin* while holding the *Pitch Pin*, the pitch increases or decreases by a value of one as shown in Figure 2(a). Furthermore, the pitch of multiple switches is altered at the same time by connecting the *Pitch Pin* to the switches as shown in Figure 2(b). The user can alter the octave, tone or volume of

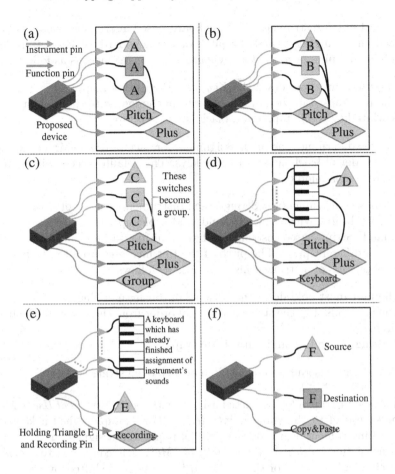

Fig. 2. Examples of function pins

a switch in the same way as that of pitch setting with the *Octave/Tone/Volume Pin*. In regard to setting of multiple switches, there are two possible methods, one which constructs a physical connection and one which constructs a virtual connection. When the user taps switches while pressing the *Group Pin*, the switches become a group. The operation of a switch which belongs to a group is applied to all the switches which belong to the group as shown in Figure 2(c).

This method is simple, but it may take a lot of time to assign a desired sound to a switch.

Musical Instrument Usage Method

The *Musical Instrument Usage Method* mimics the playing of traditional musical instruments such as the piano, guitar and drum. This allows users to create painted musical instruments that resemble traditional instruments. The method for creating a traditional-style musical instrument using the proposed system is as follows:

[Keyboard-based Instruments]   A keyboard-based instrument consists of a row of black and white keys, and the pitch of the keyboard increases from left to right. The mapping process of a keyboard-based instrument is as follows:

1. The user must hold down the *Keyboard Pin* during mapping.
2. The user must tap the keys in order from the lowest to the highest pitch.
3. A white key is one tap, and a black key is two taps.

The system determines the pitch assignment for each pin/key pair automatically from the order of black keys and white keys. The default voice is piano and the default octave is middle C.

[String-based Instruments]   String-based Instruments consist of a fret on which users control pitch with their left hand, and a pickup which is played with the right hand. String-based instruments have multiple strings, and each string is assigned a different pitch. The pitch of the fret increases from top to base. The mapping process of a stringed instrument is as follows:

1. The user must hold down the *String Pin* during mapping.
2. The user must tap the strings or frets in order from the lowest to the highest pitch.
3. A string is one tap, and a fret is two taps.

The default voice is guitar and the pitch of each open string is "E(52)", "A(57)", "D(62)", "G(67)", "B(71)" by default.

A musical instrument constructed using the *Musical Instrument Usage Method* can make use of to the *Adjustment Method*. For example, when a key of the keyboard instrument drawn on the piece of paper and assigned an instrument's sound using the *Musical Instrument Usage Method* is connected to *Pitch Pin*, the pitch of all the keys of the keyboard instrument is shifted by tapping the *Plus Pin* while holding the *Pitch Pin* as shown in Figure 2(d). Moreover, when the user connects Switch D to a key to which sound has already been assigned, as shown in Figure 2(d), the pitch of Switch D becomes the same as that of the key connected to it.

A user needs basic drawing skills and knowledge of the structure of the musical instrument in the *Musical Instrument Usage Method*. However, the user easily and intuitively understands how to adjust the instrument's sound.

Recording Method

With the *Recording Method*, a user can create an original sound source using switches to which sound is already assigned, and then assign that sound to other switches. This method enables the user to assign not only a single note but also chords and musical phrases.

To use the *Recording Method*, the user must hold down the *Recording Pin* and then press the new switch (a triangle E in Figure 2(e)) to which the user wants to assign the original sound source. The user is free to press any switch to which sound is already assigned as shown in a keyboard in Figure 2(e). When the user

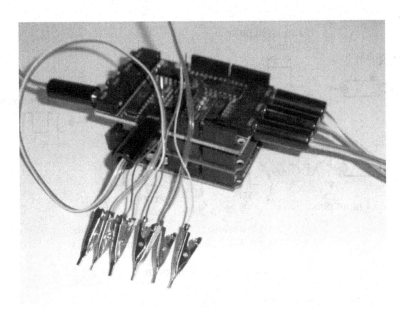

Fig. 3. Prototype device

releases the *Recording Pin* and the new switch, the system assigns the recorded sound to the new switch.

Copy&Paste Method

Copy&Paste Method is a function which assigns the sound of one switch to that of another switch.

To use the *Copy&Paste Method*, the user first presses the source switch, which is the switch that they want to copy the sound of (Triangle switch F in Figure 2(f)). After that the user presses destination switch, which is the switch that they want the sound to be copied to (Rectangle switch F in Figure 2(f)). In this way, the sound of the source switch is copied to the destination switch.

3   Implementation

We implemented a prototype of the prototyping system for painted musical instruments, as described in Section 2[1]. Figure 3 is a snapshot of the prototype device. We used an Arduino Uno as a microcomputer for the prototype device, and a Musical Instrument Shield[5] to produce sound. This shield includes 189 instrumental voices such as piano, woodwind, brass and percussion, and the shield is also capable of playing up to 127 pitches in melodic instruments. We developed an original electric circuit module to calculate capacitance as shown

---

[1] A demonstration video has been uploaded to
http://www.youtube.com/watch?v=oXgKFfHfl8s

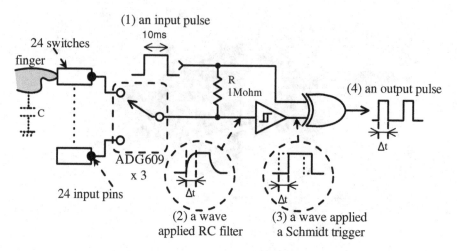

Fig. 4. Circuit diagram

in Figure 4. This module can be mounted onto the Arduino Uno directly, like the Musical Instrument Shield. The body size of the prototype device is 3" (W) by 2.2" (L) by 1" (D) inch, and the body weight is 10oz. There are various types of input pin, such as alligator clips, paper clips, pin badges, press-studs and magnet clips, as shown in Figure 5.

The capacitance module has a RC Low-pass filter which utilizes human capacitance, and calculates the value of capacitance based on reply of an input pulse. A rectangular wave shown in Figure 4(1) changes to a rectangular wave which has a time delay of Δt. The time delay of Δt becomes longer when a user touches a switch. To calculate the delay of Δt, the wave (2) is reformed by passing a Schmidt trigger circuit, and the pulse with width of Δt is made through an exclusive OR gate between wave (1) and wave (2). The capacitance value of each switch is calculated by time-sharing with an analog switch (ADG609).

The electric current that passes through the human body when using our proposed device is up to 5uA. The user does not feel electrical stimulation, since the minimum current that the human body can sense is 0.2mA (60Hz)[14].

4   Evaluation

We conducted a simple evaluative experiment to assess the usability of the proposed mapping methods with the exception of the *Recording Method*. This is because we had not yet finished implementation of the *Recording Method* when we conducted the evaluative experiment. We used a test group of eight people, all of whom are university students in their early 20s who have played the piano and the guitar for over three or four years, and thus have knowledge of musical instruments. First of all, we explained the usage of the mapping methods.

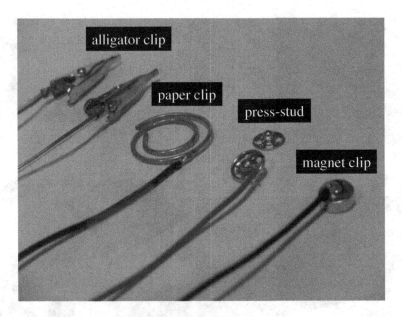

Fig. 5. Various kinds of input pins

Next, the testers drew their desired picture and assigned their favorite sounds to the switches using the mapping methods. We did not set a time limit for this evaluative experiment, and we instructed the testers to try and give equal use to each of the mapping methods. We asked the questions shown in Table 2 after the testers had finished creating their painted musical instrument.

Table 2 shows the average result for each question. The results show that all the mapping methods are very easy to use. Furthermore, the testers were satisfied with the assignment of the instrument's sound. However, we have to reduce the delay of the output sound. One tester commented after the evaluation that, especially when she played an arpeggio composed of three or four notes with the painted musical instrument that she had made, she found it sounded awkward because of the delay of the output sound.

The test group created highly original painted musical instruments. On one instrument a musical scale was output from the ears of cute characters, and on

Table 2. The questionnaires and the results

Item	Result
Did you find *Adjustment* easy to use?	4.8
Did you find *Musical Instrument Usage* easy to use?	4.2
Did you find *Copy&Paste* easy to use?	4.8
Were you able to create your desired sound?	4.6
Did you notice any sound delay?	1.9

All answers are Based on a rating scale of one to five, where one is "NO" and five is "YES".

Fig. 6. Snapshot at the exhibitions

another each circle of a polka-dot dress output a note of a different tone and pitch. All the testers commented that they could realize their desired designs due to our customize function.

5   Actual Use

We created the painted musical instruments shown in Figure 6 by using the prototype system. The designs are a huge piano, a guitar held by a cat and a tambourine held by a frog. The design and the usage of these painted musical instruments are similar to those of conventional musical instruments. We also created a painted musical instrument of new design. This instrument had a function that enabled conventional staff notation. When the user touches a black line, an area in the middle of the black lines, or an area of cloud, the appropriate sounds are output based on the rules of staff notation. There are wires on the back of the painted musical instrument, and users are able to affix stars which have tiny magnets and whose role is musical notation. The starts are held on by magnetic power. When users tap the stars, sound is output.

We have exhibited these painted musical instruments three times in the *Boston Children's Museum* and once in the *Elizabeth Seton Residence*.

The mapping of these painted musical instruments was completed with the *Musical Instrument Usage Method* described in Section 2.3. Visitors to the exhibitions, especially children, were able to enjoy playing these painted musical instruments without instruction because the usage method is the same as that of conventional musical instruments. The staff of the Boston Children's Museum passed on comments such as "Children liked the animal design, and this helped maintain their interest and relax them." Furthermore, in regard to old people, some had given up playing acoustic musical instruments as their muscles had become too weak, but they enjoyed playing the painted musical instruments since they could use them with only a light touch action.

On the other hand, there was a problematic delay between inputting action and outputting sound on the guitar instrument. This is because children often thrummed multiple strings on the guitar instrument but the prototype system has difficulty detecting multiple touches over a short time. As a result of this some children were dissatisfied with the lack of output sound. Fortunately, the delay problem can be solved by using a higher quality micro computer and by increasing the number of detectors on the string part.

6   Related Work

Capacitance Sensor

SmartSkin[6], Theremin, Freqtric Drum[7] are all examples of interactive systems which have a capacitance sensor. SmartSkin recognizes multiple hand positions and their shapes using a mesh-shaped antenna which calculates capacitance, but this does not have a mapping function because this is just an input interface. Thermin controls the pitch and volume of sound using distance calculation between two antennas, one of which is Thermin and the other the hands of the user. This system outputs a single note and does not have a function that assigns sound to multiple antennas. Freqtric Drum is an electronic musical instrument which uses Body- to-body contact, and thus enhances communication between users, but does not consider the mapping of sound as well. The above systems cannot facilitate the creation and alteration of original switches of various shapes and sizes.

In contrast, our proposed system enables the creation of a wide range of switches by using conductive ink. Furthermore, we proposed various kinds of flexible mapping methods between the switches and the sound of the instrument. However, the usage of the proposed device became more difficult than that of the aforementioned devices. Therefore, it is important to create a more highly intuitive m apping method.

Conductive Ink

DrawSound[8], DrawDio[9] , PaperPiano[1], and ElectronicOrigami[2] are interactive systems which use conductive ink. DrawSound and DrawDio transforms the electrical resistance of drawing onto a piece of paper with a regular pencil or pastel into a musical note. Several kinds of switch can be made using them, but the output sound depends on the resistance of the drawn switches. In our proposed device, the size and shape of a switch are independent of its output sound. PaperPiano and ElectronicOrigami use electronic circuits drawn in conductive ink on a piece of paper, and switch mechanisms made from folded paper. Users can make various kinds of switch, but the mapping method between the switches and the sound of the instruments is not flexible. As a result of this, creation becomes restricted.

Optics Sensor

Twinkle[10] and LiveScribe Pulse Smartpen[11] are examples of systems that output sound by using an optics sensor to recognize objects drawn on a piece of paper. Twinkle reads various kinds of mark, which may be of different colors, using an optics sensor, and represents each note by a different color. This approach lacks scalability because the number of available colors is limited so that the system can acquire high color recognition accuracy.

Pulse Smartpen combines Anoto Digital Pen[12], which has a function that recognizes drawn objects using a camera, and is capable of sound recording reproduction. The sound of the piano is output according to Smartpen's instructions meaning that it is difficult for users to make original switches which do not follow the instructions.

Tablet

UPIC[13] is a computerized musical composition tool, and represents sound using objects drawn on a tablet. This system allows users to create various kinds of switches and mapping methods with a touchscreen, but it is difficult to combine it with real world materials such as paper.

7   Conclusions

We constructed a prototyping system for painted musical instruments. The proposed system allows users to draw various kinds of switches using conductive ink, and to assign drawn switches to the instrument's sound intuitively. The results of evaluative experiments confirmed that the proposed mapping methods are useful and intuitive.

Future work will focus on the implementation of sound effects, control structures of conditional expressions and loops.

Acknowledgments. This research was supported in part by a Grant-in-Aid for Scientific Research for Young Scientists(B) (21700198) from the Japanese Ministry of Education, Culture, Sports, Science and Technology. We thank Ms. Mao Matsuda for drawing and painting various pretty painted musical instruments.

References

1. Paper and Conductive Ink Piano, http://www.flickr.com/photos/t_kondo/4725281301/
2. Electronic Origami, http://makeprojects.com/pdf/make/guide_150_en.pdf
3. LessEMF CuPro-Cote, http://www.lessemf.com/292.html
4. Y-SHIELD HSF54, http://www.yshield.eu/en/shielding-paints/HSF54
5. Web Site of Musical Instrument Shield, http://www.sparkfun.com/products/10587
6. Fukuchi, K., Rekimoto, J.: Interaction Techniques for SmartSkin. In: Proc. of the ACM Symposium on User Interface Software and Technology (2002)
7. Tetsuaki, B., Taketoshi, U., Tomimatsu, K.: Freqtric drums: a Musical Instrument that Uses Skin Contact as an Interface. In: Proc. of the 7th International Conference on New Interfaces for Musical Expression, pp. 386–387 (2007)
8. Kazuhiro, J.: DrawSound: a Drawing Instrument for Sound Performance. In: Proc. of the 2nd International Conference on Tangible and Embedded Interaction, pp. 59–62 (2008)
9. Silver, J.S., Rosenbaum, E.: Gifts for Intertwining with Modern Nature. In: Proc. of the 9th International Conference on Interaction Design and Children, pp. 340–343 (2010)
10. Silver, J.S., Rosenbaum, E.: Twinkle: Programming with Color. In: Proc. of the 4th International Conference on Tangible, Embedded, and Embodied Interaction, pp. 383–384 (2010)
11. LiveScribe, http://livescribe.com/
12. Anoto Digital Pen, http://www.anoto.co.jp/start.aspx
13. UPIC, http://en.wikipedia.org/wiki/UPIC
14. Bernstein, T.: Electrical shock hazards and safety standards. IEEE Transactions on Education 34(3), 216–222 (1991)

Reflex-Based Navigation by Inducing Self-motion Perception with Head-Mounted Vection Display

Tomohiro Tanikawa, Yuma Muroya, Takuji Narumi, and Michitaka Hirose

Graduate School of Information Science and Technology, The University of Tokyo
{tani,yuma,narumi,hirose}@cyber.t.u-tokyo.ac.jp

Abstract. Currently, many AR/MR researches and applications are based on visual information presentation with narrow field of view HMD. For example, some AR/MR systems navigate users by showing visual information signs or notification messages as needed. However, these information presentations occlude user's limited field of view with HMD and bother user's primary activities. In this study, we proposed a novel approach to navigate users by using user's inconscientious reflex motion with novel type of HMD. First, we construct Head-mounted Vection Display (HMVD) to induce self-motion perception (Vection) by presenting optical flow on peripheral vision. Next, we evaluate this effect of induced self-motion perception by observing user's walking behaviour with HMVD. The results indicate the proposed approach have possibility of automatic navigation without user's awareness and recognition.

Keywords: Vection, Self-motion Perception, Reflex movement, Head-mounted Display.

1   Introduction

In urban areas, people see huge amount of signage, signs and announcements without looking. Once someone wants to go elsewhere, he/she find proper signage from them and decide his/her action after recognizing its meaning. This process caused the stressful task in large and complex urban area. Mobile/portable devices such as smart phone provide navigation services which showing proper information according user's position and destination[1]. And many AR/MR systems are proposed to navigate user more intuitively by overlaying direction such as arrows on user's view[2]. However, these cues require user's reorganization and decision process and sometimes bother user's thinking and communication to promote awareness.

To reduce such user's stress under navigation system, many kinds of multi-modal displays are proposed. Most popular approach is utilization of haptic sensation. Many researcher proposed hand-held or wearable haptic device signals the user the directions by presenting vibration or inertial force [3-5]. Amemiya et al.[6] proposed pulling sensation device which can navigate as if someone pulls user's hand in the certain direction. However, force and tactile feedback are the main sensory inputs and these devices prevent user's main task such as talking, thinking and etc.

A. Nijholt, T. Romão, and D. Reidsma (Eds.): ACE 2012, LNCS 7624, pp. 398–405, 2012.

To overcome this disadvantage of such devices, several devices which elicit user's movement unconsciously are proposed. Maeda et al.[7] has proposed galvanic vestibular stimulation which stimulates the vestibular organs electrically to affect the user's sense of balance (vestibular sensation) for walking navigation. Kojima et al.[8] proposed portable ear-pulling device which can influence walking direction. Narumi et al. [9] proposed thermal feedback as a new channel for the transmission of imaginary characteristics.

To convey proper direction without user's awareness and recognition, AR/MR system should avoid occupying user's mainly used sensations like above mentioned approaches. In this aspect, we focus on peripheral vision as frontier for AR/MR application.

2   Reflex-Based Navigation

2.1   Vection (Self-motion Perception)

In this paper, we propose a method to navigate unconsciously by applying visual illusion. Illusion is inducted with perception process of brain. There are many visual illusions found by cognitive psychologists. Vection illusion is one of visual illusion which is induced self-motion perception visually. When the brain perceives visual motion without sufficient other cues, the brain adapted the cue as body motion.

The visual motion, called optical flow in vision field, we experience as a result of walking, running, or driving is a powerful signal to control the parameters of our own movement [10,11]. People modify their walking speed depending on optical flow. In stationary subjects optic flow induces the illusory feeling of self-movement and causes motion sickness after prolonged exposure.

In virtual reality field, many researchers have evaluated and utilized this illusion and the kinesthetic feedback. Lishman et al. [12] has demonstrated that vision is more dominant than somatic sensation with respect to controlling one's physical posture. Maeda et al. [13] have evaluated relationship between the vection produced by optical flow and that created by galvanic vestibular stimulation by measuring strength of body sway. Properly coordinated with visually produced vection can suppress motion sickness and enhance the VR experience without an expensive motion platform [14,15,16].

2.2   Our Approach

Vision provides a major source of information for the control of self-movement. Vection is important for recognizing relationship between own body and environment, and is important for controlling own posture and planning bodily motion. Furukawa et al. [17] proposed "Vection Filed" which is expected to influence walking direction as a type of intuitive walking guidance that requires no attaching or removing of any devices.

Our concept is visually augmentation of such self-motion perception on peripheral vision (Fig. 1). By using large screen or immersive display technology, researcher can present controlled visual stimulation and can evaluate the visually produced vection on both central and peripheral visual fields of view [18-21]. Results indicated that optical flow presented on peripheral vision have influence on vection.

By developing head-mounted vection display (HMVD) as shown in figure 1, the display can provide different self-motion stimulus simultaneously on both central and peripheral visual fields of user while walking in real environment. In this paper, we evaluate the influence of visually produced vection on user's walking behavior, in particular walking speed (section 3) and walking directions (section 4).

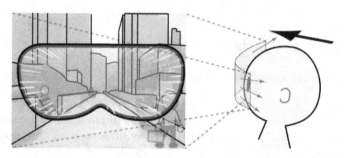

Fig. 1. Induction of self-motion perception with head-mounted vection display (HMVD)

3   Preliminary Experiment 1: Induction on Walking Speed

Based on this concept, we developed prototype system of HMVD with smart phone devices. By mounting two smart phone (Apple iPhone) on helmet as shown in Fig. 2, user can see directly on central visual field and receive generated visual stimuli simultaneously on peripheral visual field.

In preliminary experiment, we focus on relationship between walking speed and vection. As shown in Fig. 2, stripes come up to user's face smoothly. From user's viewpoint, stripes looks like edge on corridor wall. Thus, moving speed of stripes on iPhone screen is determined by distance between corridor wall and user's eyes as shown in Figure 3. Because the corridor, as experimental space, is 3 [m] width and subjects walk the center of the corridor in this experiment. For instance, when subject's walking speed is 1.5 [m/s] and presented optical flow speed is 7.5 [cm/s], user perceive synchronously self-motion stimulus on both central and peripheral vision.

We investigated how walking speed would change when the speed of the visual flow shown to a peripheral vision was changed.   In each trial, subjects walk along 50 [m] distance wearing the prototype HMVD which show still striped image or the visual flow of a speed selected out of five speed at random, 2.5[cm/s], 3.3[cm/s], 5.0[cm/s], 7.5[cm/s], 10[cm/s]. By measuring the time required for walking every 10m, we evaluated the influence of visually produced vection on subject's walking speed. The measurement was performed a total of 15 times at every 3 times of each

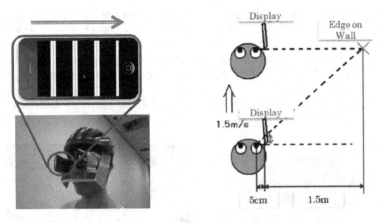

Fig. 2. Prototype 1 of HMVD for changing walking speed

speed, and five steps of speed. Also we measured the time required when still image was shown on the HMVD between intervals of each trial.

There was no definitely relationship between subjects' walking speed and presented visual flow speed. However, there was change of walking speed by presenting visual cue for perceiving vection. Thus, the proposed approach cannot control of walking speed, but have a possibility of changing walking speed induced by optical flow presentation.

4   Preliminary Experiment 2: Induction on Walking Directions

4.1   Experimental Setup

In next experiment we evaluate effectiveness of vection to walking direction, because illusionary self-rotation is more powerful [16,17]. In previous experiment, when iPhone which present optical flow are arranged obliquely downward to user's face, user perceives vection more effectively. Thus, we constructed prototype 2 of HMVD as shown in Fig. 4.

For this experiment, we generated six types of visual flow as shown in Fig. 5. These patterns are classified with two groups, random-dotted pattern and striped pattern as visual stimuli. In each group, we prepare three motion pattern, a going-straight flow, a flow from the forward right to the left rear, and a flow from the forward left to the right rear. These patterns are rendered random dots or straight lines located on the floor from subjects' viewpoint height as 3D patterns. When participants see through iPhone screen presented these patterns, they feel as if they walk straight, rightward and leftward on dot or stripe patterned floor.

To evaluate the influence of visually produced vection on user's walking directions, we investigated how the direction where a subject avoids an obstacle would change, when visual flow was changed.

Subjects reciprocated between two turn-around points 10 [m] distance wearing the prototype HMVD as shown in Fig. 5. In each trial, subject walk toward an obstacle from a starting line and avoid the obstacle freely. Patten of visual flow was changed to the right/leftward pattern from going straight pattern at the point 2 [m] far from start line. In case of random dotted pattern, visual flow was changed from type (a) to type (b/c), and in case of striped pattern, that was changed from type (d) to type (e/f).

For each five sets of flow changing pattern including control set, each subject do 20 trails. A total of 100 trials were performed 20 times for each subject, respectively. To induce subjects' unconscious motion, subjects do main tasks during walking. In experiment 2a, subjects gaze at the screen of a cellular phone as main task. And in experiment 2b, subjects do calculation task on the cellular phone as high load task.

Fig. 3. Prototype 2 of HMVD and user's view

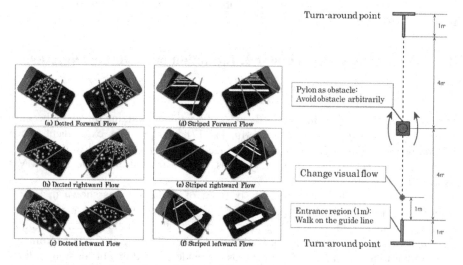

Fig. 4. Six types of visual flow on iPhone display and experimental setup

4.2   Result and Discussion

4.2.1   Experiment 2a: Walking under Low Pressure Task

First, we evaluated effectiveness of vection to walking direction under low pressure task. In experiment 2a, seven subjects do 100 trials in which visual flows changed are selected on above mentioned five sets at random. As low pressure task, subjects read text on cellar phone screen during walking. Figure 6 show the result of way for avoiding obstacle. Four subjects avoided in the same direction in all the 100 trial, and we cannot found the role decided form other three subjects' data. Also the result of questionnaire after 100 trails shows that subjects ware making intentional direction selection at the time of low pressure task.

4.2.2   Sub-experiment 2: Walking Under High Pressure Task
Next, we evaluated effectiveness of vection to walking direction under high pressure task. In experiment 2b, six subjects also do 100 trials as same as experiment 2a. And as high pressure task, subjects do a mental arithmetic test using cellar phone during walking. In this case, subjects focus on the cellar phone screen and concentrate on calculation task spontaneously. Figure 7 shows the result of experiment 2a. As compared with the trials in which a flow image is not shown on HMVD, the probability of avoiding leftward by flow presentation of the direction of the left rear went up from the method of the forward right.

4.2.3   Discussion
The result of Experiment 2b indicates that the contrary tends to become easy to avoid to a reverse side with the direction of movement of a flow similarly. Table 1 shows the percentage of subjects the tendency which becomes easy to avoid to a reverse side would be applied with this direction of movement. This means that the fitting rate of avoidance tendency under high pressure task is higher than that under low pressure task in all types of the flow presentation.

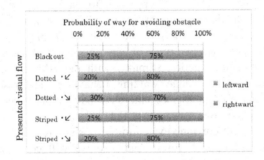

Fig. 5. Typical result of experiment 2a: walking direction under low pressure task (subject WA's 100 trial)

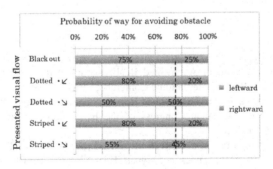

Fig. 6. Typical result of experiment 2b: walking direction under high pressure task (subject KS's 100 trial)

Under low pressure task, users of this system determine avoiding directions intentionally, and results cannot show any roles of tendency. On the other hand, under high pressure task, users walking and selecting avoiding direction unconsciously, and this tendency depend on the presented vection flows on the HMVD. Based on this result, there is possibility that walking directions of users can be guided by presenting optical flow on peripheral vision. Moreover, the score of the mental arithmetic test did not depend on types of presented optical flow (including black out). From questionnaire after each experimental case, user can do main task (reading text and doing mental arithmetic test) undisturbedly.

Table 1. Percentage of subject's trail which subject avoid to a reverse side

	Experiment 2a	Experiment 2b
Dotted	14%	100%
Dotted	14%	67%
Striped	14%	50%
Striped	29%	83%

5   Conclusion

In this study, we proposed a novel approach to navigate users by using user's inconscientious reflex motion by presenting optical flow on peripheral vision. Based on this concept, we developed Head-mounted Vection Display for inducing vection during walking. We conducted two types of experiments for observing user's walking behaviour under presenting vection stimulus with the HMVD, and evaluated the effectiveness of vection to change walking behaviour. The results indicate the proposed approach have possibility of automatic navigation, especially in selecting walking direction, without user's awareness and recognition.

In future work, we will continue evaluation of our approach in variety of walking behavior and presented optical flows. And also we will construct experiment in outdoor and wide area space. By finding versatile optical flows, our approach becomes possible to use also for an actual navigation system in daily life.

References

1. Mobile Google Map, http://m.google.com/maps/
2. Zendjebil, I., et al.: Outdoor Augmented Reality: State of the Art and Issues. In: 10th ACM/IEEE Virtual Reality International Conference (VRIC 2008), pp. 177–187 (2008)
3. Nakamura, N., Fukui, Y.: Development of Human Navigation System "HapticNavi" using GyroCube. In: XVth Triennial Congress of the International Ergonomics Association 2003, pp. 352–355 (2003)
4. Tsukada, K., Yasumura, M.: ActiveBelt: Belt-Type Wearable Tactile Display for Directional Navigation. In: Davies, N., Mynatt, E.D., Siio, I. (eds.) UbiComp 2004. LNCS, vol. 3205, pp. 384–399. Springer, Heidelberg (2004)

5. Watanabe, J., Ando, H., Maeda, T.: Shoe-shaped Interface for Inducing a Walking Cycle. In: Proceedings of the 15th International Conference on Artificial Reality and Telexistence, pp. 30–34 (2005)
6. Amemiya, T., Maeda, T.: Asymmetric Oscillation Distorts the Perceived Heaviness of Handheld Objects. IEEE Transactions on Haptics 1(1), 9–18 (2008)
7. Maeda, T., Ando, H., Amemiya, T., Inami, M., Nagaya, N., Sugimoto, M.: Shaking The World: Galvanic Vestibular Stimulation As A Novel Sensation Interface. In: ACM SIGGRAPH 2005 Emerging Technologies (2005)
8. Kojima, Y., Hashimoto, Y., Fukushima, S., Kajimoto, H.: Pull-navi: a novel tactile navigation interface by pulling the ears. In: ACM SIGGRAPH 2009 Emerging Technologies (2009)
9. Narumi, T., Tomohiro, A., Seong, Y.A., Hirose, M.: Characterizing the Space by Thermal Feedback through a Wearable Device. In: Shumaker, R. (ed.) VMR 2009. LNCS, vol. 5622, pp. 355–364. Springer, Heidelberg (2009)
10. Gibson, J.: The visual perception of objective motion and subjective movement. Psychol. Rev. 61, 304–314 (1954)
11. Nakamura, S., Shimojo, S.: A slowly moving foreground can capture an observer's self-motion – a report of a new motion illusion: inverted vection. Vision Research 40(21), 2915–2923 (2000)
12. Lishman, J.R., Le, D.N.: The autonomy of visual kinaesthesis. Perception 2(3), 287–294 (1973)
13. Maeda, T., Ando, H., Sugimoto, M.: Virtual acceleration with Galvanic Vestibular Stimulation in a virtual reality environment. In: Proceedings of IEEE VR 2005, pp. 289–290 (2005)
14. Razzaque, S., Kohn, Z., Whitton, M.C.: Redirected walking. Eurographics (Short Presentation) (2001)
15. Suma, E., Finkelstein, S., Reid, M., Babu, S., Ulinski, A., Hodges, L.: Evaluation of the cognitive effects of travel technique in complex real and virtual environments. IEEE Transactions on Visualization and Computer Graphics 16, 690–702 (2010)
16. Riecke, B.E., Feuereissen, D., Rieser, J.J., McNamara, T.P.: Self-Motion Illusions (Vection) in VR – Are They Good For Anything? In: Proceedings of IEEE VR 2012, pp. 35–38 (2012)
17. Furukawa, M., Yoshikawa, H., Hachisu, T., Fukushima, S., Kajimoto, H.: "Vection Field" for Pedestrian Traffic Control. In: Augmented Human 2011 (2011)
18. Bardy, B.G., Warren, W.H., Kay, B.A.: The role of central and peripheral vision in postural control during walking. Perception and Psychophysics 61, 1356–1368 (1999)
19. Kano, C.: The perception of self-motion induced by peripheral visual information in sittng and supine postures. Ecological Psychology 3, 241–252 (1991)
20. Johansson, G.: Studies on visual perception of locomotion. Perception 6, 265–276 (1977)
21. Watanabe, H., Umemura, H., Yoshida, C., Matsuoka, K.: Interaction between Peripheral Optical Flow and Foveal Depth Perception, The Institute of Electronics, Information and Communication Engineers, D-I, pp. 491–500 (2001)

POPAPY: Instant Paper Craft
Made Up in a Microwave Oven

Kentaro Yasu and Masahiko Inami

KEIO University 4-1-1 Hiyoshi, Kohoku-ku, Yokohama 223-8526, Japan
{yasu,inami}@kmd.keio.ac.jp

Abstract. This research proposes a postcard that transforms into a paper craft model after being heated by a microwave oven, named "POPAPY". POPAPY is made from a combination of paper, heat shrink sheet, and very thin aluminum sheet. The aluminum sheet can provide heat to the heat shrink sheet effectively, and the heated heat shrink sheet will shrink and the paper will bend, then, the paper model will stand. In this paper, POPAPY, along with an application that allows the designing of the shape of the paper figure and a simulator of the transformation are implemented. Users can make their own original POPAPY easily using the application and the simulator helps to design the bending angle of the figure by the combination of the size of the heat shrink sheet and the aluminum sheet. "POPAPY" can provide a surprising feeling to the receiver as well as amusement of sending a card to the sender.

Keywords: Paper, microwave oven, heat shrink tube, aluminum sheet, postcard, paper craft, paper figure, user interface, simulation.

1   Introduction

We often send cards. For example, greeting cards, birthday cards, Christmas cards and New Year cards. We can send compliments, thanks, delight and enjoyment by a simple message written on a small paper.

On the other hand, three-dimensional paper object like pop-up book and paper craft are widely supported. Many cards that transform to paper craft models are marketed as commercial products since early times, and still exist. Recently, there are many kinds of cards that have an electric circuit and a battery for the purpose of making music or emitting lights.

In this paper, we propose an instant paper craft card made up in a microwave oven, named "POPAPY". Everyone can enjoy making this card because it does not require any special skills to make the card. Sender can finish making the card in just five steps. Choose, print, cut, stick and write some messages. The sender can decide how much the paper will bend after heated by a microwave oven, before sending it. The finished message card can be sent by mail because the card is a very thin two-dimensional object.

Also anyone can enjoy the transformation from two-dimensional card to three-dimensional paper craft model that set up in advance by the energy from the microwave oven. It can enhance not only emotion but also surprise and entertainment of the card.

A. Nijholt, T. Romão, and D. Reidsma (Eds.): ACE 2012, LNCS 7624, pp. 406–420, 2012.
© Springer-Verlag Berlin Heidelberg 2012

Fig. 1. POPAPY: a postcard that transforms into a paper craft model after being heated by a microwave oven

2 Purpose

This study aims to realize a physically transformable paper. Planer thing like a paper is suite for an instant tangible display because of its flexibility, variety and low cost. The flexibility of the paper shows not only an ease of processing using hand or scissors but also a small actuators can bend, fold and transform.

If a control and design method of planer things is realized, paper is no longer just a media of information, but is also a media of tangible motion. We can send three-dimensional paper craft in a form of two-dimensional post card.

3 Related Works

3.1 Paper Based Works

There are some works that deal with controlling the motion of soft materials such as paper and textiles. "Sleepy Box" developed by Saul et al. is a paper robot that is made from folded cube-shaped paper of varying sizes [1]. It utilized shape memory alloy (SMA) wires to provide actuation, gold-leaf circuits to connect components, and embedded electronics to provide interactive behavior. Jie Qi and Leah Buechley at MIT Media Lab developed an interactive paper based object [2] that sparkles, sings, and moves, as controlled by switches and sensors. In order to blend the electronic components into the paper to make them as imperceptible as possible, they made switches and sensors out of pop-up mechanisms and kept the circuitry thin and flexible.

In these works, as it is necessary to include electronic components (for example, embedded sensors and actuators), the motions and the interactions of the materials are limited, and this property may also restrict the diversity of the design of these works.

3.2 Noncontact Energy Transmission

On the other hand, there is a technology to supply energy to the object contactlessly. Shibata et al developed an energy supply system for micro robots in metal pipes utilizing microwaves, consisting of rectifying circuits, a receiving antenna and Schottky barrier diodes [3]. The system supplies the energy required by micro robots through the rectification of microwaves received by the micro robot antenna. Koizumi et al developed a non-contact energy transmission system to controlling paper figure [4]. The system combines paper, SMA, retro-reflective material, and copper foil. The laser can provide energy to the paper figure precisely and wireless. The paper figure can be animated without placing any sensors or actuators.

3.3   Microwave Works

In addition to that, there is a Japanese patent on using a special kind of ink that will shrink after being heated, in order to make the paper craft in microwave oven [5]. But this patent does not contain design method of folding the paper precisely.

In this study, to establish a method of transforming in microwave oven, we clarified the relationship between the size of heat shrink sheet, aluminum sheet and bending angle of the paper to make the paper figure not only fold but also stand up from a flat state.

3.4   Origami Design Tools

To design three-dimensional objects by paper, there are some tools that help to design origami. Origamizer [6][7] can generate two-dimensional folding pattern from any types of three-dimensional polygon. ORI-REVO [8][9] can generate not only shapes consisting by straight lines like a box, but also shapes that have curved surfaces. These software provide us the really precise folding pattern. So, if we have time and nimble fingers, we can get any shapes of paper figure.

4   Method

POPAPY is a post card that will transform into a pop-up card with only 10 seconds of heating by microwave oven. All the user has to do is simply stick the heat shrink tube and the aluminum sheet onto a piece of paper. The aluminum sheet behaves like an antenna. It is controlled that the provided heat to the heat shrink sheet by changing the size and shape of the aluminum sheet.

If the heat shrink sheet is too small, it will be removed from the paper when it is heated. On the other hand, if the heat shrink sheet is too large for the paper, it fails to stand because of the weight. POPAPY is designed as a postcard, so two necessary questions needs considering, 1) maximum size and 2) repeatability.

4.1   Maximum Size

POPAPY is designed with the size of a standard post card (140mm x 100mm); therefore the maximum size of the paper figure is determined.

4.2   Repeatability

Repeatability is very important. Since In the scenario, the sender is a different person from the receiver. That means people who put the card in a microwave oven and watch the motion is a different person from the designer of the motion. If it fails or the motion is different from the motion that the sender designed, it will be unfortunate.

Fig. 2. Case of Failure. If those materials are not suite for the paper, that paper figure cannot stand and sometimes the material will come off from the paper.

4.3   Structure

POPAPY is designed with the size of a standard post card (140mm x 100mm), and made up of 4 layers: paper that will transform after heated, heat shrink sheet, an aluminum sheet that is suitable for use in microwave ovens, and the base (Figure 3).

The card does not need any batteries, lines or processors which add hardness and weight, that interrupts paper's motion, because the microwave oven provides the energy required for changing the shape of the paper remotely. Accordingly, this movable paper does not have to consider about the battery weight. The paper only has to put small material that changes its shape with temperature as an actuator. This method realized wireless control of paper.

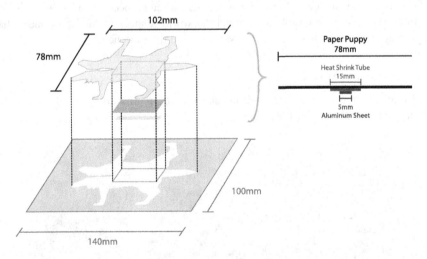

Fig. 3. Structure of POPAPY. POPAPY is designed with the size of a standard post card (140mm x 100mm), and made up of 4 layers: paper that will transform after heated, heat shrink sheet, an aluminum sheet that is suitable for use in microwave ovens, and the base.

The top layer of the card is a piece of paper (Gramm age: 80g/m2).

The second layer is a cut opened piece of heat shrink tube which is a material that is made of nylon or polyolefin. Heat shrink sheet shrinks when heated, and do not return back to their original shape. In this research, heat shrink tubes manufactured by "Sumitomo Electric Fine Polymer, Inc." (Sumitube TM B2, No. 826) was used. The minimum radial shrinkage ratio is 50%, and the longitudinal shrinkage ratio is +/-15 %. The tube will be completely shrunken once the heating temperature reaches around 90℃ [10]. Based on this longitudinal shrinkage ratio, strips are cut with the length of the tube and taped horizontally onto the first layer of paper with double-sided tape. When heated with a heating device, the paper curves and bends with the tube.

The third layer is a piece of aluminum sheet. This very thin aluminum sheet does not make any spark or fire because this sheet is produced as a commercial product that is usually used to roast pizzas and fish in a microwave oven [11][12]. It is designed for more than 20 minutes baking in microwave oven. By using this aluminum sheet, the heat shrink tube is able to shrink faster, thus shortening the heating time from 1 minute to 10~20 seconds (heated in a 500W microwave).

Finally, the fourth layer is the base of the postcard with a piece of thicker paper that is thicker than the first layer, where the sender can write a message.

Paper has a very quick response speed to heat because plane object has an extremely high ratio of surface area to volume compared with a solid object. Thus, we can touch it with our bare hands instantly because it is not scalding hot even if it is immediately taken out after heating by microwave oven.

There are a few reasons why we chose microwave oven as the heating device.

First is safety. Microwave oven is a product that is conformed to standards of safety. It can provide high density of energy in a box that has firm steel guard for microwave.

Second is prevalence. Microwave oven has already become a common home electronic appliance at households around the world. Especially in Japan, more than 90 percent of households have a microwave oven in their kitchen.

4.4   Simulation Model

The shrinkage ratio of the heat shrink sheet used in this study is 50%, and the thickness gets doubles after the heating.

Fig. 4. The Bended Heat Shrink Sheet and Aluminum Sheet

Accordingly, a lattice model of the heat shrink material is designed as pictured in the (fig. 5).

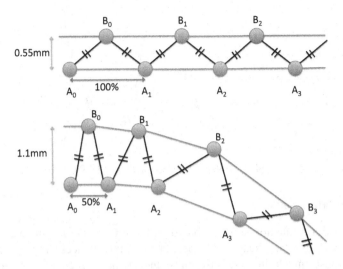

Fig. 5. Simulation Model

Additionally, a virtual heat source is set at the point of the center of the surface of the heat shrink material (A0) , to make the calculation simple. After 10 seconds of heating by microwave oven, the center of the heat source gets a temperature (Ta0), and the temperature is calculated from the following formula. The bigger the aluminum sheet (Al) is, the higher the temperature.

$$T_{max} \propto Al \tag{1}$$

$$k = T_{max} \div Al^2 \tag{2}$$

$$T_{an} = T_{max} - kr^2 \tag{3}$$

Depending on the temperature of the heat source and the distance from the heat source, temperature of each point (Tan, Tbn) is determined. As a result, the distance between the two heated points on interior surface (An - An+1) gets reduce at the rate of the data sheet. But, for the cause of the anisotropy of the material, distance between the interior point and exterior point is fixed.

Simultaneously, the model is designed that the difference between the temperature of the point on exterior side and interior side (Tan - Tbn) determines the bend angle (αn) of the interior surface with careful consideration of the inhomogeneous shrinkage ratio. Because the heat shrink material is in the shape of a tube originally, the shrinkage ratio is slightly different between inside and outside. The constant of proportion is defined based on actual measured value.

$$\alpha_n \propto \left(T_{a_n} - T_{b_n}\right) \qquad (4)$$

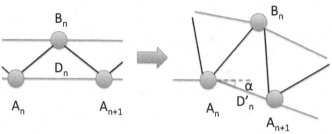

Fig. 6. Model of Bending Angle Variation

4.5   Simulation Software

We developed a simulation software based on these formulas and the data. User can change the size of paper, heat shrink sheet and aluminum sheet and see the way that the paper transforms during the 10 seconds, and see the shape and angle after the 10 seconds.

When the size of heat shrink sheet is too small compared to the aluminum sheet, an error message that says, "stripped" will appear.

When the size of aluminum sheet is too large and the system judges the paper figure cannot stand, "fallen" will appear.

User can know the most suitable size of heat shrink sheet and aluminum sheet for the paper figure.

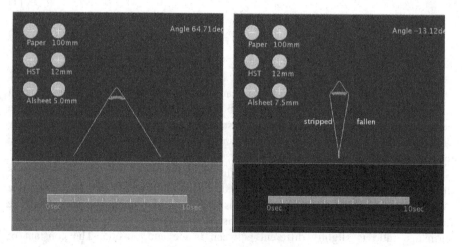

Fig. 7. POPAPY simulator

5   Evaluation

To evaluate the performance of the simulation software, we designed an experiment for comparing between theoretical value and actual measured value. The experiments were conducted under several conditions described below.

5.1   Condition

We set nine conditions for the experiment and the numbers of trials are five times for each condition. In this experiment, the size of the paper is fixed and the size of heat shrink sheet and aluminum sheet is changed because this experiment is designed for clarifying the relationship of the size of those materials and the fold angle of the paper. The POPAPY under the test was heated 10 seconds by 500W microwave oven on the cardboard with the surface that the heat shrink sheet attached down.

5.1.1   Size of the Paper
The size of the paper is fixed to 40mm by 80mm.

5.1.2   Heat Shrink Sheet and Aluminum Sheet
We prepared 3 different widths of heat shrink sheet; 3mm, 5mm, and 7mm, and 3 different width of aluminum sheet; 9mm, 15mm, and 21mm. All sheet are the same in length; 40mm, the same as the length of the paper. So, the test material sheet was attached in the middle of the paper (Fig. 8).

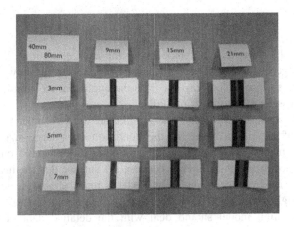

Fig. 8. POPAPY Under the Experiment

5.1.3   Measurement
After heated, the folded paper taken out from the oven was shot by a camera orthogonal oriented, to measure the angle folded. The images taken by the camera

Fig. 9. Test of Transforming of POPAPY

Fig. 10. Measurement of the Angle

was analyzed and calculated average and variance score of the bending angle of the paper.

5.2   Result

These three graphs show that the angle under the each conditions. The blue dot ◆ shows the average of the experiment result, and the red dot ■ shows the angle that simulated by the software. The gray dot ■ is the angle that the simulation calculates with an error message of "stripped" or "fallen".

It is clear from these graphs that the simulation worked under the condition of narrow width of aluminum sheet. In the condition of a large size of aluminum sheet, the experimental value is smaller than simulated value. It would appear that frictional influence or weight influence because the surface that the heat shrink sheet attached down. The developed simulation model is really simple. It does not include friction and weight influence. To make more precise simulation of more complex figure, the simulation model should deal with the detailed data of materials and environment.

The variance shows that accuracy of the simulation is low under the conditions that the heat shrink sheet size is large. It is thought to be aftereffects of dispersion of the heat shrink material and the microwave. Though this simulation software does not alert that "this heat shrink sheet is too long", it is better to inform the users to that the relationship between accuracy and the length of the heat shrink sheet.

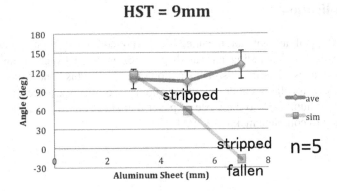

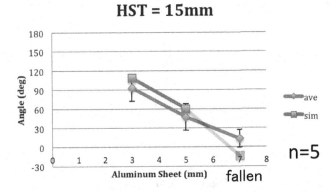

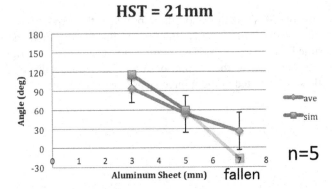

Fig. 11. The Experimental value and the Simulation value

6   Application

We also developed an application named "POPAPY editor". User can create his own POPAPY image file including animal-shaped Bezier curve by choosing parts and background images. User can also detach along the line by his hand from the printed image, user can use laser cutter or cutting plotter. To attach a piece of heat shrink sheet and aluminum sheet to the piece of paper that is cut out from the printed image is the last step to complete making POPAPY.

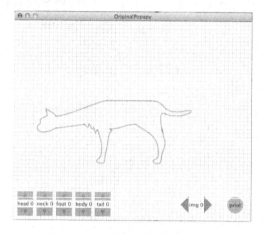

Fig. 12. POPAPY editor

Combined use of the simulator and editor provides the experience of designing motion and shape of the card instantly. Because of the making time and originality, POPAPY is suited for workshops. The participants can make an original pop up postcard and can take that to their home or send it to their family or friends. The creation workflow is separated to these three steps (fig. 13).

1. WORK STATION

design your original POPAPY.
choose from a variety of papers.
cut the paper using the cutting
plotter.

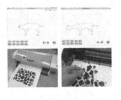

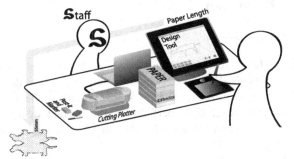

2. CRAFTS SHOP

simulate the motion on iPad.
cut Heat Shrink Tube.
cut Aluminum sheet.
stick them on the paper.

3. MOTION STUDIO

stick the paper on the base.
you can use the plastic bag to bring
it home.
you can also try the motion here.

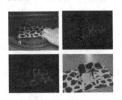

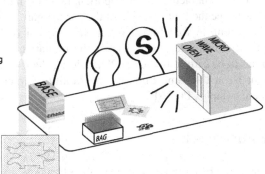

Fig. 13. The workflow of POPAPY workshop

7   Discussion

7.1   Benefits

The benefits of this method are instancy, cheap prices, and safety. Anyone can have fun with POPAPY in safety and it only costs less than 1 dollar per a piece of POPAPY. And there are so many kinds of paper in the world. If it is not too heavy to fold and the paper have perforation, the bended figure will be stronger. And the shrunk sheet is harder than before heating. That helps maintain the shape of the folded paper figure.

Additionally, the most characteristic point is that the process of making paper object is divided to an experience of the sender and that of the receiver.

The sender can design the shape of the paper figure, and bending angle. Furthermore, using a printer and thermochromic ink, sender can design a message that appears only after heated. But, the receiver only have to do is to heat that in a microwave oven. The receiver can get a three-dimensional paper object in few seconds, in safety.

7.2   Limitation

The size of the paper figure is limited by the size of a microwave oven. Also the heating time depends on the power of a microwave oven. The simulation model is designed for 10 seconds heating in 500 W. But the power and microwave exposure depends on the manufacturer. It is important to adjust the heating time by looking into the window to see the folding angle of the paper figure.

In this system, to fold folded paper like origami is difficult because the shrunk sheet is too hard to fold again. That is the limitation of designing paper craft. The designer has to be careful to the conflict, folding shape and folding sequence.

But that is, at the same time, the possibility of improvement of a tool that can design more complex POPAPY.

8   Future Work

In this paper, the bending angle is controlled by the width of the aluminum sheet and heat shrink sheet. But we already confirmed the energy conversion efficiency depends on the length of the aluminum sheet because the aluminum sheet is a kind of antenna to catch the microwave. By changing the length of the antenna, we can control bending timing and design bending sequence, and can design more complex paper craft (fig. 14). We will be able to control the motion of paper time frequency as well as spatial frequency before too long.

In this system, transformation is only one time because of the feature of the actuator. Also, it is known that SMA can shrink in microwave oven if its length is enough. SMA can return to the previous shape after being cooled. Combination of these two materials expands the range of transformation.

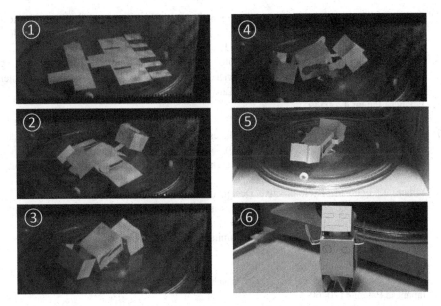

Fig. 14. Example of Complex Figure : Robot

This POPAPY technology can apply to postcards, advertising media and toys, as well as packages of food. If the frozen food package transform and some handgrips pop up, we do not have to bear the heat of the food.

9   Conclusion

This research proposes a postcard that transforms into a paper craft model after being heated by a microwave oven, named "POPAPY". In this paper, we developed a simulation software and compared with actual angle of the folded paper.

Additionally, We developed an application named "POPAPY editor". User can create his/her own POPAPY by choosing parts instantly.

Acknowledgement. This research is supported by the Japan Science and Technology Corporation (JST) under the CREST project, Foundation of Technology Supporting the Creation of Digital Media Contents."

References

1. Saul, G., Xu, C., Gross, M.D.: Interactive paper devices: end-user design & fabrication. In: Proceedings of the Fourth International Conference on Tangible, Embedded, and Embodied Interaction (TEI 2010) (January 2010)
2. Qi, J., Buechley, L.: Electronic popables: exploring paper-based computing through an interactive pop-up book. In: TEI 2010, Cambridge, Massachusetts, USA, January 24-27, pp. 121–128. ACM, New York (2010)

3. Shibata, T., Tashima, T., Tanie, K.: Emergence of Emotional Behavior thruough Physical Interaction between Human and Robot. In: Proceedings of the 1999 IEEE International Conference on Robotics and Automation, ICRA 1999 (1999)

4. Koizumi, N., Yasu, K., Liu, A., Sugimoto, M., Inami, M.: Animated Paper: A Moving Prototyping Toys. In: 7th International Conference on Advances in Computer Entertainment Technology (ACE 2010), Taiwan, November 17-19 (2010)

5. Japanese Patent 4260549

6. Origamizer, http://www.tsg.ne.jp/TT/software/index.html#origamizer

7. Tachi, T.: Origamizing Polyhedral Surfaces. IEEE Transactions on Visualization and Computer Graphics 16(2), 298–311 (2010)

8. ORI-REVO, http://mitani.cs.tsukuba.ac.jp/origami_application/ori_revo_morph/

9. Mitani, J., Igarashi, T.: Interactive Design of Planar Curved Folding by Reflection. In: Pacific Conference on Computer Graphics and Applications - Short Papers, Kaohsiung, Taiwan, September 21-23, pp. 77–81 (2011)

10. Sumitomo Electric Fine Polymer, Inc., Sumitube B2, http://www.sei-sfp.co.jp/products/pdf/SUMITUBE-B2.pdf

11. KOBAYASHI Pharmaceutical Co., Ltd., http://www.kobayashi.co.jp/seihin/tn_ksp/index.html

12. Japanese Patent 4170460

Games Bridging Cultural Communications

Adrian David Cheok[1], Narisa N.Y. Chu[2], Yongsoon Choi[1], and Jun Wei[3]

[1] Keio University, Japan
[2] CWLab International, USA
[3] National University of Singapore, Singapore
nchu@cwlabi.com,
{goodsoon96,weijun924,adriancheok}@gmail.com

Abstract. This paper presents Phase I development and Phase II enhancement of a Game platform for inter-generation cultural communication. The first application is demonstrated in a game called Confucius Chat which teaches family responsibility in conjunction with Singapores government policy. Phase I has been tested with positive and encouraging acceptance from parents and children. The purpose of Phase II development is to engage social media picture exchange and to build database learning into the system for catering to younger generations.

Keywords: user interface, intergeneration communication, database system learning, cultural promotion via social networking.

1 Introduction

The effort to introduce Confucius Computer for intergeneration communication started in 2006, in response to social needs in Singapore, advocating family responsibility [1–3]. Confucius(551 479 B.C) teaching has been well established in many Asian countries with Chinese cultural background advocating a harmonized society/government. Significant research and development results have been demonstrated in an interactive computer game: "Confucius Chat" Phase I, where a child player is joined with a parent or a teacher. This paper elaborates the on-going effort, taking into account trial feedback to improve acceptance particularly among children, evolving into a Phase II study. Multimedia interface is enabled to make the user both philosophically and practically engaged. Many layers of processing are used to digest and translate ancient philosophies such as Confucius to a form that is easier for children to comprehend. These enhancements are essential particularly when virtue learning is competing with prevailing temptations of numerous computer entertainment options which can present the opposite value of Confucius sayings.

Of noted difference between Phase I and the continuing endeavor, Phase II, is the structure that allows interpretation of the ancient Confucius wisdom with explicit pictures and stories in many forms, away from abstract and condensed formal text statements. Chapters in The Analects of Confucius, etc., are employed as the fundamental database of the interactive chatting. However, it also

A. Nijholt, T. Romão, and D. Reidsma (Eds.): ACE 2012, LNCS 7624, pp. 421–428, 2012.

attempts to realize the evolving value resulting from various interpretations from specialized scholars dedicated to Confucius teaching over the last 2500 some years. Furthermore, as most interpretations are of an academic nature, stories and pictures are necessary to relate with plain meaning in a dynamic changing time. The effort of such elaboration in plain terms is important as the traditional Chinese communication style, both in terms of oral and written formats, tends to be abstract, and thoughts are more implicitly presented rather than explicitly, to provoke pondering, or simply due to the Chinese custom of humbleness and obedience. Precision is often deliberately swayed and meaning is subtly hidden to avoid confrontation, sometimes discouraging critical thinking. Many thoughts are inherently hard to apply to modern lives without decent scholastic training. Confucius, so much practiced throughout Chinese societies, however, has carried a distinctive difference between philosophy and religion, partially because of its various derivations by different dynasties with political purposes; yet its fundamental value has been preserved through openness and balance. Thus, the objectives of our game research are meant to overcome these challenges of literacy pre-requisites and historical complexity, and to foster a friendly family dialog without indifference or abandonment by the young generation.

The digital game, Confucius Chat, has been verified by a few trials that relevance is more important than accuracy. This important finding directs the Phase II effort to focus on use of pictures and parental feedback in making the knowledge database learn and grow.

2   Core Knowledge Manifestation

Phase I development of Confucius Chat incorporates Confucius knowledge database. Chapters in the Analects of Confucius and other related books can be primarily grouped into universal concepts: starting from loyalty, filial piety, benevolence, devotion, leading to a life-long practice of a gentle human, with ritual. Adding 4 more pursuits: trust, justice, harmony and peace, Confucius sayings have been credited as a superb stabilizing philosophy for an utopian society. These concepts are populated into a flat database and fed into 23 topics shown in Figure 1.

Each topic, further equipped with 108 entries, can contain many layers of interpretation. Phase I work, based on software elements shown in Figure 2, has demonstrated the game of Confucius Chat with trial results of a selective

1. Parents	2. Marriage	3. Sibling	4. Youth	5. Elderly	6. Ancestors
7. Rites and ceremony	8. Obedience/Conduct	9. Conflict or Harmony	10. Love	11. Respect or Reverence	12. Treat/Serve others
13. Death	14. Morally Upright	15. Children in the family	16. Food	17. Knowledge Transmission/Acquisition	
18. Money	19. Filial	20. Relatives or Neighbors	21. Family	22. Health or Well-being	23. Friends or Peers

Fig. 1. 23 topics in the database

group [2]. User's web browser, working through the web server and chat server to access 3 databases that contain Confucius knowledge, chat history and chat rating. The core database, Confucius knowledge is built based on work of 5 selected Confucius scholars with their combined experts interpretations.

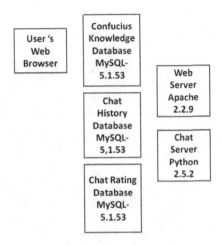

Fig. 2. Software Elements in Confucius Chat - Phase I

It is experienced, without surprise, that Confucius answers, although authentic and academically superb, are not exciting to children. For example:

```
Input: What would cause the instability of a family and how should we stay united?
Output: A family must first destroy itself before others can destroy it.
```

This answer, in full text form, is difficult for a child of 7 - 1 years old (target group) to comprehend. It also demises chances for adults to re-tune themselves if they have not adhered to Confucius teachings in prior lives. Another example:

```
Input: What kind of action should a son uphold for him to be considered filial?
Output: If the son for three years does not alter from the way of his father,
he may be called filial.
```

This answer is no fun as the task seems insurmountable by todays standards. There has to be more of an interactive mode in teaching to allow kids to ask straight-forward questions and get an answer that is less rigid and ambiguous, e.g.,

```
Input: Why do my parents argue with each other?
Output: Maybe you would beg your parents to compromise for the family goodness as a
whole. Suggest to your parents that you need a harmonized family to do yourhomework.
Help out with more family chores to ease their stress level.
```

Phase I carries the ancient face of Confucius appearing on the opening user interface. It is not appealing to kids. Without parents "forcing" them to play, it is unlikely for kids to be drawn into this Confucius Chat game. Phase II thus introduces a cartoon version of Confucius, resembling the Santa Claus, in Chinese costume in the opening page.

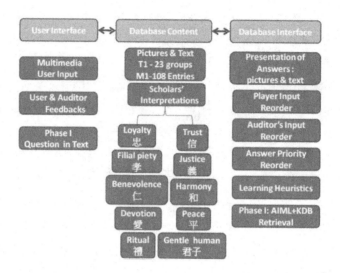

Fig. 3. Software Modules in Confucius Chat - Phase II

Phase I system is evaluated as capable to identify the keywords and topics with an accuracy of 88.72% and 81.20%, respectively. With the size of code and processing power, this is considered remarkable and economical [4] as per the finding below that relevance is more important than accuracy.

The positive correlation between relevance and enjoyment is indicated when user ratings for relevance increase, the enjoyment ratings also increase. It behooves us to work on improvements of relevance where more friendly user interface is necessary together with guidance feedback from a parent or a teacher. Multimedia user inputs are to be instilled into the Confucius knowledge database to make it smarter, more fun and relevant.

3   System Internals

A virtual Confucius is created by working with a few noted Confucius scholars who have the domain knowledge to build a knowledge base containing all the sayings by Confucius from the classics the Analects, the Mencius, the Book of Rites and the Classic on Filial Piety. A Confucius thinking engine is developed utilizing various Natural Language Processing (NLP) techniques to analyze user inputs and extract answers from the knowledge database. An adapted A.L.I.C.E (Artificial Linguistic Internet Computer Entity) program [5] was used to handle small talk. This method relies on pattern matching to find a suitable reply in pre-stored question and answer pairs. If user enters long questions, a grammatical parser [6] is applied to understand the structure of the sentence, extract the important words in the sentence [7], and match their semantic closeness [8, 9] with the topics in the Confucius knowledge database, with the help of a lexical database called WordNet [10]. The entry with the closest similarity is calculated and the answer string is selected as the output. In addition, a simple word-matching module was also implemented, to cover situations where A.L.I.C.E. and WordNet failed to find an answer.

4   Test Results Led to Phase II Specification

Initial trials indicated that adult users acceptance out-weighs childrens. This finding does not advance the purpose of aiding the government social responsibility policy. Two areas are observed as key factors to improve the games attractiveness: user interface and system self-learning based on user feedbacks.

Phase II thus architects elaborate user interface to introduces pictures in conjunction with Confucius reply in text [11]. As illustrated in Fig. 3, direct quotes from Confucius are still placed in text form, however, greatly manifested with pictures that reflect stories associating with positive and negative behaviors for more lively interactions. Further user self-expression will be incorporated via brain computer interface and smartphone bump tools. Fig. 3 shows the software enhancement modules and elaborate interfaces of the entire Phase II plan.

The user is guided to interact with the multimedia database through database interface modules. When database interface processing result presents the authentic Confucius statement with an associated picture, the user is perceived as having explored with interest in accepting Confucius teaching and confirmation is sought together with feedback from the parent/teacher. Every interexchange of Q&A, in the form of text or graphic form, is saved and the database is re-ordered and relevance enriched accordingly. The database is able to learn based on user input and rating choices to improve the acceptance of the answers.

5   User Interface

As user interface is one of the 2 key factors motivating Phase II study, its intricacy is summarized below, which includes text input and output, plus rating input buttons.

5.1   Phase I User Interface

As shown in Figure 4, Confucius Chat has gone through a few modifications from the initial text based version to a smart phone display where user can input a rating of "top", "funny", "profound", and "bad" [2, 3].

Fig. 4. User interface snapshots for Phase I Confucius Chat game

5.2   Phase II User Interface

Phase II User input is upgraded with picture input to allow fun interaction with children. The answer to a question is delivered in text and picture format. Continuing dialog is encouraged by prompting "Whats on your mind?" or the like, when the question is answered. Fig. 5 shows the opening of the chat.

6   System Learning

Phase I answer retrieval is built on Artificial Intelligence Markup Language (AIML), a natural language parsing technique and scoring evaluation. A Similarity module calculates the highest similarity score.

Questions can be input in any form, not necessarily follow our Topic grouping. Thus, Stanford Parser is used for identification of keywords in a casual text string, aided by Inverse Term Frequency method. User input is parsed through Word Sense Disambiguation, followed by a WordNet::Similarity comparison. Retrieval of Knowledge database is based on k-NN classification algorithm [12].

Test results show accuracy hovered around 80%. This is challenging, however, it is also found the answer with relevance is more important than with accuracy. Phase II design is thus focused on how to increase relevance of the answer based on user inputs and feedbacks. The rating inputs in Phase I: "top", "funny", "profound", and "bad" are simplified to "agree" and "disagree" in Phase II. Pictures are presented in conjunction with answering each question in text to avoid abstraction and to draw relevance. The picture that receives feedback as "agree" will be reordered to the top of the database. The player's input picture, which is obviously relevant, will be included in database updates as

Fig. 5. Starting a Confucius Chat

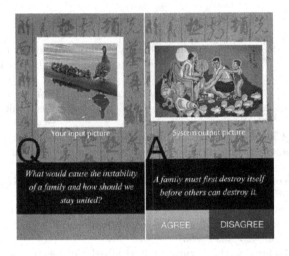

Fig. 6. Phase II interface with both pictures and text

"agree" element, carrying a basic value of "1". The rating of the parent/teacher's feedback, carrying the highest value of N, where N is the number of pictures stored in the Topic, will be constantly updated in the database.

As no single tool can recognize the content of a picture easily, on-line feedback from the parent/teacher is crucial in making database learn for ever increasing relevance. This learning scheme starts with simple evaluating value from the players and their parent or teacher, however, further enhancements are expected based on experiments and trails we run. Initially, we take advantage of the entertaining nature of pictures, not to be too much concerned about whether they match exactly with the theme of Confucius sayings. It is served as an amusing tool to the player and convincingly a fashionable communication tool with the popularity of Facebook, YouTube, etc. The traditional philosophy/culture discussion can be then perceived as a fun, positive experience with the children.

7   Conclusion

Intergeneration communication through mediated experience is demonstrated in the digital game of Confucius Chat, Phase I and II. As its trial performance evaluation reveals that relevant chats are worthy more than precise (accurate in a scholars judgment) chats, Phase II of this game platform research has been elaborated to introduce multimedia user interface for the young age and system learning capability to enlighten the ancient Confucius culture.

Said platform and approaches are expected to be applicable for other cultural promotion, not limited to Confucius teaching, for reaching the majority of the population who is often engaged in social networking. Measurement of success is yet to be addressed, but game technology application is a sure promise to foster intergeneration culture exchange and communications.

References

1. Cheok, A.D.: Reviving Traditional Chinese Culture through an Interactive Chat Application. ART, ACM Computers in Entertainment 8(4), Article 1 (December 2010)
2. Cheok, A.D.: Confucius Chat: Bridging Intergenerational Communication Through Cultural Play. In: Proceedings of the IEEE Consumer Electronics Society IGIC 2012 (2012)
3. Khoo, E.T., Cheok, A.D., Liu, W., et al.: Confucius Computer: bridging intergenerational communication through illogical and cultural computing. Virtual Reality 15(4), 249–265 (2009)
4. Baker, S., Jeopardy, F.: Man vs. Machine and the Quest to Know Everything. Houghton Mifflin Harcourt, Boston (2011)
5. A.L.I.C.E. Artificial Intelligence Foundation, http://www.alicebot.org/aiml.html; Klein, D., Manning, C.D.: Accurate unlexicalized parsing. Proceedings of ACL 2003, pp. 423–430 (2003)
6. Klein, D., Manning, C.D.: Accurate unlexicalized parsing. In: Proceedings of the 41st Annual Meeting on - ACL 2003, pp. 423–430 (2003)
7. Huang, Z., Thint, M., Qin, Z.: Question classification using head words and their hypernyms. In: Proceedings of EMNLP 2008, p. 927 (2008)
8. Pedersen, T.: WordNet:: Similarity - Measuring the Relatedness of Concepts. In: Proceedings of the 19th National Conference on Artificial Intelligence (AAAI 2004), San Jose, CA, pp. 1024–1025 (2004)
9. Pedersen, T., Kolhatkar, V.: WordNet:: SenseRelate:: AllWords - A Broad Coverage Word Sense Tagger that Maximizes Semantic Relatedness. In: Proceedings of the NA Chapter of the ACL - Human Language Technologies 2009 Conference, Boulder, CO, pp. 17–20 (2009)
10. Fellbaum, C.: WordNet: An Electronic Lexical Database. MIT Press, Cambridge
11. Qiyu, L.: Zhongguo da baike quanshu. Zhongguo da baike quanshu chubanshe, Beijing/Shanghai (1992)
12. Soucy, P., Mineau, G.: A simple knn algorithm for text categorization, pp. 647–648

Existential Waters: On Employing a Game Engine for Artistic Expression within a Theater Play, and on the Implications of This towards Existential Games

Ido Aharon Iurgel[1,2] and Mário Pinto[2]

[1] Rhine-Waal University of Applied Sciences
Kamp-Lintfort, Germany
[2] CCG & [1] EngageLab (Centro Algoritmi)
[2] UMinho, Portugal
Ido.Iurgel@hochschule-rhein-waal.de,
mariojgpinto@gmail.com

Abstract. Water possesses an extraordinary expressive power, which has already been extensively exploited in the arts and in common sense thinking. Water can evoke deep feelings of purity, unity, and happiness, but also of dirt, drowning, and despair. We have explored this expressive power for a theater play, with an interactive simulation of water that was set into motion by the actor, and that expressed the inner feelings of his soul. We have employed the Ogre game engine for the simulation. We also believe that virtual reality technologies possess yet uncovered expressive potentials, among others for creating "existential games", which means games where only main existential vectors such as life, beauty, death, love are represented.

Keywords: Computer Graphics in Theater, Computer Art, Interactive Storytelling, Games as Philosophy, Emotional Computing.

1 Introduction

Think of a painting by William Turner or Caspar David Friedrich, cf. Figure 1. You may want to recall certain videos of Bill Viola, images of "the Room" in Tarkowski´s Stalker, or simply Titanic with DiCaprio, by James Cameron. There are countless examples in all other art forms as well, and we all know of numerous proverbs like "still waters run deep". Thus, many examples can be found where water is employed as a means of expression, creating and evoking emotions and existentially dense situations.

Our immediate challenge has been to transpose this expressive power into the digital, interactive realm, in order to obtain an expressive artwork that better accompanies the story of a theater play than a non-digital artifact would be able to. We will present our response to this challenge in the following paragraphs. Additional fascinating and demanding opportunities for exploiting the expressive power of computer graphics simulations lie ahead. At the end of this document, we will present the creation of "existential games" as an example.

A. Nijholt, T. Romão, and D. Reidsma (Eds.): ACE 2012, LNCS 7624, pp. 429–436, 2012.

Fig. 1. Water in paintings of C. D. Friedrich and W. Turner

2   Related Work

There are many examples of digital art being employed within theater and dance, e.g. by Tamiko Thiel [11], João Martinho [3], or SIRO-A [12]. However, we are not aware of any interactive video installation dedicated to a theater play that had a focus on speech, in our case being even a monologue, and that would have employed the interactive projection as a "mirror of the soul" of a story person, commenting on and unveiling his/hers inner states according to the narrative. Our projection is more than only an amplification of movements or of a dance. We also do not know of any similar approach that would have had recourse to the expressive power of the digital elements such as water, fire, wind, etc., to express meaning and story, in an attempt to induce feelings as immediately as possible. Our artwork wants to employ the computer graphics of a game engine for novel and powerful atmospheric instruments to be used in theater, complementing traditional stage means such as music or lighting. But we also believe that such instruments will at the end possess a much wider range of applications.

Our main inspiration source was fine arts (some references are mentioned in the Introduction) and literature; most important have also been some video works by Bill Viola [1], the work of Gaston Bachelard on the psychological meaning of the elements, in particular [2], and works of phenomenological ("existential") philosophers such as Heidegger or Lévinas (e.g. [4] and [5]), who set out for a description of the main features of human existence and arrived at a language full of expressive, poetic, invocative figures of speech.

3   Expressing the Soul of the Cannibal

The original theater script is named "Un Acto de Comunión", by the Argentinian author Lautaro Vito, and the enactment was in Portuguese, which amounts to "Um Acto de Comunhão". This is the narration of the life of Armin Meiwes, the "Cannibal of Rotenburg", who himself recalls it in the first person, chronologically, in a monologue.

Mr. Meiwes is German and has acquired international prominence by arranging a meeting with a certain Mr. Brandes, in order to eat the later, by mutual consent.

Mr. Meiwes has then eaten the flesh of the corpse of Mr. Brandes over many months, until he was arrested when looking for his next victim.

The enactment is an initiative of the well-known artist Marcos Barbosa, who took over both the roles of director and of actor. The premiere was in Guimarães, Portugal, in October 2011, and the play has since then been presented in Felgueiras and Porto, here as part of the international theater festival FITEI; further releases are expected to be set into scene in Lisbon.

In this drama, the author does not depict Mr. Meiwes as a monster. He shows a certain inner logic of the act of cannibalism, and the script tries to unveil these reasons. The director has chosen to stress this aspect of the naturalness of the act, which, from the murderer´s point of view, was beautiful.

The authors of the present document were in charge of the digital art for this drama. Because this was a monolog, the digital art was expected to create some additional movement and to inspirit the enactment, without bringing itself into the frontal plane too often, which would distract from the story and the acting.

We have decided to focus, with the digital art, on the rather shocking aspect of the subjective normality and intelligibility of the act of cannibalism, as suggested by the script. We wanted our digital artifact to express this, and to present this very peculiar point of view of the story person to the spectator, where cannibalism is a sexually overloaded necessity. We wanted to evoke feelings of an emotional catharsis in the spectator; we wanted him to feel empathy with the rejoicing that the act of eating another man must have meant to Mr. Meiwes, and with the beauty and purity which this horrifying act must have possessed to him. We wanted the digital art to be the mirror and representation of his soul, as it emerges from the script, without commentaries, distance, or moral judgment.

4   Digital Water as Mirror of the Soul

We have decided to place the rear projection at the back of the stage, occupying a prominent visual place. The light emitted by the projection was not exclusive, but it provided usually most of the illumination of the stage, so that color and intensity of the water dominated the lighting. We have chosen to place the virtual camera of the virtual world strictly at a right angle looking down at the water, and not to move it. This results into an intentionally artificial, minimalist perspective that keeps only the expressive power of the water, and that disregards any horizon, any "beyond the water"; the spectator looks frontally at the surface of the water all the time. This artificiality should also facilitate the interpretation of the water as mirror and representation.

The motions of the actor, captured by a camera, subtly set the water into motion; his profile and the contour of the movements could be discerned as the source of the surface disturbances that propagated as waves through the screen, cf. Figure 2. This was intended to establish a link between actor and water, and show that this was "his" water, that they belonged together.

Fig. 2. Different expressive states on stage, set into motion through movement

The main expressive parameters of the water were its color and color properties, the texture of its surface and of the water ground, the viscosity of the surface, the velocity of propagation of the waves, and their size. We have discerned around ten main parts of the piece that required a different setting of the principal parameters to represent and express the emotional meaning of the story situation, and the transition from one part to another required exact synchronization to the events on stage. An assistant was responsible for triggering the correct parts at the right moment. Between, but also to certain extend within these parts, the parameters changed gradually. For example, at the beginning of the enactment, assuming purity of early childhood, the water is shining blue, transparent, and its movements are free and agile. After the passage through some of the major of Mr. Meiwe´s life´s burdens, when he speaks of the death of his mother, the water becomes dark, turbid, slow, numbed. We wanted the difference between the states of the water to be strong and clearly perceptible to the spectators, but the transitions to be nevertheless in the sum subtle and gradual; it should be discernible that the expressive transformations of the water are accompanying exactly the paths and the timing of the narrative. Figure 4 depicts some more water states belonging to different story situations.

The climax of the piece is the eating of the other, and the catharsis that this represents to Mr. Meiwe´s, as he is seen here. To express this transformation though cannibalism, this "act of communion", from the dead waters of before to the happiness of after, we needed an appropriate transition effect that would reinforce this process of a peculiar self-cleaning, which should be accompanied by purifying soul turbulences. At the end of this step of personal conquest, we wanted to show again the rejoicing purity of the beginning of life that was achieved again.

In order to express this transition, the climax of a life, we have made the water to produce a visual celebration of this "glorious moment", with symmetric forms of rhythmically varying velocity, as in a dance or in a romantic fountain. This feast of the water was to be very artificial, in the sense that the water did not behave according to physical laws at this moment, as if it could now finally transcend its elemental limitations. This is the only situation where we have decided, upon consultation with the director, to employ figurative means. Out of this rejoicing water, slowly, and elaborately, a hanging, swaying cadaver emerged, cut as if it where meat at the butcher´s – but even here, when depicting in huge size an allegedly authentic gore picture of the real events that we had found in a dark corner of the internet, we have chosen to manipulate the photography to produce a most beautiful presentation, with vivid colors and smooth forms, in order to not challenge the loyalty of the water to the master it represents – we had to think of paintings of Francis Bacon under this circumstance, with their combination of horror and decorativeness. After its long, festive emerging, the cadaver stays fully visible only for a few seconds, and then dilutes into the water, becoming part of it, and the transubstantiation, the integration, the "communion" of the other, is then accomplished and over. Towards the end of the enactment, the water is again pure, calm, and shining. Cf. Figure 3 for examples of the catharsis, with a view of the stage.

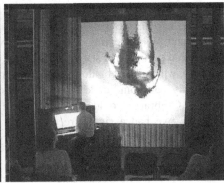

Fig. 3. The catharsis of the cannibalistic communion

This human corpse amidst an abstract representation focuses the visual narrative on the climax of the act of cannibalism, and suggests a first-time surpassing of a life-long solitude.

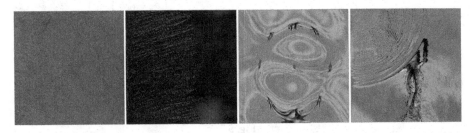

Fig. 4. Very different water states represent different story situations

Informal feedback from spectators on the digital art and its effects, including a public discussion after an enactment at the theater festival FITEI, and expert verdicts from the involved theater professionals, including principally the director, was very encouraging and positive. Up to now, it seems that indeed feelings can be transmitted and atmosphere for a theater play can be created with the help of virtual elements.

Possibly, we might need to readjust the parameters for the link between water movement and actor motion, in order to increase the effect, because some spectators reported that they were not aware of this correlation – it would have been very interesting to study possible subliminal effects of this link that we would indeed expect to exist.

5   Reproducing the Technologies

We have employed the Ogre3D [8] graphics engine for rendering, and our water simulation software had its start at the examples that can be downloaded together with Ogre. We have chosen Ogre because of these examples, and because it is open source, thus allowing us to manipulate any required detail. We are not aware of any comparable cost-free alternative for this task. The computer vision was accomplished with the help of the JMyron [7] libraries for Processing [10], which we used for motion and blob detecting. Cf. Figure 5 for a scheme of the technical configuration. There is no particularly strong justification for our choices related to computer vision software, which brought along additional complications of integrating Java and C++ – we simply had some code ready for JMyron, and time was short. OpenCV [9] or another C-library would otherwise have been a more natural choice here. As hardware, we had a single, recent laptop with a dedicated graphics card, a cheap webcam, and a projector together with a large back projection screen.

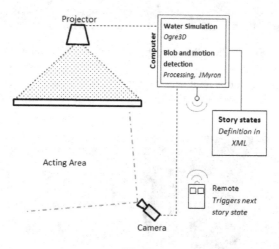

Fig. 5.

We had little more than one month only to carry out this project, from concept to premiere, and our joint efforts might have amounted to a total of six man-weeks of work for concept, programming, designing, fine tuning, and testing. The visual effects resulted from a combination of creating and adapting water textures and their image properties, and of programming and defining the simulation parameters. Most of the programming effort was invested into developing beautiful transitions between different water states, but there were also other demanding C++ tasks on the way. For triggering the transition between one state and another during the play, an assistant had to press a key in the right moment (for this we connected an off-the-shelf remote that usually controls presentations to the computer). We developed a XML-script that defined the narrative, i.e. the sequence of water states and textures, the transitions between them, and eventual special effects. The script contained at the end dozens of sub-states and transitional states, grouped together by around ten main parts (cf. above). The water simulation that we employed consisted only of surface effect algorithms, and did not allow for "entering" into the water. Originally, we intended to employ the Ogre plug-in Hydrax [6] at the beginning and end of the story, which would have allowed for "emerging" from the water at the beginning, and "entering" and "dwelling" into it at the end, but we could not finish in time for this.

6   The Challenge of Existential Games

We believe that it is possible to further exploit and intensify the individual experience of the virtual elements, in different contexts. For example, this could be done by introducing responsibility for their states, and failure and success when influencing their course, i.e. by devising novel kinds of games; such an existential game world would consists only of highly expressive elements such as the virtual water, and would represents, more immersively and with greater emotional intensity than ever before, existential situations. Thus, the expressive power of the digital elements is certainly not confined to being a visual commentary to a story. Games could build upon the expressive power of the elements, and they would touch the players and create sensations of immersion in yet unknown ways. We can only roughly sketch the ideas here.

A game requires mechanisms of responsibility (or "agency") for the user. For example, this may mean that the user has to thrive not "to drown" into the simulated water, but to "emerge" from it, and at the end of the game to bath into it, to enjoy it. The game play then becomes a metaphor for (aspects of) life, if the responsibility for the elements reflects real dependencies. It becomes a kind of "philosophy" of life.

For instance, we may want to represent how man can get lost in too much irrelevant information, publicity, and others stealing one´s attention and time; and how it is possible to regain focus and thrive at a substantial, sensible individual perspective. We can think of a simple game that implements this: Imagine drowning into the water of a storm, and each beating of a wave is accompanied by such an irrelevant but loud, dissonant voice or scream. Imagine that there is a single relevant, harmonic, authoritative voice amidst this. The challenge is to focus on this particular voice (for example on its ever changing directions) – when this succeeds for a time, the storm evades, and peace, the horizons and directions emerge again.

This sketch is based on [4]. For it, we have taken up the theme of Heidegger´s analysis of "being lost in the Man", of recognizing the "voice of one´s conscience", and such regaining "integrity" (Ganzheit). We believe that the expressive power of the elements will eventually lead to games that are "philosophical", if the game logic succeeds in representing existential structures and responsibilities, and in evoking feelings of existential situations. When this happens, we are confronted – not with an illustration of a philosopher´s philosophy, but with a true philosophy and philosophical experience for the player – something that extends and continues certain philosophical traditions technologically, and is able to create experiences that refresh and clarify our understanding, feelings, and options.

7   Conclusions

Our running example was based on the simulation of water. This simulation will have its own rules that need not be realistic; the water may speak, change colors, or even "fall up"; the metaphor may mix with other figures and elements, if required by the figurative logic that we create. And water is certainly only an example among many, albeit an important one; but an "element" in the present context can be virtually anything, or any aspect of being, that can evoke deep feelings, and that can be adapted as a metaphor for complex expressions – earth, fire, up, front, weight, equilibrium, the body and face of the other.

We believe that recent advances in computer graphics, computer vision, and other technologies, open up opportunities for employing "the elements" as means of emotional expression, both illustratively, as in the theater piece "Un Acto de Comunión", as well as in "philosophical" games, where the user is immersed into these elements and deals with them. There are many other possible usages, though, for instance as an "intelligent ambient" that reflects and influences emotions. But since the technologies are very recent, in a cultural perspective, we believe that there is still some way to go until we learn how to best use and adapt them within different contexts, and until we have learnt how to exploit their full expressive potential.

References

1. Ross, D.A., Viola, B., Hyde, L., Perov, K.: Bill Viola. Whitney Museum of American Art with Flammarion (1997)
2. Bachelard, G.: L'eau et les rêves: Essai sur l'imagination de la matière. Le Livre de Poche (1993)
3. Moura, M.J., Barros, N., Marcos, A.F., Branco, P.: NUVE – Dancing with a Digital Virtual Body. IJCICG (2011)
4. Heidegger, M.: Sein und Zeit. Niemeyer (2006)
5. Lévinas, E.: Totalité et infini: essai sur l'extériorité. Le Livre de Poche (1990)
6. Add-on for Ogre to render water scenes,
   http://www.ogre3d.org/tikiwiki/Hydrax
7. JMyron – Computer Vision and Motion Tracking,
   http://webcamxtra.sourceforge.net/
8. OGRE – Open Source 3D Graphics Engine, http://www.ogre3d.org/
9. OPENCV – Open Source Computer Vision,
   http://opencv.willowgarage.com/wiki/
10. Processing – Open Source Programming Environment, http://processing.org/
11. Thiel, T.: In the Land of Babari-an, http://www.mission-base.com/tamiko/babarian/index.html (retrieved on July 08, 2012)
12. http://www.siro-a.de/

Reframing Haute Couture Handcraftship: How to Preserve Artisans' Abilities with Gesture Recognition

Gustavo Marfia, Marco Roccetti, Andrea Marcomini,
Cristian Bertuccioli, and Giovanni Matteucci

Alma Mater Studiorum - University of Bologna
Mura Anteo Zamboni 7, 40127 - Bologna, Italy
{gustavo.marfia,marco.roccetti,andrea.marcomini,
cristian.bertuccioli,giovanni.matteucci}@unibo.it

Abstract. Computer gaming has often represented a fertile ground for the implementation and testing of novel and engaging human-computer interactions systems. Such phenomenon has occurred first with mice and joysticks and keeps on going, increasing in complexity and realism, with body-based interfaces (e.g., Wii, Kinect). Now, many fields and applications could benefit from these advances, starting with those where interactions, rather than physical objects, play a key role. Relevant exemplars can be found within many specimen of intangible cultural heritage (e.g., music, drama, skills, craft, etc.), whose preservation is possible only thanks to those tradition bearers that patiently bestow their knowledge upon new generations. Italian luxury crafts, which range from sports cars to high-end clothing, for example, often obtain their high quality and consequent reputation from a mix of intangible artistic and technological skills. The preservation of such skills and the persistent creation of such handcrafts has been possible, in time, thanks to those "master-apprentice" relations that have retained the quality standards that stand behind them. Nowadays such type of relations remain no longer easy to implement, as creation and production paradigms have undergone radical changes in the past two decades (i.e., globalization of production processes), making the transfer and preservation of skills challenging. Inspired by the advances made in human-computer interaction schemes for gaming, in this work we propose a non-invasive encoding of artisans manual skills, which, based on a set of vision algorithms, is able to capture and recognize the gestures performed by one or both hands, without needing the use of any specific hardware but a simple video camera. Our system has been tested on a real-world scenario: we here present the preliminary results obtained when encoding the gestures performed by an artisan while working at the creation of haute couture shoes.

Keywords: Algorithms, Design, Performance, Experimentation.

A. Nijholt, T. Romão, and D. Reidsma (Eds.): ACE 2012, LNCS 7624, pp. 437–444, 2012.
© Springer-Verlag Berlin Heidelberg 2012

1 Introduction

Craftsman skills are the result of experience and technique learned over time through consolidated careers in designing and manufacturing a specific product, where tradition is often mixed with art and the use of new technologies, just as envisioned long ago by the Bauhaus scholars [1]. However, the "master-apprentice" teaching model, which has been at the basis of the transfer of such skills, is no longer as common as in the past. Hence it is not easy to teach and pass on knowledge and skills learned by specialized craftsmen who create and develop sophisticated and unique craft products, in a perfect balance between tradition and modernity. For these reasons, it is clear that, within a crafting enterprise, it is very important to find ways of archiving the most relevant collections of intangible assets and knowledge. This is a process where technologies that have been devised in the realm of computer gaming can make a difference and lead to the preservation, through digital encodings of gestures and movements, of the knowledge and experience required in the craft industry [2].

Such benefits, in addition, can be extended beyond the preservation of knowledge, and also be utilized to analyze and assess the processes and gestures that are employed to design and create particular products, for example. Also for this reason, the use systems that can track and recognize human movements within the context of handcrafting opens up to a new range of opportunities and applications that would have been unimaginable before now.

Now, the contribution of this work is the design and implementation of a system capable of tracking and encoding the actions performed by an artisan at work. It operates in two steps. The first is that of recognizing and tracking the features of a human body, while performing coarse movements. The second is the recognition and tracking of the actions performed by one or both hands, while making fine, but also fast, gestures within a restricted area. With these two steps we are able to follow the complete set of movements and gestures, which an artisan can perform while working.

Before ours, a few works have been proposing the idea of preserving cultural heritage with the use of modern technologies, for example in the context of knitting [3]. However, the cited stream of work principally leveraged on all those technologies that can support and emphasize the social aspects that intervene while crafting (e.g., exchange of information with social networks) rather than on obtaining, through the tracking and recognition of gestures, a digital coding of experiences and skills. An interesting technique, in this latter sense, has been proposed in [4], [5], where the authors demonstrated the feasibility of tracking and recognizing handmade gestures with the sole use of a video camera and a pair of special gloves, specifically customized (i.e., colored with a give pattern) for such purpose. However, when applied to haute couture crafting enterprises, the requirement of wearing special gloves can represent a disturbing factor for an artisan, thus jeopardizing the performance of the natural gestures executed while creating.

Following the recent achievements that have been got in the field of gestural gaming interfaces, in the remainder we will show that it is possible to encode and maintain the knowledge of craft skills through a gesture recognition system based on non-invasive technology. Starting from the idea that any interaction with our system must be realized without the use of any tangible device or equipment, i.e., without using dedicated and specialized hardware ([2], [6]), we realized a system that can encode craft gestures, with the sole use of a single video camera and a set of specialized software algorithms. As we shall shortly see, such system has been successfully applied to the tracking and recognition of the gestures involved in the creation of haute couture shoes.

2   Our Approach

The actions performed by any artisan can be roughly of two types, depending on the gesture that it performs: fine and coarse. Intuitively, actions that involve fine gestures are performed in all those cases where a high degree of precision is required, as in the cases where a shoe is stitched or when a mechanical wristwatch is tweaked, for example. We consider coarse all the remaining actions where, instead, the same precision is not mandatory (e.g., moving an object from one end to another of a lab). In the following we will first focus on how fine-grained gestures can be tracked and recognized, and then move on to how coarse ones can be followed as well, in the context of the production of haute couture shoes. The production of shoes involves a long set of steps which range from, choosing the leather of which they will be made of to stitching together the midsole, the sole, the vamp and the heel sections that compose them. Among all the possible actions, we selected two significant gestures in the production of shoes: carving and stitching a sole (Figs. 1.a and 2.a). These two actions are typically performed in a sequence, one after the other: at first, a sole is carved in order to create a groove; then the obtained groove is used as a track to sew together the remaining leather parts of the shoe to the given sole. The coding of these gestures lies in the determination of: (a) the number of times that a particular gesture is repeated and (b) the path that is followed while performing that gesture. Our system supports this type of coding through the tracking of the hand movements of a craftsman at work (Figs. 1.c and 2.c).

Technically, our system operates as follows. A video camera is placed in front of the areas where an artisan works, at a close distance from where gestures and movements are typically performed (we tested our system with this distance set to 50 cm and to 120 cm). After capturing two consecutive video frames,

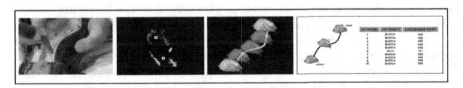

Fig. 1. Left to right: (a) carving the sole, (b) distance of the center of clusters, (c) tracking one hand, (d) system performance while carving

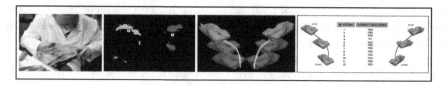

Fig. 2. Left to right: (a) sewing leather to a sole, (b) distance of the cluster centers, (c) tracking two hands, (d) system performance while sewing

the system first of all applies a Gaussian filter to remove any high-frequency noise. Every second frame is then subtracted from the first one in order to obtain the difference frame between the two. Such frame, in fact, contains the information pertaining any change that occurred in time, between the moment when the first frame was captured and that when the second was acquired. Within the difference, hence, our system searches for any macro area where the two frames effectively differ, as this may be indicating that, single movements, or also multiple movements, have been performed. This step is performed dividing the difference frame into a grid where a square becomes active when it contains an active macro area. However, an active square may not represent a solid indication of motion, if it lies in an isolated position (the motion of one hand also involves the motion of the connected arm, for example). For this reason we also apply a filter that eliminates all those active squares that fall into isolated positions, since they cannot be representing significant movements.

Now, once the areas where motion has occurred have been individuated, an interesting problem is that of determining whether an artisan is working, utilizing one or both of its hands. In order to detect whether both hands are used, we adopted the following approach. In particular, we first utilize a k-means clustering algorithm (with k equal to 2) that takes as an input all active squares in order to separate them into two clusters. In fact, with k = 2 we are considering, a priori, that any movement may have been performed by two hands. Obviously this is not always the case: in fact, there may be actions, which require a single hand and others, which require both. Hence, in order to discriminate whether one or both hands accomplished a given movement, we adopted the following heuristics based on the distance between the two cluster centers that have been individuated at the preceding step (Figs. 1.b and 2.b): a distance that exceeds a given threshold value indicates that both hands accomplished a movement (Fig. 3.a, frames 1 through 7), while if that distance is less than that threshold value the movement is probably performed by a single hand (Fig. 3.a, frame 8, and Fig. 3.b). Finally, after having determined whether one or two hands are moving in front of the camera, their position is computed as follows. If only one moving hand is detected, its position will be identified as the cluster center positioned higher in the grid (Fig. 3.b); otherwise, if two hands are in motion, their positions will be estimated as the center of the two separated clusters. Clearly, with such approach discontinuities may appear, yielding situations where, due to a number of reasons (e.g., illumination level), first one and then two hands are detected, and vice versa; to overcome such type of problem, we integrated

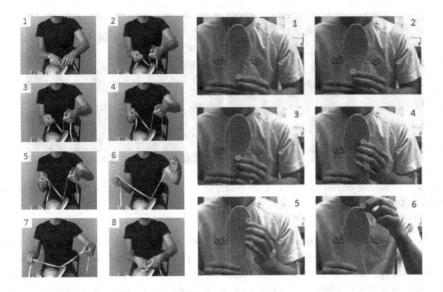

Fig. 3. Left to right: (a) tracking two hands, (b) tracking one hand

a Kalman Filter in our system, whose role is that of tracking consistently and gracefully the trajectories along which a particular movement is carried out.

Now, the tracking and recognition of any coarse gesture can be performed utilizing a video camera that is placed at some distance from an artisan, hence capturing its whole figure. The algorithm that we implemented to carry out this task lies along the lines of the one that has been presented in [7] and works as follows. The basic idea that is implemented is that of determining the position of five crucial points of the human body: the head, the hands and the feet of a person (Fig. 4.a). In brief, this is performed by first determining the positions of the two feet, which may be detected as the two minimum points of a human blob which has been separated from the static background. After this first step, and utilizing anatomical proportions, the same human blob is divided into four sectors (Fig. 4.b), two that include its bottom part (i.e., below the hip line) and two that, instead, incorporate its top (i.e., above the hip line). Within the top sector, our algorithm proceeds searching for three maxima: if these are successfully found our algorithm has detected also the hands and the head of the moving person. If not, our algorithm assumes that the global maximum represents the head of the person and adopts additional strategies to find the remaining positions (i.e., those of one or both hands), again leveraging on the idea of searching for the maximum of the blob in a given direction. This said, this methodology can be adopted to track and recognize a wide set of actions that are performed when crafting a shoe, ranging from those where an artisan transports any leather or other material to its workstation, to those that are executed while interacting with different machinery and tools (e.g., automatic stitchers, leather polishing machines, etc.).

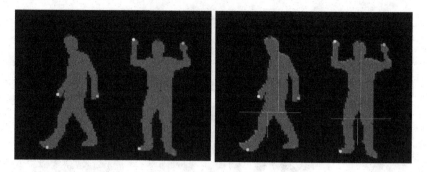

Fig. 4. Detecting coarse actions. Left to right: (a) detected points, and, (b) human body sectors

Obviously, once the data has been obtained, the goal can be twofold: (a) use this as a benchmark and compare it against individuals for performance feedback, and, (b) use the acquired information as a training set that can be adopted by unskilled apprentices. All this leaves an open set of questions unanswered, which require further research and investigation. In fact, how could it be possible to efficiently compare the gestures performed by two different artisans working at the same task? These gestures comprise actions that are not only based on simple repetitions, but also synthetize creativity aspects that could give different, but similarly remarkable, results. To this date, our approach to this problem has only relied on a geometrical analysis and comparison of the trajectories that are returned by our tracking activities. In particular, two gestures are considered to be similar, if their corresponding trajectories begin (and end) in nearby areas. More precisely, our algorithm recognizes as correct all those trajectories that flow within a stripe of a given size (the idea is that a certain degree of tolerance is admitted to capture any difference produced by creativity). Finally, each given trajectory must terminate within a given period of time, after which that gesture has been performed too slowly to be considered correct. This mechanism was devised to make our recognizer able to consider as correct a wider set of movements with slightly different trajectories that differentiate only on the basis of a few geometric differences, nonetheless there is awareness on our side that this methodology is rough and needs to be refined, for example inspired by relevant intuitions provided in [3].

3   Empirical Results

The performance of our system has been assessed in reality, thanks to the collaboration with a renowned Italian haute couture shoe brand. In particular, we were able to assess how our system behaved while performing fine gestures when two different actions were being carried out: (i) carving the sole of a shoe, which required the movement of a single hand, and, (ii) sewing the leather to a sole, which, instead, required the use of two hands.

Table 1. Single hand

Euclidean distance (pixel)	Camera distance (cm)	Match (%)	Uniqueness point (%)
35	50	96.65	98.08
35	120	96.8	100
45	50	96.15	100
45	120	93.57	100

All the results discussed in this Section were obtained utilizing a camera whose frame rate was set to 30 fps. The performance figures pertaining our algorithm while the first movement was executed are shown in Table 1. In particular, when dealing with a single hand, we notice that it is possible to encounter situations where, erroneously, two hands are detected. However, when choosing a threshold value for the distance between the two centers that fell in the 35 to 45 pixels range, we obtained a very close match and a good estimate in determining the movement of a single hand (Fig. 1.d).

Table 2. Two hands

Euclidean distance (pixel)	Camera distance (cm)	Match (%)
35	50	94.54
35	120	84.78
45	50	83.82
45	120	90.9

The results pertaining movement (ii) are, instead, shown in Table 2. Also in this case the threshold value between the cluster centers (i.e., distance between the two hands) plays an important role. In particular, the closer are the hands to a camera, the larger is the size of the motion-sensible areas. As a consequence, the distance between the cluster centers will be small/large when the hands are close/distant from the camera. This means that the threshold value needs to be small in all those cases where the camera is kept close to an artisan, and large in all other cases. We hence can better determine if we have one or two hands involved during the performance of a given movement (Fig. 2.d).

4   Conclusion

We implemented a prototype, which, with sole use of a webcam, is able to track and encode the trajectory of a movement made by a craftsman at work. Our first results indicate that there is a good accuracy in following fine gestures, as well as coarse ones, when a video camera is both close or far from a craftsman at work. What is relevant is that all this has been made possible thanks to techniques and experiences drawn from the computer gaming field and allied technologies [8], [9], [10], [11].

Acknowledgements. The authors wish to thank the ALTER-NET Project for the financial support.

References

1. Maulsby, L.M.: Bauhaus Modern and Bauhaus Culture: From Weimer to the Cold War. Wiley Journal of Architectural Education 63(1) (2009)
2. Roccetti, M., Marfia, G., Zanichelli, M.: The Art and Craft of Making the Tortellino: Playing with a Digital Gesture Recognizer for Preparing Pasta Culinary Recipes. ACM Computers in Entertainment 8(4) (2010)
3. Rosner, D.K., Ryokay, K.: Reflections on Craft: Probing the Creative Process of Everyday Knitters. In: 7th ACM Conf. on Creativity and Cognition, Berkeley, pp. 195–204 (2009)
4. Wang, R.Y., Popovic, J.: Real-time Hand-Tracking with a Color Glove. ACM Trans. Graph. 28(3) (2009)
5. Palazzi, C.E., Roccetti, M., Marfia, G.: Realizing the Unexploited Potential of Games on Serious Challenges. ACM Computers in Entertainment 8(4) (2010)
6. Marfia, G., Roccetti, M., Matteucci, G., Marcomini, A.: Technoculture of Handcraft: Fine Gesture Recognition for Haute Couture Skills Preservation and Transfer in Italy. In: 39th ACM International Conference and Exhibition on Computer Graphics and Interactive Techniques Posters, Los Angeles (2012)
7. Roccetti, M., Marfia, G., Bertuccioli, C.: Day and Night at the Museum: Intangible Computer Interfaces for Public Exhibitions (submitted for publication, 2012)
8. Palazzi, C.E., Ferretti, S., Roccetti, M., Pau, G., Gerla, M.: How Do You Quickly Choreograph Inter-Vehicular Communications? A Fast Vehicle-to-Vehicle Multi-Hop Broadcast Algorithm, Explained. In: 4th Annual IEEE Consumer Communications and Networking Conference, pp. 960–964 (2007)
9. Aldini, A., Gorrieri, R., Roccetti, M., Bernardo, M.: Comparing the QoS of Internet Audio Mechanisms via Formal Methods. ACM Transactions on Modeling and Computer Simulation 11(1), 1–42 (2001)
10. Leontiadis, I., Marfia, G., MacK, D., Pau, G., Mascolo, C., Gerla, M.: On the effectiveness of an opportunistic traffic management system for vehicular networks. IEEE Transactions on Intelligent Transportation Systems 12(4), 1537–1548 (2011)
11. Marfia, G., Roccetti, M.: TCP at last: Reconsidering TCP's role for wireless entertainment centers at home. IEEE Transactions on Consumer Electronics 56(4), 2233–2240 (2010)

PURE FLOW: Gallery Installation / Mobile Application

Duncan Rowland[1] and Katy Connor[2]

[1] School of Computer Science, University of Lincoln, Lincoln, U.K.
`drowland@lincoln.ac.uk`
[2] Studio 94, Spike Island, Bristol, UK
`info@katyconnor.com`

Abstract. This paper describes the two phase development of the digital art piece PURE FLOW. The first deployment of this work was as a gallery based exhibit in which digital noise sampled from the Global Positioning System was exposed as dynamic sound and projected visual displays. The second piece extended these initial themes onto a handheld platform (iPhone) whereby the user could continually sample digital noise from positioning systems at their surrounding environment and generate an audio and visual experience specifically created for their immediate location. Aesthetic considerations are described along with implementation details leading to general reflections relating to collaborations between artists and technical specialists.

Keywords: Visual Arts, Sound and Music Design, Aesthetics, Mobile and Ubiquitous Entertainment, Cultural Computing.

1 Introduction

1.1 Artist's Statement

From the artist's website (Connor 2011):
"PURE FLOW reveals the noise generated between GPS data systems and multiple satellites, 3G networks and Wifi hotspots as a tangible presence in the environment.

The APP visualises the instability and fragility of Live signals, passing through cloud cover and urban architecture; absorbed by bodies, reflecting off concrete and refracting through glass. The user can directly manipulate the outcomes, by touching the visual and sonic patterns triggered by fluctuations in the data. Once activated, PURE FLOW reveals these signals as a sliver of fluctuating white noise, responding directly to the movement and immediate environment of the device.

PURE FLOW subverts the use-value of GPS as a surveying and navigational tool; revealing these invisible data streams and highlighting their increasing ubiquity, as sophisticated military technologies become key components in daily life."

The artistic desire here is clear. There is, around us, an invisible field created by the many wirelessly collaborating technical devices, and the artist would like this exposed. This feeling is not new, and there is a good deal of previous work in this area. Indeed, it is general human nature to dislike things being hidden from us, and so it is therefore not surprising that there is this pervading wish for such invisible forces to be revealed.

A. Nijholt, T. Romão, and D. Reidsma (Eds.): ACE 2012, LNCS 7624, pp. 445–452, 2012.
© Springer-Verlag Berlin Heidelberg 2012

1.2   Background

Since the late 1970s Christina Kubisch has produced a series of sound installations based on the sonification of electromagnetic fields [1, 2]. In some pieces, electric wire is deliberately positioned around a space and used to construct fields based on pre-defined audio material. As the sounds are 'played' down the wires, the visitor is able to wirelessly 'mix' between the different sources by altering his location and orientation. To generate the audio, early implementations required the visitor to manipulate a small cube containing an inductance-coil and a loudspeaker. Later, Kubisch developed wireless headphones that better succeed in centring the user within the experience, "[where] every movement, even a slight turn of the head, results in a different sequence of tones". The headphones contain a built-in inductance coil which picks up not only the intended signal emanating from the wires, but also noise produced by unrelated nearby electrical activity ('naturally' occurring fields such as those produced by lights, transformers and indeed most modern electrical equipment). Originally Kubisch sought to filter out the hum of this electromagnetic interference, but in 2003 the continual increase of this 'noise' in the environment forced a reconceptualisation of her work [3]. She began to treat these fluctuations as 'signal', revealing these hidden fields as sounds as the user progressed along an 'Electrical Walk'.

More recently, two projects by Timo Arnall et al have explored the visualisation of fields associated with RFID and WiFi technologies [4,5]. Both projects use long exposure photography together with a probe to record properties of the field at various locations. As the probe is moved through space it reacts to the signal at its current locations and emits light designed to reflect this. This allows a picture of the field to be built-up over time as the probe is relocated to multiple positions. The probe "Immaterials: the ghost in the field" consisted of an RFID reader and green led configured to illuminate when within readable range of the RFID tag. This allowed the image of a "readable volume" to be produced, i.e. the volume surrounding the RFID tag within which its data could be read. In a subsequent project, "Immaterials: light painting WiFi", a series of lights were placed along the length of a long pole and configured to sequentially illuminate in proportion to the available WiFi signal strength (in a way analogues to the signal strength bars on a laptop or phone, only with more precision). This pole was carried vertically through an environment such that the long exposure image recorded a glowing bar-chart like graph embedded in the environment.

PURE FLOW draws on both collections of projects for context and relates to their goals in the following ways:

Analogue Immediacy vs. Digital Mediation

In Kubisch's audio creations there is a direct analogue mapping between the fields present in the environment and the sounds generated as an associated sonification. There is no digital signal processing, there is no analogue to digital conversion. This close mapping affords the sense of immediacy indicated by the claim that a "slight turn of the head" affects the quality of the sound. Although with updated technology it may now be possible to sense the field strength, convert this to a digital value and subsequently use this to produce an audio rendition. This may introduce delay, losing the sense of immediacy, but more importantly the direct mapping would be effectively lost, since the digital value could be used to trigger any variety of events. In contrast, the digital approach employed by Arnall et al has no such sense of immediacy. Whilst during the production of the images there are points in time when the light is either on or off (corresponding to whether a signal is either detected with sufficient strength or not), but during the long exposure this temporality is lost. Also, the mapping of signal strength to LED activation is entirely arbitrary, and exists solely for the production of the final image. Since this image is built over time, the image is effectively recording (or 'buffering') the data and representing it as an instance collapsed across the sampling period. A key consideration here is the amount of information available for sonification or visualization (i.e. the analogue and digital bandwidth). In the analogue case, Kubisch has at her disposal such a large amount of information that it can be streaming in real-time through the headphones straight to her visitor's ears. This is not the case in Arnall et al's digital environment where the data flow is so small it takes a good deal of time to build up even a single image. A contrast could be drawn with the often sonified Geiger–Müller tube, where the detection of ionizing radiation is used to generate a popping noise. The more radiation, the more pops, up until a point whether there are enough pops to generate a crackle with a discernable pitch. In the case of RFID and WiFi signal strength the available data is the result of a good deal of signal processing and updates are in the order of one data point every few seconds. In terms of our Geiger counter this will correspond to a frequent pop, but nothing that would be interesting to view or listen to. As a consequence the data needs to be buffered although this results in an inevitable loss of immediacy. The case is even more severe for Global Positioning System signals.

The Global Positioning System (GPS)

Initially developed for military purposes, GPS applications are now commonplace. From SATNAV routing systems on vehicles and the geo-tagging of images on smart-phones, to more esoteric pursuits such as mobile and pervasive media art (for example, Blast Theory's 'Can You See Me Now?' and 'Uncle Roy All Around You' [6]), the uses for accurate positioning data is growing. In essence the system is very straightforward. A number of satellites orbiting the earth are constantly broadcasting the current time and their present location. When this message is received, the time elapsed since it was sent tells the listener how far they are away from that specific satellite. This process is repeated for multiple satellites so that the location of the listening device can be estimated. Error appears in this estimation from a number of sources including: inaccurate values sent from the satellite (although these values are known to a very high degree of accuracy, it is possible the values are deliberately distorted), noise in transmission (i.e. something that interferes with the signal on route, such as it bouncing off a building or being blocked totally by a wall), however, one of the largest source of error is likely the GPS receiver's own clock which is considerably less accurate that the atomic clock on the satellites.

By watching the fluctuations of the values of a stationary GPS receiver is it possible to suggest that this is 'noise' in the data, and indeed, this is the very information which PURE FLOW uses in its visualizations. However, it is not possible to say exactly where this noise has come from, indeed our conceptualization of "noise" here is at the holistic level and so we do not even know (nor mind) if the noise stems from an analogue or digital source. An alternative solution would be to directly use the analogue signal (cf. "radio field") to generate the visualization as opposed to the digital data (cf. "readable volume") in a manner more similar to Kubisch's work. This may indeed produce interesting possibilities for RFID and WiFi and it is definitely possible to 'listen' to the GPS signal directly (as opposed to the pattern produced by the digital error). Unfortunately, this technique would require specialist hardware and so would not be deployable on a consumer phone.

Signal, Noise and Error

Katy Connor has previously exhibited a video installation "Snow, TV Snow" in which two identical black and white televisions show 'noisy' visuals [7]. One screen displays a looped video footage of swirling snow, with eddies and circling birds, while the other shows contrasting TV static.

PURE FLOW attempts to generate a similar visual aesthetic by generating a 'noisy looking' pattern from the error in GPS data. The guiding principle for the implementation is that the algorithms deployed should not introduce any random elements; rather all displays (audio and visual) should be driven solely by the detected error. This is rather a fine point, since a system could be implemented that uses the error as a seed for some non-deterministic function. During discussions with the artist it was not felt that this was in the spirit of the piece (exposing that which is hidden) since the display would have little correlation to the error data. Instead, the small amount of available error data should be reused in multiple ways to create sounds and images that are directly connected to the source, hence the algorithms deployed are predictable in the intuitive sense and do not introduce any pseudo-randomness. In his work on Algorithmic Information Theory (AIT), Gregory Chaitin provides a meaningful working definition for randomness [8], but as Kubisch illustrates, both signal and noise are entirely context dependent and antithetical (signal is that which is not noise, and conversely, noise is that which is not signal). In the design of PURE FLOW the goal was to expose the error without introducing noise (randomness), hence stochastic algorithms were rejected.

2   Implementation

From the design remit and aesthetic considerations two pieces were created via remote collaborations. The first, as a gallery installation, was created entirely remotely (with the exception of an initial introductory meeting) with sporadic discussions taking place via Skype as required and much 'remote debugging' performed by logging into and controlling the artist's Macbook through iChat. The second, as an iPhone app, involved two additional meetings with the artist to fine-tune the look-and-feel of the application.

2.1   Gallery Installation

To collect the GPS error information, the gallery installation made use of a Bluetooth GPS device (Holux M-1200). This was situated such that it regularly obtained a good GPS signal, but was close enough to the Macbook running the display for a reliable Bluetooth connection to be established and maintained. The Macbook drove a projector which cast an image onto a suspended semi-opaque Perspex sheet. This provided a direct visual image from the projector but also reflected a portion of the received light to generate a back-projection. As a result, a visitor situated in the space was enveloped in the light-field (to reflect the manor in which the GPS signal permeates space).

Visual Programming

Pure Data (Pd-extended) is a free visual patch programming environment for creating audio/visual displays [9]. It was selected partly for the ease with which it can be used to create synchronized audio and visual displays, but mainly as a method through which system functionality could be exposed to the artist in a familiar way (i.e. both through a visual representation of the system and its data flow, as well as through parameter control via sliders and other standard interface elements).

The Macbook ran a bespoke native application to collect the positional error from the stationary GPS device and generate 512x512 grayscale images. The image data (normalized error information) was used by the Pd patch in a number of ways. The texture information was displayed six times on the screen (with various degrees of transparency and transformation). Translation was used to create a rapid flickering effect by sequentially using the values present in the gray-scale image to control the horizontal and vertical offsets of the texture. The frame-rate (and rate with which each pair of pixel values were read from the image) was set by the artist via a slider, as were the rotation, transparency and scale of the textures. A similar technique was used in the generation of the audio where a series of interlinked oscillators had various parameters controlled by the values of the gray-scale image data. The same values are used synchronously as those employed to control the texture offset, and this ensures the visual movements on the screen are mirrored by the fluctuations in the sounds.

Post-mortem

Although the gallery piece was well received [10, 11] (as it helped secure funding for the subsequent mobile development) there were several issues that arose during the implementation that were not foreseen. Remote working was more of a hindrance that expected, particularly during demonstrations where showing work-in-progress was hampered because the development environment was not easily portable, and due to bandwidth/frame-rate limitations remotely logging into a Macbook did not accurately reflect what the display was showing. Ultimately the solution employed was to courier the Macbook to the developer, install the software, configure it for the gallery and then courier it back. This worked well except for late problems that occurred in the gallery itself when the Macbook totally failed and needed to be replaced (it is possible that couriering the Macbook about may have contributed to its demise).

Although the goal of using Pd was to develop a solution that could be adapted by the artist after development had finished, ultimately this was only achieved through the use of sliders. The complexity of the Pd patch made it unmaintainable, possible mostly through the inexperience of the developer with the medium, but also down to inadequacies of the visual programming system itself which did not seem to scale well and appeared difficult to debug. For the second implementation it was resolved to rely on text-based (rather than visual) coding, to deploy on a standard platform well known features, to use appropriate project management tools, and to meet more often.

2.2   Mobile Application

A second implementation "PURE FLOW [mobile edition]" sought to relocate the experience out of the gallery setting. Just as "Electrical Walks" and "Immaterials" reveal the fields present in every day places, the new work exposes the pervasive nature of GPS data. Apple's iOS platform was selected for deployment because it provided an established user-base with known features and a well understood interface paradigm. Although it was not possible to exactly replicate the functionality of the gallery piece (the iPhone application uses fluctuations in the accelerometer values in place of GPS noise) the essence of the experience is maintained through the artistic framing (if not through the actual mechanical operation of the implementation).

3 Discussion

The technical goals of PURE FLOW were twofold: first to sense the electromagnetic 'noise' in the environment created by navigation systems; and second, to create an audio/visual display that exposed this according to a given aesthetic. This was successfully achieved for the initial gallery artwork, and a workaround using accelerometer noise meant the mobile edition was accomplished as a reasonable compromise. Because of the small amounts of sensor information, all solutions required the buffering of data in order to produce a visual display and associated sounds capable of generating interest in the viewer. This produced an inevitable lack of immediacy in the experience. Alternative solutions to access GPS satellite transmissions directly would require bespoke hardware to be constructed and so would not be reasonably deployable to consumer phones; however, this is clearly an interesting avenue for future work in a gallery setting. Contemporary art has always used contemporary materials in its practice, and at present there is a growing interest in the use of modern electronic technology [12] (take for example, the expanding international network of dorkbot events [13], for "engineers who want to be artists, or artists who want to be engineers, or the otherwise confused"). This trans-disciplinary (or post-disciplinary) thinking has fostered an emergent culture of collaboration where the distinction between artist and technology specialist is becoming blurred. Artists are keen to understand the capabilities afforded by the new media and technical experts benefit from exposure to new use scenarios. Culturally though there can be very different expectations and an attempt to simultaneously progress knowledge in different disciplines (satisfying multiple, often conflicting agenda) can be difficult to accomplish (e.g. with credit often not given to the technical role in the creative process and *vice versa*). Attempts to repurpose the novel functionality of a new technology platform through artistic collaborations needs careful orchestration. A technical expert will often present technology in the way that it is traditionally understood in their field, and an artist new to the area may have unrealistic preconceptions about any capabilities. In addition, to push technology into new areas an artist must often gain a high level of technical knowledge to converse meaningfully and this can be counter productive as interest is forced away from artistic concerns. The games industry has recently begun employing 'technical artists' to bridge this gap [14], and as the middle-ground between art, science and technology opens up more roles can be expected in this boundary-crossing area of facilitation.

4 Conclusion

Participation in an artistic collaboration such at PURE FLOW is a rewarding outlet for technical creativity - free from the constraints of more prescriptive projects - there are sure to be areas of cultural discord, but with experience these can be foreseen and planned for with careful role definition and expectation management. Post-disciplinarily collaborations are now common, with collaborative working practices empowering artists through the democratisation of technology, and the engagement of technical experts with the more human concerns of art and its practitioners. Ideally, all contributors benefit from these collaborations where traditional discipline boundaries are transgressed to broaden the experience of all involved. PURE FLOW is a successful example of such a post-disciplinary project.

Acknowledgements. PURE FLOW is supported by the National Lottery through Arts Council England, UK, and was developed with support from the University of Lincoln's UROS Scheme; we thank Joshua O'Rourke for his assistance developing the iPhone app.

References

1. Works with Electromagnetic Induction, http://www.christinakubisch.de/english/install_induktion.html (retrieved May 23, 2012)
2. Kubisch, K.: Electrical Walks: Samples of Raw Sounds Cabinet Magazine, Issue 21 (Spring 2006) Electricity, http://www.cabinetmagazine.org/issues/21/kubisch.php (retrieved May 23, 2012)
3. Cox, C.: Invisible Cities: An Interview with Christina Kubisch. Cabinet Magazine (21) (Spring 2006); Electricity
4. Arnall, A., Martinussen, E.S., Schulze, J., Knutsen, J.: Immaterials: the ghost in the field (October 2009) http://www.nearfield.org/2009/10/immaterials-the-ghost-in-the-field (retrieved May 23, 2012)

5. Arnall, T., Knutsen, J., Martinussen, E.S.: Immaterials: light painting WiFi (February 2011), http://www.nearfield.org/2011/02/wifi-light-painting (retrieved May 23, 2012)

6. Benford, S., Flintham, M., Drozd, A., Anastasi, R., Rowland, D., Tandavanitj, N., Adams, M., Row Farr, J., Oldroyd, A., Sutton, J.: Uncle Roy all around you: implicating the city in a location-based performance. In: Proceeding of. Advanced Computer Entertainment (ACE 2004). ACM Press, Singapore (2004)

7. Connor, K.: Snow, TV Snow (2009), http://www.katyconnor.com/snow_tv_snow.html (retrieved May 23, 2012)

8. Chaitin, G.J.: Algorithmic Information Theory. Cambridge University Press (1987) Cambridge Books Online, http://dx.doi.org/10.1017/CBO9780511608858

9. pd~ Home: Pure Data (2012), http://puredata.info/ (retrieved May 23, 2012)

10. Becker, E.: Pure Flow Turns GPS Noise into Art, Right in the Palm of Your Hand, The New iPad Owner's App Buying Guide (August 2011), http://appadvice.com/appnn/2011/08/quickadvice-pure-flow (retrieved May 23, 2012)

11. Digital artist with her show Pure Flow, BBC World Service: Click – 4 (August 2011), http://www.bbc.co.uk/programmes/p00k404s (retrieved May 23, 2012)

12. Wilson, S.: Information Arts – Intersections of Art, Science, and Technology. The MIT Press (2002) ISBN 0-262-23209-X, http://www.arts.rpi.edu/~ruiz/AdvancedIntegratedArts/ReadingsAIA/WilsonArtScienceCulturalActs.pdf (retrieved May 23, 2012)

13. dorkbot: people doing strange things with electricity, http://dorkbot.org/ (retrieved May 23, 2012)

14. Hayes, J.: The Code/Art Divide: How Technical Artists Bridge The Gap (August 2008), http://www.gamasutra.com/view/feature/1651/the_codeart_divide_how_technical_.php (retrieved May 23, 2012)

Juke Cylinder: Sound Image Augmentation to Metamorphose Hands into a Musical Instrument

Masamichi Ueta[1], Osamu Hoshuyama[2], Takuji Narumi[1], Sho Sakurai[1], Tomohiro Tanikawa[1], and Michitaka Hirose[1]

[1] The University of Tokyo
7-3-1, Hongo, Bunkyo-ku, Tokyo, Japan
{ueta,narumi,sho,tani,hirose}@cyber.t.u-tokyo.ac.jp
[2] NEC Corporation
1753, Shimonumabe, Nakahara-Ku, Kawasaki, Kanagawa, Japan
houshu@bp.jp.nec.com

Abstract. This paper proposes a piece of interactive art installation named the "Juke Cylinder" to augment sound images through hand interaction and to metamorphose hands into a musical instrument. To augment a sound image onto users' hands, we used a parametric loudspeaker because it can localize a sound image on a reflecting surface. When users interact with our system, they perceive that their hands are metamorphosed into various musical instruments such as a guitar, a piano, or a synthesizer. Users can control the pitches of the sounds depending on their hand interactions such as with real musical instruments. In a demonstration at a media art exhibition, this system provided visitors with extraordinary sound experiences, and we received positive feedback from them.

Keywords: Sound image localization, Parametric loudspeaker, Musical instrument, Media art.

1 Introduction

If a person strikes an object, a sound is produced and a sound image is localized on the place where he does. However, when people play some electronic musical instruments such as synthesizers, a sound comes from loudspeakers and a sound image is not localized on the place where they interact. For users, it is natural that the sound comes from the place where they interact.

The parametric loudspeaker makes it possible for people to feel that the sound comes from actions or objects that would not produce audio output, because the parametric loudspeaker can localize a sound image on a reflecting surface and virtually produce audio output from any actions or objects[1][2]. By using a parametric loudspeaker, the sound image can be localized where people interact. A parametric loudspeaker works in entirely differently from a conventional loudspeaker. It generates ultrasound which travels outward in a narrowly focused

A. Nijholt, T. Romão, and D. Reidsma (Eds.): ACE 2012, LNCS 7624, pp. 453–460, 2012.

column analogous to a flashlight beam. When it strikes a surface, it turns into ordinary sound that people can hear.

In the field of virtual reality, various virtual objects are augmented into the real world. However in many cases, the objects are augmented only visually. Using a parametric loudspeaker, one can produce a sound spot and localize the sound image at a given position.

We developed a prototype system as a piece of interactive installation art named the "Juke Cylinder," which can localize sound images on users' hands and play various tones depending on their actions. By localizing sound images on users' hands with a parametric loudspeaker, the sound image is augmented onto their hands, and they perceive that their hands metamorphose into sound sources. In the demonstration at the "iiiexhibition13" media art exhibition held at the University of Tokyo, this system was highly acclaimed.

2   Related Work

Dobler et al. proposed augmented sound reality (ASR) [3]. ASR enables one to place sound sources in a virtual or real room, and three-dimensional sound is created there by a stereophonic sound system. However, the sound image is virtual and not real. Our attempt is to augment a real sound image onto the position where users interact.

Parametric loudspeakers have found several applications. Nishimura et al. developed the "Bird of Luggage" system and exhibited it in a baggage claim area at the Haneda Airport, one of the biggest airports in Japan[4]. This artwork uses a parametric loudspeaker and a projector to project a fluttering sound along with bird images onto luggage. The sound projected onto the luggage is reflected, and people can hear a fluttering sound coming from it. However, this system is not designed to interact with users.

Kimura et al. developed a visualization system for interaction with transmitted audio signals (VITA)[5]. VITA uses LEDs to provide visual feedback to the user in real time in the same space and enables the interaction between the user and the sound by detecting ultrasonic sound beams from a parametric loudspeaker. In this system, the parametric loudspeaker is used to convert the sound wave into electrical energy, and it is not used to augment the sound image.

Alexis et al. proposed Invoked Computing, which is a multi-modal ASR system that enables the use of everyday objects as computer interfaces or communication devices by simply using a projector and a parametric loudspeaker[6]. For example, by localizing the sound image on a banana, people are able to use the banana as a phone. However, in the case of invoked computing, users cannot control the content of the sound by themselves.

The parametric loudspeaker can be useful for some interfaces. Harrison et al. proposed wearable computer interface called the "Omnitouch"[7]. This system allows the surfaces of everyday objects to be used for graphical multi-touch interaction. For example, users' hands can become the input interface. Wilson et al. proposed "LightSpace," an interactive system that allows users to interact on, above, and between interactive surfaces in a room-sized environment[8]. By adding parametric loudspeakers to these systems, users can project visual as well as audio information.

3   Proposed System

In this study, to augment sound images with interaction we propose the localization of sound images on users' hands. By localizing sound images on users' hands using parametric loudspeakers, users perceive that their hands are metamorphosed into sound sources.

3.1   System Concept

The concept of our study is to metamorphose hands into sound sources by localizing sound images on the hands and to make it possible for users to control the content of the sound. For the contents of the sound, we selected the sounds of various musical instruments. When users interact with our system, a sound image is localized on their hands, and they perceive that their hands are metamorphosed into various musical instruments such as a guitar, a piano, or a synthesizer. In addition, they can control the pitch of the sound as with real musical instruments.

There are two requirements for this system. First, the sound images must be localized on the users' hands. To localize the sound images on their hands, parametric loudspeakers are installed where they can project audio output onto the users' hands. Secondly, the pitch of the sounds is controlled by detecting the position of the users' hands.

3.2   Implementation

We developed a piece of interactive installation art called the "Juke Cylinder" which can localize a sound image on users' hands and play various tones depending on hand position. Figure 1 and Figure 2 show the whole view and the structure of Juke Cylinder respectively.

The Juke Cylinder consists of four parametric loudspeakers, two Microsoft Xbox Kinect game consoles (henceforth referred to as Kinects), eight dimmable LEDs, and four humidifiers. All parametric loudspeakers, all Kinects, and 4 of the 8 LEDs are installed in the upper part, and the other components are in the lower part.

Design of Interaction. Figure 3 illustrates how to interact with the Juke Cylinder.

There are three steps in the interaction. First, users hold their hands up to the light. Second, the parametric loudspeakers project the audio output of the assigned musical instruments. Finally, users move their hands up and down. Figure 4 is a photograph of a user interacting with the Juke Cylinder.

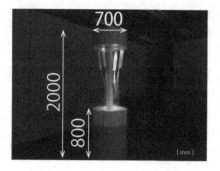
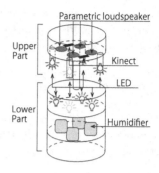

Fig. 1. Whole view of Juke Cylinder   **Fig. 2.** The structure of Juke Cylinder

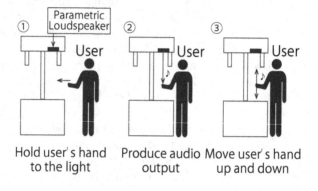

Fig. 3. How to interact with Juke Cylinder

To enable users to hold their hands to the light, the rays from LEDs are visualized at the humidifiers. The mist diffused from users' hands makes it appear that the sound is emanating from them. This effect lets users recognize that the sound image is located on their hands. The parametric loudspeakers project audio output onto users' hands, and the sound spreads from their hands.

When users play musical instruments with other people, it is considered pleasant to act in concert. One to four users can play the Juke Cylinder simultaneously. When multiple users play the Juke Cylinder, a drum sound is generated with the assigned sound from the parametric loudspeakers. Thanks to the drum sound, the users feel a sense of cooperativeness with each other.

Hand Detection. The Kinects are used to detect the depth of the users' hands. When users hold their hands up to the light, the Kinects obtain depth data from them. Figure 5 shows an image taken by one of the Kinects. The black areas in Fig. 5 are the error data. The depth data has a lot of noise contamination due to the mist.

Fig. 4. A user interacting with Juke Cylinder

To obtain depth data from the hands, the depth data window is divided into 16 sections. In Fig. 6, the red circles indicate the positions where users can hold their hands. The positions of users' hands are acquired by taking the average depth of the white areas in each window.

Fig. 5. A depth data image taken by one of the Kinects

Fig. 6. The divided windows and the positions that users will hold their hands

Audio and Visual Output. The pitch of the sound and the brightness of the dimmable LEDs are determined based on the depth data. In the case of audio output, the scale of the depth data is converted to a MIDI note number from 60 to 80 every 200 milliseconds. If the depth data is lower than the threshold, audio output is produced. Each parametric loudspeaker is assigned an output sound of a software instrument such as a guitar, a piano, or a synthesizer.

For the visual output, the scale of the depth data is converted to an integer which is sent to a dimmer. Each instrument is assigned to a red, yellow, green, or blue LED.

4   Experiment

4.1   Exhibition

We demonstrated our system at the "iiiexhibition13" media art exhibition held at the University of Tokyo from December 2 to 7, 2011, as shown Fig. 7. Our

Fig. 7. Users playing with Juke Cylinder

system was set up in an exhibition room at the university. Ambient sound or the sound from other exhibits did not affect our system as long as it was not too loud. At least one employee was beside the system during the exhibition to describe the system to visitors. More than 800 visitors came to the exhibition. We distributed a questionnaire and observed their reactions.

4.2   User Study

The visitors enjoyed the experience that their hands were metamorphosed into musical instruments. There were some visitors who played the Juke Cylinder with their friends and enjoyed the harmony.

A questionnaire of free description was distributed to the visitors, and 62 visitors answered it. Approximately 90% (56 visitors) were positive as follows:

- The experience that the sound comes from my own hands is weird and pleasant.
- The experience of this system is novel.
- The relationship of the pitch of the sound and the position of my hands is interesting.
- This system can be used as a musical instrument.
- I want to see the commercialized version.

However, approximately 10% (6 visitors) suggested further improvements as follows:

- If more interactive functions were included, the project could be more attractive.
- If it were possible to detect the detailed movement of hands, this system could be more interesting.
- If the reaction speed were slightly faster, this system could be more interesting.

4.3 Discussion

We observed the reactions of more than 800 visitors. They were surprised at the experience that audio output was produced from their hands and that their actions controlled the sound. There were some visitors who checked the difference of the sound reflection depending on the angle of their hands.

According to the feedback, most of the visitors described the experience of audio output being produced from their hands was novel, and the mechanism that the height of their hands could control the pitch of the sound was very interesting. Some visitors wrote that their hands metamorphosed into a musical instrument. From this, it could be said that the aim of this project, to project a sound image onto users' bodies and to produce audio output depending on their actions, was achieved.

Furthermore, some visitors said our system could be used as a musical instrument and played with their friends or other visitors simultaneously. This showed that our system not only provided visitors with a novel experience, but it could also be used as a musical instrument. According to the feedback, more interactive functions and faster detection are required, but most visitors enjoyed playing our system.

5   Conclution

We developed a piece of interactive installation art called the "Juke Cylinder" to augment a sound image through hand interaction and metamorphose hands into musical instruments. When users interacted with our system, the sound image was localized to their hands, and they could control the pitch of the sound. Parametric speakers were used to localize the sound source on users' hands, and Kinects were used to detect the depth of users' hands. By holding their hands up to the light and moving them up and down, users could interact with the Juke Cylinder.

We demonstrated our system at a media art exhibition held at the University of Tokyo, and 62 visitors answered our questionnaire. According to them, it could be said that the sound image was projected onto their hands, and they felt that their hands were metamorphosed into musical instruments. The parametric loudspeaker provided users with extraordinary sound experiences and could contribute to new computer entertainment systems.

References

1. Pompei, F.J.: The use of airborne ultrasonics for generating audible sound beams. J. Audio Eng. Soc. 47(9), 726–731 (1999)
2. Gan, W.S., Tan, E.L., Kuo, S.M.: Audio projection. IEEE Signal Processing Magazine 28(1), 43–57 (2011)
3. Dobler, D., Haller, M., Stampfl, P.: ASR: Augmented sound reality. In: ACM SIGGRAPH 2002 Conference Abstracts and Applications, p. 148 (2002)
4. Nishimura, K., Kimura, K., Yamazaki, M., Suzuki, Y., Tanikawa, T., Hirose, M.: Public art at a baggage claim at haneda airport: Bird of luggage. Transactions of the Virtual Reality Society of Japan 15(3), 467–470 (2010)
5. Kimura, K., Hoshuyama, O., Narumi, T., Tanikawa, T., Hirose, M.: Sound-power visualization system for real-world interaction based on ultrasonic power transmission. In: Proceedings of the 8th International Conference on Advances in Computer Entertainment Technology, ACE 2011, 60:1–60:8(2011)
6. Zerroug, A., Cassinelli, A., Ishikawa, M.: Invoked computing: Spatial audio and video ar invoked through miming. In: Proceedings of Virtual Reality International Conference, LAVAL VIRTUAL 2011, pp. 31–32 (2011)
7. Harrison, C., Benko, H., Wilson, A.D.: Omnitouch: wearable multitouch interaction everywhere. In: Proceedings of the 24th Annual ACM Symposium on User Interface Software and Technology, UIST 2011, pp. 441–450 (2011)
8. Wilson, A.D., Benko, H.: Combining multiple depth cameras and projectors for interactions on, above and between surfaces. In: Proceedings of the 23rd Annual ACM Symposium on User Interface Software and Technology, UIST 2010, pp. 273–282 (2010)

Puppet Theater System for Normal-Hearing and Hearing-Impaired People

Takayuki Adachi[1,*], Masafumi Goseki[1], Hiroshi Mizoguchi[1], Miki Namatame[2], Fusako Kusunoki[3], Ryohei Egusa[4], and Shigenori Inagaki[4]

[1] Tokyo University of Science, 2641, Yamazaki, Noda, Chiba, Japan
{j7512602,j7511629}@ed.tus.ac.jp, hm@rs.noda.tus.ac.jp
[2] Tsukuba University of Technology, 4-3-15, Amakubo, Tsukuba, Ibaraki, Japan
miki@a.tsukuba-tech.ac.jp
[3] Tama Art University, 2-1723, Yarimizu, Hachioji, Tokyo, Japan
kusunoki@tamabi.ac.jp
[4] Kobe University, 3-11, Tsurukabuto, Nada, Kobe, Hyogo, Japan
126d103d@stu.kobe-u.ac.jp, inagakis@kobe-u.ac.jp

Abstract. We are developing Puppet Theater system which enables both the hearing impaired and the normal hearing to enjoy a puppet show. This system projects puppet's lines in balloon on the background. In addition, the system has a function that presents branches of the story to audience and allows them to select. We performed the system to elementary school pupils with hearing impairment and found that the pupils enjoyed it. Effects of the function were investigated with questionnaire. This paper describes the function and the result of questionnaire.

Keywords: word balloon, interactive content, Kinect sensor, body movement.

1 Introduction

Puppet show is effective in language education and emotional education of children. Thus it has been incorporated into the field of education. But it is very difficult for the hearing impaired to enjoy the contents of the puppet show as the normal hearing. The hearing impaired gets the contents of the conversation from shape of face and mouth. In normal puppet show, they can't get information about shape of face and mouth.

Therefore, we are developing Puppet Theater system to entertain both hearing impaired and normal hearing [1]. In this system, the lines are displayed as letters with voice. The system enables the hearing impaired to understand the contents [2]. Figure 1 shows overview of the Puppet Theater and Figure 2 shows a stage. In addition, the system has a function that presents branches of the story to audience and allows them to select.

We performed Puppet Theater to elementary school students with hearing impairment and investigated effects of the function. In this paper, we describe the function and the experiment.

---

* Corresponding author.

A. Nijholt, T. Romão, and D. Reidsma (Eds.): ACE 2012, LNCS 7624, pp. 461–464, 2012.
© Springer-Verlag Berlin Heidelberg 2012

Fig. 1. Overview of Puppet Theater

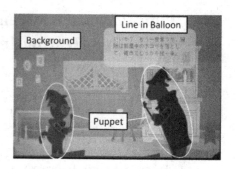

Fig. 2. Stage of Puppet Theater

2   Puppet Theater

2.1   Branch of the Story

In the Puppet Theater, the scene to branch of the story is presented to audience. One person is chosen from among the audience. He or she selects a favorite choice from four choices in Figure 3. Then, the story that corresponds to the choice starts and puppet show return to the scene presents branches again. After all four stories were chosen, puppet show lead to the end of story.

In the scene story to branch, representative of the audience make a selection by body movements.

2.2   Select of the Story

The audience can participate in the puppet show through body movements. To measure the body movements, Puppet Theater uses the Kinect sensor of Microsoft. The reasons for using this sensor are the human body can be detected even in a dark room, people do not need to have hardware, less expensive than other sensors and easy installation.

Kinect sensor can get the distance information by infrared rays and measure the body movements of people from that information. So measurement of body movement is not affected by the illumination. Therefore, Kinect sensor is suitable for Puppet Theater that dims the room in order to clear the projection.

By using OpenNI which is an open source library, when a person moves his hand toward the Kinect sensor, the sensor can measure the 3D position of the hand.

In addition, NITE middleware can detect hand gesture such as left and right movement or back and forth movement. In Puppet Theater, audience selects a branch of story by hand gesture which a person push the hand forward. Figure 5 shows a system configuration of function to select branch of the story. Through a router, information of the 3D position and gesture of hand are sent from server PC to manipulate Kinect sensor to client PC to manipulate the Flash animation.

When hand is detected, a cursor is displayed in the Flash animation based on the location of the hand. The cursor on the screen moves in conjunction with the position of the hand. This makes it possible for audience to freely move the cursor on the screen by the movement of the hand. When the cursor overlaps an icon, an icon moves. The audience can visually understand that which icon is selected. If the cursor is on an icon, audience can select an icon by push gesture. If the cursor is not on an icon, audience cannot select any icon.

2.3   Experiment

We performed Puppet Theater to 12 elementary school pupils with hearing impairments. In the Puppet Theater, the students experienced the function to participate in story by using body movements. After watching, a questionnaire was carried out to investigate effects of the function. The questionnaire was a five-point Likert scale :"strongly agree", "agree", "neither agree nor disagree", "disagree," and "strongly disagree".

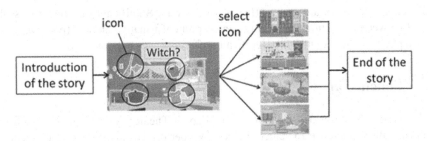

Fig. 3. Branching of the story

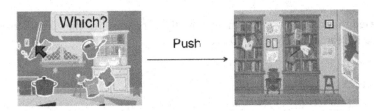

Fig. 4. Select of the story

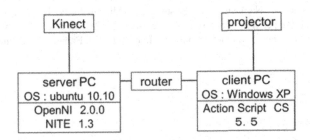

Fig. 5. System configuration

Table 1. Response of children to participate in the story using body movement

Items	SA	A	N	D	SD
It was interesting to select story by body movement.*	6	3	1	1	1
It was easy to select story by body movement.	2	6	3	1	0

*$p<0.05$ SA:Strongly Agree   A:Agree   N:Neither agree nor disagree
D:Disagree   SD:Strongly Disagree

Data obtained from the Likert evaluation was divided into two groups: positive evaluations and neutral or negative evaluations. The difference between the positive and neutral/negative evaluations was computed using Fisher's Exact Test (1 x 2). Results are summarized in Table 1.

For affective, there are many affirmative answers. Significant difference was observed between the neutral or negative answer and affirmative answer ($p < 0.05$). For the simplicity of how to use, the significant difference was not observed.

3   Conclusion

In this paper, we described the function of Puppet Theater system which branch the story and allow audience to select choices. We performed this system to elementary school student and investigated effects of this system by questionnaire. The results of questionnaire show that the function entertains the audience.

Acknowledgmants. This research was partly supported by the Grants-in-Aid for Scientific Research (B) (No. 23300309).

References

1. Egusa, R., Wada, K., Namatame, M., Kusunoki, F., Mizoguchi, H., Inagaki, S.: Learning Support System Based on Inclusive Desighn Method for Story Comprehension. In: The 35th Annual Meeting of JSSE, pp. 456–457 (2011)
2. Wada, K., Egusa, R., Namatame, M., Kusunoki, F., Mizoguchi, H., Inagaki, S.: Evaluation of the Universal Puppet Theater based on Inclusive Design Method. In: The Fourth IEEE International Conference on Digital Game and Intelligent Toy Enhanced Learning, pp. 135–137 (2012)

Creative Design: Exploring Value Propositions with Urban Nepalese Children

Alissa N. Antle and Allen Bevans

School of Interactive Arts & Technology
Simon Fraser University, Central City, Surrey, B.C. V3T 0A3 Canada
{aantle,alb19}@sfu.ca

Abstract. Interactive technologies are being introduced into urban children's lives in developing countries. It is critical that these children have an active voice in the process of developing such technologies. Towards these aims we describe the research goals, process and outcomes for an action research project. The overarching goal of the research is to investigate and better understand how edutainment-based interactive technologies might change or improve the lives of urban Nepalese children, their families and their communities. In this paper, we describe the preliminary phase of the research in which in which we design and run a creative design workshop with Nepalese children.

Keywords: action research, empathic design, design for developing countries, participatory design for children.

1 Introduction

Involving children in developing countries in the design of interactive technologies can improve the likelihood that applications and products will address challenges and needs faced by these children, their families and communities. However, children's ideas and input must be carefully elicited to ensure they accurately reflect real opportunities and inform the production of viable solutions. In this short paper, we present our action research approach to a creative design workshop for urban Nepalese children. The focus of the research is to elicit and capture value propositions about how challenges and needs in urban Nepalese children's lives may be improved through edutainment-based interactive technology. In line with action research, our intention is to lay the foundation for a lasting relationship between the research participants and researchers. We will also obtain information that can be represented in child-personas and used in subsequent design and evaluation of edutainment applications for this audience (see [1] for information on this type of child-persona development).

2 Research Goals

The primary goal of the research is to elicit and understand issues of importance to Urban Nepalese children that may be enabled, enhanced or augmented with

A. Nijholt, T. Romão, and D. Reidsma (Eds.): ACE 2012, LNCS 7624, pp. 465–468, 2012.
© Springer-Verlag Berlin Heidelberg 2012

edutainment-based interactive technologies. Specifically, we aim to determine one to three ways that interactive technology applications may improve urban Nepalese children's lived experiences informed by the children's own reflections. We also aim to compile a set of personas that can be used to inform the design of working prototypes once the research team returns to Canada.

In order to support an action research paradigm, our approach includes several goals related to relationship building and the processes of working with children in a developing country. One goal is to create an ongoing bridge between our research team (which may include Canadian children) and the Nepalese children we are working with, developing relationships intended to strengthen the impact and efficacy of our research. Another goal is to enable Nepalese children to participate in a creative process of ideation and expression in ways that they find meaningful and authentic. A meta goal related to these two goals is to better understand the challenges of participatory designing with children in developing countries.

Preliminary Research Process

The research process will begin with several key activities working directly with Nepalese children on our first visit. Building on the outcomes of this preliminary process (outlined below), we will determine the next phase of the research.

The preliminary process of working with the Nepalese children will begin with a survey to determine language background, education level, and technology experience in order to better customize our initial workshop and future research phases. Data from these surveys will be used to organize a participatory design workshop for eight to sixteen Nepalese children aged eight to twelve. The main outcome for the workshop is a shared understanding of issues that are important to the children, families and communities of the workshop participants, as well as an understanding of which of these issues could be addressed with edutainment-based interactive technologies.

The workshop will begin with a relationship building exercise. The activity will involve each participant and researcher telling the group about the best and worst part of a typical school or work day, what they want to do when they grow up, and something they think the other cultural group wouldn't know about their community or culture. The process will involve the group taking turns talking, and/or drawing part of the answer with simple art materials. This activity is an important step to begin finding common ground between ourselves, local helpers, and workshop participants, and to set the stage for the creative and discursive group activities that will follow.

The second workshop activity will involve working in small groups to discuss challenges and needs from children's daily lives. We will spark conversation and seed reflection using information from the previous relationship building exercise. We will also look for commonality between children (e.g. who else has faced this challenge?). Children will be especially encouraged to discuss challenges that relate to an issue of importance to them in their personal lives.

The third workshop activity will involve an interactive technology demonstration. We will show several iPad edutainment applications (e.g. a literacy game, a memory/matching game, an art application) with a focus on the activities and experiences that interactive technology can provide. For example, we will discuss how these technologies can enable kids to learn new things, to communicate with others across the world, and it can be used to express ideas. The final workshop activity will involve working in small groups to ideate how interactive technology might be used to enhance children's lives based on a challenge or need they expressed in the second activity. We will guide each group to express and capture the essence of their idea with a visual storyboard. These storyboards may involve drawings, collage (cutting and pasting pictures), photos and words that express how the challenge or need might be addressed. The children will leave with paper (and/or digital) post-cards with follow-up questions, which they will be asked to work on later and mail (or email) to us. This may help transition the relationship from a face to face one to a remote one.

After the workshop, we will summarize 1-3 key ideas that emerged from the children's participation in the workshop. We will also use observations and information from all the activities to design a set of basic child-personas. For example, information about children's daily lives, challenges, needs and ideas about how they would like to use interactive technologies will be included in the personas. We will also capture children's ideation and design process in order to better understand the challenges of participatory design with children from developing nations. This will complete the preliminary phase of the research.

3   Research Challenges

Our creative design workshop is informed by participatory design practices developed by the author and others for working with children (e.g. [1, 2]). The workshop design is also informed by practices from empathic design and experience design [3]. The workshop is intended to enable workshop participants to express themselves through a structured creative process. The workshop structure includes key "triggers" that support the elicitation of propositions that are both empathetic to the lives of participants and aligned with possibilities afforded by interactive technologies. Our approach is also consistent with Wright and McCarthy's discussion of designing with a dialogical understanding of empathy that embraces both the designer's goals and perspectives, while enabling expression and understanding of the participant's perspectives [6].

One of the key workshop challenges cited in previous literature is the unequal power differential between adults and children. This may be heightened by cultural differences. Inadequately addressing this challenge will hinder building an effective design relationship [2, 5]. We have structured the workshop to build on an initial relationship building activity by repeating some of the relationship-building structure in subsequent activities (e.g. sharing personal stories, drawing/using pictures to represent ideas). We will also use activities that children are already familiar with (e.g. sharing stories from their lives, creating pictorial representations of ideas) rather than asking them to work with new technologies or new forms of expression.

Further challenges identified in the literature are that children often try to satisfy the expectations of adults and have difficulty expressing their own ideas in co-design processes [4]. In general, this is a result of being given too little structure and having too few boundaries within which to work. We will address this challenge by following a well-structured creative process of context setting, problem identification, opportunity and constraint setting, and ideation.

4   Research Outcomes

The workshop outlined here is intended to create a bridge between the research team and the child workshop participants, which may be built on with future work. It provides the workshop participants with an active voice in articulating their needs and issues of importance; a supportive creative process in which to express those needs; and an introduction into an active role in interactive technology development. The workshop participants will also benefit from being exposed to a creative design process and to forms of interactive technology that may be new to them (e.g. iPad) and which may be more feasible options for personal, family and community computing than traditional desktop based systems. The workshop will enable us to better understand the daily lived experiences of the participants, capture these in personas, and come away with potential avenues for technology applications. The preliminary phase will set the stage for a working relationship between the research team and the child participants. It will provide several seed ideas for ways that interactive technologies can improve urban Nepalese children's lives. Another key outcome will be a rough cut of a set of child-personas, focusing on abilities, needs and experiences that can be used in future design.

References

1. Antle, A.N.: Child-based personas: need, ability and experience. Cognition, Technology & Work 10, 155–166 (2008)
2. Druin, A.: Cooperative inquiry: developing new technologies for children with children. In: Conference on Human Factors in Computing Systems, pp. 592–599. ACM Press, New York (1999)
3. Ehn, P.: Work-oriented Design of Computer Artifacts. Arbetslivscentrum, Stockholm, Sweden (1989)
4. Jones, C., McIver, L., Gibson, L., Gregor, P.: Experiences obtained from designing with children. In: Conference on Interaction Design for Children, pp. 69–74. ACM Press, New York (2003)
5. Kam, M., Ramachandran, D., Raghavan, A., Chiu, J., Sahni, U., Canny, J.: Practical considerations for participatory design with rural school children in underdeveloped regions: early reflections from the field. In: Conference on Interaction Design for Children, pp. 25–32. ACM Press, New York (2006)
6. Wright, P., McCarthy, J.: Empathy and experience in HCI. In: Conference on Human Factors in Computing Systems, pp. 637–646. ACM Press, New York (2008)

DriveRS: An In-Car Persuasive System for Making Driving Safe and Fun

Anne Bergmans and Suleman Shahid[1]

Department of Communication and Information Sciences, Tilburg University,
5037 AB, Tilburg, The Netherlands
acmbergmans@gmail.com
[1] Tilburg center for Cognition and Communication, Tilburg University,
5037 AB, Tilburg, The Netherlands
s.shahid@uvt.nl

Abstract. This paper presents a solution to the growing problems connected with bad driving specially with over-speeding. This paper outlines a persuasive mobile solution 'DriveRS' that is designed to change the speeding behavior of male novice drivers in a persuasive manner. The 'DriveRS' application targets both weak and strong habit young male drivers between the age of 18 and 26 by giving them various incentives to change their speeding behavior. Results show an overall acceptance of the application, mainly due to its unique rewarding mechanism, and its ability to demonstrate the actual speeding behavior with major impact on safety, fuel cost and possible fines. Results also indicate behavior change for weak habit users and attitude change for strong habit users.

Keywords: Speeding behavior, persuasive technology, mobile persuasion.

1   Introduction

Speeding behavior is at least partially responsible for one out of three accidents that end in death. It also significantly increases injury severity for all parties involved in an accident [1]. In the Netherlands, men between the age of 18 and 26 are six times more likely to get involved into accidents than older drivers and females [2]. The current measures of the government to stop speeding largely consist of punishment. Drivers receive fines, or a more severe punishment when they excessively break the speed limit (e.g. jail sentence). On the other hand, rewarding proves to be an effective measure to change driving behavior but it does not make drivers understand why their behavior is bad, nor does it change behavior permanently [3]. In 2011 7,403,549 fines were issued [4] and this huge number shows that the current measures to discourage bad driving habits particularly over-speeding are not working properly.

Currently there exist a number of mobile applications, and research initiatives that focus on inappropriate driving behavior of drivers but other than few exceptions where researchers focused on in-car feedback based on driving behavior [5], most of these systems largely aimed at stopping distracted driving by mainly taking a long-term approach [6]. There is hardly a solution either short-term or long-term, which is

A. Nijholt, T. Romão, and D. Reidsma (Eds.): ACE 2012, LNCS 7624, pp. 469–472, 2012.
© Springer-Verlag Berlin Heidelberg 2012

designed for monitoring the in-car speeding behavior, for intervening and assisting in changing behavior at the right time by giving immediate persuasive feedback. Furthermore, hardly any existing solution provides an opportunity to reflect and learn from mistakes after a bad driving session. This article therefore presents an approach through persuasive technology, aimed to persuade drivers into willingly changing their speeding behavior and as well as gaining awareness of their bad behavior.

2   User Research

An extensive user research was conducted to investigate rationales for speeding, attitude towards speeding, and actual speeding behavior. Semi-structured interviews and a diary study based on the Speeding behavior model [7] were used as user research methods. Seven over speeders were selected based on their age and speeding behavior (i.e. habits of receiving fines), and subsequently participated in the three phases of the user research: 1) a detailed interview, 2) longitudinal diary keeping and 3) a follow-up interview with questions regarding the diary. The main results showed that participants' attitude towards speeding was careless, although they did set boundaries for not speeding excessively (up to 30 km per hour). Most of them experienced positive feelings when speeding (e.g. satisfaction), and appeared immune for social influence from significant others. Most participants had a weak habit of speeding and couple of them had a strong habit of speeding. All participants were particularly worried about negative consequences of speeding (e.g. accidents), but did not see any harm in their speeding behavior. According to them, they only speed when they feel the situation is safe. Furthermore, a comparison between the diary and statements from the first interview confirmed their reliability; statements were equal to actual speeding behavior recorded over time. Participants found it easy to keep the diary, and for some it even gave them a new insight into their speeding behavior. Thus, not all participants were as aware of their speeding behavior as they assumed.

3   Design and Implementation

Design requirements were derived from findings of the user research and literature. Based on those requirements, five design alternatives were developed to use during driving ('in-car') and 'after a driving session'. Based on user evaluation, multiple concepts from these alternatives were combined which resulted in the final design. The final design was developed as a paper prototype and tested with end users to evaluate the usability of the interface. Subsequently, findings from this test were processed in a high fidelity design (Figure 1), which was developed for an iPhone (to use in-car and for reviewing the driving session outside car) and iPad (for reviewing a driving session outside car). The main purpose of the "DriveRS" application is to discourage speeding behavior by stimulating users. The app runs on a smartphone and users can interact with the system whenever they want. The design of the app requires drivers to take the smartphone with them in the car to track their speeding behavior. The main screen shows four key goals to be achieved in order to obtain a reward and these goals are *CO2 emissions*, *overview fines costs*, *petrol costs*, and *chance for an accident*. The main goals show both positive and negative consequences of speeding; they communicate negative feedback when users do not adjust their behavior (e.g. damage to environment), and positive feedback when users do adjust their behavior (e.g. saved petrol costs).

The in-car 'live screen' shows real-time goal progress while driving, possible fine cost at the current speed, damage at the current speed represented by a dented car, and possibility to personalize the car. This 'live screen' is the most important aspect of this app, as it tracks actual speeding behavior and presents it to users who can immediately change their behavior if necessary. The app has five other features or visual sections and out of five only one feature is designed to use in the car namely *tracking speeding behavior*. The hands-on interaction with the app in the car is extremely limited. Other sections consist of a *traffic game* as fun-factor, *profile* including inviting friends, overall goal *progress* and previously obtained *rewards*.

Fig. 1. "DriveRS" sections: main screen and tracking speeding behavior

4   User Evaluation and Results

A combination of usability test, usage diary, semi-structured interviews were used for user evaluation with seven participants. The technology acceptance model and behavior change framework were used for this evaluation. Before handing over the application for actual use to end users, users performed an exercise to get acquainted with the operations of the app. The evaluation consisted of tasks execution and a post-test semi-structured interview. The post-test interview measured evaluation in terms of perceived ease of use, perceived usefulness, and perceived acceptance. Results show an overall positive evaluation of the app. Users had no major problems while interacting with the app and they overall liked the simplicity of the interface. They were willing to evaluate it on long-term basis.

After the preliminary round, actual behavior-change assessment was done with same users. Results show that users rated the app quite positive, mainly because of its usefulness. Users were the most influenced by the reward and the four goals. They liked the idea of 'four key goals' on the main screen and they reported that 'dented car' picture and impact of bad driving on the 'wallet' really persuaded them. The impact on environment is a good add-on, though not the primary factor. They informed evaluators that they would also recommend the app to others based on the fun-factor, competition with friends, and reflection (learning from mistakes) factor. Users stated they had more control over their speeding behavior (i.e. confronts users with their actual behavior), which subsequently makes it easier for both weak and strong habit users to adjust their behavior. The app additionally stimulated less speeding because of anticipated regret such as 'points deduction'.

5   Discussion and Conclusion

The aim of this study was to investigate whether a persuasive application could change the speeding driving behavior of 18 to 26 year old male novice drivers. The evaluation results support this, as the app influences all types of users through the different sections. Every user had a preference for at least one section or goal. Although weak habit participants were more persuaded to immediately change their behavior, strong habit participants experienced a change in attitude. The latter could eventually lead to less speeding. The four main goals and reward particularly made participants see the value of the app, but other aspects such as competition with friends and the game also contributed to the overall positive evaluation. Users were no longer neglectful towards their behavior, but perceived it as a type of bad behavior.

The "DriveRS" application differs from existing solutions because it uses a multi-level approach for changing behavior, rather than solely focusing on punishing or rewarding. Moreover, rather than merely influencing the user while driving, the app influences users outside the car by giving them an opportunity to reflect on their driving habits. Finally, this work is still in progress and only short-term user evaluations were performed in the first round. In future, it would be interesting to run an in-car long-term user evaluation for monitoring the behavior change over weeks.

References

1. SWOV-factsheet De relatie tussen snelheid en ongevallen (2012),
   http://www.swov.nl/rapport/Factsheets/NL/Factsheet_Snelheid.pdf (retrieved)
2. SWOV-factsheet Jonge beginnende automobilisten (2010), http://www.swov.nl/rapport/Factsheets/NL/Factsheet_Jonge_automobilisten.pdf (retrieved)
3. SWOV-factsheet Beloningen voor verkeersveilig gedrag (2011), http://www.swov.nl/rapport/Factsheets/NL/Factsheet_Belonen.pdf (retrieved)
4. Minder verkeersboetes in 2011 (2012),
   http://www.om.nl/onderwerpen/verkeer/actueel/@58260/minder/
5. SWOV-factsheet Intelligente Snelheidsassistentie (ISA) (2010), http://www.swov.nl/rapport/Factsheets/NL/Factsheet_ISA.pdf (retrieved)
6. McKnight, A.J., Peck, R.C.: Graduated driver licensing and safer driving. Journal of Safety Research 34, 85–89 (2003)
7. De Pelsmacker, P., Janssens, W.: The effect of norms, attitudes and habits on speeding behavior: Scale development and model building and estimation. Accident Analysis and Prevention 39(1), 6–11 (2007)

When Away Applaud Anyway

Pedro Centieiro[1], Teresa Romão[1], and A. Eduardo Dias[1,2]

[1] CITI, DI-Faculdade de Ciências e Tecnologia/Universidade Nova de Lisboa
2829-516 Caparica, Portugal
{Pcentieiro,aed.fct}@gmail.com, tir@fct.unl.pt,
[2] bViva International, B. V.
Romanovhof 9, 3329 BD, Dordrecht, Netherlands
edias@bviva.com

Abstract. WeApplaud is a multiplayer mobile game that takes remote users to participate in the applauses happening in a sport event venue, increasing their levels of fun and immersion while remotely watching a live event. Through the use of persuasive technology concepts, WeApplaud encourages fans to applaud their favourite sports team during specific key moments of a match.

1 Introduction

The level of thrill and excitement felt during live sports is a unique experience: performance happens in front of our eyes in real time and we can cheer, chant and support our team. We can perform similar supporting actions at home; however, we do not have the same feeling of connection with the performers and the in-venue fans, therefore not reaching the same emotional level. Moreover, our home actions are not reflected in the live event, so the objective of supporting our team is never really accomplished.

Since there are usually much more spectators remotely watching a match, at home or in a café, than at the live venue, we feel that there is room to introduce a new paradigm to bring the venue atmosphere, its immersion and emotional level to the users' homes. This concept would increase remote fans' interest to watch sports events. To achieve the previous goals, we started by developing WeApplaud, a multiplayer mobile game that takes users to participate in the applauses happening in the stadium. WeApplaud is strongly based on two persuasive technology concepts: social facilitation and competition [1]. Social facilitation suggests that allowing observation of the owner's performance by others increases the effectiveness of persuasion [1]. Competition motivates users to adopt a target attitude or behavior by leveraging human beings' natural drive to compete [1]. Thus, our system allows remote users to use their mobile phone to choose one of two teams, and applaud their team during key moments taking place in the sports event. WeApplaud aims to study if this concept helps people remotely watching a sports event to have more fun and feel more engaged in the stadium experience and atmosphere, as mentioned before.

A. Nijholt, T. Romão, and D. Reidsma (Eds.): ACE 2012, LNCS 7624, pp. 473–476, 2012.

2   Design and Gameplay

We aimed to provide an intuitive and non-intrusive as possible interaction, allowing users to just clap. By using a mobile phone while clapping, for example by holding a mobile device on one hand, and then moving the device as if we would hit the palm of the other hand Figure 1 (a)), it is possible to detect claps by combining sound analysis and accelerometer data (more details about this on Section 3). This can be done by using either the front or back side of the device while clapping.

In the current version of WeApplaud we created a multiplayer mobile game where players are challenged to applaud during key moments of a football match. There are two different kinds of challenges included in our prototype, involving two kinds of applauses: free and synchronized applauses. During free applauses, players just need to keep clapping, like they would do in a normal applause action, to be rewarded with points. During synchronized applauses, like in rhythmic games, players need to be synchronized with the tempo to score points. Examples of synchronized applauses are the slow clap (which happens often on the triple jump, or before a free kick in football) and the claps that mark the rhythm of some football chants. These challenges are triggered by the application at key moments of a match when fans at the venue would start performing the same action. In a real life environment, the number of triggered key moments is determined by a human operator (which can be at the stadium to have a better perception of the crowd's actions), in order to not become a tiring action for users.

While watching a sport event (a football match in this case, both teams of supporters are presented with the two kinds of challenges. Each time a team member performs a correct clap, the team is awarded points and a consecutive streak count is started. The consecutive streak count is associated with a score multiplier, intended to reward the team that is synchronized with the tempo during a period of time. The developed prototype simulates a football match broadcast, displayed on a TV screen, or projected on a wall, complemented with additional interface elements that point out the key moments, challenge users to applaud, and reveal results (Figure 1 (b)).

Fig. 1. (a) Game screen on the main display and (b) clapping action

The mobile devices are used for user interaction, allowing claps recognition and count. To visualize the supporter teams' performance we have added two bars to the display: one for the red team and other for the blue team. Each time users win points for their team the score bar increases accordingly. The team that fills the score bar quicker wins the challenge. To win the game, a team needs to have more points than the other team, at the end of the simulated broadcast. This is intended to motivate users not to give up, because there is always a chance to win, even after losing some of the challenges.

To make users aware of a current challenge (alert users when they should applaud), we use three kinds of feedback mechanisms: a visual message on the top of the video (match displaying window), a hand inside a circle that keeps spinning on the mobile device display until the end of the challenge and we set the mobile device to vibrate, so it can get user's attention in a simple and seamless manner. Furthermore, during the first moments of the synchronized challenges, we have also synchronized the vibration with the rhythm that users are required to follow.

To better explain how a game unfolds, we present the typical game flow:

1. Users are initially presented with the instructions on the main display. During this phase, users can select one of the two teams of supporters on their mobile devices.
2. After everyone has chosen theirs teams, the game starts.
3. The video is displayed on the main display. After a short time, the first challenge appears, where users are prompted to applaud after a dangerous attacking play. We started with a simple challenge, since it would allow users to understand the concept of the game.
4. When the key moment ends, a message stating which team won that challenge appears on the main display, while on the mobile devices a message shows how many points the their owners won in the challenge.
5. The video keeps playing until another challenge appears (either a free or synchronized applause challenge).
6. The process repeats until the video ends.
7. A final screen appears showing the final results, both on the display and on the mobile devices. The main display shows more detailed information regarding both teams of supporters, while on the mobile devices users can see how many points they won for their team.

3   Clap Detection

We took three approaches to identify claps on the mobile devices: by analyzing accelerometer data, by sound analysis and by merging both methods. We started by following the approach implemented in [2]: to use the mobile device accelerometer to detect whether there is a movement in a particular direction. While this approach works, users would be able to do a "clap" without the need to hit the other hand, just by wagging the mobile device. Next, we decided to analyze the sound to detect a clap. Every time there would be a volume peak, we would count as a clap. However, this approach has also its flaws, because a loud noise, like talking aloud, blowing into the microphone or snapping the fingers, would also count as a clap.

Both of these approaches also have a common issue: it is necessary to find some good values as thresholds to tweak the algorithms, in order to have good rates of clap detection. This means that both of these approaches are very rigid, because they do not leave much room for error. Therefore, we combined the two previous approaches so they could complement each other. In this new approach, when the mobile device detects a sound peak, it checks if there was a recent movement in a particular direction. If so, then it is counted as a clap, otherwise it is not. This way we have a more flexible system, where we do not resort so heavily on thresholds.

4   Implementation

WeApplaud was developed in Objective C and the client application was developed to be compatible with iOS 5.0 (or higher) running on iPhone 3GS, 4 and 4S and iPod Touch (4th generation). The server application was developed to be compatible with Mac OS X 10.7 (or higher).

WeApplaud is based on a client-server architecture, which allows to quickly notify clients so they acknowledge when to interact with the system. We used the Bonjour protocol to quickly identify the clients and the server. This means that this version of the prototype only works if both the server and the mobile devices are on the same wireless network. In order to not be dependent on third-party networks and to keep the process simple, the computer running the server application creates a wireless network for the clients to connect to. To handle the network communication, we used the UDP protocol through CocoaAsyncSocket (a TCP/IP socket networking library).

5   Conclusions

We described a new concept of using mobile devices to remotely interact with live sports. This demo constitutes an important milestone within our global project for enhancing the users' experience during a sports event, creating a connection between the fans at the venue and the ones watching on TV.

Acknowledgments. This work is funded by CITI/DI/FCT/UNL (PEst-OE/EEI/UI0527/2011). The authors thank Bárbara Teixeira for her contribution on the graphic design.

References

1. Fogg, B.J.: Persuasive Technology: Using Computers to Change What We Think and Do. Morgan Kaufmann, San Francisco (2003)
2. Sega Sports Japan Mario & Sonic at the London 2012 Olympic Games (2012), http://www.olympicvideogames.com/mario-and-sonic-london-2012/ (accessed June 14 , 2012)

Making a Toy Educative Using Electronics

Edwin Dertien, Jelle Dijkstra, Angelika Mader, and Dennis Reidsma

University of Twente, The Netherlands
{e.c.dertien,a.h.mader,d.reidsma}@utwente.nl

Abstract. We present building blocks equipped with electronics for educational purposes. The blocks have changeable colors, a simple LED screen, and a mechanism for decentralized communication between blocks that touch each other. Using these simple elements, we introduced functionality to implicitly support the development of *prenumerical skills* of preschool children without detracting from the primary value of the toys: building towers and structures of blocks.

1 Introduction

When designing an educational toy there is a basic decision between the design of a new, dedicated toy that focusses on a learning objective, or the design of a regular toy in which the educational content comes in addition to a well proven playing aspect.

We discuss how we equipped robust *building blocks* with technology to implicitly support development of prenumerical skills in preschool children (aged 5-6), in such a way as to not interfere with the basic play functionality of the blocks. Usability was a key concern, not only for the children but also for the teachers who have to work with the blocks. We aim at simple, off-the-shelf usability, without the need for a central server PC, and no complicated installation or configuration processes. The toy is implemented in such a way that it is feasible to make it into a commercial product. This includes aspects such as robustness, battery life, producability and manufacturability. The various elements of the design should lend themselves to large scale manufacturing and the components should be affordable.

2 Related Work

Playing blocks and electronics are a popular combination in related research. Here, we discuss a small, representative collection of related work.

TileToy[1] — TileToys are a dynamic, electronic platform for tangible LED games. They consist of tiles with a LED matrix to display simple images and shapes, communicating with each other by wireless radio through a host computer. Various games such as word games and jigsaw games are available.

---

[1] http://tiletoy.org

A. Nijholt, T. Romão, and D. Reidsma (Eds.): ACE 2012, LNCS 7624, pp. 477–480, 2012.

The authors also describe a game in which the tiles show numbers and have to be grouped in order to sum up to a desired outcome.

MB Led[2] — The MB Led toy originated from the idea to create a dynamic jigsaw, where an animation instead of a static picture has to be formed. The difference with TileToy is that communication is done through IrDA transceivers at the edges and therefore does not rely on a host computer, and that a speaker is included. Games available include a dynamic puzzle, a snake game where the tiles need to be repositioned in order to avoid the snake touching an edge and a tetris game where the falling blocks are controlled by blocks at the sides.

Siftables [3] — Siftables are square tiles with a graphical display instead of a LED matrix, which allows for more flexible visualization. Interaction with Siftables relies on gestures such as shaking and tilting, in addition to the 2D layout of the blocks next to each other. Communication is also through IrDA transceivers at the edges of blocks. The flexibility of the product has led to a huge variety of mostly educational applications.

Interactive Tiles [4] — "Interactive Tiles" are toys for children about 3-4 years old. Their goal is to encourage and support social interaction between playing children. The toys are robust tiles with different colors lighting built in. The different colors are activated by applying different pressures on the tile. Tiles can be combined to build stacks, pathways, floors, etc. An important aspect of the design is the fact that there are no predefined game rules imposed on the children. All 'games' that the children played with the tiles emerged naturally from their playful exploration of the possibilities of the tiles.

3 Design

We chose to work in the area of mathematical skills. The mathematical ideas that preschool children are taught are called "pre-numerical skills", and can be classified in awareness of numbers and counting, quantities and quantity-in-variety ("two half cookies are not more cookie than one whole cookie"), sorting and grouping, series, memory, and spatial vision [2].

It has been shown that realistic objects motivate children to reenact real-life scenarios, whereas geometric objects encourage abstract thinking [1]. We chose to work with *building blocks* (abstract geometrical objects such as cubes, cuboids, cylinders, arcs, and triangular prisms), because they are popular, well known and understood, can be used in large amounts at the same time (useful to present quantities), are rearranged frequently (useful for sorting and grouping concepts), and are large enough to fit electronics.

The concept of quantities and of classification/grouping are very important for children at this age. Quantities are of course very easy to emphasize with *blocks as units*. Our blocks can change color, which makes it possible to distinguish blocks from each other, better facilitating concepts of classification and

---

[2] http://mbled.wordpress.com/

grouping. Detecting when blocks form a group requires "neighbor sensing" and communication between the blocks. The blocks can deliver feedback in various ways. They can signal "right or wrong" (e.g., activated/not activated). They can also "point out information", by showing a number on a screen denoting the sum of all blocks connected in a group.

Fig. 1 shows a photo of our prototypes. They are cubic in shape, because this yields the most possibilities in building structures, and are about 6x6x6 cm. The blocks are semi-transparent and can shine in different colors. Tapping a block will make it change color. All blocks are equipped with a display. This display always shows the number of blocks grouped together with the same color. Groups are formed by blocks of the same color, partially or fully connected to each other (side by side or stacked, see Fig. 1(a)).

(a)   Stacked   and   (b) Pre-school children playing
grouped   with the blocks

Fig. 1. The prototype blocks

4   Implementation

The electronic system consists of microcontroller, communication system, tap and orientation sensing, RGB LEDs, LCD display and power section. The blocks are controlled by an Atmel AVR series microcontroller.

A contact detection mechanism and protocol has been developed that allows for detecting not only when blocks are fully aligned, as with the IrDA solutions of related systems, but also when blocks are connected only on half or quarter of the surface of one side (see also the purple blocks in Fig. 1(a)). The blocks use six inductive wire loops, one loop on every face of the block, allowing for 3D constructions, instead of the 2D layouts allowed for in the related works. The wire loops allow for short distance (face-to-face) communication between blocks. Bits of data are transferred by modulating the bit signal on a 1Mhz carrier. The loops are wound according to Fig. 2, to also allow half-sided and quarter-sided communication. Stacking the blocks pyramid wise, three of even five different blocks can talk to each other on the same loop connection. A decentralized communication protocol allows the blocks to know when they are

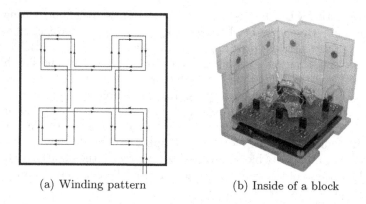

(a) Winding pattern   (b) Inside of a block

Fig. 2. Implementation of the wire coils used for communication

grouped with other blocks of the same color. Therefore, in contrast to related work, this communication does not require additional communication with a central host.

5 Discussion and Evaluation

We designed and built blocks that can be used for "regular" play, but that also implicitly support the development of prenumerical skills of preschool children. In a small, first evaluation, several pairs of children (aged 5-6) played with the blocks, and their play behaviour was observed (see also Fig. 1(b)). Questions of interest were whether the children understood the interaction concept, understood the counting mechanism, used the building blocks also for "normal" construction, and whether they mentioned the counting aspects in their play. Although the evaluation was preliminary, all of these questions could be answered affirmatively from the pilot observations, leading us to believe that the basic concepts behind this project are viable.

References

1. Berk, L.E.: Child Development, 8th edn. Allyn & Bacon (2008)
2. Merdian, G.: Kindergartenpädagogik - Training mathematischer Vorläuferertigkeiten im Vorschulalter, http://www.kindergartenpaedagogik.de/489.html
3. Merrill, D., Kalanithi, J., Maes, P.: Siftables: Towards sensor network user interfaces. In: First Int. Conf. on Tangible and Embedded Interaction (2007)
4. Wesselink, R.: Interactive tiles - design report. Course report, University of Eindhoven, Industrial Design, Eindhoven (January 2006)

Enhancing Tactile Imagination through Sound and Light

Hideyuki Endo and Hideki Yoshioka

Tokyo University of Technology, Hachioji, Tokyo, Japan
endotut@gmail.com, yoshioka@stf.teu.ac.jp

Abstract. Drive Mind is a unique electro-acoustic system, which offers an audience a new sonic experience produced by the refraction of light. The main feature of this system is to visualize abstract figures of sound using a ray of LED light and to manipulate the system using acrylic objects. By this manipulation, the system creates a refraction of light and attendant positional data. This positional data is used to produce sound. The complexity of refraction of the light and the frame rate of the camera cause subtle fluctuations and produce distinctive sounds. The object is to enhance an audience's imagination by enabling them to identify with the performer's action visually, and help understanding of complex digital expression, using not only physical material but also physical phenomena when operating the system. This system helps the audience to become familiar with complex digital expression and experience the new possibilities of sound art.

Keywords: sound art, tangible bits, Max/MSP/Jitter, electro-acoustic, sonification, sound sculpture, media art.

1 Introduction

The computer has become an indispensable part of modern life. Furthermore, the computer has now become a tool that can enrich human life imaginatively and creatively. Based on these facts, this research aims to explore a new expressive method for music, which has the audience experience something new.

2 Background

Advances in computing have led to achievements in complex virtualization. Also, with the development of peripheral devices, such as touch panel screens and remote controllers, it has become easy for anyone to have a virtual experience. These tools are actively utilized in the field of media art.

One such tool is called reactable [1], which enables users to physically control sound with their hands and with objects. The objects have some marks to identify them, and the system recognizes which object is moved by these marks. The user can understand how the sound is changing through movement or the distance between

A. Nijholt, T. Romão, and D. Reidsma (Eds.): ACE 2012, LNCS 7624, pp. 481–484, 2012.
© Springer-Verlag Berlin Heidelberg 2012

objects. Data produced by the manipulation is abstracted as computer graphics and displayed on a table.

However, operation for modulations and the changing parameters of the sound is manipulated by a GUI, where displayed on the table. The display on this GUI is similar in appearance and operation to a basic software synthesizer like a slider. For this operation, the user has to understand what kind of shapes or signs (ex. slider) are connected to the parameters. Also, this system requires knowledge of how to manipulate a typical software synthesizer, which uses a controller like a touch panel.

Another example of a tool is FLEXIBILITY EXPERIENCE [2]. This system uses Microsoft Kinect [3] and it has been used in the promotion of Nike sportswear. The basic operation of this system merely involves the moving of the operator's own body. When the user is standing on a specific point, the system plays music. In this position, when the user moves his or her body to the music, the avatar on the screen moves like the user, and produces some visual effects generated by the movement of the user's body. This means that it is the user who is the controller of the avatar on the screen. The user does not require any other devices, because the camera and sensor in Kinect has caught the movements of the user.

3   Aim

Despite these advances in virtualization none of the tools have been able to expand the audience's understanding. The important thing is for the audience to understand what kind of data has been used for the performance, although in reality most of the data for the operation is invisible or too complex to grasp [4].

In addition, in order to help an audience's understanding, the system has to give the concrete tactile and visual information. For example, when a user is using gestures while performing an operation with motion graphics, ideally the user should feel the weight of the operation, not just air resistance.

At present, there is not enough information provided for easy recognition and understanding if one is just viewing the operation. Because of these problems, an audience has difficulty empathizing with the performer or system and does not have a full experience that can be expanded by their own imaginations.

In order to solve these problems, the performer has to manipulate objects physically, and the system has to use more familiar physical phenomena for the audience's understanding. To overcome these difficulties I have developed an electro-acoustic system named Drive Mind.

4   Approach

In Drive Mind, the abstract figure of sound takes concrete shape by using a shining ray of light in the darkness, which is made up of an LED light. The system is manipulated physically through the use of a number of acrylic objects placed in the path of the ray of light. The acrylic objects have to be moved or rotated to manipulate the

Fig. 1. An LED light and acrylic objects

system. With this manipulation, the ray of light is refracted into complex shapes. This refraction of light is a visual metaphor for the changing figure of the sound, and creates positional data for sonification.

5   Implementation

The input to this system is an image taken with a web camera. The ray of light is projected onto a panel and the camera shoots an image onto that panel. When the acrylic objects move, the ray of light gets refracted; in effect, the position of the light on the panel changes. The moving light on the panel is tracked by an application called Max/MSP/Jitter [5], and produces positional information for the light in the application's video window. This positional information is converted to MIDI [6] information, which is used by a software synthesizer called Reason [7] to produce a variety of sounds.

The application tracks the region of higher brightness from the input data and constantly changes the tracking with the interference of other brighter light. The brightness is controlled by focusing produced by the acrylic objects. The LED light is magnified by a round acrylic object supplemented by another round acrylic object to produce the focus. These two round acrylic objects act as lenses between the two objects. In this state, a square object is set up between the two round objects.

When twisting the square object as if manipulating a knob, refraction of light occurs around the objects. Through this action, the focus is also moved around and it makes the brightness of the focus and tracking position change. The process of tracking results in the application producing two kinds of numbers, which include information on horizontal and vertical movements.

A wavetable synthesizer, FM synthesizer, and noise oscillator produce the timbre. The horizontal moving numbers control the pitch of the sound, the modulation of the FM oscillator, the superposition of noise, and the vowel type of formant filter. The vertical moving numbers control the timing of sound emission, the type of waveform, the start position of the waveform, and the frequency of the formant filter. With these modulations, the software synthesizer plays an irregular beat through the speakers.

6   Solution

This system provides the user with a way of understanding the connection between tactile, hearing and visual sensations by providing visualized data and tactile information for easy recognition by both performer and audience of the manipulated digital data.

The important factor is that the performer can imagine the next step of how to compose with sound using tactile sensations at the moment of playing. This means that at the very least the system stimulates the performer's imagination with information derived by touch.

Regarding content matter, the LED light and the frame rate of the camera have a cyclic pattern. Furthermore, each pattern has a different cyclic pattern of its own, and mostly these patterns will never be synchronized. This arrhythmic rhythm, produced by cyclic patterns, gives subtle fluctuations to the sound. The sound produced gives the audience the illusion of becoming an engine of combustion derived from its own energies.

Acknowledgments. I would like to give special thanks to Dr.Yuta Uozumi and Tomoko Nakai for their creative advice. I would also like to thanks   Paul Brocklebank and Dr. Akemi Iida for proofreading this paper. I would also like to thank Akinori Ito for informational support.

References

1. Reactable, http://www.reactable.com/products/live/
2. NIKE FREE FLEXIBILITY EXPERIENCE, http://vimeo.com/43248674, http://public-image.org/
3. Microsoft. Kinect, http://www.xbox.com/
4. Hiroshi, I.: Fusion of Virtual and Real: Tangible Bits: User Interface Design towards Seamless Integration of Bits and Atoms. IPSJ-MGN430305. MIT Media Lab (2002)
5. Cycling'74. Max, http://cycling74.com/
6. Curtis, Roads. The computer music tutorial. Massachusetts Institute of Technology (1996)
7. propellerheads. Reason, http://www.propellerheads.se/

Streaming DirectX-Based Games on Windows

Alexander Franiak, Yohann Pitrey, Christoph Czepa, and Helmut Hlavacs*

University of Vienna, Research Group Entertainment Computing

Abstract. We present a framework that allows for simulating a cloud gaming architecture with any DirectX-based video game. The gamer's screen is captured and compressed as a video stream using the VP8 codec and sent over the network using UDP. We use this framework to evaluate the influence of frame-rate and encoding bit-rate on the Quality of Experience, as perceived by a panel of human test subjects.

Keywords: Cloud gaming, Quality of Experience, Video coding, VP8.

1 Introduction and Related Work

Cloud gaming is a new alternative for online gaming that does not require the user to buy expensive hardware or specific gaming consoles. The game is no longer executed locally, but on a distant host with dedicated hardware in a large data center [1]. The graphical output is encoded using a video codec and sent via the Internet to the gamer. The gamer only needs a simple low-power terminal to receive and present the video stream. The client then collects the user input and sends it back to the game in the data center, which can react by changing the game environment.

Cloud gaming is gradually developing into a serious industry branch, targeting at millions of casual gamers [1]. However, the limited resources on the server side in terms of processing power as well as network restrictions might affect the QoE on the gamer's side. For instance, the delay in the interactions between the game server and the client is known to be perceived as annoying by the end-user. Currently, the best cloud gaming providers such as OnLive[1] add delays up to 240 ms [4]. The second main factor affecting QoE in cloud gaming is the limited bandwidth. The encoding configuration, and more precisely the tradeoff between frame resolution, temporal frame-rate and overall encoding quality have an impact on the end-user experience. In practice, OnLive uses a proprietary video codec and a bandwidth on average around 2 Mbit/s [7].

As of today, only few contributions exist regarding QoE in cloud gaming. From 2006 to 2010, a European FP6 Project named *Games@Large* was conducted aiming at developing new platforms for gaming in the home environment [2]. A video-based approach was considered to address low processing power devices such as mobile phones. QoE was not really addressed and remained in the

---

* The authors would like to thank the WWTF Viennese Science Fund for funding this research.

[1] http://www.onlive.com/

A. Nijholt, T. Romão, and D. Reidsma (Eds.): ACE 2012, LNCS 7624, pp. 485–489, 2012.

concluding remarks of the project as an opportunity for future work. In [3], a metric was proposed, aiming at estimating the QoE based on the video encoder configuration, the transmission delay and the packet loss rate. This contribution used a custom built cloud gaming architecture and was based on an early video codec which does not reflect current state-of-the-art compression techniques such as MPEG-4 AVC/H.264 or VP8. In [5], the authors analyze the influence of network and Quality of Service (QoS) parameters such as the propagation delay and the amount of packet loss on the QoE. The main outcomes of this first study show that user experience depends on a complex mix of network performance, type of game, and also user personal preference. In [6], the same authors research on key influence factors of cloud gaming, most notably delay and packet loss, and evaluate the resulting QoE.

In this paper, we first present a simple framework that simulates a complete cloud gaming archiecture. The graphical output of any DirectX 9-based video game can be captured, compressed using the VP8 video codec and transmitted over a network using a UDP link. The gamer's input is collected and sent back to the hosting computer, to close the interaction loop. Secondly, we use this framework to study the impact of encoding bit-rate and frame-rate on the perceived quality, for two types of games. We report the results of a controlled subjective experiment identifying the transition points between good, acceptable and not acceptable quality for both parameters.

2   Cloud Gaming Architecture Description

To simulate a complete cloud gaming architecture, we hooked a VP8 video encoder inside the DirectX 9 rendering engine. Instead of being sent to a local screen to be displayed, each frame is captured and compressed using the video codec. Each encoded frame is then sent to the client over a UDP link. On the client's side, the received and decoded frames can then be drawn on the screen. Then, the user input is sent back to the server so that the game environment can be modified. To this end, we used the XInput API for DirectX 9, designed to communicate with game controllers. By hooking the code of XInput with custom input functions, our framework allows using various input devices such as traditional game controllers, keyboards and mice, or even mobiles phones using the orientation sensors and touch screen available on most current smartphones. For the current demonstration, we used an Android-operated smartphone converted into a game controller, using a custom application. The application emulates the basic buttons and steering devices (*e.g.* steering wheel and throttle) needed for the two games used for our evaluation.

In the next section, we demonstrate the power and flexibility of our framework by building a subjective experiment aimed at evaluating the influence of encoding bitrate and frame-rate on the quality perceived by human test subjects.

3   Subjective Evaluation

We evaluate the influence of the number of frames per second (FPS) and the encoding bitrate on the quality of the gaming experience, as perceived by human subjects. These two parameters affect both the gaming experience and the amount of data to be transmitted over the network, and are therefore of great interest from both technical and user points of view.

We conducted a subjective experiment under controlled conditions in order to present a reliable evaluation of the considered parameters. Our framework was extended to be capable of changing the FPS and the encoding bitrate dynamically, without interrupting the game. Two types of games are involved: a first person shooting game and an adventure game. The first person shooting game is based on quick movements of the main character, with relatively few details in the images. The adventure game is based on more static images with a high amount of details.

The experiment starts with a free-play phase for 5 minutes on each game, for the participant to get used to the game itself. Next, the experiment consists in progressively decreasing or increasing the two parameters, first separately, then jointly. Our goal is to determine the transition points between three levels of quality of the gaming experience. In the first scenario, the FPS only is varied. The game starts with the FPS set to 40 Hz and the bitrate set to 1600 kbps. Based on our observations, these values give a visual quality equivalent to that using a local hardware-based version of both games. The FPS is progressively decreased by the experimenter. The test person is asked to state when the quality of the game changes from *good* to *acceptable* in his opinion. At this point the experimenter stops the decrease and reports the corresponding FPS value. Then the decrease is continued, and the test person is asked to state when the quality changes from *acceptable* to *not acceptable*. The second FPS value is reported. The FPS is then set to a very low value (*i.e.* 5 Hz), and progressively increased. A symmetric process is repeated, increasing the FPS and reporting the transition values. The second scenario obeys the same structure, while the bitrate only is varied, starting from 1600 kbps, down to 160 kbps (the FPS is set to 40 Hz). In the third scenario, both the FPS and bitrate are varied simultaneously, using the same procedure. In order to avoid order effects, we varied the presentation order of the three scenarios from one test subject to another, as well as that of the decreasing and increasing phases and the type of game. The experiment was conducted with five test subjects, including males and females, with gaming affinity ranging from none to high. The hardware configuration of the game server and the client caused no uncontrolled impairments.

Figure 1 presents the transition points between the three levels of quality for each game and each parameter. The values are averaged over each scenario and over test subjects. The transition point between good and acceptable quality is referred to as the high transition point, whereas the transition between acceptable and not acceptable is referred to as the low transition point.

On Figure 1 (a), the low transition point is equivalent for the two games. The high transition point appears slightly lower for the adventure game, showing

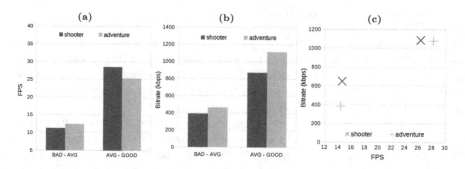

Fig. 1. Influence of bitrate and FPS on gaming quality. (a): FPS only, (b): bitrate only, (c): joint. The plots display the average values over the five test participants.

that it suffers slightly more from a decrease in FPS than the adventure game. Fluidity is indeed a critical feature in the shooting game, so the gamer can react to the fast changes in his environment. On the opposite, the adventure game can afford a slightly lower FPS value, as the amount and importance of motion included in the game is lower. Nevertheless, we observed a relatively high variation in the transition points between test subjects, as well as a dependency to the presentation order between decreasing and increasing quality. Reconducting the experiment with more test subjects should allow us to verify the significance of these results using statistical tools such as the student t-test.

On Figure 1 (b), we observe that the shooting game can afford lower bitrates than the adventure game. The image quality is more important in the adventure game, where the environment contains small details are useful for the gamer. On the opposite, the shooting game can afford lower bitrates, as the main action appears to be focused on motion fluidity rather than on image quality.

Figure 1 (c) illustrates interesting behaviours for the two games. As the bitrate and the FPS are varied at the same time in this scenario, one could expect the transition points to move towards higher values, in order to compensate for the more drastic quality changes. However, we observe that the transition points for the adventure game only slightly move towards higher FPS values, whereas the bitrate values do not change. For the shooting game, both transition points move towards higher bitrate. The low transition point moves towards higher FPS values, whereas the high transition point moves towards lower values.

4   Conclusion

In this paper we describe a framework providing a high level of control on cloud gaming. We use this framework to conduct a subjective experiment evaluating the influence of bitrate and frame-rate on the perceived quality of experience. The results show that both parameters have an impact on the quality, and call for more detailed investigation on their joint influence, as well as the inclusion of other parameters such as the delay between the client and the server, the frame resolution and variable bandwidth conditions.

References

1. Ojala, Tyrvainen: Developing Cloud Business Models: A Case Study on Cloud Gaming. IEEE Software (2011)
2. Nave, D., et al.: Games@large graphics streaming architecture. In: Int. Symp. on Consumer Electronics (2008)
3. Wang: Modeling and characterizing user experience in a cloud server based mobile gaming approach. In: IEEE Global Telecomm. Conf. (2009)
4. Chen, Chang, Tseng, Huang, Lei: Measuring the latency of cloud gaming systems. ACM Multimedia (2011)
5. Jarschel, Schlosser, et al.: Gaming in the clouds: QoE and the users perspective. Mathematical and Computer Modelling (2011)
6. Jarschel, S., et al.: An Evaluation of QoE in Cloud Gaming Based on Subjective Tests. In: Int. Conf. on Innovative Mobile and Internet Services in Ubiquitous Computing (2011)
7. OnLive Technical FAQ. OnLive (retrieved July 17, 2010)

Autonomously Acquiring a Video Game Agent's Behavior: Letting Players Feel Like Playing with a Human Player

Nobuto Fujii, Yuichi Sato, Hironori Wakama, and Haruhiro Katayose

Graduate School of Science and Technology, Kwansei Gakuin University
2-1 Gakuen, Sanda, Hyogo, Japan
{nobuto,katayose}@kwansei.ac.jp

Abstract. Designing behavior patterns of video game agents (COM players) is a crucial aspect of video game development. While various systems aiming to automatically acquire behavior patterns has been proposed and some have successfully obtained stronger patterns than human players, the obtained behavior patterns looks mechanical. We present herein an autonomous acquisition of video game agent behavior, which emulates the behavior of a human player. Instead of implementing straightforward heuristics, the behavior is acquired using Q-learning, a reinforcement learning, where, *biological constraints* are imposed. In the experiments using Infinite Mario Bros., we observe that behaviors that imply human behaviors are obtained by imposing *sensory error, perceptual and motion delay*, and *fatigue* as biological constraints.

Keywords: Strategy acquisition, Biological constraints, Video game.

1 Introduction

It is no exaggeration to say that the video game agent's "strategy" and "behavior" determine the player's experience when playing the video game. Conventionally, game programmers have elaborately programmed the agents' "behavior" and "strategy" including "getting higher scores" and "avoiding enemy characters," using the cut-and-trial approach, as those simulate human players' approaches. In addition to following video game level design, programmers are obliged to engage in extremely complicated and difficult tasks. In recent game design, an automated method called "procedural technology" has received attention as a method to lower the programmers' burden. Introducing machine learning algorithms is a promising and rational way to automate designing the agents' "behavior" and "strategy." Studies about automatically acquiring "behavior" and "strategy"" contain following related works, the approach using path finding for contest where algorithms compete behavior patterns in "Infinite Mario Bros." [1], the approaches using reinforcement learning for "Hearts[2]" and "trading card games[3]." However, strong algorithms do not always create realistic human players feel like playing with a human player. It is more difficult to make algorithms human-like than

A. Nijholt, T. Romão, and D. Reidsma (Eds.): ACE 2012, LNCS 7624, pp. 490–493, 2012.
© Springer-Verlag Berlin Heidelberg 2012

strong, because subjective criteria should be accessed for this goal. We must determine other tactics, i.e., realizing human-like "behavior," with as few required exhaustive heuristics as possible.

This study seeks to realize the autonomous acquisition of video game agents' "behavior" and "strategy," thus making its players feel like they are playing with a human player, instead of implementing straightforward heuristics. We set a hypothesis that "biological constraints" are the origin of "behavior" that looks human-like in its appearance. In this paper, we examine how human-like behavior emerges based on machine learning techniques, where "biological constraints" are introduced. *Sensory error, perceptual and motion delay*, and *fatigue* are considered biological constraints in the reinforcement learning evaluation process.

2   Reinforcement Learning Algorithm and Learning Target

We adopt the reinforcement learning approach i.e. Q-learning, to make a video game agent's acquire behavior patterns as if human player plays a video game, and we use the input information considered "biological constraints," i.e., *Sensory error, perceptual and motion delay*, and *fatigue*.

A learning target with the following factors is desirable: the human player must control a character in real time under an environment in which "sensory error" and "perceptual and motion delay" occur, though the game can regenerate situations. In our study, we adopt the action game "Infinite Mario Bros." as a learning target.

3   "Biological Constraints" Definition

"Sensory error", "perceptual and motion delay", "fatigue" are defined as follows.

1. **"Sensory error" of observable placement information**
   It is difficult for a human player to precisely recognize the position (coordinates) of a character; a sensory error is thus included in the observable placement information. The video game agent can observe the coordinates, i.e., placement information, given a Gaussian noise for the correct coordinates of Mario and enemy characters.
2. **"Perceptual and motion delay" of key input**
   "Perceptual and motion delay" occurs until a human player moves, after observing and recognizing the game state. The observable information becomes the past information when the human player inputs the key. The video game agent can observe the game state in several previous frames.
3. **"Fatigue" by key control**
   The human player should be tired when he/she controls a key in succession while short time. The video game agent can learn strategy to get better score with less key controls.

4   Behavior-Acquisition under "Biological Constraints"

To implement behavior-acquisition system under "biological constraints", our system must learn about behavior patterns in non-ideal environments where our system cannot observe the precise game states. In this chapter, we propose a method to acquire such patterns despite this difficulty. We present how "biological constraints" are handled in our reinforcement learning framework.

4.1   Feature Extraction from Mario and Observable Information

Our system extracts features from Mario and observable information thus. The game state dimensions are reduced, and our system can learn behavior patterns using Q-learning in realistic learning time.

- **Ground information of the neighborhood within 7×7 blocks of Mario**
- **Enemy characters in the neighborhood within 7×7 blocks of Mario**
- **Either "Super Mario" or "Small Mario"**
- **Mario's moving direction.**

4.2   Reward Function

The video game agent must obtain a higher score by capturing a longer stage more quickly. Therefore, our system gives positive rewards for capturing a stage and negative rewards for factors that obstruct capturing a stage, including damaged and dying. Furthermore, our system gives negative rewards for key control causing the fatigue.

$$reward = distance + damaged + death + keyPress \tag{1}$$

In Formula 1, *distance* indicates positive rewards that Mario go ahead a stage by his action, *damaged* denotes negative rewards, as when Mario is damaged by clashing with enemy characters in an action. *death* means negative rewards that Mario is dead after an action, and *keyPress* means negative rewards when the agent changes key control from previous frame. The parameters, used here, are those adjusted based on preliminary experiments executed before this experiment, i.e., *damaged* equals −50.0, *death* equals −100.0, *keyPress* equals −5.0 in our system.

5   Experiments and Discussion

We compare an agent in an ideal environment with an agent considering "biological constraints," and we examine differences in the behavior patterns that the agent acquires. We compare the patterns without biological constraints and with biological constraints. Each agent learns the patterns on an invariable stage generated by the same seed parameter every game to compare optimum behavior patterns. Each learning trial has 100,000 games, and we sample the play when each agent can obtain the highest score in a learning trial.

Pictures of Figure 1 show difference in behavior pattern tendency when Mario captures an enemy character that he cannot defeat. Though Mario without biological constraints can capture this stage with minimal jumping and non-stopping, Mario with biological constraints captures this enemy character with a big jump and a motion that requires stopping.

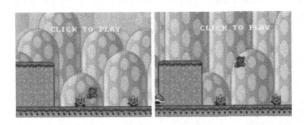

Fig. 1. Comparison of the agent without biological constraints (Left) and with biological constraints (Right) when the agent avoids untouchable enemies

6   Conclusion

In this paper, we proposed an autonomous behavior-acquisition system to obtain the "behavior" and "strategy" of a video game agent that plays a video game like a human player. Instead of enumerating heuristics, we realized the system by introducing "biological constraints" in the reinforcement learning framework. Experimental results of the simulation explored for an action game showed that the proposed system can acquire appropriate behavior patterns that are adaptive to the game world. When "sensory error", "perceptual and motion delay" and "fatigue" are introduced as biological constraints, behavior patterns that look like those of a human player are observed.

We verified the possibility that reinforcement learning through introducing "biological constraints" acquire rational and robust behavior patterns, and that human players feel them as if those of human player's. In future works, we would like to conduct more detailed experiments, changing the "sensory error" "perceptual and motion delay," and "fatigue factor" parameters and apply this method to various game genres.

References

1. Baumgarten, R.: The 2009 mario ai competition. In: 2010 IEEE Evolutionary Computation (CEC), pp. 1–8 (2010)
2. Fujita, H., Ishii, S.: Model-based reinforcement learning for partially observable games with sampling-based state estimation. Neural Computation 19, 3051–3087 (2007)
3. Fujii, N., Hashida, M., Katayose, H.: Strategy-acquisition system for video trading card game. In: ACE 2008, pp. 175–182 (2008)

Chop Chop:
A Sound Augmented Kitchen Prototype

Veronica Halupka, Ali Almahr, Yupeng Pan, and Adrian David Cheok

Keio University Graduate School of Media Design,
4-1-1 Hiyoshi, Kohoku-ku, Yokohama-city, Kanagawa, Japan 223-8526
{veronica,alia,yupengpan,adriancheok}@kmd.keio.ac.jp
http://www.kmd.keio.ac.jp/en/

Abstract. In our fast evolving, highly technological world, sometimes we don't spend quality time cooking or eating together because our attention is split. How can we find a way to bring fun back into the kitchen, re-engaging people with cooking?

The aim of this research is to use Media Design to engage people with food experiences by bringing fun into cooking and eating. Through the design and implementation of a sound augmented kitchen prototype, we have attempted to address this question.

Chop Chop is a sound augmented kitchen prototype system. It consists of very simple commercially available hardware; A computer or mobile device, headphones, a cutting board and knife. As a user performs a simple everyday cooking task, chopping food, the sound is enhanced with filters and combo events, allowing the user to experience the act of chopping in a novel and exciting way.

Through demonstrations, surveys and user experience analysis, we have tested our prototype and shown that using our Augmented Reality system in a kitchen setting has no detriment over traditional tools and techniques, and enhances user experience and positive affect.

Keywords: Augmented Reality, Multi-Sensory, Food Media, Sound, Kitchen.

1 Introduction

The setting for this research is a new and exciting field, Food Media. The Food Media landscape is diverse, and through the introduction of new technology and methods, is changing rapidly. Food Media is a common ground between the food sciences, media and culture, a step beyond pure gastronomy into a new multi-disciplinary field.

Previous Mixed and Augmented Reality kitchen prototypes have been largely focussed on improving efficiency. Our prototype is different, in that we aimed to enhance fun and entertainment and improve cooking experiences. Chop Chop uses very simple off the shelf hardware, which we have employed in a novel way.

A. Nijholt, T. Romão, and D. Reidsma (Eds.): ACE 2012, LNCS 7624, pp. 494–497, 2012.
© Springer-Verlag Berlin Heidelberg 2012

2 System

2.1 Related Works

Cooking Games. In early infancy, we learn to play with our food. You may remember your mother encouraging younger brothers or sisters to eat by saying "Here comes the airplane!" accompanied by plane sounds and actions. This kind of game is one of the first play interactions we have with our food. This is not just for fun or to calm a cranky or fussy infant. Instinctively, mothers know (or learn from their own mothers) that this is a good way to encourage healthy eating behaviours. In fact, mothers who have good play interactions with their babies are more likely to have infants with better and healthier eating habits[1].

In creating the Chop Chop prototype, we took inspiration from various existing cooking simulation games, such as Cooking Mama[2], Diner Dash[3] and Cake Mania[4]. Our goal is to incorporate a fun element into every-day cooking scenarios, drawing inspiration from these childhood games, and realising features from cooking simulations. We want to encourage people to enjoy cooking more, and perhaps even inspire them to cook more often.

Augmented Kitchen Systems. We examined several existing augmented kitchen systems during the design process for our prototype. What we found in common amongst these systems was that mostly they are aimed at improving kitchen processes and efficiency. While our goal is different, we were able to learn several important points that influenced the design and implementation of our system, for example, that users are willing to engage with augmented interfaces and find them no more difficult to use (if well designed) than a traditional kitchen[5][6][7].

Our related previous augmented kitchen work, a flavour visualisation system [8], used visual feedback to improve the user's cooking experience and communication with a remote cooking partner.

2.2 Chop Chop - Design and Specifications

The hardware component of our system is simple and available off-the-shelf to any end user. The system consists of an input device (microphone), processing (computer or mobile device), output (headphones) and tools (chopping board and knife).

The chopping sounds picked up by the microphone are processed by the computer using a simple set of custom filters to change the sound. A flash-based combo system rewards the user for sound sequences or "combos" with a special sound event.

2.3 User Testing

Our concept itself is very simple, cute, and straightforward. But the results we achieved were far beyond what we first anticipated. Users were very engaged

Fig. 1. Chop Chop Preliminary User Testing

with the system, and expressed surprise and delight. What was a simple idea actually had a big impact.

We conducted preliminary user testing with 12 real users by giving them a chopping scenario: cut the cucumber, crosswise into circles. The user performed the test twice, with and without the audio feedback, and filled out a worksheet including a standardised measure of positive and negative affect (I-PANAS-SF)[9] to assess their emotional state. We concluded from our results that while chopping vegetables in general decreases negative affect, chopping with our sound augmented system increases positive affect. Users rated chopping with sounds as more fun than chopping without, and also reported that using the sound augmented system had no negative effect on chopping difficulty.

3   Conclusions

The Chop Chop sound augmented kitchen prototype is designed to make the task of chopping more fun and entertaining. It consists of off-the-shelf hardware and uses software processing to modify and enhance the sound of chopping using custom filters and combo rewards.

We have made several conclusions about this system from the testing of our prototype:

1. We can make the experience of cooking more fun and enjoyable using AR technology;
2. While we have not yet proven that these systems can improve cooking skill, we see no detrimental effect - that is to say, our AR kitchen scenario is no worse than traditional tools and methods;
3. The activity of cooking in itself improves mood, and cooking with our AR system enhances this effect.

References

1. Chatoor, I., Egan, J., Getson, P., Menvielle, E., O'Donnell, R.: Mother–Infant Interactions in Infantile Anorexia Nervosa. Journal of the American Academy of Child & Adolescent Psychiatry 27(5), 535–540 (1988)
2. Cooking Mama, Taito (2006), http://www.taito.co.jp/csm/cooking_mama_portal/
3. Diner Dash, Playfirst (2005), http://www.playfirst.com/diner-dash
4. Cake Mania, Digital Chocolate (2011), http://www.digitalchocolate.com/sandlot-games/
5. Bonanni, L., Lee, C.H., Selker, T.: Counter Intelligence: Augmented reality kitchen. In: Proc. CHI, vol. 2239, p. 44 (2005)
6. Hashimoto, A., Mori, N., Funatomi, T., Yamakata, Y., Kakusho, K., Minoh, M.: Smart kitchen: A user centric cooking support system. In: Proceedings of IPMU, vol. 8, pp. 848–854 (2008)
7. Chen, J.H., Chi, P.P.Y., Chu, H.H., Chen, C.C.H., Huang, P.: A smart kitchen for nutrition-aware cooking. IEEE Pervasive Computing 9(4), 58–65 (2010)
8. Choi, Y., Cheok, A.D., Halupka, V., Sepulveda, J., Peris, R., Koh, J., Xuan, W., Jun, W., Dilrukshi, A., Tomoharu, Y., et al.: Flavor visualization: Taste guidance in co-cooking system for coexistence. In: 2010 IEEE International Symposium on Mixed and Augmented Reality-Arts, Media, and Humanities (ISMAR-AMH), pp. 53–60 (2010)
9. Thompson, E.R.: Development and validation of an internationally reliable short-form of the positive and negative affect schedule (PANAS). Journal of Cross-Cultural Psychology 38(2), 227–242 (2007)

Time Telescopic Replay of Tactile Sensations

Yuki Hashimoto

Osaka University / Japan Society for the Promotion of Science
Osaka Japan
y.hashimoto@ist.osaka-u.ac.jp

Abstract. We daily enjoy the visual effects of slow and fast motion content. Time telescopic techniques are useful in scientific research and provide new possibilities in art and entertainment. We suggest that tactile sensations can also benefit from the effect of time telescopic replay because of knowledge that we can generally recognize texture regardless of the stroking speed. We confirmed which resembles the visual during slow motion in previous research. In this pa-pef, we report a new system design to measure and present tactile phenomena accurately. We also describe some application ideas to enjoy immersion in the time telescopic world.

Keywords: Tactile Sensation, Time Telescopic Replay, Collision.

1 Introduction

A technique that expands and contracts information in a time-wise manner has already been widely used in the analysis of various phenomena [1][2][3] and art and entertainment. Slow or fast motion is a popular visual effect in many movies and provides new perceptions [4][5][6]. However, this time expansion technique is currently limited to visual information. For audio information, since simple time expansion results in odd or inaudible sounds, this technique can only be used for such limited situations as dance training.

The time expansion and contraction of tactile information raise interesting issues. We believe that with tactile sensations, the slow/quick motion effect may provide useful benefits for the following reasons. When we stroke a textured material, we can generally recognize its texture regardless of the stroking speed. Research has also developed tactile displays that respond to hand movements [7][8]. This suggests that we can use the effect of time expansion and contraction to acquire tactile information. We verified this hypothesis from the time expansion aspect and confirmed that the effect of tactile slow motion resembles visual slow motion.

In this paper, we describe a new system to realize slow/quick motion replay and show some entertainment application ideas for these effects. We focus on collision phenomena as examples, since they are one of the most popular situations in visual slow motion content.

A. Nijholt, T. Romão, and D. Reidsma (Eds.): ACE 2012, LNCS 7624, pp. 498–501, 2012.
© Springer-Verlag Berlin Heidelberg 2012

2   Princeple

The principle of the time telescopic replay of tactile sensations is simple. First, the tactile phenomenon is recorded at a high sampling rate. Next, a tactile display replays the recorded data at a different sampling frequency. For instance, if the recording was done at a 50 kHz sampling frequency and the replay was at 5 kHz, the user will experience a 10 times slower tactile sensation. If the replay was done at 500 kHz, the user will experience a 10 times slower tactile sensation.

3   System Design

3.1   Overview

In the previous research [9], we developed a record and replay system for tactile slow motion replay. However, this system has several problems that must be solved before it can be used for tactile fast motion replay.

The first is that it can't record slight pressure because of its measuring method. In the previous recording system, objects were dropped onto plastic boards whose vibrations were recorded. This system depends on the bend of the board. Therefore, if slight pressure is added to the board, it is very hard to measure the bend of the board.

The second is that the previous system had to record the board's physical properties. Users experienced the collision sensation of objects and the board, but not the skin.

The third is that we could not control all the devices from a one PC because the record and replay systems were separate. The high-speed camera wasn't even connected to a PC. Therefore, we manually combined video and vibration data from a sensor. However, this way is not accurate.

We designed a new system to solve these problems (Fig.1). The details of each part are described below.

3.2   Recording Part

The recording part is composed of a pressure sensor (Nitta Corporation, FlexiForce A201-1), a high-speed camera (DITECT Corporation, HAS-L1), and an analog-to-digital converter in a micro-computer (NXP, mbed LPC1768).

The pressure sensor was covered by a human skin gel (Exseal Corporation, H0-2K) to record similar phenomena as is done by the human skin. The sampling rate of the pressure sensor was 50 kHz, and the camera's sampling rate was 1000 fps (400 x 300 pixels).

3.3   Replay Part

The replay part (Fig.2) is composed of a tactile display, an LCD display, an amplifier (RASTEME SYSTEMS CO., LTD., RSDA202), and a digital-to-analog converter in a micro-computer (NXP, mbed LPC1768).

The tactile display is composed of an audio speaker that faces down. The user covers the speaker with her palm while the speaker vibrates air between the speaker and the palm and feels various vibrations from the air pressure. The effectiveness of this method was confirmed by our previous study [10][11].

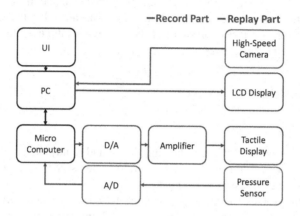

Fig. 1. Block diagram of our system

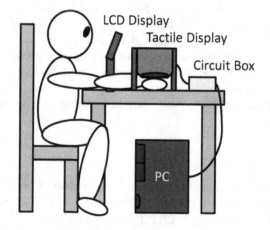

Fig. 2. Replay part setup

4   Application Ideas

We believe that our method can be applied to most of the applications that have already been used in the field of vision, especially entertainment uses. We previously confirmed that tactile slow motion replay has an emotional effect [9]. Based on this knowledge, we are making several applications. For example, when a user watches a movie with our system, it presents time telescopic tactile sensations that match the video's slow or fast motion. As another example, when we slowly or quickly move and interact with objects as if in a fantasy world, our system presents tactile feedback to the movement speed.

These examples will enhance the feelings of immersion in the time telescopic world and provide pleasure to discover new phenomena which we can't notice for a sense of the time of the real world.

5   Conclusion

In this paper, we proposed a new application field for tactile display called time telescopic motion. After describing the problems of our previous system, we showed a new design of a record and replay system that can record similar vibration phenomena as done by the human skin using a pressure sensor covered by a human skin gel. Since all of the devices were controlled by one PC, we can easily exhibit our system. We also showed application ideas using it. Our next step is to verify a performance of the new system. We will also confirm the effectiveness of tactile fast motion replay and develop an appropriate system for art and entertainment.

Acknowledgements. Grant-in-Aid for Creative Scientific Research.

References

1. Labous, L., Rosato, D.A., Dave, N.R.: Measurements of collisional properties of spheres using high-speed video analysis. Physical Review E 56, 5717–5725 (1997)
2. Reinschmidt, C., van den Bogert, A.J., Nigg, B.M., Lundberg, A., Murphy, N.: Effect of skin movement on the analysis of skeletal knee joint motion during running. Journal of Biomechanics, 729–732 (1997)
3. Larsson, H., Hertegård, S., Lindestad, P.A., Hammarberg, B.: Vocal Fold Vibrations: High-Speed Imaging, Kymography, and Acoustic Analysis: A Preliminary Report. Laryngoscope 110(12), 2117–2122 (2000)
4. Palma, D.B.: The Fury, Twentieth Century Fox Film (1978)
5. Wachowski, L., Wachowski, A.: The Matorix, Silver Pictures (1999)
6. Snyder, Z.: 300, Legendary Pictures (2007)
7. Misky, M., Ouh-Young, M., Steele, O., Brooks, F.P., Behensky, M.: Feeling and seeing. Issues in force display. Computer Graphics 24(2), 235–243 (1990)
8. Konyo, M., Akazawa, K., Tadokoro, S., Takamori, T.: Tactile Feel Display for Virtual Active Touch. In: Proc. IEEE/RSJ International Conference on Intelligent Robots and Systems, pp. 3744–3750 (2003)
9. Hashimoto, Y., Kajimoto, H.: Slow Motion Replay of Tactile Sensation. In: ICAT 2010, pp. 51–56 (2010)
10. Hashimoto, Y., Nakata, S.: Novel Tactile Display for Emotional Tactile Experience. In: Int. Conf. on Advances in Computer Entertainment Technologies (2009)
11. Hashimoto, Y., Kajimoto, H.: A novel interface to present emotional tactile sensation to a palm using air pressure. In: CHI 2008 Extended Abstracts on Human Factors in Computing Systems, pp. 2703–2708 (2008)

Compact Ultrasound Device for Noncontact Interaction

Takayuki Hoshi

Nagoya Institute of Technology, Aichi-ken, Japan
star@nitech.ac.jp

Abstract. This paper introduces a compact device for noncontact interaction. It can push objects from a distance by utilizing focused ultrasound. The maximum output force at the focal point is 16 mN. The position of the focal point can be moved quickly and precisely. The device is small (19×19×5 cm^3), light (0.6 kg), and compact so that one can pick it up with one hand and install it at various places. This easy-to-use device would lead to a wide variety of applications.

Keywords: Noncontact interaction, Ultrasound, Acoustic radiation pressure.

1   Introduction

Noncontact interaction attracts a lot of attention of ordinary people and such a technology is expected to lead to a novel type of physical interface. Some tabletop systems with different principles are demonstrated in these years. Air jets are used in [1]. Three air jets surrounding an object moves it on a flat surface. ZeroN system [2] uses a solenoid coil attached on an XYZ stage. This system holds a spherical magnet in mid-air and moves it three-dimensionally. Ultra-tangibles system [3] utilizes focused ultrasound to control multi objects simultaneously. Four arrays of ultrasound transducer surround the workspace and move the objects two-dimensionally.

In a noncontact interaction system, actuators (e.g. air jets, solenoid coils, and ultrasound arrays in the systems introduced above) are usually built in the surrounding structures mainly because a large space is occupied by their own bodies, driving circuits, and wirings. It is not easy for other people, especially who are not familiar to electronics, to give it a try to use such actuators for their own issues. The application area of nonlinear interaction (including entertainments) would widely expand if the actuators become smaller, lighter, and more compact.

Our research group originally developed an ultrasound-based noncontact interaction device for the purpose of producing tactile stimulation from a distace [4]. The device pushes the surface of human skin by focusing airborne ultrasound. We call it "AUFD (Airborne Ultrasound Focusing Device)" hereafter. One of the most strengths of the AUFD is that it is noncontact and hence users do not need to wear or have stimulating devices on their hand. Additionally, the spatial and the temporal resolutions are both high and so various patterns of tactile feelings can be reproduced. The maximum output force is several dozen mN.

This paper introduces a compact device of AUFD (Fig. 1) smaller and lighter than the previsou one in order to explore its application other than tactile display. Its size and weight are 19×19×5 cm^3 and 0.6 kg, respectively.

A. Nijholt, T. Romão, and D. Reidsma (Eds.): ACE 2012, LNCS 7624, pp. 502–505, 2012.

(a) Flipping up paper strips.   (b) Vibrating water surface.

Fig. 1. Examples of possible applications of developed ultrasound focusing device

2   Principles

2.1   Acoustic Radiation Pressure

The acoustic radiation pressure, which is a nonlinear phenomenon of ultrasound, is utilized to push objects in midair. When an ultrasound beam is reflected vertically at an object surface, the surface is subjected to a constant vertical force in the direction of the incident beam. Assuming a plane wave, the acoustic radiation pressure P [Pa] is described as

$$P = \alpha E = \alpha \frac{p^2}{\rho c^2} \tag{1}$$

where E [J/m^3] is the energy density of ultrasound, c [m/s] is the sound speed, p [Pa] is the RMS sound pressure of ultrasound, and ρ [kg/m^3] is the density of medium. α is the constant depending on the reflection coefficient at the object surface and α is equal to 2 in the case of total reflection. Equation (1) suggests that the spatial distribution of the radiation pressure P can be controlled by synthesizing the spatial distribution of the ultrasound p.

2.2   Phased Array Focusing

The phased array focusing technique is used to produce the radiation pressure up to several dozen mN. The focal point of ultrasound is generated by setting adequate phase delays of multiple transducers. In addition, the focal point can be moved to an arbitrary position by controlling the phase delays.

The spatial resolution and the array size are in the relationship of trade-off. It is theoretically derived that the spatial distribution of ultrasound generated from a rectangular transducer array is nearly sinc-function shaped. The width of the main lobe (w [m]) parallel to the side of the rectangular is written as

$$w = \frac{2\lambda R}{D} \tag{2}$$

where λ [m] is the wavelength, R [m] is the focal length, and D [m] is the side length of the rectangular array.

3   Prototype

The developed compact device (Fig. 1) consists of two circuit boards. One is an array board of ultrasound transducers and the other is a controller board including an FPGA and amplifiers. Both boards are 19×19 cm^2. They are connected electrically to each other by pin connectors instead of wirings.

285 pieces of ultrasound transducers (10 mm diameter, T4010A1, Nippon Ceramic Co. Ltd.) are arranged in a rectangular area whose D is 17 cm. As shown in (2), D is related to the resulting size of the focal point. The resonant frequency of the transducers is 40 kHz (i.e. $\lambda = 8.5$ mm). Then, w is 20 mm when R is set at 20 cm. The maximum output force is 16 mN (measured).

4   Possible Applications

4.1   Tactile Feedback

The AUFD provides noncontact tactile feedback in mid-air. It is suitable to be combined with aerial image displays [5] and aerial interface systems [6]. Besides, the stimulation of the AUFD moves finely (sub-mm resolution) and so it can reproduce handwriting strokes as tactile stimulation [7]. This kind of tactile stimulation may be utilized for transmitting non-verbal information, giving passwords more safely than displaying them on a screen, and showing characters instead of braille. Furthermore, it could be utilized to "make sound touchable" as demonstrated in [8].

4.2   Entertainments and Arts

The AUFD also has possibility to be used in the field of entertainments and arts. The output force is several dozen mN and so it can operate soft and/or light objects such as paper, smoke, water, particles [3], bubbles, balloons, etc. from a distance (Fig. 1). Mysterious and attractive effects would be demonstrated by using the AUFD.

It is easy to install the compact AUFD on the ceiling, the walls, etc. because it is compact. It is even possible to make it wireless if the USB module is replaced with a wireless module and a battery is mounted. This is optional and depends on user's electronic skill.

4.3   Measurements

The AUFD may contribute to develop a new measurement method in which the material surface is deformed or vibrated. It is used to deform the surface of elastic material and the deformation is measured by a laser displacement sensor to obtain the compliance distribution [9]. For another example, it is expected that the sound-based static electricity measurement [10] is expanded to 2D scan by employing the AUFD.

5   Conclusion

A compact ultrasound device for noncontact interaction was introduced. It is small and easy to pick up, bring, and install anywhere. The principles were explained and the possible applications were discussed.

It is expected that this compact device increases the user population and expands its application area. We are planning to lend the compact devices to researchers who want to give it a try to use the ultrasound-based noncontact interaction device.

References

1. Iwaki, S., Morimasa, H., Noritsugu, T., Kobayashi, M.: Contactless Manipulation of an Object on a Plane Surface Using Multiple Air Jets. In: ICRA 2011, pp. 3257–3262 (2011)
2. Lee, J., Post, R., Ishii, H.: ZeroN: Mid-Air Tangible Interaction Enabled by Computer Controlled Magnetic Levitation. In: UIST 2011, pp. 327–336 (2011)
3. Marshall, M.T., Carter, T., Alexander, J., Subramanian, S.: Ultra-Tangibles: Creating Movable Tangible Objects on Interactive Tables. In: CHI 2012, pp. 2185–2188 (2012)
4. Hoshi, T., Takahashi, M., Iwamoto, T., Shinoda, H.: Noncontact Tactile Display Based on Radiation Pressure of Airborne Ultrasound. IEEE Trans. Haptics 3(3), 155–165 (2010)
5. Hoshi, T., Takahashi, M., Nakatsuma, K., Shinoda, H.: Touchable Holography. In: SIGGRAPH 2009, Emerging Technologies, article no. 23 (2009)
6. Hoshi, T.: Development of Aerial-Input and Aerial-Tactile-Feedback System. In: IEEE World Haptics 2011, pp. 569–573 (2011)
7. Hoshi, T.: Handwriting Transmission System Using Noncontact Tactile Display. In: IEEE Haptics Symposium 2012, pp. 399–401 (2012)
8. Ciglar, M.: An Ultrasound Based Instrument Generating Audible and Tactile Sound. In: NIME 2010, pp. 19–22 (2010)
9. Fujiwara, M., Nakatsuma, K., Takahashi, M., Shinoda, H.: Remote Measurement of Surface Compliance Distribution Using Ultrasound Radiation Pressure. In: IEEE World Haptics 2011, pp. 43–47 (2011)
10. Development of Technology for Measuring Static Electricity Using Sound Waves, http://www.aist.go.jp/aist_e/latest_research/2012/20120210/2 0120210.html

Pillow Fight 2.0: A Creative Use of Technology for Physical Interaction

Anne Sofie Juul Sørensen

Art & Technology
Aalborg University
9000 Aalborg, Denmark
asjuuls@hotmail.com

Abstract. This paper describes Pillow Fight 2.0, a physical game made as a suggestion on how to use technology to encourage physical human to human interaction in entertainment.

Firstly the theoretical and social background and motivation for creating the game is introduced. Then follows a presentation of the implemented technological system and the final design. Hereafter comes an analysis of user behavior observed during the implementation of the game along with technological observations. Finally comes a brief description, evaluation and reflection upon the observed interaction and possible solutions and suggestions for the future development of the game are put presented.

Keywords: Interaction Design, First Hand and Second Hand Experiences, User Centered Design, Creative Use of Technology, Entertainment.

1   Introduction

Technology is an essential part of modern life and is enabling us to do things we did not think possible 50 years ago. It supports and facilitates our general everyday life and provides new, staggering possibilities wherever implemented. Both science, research, communication and digital experiences—just to mention a few—have in the recent decades breached new grounds due to technology. But at the moment, when using technology for communication and entertainment, users are being separated by the interface—in most cases a screen—which causes immediate emotional response, touch and intimacy to be left out. Pillow Fight 2.0 is a suggestion on how to use technology to give its users a First Hand Experience when using technology for entertainment and aims to keep the face to face social aspect present in the game. It is hoped that the project will inspire others to implement higher levels of physical interaction in games. Pillow Fight 2.0 is made as a Bachelor project in Art & Technology at Aalborg University, Denmark by Anne Sofie Juul Sørensen with supervision of Daniel Overholt and exhibited at PlayForm Mobile Exhibition in Denmark.

2   Theory

The terms *First-Hand* and *Second-Hand Experiences* are presented by Associate Professor of Psychology at Franklin and Marshall College, Edward S. Reed, who gives

A. Nijholt, T. Romão, and D. Reidsma (Eds.): ACE 2012, LNCS 7624, pp. 506–512, 2012.
© Springer-Verlag Berlin Heidelberg 2012

a constructive point of view in the discussion of the influence of technology in his book the Necessity of Experience. A primary experience is the ecological source from which the meaning of secondary experience derives from and is dependent on. [1] In general Reed encourages and requests a relation between the primary and secondary experiences where the balance is tilted towards the primary, which he exclaims "*has been disrupted and degraded by modern life*". (Reed, 1996, p. 2) Pillow Fight 2.0 aims to give its users a primary experience by using implemented technology to encourage people to play face to face.

3   Conceptual Design

The use of social networks and mobile phones is allowing us to decrease the necessity of our physical, and to some extent mental, presence in non-virtual life. But texting and chatting only serves as simulations and representations of life and leaves out immediate emotional response, touch and intimacy. As Marco Trevino, Interaction Designer at IDEO explains: "*while we are growing more comfortable with this latter way of communicating we are left with technology that creates a gab especially with the people we are closer to*". [2] His final project from Copenhagen Institute of Interaction Design, an application called "Feel Me", touches on the subject. The app aims to facilitate interaction by opening a real-time channel that allows two people to show each others presence while texting. [2]

Supporting the same viewpoints as Reed is Professor of the Social Studies of Science and Technology at MIT, Sherry Turkle. In her TED talk "Connected, but Alone?" she acknowledges the thrill that our experimenting and explorational life on the internet gave us back in 1996 but also states that today we are letting it take us places that we do not want to go. [3] She explains that technology is providing an environment where we are able to take control, by editing and deleting, and present ourselves as we want to be. [3] She points out that technology may work for telling your special someone that we are thinking about them or even that we love them but it can not replace—especially for children growing up—the experience and skills that you gain from interacting in *real* life. [3] As a social individual it is important to be able to know and understand the people and environment that surrounds you and therefore we must not let second hand experiences become the priority. [3] According to Turkle we are, unnecessarily, using technology to clean up our human relationships and by doing that we sacrifice conversation for mere connection. This is how digital technology is influencing our social life at the moment but it is still early days in the development and there is plenty of time for us to reconsider how we use it. [3] Therefore we as developers and creators have the responsibility to be critical about how we are letting technology influence social life, our relations and life in general and create and develop—not only with financial profit in mind—but also with the wellbeing of *real* experiences and the users of our designs.

4   The System

The game consists of six pillows equipped with resealable pockets made to fit a foam-padded Nintendo Wii Remote. It is programmed in Max/MSP [4] and uses the freeware "Darwiin Remote Extension" [5] and the Open Sound Control upsend/receive object in Max/MSP to get the data from the Wii Remotes. To connect the remotes to the receiver— a MacBook— the build-in Bluetooth function is used. See concept drawing below.

Darwiin Remote sends Open Sound Control data and by using the upsend/receive object the data can be received by Max/MSP. To establish connection between multiple remotes and the MacBook multiple copies of Darwiin Remote must be downloaded and opened one at a time. To distinguish one remote from the other a number from 0-5 is written both in the name of the copy of Darwiin Remote and directly on the remotes.

When connection is established the accelerometer inside the remote will send x, y and z coordinate data. This data is used to control the *hit count* and the *reset function* in Max/MSP. For the hit count the peaks in the accelerometer data are set to trigger the score on an external flatscreen/projector and increase the number by one digit. One hit gives one point. To reset the score simply throw the pillow into the air—the accelerometer detects free fall, triggers a "bang" in Max/MSP and resets the score. The photo below is taken during the test of the prototype.

5 Design Rationale

The game had to be self-explanatory and grasp a wide user group. Therefore Donald Norman's six design principles [6] played an important role in the concept development. In relation to Norman's principles *Visibility, Affordances* and *Mapping* using a well-known everyday object—a pillow—and adding a lucid name should help people associate the pillows with play. To let users know that their actions affect a technological environment they receive visual *Feedback* in the form of a drawn comic sound effect appearing on the flatscreen/projector when they hit something with the pillow. The image below shows the initial sketches.

In terms of *Constraints* and *Consistency* the game is designed button-free and wireless to make it more durable and easy to use. All the pillows have the same color and the same typography which helps keep the design simple and consistent. The name is inspired by software upgrades and refers to the original Pillow Fight now with a technological upgrade—therefore it is named 2.0.

6   Analysis

Ideally the game would be at a level of understanding where a wide group of users have a chance to participate regardless of their technological understanding. Most people understood how to use the game easily and nearly every age group was playing during the exhibition. Even very small children expressed that they would like to play as they reached out for the pillows. When a grownup handed them a pillow they instantly attempted to beat up a person familiar to them while squeaking of delight. To small children the implemented technology was insignificant but to children old enough to understand the system: *hit, get points, win* the technology became a factor of prestige—*the higher score the better!* To adolescents the technology provided the opportunity to set a goal—*let's play to 100!* which enabled them to define when a fight was over. People investigated the pillows by feeling them through and tried to figure out how they were able to detect the hits. Those who knew of accelerometers and understood the underlying technology called the use of the Wii Remote "fascinating", "creative", "fun" and "innovative", while people with extended technology knowledge showed a hint of disappointment. They explained that they had hoped that the tracking was done by new astounding technology or at least with the Microsoft Kinect Camera. To those who did not know of the underlying technology, or could not comprehend how it was used, it seemed like the pillows were magic. When explained about the implementation of the Wii Remote some even asked if it was illegal.

Some players found themselves out of breath after playing and laughing intensely for a couple of minutes. In general signs such as smiles, laughter and triumphant outbursts were observed amongst the users and it is therefore assumed that people were having fun. It was also clear that most people would only play against someone familiar. Some users suggested that the score could correspond to the power of the strike. However this feature is deliberately avoided as it would probably add aspects to the game—including severe pillow smacking—that neither the pillows nor the users would benefit from in the long run.

From time to time a pillow would not reset. The minor malfunction was mostly caused by throwing the pillow so that the accelerometer could not detect the free fall—for instance by spinning it. The malfunction could be fixed by re-throwing. However not knowing the conditions, that the program needs fulfilled, people would simply re-throw in the same manor until they by accident matched the conditions needed for a reset.

Every once in a while the remotes would be disconnected for no particular reason and difficulty in maintaining a stable connection would continue until the system had been rebooted. And even then a stable connection was not guaranteed. Five remotes seems to be the absolute maximum for a stable connection. The most rational explanation to the malfunction seems to be that the Bluetooth connection between the MacBook and the Wii remotes is interrupted by other devices that use Bluetooth.

7   Discussion and Reflection

To be able to use the game to its full extent a 3-step guide is printed on the backside of the pillows.

To encourage creativity no further rules or regulations are put down. The players therefore have freedom to create their own rules and frames for the game and play as they wish. This can however cause limitation and frustration in individuals who are seeking rules.

HOW TO PLAY:

Please Note: You Play at Your Own Risk

Reset Your Pillow
Throw it about one meter into the air and catch it. Your score is now reset and you are ready to play.

Hit Your Opponents With the Pillow
Every time you strike an opponent you receive one point.

View Your Score
Your score is displayed on the flatscreen TV located near the pillows and can be viewed at any time during your game.

You can play against as many as you please.

Most importantly:

HAVE FUN

512 A.S. Juul Sørensen

To be able to connect six or more Wii Remotes to the MacBook a more stable, lighter and smaller alternative to the remotes would be preferred. However using only four remotes might also solve the disconnection issue. If the Wii Remotes are to be used for a commercially available version a more solid alternative to the foam cores is to be preferred. At the moment wear and tear can over time expose the Wii Remote and cause a severe safety hazard.

People interacted with each other—Human to Human, in stead of Human to Computer—which was the aim of the project. However they did not interact with people they did not know in advance. This could be overcome by adding different colors to the pillows to create teams. If the players automatically join a team they might be encouraged to play against unknown opponents.

Using Donald Norman's design principles as a guide for the development helped create a concept that ties together user requirements, simple aesthetics, first hand experiences and Human to Human Interactivity.

8   Future Development

Students from Aarhus University have developed a piece of hardware/embedded software for physical interaction prototyping called DUL-radio [7]. It is wireless and communicates sensor data via FM-radio transmission but is not yet a commercially available product. To replace the Wii Remotes with DUL-radios would be a possible further development of the project.

Another possibility is to add Human Computer Interaction by allowing the users to preset a final score and add a preferred sound effects. This will add possibilities in terms of customizing the game.

Acknowledgments. A special thanks goes to my Bachelor Thesis Supervisor, Daniel Overholt, from AAU for skilled supervision throughout the project. Also thanks to those who have partaken in the realization of the project through feedback, discussions and tests.

References

1. Reed, E.S.: The Necessity of Experience. Yale University Press (1996)
2. Triverio, M.: Feel Me [video] Denmark: Copenhagen Institute of Interaction Design (2012), http://ciid.dk/2012/05/11/feel-me-by-marco-triverio/ (accessed: July 07, 2012)
3. Turkle, S.: Connected, but alone? [Video] TED - Ideas Worth Spreading (2012), http://www.ted.com/talks/lang/en/sherry_turkle_alone_together.html (accessed: July 07, 2012)
4. Max/MSP - Software for the Interactive Arts, http://cycling74.com/ (accessed: July 07, 2012)
5. Darwiin Remote with OSC Extension for OSX, http://code.google.com/p/darwiinosc/ (accessed: July 07, 2012)
6. Norman, D.A.: The Design of Everyday Things, second printing, 1st edn. The MIT Press, United States of America (1988)
7. DUL radio, Århus University, Denmark - Digital Urban Living, http://www.digitalurbanliving.dk/news/news/dul-radio.php(accessed: July 07, 2012)

Immobile Haptic Interface Using Tendon Electrical Stimulation

Hiroyuki Kajimoto

The University of Electro-Communications / Japan Science and Technology Agency
kajimoto@kaji-lab.jp

Abstract. For whole-body interaction for computer entertainment, I propose applying electrical stimulations to tendons to create an illusory motion of the limbs so that real motion becomes unnecessary. Strong vibrations to joints induce the well-known kinesthetic illusion, but electrically inducing this illusion has been rarely explored. An experiment is described showing that this illusion can be generated by electrical stimulation of the tendon, and suggesting a role of the Golgi tendon organ in the illusion.

Keywords: Golgi Tendon Organ, Haptic Display, Kinesthetic Illusion, Muscle Spindle, Tendon Electrical Stimulation, Virtual Reality.

1 Introduction

Whole-body interaction is an intuitive and promising form of computer interaction for entertainment and virtual reality systems. In particular, in the computer entertainment field, the recent successes of the Nintendo Wii and Microsoft Kinect impressed the importance of this form of interaction.

However, requiring input from movements of users is sometimes undesirable, because of limited workspace and physical capability or fatigue of the user. In such cases, the presentation of a kinesthetic sense without real motion is preferable (Fig. 1). Furthermore, the artificial generation of a kinesthetic sense might open the door to a new super-natural sensation, which should contribute to the field of computer entertainment.

Fig. 1. Immobile haptic interface by kinesthetic illusion

A. Nijholt, T. Romão, and D. Reidsma (Eds.): ACE 2012, LNCS 7624, pp. 513–516, 2012.

The kinesthetic illusion, a well-known phenomenon, which is created by vibratory stimulations to a tendon, and is thought to stimulate muscle spindles[1,2,3]. This phenomenon seems ideal for producing this illusory sense of motion. Roll et al. used numerous vibrators around the lower limb and induced 2D motion[4]. Collins et al. proposed combining the illusion with cutaneous sensations to enhance the illusion[5]. Yaguchi et al. proposed stimulating both ends of the muscle simultaneously so that the illusion is more distinct[6]. However, heavy actuators required to produce strong mechanical vibrations and the accompanying noise impede its practical use.

2   Tendon Electrical Stimulation

Here, I propose to use electrical stimulation to generate the illusion. If it is applicable, issues related to size and noise will be resolved. Furthermore, kinesthetic receptors could be selectively stimulated without generating unnecessary sensations.

However, electrical stimulation has rarely been used to induce the illusion, possibly because of the presumed underlying mechanism. The illusion was thought to be generated by the activity of the muscle spindles, which are indirectly stimulated by vibratory input to the tendon. If that were the case, electrical stimulation would seem difficult because it would inevitably stimulate muscle efferent nerves that cause motion. On the contrary, if the Golgi tendon organ, residing in the tendon, is at least partially responsible for the illusion, electrical stimulation of the organ without stimulating muscle becomes possible by placing electrodes on tendon. See Fig. 2 for a schematic drawing.

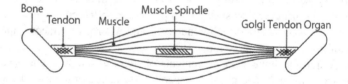

Fig. 2. Location of kinesthetic receptors

In support of this idea, literatures exist implying the possible involvement of the Golgi tendon organ in the illusion. Macefield et al. electrically stimulated single nerve fiber of the muscle spindle, joint receptor, Golgi tendon organ, and skin mechanoreceptor[7]. They found that single nerve activation of the muscle spindle did not elicit the illusion, whereas that of the joint receptor and Golgi tendon organ did (We must note that the sample number of nerves from the Golgi tendon organ was quite limited.). Furthermore, during the 1980s and 90s, many reports stated that the muscle spindle receptors have much lower threshold than other receptors[8], but recently Fallon et al. found that the threshold among receptors is actually not so significant[9].

Given the above implications, I assert the following two hypotheses:

- H1: The Golgi tendon organ plays a partial role in the kinesthetic illusion.
- H2: Given H1, the illusory motion is possible by tendon electrical stimulation.

3   Experiment

Transcutaneous electrical stimulation of Golgi tendon organ itself has already been done to investigate the Golgi tendon reflex[10, 11]. Experiments were conducted to establish H2.

Fig. 3 shows the setup for electrical stimulation of the arm tendon. Two electrodes (Nihon-Kohden Corp., F-150S) were attached 3 cm above the elbow joint over the bicep and tricep tendons of the right arm. The electrode size was 18 mm × 36 mm; the main axis of the electrodes was set at right angles to the arm.

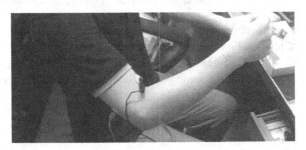

Fig. 3. Electrical stimulation to arm biceps and triceps tendons

The electrical stimulation was a current-controlled rectangular pulse with 200 μs pulse width, up to 20 mA pulse height, and 100 Hz pulse frequency. The voltage ranged from 0 to around 150 V, depending on conditions on the skin. With the left hand, participants themselves controlled the pulse height. The pulse was monophasic, meaning that one electrode functions as an anode and the other as a cathode.

The participants were four adults, including the author, aged 22–36 years. Participants were told that the experiment was about illusory motion. With closed eyes during electrical stimulation, each was asked to provide the directional sense of motion. For each participant, test was conducted twice with the polarity of the electrodes exchanged for the second test.

4   Results and Discussions

All participants reported that when the bicep electrode was the cathode, their arms moved outward. Conversely, when the tricep side electrode was the cathode, their arms moved inward. All participants were surprised upon opening their eyes to find that their arms had not actually moved.

It is well-known that in ordinary electrical stimulations, the cathode functions as a stimulating electrode. Therefore, the results clearly showed that the illusory motion was contrary to the stimulation side. This direction agrees with the kinesthetic illusion induced by mechanical vibration of the tendon, suggesting that both are basically one and the same phenomenon.

As the electrode positions were close to the elbow joint, stimulation of the muscle spindles, as well as muscle efferent nerves, is not possible.

In summary, the experimental results established that the illusory motion by electrical stimulation of the tendon is possible (H2), and the Golgi tendon organ does play a role in kinesthetic illusion (H1).

5   Conclusion

To achieve whole-body interaction without motion, this paper proposed using electrical stimulation to tendons to generate illusory sense of motion. This kinesthetic illusion, a well-known phenomenon, is commonly created by vibratory, rather than electrical stimulation.

The experimental result showed that this illusion can be generated by electrical stimulation of the tendon. Furthermore, the direction of illusory motion is the same as for the kinesthetic illusion, suggesting that our illusion caused by electrical stimulation of the tendon is one and the same phenomenon. The possible contribution of the Golgi tendon organ to the illusion is also suggested.

References

1. Goodwin, G.M., McCloskey, D.I., Matthews, P.B.C.: The contribution of muscle afferents to kinesthesia shown by vibration induced illusions of movement and by the effects of paralyzing joint afferents. Brain 95(4), 705–748 (1972)
2. Jones, L.A.: Motor illusions: What do they reveal about proprioception? Psychological Bulletin 103(1), 72–86 (1988)
3. Naito, E.: Sensing Limb Movements in the Motor Cortex: How Humans Sense Limb Movement. The Neuroscientist 10, 73–82 (2004)
4. Roll, J.P., Albert, F., Thyrion, C., Ribot-Ciscar, E., Bergenheim, M., Mattei, B.: Inducing Any Virtual Two-Dimensional Movement in Humans by Applying Muscle Tendon Vibration. J. Neurophysiol. 101, 816–823 (2009)
5. Collins, D.F., Refshauge, K.M., Todd, G., Gandevia, S.C.: Cutaneous Receptors Contribute to Kinesthesia at the Index Finger, Elbow, and Knee. J. Neurophysiol. 94, 1699–1706 (2005)
6. Yaguchi, H., Fukayama, O., Suzuki, T., Mabuchi, K.: Effect of simultaneous vibrations to two tendons on velocity of the induced illusory movement. In: Proceedings of IEEE International Conference of Engineering in Medicine and Biology Society (EMBC), pp. 5851–5853 (2010)
7. Macefield, G., Gandevia, S.C., Burke, D.: Perceptual responses to microstimulation of single afferents innervating joints, muscles and skin of the human hand. J. Physiol. 429, 113–129 (1990)
8. Roll, J.P., Vedel, J.P., Ribot, E.: Alteration of proprioceptive messages induced by tendon vibration in man: a microneurographic study. Exp. Brain Res. 76, 213–222 (1989)
9. Fallon, J.B., Macefield, V.G.: Vibration sensitivity of human muscle spindles and Golgi tendon organs. Muscle & Nerve 36, 21–29 (2007)
10. Burne, J.A., Lippold, O.C.J.: Reflex inhibition following electrical stimulation over muscle tendons in man. Brain 119, 1107–1114 (1996)
11. Khan, S.I., Burne, J.A.: Inhibitory mechanisms following electrical stimulation of tendon and cutaneous afferents in the lower limb. Brain Research 1308, 47–57 (2010)

STRAVIGATION: A Vibrotactile Mobile Navigation for Exploration-Like Sightseeing

Hiroki Kawaguchi and Takuya Nojima

Graduate School of Information Systems, University of Electro-Communications, Japan
kawaguchi@vogue.is.uec.ac.jp, tnojima@computer.org

Abstract. Exploration-like sightseeing is wandering around an unfamiliar place, and is a way of seeing sights and enjoying novel experiences that are not mentioned in guidebooks. However, the fear of getting lost prevents tourists from engaging in exploration-like sightseeing. Current navigation devices are capable of providing effective routes to specific places, which is not compatible for this mode of sightseeing. This is because tourists tend to focus on the recommended route displayed on the device and follow it faithfully. This prevents tourists from seeing surrounding sights. Here, we propose a new navigation method called stravigation. Stravigation is a vibrotactile mobile navigation for the tourist to be able to enjoy exploration-like sightseeing. We describe its basic concept and the results of evaluation experiments. These results show that stravigation is capable of guiding tourists to specific places correctly without the need to watch navigation devices. Furthermore, the results also show that stravigation enhances the sense of delight while wandering.

Keywords: Navigation, Exploration, Vibrotactile, Mobile Device, Sightseeing.

1 Introduction

Wandering about an unfamiliar place, which is similar to exploration, is one of the ways to enjoy sightseeing. For instance, Venice is famous for its complex network of alleyways and many bridges across canals. Many tourists have found themselves lost while walking its islands, and have become irritated when unable to reach their destination easily. However, while wandering around the city, tourists often discover something new. Wandering and exploring unknown places often lead tourists to novel experiences that are not mentioned in guidebooks. Such unique experiences underscore the enjoyment in sightseeing. In this research, we call this mode of sightseeing "exploration-like sightseeing". Although wandering itself is sometimes enjoyable for tourists, they do not want to find themselves in situations where they are unable to return, for example, to their hotel. Current navigation devices are able to display appropriate and precise route information to guide tourists to their destination; these devices comfort the mind and enable the tourist to freely enjoy the walk. However, such devices are incompatible with exploration-like sightseeing. Displaying a precise route implicitly forces tourists to stay on a specific track, requiring that they maintain their focus on the displayed route. The enjoyment of sightseeing therefore diminishes.

A. Nijholt, T. Romão, and D. Reidsma (Eds.): ACE 2012, LNCS 7624, pp. 517–520, 2012.

Using visual displays to provide navigation-related information interrupts the enjoyment of wandering because it would still require the user to watch the display. To solve the problem, we propose a new vibrotactile mobile navigation called "stravigation". The basic concept of stravigation has two components. The first is reducing the amount of information. Too much information can annoy tourists and impede seeing the surrounding sights. Thus, only distance and direction to a specific place are provided by stravigation. This represents the minimum amount of information needed to prevent tourists from getting lost. The second is making use of vibrotactile sensation. Stravigation provides distance and direction by using vibrotactile signals enabling tourists to free their attention from their navigation devices.

2   Related Works

Much research related to vibrotactile navigation has been done. That research can be grouped into two methods: turn-by-turn or relative position-based. The turn-by-turn method indicates the correct direction every time the user reaches a specific waypoint or an intersection [1,2]. These systems are able to provide precise route information. However, vibrotactile signals at every intersection could annoy tourists. The relative position-based method only indicates spatial relationships, such as direction and distance, between current location and destination [3-5]. This method does not provide precise route information. However, users are able to understand these spatial relationships, enabling them to choose between routes to a destination freely, engaging in what we term exploration-like sightseeing. Most systems based on this method are able to provide direction to the destination by having the user scan the surroundings with the device. A vibrotactile signal is generated only when the device points towards the destination. Stravigation is based on the same concept as this relative position-based method. However, previous systems do not have sufficient capability for navigation, and some are unable to provide distance information. This is not only essential for estimating time of arrival, but also directly affects reliability of such systems. The transition of such information, based on the tourist's walking, is the basis for them knowing whether the system is working. In addition, the accuracy of directional information of these previous systems is almost ±30 [deg], which is far from being satisfactory. Stravigation is capable of providing distance information as well as providing directional information with an accuracy of ±5 [deg].

3   System Summary

When providing directional information, stravigation indicates the angular deviation between the device's axial direction and the direction to the destination. This means that specific vibration occurs according to the angular deviation (Figure 1 Left). If the angular deviation is greater than ±30[deg] [6], the device does not provide any vibrational feedback. If the angular deviation is between ±15[deg] and ±30[deg], the device vibrates with a low frequency; an intermediate frequency is generated when the

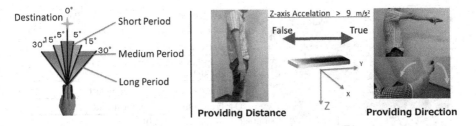

Fig. 1. Left: The angular deviation and vibration period, Right: Switching information by using device orientation

angular deviation angle is between ±5[deg] and ±15[deg]. If the angular deviation is less than ±5[deg], a rapid frequency vibration is generated. The same principle provides the distance information; specific vibrations are generated according to distance.

Distance and directional information is provided through the same vibrotactile signal. Some sort of practical means is required for users to identify easily which information is provided. To solve this problem, we make use of the orientation of the device. By using a 3-dimensional accelerometer, we can determine whether the surface of the device is parallel to the ground (Figure 1 Right). The users are able to switch information modes by gesturing. If its surface is parallel to the ground, the device switches to the direction-providing mode in which the user swings the device left and right to find the direction; otherwise the device switches to the distance-providing mode.

4   Evaluation Experiments

4.1   Navigation Capability

We performed an experiment to confirm the practicality of stravigation. Subjects were asked to walk towards a specific place, which was 400 [m] away from their starting position, using stravigation. They were not informed where the place was. The tracked routes and times taken are shown in Figure 2 Left. The result shows that stravigation has sufficient capability to guide users to a specific place.

4.2   User Test

User tests were performed to confirm that stravigation is able to put users in an exploratory-like mood while walking. We compared stravigation with a conventional map-based visual navigation system (Google Maps). The participants were asked to answer a questionnaire after using these two navigation methods. The number of participants was 4. All participants use both stravigation and Google Maps two times each. The results are shown in Figure 2 Right. The result for Q2 indicates that our system received better scores than navigation using maps. This means that stravigation does not

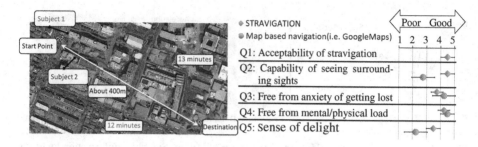

Fig. 2. Left: Time taken and tracked route walked by subjects, Right:Questionnaire responses

hinder tourists from seeing the surrounding sights. At the same time, the result for Q5 indicates that using stravigation is more exciting than using conventional systems. As a result, tourists should be able to enjoy wandering without losing their way.

5   Conclusion

In this research, we propose a new navigation method, stravigation, for tourists to enjoy exploration-like sightseeing. The experimental results show that stravigation has higher accuracy in providing directional information. Also, stravigation had suffi-cient capability as a navigation aid and reliability to enable tourists to enjoy explora-tion-like sightseeing. In the future, we will deliver stravigation via the web to conduct larger-scale user tests.

References

1. Pielot, M., Poppinga, B., Boll, S.: PocketNavigator: vibro-tactile waypoint navigation for everyday mobile devices. In: 12th International Conference on Human-Computer Interac-tion with Mobile Devices and Services, pp. 423–426. ACM Press, New York (2010)
2. Rümelin, S., Rukzio, E., Hardy, R.: NaviRadar: a novel tactile information display for pedestrian navigation. In: 24th Symposium on User Interface Software and Technology, pp. 293–302. ACM Press, New York (2011)
3. Williamson, J., Robinson, S., Stewart, C., Murray-Smith, R., Jones, M., Brewster, S.: Social gravity: a virtual elastic tether for casual, privacy-preserving pedestrian rendezvous. In: 28th International Conference on Human Factors in Computing Systems, pp. 1485–1494. ACM Press, New York (2010)
4. Robinson, S., Jones, M., Eslambolchilar, P., Murray-Smith, R., Lindborg, M.: "I did it my way": moving away from the tyranny of turn-by-turn pedestrian navigation. In: 12th Inter-national Conference on Human-Computer Interaction with Mobile Devices and Services, pp. 341–344. ACM Press, New York (2010)
5. Szymczak, D., Magnusson, C., Rassmus-Gröhn, K.: Guiding Tourists through Haptic Inte-raction: Vibration Feedback in the Lund Time Machine. In: Eurohaptics Part II, Tampere, Finland, pp. 157–162 (2012)
6. Strachan, S., Murray-Smith, R.: Bearing-based selection in mobile spatial interaction. Jour-nal of Personal and Ubiquitous Computing 13(4), 265–280 (2009)

Earth Girl: A Multi-cultural Game about Natural Disaster Prevention and Resilience

Isaac Kerlow, Muhammad Khadafi, Harry Zhuang, Henry Zhuang,
Aida Azlin, and Aisyah Suhaimi

Earth Observatory of Singapore, Nanyang Technological University, Singapore
{isaac,mkhadafi,hwfzhuang,hwgzhuang,aidaazlin}@ntu.edu.sg,
aissumi@gmail.com

Abstract. *Earth Girl: The Natural Disaster Fighter* is an edutainment digital game featuring a girl who can save her family and friends from natural hazards. The scenario and game play are inspired by the challenges faced by communities living in the Asian regions prone to earthquakes, tsunamis, flooding and volcano hazards. The Earth Girl game is meant to help players to gain a better understanding of natural hazards through imaginative and fun game play. The game was developed in English and translated to Indonesian, Japanese and Chinese. It runs on any Flash-enabled browser and was user-tested in Southeast Asia with positive results and feedback.

Keywords: Earth Girl, natural hazards, disaster prevention, computer game, edutainment, serious games, casual games, game play, non-traditional education, game prototype, character design, character animation, emotional connection, pre-teens, Asia, cultural traditions, community, sustainability, resilience.

1 Introduction

The Earth Girl digital game was developed for a mainstream non-scientist audience of all ages and particularly for children between the ages of 7-12. The game seeks to increase the regional awareness of natural hazards while providing simple but engaging game play that is as culturally sensitive as it is fun. (Fig. 1). The project was inspired and informed by our 2009-2012 trips to resilient communities in The Philippines, Indonesia, Thailand and China. The main goal of *Earth Girl: The Natural Disaster Fighter* is to provide players of any culture with a better understanding of natural hazards through simple but engaging and fun game play. The game is coded in Flash and can be played on a Flash-enabled browser. Earth Girl is a village girl who can save her family and friends from natural disasters. This fictional character is inspired by people who live in hazardous areas throughout Asia yet manage to find a way to survive by being in tune with Nature.

The Earth Girl game is not a traditional science game but it is inspired by science. It is an initiative of the Artist-in-Residence group at the Earth Observatory of Singapore (EOS), a Research Center of Excellence located on the campus of the

A. Nijholt, T. Romão, and D. Reidsma (Eds.): ACE 2012, LNCS 7624, pp. 521–524, 2012.

Nanyang Technological University. The mission of EOS is "to conduct fundamental research on earthquakes, volcanic eruptions, tsunami and climate change in and around the region, toward safer and more sustainable societies" [1]. Interdisciplinary collaboration is at the core of this mission, and creating a game for children is a step in that direction. For project updates visit www.earthgirlgame.com.

Fig. 1. (Left) Main menu where players can choose a disaster. (Right) School girls in Banda Aceh, Indonesia, discussing the best strategy for rescuing a villager floating in the flood.

2   The Game Paradigm

The game paradigm of Earth Girl combines skill and knowledge. *Earth Girl: The Natural Disaster Fighter* is a game of awareness, preparedness and survival. It offers three levels of side-scrolling action, plus factual information delivered in the form of quizzes. Each one of the three levels presents a different hazard scenario (tsunami, flooding and volcano) and starts with a cinematic animated introduction that helps to contextualize the action.

Players move forward through the first part of each level by rescuing villagers. This is followed by a quiz that presents multiple-choice questions relevant to the hazard being played. Correct answers enhance the players' scientific knowledge and also provide Earth Girl with additional health to save villagers more effectively and/or special skills or super-powers to combat the hazard. Multiple explorations were required during the development process before a suitable game play paradigm was found, one that splits each game level into three parts. The first and last parts are action oriented, and the middle one consists of a quiz that provides objective information about the hazard at hand.

One of the biggest challenges of this project was finding the right tone to tell a story that can range from success to disaster. Players of the game, through Earth Girl, are able to save the villagers from death, or lose them all to a natural disaster. We stayed away from overly didactic or technical scenarios and naturally gravitated towards action-based dramatization. We were sensitive to depictions of death, touch on issues of preparedness and awareness, and occasionally infuse some dramatic situations with bits of humor when appropriate.

Another early challenge was finding the best way to present scientific facts about natural hazards to a mainstream audience in the context of fun and simple game play.

We were interested in the tradition of edutainment and not in the traditional lecture/lab scientific game. We believe that the game provides engaging entertainment and it also fulfills an educational mission by reminding players the important role that awareness and preparedness play in surviving natural hazards.

Unlike the traditional educational formats of geography or science lectures this game focuses on the emotional experience of the player, an approach discussed in [2, 3]. The Earth Girl game uses emotional impact as a teaching tool instead of relying on a purely rational understanding of the issues. Placing emotion above knowledge might seem like an unorthodox design approach for a serious game. But we found it to be an effective approach since the essence of the game is about saving people. Emotion and instinct are oftentimes as powerful as rational intellect when it comes to pulling people out of harm's way. Adrenaline provides an immediacy that technical explanations cannot.

3   User Testing and Feedback

We conducted three stages of user testing and feedback, and throughout it we learned many valuable lessons. During the first stage of testing we watched children and adults play the game. This stage of testing took place in Singapore where children and pre-teens are used to interacting with hand-held devices, particularly Apple iPhones, and tablets. This early stage of testing helped us to fine-tune the level of difficulty regarding speed and intensity of challenges, and the number of keys required to play the game.

The second stage of testing was mostly about gathering feedback from the science experts at EOS. For these feedback sessions we used the early prototype of the tsunami level and in-progress versions of the flooding and volcano levels. We had talked to scientists informally earlier in the development process but this stage represented a more formal setting for exchanging opinions and points of view about our specific implementations of the original idea. These feedback sessions proved to be a good and fruitful exercise in interdisciplinary collaboration between sometimes clashing cultures. The majority of the feedback focused on scientific issues as the scientists' first-hand experience and understanding of games was limited. One of the scientists' main concerns was the issue of providing flawed information in the game that could lead players to making wrong assumptions about earth hazards. We made two significant changes to the original idea.

The first change was a compromise. We split each level in two halves, and we allowed some super-powers in the second half but not in the first half. This way we could offer a feature that is standard in most action games but we would tie it to the reality of survival. We made the amount of super-powers conditional on the percentage of villagers saved in the first half of a level. We also minimized the force of the super-powers so that in the volcano level for example players cannot defeat the hazard with super-powers alone, they must also directly save villagers. Fine-tuning the right amount of fantasy and reality eventually helped to make the Earth Girl game engaging to play. The second change was an improvement. We enhanced the game cinematics in order to provide contextual information about the hazard.

The third stage of user testing and feedback took place when most of the functionality in the three levels was completed. This testing focused on playability, language and conceptual comprehension and it took place with school children in Singapore, Banda Aceh in Indonesia and rural Yunnan in China. Testing the game in Banda Aceh was an unforgettable experience as we knew that many of the kids in the classrooms were likely to have lost relatives in the 2004 Indian Ocean tsunami. We observed that children liked the flooding level because it provides for extended game play and it requires some strategizing in addition to action skills. The majority of the advanced players seem to enjoy the volcano level (Fig. 2). We translated the original game from English to Indonesian, Japanese and Chinese, and we had to work through a few language comprehension issues. This localization effort was significant and important to the overall strategy of reaching the widest possible audience.

Fig. 2. (Left) In the volcano level cinematic Earth Girl sounds the alarm for the villagers to evacuate. (Right) The stylized representation of the flaming lava is not scientifically accurate but it helps to dramatize a volcano eruption in the context of a casual action game.

References

1. Retrieved on July 2012 from the Earth Observatory of Singapore's website at http://www.earthobservatory.sg/about-us/mission.html
2. Schell, J.: The Art of Game Design: A Book of Lenses. Morgan Kauffman, Burlington (2008)
3. Dillon, R.: On the Way to Fun: An Emotion-Based Approach to Successful Game Design. A. K. Peters, Natick (2010)
4. Crawford, C.: The Art of Computer Game Design: Reflections of a Master Game Designer. Osborne/McGraw-Hill, New York (1984)
5. Fullerton, T.: Game Design Workshop, 2nd edn. Morgan Kaufmann, Boston (2008)
6. Kerlow, I.: Earth Girl Saves the Day: A Computer Game Prototype about Earth Hazards. In: Proceedings 2nd Conference on Culture and Computing, Kyoto, Japan, October 20-22 (2011)

PowerFood: Turns Fruit Eating into Fun and Makes Snacks Not Done

Lies Kroes[1] and Suleman Shahid[2]

[1] Department of Communication and Information Sciences, Tilburg University,
5037 AB, Tilburg, The Netherlands
lieskroes@hotmail.com
[2] Tilburg center for Cognition and Communication, Tilburg University,
5037 AB, Tilburg, The Netherlands
s.shahid@uvt.nl

Abstract. This paper provides an outline of the persuasive mobile application 'Krachtvoer' (In English: PowerFood) that encourages adolescents with moderate overweight to eat more fruit and fewer snacks. The key features of this solution are dynamic goal setting, personal reminders, progress monitoring, social interaction and competition with friends. Results of the evaluation indicate that the app enhances the user's attitude and self-efficacy towards eating fruit and healthy food. In addition, social influences encourage users to eat more fruit and less unhealthy snacks.

Keywords: Persuasive technology, overweight, adolescents, behavior change.

1   Introduction

According to the National Institute for Public Health and the Environment, 40 to 50% of the Dutch population is overweight, and approximately 10% is obese [1]. One of the major problems contributing to overweight in the Netherlands is the unhealthy food consumption of adolescents, which mainly regards low fruit consumption, skipping breakfast and consuming many high-fat snacks. Especially adolescents between the age of 12 and 15 with a lower socio-economic position are vulnerable for overweight [2].

A substantial amount of research has already been conducted on the improvement of nutritional habits using mobile technology [3, 4], although not focusing on this specific target group. Adolescents who are just above their healthy weight (i.e. moderate overweight) are most relevant in this regard, as they have problems with their health but excessive overweight and clinical intervention can still be prevented. The goal of this study is to create a persuasive intervention that assists young adolescents in healthier food choices in fun manner. In particular mobile applications have great potential to influence adolescents at the appropriate moment. The hereby presented persuasive intervention focuses on causing an increase in fruit consumption and a decrease in snack consumption.

A. Nijholt, T. Romão, and D. Reidsma (Eds.): ACE 2012, LNCS 7624, pp. 525–528, 2012.
© Springer-Verlag Berlin Heidelberg 2012

The conceptual framework of the study is primarily based on three theories. The ASE model states that an individual's attitude, social influence and perceived efficacy influence the intention to perform a given behavior, which in turn determines the actual behavior [5]. Fogg's behavior model further states that motivation, ability and triggers must all be present at the same time for behavior to occur [6]. Finally, the theory of change implies that people undergo several stages while changing addictive behavior, which are pre-contemplation, contemplation, preparation, action and maintenance [7]. Adolescents with moderate overweight are generally in the stage of contemplation, and this study aims to assist them up until the action stage.

2   User Research

A combination of interviews and longitudinal food records in the form of personal diaries, has been used for user research. A semi-structured interview was used to assess the determinants for fruit and snack consumption of the ASE model (i.e. attitude, social influence and efficacy). After participants had been interviewed, they were asked to record their fruit and snack consumption for seven consecutive days. After this longitudinal diet record, they were contacted for a second interview in which their awareness of the behavior and need for triggers, ability and motivation were assessed. Results show that participants are often tempted to eat snacks and they do not achieve the Dutch recommendations of two pieces of fruit per day.

Findings of the interviews indicate that participants have a positive attitude towards fruit. However, adolescents often forget to eat fruit and prefer the taste of snacks. In addition, snacks are easier available compared to fruit, which especially applies to school situations. The positive attitude towards the ease and availability of snacks should make place for reminders to eat fruit. The motivation of participants is greatly determined by the availability and social influences of eating fruit and snacks.

In general, fruit is not triggered at all, while there are too many triggers for snacks. Furthermore, participants are restrained in their ability to eat fruit because it is often not available at school and they forget to bring it with them. Participants generally find themselves between the stage of pre-contemplation and contemplation. They know why it is important to eat healthy but most of them do not have sufficient knowledge of the Dutch recommendations regarding fruit and snacks. Participants are generally aware of their own consumption, although many of their expectations differed from the outcome of their diaries. Keeping track of their habits helped them to create this awareness.

3   Design

Based on user research and literature, design requirements were derived and design alternatives were developed. Subsequently, a paper prototype test was performed. Based on the results of this test, a final functional design for an iPhone (extendable to iPad) was developed which was a combination of multiple concepts. The final design consists of a real life kitchen with multiple items that users can click on. Based on user research, these buttons contain several triggers to encourage healthy behavior.

These triggers include 1) an alarm as reminder, 2) a planner that includes adaptive goal setting and an agenda, 3) a fruit bowl and candy jar to enter snacks and fruit, 4) consequences of good/bad eating behavior in a mirror, 5) feedback through messages from friends and the system, 6) tips to improve behavior and 7) game-like interface for competition with friends. The app includes a game-like point system, which means that users earn points according to their snack and fruit behavior.

Different functionalities of the app, such as the appearance of users and their ranking compared to friends, interact with this point system. The app is called the Krachtvoer app as it connects to an offline school program called *Krachtvoer*, which focuses on a similar target group and problem. This connection is unique as it is ensures support of an existing well-established program and creates behavior change both online and offline. The home screen and one of the sub screens of the Krachtvoer app is presented in Figure 1.

Fig. 1. Home screen (left – colour icons are clickable) and screen to enter snacks

4   Evaluation

The final evaluation consisted of a usability test, usage diary, a post-interview and an online questionnaire with seven participants. Measurements were obtained regarding the attractiveness of the design, information quality, the ASE model, openness to influence, perceived ease of use and perceived usefulness. Results of the evaluation show that participants perceive the app as easy to use and useful. They are positive about the design and find information relevant and reliable. Some alterations need to be made in the next version, which are primarily regarding the much richer integration of social media platforms with the app. After a short-term use, participants expect that in long term they will have a more positive attitude towards eating fruit and a more negative attitude towards snacks as they can already see a positive change in their behavior.

Confrontation with negative consequences and positive social influence especially contribute to this predicted shift in attitude. Furthermore, participants feel that the app makes the behavior easier to perform because of subtle and fun reminders available in the app. Hence, all constructs of the ASE model have been either partially or fully supported by the evaluation. The point system also contributes on this part, as it serves as a point of reference and as a challenge for users. Finally, participants indicated it would be beneficial for credibility and brand awareness if school, which indicates the value of the connection to Krachtvoer, promoted the app.

5   Discussion

Findings from this study support the fact that the Krachtvoer app is able to change the attitude and behavior of young adolescents. The design of this app results from long-term interaction with the target group, whose input was essential. Existing applications focus on different target groups, media or problems and often focus on slimming, emphasizing the negative side of reducing overweight. The Krachtvoer app engages adolescents in a playful manner and assists them in choosing the healthy alternative. In the first development round, only the major concept of the application was developed and short-term evaluation was performed. In future, we would like to perform a longitudinal evaluation of one month, measuring actual behavior change. What the Krachtvoer app will eventually bring about for young adolescents in real life remains to be proven, but the hereby presented design and analysis create a strong foundation for the further development and evaluation of the Krachtvoer app.

References

1. Van der Lucht, F., Polder, J.J.: The Dutch 2010, Public Health Status and Forecasts Report. The National Institute for Public Health and Environment. Bilthoven, The Netherlands, 1–94 (2010)
2. Martens, M.K., Assema, P.V., Brug, J.: Why do adolescents eat what they eat? Personal and social environmental predictors of fruit, snack and breakfast consumption among 12 - 14-year-old Dutch students. Public Health Nutrition 8(8), 1258–1265 (2005)
3. Anderson, I., Maitland, J., Sherwood, S., Barkhuus, L., Chalmers, M., Hall, M., Brown, B., Muller, H.: Shakra: tracking and sharing daily activity levels with unaugmented mobile phones. Mob. Netw. Appl. 12, 185–199 (2007)
4. Arteaga, S., Kudeki, M., Woodworth, A., Kurniawan, S.: Mobile system to motivate teenagers' physical activity. In: Proceedings of the 9th International Conference on Interaction Design and Children, pp. 1–10 (2010)
5. De Vries, H., Dijkstra, M., Kuhlman, P.: Self-efficacy: the third factor besides attitude and subjective norm as a predictor of behavioural intentions. Health Education Research 3, 273–282 (1998)
6. Fogg, B.J.: A behavior model for persuasive design. In: The Proceedings of the Persuasive Technology (2009)
7. Prochaska, J.O., DiClemente, C.C., Norcross, J.C.: In search of how people change. Applications to addictive behaviors. The American Psychologist 47(9), 1102–1114 (1992)

City Pulse: Supporting Going-Out Activities with a Context-Aware Urban Display

Mohammad Obaid[1,2], Ekaterina Kurdyukova[2], and Elisabeth Andre[2]

[1] HITLab New Zealand, University of Canterbury, Christchurch 8140, New Zealand
[2] University of Augsburg, Universitätsstr. 6a, 86159 Augsburg, Germany
mohammad.obaid@hitlabnz.org,
{katja.kurdyukova,andre}@informatik.uni-augsburg.de

Abstract. In this paper, we describe a concept of City Pulse, an urban public display that helps people find going-out locations of their taste. Relying on mobile context collected by going-out citizens, the display visualizes the immediate situation in city locations. The sensors integrated into the citizens' mobile phones gather data on people's motion, pulse, and sound around. Based on this data, City Pulse display shows, for instance, how crowded and how loud the locations are, which music is playing, whether people dance or drink. In addition, users can request the display to highlight the places matching their preferences, such as specific cuisine or music style. It also allows finding locations where the user's friends are currently going out. We present design and of City Pulse display, motivating the concept by the user study conducted with 20 international participants.

Keywords: Public displays, context awareness, mobile context.

1 Motivation

The advent of Web 2.0 [1] has significantly improved the way people plan their leisure time activities. Relying on the user-generated content, such as online forums, eased and diversified the way we choose the locations for travelling, sightseeing or going out. In this work we focus on going-out activities in public locations, such as bars, cafés, restaurants, clubs, or discos. A public display reflecting the current situation in city locations can solve the problem. In this work we present City Pulse, an urban public display that visualizes the immediate situation in city locations. The display relies on real-time context data provided by the visitors of city locations. The context data is implicitly collected from sensors integrated into mobile phones of visitors. The data collected from numerous visitors going out in the city, is reflected by the display content.

Considering people as ubiquitous sensors, "People are eight billion sensors" [2], enable modern technology to collect and generate large amounts of urban data. Such user-generated data can be used to understand and improve the situation in the cities.

Most work doesn't rely on real-time information but rather on the analysis of *previously collected* data, e.g. [3]. Often there is a necessity to have an urban picture based on *real-time* information.

A. Nijholt, T. Romão, and D. Reidsma (Eds.): ACE 2012, LNCS 7624, pp. 529–532, 2012.
© Springer-Verlag Berlin Heidelberg 2012

City Pulse display, presented in this paper, utilizes various mobile sensors to collect the data on immediate situation in the city. Collecting the data on people's motion, pulse, location, and loudness, it visualizes the current situation in going-out locations.

2   City Pulse Design

City Pulse is designed based on the insights gained from interviewing 20 participants, where the aim was to capture criteria to decide on the going-out location, difficulties people have when looking for a location, and their vision of the City Pulse display. The semi-structured interviews were conducted individually, in a form of a moderated discussion.

We designed the visualization of City Pulse display to provide two views: standard and personalized view. The standard view presents the data critical for the majority of people (based on interviews). The opened locations are overlaid over the city map covering the neighborhood areas. For each location the display shows the density of people, loudness, people motion (dancing, standing or sitting), and alcohol consumption. The design is illustrated with the example, Figure 1, of downtown Munich, Germany.

Fig. 1. City Pulse display: downtown Munich

The personalized view is shown when users interact with City Pulse display. The users can make a request according to their preferences, for example, highlight all Japanese restaurants, or request to highlight the locations of their friends. The requests can be done by means of a mobile client. The requests can include price category, music style, non-smoking places, etc. Since such preference-based highlights are relevant only for the current requesting spectators, they appear only by demand, on the personalized view. Below we describe the solution we chose for the visualization of City Pulse display.

The standard view of City Pulse shows the downtown map in black and white. The location of the user (and the display) is marked with a contrast magenta icon. Colored spots, overlaid on the map, depict the context data obtained from the citizens.

Density of people inside the location is mapped to the size of the colored spot: the smaller the spot, the less density inside. If the spot goes out of the building silhouette, the place is overcrowded.

Loudness is mapped to the opacity of the spot. The opacity of 100% corresponds to a very loud place, while 0% makes the spot almost invisible. Indeed, if the loudness is registered as zero, the place is absolutely empty and is probably closed. Thus, there is no need to display it on the map (Figure. 2 (left)).

Motion of people is presented by animation. Their activity reflects on the corresponding spot, i.e. if people are active (dancing), the spot pulsates with high frequency, on the contradictory, if they are standing the spot pulsates slowly.

The consumption of alcohol is encoded in color. A place with low alcohol consumption is depicted with a yellow spot. The redder the spot, the higher alcohol consumption (Figure. 2 (right)).

Fig. 2. Loudness is depicted by opacity of the spot (left), Alcohol consumption is encoded in color (right)

The personalized requests are shown with contrast magenta highlights. For instance, Figure 3 illustrates the request of Bavarian breweries in the downtown Munich. Such highlights provide a quick overview of the necessary places. A request to highlight the locations of friends yields the display of colored dot. Each dot stands for one friend, hiding however any information on the friend's personality as illustrated in Figure 3.

3   Conclusion and Future Work

We presented the concept and design of City Pulse display, an urban public display which supports people in their going-out activities. The design of City Pulse was guided by the user study conducted as interviews with 20 international participants. The interviews inspired the design solution of City Pulse. We described the visualization design of the system.

Fig. 3. Example of locations that match a personalized request and friends' locations

Future directions are put towards conducting a user evaluation of the presented concept to validate its use in public. In addition, we plan to integrate a recommender system that may initiatively propose locations based on the user's previous going-out history, the preferences of the user, and/or the preferences of their friends. The recommender system can also consider the environmental context, such as the weather, events in the city and daytime. Thus, in a cold winter day the display would rather propose cozy cafés, and in a hot summer evening – an opened terrace or a beer garden. Finally, the recommender system may take into account the emotional and social context. For example, it would propose a loud social place with many friends inside, when the user is sad and alone; or a romantic place when the user is happy, accompanied by their partner.

References

1. O'Reilly, T.: What is Web 2.0? Design Patterns and Business Models for the Next Generation of Software (2005), http://www.oreillynet.com/pub/a/oreilly/tim/news/2005/09/30/what-is-web-20.html
2. Goodchild, M.F.: Citizens as voluntary Sensors: Spatial Data Infrastructure in the World of Web 2.0. International Journal of Spatial Data Infrastructures Research 2, 24–32 (2007)
3. Ratti, C., Pulselli, R.M., Williams, S., Frenchman, D.: Mobile Landscapes: Using Location Data from Cell Phones for Urban Analysis. Environment and Planning B 33(5), 727–748 (2006)

Physiological Signals Based Fatigue Prediction Model for Motion Sensing Games

Ziyu Lu, Ling Chen, Changjun Fan, and Gencai Chen

College of Computer Science, Zhejiang University, China
lvziyu@yahoo.cn, {lingchen,chengc}@cs.zju.edu.cn,
daringpig@zju.edu.cn,

Abstract. We present a fatigue prediction model for motion sensing games, dependent on the change of physiological signals including blood volume pulse, skin conductance, respiration, skin temperature and electromyography (EMG). After extracting a range of features followed by using sequential floating forward selection (SFFS) to select features, support vector regression (SVR) was used to construct our prediction model that can predict how long participants enter fatigue states. The root mean square error (RMSE) and the relative root square error (RRSE) of our model are respectively 198.36s and 0.51 for subject-dependent, and 522.94s and 0.97 for subject-independent. The results indicate each subject has individualized physiological pattern when they felt fatigue.

Keywords: Physiological signals, fatigue, prediction, motion sensing games.

1   Introduction

Motion sensing games, e.g. Nintendo Wii and Microsoft Kinect etc., extends and combines gaming experience from digital world to physical world seamlessly. Also, players could easily experience some physiological states such as fatigue during motion sensing games. Motion sensing games intend to render people a healthier way for exercise but not excessive exercises. Therefore, predicting fatigue states is vital for improvements of motion sensing games.

Currently, many literatures have focused on fatigue model applied to a range of directions. And physiological measures have been wildly used for studying the level of fatigue and intensity of activity [1-2]. Especially, our preliminary work [3] has studied the change of physiological signals during playing motion sensing games and proposed a discriminate model to recognize players' fatigue states.

However, these works mainly focused on fatigue recognition. To our best knowledge, no studies have proposed a fatigue prediction model. In this paper, we constructed a fatigue prediction model for motion sensing games, based on physiological measures. It can play a vital role in designing adaptive interactions of responding to the upcoming fatigue states.

The main contributions of our work are: (1) proposed a fatigue prediction model especially for motion sensing games; (2) designed an experiment to collect a data set of physiological signals; and (3) performed evaluation for our model, based on the data set.

A. Nijholt, T. Romão, and D. Reidsma (Eds.): ACE 2012, LNCS 7624, pp. 533–536, 2012.

2   Method

Figure 1 shows the overview of our fatigue prediction model.

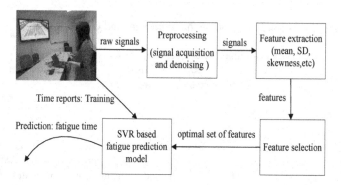

Fig. 1. Overview of the fatigue prediction model

After the preprocessing stage, features are extracted and selected. Then, SVR was used to construct our fatigue prediction model which could output the real-time deviating time that defines how long it will take to enter the fatigue state.

2.1   Feature Extraction and Feature Selection

From the five original physiological signals (blood volume pulse (BVP), temperature, skin conductance, respiration and EMG), we calculated features from various analysis domains such as conventional statistics, time and frequency domain.

In conventional statistics, the mean value (mean), standard deviation (SD), skewness and root mean square of successive differences (RMSSD) of physiological signals were computed. In addition, as heart rate variability (HRV) was widely used as an indication of fatigue in adults, we further explored extra features of HRV from time and frequency domain, including power spectral density, consecutive beats that differ by more than 50 millisecond (pnn50) as well as fast and low power computed by detrended fluctuation analysis (hrdfa). Then SFFS were used to select the optimal features due to its consistent success in related works. Finally, we had 27 features as our physiological measures.

2.2   Fatigue Prediction Model

Unlike fatigue recognition models that detect users' fatigue states, we predict how long it might take to reach the fatigue state. SVM regression was employed as it had been successfully applied for various problems. SVR can perform linear regression in high-dimension feature space by minimizing the ε-insensitive loss [5]. Introducing slack variables ξ_i to measure the deviation of training samples outside ε-insensitive zone, SVR is formulated as minimization of the following function:

$$\frac{1}{2}\|\omega\|^2 + C\sum_{i=1}^{n}(\xi_i + \xi_i^*) \tag{1}$$

Subject to
$$\begin{cases} y_i - f(x_i, \omega) - b \le \varepsilon + \xi_i^* \\ f(x_i, \omega) + b - y_i \le \varepsilon + \xi_i \\ \xi_i, \xi_i^* \ge 0 \end{cases} \tag{2}$$

where C is a positive constant. The formulation were transformed into dual problem, and the solution is given by

$$(x) = \sum_{i=1}^{n}(a_i - a_i^*) K(x_i, x) + b \tag{3}$$

Based on the theory of SVR, we used selected features as training data and the corresponding deviating time as labels to train our fatigue prediction model.

3   Performance Evaluation

We have designed an experiment to collect a high-quality dataset of physiological signals where Nintendo Wii tennis sports were our induction game. At the first of our experiment, participants relaxed for roughly five minutes. Then they endeavored to play the tennis game, reported fatigue to the experiment administrator who wrote down the fatigue time and stopped playing after three more minutes since the report. Physiological signals of participants were recorded from the start to the stop. Using window length of 10 seconds with overlap of 9 seconds, we segmented the signals into about 23400 samples as our data set.

For evaluating our fatigue prediction model, two prediction error indices are computed, including RMSE (root mean square error) and RRSE (relative root square error). These indices are defined as:

$$RMSE = \sqrt{\frac{1}{N}\sum_t \left(x(t) - \hat{x}(t)\right)^2} \tag{4}$$

$$RRSE = \sqrt{\frac{1}{\sum_t x(t)}\sum_t \left[\frac{x(t) - \hat{x}(t)}{x(t)}\right]^2 x(t)} \tag{5}$$

in which N is the number of samples, x(t) is value of a sample's deviating time from the fatigue report time and $\hat{x}(t)$ is the predicted value of x(t). RMSE indicates the mean value of all samples' prediction error while RRSE illustrates the relative prediction error, taking each sample' prediction error and deviating time in consideration.

Table 1 shows the results of prediction error indices for user-dependent and user-independent. We can see that the prediction error indices are significantly different when comparing the results of two different validation methods. For user-dependent results, RMSE by tenfold cross validation is about 27% larger than that by self-validation while RRSE is roughly 45% larger. It might be because that RRSE takes each simple's deviating time into account and regards samples individually. In comparison, the results of RMSE for user-independent by using tenfold validation are both about 12% larger than those by using self-validation. It might be because user-independent results originally present the general performance of our model and to some extent reduce influences caused by samples' different periods.

Table 1. Results of prediction error indices for user-dependent and user-indepedent

Validation method	user-dependent		user-independent	
	RMSE (s)	RRSE	RMSE (s)	RRSE
self- validation	155.96	0.37	466.37	0.86
tenfold cross-validation	198.36	0.51	522.94	0.97

4   Conclusions and Future Work

In this paper, we presented a fatigue prediction model for motion sensing games, based on physiological signals. For evaluating our model, two prediction error indexes (RMSE and RRSE) were computed. The significant difference in the results between user-independent and user-dependent to some extent indicates that the fatigue states during playing motion sensing games are individualized and different users may have different physiological patterns. As our model is at the first stage, much work remains to be done. We will discuss the selection of parameters and their effects on performance of our model. In addition, we will extend our model to multiple applications such as sports and virtual training.

Acknowledgements. This work was funded by the Ministry of Industry and Information Technology of China (No.2010ZX01042-002-003-001), Natural Science Foundation of China (No. 60703040), and Science and Technology Department of Zhejiang Province (Nos. 2007C13019, 2011C13042).

References

1. Chattopadhyay, R., Sethuraman, P., Gaurav, P.: Towards fatigue and intensity measurement framework during continuous repetitive activities. In: I2MTC (2010)
2. Yang, G., Lin, Y., Bhattacharya, P.: A Driver Fatigue Recognition Model Based on Information Fusion and Dynamic Bayesian Network. Information Sciences 180, 1942–1954 (2010)
3. Ruan, S.S., Chen, L., Chen, G.C.: Study on the change of physiological signals during playing body-controlled games. In: Proc. of International Conference on Advances in Computer Entertainment Technology, pp. 349–352 (2009)
4. Vapnik, V.: The nature of statistical learning theory, 2nd edn. Springer, Berlin (1999)

JECCO: A Creature-Like Tentacle Robot

Haipeng Mi and Yoichiro Kawaguchi

Interfaculty Initiative in Information Studies, University of Tokyo,
7-3-1 Hongo, Tokyo, Japan
{mi,yoichiro}@iii.u-tokyo.ac.jp
http://yoichiro-kawaguchi.com

Abstract. This paper presents a creature-like tentacle robot, JECCO, which is inspired by an imaginary artwork series. JECCO robot has five robotic tentacles and a novel creature-like interaction mechanism. JECCO responds to a user's contact gestures and provides to users a sense of a living creature. The tentacle expression of JECCO robot provides a unique interaction style and impressive experiences.

Keywords: Interactive art, Robotic art, Interaction style.

1 Introduction

With the fast development of innovative technology, robots are becoming pervasive in factories, schools, museums and homes. Robots are now not only designed for conducting a specific task instead of us, but also for emotional interaction with us. There are many researches investigating different emotional interaction styles between robot and human. Some robots are assigned psychological reactions such as shyness[2]; Some robots are designed like a real plant[1]; While some other robots can react to people's intention and smile[3].

In this paper, we presents a creature-like tentacle robot, JECCO, which combines artistic concept and engineering technology. We introduce the concept and implementation of JECCO robot, and also discuss interactions with JECCO for interactive artwork and entertainment purpose.

2 JECCO

2.1 Background

"JECCO", which means "Jellyfish in Cosmos" , is a CG and installation artwork series that illustrates imaginary alien tentacle creatures (Fig. 1: Left). JECCO series was created under an experimental CG simulation project, which assumes alien creatures from an undiscovered planet have some biological features that are similar to earth creatures such as jellyfish tentacle and butterfly wings. JECCO was initially born in a computer simulation and later had a physical installation representation. However, both CG and physical installations have limitations. CG artworks lack of sense of realism and presence, while installation artworks

A. Nijholt, T. Romão, and D. Reidsma (Eds.): ACE 2012, LNCS 7624, pp. 537–540, 2012.

Fig. 1. Left: An installation artwork of JECCO; Right: JECCO robot prototype

lack of vitality. Combining the artist concept and engineering technology, we are able to create a creature-like robotic installation of JECCO, which has a better sense of living organisms (Fig. 1: Right).

2.2 Concept of JECCO Robot

As an imaginary alien creature, it is challenging but important to make the JECCO robot provides a perception of a real creature. As the most important parts, tentacles of JECCO should behave like a natural creature's organ, being able to not only sense and move, but also express emotions. Biologically speaking, unlike a higher mammal animal, a lower cephalopods creature has less ability of thinking. However, it should respond appropriately to environment change. This kind of "stress response" is one of the most important biological identities of lower creatures. Tentacles and the ability of stress response are the two fundamental biological identities of a JECCO robot.

3   Implementation

JECCO is a creature-like robot, which has five robotic tentacles on its swinging body. It has a self-contained design that all sensors, actuators, controllers and power supply are integrated together.

3.1   Robotic Tentacles

The design and development of robotic tentacles are inspired by cephalopods. The tentacle of cephalopods consists of a tightly packed three-dimensional array of muscle fibers. The musculature of the arms of octopus not only generates the forces required for movement, deformation and changes in stiffness, it also provides the required skeletal support. Inspired by this mechanism, we designed a string-spring structure for the robotic tentacle. Each tentacle consists of a number of alternately placed springs and metal plates. In each metal plate, three holes are drilled near the circumference and set 120° apart. Three metal strings are thread through all the springs and metal plates in order to link them together. The metal strings work like muscle fibers in the cephalopods tentacles. Each metal string is tied to a retractor, which is driven by a cam. Once the retractor drags a metal string, it bends the tentacle to the direction of the dragged string. By separately controlling the three retractors, it is possible to bend the tentacle to any direction.

3.2 JECCO Robot

We developed a simple swing mechanism for JECCO robot body. Two cams are installed to a rotation axle with a angle difference of 180°. When rotate, they can alternatively promote two pillars of the upper body so that the body swings left and right continuously. The swing margin is about ±5°.

Five robotic tentacles are installed onto the swing body, each of which is driven by a rotating cam. Once the cam rotates, it pushes the three retractors of each tentacle one by one. As a result, the tentacle performs like it is exploring the surrounding environment. A compact control unit with micro controller is used to control both motors to generate appropriate behaviors of the robot. A number of sensors are embedded into the robot in order to sense users's touch. Sensors and the motor controller are connected by a small circuit, which employes a certain algorithm to realize creature-like interactions with users. The whole system is powered by a 12V battery, which can last running for more than four hours after a fully charge.

4 Interaction

JECCO robots has five robotic tentacles, which provide unique expressions. The embedded capacitive sensors can sense a human's contact gesture such as a touch or a grasp. In order to provide to users a sense of a living creature, we have implemented a simple "stress response" interaction mechanism for JECCO robots. The idea of this interaction mechanism is to make the robot respond to external stimuli such as human's touch and grasp. Based on this concept, we have developed a simple interaction scenario.

Usually, the JECCO robot stays quietly just like it is sleeping. When there is someone touches it, it starts to swing its body and tentacles just like it is waken up by the user. After the user's hand left the robot, it then calms down slowly and falls into sleep again. However, if the user continuously grasps the tentacle of the JECCO, the robot swings faster and faster, just like it is getting rid of the user's grasping (Fig. 2).

Fig. 2. Interaction with JECCO robot

5   Conclusions and Future Work

We have presented a creature-like robot, JECCO, which has five robotic tentacles on its swinging body. A "stress response" interaction mechanism is implemented to provide a sense of a living creature. The tentacle robot provided unique interaction experiences, and received surprise and high interests. However, the limited number of actuators did not fully demonstrate the expression. In the future, we plan to improve the expression mechanism of the tentacle robot. We also plan to explore the possibility of applying JECCO robot for entertainment purpose such as creating mixed-reality games. Furthermore, it is worthy to study human interactions and perceptions regarding to a organic creature-like robot.

Acknowledgments. We thank Akiya Kamimura and Tatsuya Murakawa, who helped developing and fabricating the JECCO robot; and Ai Ueda, who helped making the video.

References

1. Nakayasu, A.: Himawari: Shape Memory Alloy Motion Display for Robotic Representation. In: Proc. of CHI EA 2010, pp. 4327–4332. ACM Press, New York (2010)
2. Lee, C.J., Breazeal, C., Kim, K., Picard, R.: Shybot: Friend-Stranger Interaction for Children Living with Autism. In: Proc. of CHI EA 2008, pp. 3375–3380. ACM Press, New York (2008)
3. Nam, H.Y., Choi, C.: Artistic Robot Please Smile. In: Proc. of CHI EA 2012, pp. 967–970. ACM Press, New York (2012)
4. Kawaguchi, Y.: JECCO, http://yoichiro-kawaguchi.com/archives/399

Yusabutter: A Messaging Tool
That Generates Animated Texts

Mitsuru Minakuchi, Shougo Kinoshita, and Yu Suzuki

Kyoto Sangyo University, Faculty of Computer Science and Engineering,
Kamigamo-motoyama, Kita-ku, 6038555 Kyoto, Japan
mmina@acm.org, {fg0846741,suzug}@cse.kyoto-su.ac.jp
http://mmil.cse.kyoto-su.ac.jp

Abstract. Text messages sometimes fail to communicate feelings appropriately and cause flaming. To solve this problem, we propose a messaging tool, named "Yusabutter[1]," that conveys the sender's feeling through animated texts, i.e., kinetic typography. The sender can make texts move by shaking a handy terminal with a builtin accelerometer. We have also implemented a Yusabutter server that generates a Web page containing the animated message and posts the message along with the URI of the page on Twitter. Experiments showed that the senders' feeling attached to messages by shaking the terminal and the receivers' feeling upon reading the messages were approximately equivalent. This result suggests that the proposed method can convey feelings appropriately, easily, and pleasingly.

Keywords: Communications applications, emotion, kinetic typography.

1   Introduction

Text messages, such as those in e-mails, forums, and chat systems, are a popular means of communication. However, misunderstanding and flaming often occur since it is difficult to express actual feelings. Face marks and emoticons are used to complement nuances of emotion, but it is troublesome to select the intended marks. Kinetic chat that attaches motions to text messages by using a GSR sensor [1] has been proposed, but it is not convenient to attach a sensor to the user.

We thus propose a messaging application that attaches motion to text when a user shakes a motion sensor embedded in a smartphone. The shaking operation is simple but highly flexible for expressing emotions. In addition, physical performance may be entertaining.

2   Implementation

We implemented the client software for iOS, runnable on iPhones, iPod touches, and iPads. Figures 1 and 2 show screenshots of the client. The white box in the

---

[1] "In Japanese, yusa-buru" means sway or bump.

A. Nijholt, T. Romão, and D. Reidsma (Eds.): ACE 2012, LNCS 7624, pp. 541–544, 2012.

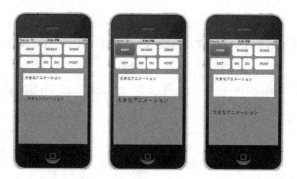

Fig. 1. Example of large motion

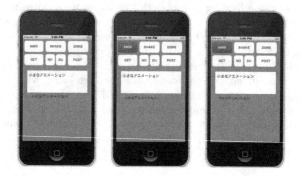

Fig. 2. Example of small motion

middle is the text area for editing a message. The lower half of the screen is the preview area for an animated message. The user edits a message and shakes the terminal. Subsequently, the user confirms the animated message and sends it.

The motion of a text is determined by the motion sensor (accelerometer) data. Movements of the motion sensor in the left-right and top-bottom directions control the text motion, while movements in the forward-backward direction control the text size. The intensity of the accelerometer data is reflected in the intensity of text motion. The accelerometer data are obtained for $3.125s$ ($= 1/2^6s \times 200$), and the 50 data at the beginning are discarded in view of the time lag between the time when the user taps the shake button on the screen and the time when he or she actually shakes the terminal. Figures 1 and 2 show examples of animated text.

Figure 3 shows a diagram of the system architecture. A sender client posts a message and motion data to the server. A receiver client gets the message and motion data from the server and displays the animated message. The server also generates a Web page containing the animated message and posts the message along with the URI of the page on Twitter. Twitter users can access the page via the tweet and see the animated message.

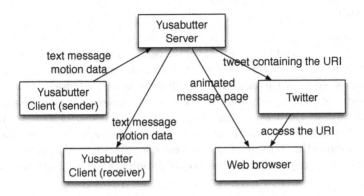

Fig. 3. System architecture

3   Evaluation

We evaluated the effectiveness of animated text in communicating feelings.

3.1   Procedure

The participants in the evaluation experiment were 10 undergraduate students. They were grouped into five sender-receiver pairs.

First, the sender prepared a message according to a given situation. We suggested the following situations corresponding to the three elemental feelings happiness, anger, and sadness: tell your friend that you passed a certification exam (happiness), convey your displeasure to your friend for him or her being late by 20 min for a rendezvous (anger), and tell your friend about the death of your dog (sadness).

Next, the sender shook the terminal to add motion to the message. The participants practiced preparing messages before the experiments, but we did not instruct them on how to shake the terminal.

Then, the subject sent the message. At this time, the actual motion attached to the message was one of the following three patterns: (1) original motion: use the motion generated by the sender; (2) no motion: discard the generated motion; and (3) dummy motion: replace with a previously prepared motion that expresses strong happiness.

After the receiver read the message, we asked them to rate the intensity of feeling using scores of 1 (not felt) to 5 (strongly felt) for each of the three feelings (happiness, anger, and sadness).

Each participant performed both the sender role and receiver role. The combination of the situation and the attached motion was varied in consideration of counterbalance.

3.2 Result

Table 1 summarizes the results. We did not apply a statistical test because the amount of data was insufficient. Low average values of the differences in the scores for the three feelings between the sender and the receiver indicate a good result, that is, the receiver felt the exact feelings that the sender intended. The fact that the value for pattern 2 (no animation) was small implies that the message itself could communicate the basic feeling. However, in comparison, the value for pattern 1 (original animation) was smaller and the value for pattern 3 (dummy data) was larger. This shows that motion of text can complement the feeling in the message. The results thus suggest that the proposed system is efficient in communicating feelings.

Table 1. Results of the experiment

Actual motion attached to the message	Average of the differences in scores	Standard deviation
(1) Original motion	0.50	0.45
(2) No motion	0.57	0.45
(3) Dummy motion (excluding data for the happiness situations)	0.57 (0.81)	0.67 (0.66)

In interviews conducted after the experiments, many participants stated that they were satisfied with the generated animated messages (23 of the 30 trials) but that they sometimes found it difficult to provide small motion for sadness. All participants found the operation of (shaking) the terminal to be enjoyable and easy.

4 Conclusion

We have proposed a novel messaging system that conveys feelings through animated text generated by shaking a terminal. An evaluation suggests that users find the system convenient and enjoyable to use for expressing feelings.

Acknowledgement. A part of this work was supported by JSPS KAKENHI grant number (24603028).

Reference

1. Wang, H., Prendinger, H., Igarashi, T.: Communicating emotions in online chat using physiological sensors and animated text. In: CHI 2004 Extended Abstracts on Human Factors in Computing Systems, CHI EA 2004, pp. 1171–1174. ACM, New York (2004)

HomeTree – An Art Inspired Mobile Eco-feedback Visualization

Filipe Quintal, Valentina Nisi, Nuno Nunes, Mary Barreto, and Lucas Pereira

Madeira Interactive Technologies Institute, University of Madeira, Caminho da Penteada,
Funchal, 9020-105, Madeira, Portugal
{Fquinta,mary.barreto,lucas}@m-ti.org,
valentina.nisi@gmail.com, njn@uma.pt,

Abstract. This paper presents HomeTree a prototype of an art-inspired mobile eco-feedback system. The system is implemented on a tablet PC and relies on a non-intrusive energy-monitoring infrastructure to access consumption and power event information. Our prototype addresses an important problem in eco-feedback, which is the fact that users loose interest about their energy consumption after a period of several weeks. To accomplish this HomeTree implements a dual visualization strategy. Initially HomeTree presents users with a screensaver that shows energy consumption mapped in a dynamic illustration of the local forest. Through this strategy we leverage the emotional connection between the short-term energy consumption and the long-term effects on nature through the local depicted landscape. In a second mode of operation users can interact with HomeTree directly by checking the historical records of their consumption data, and check which days or weeks they have reduced or increased consumption. Furthermore a comparison with a more objective baseline, such as the city of Funchal energy consumption is provided, in order to give users a sense of the level of their consumption in a wider context.

Keywords: ffective computing, Sustainability, Aesthetics, Art driven Eco-feedback, User Interfaces, Prototyping.

1   Introduction

Eco-feedback technology is defined as technology that provides feedback on individual or group behaviors with the goal of reducing environmental impact [1]. Many studies argue that providing users with real-time energy feedback is an effective way of changing consumption behaviors. Savings reported in the literature range from 5% to 10% energy consumption [2]. To maximize the potential of the eco-feedback technology, information must be easy to understand, presented in a way that attracts attention and is remembered, and also delivered as close as possible to the time of the decision [3]. However, researchers also found that attention in eco-feedback systems tend to decrease over time [4], and that can compromise the long-term effect of eco-feedback technology. Inspired by this challenge we designed HomeTree, an art-inpired eco-feedback visualization based on changes happening over a landscape depicting the local endemic Forest (see Fig. 1).

A. Nijholt, T. Romão, and D. Reidsma (Eds.): ACE 2012, LNCS 7624, pp. 545–548, 2012.

2   Designing an Eco-feedback System

Under the context of a sustainability research project we conducted three real world deployments across more than 20 households during 18 months in Funchal, Portugal. The system presented here is the result of reflection and design based on the experience, interviews and other qualitative studies with users of these deployments. Previously [4,5] the eco-feedback system was based on a netbook acting both as the non-intrusive energy sensor and the visualization device. For this version we opted to separate the sensor system from the visualization component that is implemented using a tablet PC that could be easily moved across the house, and accessible by all family members. Furthermore, this new version couples energy consumption with natural elements of the endemic forest in an attempt to leverage the emotional connection to keep users engaged with the eco-feedback. The system also provides detailed historical consumption reports as well as simple tips about energy conservation and best practices promoting sustainable behavior change. Finally our eco-feedback system provides a way for users to classify power events detected by the low-cost non-intrusive single-point sensor enabling the disaggregation of consumption per appliance (a power event is a change in the energy consumption, normally associated with an appliance ON/OFF transition).

3   The Hometree System

HomeTree is an art inspired eco-feedback visualization based on a low-costs non-intrusive energy sensing platform developed under the context of an HCI sustainability research project. The sensing platform is capable of calculating electricity consumption from a single point sensor in the house by detecting when an appliance is turned ON or OFF once a set of training data is given. The framework is responsible for acquiring, storing and providing data via web-services to multiple eco-feedback visualization systems, including HomeTree.

3.1   Implementation

HomeTree is implemented in a 7'' android tablet using the android native SDK. It receives real-time consumption, power events and historical data from the sensing framework. This communication is made using sockets and a specific communication protocol. It requires the tablet to be connected to the Internet in the same local network.

3.2   Operation

The system has two main modes of operation. When it is not used for two minutes it goes to the energy awareness mode that shows the consumption mapped as an digital illustration of the local endemic forest. Once the user interacts with the tablet, by removing it from a stationary position, or pressing the back soft key the system goes to detailed consumption mode and shows daily, weekly and monthly information about the home energy use.

Energy Awareness Mode

In this mode we aim at leveraging the emotional connection between natural elements of the local landscape and the energy consumption in the household. In this mode, the tablet resembles a digital photo frame displaying a digitally generated landscape depicting a real place in the local endemic forest. The color of the landscape will alert the user about the energy consumption ranging from green (low consumption) to a brownish red color, indicating very high levels of energy consumption (see Fig. 1). The consumption displayed here is a combination between real-time consumption and historical baseline data.

Fig. 1. Energy awareness mode at extreme levels of consumption, low at the left and high at the right

Detailed Consumption Mode

This mode is triggered when the user grabs the tablet from a stationary position or presses the device back button. As a consequence the system presents a tabbed menu with four options: "Home", "Day", "Week" and "Events". The "Home" (Fig. 2. Left) tab shows a summary of the overall consumption as well as the current consumption. The summary contains aggregated consumption of the current day/week and month, and comparisons between homologous periods. Also in this tab the user is presented with a tip of the day with general sustainable actions. The "Day" (Fig. 2 Right) "Week" and "Month" tabs present a chart displaying the consumption over that period and the total aggregated consumption. It also informs the user of where the peak consumption happened. By default the information presented here refers to the current day/week/month but the user can select previous periods.

Finally, the "Events" tab presents information about the power events. The events are displayed as circles in a chart, the position on the vertical axis represents the consumption of that event, and the horizontal position represents time. The circle's color expresses if our framework has enough training data to estimate which appliance caused that event. If the user selects an event in the chart the system displays its consumption, the time when it happened and which appliance triggered it. The user can always correct the system's guess or identify the appliance (if the system did not have any guess). Doing this will produce more accurate estimates over time. By default the system only displays the last 10 events (but the user can change that value).

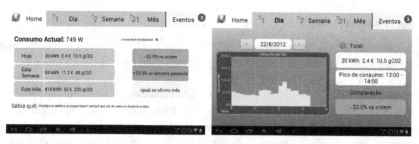

Fig. 2. Ont the left the home view of the system, and on the right the tab with the consumption of the current day

4   Conclusion

This paper we presented an innovative eco-feedback system that attempts to overcome an important limitation of this technology related to the fact that people loose interest about their energy consumption after some weeks. Starting from a low-cost single point non-intrusive energy sensing infrastructure and based on two years of experience with eco-feedback deployments, we designed a new visualization that leverages the emotional connection between users and elements of the natural forest. We argue that our prototype will be more effective in retaining people's attention over time while also providing a way of enabling people to train the non-intrusive sensing system.

References

1. Froehlich, J., Findlater, L., Landay, J.: The design of eco-feedback technology. In: Proceedings of CHI (2010)
2. Parker, D., Hoak, D., Meier, A., Brown, R.: How much energy are we using? Potential of residential energy demand feedback devices.:Summer Study on Energy Efficiency in Buildings (2006)
3. Brewer, G., Stern, P.: Panel on Social and Behavioral Science Research Priorities for Environmental Decision Making Committee on the Human Dimensions of Global Change National Research Council, 160 S (2005)
4. Nunes, N.J., Pereira, L., Quintal, F., Bergés, M.: Deploying and evaluating the effectiveness of energy eco-feedback through a low-cost NILM solution. In: Proceedings of the 6th International Conference on Persuasive Technology (2011)
5. Pereira, L., Quintal, F., Nunes, N.J., Berges, M.: The Design of a Hardware-software Platform for Long-term Energy Eco-feedback Research. In: Proceedings of EICS (2012)

Augmenting Trading Card Game: Playing against Virtual Characters Used in Fictional Stories

Mizuki Sakamoto, Tatsuo Nakajima, and Todorka Alexandrova

Department of Computer Science and Engineering, Waseda University
{mizuki,tatsuo,toty}@dcl.cs.waseda.ac.jp

Abstract. We present Augmented Trading Card Game that enhances remote trading card game play with empathetic virtual characters used in fictional stories like popular animation and game stories.

1 Introduction

Augmented Trading Card Game (Augmented TCG) for playing the Yu-Gi-Oh! Trading Card Game (http://www.yugioh-card.com/en/) between two players who are located in different places is presented in this paper.

We use popular virtual characters that have been used in Japanese animations and games as opponent players in Augmented TCG. The virtual characters replace real players whose movements are synchronized with the virtual characters. Especially, the Yu-Gi-Oh! TCG has been originally introduced in the Yu-Gi-Oh! comic and animation. One of the reasons why Yu-Gi-Oh! TCG is popular in Japan is the fact that almost all young people have first enjoyed the animation and comic story and then learnt how to play the game from the story. Moreover, the story teaches some important ideological concepts such as the importance of justice, friendship, bravery, positivity, and thoughtfulness. That is why we believe that the characters of the animation story can be used to enhance the playing style of the game through the stories they carry and recall. We conducted a user study in which we observed the participants' behavior during the play, and interviewed them after that.

In the current study, we adopted virtual characters used in game and animation stories in three ways. The first way is to use a favorite character unrelated to trading card game. The second way is to use a character appeared on a trading card. Finally, the third way is to use the characters that are appeared in the *YuGiOh!* animation story. Especially, the third way is useful to increase human positive attitude and to enhance their self-efficacy to make a progress of their gaming skills.

There are several other systems that support remote TCG play. Duel Accelerator (http://www.yugioh-online.net/v3/newvisitors/) is an online-based Yu-Gi-Oh! TCG where each player chooses an avatar that identifies him/her from the other players. Also, *The Eye of Judgment* (http://en.wikipedia.org/wiki/The_Eye_of_Judgment) uses augmented reality technologies to show special effects on real trading cards.

A. Nijholt, T. Romão, and D. Reidsma (Eds.): ACE 2012, LNCS 7624, pp. 549–552, 2012.

2   Augmenting Trading Card Game

Augmented TCG enhances the remote trading card play performed by two persons. As shown in Figure 1, the two players are located in different places. Each player's cards in his/her battle field on the table in front of him/her are captured by a camera and projected on the opponent player's table. Also, each player is represented as the 3D model of a virtual character used in popular animations and games, and this character is shown to the opponent player. In the current implementation, MikuMikuDance (http://www.geocities.jp/higuchuu4) is used to show the 3D models of virtual characters. The virtual character is controlled using MS Kinect, its movement is synchronized with the movement and the behavior of the player. In the current Augmented TCG, a player can choose one of three virtual characters that are *Yugi* and *Kaiba* from the Yu-Gi-Oh! animation story, and *Link* from *The Legend of Zelda* (http://zelda.com/). In the Yu-Gi-Oh! animation story, *Yugi* is always surrounded by many friends and his winning success is a result of his strong bonds with his friends who love the trading card game. *Kaiba* is a lonely hero and he always seeks the strength in the game, but he does not accept other person's help even if he is in a critical situation. However, he also finally understands the importance of friendship. Most young boys want to follow either of these two characters because they have very typical ideal personalities that are very attractive to most boys. The reason to choose *Link* as the third character in our experiment is that we would like to investigate how a favorite character from another unrelated to TCG story affects the attitude of a player. Also, while playing the game, another virtual character depicted on one of the player's cards appears on a small display near the player once that card is drawn out of the deck, and supports and encourages him/her to win the game until the end of the game.

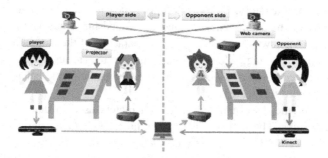

Fig. 1. Augmented TCG System

For the experiments presented in this paper, we have created a special deck as the participants have used the cards in a controlled manner and the rules have been simplified for making the duels shorter. We are also very familiar with the animation story, and know how each character structures the deck and uses the cards in the animation. So, the deck used in the experiment has been structured depending on the character that the player has chosen to play with. However, in the current experiment, the virtual character's behavior does not reflect the real behavior of the opponent player exactly. Another person imitates the behavior of the opponent player and this behavior is sometimes over-reacted in order to be closer to the actual character's behavior in the animation.

In the current prototype configuration, on a large display, a virtual character which behavior is synchronized with the behavior of the person who imitates the opponent player is shown. A camera is setup behind a small display near the participant, and captures the image of the cards. The opponent player's cards are projected by a projector that is installed on the table. A small display shows the other virtual character depicted on one of the player's cards, which in this case is the one of most powerful cards in the participant's deck.

Most of the five Japanese participants in our experiments have more than three years' experience in Yu-Gi-Oh! TCG and they know the characters that appear in the animation stories very well. During the experiments, we observed each participant's play and conducted interviews with them after their plays. Before the experiments, none of the participants knew about Augmented TCG, and they were told how the rules were simplified right before the experiment.

We did two experiments for playing Augmented TCG with a virtual character representing the opponent player. In the first experiment, participants could choose either *Yugi* or *Kaiba* according to their preferences.

After the play, we interviewed the participants. One of them said: "*I could feel I am playing against Yugi, but Yugi used in the experiment does not offer enough reality*". Especially, the movement of the character was sometimes not like the real movement of *Yugi*. He said: "*I will definitely enjoy more the game against Yugi, and would like to win the game if the movement is more realistic*". However, another participant said: "*The face expression of the character is poor and it is a very important issue while playing a game against a real person*". Also, one of the players told us: "*The voice should be the same as the actor's voice of the character in the animation story*". Especially, if the opponent player was a female, some participants felt strange since both *Yugi* and *Kaiba* were male characters.

In the animation story, players usually play TCG while standing, that is why we choose that the characters are always standing during the play, but in the real situation, a player usually sits down on a chair. Some participants feel the unreality on the behavior of the characters, but if the characters just sit down all the time, the participants also feel the inconsistency with the *Yugi* and *Kaiba*'s personality.

In the second experiment, *Link from The Legend of Zelda* was used as a character representing the opponent player. The results in this case were completely different depending on whether the participants liked this character or not. If the participants were not interested in *Link*, they usually did not care about the presence of Link, but if *Link* was their favorite character, then they found playing the game with *Link more enjoyable*. One of the male participants also told us: "*If the character is a pretty girl, I may be more excited to play the game*". Also, a female participant told us: *I feel that Link is my boy friend, so playing with him increases my pleasure and positivity*".

In the next experiment, a small display on the table shows the virtual character depicted on one of the cards used by the participant. We have selected *Dead Master* from *Black★Rock Shooter* (http://blackrockshooter.wikia.com/) as a character to be depicted on the card because we feel that the character does not contradicts with or violate the atmosphere of Yu-Gi-Oh!.

In this experiment, we structured a special deck in advance, and all participants used the same deck. Then, in the duel, the participant always drew the card depicting *Dead Master* at the beginning of the game. Once that card has been drawn out of the deck a small display next to the player showed *Dead Master* that remained present until the end of the duel. *Dead Master* supported and encouraged the player during the game by using a body gesture for encouraging people and its behavior was controlled by a person who operated MS Kinect.

After the experiment one of the participants said: *"It is desirable that the card depicting Dead Master does not lose from the attack of the opponent player"*. However, another player who was not interested in the character told us: *"It is more enjoyable if the participant's favorite character encourages him"*. One of the other participants said: *"I feel that the character does not encourage me enough using only gesture. It is better that the character talks or advises me. He also told us: "It is desirable that the character behaves like a cheerleader".* Dead Master is a serious character, so if that character just behaves as a cheerleader, some players may feel the unreality due to the loss of the consistency with its animation story. Also, another participant told us: *"The encouragement should be like the one in the animation story"*. Most participants said: *"The presence of the character increases the pleasure, but it is hard to consider winning the game just from that encouragement"*. The participants' comments showed that they were aware that exactly the character depicted on one of their cards appeared on the small display without them being informed in advance about this feature of the system.

3   Future Direction

If people are familiar with the story of an animation or a game, virtual characters in the story recall the leitmotif of the story with a little information by performing some action/interaction with the character. We believe that this observation is important when using virtual characters in various future information services in the real world. The proposed approach will be integrated to other design approaches [1, 2] to design attractive information services that regulate human attitude and behavior.

References

1. Sakamoto, M., Nakajima, T., Alexandrova, T.: Value-Based Design for Gamifying Daily Activities. In: Herrlich, M., Malaka, R., Masuch, M. (eds.) ICEC 2012. LNCS, vol. 7522, pp. 421–424. Springer, Heidelberg (2012)
2. Sakamoto, M., Nakajima, T., Alexandrova, T.: Analyzing the Effects of Virtualizing and Augmenting Trading Card Game based on a Player's Personality. Distributed and Ubiquitous Computing Lab. Technical Report (2012)

Changing Environmental Behaviors through Smartphone-Based Augmented Experiences

Bruno Santos[1], Teresa Romão[1], A. Eduardo Dias[1,2], Pedro Centieiro[1],
and Bárbara Teixeira[1]

[1] CITI, DI-Faculdade de Ciências e Tecnologia/Universidade Nova de Lisboa
2829-516 Caparica, Portugal
bmsjobs@me.com, tir@fct.unl.pt,
{aed.fct,pcentieiro,anabarbarateixeira}@gmail.com
[2] bViva International, B.V.
Romanovhof 9, 3329 BD, Dordrecht, Netherlands
edias@bviva.com

Abstract. A significant part of the population is still not aware of the sustainability problems that our planet is facing, so it is important to inform people about the theme while persuading them to change their behavior and acquire pro-environmental attitudes. This work intends to alert citizens to these issues in a fun and immersive way through the use of mobile devices, more specifically smartphones, and augmented reality technology which will provide the user with informative insight about the surrounding environment, while highlighting the environmental threats. This paper presents a system that works like an environmental scanner, allowing users to inspect their surroundings with their mobile devices in search of pollution sources. When detected the system provides users with additional information and allows them to virtually clean these pollution sources. In addition it is intended to positively reinforce pro-environmental actions using a system of rewards and a virtual character that will interact and motivate the users.

1 Introduction

The modern society has evolved in many aspects in the recent years, but people still lack routines and behaviors that support and help the environment. The concept of sustainability is often ignored, or simply unknown, by many people on developed nations meanwhile consumption of natural resources far exceeds the planet capacity to produce them [1]. In our everyday life we are confronted with situations which directly damage our planet's sustainability, sometimes without even noticing them. Making people aware of this kind of situations is crucial to change their perspective, concerns and attitudes. Having this in mind eVision, an application which tries to persuade the users to change their pro-environment behavior, was conceived. The previous is achieved by providing informative environmental insight about the users' surroundings regarding environmental threads and offering a game-based activity where they are rewarded when they complete some tasks of interest. To keep the users engaged, the application also offers a customizable virtual character that mentors and motivates the users throughout the experience.

A. Nijholt, T. Romão, and D. Reidsma (Eds.): ACE 2012, LNCS 7624, pp. 553–556, 2012.

2   System Overview

As aforementioned, eVision is a persuasive mobile game designed to change people's attitudes or behaviors towards environment in a fun and immersive way, through the use of mobile devices, augmented reality and persuasive technology [2]. eVision works like an environmental scanner, allowing users to use mobile devices to detect and gather information regarding air quality and environmental threatening structures around their current geographical position. Users are invited, by the eVision mascot, to participate in an activity that consists in detecting and cleaning environmental threats, such as cars, airplanes and factories, which will then be automatically overlaid with pro-environmental objects (e.g.: overlaying a car with a bicycle). For this cleaning operation, the users just need to use their finger to rub the mobile phone display over the detect threat (see Figure 1). When completing each activity, users are awarded with points and leaves (eVision virtual currency) as well as with environmental information regarding the corresponding threat.

The eVision activity game and persuasive design was created having different concepts and objectives in mind. One key point is the presentation of general information about environmental offensive agents through Augmented Reality (AR), making the user wonder about the sustainability problems of our planet. Using the same AR technology, eVision also provides the ability to make landscape changes presented on the mobile device screen. This type of feedback keep the users interested on the activity while being pleased with the alterations he is virtually performing on his surroundings. In addition, positive reinforcement techniques are also used to keep the user engaged. This aspect is very important and it is achieved with the assistance of the virtual character, SnowKin, by establishing motivating and pro-environmental dialogues every time the users clean a threat. The virtual character interaction with the users along with the on-screen score gauge are intended to encourage the users to scan their surroundings and complete their tasks without giving up.

One more aspect to take into account is the reward system. When a user finishes cleaning an area he is awarded with a final score and an amount of eVision money (illustrated as green leaves) based on his performance. Afterwards, the user can spend the earned green leaves in the in-game store, buying items that can be used to customize the virtual character, turning it into an avatar that represents all virtual pro-environmental actions and progress performed by the user over time. This is intended to help the user to create an emotional relationship with the personalized eVision mascot and consequently engage the user in the game activities. Therefore, the interaction between the virtual character and the users is a key point on the persuasive design. The longer the user keeps playing the more information about environmental issues can be conveyed to him, improving the results of the persuasive process. Besides what was previous mentioned, the fact that the user puts some amount of work and dedication building the virtual character's appearance will create a "bond" between them, making the user more likely to follow the character's advices and recommendations about the environment.

Even though the user is not actually doing anything "real", he is being induced to adopt better environmental behaviors by being informed about the real impact of the pro-environmental actions while being motivated and rewarded with virtual assets.

Users activities and achievements while using eVision can also be disseminated through social networks (Facebook). This process enables a very powerful type of advertising and persuasion through social networks [2], because people tend to trust or show interest in content generated by those they have accepted as friends.

Fig. 1. User Interaction: (1) Detection, (2) Cleaning, (3) Overlaying of the Environmental Thread

From a more technical standpoint eVision was developed mainly for the Apple's iPhone® giving us the possibility to use and exploit the touch-based gestures, camera, compass, GPS and Wi-Fi capabilities of the device. The implementation can be described essentially in three modules: Main Application (using Objective-C), Image Processing module (using OpenCV) and Information Sharing module (using Facebook API). The detection of environmental threats is achieved as follows: car detection is based on plate detection and recognition through their fundamental features and disposition; airplane detection is based on the contrast of their shape against the sky background; and factories are identified by their geographical position. Other detection methods for other types of environmental threats can also be easily added in the future.

3   General Interfaces

Figure 2 (left) illustrates the eVision's main menu interface where the users can navigate through all the features of the application. The menu Help gives the user an introduction and tutorial about the eVision application. The Scanner menu, as already described, leads the users to where the eVision's core experience takes place. The eShop and SnowKin (Figure 2 - right) menus are related to the customization of the virtual character. The first allows the users to buy items for the character (with the green leaves earned) and the second allows the users to customize the SnowKin with the items already bought. The Statistics menu allows users to keep track on their game progression and access data related to the application. Facebook menu gives the user the possibility to connect and share his information through the social network with the same name.

Fig. 2. eVision: (left) main Menu; (right) SnowKin customization tool

4   Conclusions

eVision is making a contribution to increase people environmental awareness through a fun, immersive and engaging experience. eVision conveys information about environmental threats in the users' surroundings and provides new and amusing ways of interaction, stimulating and driving users to become more aware of environmental sustainability problems, while persuading them to adopt pro-environmental behaviors in favor of a better future.

Future work will include the detection of additional environmental threats as well as the improvement of existing detection methods and algorithms. Finally, eVision will also be capable of connecting to other social networks besides Facebook.

Acknowledgments. This work is funded by Fundação para a Ciência e Tecnologia (FCT/MEC), Portugal, in the scope of project DEAP (PTDC/AAC-AMB/104834/2008) and by CITI/DI/FCT/UNL (PEst-OE/EEI/UI0527/2011).

References

1. World Wildlife Fund 2010. Living Planet Report 2010, http://assets.panda.org/downloads/lpr_summary_booklet_final_feb_2011.pdf (accessed July 5, 2012)
2. Fogg, B.J.: Persuasive Technology: Using Computers to Change What We Think and Do. Morgan Kaufmann, San Francisco (2003)
3. Fogg, B.J.: Mass Interpersonal Persuasion: An Early View of a New Phenomenon. In: Oinas-Kukkonen, H., Hasle, P., Harjumaa, M., Segerståhl, K., Øhrstrøm, P. (eds.) PERSUASIVE 2008. LNCS, vol. 5033, pp. 23–34. Springer, Heidelberg (2008)

flona: Development of an Interface That Implements Lifelike Behaviors to a Plant

Furi Sawaki, Kentaro Yasu, and Masahiko Inami

KEIO University 4-1-1 Hiyoshi, Kohoku-ku, Yokohama 223-8526, Japan
{furi,yasu,inami}@kmd.keio.ac.jp

Abstract. In this paper, we propose the use of a plant as a new interface by superimposing its static lifelike traits such as texture and growth, with dynamic lifelike traits. In order to improve the affinity and to promote smoother communication between a man and a robot, researchers have tried raising lifelike traits by modeling a domestic robot's operation, form, and texture on a living entity. A plant exists as a static entity having features peculiar to living entity such as texture and growth. Although plant is a living entity, it does not have the capability to move on its own unless living entity compelled by external forces. Therefore, in this research, we give lifelike behaviors to the plant by attaching an actuator to it.

Keywords: Plants, interface, lifelike traits.

1 Introduction

Human is capable of acquiring various information from any living entity that he or she comes in contact with, regardless of it being an animal or a plant. For example, the softness and the heartbeat of a dog which is being held, the size of the big tree gazing up upon or even the veins of a leaf may sometimes leave an impression. There has been many researches regarding this 'feeling of vitality felt from a living entity', in other words, 'lifelike traits' done from various angles. However, plants are static living entities. Although plant grows as same as animals, most plants do not have the capability to move. Besides that, a plant has similar texture to human and animal. Therefore, this research aims to generate lifelike behavior in a plant, by implementing animal's dynamic living traits into a plant's static traits.

2 Purpose

In this paper, a lifelike trait with a high rate of a high frequency composition felt in the time-space domain is defined as "dynamic living trait", while a lifelike trait such as texture or growth is defined as "static living trait".

In this research, we give the plant the capability of moving like a robot in order to adapt themselves in human's life. And by superimposing dynamic traits on static

A. Nijholt, T. Romão, and D. Reidsma (Eds.): ACE 2012, LNCS 7624, pp. 557–560, 2012.

living traits in plants, it is possible to materialize a simple implementation of lifelike behavior onto artificial creation. By this research, a new existence, "flona: the plant which moves" will be materialized. It is expected that "flona" will cover the domain which was not able to be realized by domestic robots or home- grown plants, such as a foliage plant.

3   Related Researches

There are two types of related researches regarding this implementation of lifelike traits; one at aiming at presenting dynamic lifelike traits and another aiming at presenting static lifelike traits.

These are examples which gave dynamic lifelike traits to artifacts in the form of imitated plants "Pekoppa" (made by SEGA TOYS CO., LTD.) performs a nod reaction with sufficient timing based on man's utterance sound [1]. Moreover, Kawakami and others researched on robotizing a pot which performs an interaction with man by moving the plant to a place depending on the situation, such as under the sun, or close-by to human [2].

Also there are examples that aiming to present static lifelike traits. By operating a dry flower gently, David Bowen expressed the situation as if the plant was completely swung by a visualized wind [3]. Moreover, There are examples which pursued static lifelike traits which a texture has. Nakata and others showed change of lifelike traits by the difference in a feeling of a texture by showing tactile lifelike traits, and it has described improvement in the feeling of vitality by passing a texture [4].

And as a robot which pursued both dynamic and static lifelike traits, Shibata and others developed seal type mental commitment robot "PARO" [5]. This robot has dynamic lifelike traits of reacting by operation or blink to influence of man. Furthermore, static lifelike traits such as tactile feeling and warmth are also taken into consideration by this robot. Otherwise, "Geminoid" by Ishiguro and others is developed in pursuit of man infinite until it results in a robot's form, operation, or textures [6].

4   Realization Plan

It is shown that dynamic lifelike traits can be obtained by moving an artificial thing like a robot or a toy from precedence research.

On the other hand, it is shown by bringing the texture of the artificial thing close to organic matters, such as man and an animal, that it is also possible to raise static lifelike traits. However, bringing a robot close to a living entity infinite becomes a cause which the uncanny valley phenomenon produces simultaneously. it has too many elements that a robot copies all elements other than operation of a living entity.

Then, in this research, We superimpose dynamic lifelike traits on static lifelike traits which a plant has. As a living entity model for giving dynamic lifelike traits, we decided to copy a motion of the antenna of an insect this time. The reason for having chosen the antenna is that modeling is easy, and an expression of operation is possible at few joints.

5   Imprementation

We describe the concrete implementation technique. At first, it referred to what analyzed operation of the antenna of the stick insect by Andre F. Krause and others [7] as a model of the operation made to show a plant this time. According to Krause and others, the antenna of the stick insect consists of two hinge type joints, and the stick insect is moving the antenna actively in the combination of the motion of these joints [Fig. 1]. According to their analysis, the antenna of a stick insect is operating on the angle and time-axis which are shown in a [Fig. 2].

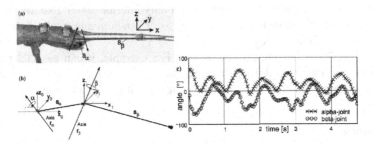

Fig. 1. Construction of a stick insect antenna and conventions for a generic model of an antenna with two hinge joints. (according to reference [7]).

Fig. 2. Joint angles calculated using inverse kinematics. (according to reference [7])

Then, like the antenna of the stick insect made into a model, the string was attached to two places of one plant's branch, and we implemented the mechanism which pulls each by a stepping motor [Fig. 3]. We mapped the motion of the antenna of a stick insect on each of this motor. As the technique of this mapping, we deduced minimum and maximum range of an angle and a time- axis of operation data which Krause and others analyzed, and set up so that operation might occur at random within the limits of this. We prevented a plant repeating the same operation mechanically in conformity with model data by carrying out like this.

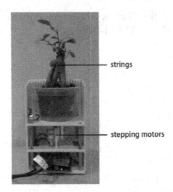

Fig. 3. System overview. the actuators that were attached to the plant.

6   Conclusion ·

In this implementation, we used a plant as an equipment. By this technique, the effect that the robot has so far copied and got operation of an animal does not change. Furthermore, we were able to implement the interface which has lifelike traits without presenting static lifelike traits artificially.

In this paper, we stated the fundamental concept of this research. From now on, we would like to consider definition of lifelike traits and concrete applications. For example, "flona" can becomes a new pet. Because of the reason of healthy, or a domestic situation of them, there are some people who can not keep pets. However they may be able to keep plants. "flona" is not only interior design like foliage plants but also living entity which has lifelike traits. So it can communicate with human by using movement of entire body.

Next, "flona" can becomes a new media. For example, it can be a telepresense robot which transmits the information of man in a remote place. "flona" is suitable for transmitting the information on living entity. Because it has lifelike traits.

References

1. SEGA TOYS CO., LTD. Pekoppa, http://www.segatoys.co.jp/pekoppa/
2. Kawakami, A., Tsukada, K., Kambara, K., Siio, I.: PotPet: Pet-like Flowerpot Robot. In: Proceedings of 5th International Conference on Tangible, Embedded, and Embodied Interaction (TEI 2011), pp. 263–264 (2011)
3. Bowen, D.: Tele-present wind. MIT Press Journals 44(4), 358–359 (2011)
4. Nakata, S., Hashimoto, Y., Kajimoto, H.: The University of Electro-Communications. Qualitative repletion of presentation of the feeling of living matter by presenting tactile sensation (2009)
5. Shibata, F.: The mental commitment robot "PARO"which enriches people's mind (2009), http://www.sonpo.or.jp/archive/publish/bousai/jiho/pdf/no_231/yj23144.pdf
6. Ishiguro, H.: Differences among Android, Geminoid, Human(<Spectal Features> Research on Human Information Processing Using Robotic Media). Information Processing 49(1), 7–14 (2008)
7. Krause, A.F., Dürr, V.: Tactile efficiency of insect antennae with two hinge joints. Biol. Cybern. (2004), doi:10.1007/s00422-004-0490-6©

HOJI*HOJI:
The Hole-Type Interactive Device
for Entertainment

Yuta Suzuki, Yusaku Okada, Hiroki Kawaguchi, Takashi Kimura,
Yoichi Takahashi, Kodai Horita, Takuya Nojima, and Hideki Koike

Graduate School of Information Systems,
The University of Electro-Communications,
1-5-1 Chofugaoka, Chofu, Tokyo, Japan
hojihoji@vogue.is.uec.ac.jp
https://sites.google.com/a/vogue.is.uec.ac.jp/hoji-hoji/home

Abstract. Holes often excite our curiosity and eventually people will
want to look inside them. In this research, focusing the attention on this
"hole exploration" and corresponding actions as an element of interactive
entertainment, we developed a hole-type device named "HOJI*HOJI".
HOJI*HOJI is equipped with a hole that can recognize finger position
through the use of pressure sensors. Force feedback is also implemented
within the device for realizing interaction between the 'hole' and the
user's finger. For proof of concept, an interactive game application was
made for HOJI*HOJI and was exhibited at 2 events to confirm whether
this 'hole' can attract people's curiosity.

Keywords: entertainment system, interactive interface, tactile feedback.

1 Introduction

We, as humans, are naturally curious of the unknown. Upon discovering a door
to the unknown, such as a hole, we are driven to action to discover more about
its contents. We both experience unease as to what is inside the darkness, but
fight this off with our curiosity. This research regards this action as a base
for entertainment that stimulates human curiosity. In order to reproduce the
action, we have developed a hole-type interface which can provide a virtual
"hole picking" experience by realizing interaction between the hole and the user
through feedback to the fingers.

2 Related Work

The example of a system measuring finger motion within a hole and presenting
feedback is The Poking Box [1]. This box type device has a hole which the user
can insert his/her finger in and the motion will be displayed on the front LCD.
The user can then interact with the character on the display with the 'virtual'

A. Nijholt, T. Romão, and D. Reidsma (Eds.): ACE 2012, LNCS 7624, pp. 561–564, 2012.
© Springer-Verlag Berlin Heidelberg 2012

finger displayed on LCD. However, while using this device, one's finger does not touch anything, but may perceive your finger touching the virtual character. But, since this sensation is created by visual information, it is difficult for the device to provide haptic, tactile feedback to the user's finger.

3   System

The system overview and composition of HOJI*HOJI is shown in Figure 1.

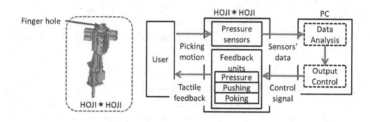

Fig. 1. System overview (left) and composition (right)

3.1   The Sensing Unit

In order to recognize finger motion inside the hole, we developed a sensing unit for HOJI*HOJI. The overview of the unit is shown in Figure 2. The unit is composed by 8 pressure sensors, outer and silicone gel lining. Pressure sensors are arranged in array on four position of inner wall and the gel is used to diffuse the pressure from the finger for efficient pressure detection by the 8 pressure sensors.

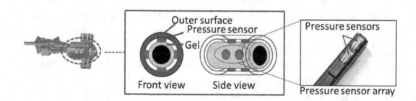

Fig. 2. The sensing unit

3.2   The Feedback Units

For the interaction with the hole, we made 3 Force Feedback units the Pressure unit, Pushing unit, and Poking unit. We describe about these units in this section.

Pressure Unit. The Pressure unit applies pressure to around the inserted finger through the gel. Figure 3 left shows this Pressure unit in action. The unit consists of 8 pressing cells which are each composed of a servomotor and rack gear and these pressing cells are arranged in array between sensor arrays (Figure 3 right). The servomotors used for this were "GWS PICO STD (Grand Wing Servo-Tech Co)".

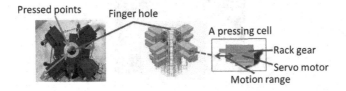

Fig. 3. Pressure unit

Pushing Unit. This unit provides impact to the tip of a finger from the bottom of the hole reproducing the feeling that something exists within the hole by pushing back giving deeper expression of the 'depth' of the hole. Much like the Pressure unit, this unit is created by a rack gear and a servomotor (Figure 4), however the servomotor used for this unit is a "HS-322HD (Phidgets Co)".

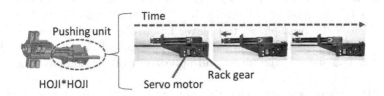

Fig. 4. Pushing unit

Poking Unit. This unit reproduces a feeling that something is prodding or attacking the finger from within the hole. This unit consists of a solenoid "S-05S03PUSH (SHINDENGEN MECHATRONICS CO., LTD)" and installed on the Pushing unit as shown in Figure 5.

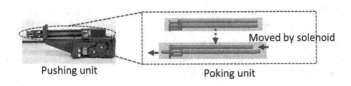

Fig. 5. Poking unit

3.3   Application

The application we made is an interactive game called "Tree Stump Insect Hunter (Figure 6)". The purpose of this game is dig out an insect by picking the hole of the stump.

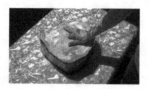

Fig. 6. Overview of the application

This game has 3 phases. The 1st phase is named "Hole Excavation". In the beginning of the game, since the hole of the stump is too narrow to put a finger into it, player has to widen the hole by expanding the inside wall of the hole to access the deeper areas. The "narrow hole" effect is produced by the Pressure units. The 2nd phase "Insect Nest" is begins once the hole has been excavated. In the depths of this hole, there is a nest of insects and player can literally 'feel' these insects with his/her finger remains in the hole. These sensations are reproduced by the Pushing unit and the Pokint unit collectively. In the 3rd phase, which is the final phase, the player has to dig out the insect from the hole by picking at the hole while withstanding attacks from the insect. When the hunting is a success, the insect will appear out of the hole and the player wins.

HOJI*HOJI was exhibited with this application at 2 events. One is the International Virtual Reality Contest (IVRC), and the other is Digital Contents Expo (DCExpo). During these events, many people showed interest while experiencing HOJI*HOJI. Considering this fact, we can say it was confirmed that, as intended, a hole can attract people's curiosity.

3.4   Conclusion

In this paper, we described a hole-type device "HOJI*HOJI" which can provide virtual hole picking experience using finger position sensing and force feedback to respond to finger movement. Additionally, an application for HOJI*HOJI was developed in the form of Insect Hunting and was exhibited at 2 events. Through these events, we confirmed that a hole might certainly attract interest and then provide an interesting, exciting experience.

Reference

1. Poking Box, http://www.asovision.com/tuttuki/about.html

t-words: Playing with Sounds and Creating Narratives

Cristina Sylla[1], Sérgio Gonçalves[1], Pedro Branco[2], and Clara Coutinho[1]

[1] engageLab/CIEd, University of Minho, Braga/Guimarães, Portugal
{sylla,sgoncalves}@engagelab.org, ccoutinho@ie.uminho.pt
[2] engageLab/Dep. of Information Systems, University of Minho, Guimarães, Portugal
pbranco@dsi.uminho.pt

Abstract. We present t-words an interface for children to playful explore sounds, words and sentences while developing pre-literate skills. The interface consists of rectangular blocks in which children can record and then play the recorded audio. Additionally children can personalize the blocks by drawing on their surface. Children can engage in different literacy related activities such as building rhymes, playing with sounds and words as well as trying out different combinations of sentences while engaging in storytelling. Since the interface targets audio skills it may foster the development of phonological awareness and sensitiveness, helping to promote children's early literacy.

Keywords: Tangible Interfaces, Story Listening System, Storytelling, Children, Emergent Literacy, Phonological Awareness.

1 Introduction

Emergent literacy, a term first coined by Clay [3] sees reading and writing as a continuous process that begins in the early years of childhood, through children's exposure to environments where literacy is present. This means that children have contact with books, for instance through shared reading, listening to and telling stories, or by engaging in language games. *Emergent literacy* consists of the skills that lead to the development of reading and writing. From this perspective, reading, writing and language development are developmental processes that are intertwined with each other. *Inside-out and inside-in skills* [7] are two domains of *emergent literacy*. *Inside-out skills* refer to phonological awareness, and letter knowledge, it presupposes the ability to map letters to sounds and sounds to words. *Outside-in skills* refer to the knowledge of the narrative's conceptual and semantic context, which implies knowing the words that are used and the context in which the narrative takes place. Studies suggest that reading in the 1st and 2nd grades is strongly determined by the *inside-out skills* that children have acquired at the end of pre-school [7].

2 Background

The idea behind t-words was to develop an interface where children can playful engage with sounds and words, that can be used to deepen young children's

A. Nijholt, T. Romão, and D. Reidsma (Eds.): ACE 2012, LNCS 7624, pp. 565–568, 2012.

phonological awareness and sensitivity, promoting the acquisition of new vocabulary and ultimately develop their early literacy skills. Additionally the interface should encourage collaborative work and team spirit, as well as promote exchange of experiences and knowledge. There are numerous systems where children can play with language elements, while engaging as story authors [1,4,5,6]. t-words positions itself in between TellTale [1] and the Siftables [4]: each piece can record audio and be written and drawn on the surface and all the pieces can be connected together to playback the recorded sounds, furthermore t-words has no screen or need of a computer, thus facilitating digital inclusion in contexts with less technological infrastructures.

3   The Interface

The t-words interface comprises a set of different sized blocks capable of recording and playing sounds, words or sentences. The blocks can either have the same or different sizes. Children can customize the blocks with their drawings, which can be drawn on top of the blocks' surface. Each block has a recorder embedded except the player-block, which has a player instead (Fig.1). Every block has a button to start and stop recording and a light bar that gives the user information about the recording and playback sound level.

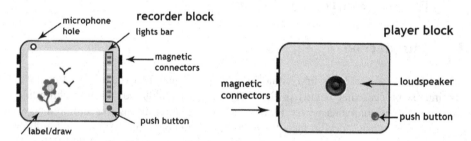

Fig. 1. Recorder-block (left), player-block (right)

The player-block has a loudspeaker, and an electronic system that gathers information from the recorder-blocks. The communication between the blocks happens through magnetic connectors, which allows building a well-aligned sequence of recorder-blocks and player and simultaneous permits the electrical communication between them (sending/receiving data signals as well as power supply). Children can record audio in one or more blocks depending on the proposed activities. To play the recorded audio children snap the player-block to the block or block sequence in which they have recorded the audio. In case the audio is recorded in more than one block, the recorded blocks have to be snapped together with the player-block at the end (Fig.2).

Fig. 2. Sequence with recorder-blocks and a player-block

3.1 Technical Description

The recorder has an embedded microphone, which is connected to a microcontroller through an analog-to-digital converter (Fig.3 left). The microcontroller is an Arduino [2] compatible very small and low power microprocessor. A flash memory, which is connected to the microcontroller, is used to store the recorded audio in digital format. A touch button triggers the start and stop of recording. When switched in the playing mode, the different microprocessors from the different recorders must detect the order in which they are arranged, to identify the first one, as well as the order of the whole sequence, to send their respective data to the player. Each recorder is power supplied by a small rechargeable battery that charges automatically when connected to the player.

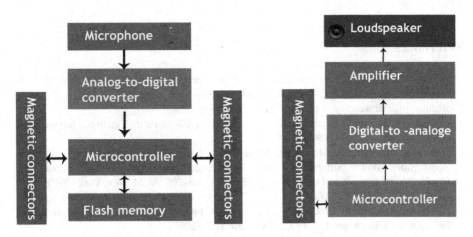

Fig. 3. Diagram of a recorder block (left) and of a player -block (right)

The player has a microcontroller that receives the audio in digital format from the recorders, and then sends it to a loudspeaker through a digital-to-analog converter and a sound amplifier (Fig.3 right). The audio data is requested from the recorders as needed. The player's power is supplied by a set of non-rechargeable batteries, capable of supplying the entire system. The communication protocol is serial-based allowing pieces to connect to each other, through magnetic connectors. Among a subgroup of pieces there is always just a single masterpiece, the remaining others are slaves, the master's function is to retain the information about the relative order by which the pieces are connected. When the player is added, it automatically becomes the master and manages the entire row, requesting the necessary data from the corresponding recorders. The blocks can be arranged and rearranged so that children can playful engage in trying out different possibilities.

4   Conclusions

Teachers can use t-words to propose a wide range of activities that can help children to foster early literacy and language development through improvement of phonological sensitiveness, and creatively engaging in storytelling. They may create rhymes that match a certain word; record words or sentences about a certain subject, or create a narrative. Additionally the design of the interface encourages children's collaboration, as they have to handle the best way of bringing the different blocks together.

Acknowledgements. This work is funded by FEDER through the Operational Competitiveness Factors Program - COMPETE and by National Funds through the FCT – Portuguese Foundation for the Science and the Technology within the Project: PTDC/CPE-CED   /110417/2009, and the Doctoral Grant: SFRH /BD / 62531 / 2009.

References

1. Ananny, M.: Telling Tales: A new toy for encouraging written literacy through oral storytelling. In: Society for Research in Child Development, Minneapolis (2001)
2. Arduino official web site, http://www.arduino.cc/
3. Clay, M.M.: Emergent Reading Behavior. Unpublished doctoral dissertation, University of Auckland, New Zeland (1996)
4. Hunter, S., Kalanithi, J., Merrill, D.: Make a Riddle and TeleStory: Designing Children's Applications for the Siftables Platform. In: Proceedings of the 9th IDC International Conference on Interaction Design and Children, pp. 206–209. ACM, New York (2010)
5. Raffle, H., Vaucelle, C., Wang, R., Ishii, H.: Jabberstamp: embedding sound and voice in traditional drawings. In: Proceedings of the 6th IDC International Conference on Interaction Design and Children, pp. 137–144. ACM, New York (2007)
6. Sylla, C., Gonçalves, S., Brito, P., Branco, P., Coutinho, C.: t-books - Merging Traditional Storybooks With Electronics. In: Proceedings of the 11th IDC International Conference on Interaction Design and Children, pp. 323–326. ACM, New York (2012)
7. Whitehurst, G.J., Lonigan, C.J.: Child Development and Emergent Literacy. Child Development 69(3), 848–872 (1998)

Semi-transparent Augmented Reality System

Tomoya Tachikawa[1], Takenori Hara[1], Chiho Toyono[1], Goro Motai[1], Karin Iwazaki[2],
Keisuke Shuto[2], Hiroko Uchiyama[2], and Sakuji Yoshimura[3]

[1] Dai Nippon Printing Co., Ltd, Tokyo, Japan
Tachikawa-T3@mail.dnp.co.jp
[2] Joshibi University of Art and Design, Tokyo, Japan
[3] Waseda University, Tokyo, Japan

Abstract. We have developed a new Semi-Transparent Augmented Reality
(AR) system that displays the inner structures of objects by making their surface semi-transparent. In this system we combine the live video of the object of
interest and 3D computer graphics (3DCG) models with appropriate transparency and in proper order using AR technology. This system shows the 3DCG
models of inner structures as if they existed inside the object.

Keywords: AR, Transparency, Exhibition.

1 Introduction

We have developed a new Semi-Transparent Augmented Reality (AR) system that
shows three-dimensional inner structures of objects by making their surface semi-
transparent. When the user points the camera of a mobile device which is part of the
developed system, toward the object, he/she can interactively see 3D computer graphics (3DCG) models of inner structures of the object (Fig. 1).

Fig. 1. Semi-Transparent Augmented Reality System

A. Nijholt, T. Romão, and D. Reidsma (Eds.): ACE 2012, LNCS 7624, pp. 569–572, 2012.

2   Research Background and Feature

2.1   Research Background

Nowadays, AR technology is used in various fields. Most systems based on this technology show 3DCG in front of the target objects on live videos. On the other hand, there are AR systems that can see through the target object and show background images. Examples are the AR X-ray system [1] and the Optical Camouflage system [2]. These systems make part or the whole of target objects (for example, a wall) transparent and show live images behind them. These systems cannot show the inside of target objects, and they are not suitable for showing inner structures intelligibly. Therefore, we developed a system that shows inner structures of the target object intelligibly with the aid of 3DCG by making the outer surface of the target object semi-transparent.

2.2   Research Feature

The developed system shows three-dimensional inner structures through the semi-transparent outer surface of the target object. In the system, the target object is regarded as a cavity box and its inner structures are displayed with the aid of 3DCG models. By combining models with appropriate transparency and in proper order with live video from the camera, this system shows the inner structures as if they existed inside the target objects. We use a marker-based AR technology to estimate the camera position and suitably position 3DCG models on target objects.

3   Description

3.1   System Overview

The proposed system consists of an AR system and 3DCG models. We used the Samsung Galaxy Tab with the Android 2.3.3 operating system.

AR System. We used a marker-based AR system to estimate the position of the camera from the target object and to show 3DCG models at proper positions. This time we used Vuforia (Qualcomm) [3]. We put a marker just beside the target object to align the positions of 3DCG models and live video from the camera.

3D Computer Graphics Models. To display the inner structure through the outer surface of the target object, we combine three types of 3DCG models. One is an outer surface model. This has the shape of the target object and a semi-transparent texture, and it is copied from part of the live video. Another type of model is an inner structure model. The third one is a backplane model. As we regard the target object as a cavity box, this model represents the shape of the target object, but with only the backplanes of the surface by using front-face culling. To show these models in the AR system, we use Unity[4] as the real-time 3DCG rendering engine.

Description of System Behavior. First, this system recognizes the marker beside the target object and estimates the pose and position of the target from the camera. It then shows the backplane model over the target on the live video. Subsequently, the inner structure model is placed on the model. Finally, the semi-transparent outer surface model is shown above these models. When the user sees these models shown on the mobile device and changes his/her viewing position, he/she can perceive the relative movement of each element, and the inner structures are seen as if they existed inside the target object.

Application. We are currently exhibiting an AR guidance system at "Sakuji Yoshimura's Seven Ancient Civilizations Exhibition." which is being held in Japan since June 2011[5]. We superimposed real-time 3DCG explanatory content (for example, an excavated and restored model of the Solar Boat) in front of a precise 1:100-scale diorama of the Pyramid of Khufu (Fig. 2). We combined the proposed system and the AR guidance system to improve the latter system.

Fig. 2. 1:100 scale diorama of a pyramid

Description of Contents. During this exhibition, we performed a few user surveys. We found that many users like to know how the inside of the pyramid looks. This is the reason why we developed the system to describe the inner structure of the pyramid three-dimensionally. To obtain the 3D inner structure of the pyramid, we prepared three computer graphics models of the pyramid. One was an outer surface model of the pyramid shape (left-hand-side figure in Fig. 3) as an inner structure model, which represented the corridors and chambers precisely (middle figure in Fig. 3). The third model was a backplane model (right-hand-side figure in Fig. 3). We then combined these models with appropriate transparency and in proper order with live video, as described in section 3.2. The user could see the inner structures as if they existed inside the pyramid (Fig. 4).

Fig. 3. 3DCG models of the pyramid

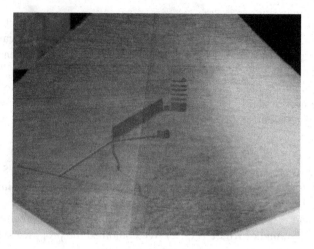

Fig. 4. Resulting image

4   Conclusion

In this paper, we have proposed a new method for displaying the inner structure of an object intelligibly through the semi-transparent outer surface. This method will be used to make our interactive exhibits more intelligible in future exhibitions. We can also apply this system at historic sites. For example, using this system, we can see a mummy lying in a coffin in a grave from outside. Usually, archaeological excavation causes physical and chemical degradation of treasure troves. Therefore, non-destructive examination methods are needed, such as those involving the use of a ground-penetrating radar or X-ray camera. In addition, non-invasive observation methods are also needed. We can construct a non-invasive observation system by using our method and visualize data obtained by non-destructive examination methods. This system can be effectively used for observation at the sites like World Heritage since it is conducive to maintaining the sites in a good state.

References

1. Sandor, C., et al.: An Augmented Reality X-Ray System Based on Visual Saliency. In: Proceedings of IEEE International Symposium on Mixed and Augmented Reality, Seoul, Korea (October 2010)
2. Kawakami, N., et al.: Study for the Reality Fusion(II) -The Design and Implementation of optical camouflage. In: Proceedings of Annual Conference of the Virtual Reality Society of Japan, vol. 3 (1998)
3. Vuforia, http://www.qualcomm.com/solutions/augmented-reality
4. Unity, http://unity3d.com/
5. Yoshimura, S.: Seven Ancient Civilizations Exhibition, http://www.egypt.co.jp/

Awareness Support for Remote Music Performance

Hiroyuki Tarumi, Keiichi Akazawa, Masaki Ono, Erina Kagawa,
Toshihiro Hayashi, and Rihito Yaegashi

Kagawa University, Takamatsu, Kagawa 761-0396, Japan
tarumi@acm.org

Abstract. Internet live streaming services are now popular. Music live performances are one of the best contents for live streaming. However, remote audience cannot enjoy the performance as well as local audience due to the lack of mutual awareness. In this paper, we define some challenging problems with streaming services for music live performances, and give a basic system design towards solving the problems.

Keywords: music performance, live streaming, awareness.

1   Introduction

Internet streaming of live entertainment activities like sports and music performances is now popular. UStream or NICO NICO LIVE are examples of well-known streaming services.

However, streaming services are almost one-way communication. Audience can simply send texts to the performers, but they can hardly read them during the performance. This means that two-way communication between the performer and remote audiences is very poor. Moreover, remote audiences cannot feel the atmosphere of the live venue well. In other words, only poor awareness is given between remote audiences and performers or audiences at the live venue.

Awareness was first defined in the context of cooperative work[1], but later it has been extended to refer to non-verbal and implicit (and often unconscious) communication in any contexts.

We are trying to design a system to support internet streaming of entertaining performances by giving more mutual awareness (i.e., two-way communication). We have already defined problems and shown a design and evaluation of a system for sports entertainment[2]. In this paper, we will define problems and show a concept design to support streaming services for music performances.

2   Problem Analysis

2.1   Modeling

Figure 1 illustrates a model structure of communication in case of music performances with live streaming services. Here, *in-house audiences* refer to the audiences in the live venue like live houses or concert halls. Performers and in-house

A. Nijholt, T. Romão, and D. Reidsma (Eds.): ACE 2012, LNCS 7624, pp. 573–576, 2012.
© Springer-Verlag Berlin Heidelberg 2012

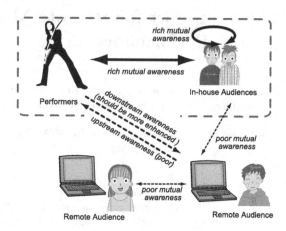

Fig. 1. Communication structure between performers and audiences

audiences already have rich mutual awareness. *Remote audiences*, however, cannot enjoy rich two-way communication with performers or in-house audiences. They do not have mutual awareness with each other, either. From performers to remote audiences, one-way communication by means of the streaming service itself is given, but it is not so rich as the case of in-house audiences.

The model given in Figure 1 suggests that we have many problems to solve. Here we focus on the problem of supporting upstream communication from remote audiences to performers.

2.2   Analysis

The problem analysis has been conducted informally, based on the experiences of the first author. He visited and observed 258 live music events from January 2008 to August 2012, covering various genres including popular, rock, jazz, and ethnic music. They were mostly in Japan, but experiences in USA, Italy, Hong Kong, Taiwan, and Thailand are also included.

The style of communication between in-house audiences and performers differs depending on the genre of music, and even depending on individual musicians or bands. Mutual communication between performers and in-house audiences is most active in case of popular and rock music. Thus we focus on them.

In case of these styles of music, performers are not only playing music, but also trying to communicate with the audience by body actions, face expressions, and even gazing or glances. Performers often request audiences to react to the music or to the body actions taken by the performers.

Forms of the reactions by audiences vary depending on local cultures of the community of each artist's fans. However, typical patterns of reactions are common to most fan communities. They are shown in Table 1. These reactions are observed during the play of music. Reactions observed between songs are omitted here.

Table 1. Typical reactions from in-house audiences to performers

Reaction type	Description
voice action	To say a short word (e.g. "Yeah!", "Oi!") or sing short phrases of the song altogether.
hand waiving	To lift a hand and wave it left and right with an open palm that is shown to the performer, synchronized with the rhythm of the music.
hand clapping	To clap hands synchronized with the rhythm.
hand joggling	To lift a hand and joggle it, without moving one's arm widely. The shape of the hand is probably — (1) a fist but only one finger (often the index finger) is stretched, or (2) a relaxed open palm that.
push up	To push up (and down) one's hand synchronized with the music. The shape of the hand is probably (1) a fist, or (2) a relaxed open palm that is faced to the ceiling.
towel swinging	To swing a towel (like a helicopter's propeller) above one's head.

These reactions have effects to performers and also to other audiences. To performers, the reactions encourage the performer; to other audience, they generate a sense of unity among audiences.

Therefore, designing a system that can transmit reactions shown in Table 1 from remote audiences to performers (and in-house audiences) will be a solution of the upstream awareness problem we have shown in section 2.1.

3 Design

Our design policy is not to send reactions of remote audiences as audio/video data, but to symbolize reactions. One of the reasons of symbolization is, of course, to reduce the bandwidth and computer power required to transmit data from (possibly) hundreds of remote sites and process them. Another reason is the delay of downward/upward communication. We cannot avoid the communication delay in case of internet streaming. Most of the reactions are taken synchronized with the music. If the reactions are treated as audio/video data, they will never be synchronized with the music. Hence we symbolize the reactions by remote listeners, let the server at the performers' side receive them, and show them to the performers (and/or in-house audiences) by animation synchronized with the music. At the remote side, reactions are detected by using $Kinect^{TM}$ or simply by mouse. Currently, voice actions are excluded from the implementation.

At the performers' side, the collected reactions should be shown to the performers. A basic policy for this design is not to disturb or badly affect the live performance itself. We should respect the in-house audiences, performers, and stage staffs including the lightning and sound technicians. Our current design is to use a LCD display without sound.

Another important design decision at the performers' side is how to represent reactions from many remote audiences and how to identify (or not to identify) each remote audience. We have several design candidates for the data aggregation and representation of reactions. Due to the space limit, we do not describe each design, in this paper. They should be evaluated by real musicians and audiences in future.

4 Conclusion

In this paper, we have given a model of communication structure in case of a music event that is also on live streaming services, defined problems to enhance the quality of such communication, and also given an analysis on the reaction taken by audiences of music live events. Based on the analysis, we have given a basic design policy of a system that will provide functions to send reactions by remote audiences to performers. Currently we are implementing a system, which will be evaluated by real events in future.

Known related work includes a system to collect body actions from remote audiences and overlay them onto a stored shared video by skeleton images[3] and a machine to mechanically reproduce hand clapping by remote audiences[4].

According to the communication model in Figure 1, we still have many derived problems, including communication between remote audiences, enhanced communication from performers to remote fans, enhanced communication between in-house audiences, and enhanced communication between performers and in-house audiences. Designs of solution will vary depending on type of music. Even in cases of jazz or classic music, with which body actions are less active, we can expect some system designs to enhance mutual awareness. We have quite a lot of future work.

Acknowledgments. This research was partially supported by KAKENHI (22500109).

References

1. Schmidt, K.: The problem with 'awareness'. Computer Supported Cooperative Work 11-3, 285–298 (2002)
2. Izumi, T., et al.: An Experimental Live Streaming for an Ice Hockey Game with Enhancement of Mutual Awareness. In: Proceedings of Collabtech 2012, IPSJ (2012)
3. Yoshida, A., Miyashita, H.: Video Sharing System that Overlays Body Movement for the Sense of Unity. In: Proceedings of Interaction 2012, IPSJ, pp. 527–532 (2012) (in Japanese)
4. Takahashi, M., et al.: Remote Hand Clapping Transmission Using Hand Clapping Machines on Live Video Streaming. In: Proceedings of Entertainment Computing 2011, IPSJ, 06A–06 (2011) (in Japanese)

GENIE: Photo-Based Interface for Many Heterogeneous LED Lamps

Jordan Tewell[1], Sunao Hashimoto[1], Masahiko Inami[1,2], and Takeo Igarashi[1,3]

[1] JST ERATO, Tokyo, Japan
{jordan,hashimoto,inami,takeo}@designinterface.jp
[2] Graduate School of Media Design, Keio University, Yokohama, Japan
[3] Computer Science Department, The University of Tokyo, Tokyo, Japan

Abstract. We present an interface to allow for easy selection and creative control of color changing lamp fixtures in the home, using the analogy of taking a snapshot to select them. The user is presented with a GUI on their mobile phone to control light attributes such as color, brightness, and scheduling and is provided a means to specify a group of lights to be controlled at once. This is achieved using an IR filter switcher on the phone to capture IR blobs pulsating from inside the lamps and uses a central server to communicate between the two. The system can operate under normal, indoor lighting conditions and is concealed inside the lamps without any need to place fiducials or other obscuring means of identification in the environment.

Keywords: Infrared, lighting control, mobile, LED, photo-based interface.

1 Introduction

We expect contemporary lighting technology, such as incandescent and fluorescent fixtures, to be obsolete within the next decade. LED lighting will be used solely for everyday illumination due to decreased power consumption and the creative possibilities of changing the color. Dozens, and even hundreds of lights could be embedded seamlessly in the environment, as seen the experimental Vos Pad complex [1]. However, using such standard lighting controls such as light switches will be inadequate due to the sheer number of controls to select from.

We propose a system where a user can group control of the lights themselves by taking a photo of them. Since the user might unintentionally capture lights they didn't want to change, we provide them the ability to disable lights in the shot by overlaying controls over the photo. The user is then free to modify all the lighting attributes that LED technology provides, in addition to additional functionally for scheduling power. We achieved this by constructing three components. First we built an accessory for the mobile phone to allow IR optical communication. Next, we fabricated special light control modules in each of our lamps to identify them. We then wrote a server that mediates data between the two.

A. Nijholt, T. Romão, and D. Reidsma (Eds.): ACE 2012, LNCS 7624, pp. 577–580, 2012.

2   Previous Work

There have been a great number of proposals in lighting system design research. The most promising we found is suggested in [2] where a remote senses the light contribution from an above ceiling array by embedding a light ID within the LED's PWM wave. However, this is not a heterogeneous system. Commercially, there are a number of multicolor LED bulbs available that are controlled with an IR remote. However, we found the interface of these remotes difficult to understand immediately. Also the spread of the IR beam inadvertently changes lights that in close proximity to one another. Philips offers their Living Colors brand of color changing mood lamps [3] which are controllable by Wifi remote, and multiple lights can be linked together to control at once. For individual control, however, a user must select lights via left and right arrow buttons on the remote control.

3   User Interface

To achieve selection of our lights, we use the photo-based paradigm suggested in [4] where a user points a camera at the environment and takes a picture to obtain and modify the embedded information. Since people are comfortable taking pictures with their smart phone, we decided to build our system as an app for the Android platform. Furthermore, we choose to create an interface look and feel that best replicates a camera app so it would be more familiar to users.

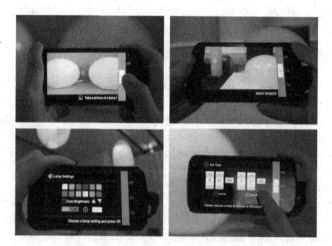

Fig. 1. Upper *Left*, user aims and takes snapshot. *Upper Right*, grouping lights in the photo. *Lower Left*, user changes light attributes. *Lower Right*, power scheduling (optional).

The breakdown of the interface is shown in Figure 1. The user is first presented with a familiar preview screen with the camera cross-hair in the center, a snapshot button, and some simple textual directions. If the snapshot is successful, and depending on how many lights they took a picture of, the user either progresses to modify the light, or they will see a light grouping selection screen. If no lights are detected, a dialogue pop-up is displayed to inform the user that they should try again.

Should the user select more than one light, they will be presented with the photo along with targets overlayed on top of the light sources. They can select which lights to change at once by toggling the targets and then press the OK button to proceed to change the group. By default, all lights are selected as the system assumes the user wanted to change all the lights, but the screen serves as a way to affirm the user of their action. It can also be accessed again if the user presses the android's back button to return to select another light source(s) instead of having to take another snapshot again.

A screen for changing the light appearance then appears. The colors can be changed by tapping on their respective button in the color pallet table. Below it are arrows the user can press and hold for changing brightness and a check box for resetting the brightness back to full. The last line of options are the power switch, a clock button for scheduling time, and the OK button to return to take a new snapshot. Scheduling takes place on another screen, and the user can specify the time range for when the light(s) should turn on and off, as well as whether each should occur daily or not.

4   Implementation

An attachable filter switcher equipped with an IR filter was mounted to an android cover. This accessory is compatible with any Android 4.0 device with an available mini USB. When the user takes a snapshot, the filter switcher closes in front of the phone's back camera, blocking all visible light. Any IR source within the camera's viewing frustum is detected and is analyzed using a blob detection algorithm optimized for monochromatic images. The detection is adjusted to eliminate the camera noise, and the exposure compensation is also changed during the IR capture state to ignore weak sources of IR radiation in the environment which can interfere with our detection. Using a lamp shade effectively blocks the radiation emitted from LED bulbs, but not as well for non-LED bulbs, so using other types of fixtures is not recommended with this system.

The android connects to a server using a standard wireless TCP connection. The server uses an Xbee to communicate with each light module independently. Once a light source(s) are selected, the server only commands to those lights in the XBee's network. The server communicates both ways to insure synchronicity between the pulses and the capture.

Five 5-watt IR controllable LED bulbs were installed in three different types of lamps: two table lamps, one floor lamp, and two ceiling-hung lamps. Installed in each lamp is a module consisting of a controller attached to its own XBee and two IR LED array outputs. The small array of IR lights is use to command the light bulb using deciphered IR codes obtained from the remote control packaged with the bulb. The other, larger array of IR LEDs are used to pulse the ID of the light source on and off.

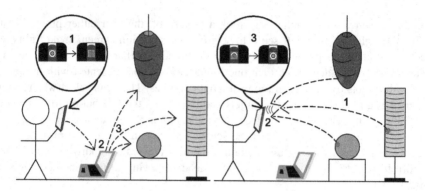

Fig. 2. Left, the IR filter switcher on the android closes to capture IR light in the environment (1); the android sends the pulsing command to the server (2); the server subsequently sends a pulsing command to all light modules in its network (3). *Right*, the lamp IR LED emitters pulse (1); the android camera senses IR contributions over a small period of time (2), and then opens the IR switcher after the pulses are completed to allow normal viewing again (3).

Each light is given an unique ID which is binary encoded to minimize the time needed to identify all the lights in the network. The IR arrays are pulsed together once in the beginning to identify where the lights are in the image before pulsing their codes.

Figure 2 shows this whole process. By processing multiple codes in parallel, we can achieve fast enough recognition so that the user is presented with the interface as soon as the filter switcher shuts off. This however, is not an instantaneous process: we must account for the time needed to complete the mechanical motion of the switcher as well as the change in exposure from normal camera viewing to the IR capture state, and then the time held by each pulse needed to uniquely identify all n light sources accurately.

5   Future Work

We could eliminate the need for a server and instead choose to install a XBee directly on our phone accessory. Also, we could fabricate a special bulb socket that would integrate our light modules to allow for easy installation for the lamps.

References

1. Vos Pad, http://www.vosled.com/projects
2. Linnartz, J.-P.M.G., Feri, L., Yang, H., Colak, S.B., Schenk, T.C.W.: Code division-based sensing of illumination contributions in solid-state lighting systems. IEEE Transactions on Signal Processing, 3984–3998 (October 2009)
3. Philips Living Colors, http://www.livingambiance.philips.com
4. Aoki, S., Iwanmoto, T., Koda, T., Maruyama, D., Suzuki, G., Takashio, K., Tokuda, H.: u-Photo tools: photo-based application framework for controlling networked appliances and sensors. In: UbiComp, Demonstration Session, Nottingham, England, NA–NA (September 2004)

Disaster Experience Game in a Real World

Sachi Urano, Peichao Yu, and Junichi Hoshino

University of Tsukuba
3M309, 1-1-1 Tennodai, Tsukuba
Ibaraki Japan, 305-8573
me@sachiurano.jp, s1020918@u.tsukuba.ac.jp,
jhoshino@esys.tsukuba.ac.jp

Abstract. We present a new game system that provides both general knowledge and regionally specific disaster risks in a fun and interesting way. Users can experience disaster simulations on the go, as the game system detects the user's position and movement using available GPS and acceleration sensors found in most current Smartphones. This application is intended to increase the user's knowledge and understanding of disaster risks while maintaining the user's motivation to continue playing and learning.

An assessment experiment of the game was clearly beneficial to understand Risk Perception and support the user's motivation of a muster drill.

Keywords: Disaster, Smartphone, Risk Recognition.

1 Introduction

On March 11 2011, a wide area of northeastern Japan was hit by one of the biggest earthquakes ever recorded. According to the Tokyo Metropolitan Police Department, 15,833 people were killed, 5,943 people were injured, 3,671 people went missing and more than 30,000 houses were fully or partially destroyed. Also, according to a variety of sources, within the next 30 years the possibility of a 7.0 magnitude earthquake in the southern Kanto region is as high as 70%; it was predicted that an earthquake of such magnitude might kill 5,600 people and injure 150,000 more. Given the great potential human cost, disaster prevention is essential [1], [2]; preparing, planning, and mapping out a response to a disaster is necessary to ensure safety and survival.

The recognition of risks in a possible disaster situation is known as "Risk Perception." Appropriate decision-making and behavioral judgment are needed, but this is not common knowledge since disaster situations do not occur frequently. Public Schools conduct evacuation drills to practice appropriate disaster response behaviors, but it is difficult to determine an escape route because participants are following instructions, not their instincts. Meanwhile, there are training lectures which teach effective decision-making skills using disaster maps and illustrations. In a manner this is an effective training method involving Risk Perception, but it has some feasibility problems to be a nationwide program because it requires many instructors with the necessary expertise and experience. It is also quite difficult to apply regionally specific Risk Perception into action.

A. Nijholt, T. Romão, and D. Reidsma (Eds.): ACE 2012, LNCS 7624, pp. 581–584, 2012.

In this paper, we propose a disaster experience game system which instructs the user about general knowledge and regionally specific disaster risks. Our system lead to recognize regionally specific risk and experience with a disaster with user's own two feet. Disaster drills are often messy and unorganized [3], but through frequent disaster drill performing, we were able to introduce a game concept that makes these drills feel a bit more fun.

2   Associated Research

An evacuation simulation tool using the Potential Model [4], "Tangible All Disaster Scenario and Simulator[6]" and a diorama [6] propose new visual-simulation systems and interfaces to enhance both Risk Perception and accuracy of predictions, but do not consider behavior and decision-making. On the other hand "Disaster Risk Finder"[7] and Komatta-Kun [8] are taken into account as well such as having a mask over the eyes, bound arms, or having to leap over objects. These disaster drills are made from typical case examples by instructors with expertise, however a real feature's disaster drill is difficult to be used world wide.

3   Disaster Experience Game System

In the system, the current location and genesis location are fixed by coordinates of longitude and latitude (Place), and display the disaster situation using images and text (Context). User's instructional information is identified by the situation (Handling), and events executed by the user are evaluated and recorded, according to **Table 1**(Reward). This evaluation is displayed graphically at the end of each game. We assume all users exist in the same world, so all the events influence each other; If the bridge is broken in someone's event, the bridge shouldn't be crossable in another user's event (Causality).

Table 1. Event evaluation items

Knowledge	Have an appropriate coping technique. e.c.How to help a person with significant hemorrhage.
Judgment	Realize and decide an decision. e.c. If the bridge broken, whether or not to across it.
Action	Move into action against the problem e.c. whether you are acting fast or slow.

There are 4 types of handling that appear in Fig. 1: choosing from selection border, touching the right place on display, entering characters, and taking necessary actions: action event, touch event, typing event and selection border event, respectively.

We developed the DEG system using the processes described in section 3. The game consists of 7 scenes as shown in Fig. 2.

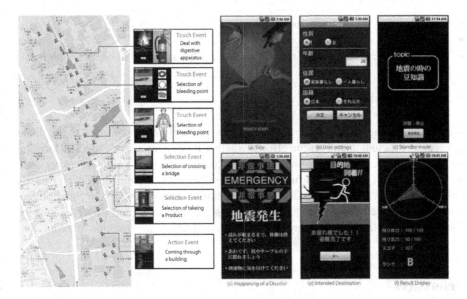

Fig. 1. List of event category   **Fig. 2.** Screenshot of application

After the Disaster event begins, the user's location is detected by GPS and the system can confirm whether the user has arrived at their final destination. If user has not yet arrived, it compares the distance between the user and each event of origin registered in the Event Database. If this distance is below a certain value, it generates an event, and if it exceeds a certain value, the user's location is required. It runs over and over again until the user arrives at the destination. To enhance the user's motivation and also to provide a feeling of tension, we introduced game over functionality if the user could not meet the necessary criteria.

4   Assessment Experiment

By using this disaster experience game, whether the user can understand risks by imaging a disaster situation and whether the user (men: 10, women: 1) can keep the fun on this game still need to be explored and we obtained following statement.

- I want to play it via a different route.
- The event of finding someone on the ground comes up too often.
- I felt like I was just walking.
- It was fun because I could move.
- I was demoralized because I am pretty new to using Android.
- It might be more fun with graphic depictions of the injured or sounds of breaking glass.
- Binding may be needed in order to feel more tension.
- The destination was difficult to find.

- I want to orient myself geographically.
- I want to play with a large group.
- If the same event happened a number of times, I became used to dealing with it.

5   Conclusion

We present a fun game system which offers precautionary measures to facilitate emergency evacuation and rescue efforts, whether it involves a user's specific location within a small area or a larger one, such as a particular region. A user can experience the simulation of a disaster while walking, as the game system detects the user's position and movement using GPS and acceleration sensors inside the Smartphone. The game-application seeks to increase the user's knowledge and understanding of disaster risks while maintaining the user's motivation to continue playing and learning.

References

1. Bureau of Development Tokyo Metropolitan Govenment: religious danger measurement survey in disaster, http://www.toshiseibi.metro.tokyo.jp/bosai/chousa_6/home.html
2. Tokyo Metropolitan Government: heavy damage report of metropolitan epicentral earthquake, Disaster Prevention Information, http://www.bousai.metro.tokyo.jp/japanese/knowledge/material_h.html
3. Yokomatsu, M.: A Game Theoretic Analysis of Risk Communication in Disaster Prevention Activity. Disaster Prevention Research Institute Abstracts for Annuals (49), 147–154 (2006)
4. Yokoyama, H., Meguro, K., Katayama, T.: Simulation Method of Human Behavior at the Underground Shopping Center 3, 160–164 (1993)
5. Kobayashi, K., Narita, A., Hirano, M., et al.: Collaborative simulation interface for planning disaster measures. In: CHI 2006, pp. 22–27 (2006)
6. Sakai, R., Yokoe, S., Kimura, A., et al.: Mixed Reality Based Information Presentation for Disaster Prevention Studies and Disaster Measures: Showing an Interactive Dynamic 3D Hazard Map Superimposed on Diorama 105(536), 201–206 (2006)
7. NIED: Development of "Disaster Risk Finder", http://bosai-drip.jp/info/1004info.html
8. Suezawa, K., Kurosaki, H., Kimura, Y., Fukumoto, S.: Development and Enforcement of General Disaster Prevention Training to Think about Together. In: ISSS, vol. (20), pp. 25–28 (2008)

Entertainment Displays Which Restore Negative Images of Shopping Center

Sachi Urano, Tetsuya Saito, and Junichi Hoshino

University of Tsukuba
3M309, 1-1-1 Tennodai, Tsukuba
Ibaraki, 305-8573
me@sachiurano.jp, e0411304@edu.esys.tsukuba.ac.jp,
jhoshino@esys.tsukuba.ac.jp

Abstract. According to data from Statistical Research on Shopping Centers (SC), the number of SC in January 2012 was 3050, which is 1.41 times that of Y2000. Despite gathering the impact on the custom absorbency power, there are some spaces with a negative atmosphere where crowds of people gather together at the same time in what could be considered as inactive dead spaces. In this paper, we propose two entertainment systems which display animations by object detection to improve these negative atmospheres of particularly large SCs. We survey the changes in customer impressions by placing these systems in SC and verify that these systems deliver better impressions on the spaces.

Keywords: Shopping Center, Negative Image, Entertainment System.

1 Introduction

There are many Shopping Centers (SC) that have been built throughout the country, a total of over 3050 in Japan [1]. They have done all sorts of things to allow shoppers enjoy their shopping experience (e.g. setting up food courts and holding of periodic events). But many of these SC also have some problems which can generate negative impressions that take away from the overall shopping experience. There has been a major issue with the appearance of dead and inactive spaces due to the increased size of SC. Additionally, the increase in visitors has resulted in congestion around these dead spaces. To make more effective use of dead spaces such as sub-entrances and areas near the restrooms, some comforts (e.g. bench, vending machine, crane game) have been installed, but it is difficult to create an appealing space for shoppers because there are not enough requirements. For example, there are restricted areas and wall surface which cover a wide range of space. Additionally, a period of waiting for something like the elevator or the line at the cash register cause boredom for shoppers as they likely have nothing to do. If the SC were to improve these atmospheres and

A. Nijholt, T. Romão, and D. Reidsma (Eds.): ACE 2012, LNCS 7624, pp. 585–588, 2012.

create a place to have fun, it may be profitable, not only in regard to the effective use of the spaces, but also as playing an important role in attracting more shoppers.

To improve characteristics of negative atmospheres in the SC, we propose two different entertainment models for shoppers' convenience and fun, taking into account both easy and inexpensive installation in the SC's environment. Both models employ the use of a projector system, which produce animation and add images through object detection (explained later). We have confirmed through experimentation, by placing these systems at rest stations and sub-entrances in SC, that these systems produce a more positive atmosphere and are effective in changing shopper's impressions of the spaces.

2   Background

SC meets shopper's value by providing the higher value of diversity of choices, convenience, comfort and amusement [1], and also it is expected to gives shoppers have a good time and brighten street image up. Then we choose "boring" which is the pair of adjectives of "bright" and examine why they expect these. We carried out a questionnaire survey for 15 examinees to determine what spaces in SC give negative impressions due to a poor atmosphere. We ask them to give examples on what environments would feel boring and why they feel bored and how they generally spend their waiting time.

As a result, we decided to propose two different interactive entertainment systems, "Jelly Canvas," which can be played without moving in a short amount of time and "Shadowgraph System," which does not hamper traffic and provides a bright and clear area for shoppers to feel comfortable, using projector systems which are cheap and easy to set up at any SC.

2.1   Related Cases

There have been various studies of public displays set up in public places and played by concurrent users. But these studies excel in terms of inducement of entry by analyzing users' responses, but are difficult to use for SC because they need to occupy a wide area and are very much a multiplayer experience. These days, interactive digital public art using computer technology to produce various sounds and images are often seen in public[6],[7],[8] are not realistic ways to hold regular exhibitions as they require long time observation, expensive implementation cost, and there is more limited space in SCs. An example of a space where people might stay for extended period of time (e.g. spaces for relaxation, benches, desks, vending machines, crane games, bulletin boards, static merchandise exhibitions, advertisements, etc.). Some vacant spaces and premises are utilized effectively, but it is difficult to create a good and appealing space for shoppers because there are not enough requirements (e.g. there are restricted spaces and wall surface which cover wide ranges).

3 Method

We develop "Jelly Canvas" and "Shadowgraph System," both of which are controlled by an object recognition system using a camera and a display object by the projector. The system goes through a complex anti-aliasing algorithm, processing the images provided by the camera. It also runs through gray-scale processing and the uses the binary data to output the difference between the images and the background. Classification of object shapes is done by template matching and is used in producing reactions.

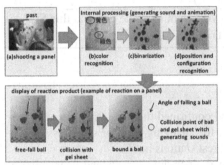

Fig. 1. Flow in Jelly Canvas

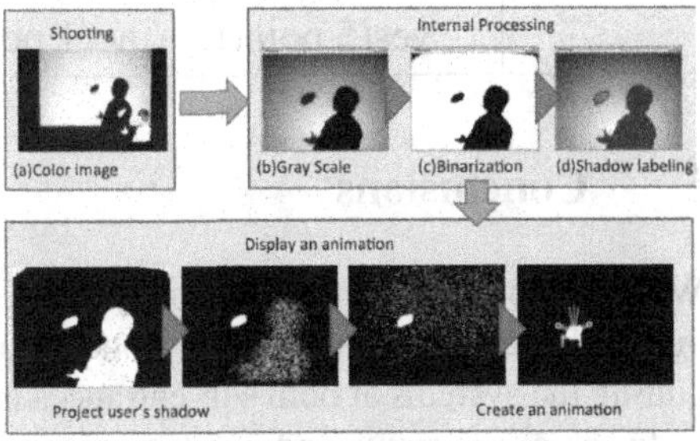

Fig. 2. Image processing in Shadowgraph System

4 Assessment Experiment

We made an exhibition experiment at a Giant SC called "iias Tsukuba" on April 14th and 29th, 2012. Fig. 4 shows the questionnaire results. In Jelly Canvas, we heard what shoppers have to say, "I like the comfort of children playing among themselves", "It is great to see children playing before my eyes." and so on. In Shadowgraph System, we also received some good feedback such as: "A system which attracts our attention like this is good", "I like the cute animations" and so on.

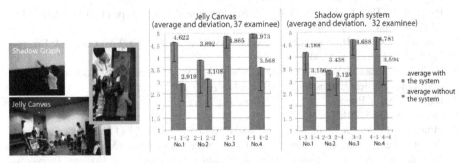

Fig. 3. The image of exhibition

Fig. 4. Comparing with and without the systems

Table 1. Evaluation Item

	Question: Positive(5 point)~Negative(1 point)
No.1	How is your current mood? fun(5 point) ~ boring(1 point)
No.2	(Setting up the system) How is this atmosphere in this space? positive(5 point) ~ negative(1 point)
No.3	How is this system? Good(5 point) ~ bad(1 point)
No.4	(Setting up the system) Do you want to come again at this SC? yes(5 point) ~ no(1 point)

5   Conclusions

We developed two entertainment systems and confirmed that the systems would produce a better space, and obtain good results for changing shopper's impressions by putting the systems at both sub-entrances and rest stations in SC.

In the experiments and exhibitions, shoppers, including parents and their children pay attention to the systems in each space. Moving forward we must try and develop more animations and special effects, especially geared toward children.

References

1. Japanese Council of Shopping Centers, The report of statistical survey of SC sales, pp. 1–2 (2012)
2. Ministry of Economy, Trade and Industry Information packet of Large-Scale Retail Store Location Act, http://www.meti.go.jp/policy/economy/distribution/daikibo/e91112aj.html (access: April 18, 2012)
3. Kato, H., Naemura, T., et al.: Textured Shadow. In: The Second Intern Symp on Mixed and Augmented Reality 2003 MR Technology Expo., pp. 352–353 (2003)
4. Pasquier, P., Han, E., Kim, K., Jung, K.: Shadow Agent, a New Type of Virtual Agent. In: ACE 2008, pp. 71–74 (2008)
5. Igarashi, T., Ogata, H.: Another shadow. In: SIGGRAPH ASIA 2009 Art Gallery & Emerging Technologies, p. 61 (2009)
6. Hashida, T., Kakehi, Y.: Ensemble system with i-trace. In: International Conf. on New Interfaces for Musical Expression (NIME 2004), 4A-10, pp. 215–216 (2004)
7. Digital Art Project, http://www.digital-public-art.org/index.php (access: April 15, 2012)
8. Miura, K., Takagi, K., et al.: 7028 Analysis of Attractive Public Road through Social Experiment in Tenjin Area. In: Summaries of Technical Papers of Annual Meeting Architectural Institute of Japan. F-1, Urban Planning, Building Economics and Housing Problems, pp.109–112 (2005)

Where Buddhism Encounters Entertainment Computing

Daisuke Uriu[1], Naohito Okude[1], Masahiko Inami[1],
Takafumi Taketomi[2], and Chihiro Sato[1]

[1] Graduate School of Media Design, Keio University
4-1-1 Hiyoshi, Kohoku-ku, Yokohama, Japan 223-8526
{uriu,okude,inami,chihiro}@kmd.keio.ac.jp
[2] Graduate School of Information Science,
Nara Institute of Science and Technology
8916-5 Takayama, Ikoma, Nara, Japan 630-0192
takafumi-t@is.naist.jp

Abstract. This special panel session provides an opportunity to discuss how entertainment computing designers create interactive media/ contents on Buddhism and also other religious practices. In this year, we have launched an exciting project designing interactive contents to be used in Todaiji temple, one of the world heritages located in Nara, Japan. In this project, we are actually collaborating with monks of the Todaiji temple, learning Buddhist rituals in this temple from the monks, and creating Augmented Reality contents working on high performance network infrastructure. This session consists of a presentation introducing our Todaiji temple project and a set of short key notes from specialists; researchers on Augmented Reality, Entertainment Computing, and Anthropology.

1   Introduction

Todaiji temple, registered as a world heritage, is one of most famous Japanese Buddhist temple. Its Buddhism religion—called *Kegon-kyo*, the Avatamsaka Sutra, or Flower Ornament Scripture [1]—has been carried out over 1200 years. The Great Buddha of this temple (Right of Figure 1) is said to represent the world of *Kegon-kyo* and known as symbolic object for sightseers. In every February, the temple holds a special ritual ceremony called *Shunie* or *Omizutori* at Nigatsu-do Hall of this temple in two weeks. Monks run around the hall's balconies, swinging large torches (Left of Figure 1). This event continuing for over 1200 years owns very important meanings for the monks and has been attracting many visitors who believe being touched by the falling sparks can make them happy.

Fortunately, we—Nara Institute of Science and Technology (NAIST)[1] and Graduate School of Media Design, Keio University (KMD)[2]—have acquired a

---

[1] http://www.naist.jp/en/
[2] http://www.kmd.keio.ac.jp/en/

A. Nijholt, T. Romão, and D. Reidsma (Eds.): ACE 2012, LNCS 7624, pp. 589–592, 2012.

Fig. 1. Left: A monk runs with swinging the torche, Right: Great Buddha of the Todaiji temple

chance to collaborate with the Todaiji temple to conduct an exciting project designing interactive contents enabling students, the visitors, and the monks to learn about Todaiji and its difficult religion *Kegon-kyo* with walking around locations in the temple. Our initial purpose is to create Augmented Reality contents working on high performance network infrastructure, which is a challenge to design a novel experience, honestly even we have not imagined yet, crossing between human's spirituality, religious rituals, and cutting edge technologies.

Our design and development team of this project consists of researchers working on Anthropology, Augmented Reality, and Entertainment Computing. Naohito Okude, a professor in KMD, is investigating rituals of *Kegonkyo* and practices in the Todaiji temple based on anthropological studies. Masahiko Inami, a professor in KMD, is one of pioneers of Entertainment Computing. Takafumi Taketomi, an assistant professor in NAIST, specializes in the field of Augmented Reality. The team of this project has been discussing with the monks in Todaiji temple many times and now constructing specific contents to be used at the sites in the temple.

At the ACE 2012 conference, we organize a special panel session that provides an opportunity to discuss how entertainment computing designers create interactive media/contents on Buddhism and also other religious practices. Firstly we introduce our Todaiji temple project as a case study of designing digital contents supporting to learn Buddhist rituals. Panelists that come from our design team provide a set of short key notes from each of their specialized backgrounds. After the short key notes, the panelists discuss future forecasts for entertainment computing with religious practices; where Buddhism encounters entertainment computing, how interactive technologies should support humans spirituality, and what are the challenges to develop these interactive contents.

2 Spirituality HCI Supported

An anthropologist Genevieve Bell firstly revealed connections between spiritual (especially religious) practices and technologies reviewing case examples from online virtual cemeteries to special mobile phone supporting religious practices at Ubicomp2006 conference [2]. After her result, some researchers have been striving to design interactive digital media supporting spiritual practices, but there is still not many design oriented works yet. For example, Wyche produced an image based mobile phone application supporting Islam practices [3]. While, Gaver designed a special physical artifact supporting nuns working at a church [4].

Our Todaiji temple project also challenges to design connections between one's spirituality and technologies, especially focusing on user experience when users—students, visitors, and young monks—walk around real locations in the temple. Our current purpose or goal in this project is to give them learnings of not only actions of rituals such as *Omizutori* but also strict meanings of *Kegon-kyo* hidden from superficial ones. Our research approach, collaborating with the monks to design contents that extends ones' experience at physical locations at the temple, will provide a forecast how HCI researchers produce contents and media for supporting people's techno-spiritual practices [2].

3 Moderator and Panelists

3.1 Daisuke Uriu (Moderator)

He is an interaction designer especially focusing on connection between one's spiritual practices and memories. His recent work "Thanato Fenestra" [5] supports Buddhist rituals to pray for the repose of the dead persons' spirits with applying candle movements to effect digital photos. In the Todaiji temple project, he is producing to develop interaction design between physical objects in the temple and religious experience of *Kegon-kyo*.

3.2 Naohito Okude

He conducts some research projects related with cultural anthropology, phenomenology, media environment. He produced a Virtual Reality content reproducing Sistine Chapel located in Vatican in 1998. In the Todaiji temple project, he is trying to design spiritual experience packaged in on-site digital application, considering religious meanings of *Kegon-kyo* with employing his anthropological background.

3.3 Masahiko Inami

He is a scientist specializing in interactive technologies such as robotics, Virtual Reality, Augmented Reality, and Entertainment Computing. In the Todaiji temple project, he is the chief technology organizer utilizing multiple technologies and bridging them to the field of spiritual experience.

3.4 Takafumi Taketomi

Takafumi Taketomi (Panelist) is developing a feature landmark based camera pose estimation method. In the Todaiji Project, he is working on vision-based markerless geometric registration outdoors. By using a structure-from motion, 3D structure of the target environment is automatically acquired.

4 Contents

This special session consists of 4 sections.

- Introduction about Todaiji temple and Todaiji temple project (20 min.)
- Panelists' talks (30min.)
- Discussion between panelists (20 min.)
- Discussion with the audiences (20 min.)

At first we will introduce Todaiji-temple and outline of our project. Secondly, each panelists will give the audiences a short talk related with his research background. Thirdly, panelists will discuss future forecasts for entertainment computing with religious practices. Finally, we reserve time to discuss the topics the panelists provide with the audience and conclude "Where Buddhism Encounters Entertainment Computing," how interactive technologies should support humans spirituality and religious experience, and what are the challenges to produce interactive contents supporting this issue.

Acknowledgments. This panel session is granted by NAIST Advanced Research Partnership Project.

References

1. Cleary, T.: The Flower Ornament Scripture: A Translation of the Avatamsaka Sutra. Shambhala (1993)
2. Bell, G.: *No More SMS from Jesus:* Ubicomp, Religion and Techno-spiritual Practices. In: Dourish, P., Friday, A. (eds.) UbiComp 2006. LNCS, vol. 4206, pp. 141–158. Springer, Heidelberg (2006)
3. Wyche, S.P., Caine, K.E., Davison, B.K., Patel, S.N., Arteaga, M., Grinter, R.E.: Sacred imagery in techno-spiritual design. In: Proc. of CHI 2009, pp. 55–58 (2009)
4. Gaver, W., Blythe, M., Boucher, A., Jarvis, N., Bowers, J., Wright, P.: The prayer companion: openness and specificity, materiality and spirituality. In: Proc. of CHI 2010, pp. 2055–2064 (2010)
5. Uriu, D., Okude, N.: Thanatofenestra: photographic family altar supporting a ritual to pray for the deceased. In: Proc. of DIS 2010, pp. 422–425 (2010)

IUstream: Personal Live Streaming Support System with Automatic Collection and Real-Time Recommendation of Topics

Keiko Yamamoto, Soya Kirito, Itaru Kuramoto, and Yoshihiro Tsujino

Kyoto Institute of Technology, Matsugasaki, Sakyo-ku, Kyoto, Japan
{kei,kirito,kuramoto,tsujino}@hit.is.kit.ac.jp

Abstract. Nowadays, it becomes much easier to perform live streaming personally via the Internet. When performers broadcast their programs, they sometimes have no idea for what they should talk. In this paper, we propose a system, named IUstream, to recommend one of proper topics which have been collected automatically. As the result of an empirical evaluation, it is found that IUstream can support performers.

Keywords: personal live streaming, topic recommendation.

1 Introduction

Sharing personal information online is popular these days. Everyone has a chance to use personal live streaming services such as Ustream[1] and NICO NICO LIVE[2]. Osker et al.[1] discussed about live streaming as a social media. The personal live streaming services make the performers broadcast their minds or actions toward general public audiences easily and freely with a computer, a webcam, and the Internet. In NICO NICO LIVE, about half of programs are for the purpose of chatting casually with the audiences about informal or not pre-defined topics. In these programs, the performers are likely to drop into situations where they become in silence because they have no idea about what they should talk.

In this paper, we propose IUstream[3] to recommend one of proper topics which have been collected automatically. Unlike traditional support systems for professional performers such as Wearable MC system[2], on personal live streaming, scripts may not be prepared for the performers because it takes time and labor to prepared scripts by themselves. Therefore, IUstream recommends the performers proper topics when they have no idea about what they should talk.

2 IUstream

Fig. 1 shows the flow of IUstream. Before broadcasting, IUstream collects articles to database automatically so as not to prepare scripts beforehand by performers.

---

[1] http://www.ustream.tv/

[2] http://live.niconico.com/

[3] "IU" is a Japanese verb that has meaning of "talk" or "say".

A. Nijholt, T. Romão, and D. Reidsma (Eds.): ACE 2012, LNCS 7624, pp. 593–596, 2012.

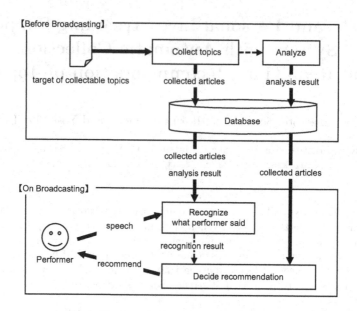

Fig. 1. Flow of IUstream

The performers tend to talk about new and interesting topics for themselves on their programs. In order to gather such topics, articles are collected from the performer's blog through a browser, and then IUstream analyzes the articles to prepare for his or her talk.

On broadacsting, IUstream recognizes what a performer is talking and decides a recommendation from articles in the database as the result of the recognition. Based on this process, IUstream shows one of proper contents for the performer in real-time. This process consists of two steps. First, IUstream recognizes the performer's speech with AmiVoice®SP. If he or she is talking about the content which is the same as some article collected in his or her database, it is highly possible that sentences in the article contains words currently talked by him or her. Therefore, IUstream recognizes sentences by comparing the words that he or she was talking with the words contained in each sentence of the article with keyword matching technology. Next, IUstream decides a recommendation. When a performer forgets contents which he or she wants to talk next in a topic, IUstream recognizes that he or she is talking with a sentence in a topic and recommends the next sentence of the topic that he or she is talking. When a performer cannot recall a next topic after finishing a certain topic, IUstream recognizes that he or she has already finished talking about a topic and recommends a latest topic that he or she has not talked about and that has not been displayed. When a performer cannot realize a topic related to comments from audiences, IUstream recognizes that he or she is not talking about a topic associated with comments from audiences in the performer's database and recommends the topic.

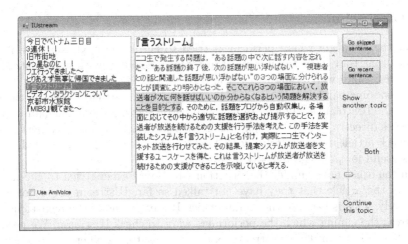

Fig. 2. Interface of IUstream

3   Evaluation

An empirical evaluation of IUstream is conducted to confirm the effect of the system. First, participants are asked to post their blog entries. They write at least seven entries each of which has at least 400 characters. Second, they broadcast their own personal live streaming programs using NICO NICO LIVE with IUstream (see Fig. 2) more than three days after posting. The experimenter lets them know that their programs are closed and the audiences are cooperators. Finally, the experimenter interviews the participants after their programs. The participants are 10 Japanese native graduate students.

Table 1 shows the use of IUstream on the streaming programs. Total number of use is 96 and all participants tried to check IUstream at least one time. The reasons why they tried to check IUstream are categorized four groups.

Table 1. The times that participants try to check topics by IUstream

Participants		A	B	C	D	E	F	G	H	I	J	Total
Can you check a next content of the article that you were talking?	Yes	5	2	2	1	5	3	2	2	3	3	28
	No	3			1	6		2			4	16
Can you check the contents of the article that you have not talked so far?	No	2	8			3	1		3		2	19
Can you check the topics associated with comments from your audiences?	Yes		1			1	1		1	1		5
	No		11						1			12
	*						1				3	4
The participant tries to check a topic from a list of the articles' titles.		4			1		3	1	2	1		12
Total		14	22	2	3	15	9	5	9	5	12	96

*: IUstream showed a topic, but the participant did not talk about it.

4   Discussion

Under the situation where performers tried to check the next contents of the articles that they were talking and the topics associated with comments from audiences, there were some cases where IUstream could support them. There were also some participants who tried to check a list of articles' titles on the left side of the IUstream's window. In this evaluation setting, the participants could not check directly an article which was in the list. In actual situation, performers can check articles immediately by clicking it. Therefore, it is expected that the list is useful for personal live streaming.

On the other hand, under the situation where performers tried to check contents of the article that they have not talked so far, IUstream could not work effectively. This is because the timing which IUstearm shows the next topic differs from the timing which the performers want to check IUstream. We need to provide the function that IUstream can show next topics whenever performers want. Under the situation where the performers tried to check topics associated with comments from audiences, two participants did not talk about the topics showed by IUstream. This is because they thought the recommendations were not sufficiently associated with comments from the audiences. If there were more articles posted, the degree of association could be expected much higher.

5   Conclusion

In this paper, we proposed IUstream, which recommends proper one of topics for performers on personal live streaming. IUstream collects articles from the performers' blogs automatically and recommends topics based on analysis of collected articles and performers' speech recognition.

In an empirical evaluation, we asked some participants to perform live streaming on NICO NICO LIVE with IUstream to confirm the effects of IUstream. As the result of the evaluation, we found that IUstream could show participants topics in 33 cases (39%) of 84 cases where they tried to check articles by IUstream. Especially, IUstream could support performers in a case where they forget contents which they want to talk next in a topic.

As a future work, we plan to evaluate that performers could get recommendation associated with audiences' comments, collecting more articles. Especially, we will improve IUstream with collecting articles from news sites because news is expected to contain information that the performer has gotten newly. Furthermore, we will apply IUstream to face-to-face communication in daily lives.

References

1. Juhlin, O., Reponen, E., Bentley, F., Kirk, D.: Video interaction - Making broadcasting a successful social media. In: Proc. of CHI EA 2011, pp. 2437–2440 (2011)
2. Okada, T., Yamamoto, T., Terada, T., Tsukamoto, M.: Wearable MC System: a System for Supporting MC Performances using Wearable Computing Technologies. In: Proc. of Augmented Human Conference 2011, pp. 25:1–25:7 (2011)

Author Index

Adachi, Takayuki   461
Akazawa, Keiichi   573
Alexandrova, Todorka   549
Alha, Kati   336
Almahr, Ali   494
Andre, Elisabeth   529
Antle, Alissa N.   465
Azlin, Aida   521

Ban, Yuki   309
Barreto, Mary   545
Bergmans, Anne   469
Bertuccioli, Cristian   437
Bevans, Allen   465
Birra, Fernando   70
Branco, Pedro   565

Centieiro, Pedro   1, 352, 473, 553
Champagnat, Ronan   246
Chan, Shih-Han   151
Chang, Chin-Chen   167
Chen, Gencai   533
Chen, Ling   533
Chen, Tai-Yun   167
Cheok, Adrian David   182, 421, 494
Choi, Yongsoon   182, 421
Chu, Narisa N.Y.   421
Connor, Katy   445
Correia, Nuno   368
Coutinho, Clara   565
Cui, Yanqing   133
Czepa, Christoph   485

Deaker, Chris   198
Dertien, Edwin   477
Dias, A. Eduardo   1, 473, 553
Dijkstra, Jelle   477

Egusa, Ryohei   461
Endo, Hideyuki   481

Fan, Changjun   533
Franiak, Alexander   485
Fujii, Nobuto   490
Fujita, Kazuyuki   17
Fukushi, Kenichiro   384

Gonçalves, Sérgio   565
Goseki, Masafumi   461
Grammenos, Dimitris   214
Grassel, Guido   133
Grønbæk, Kaj   230
Guy, Olivier   246

Hachisu, Taku   31
Halupka, Veronica   494
Hara, Takenori   569
Hashimoto, Sunao   577
Hashimoto, Yuki   498
Hayakawa, Seiho   44
Hayashi, Oribe   309
Hayashi, Toshihiro   573
Hirai, Shigeyuki   44
Hirose, Michitaka   309, 398, 453
Hlavacs, Helmut   485
Horita, Kodai   561
Hoshi, Takayuki   502
Hoshino, Junichi   262, 581, 585
Hoshuyama, Osamu   453
Howland, Robert   262
Hsu, Hung-Wei   167

Igarashi, Takeo   577
Inagaki, Shigenori   461
Inami, Masahiko   406, 557, 577, 589
Itoh, Yuichi   17
Iurgel, Ido Aharon   429
Iwazaki, Karin   569

Juul Sørensen, Anne Sofie   506

Kagawa, Erina   573
Kajimoto, Hiroyuki   31, 513
Kaneko, Kosuke   117
Kanke, Hiroyuki   57
Katayose, Haruhiro   490
Kawaguchi, Hiroki   517, 561
Kawaguchi, Yoichiro   287, 537
Kerlow, Isaac   521
Khadafi, Muhammad   521
Kidokoro, Hiroyuki   17
Kimura, Kentaro   309

Kimura, Takashi   561
Kinoshita, Shougo   541
Kirito, Soya   593
Koike, Hideki   561
Konya, Yuko   274
Korhonen, Hannu   336
Kortbek, Karen Johanne   230
Kou, Kinyo   287
Koutlemanis, Panagiotis   214
Kroes, Lies   525
Kuramoto, Itaru   593
Kurdyukova, Ekaterina   529
Kusunoki, Fusako   461

LiWei, Yang   309
Lu, Ziyu   533

Machover, Tod   384
Mader, Angelika   477
Marcomini, Andrea   437
Marfia, Gustavo   437
Margetis, George   214
Masoodian, Masood   198
Masui, Toshiyuki   297
Matsui, Yu   117
Matteucci, Giovanni   437
Mi, Haipeng   537
Mikami, Koji   117
Minakuchi, Mitsuru   541
Mizoguchi, Hiroshi   461
Møller, Claus   230
Motai, Goro   569
Mourato, Fausto   70
Muroya, Yuma   309, 398

Nagaku, Masaru   117
Nakabayashi, Toshifumi   117
Nakajima, Tatsuo   549
Namatame, Miki   461
Narumi, Takuji   398, 453
Natkin, Stéphane   151
Nielsen, Jesper   230
Nishimura, Kunihiro   309
Nishizaka, Shinya   309
Nisi, Valentina   545
Nojima, Takuya   517, 561
Nunes, Nuno   545

Obaid, Mohammad   529
Ohta, Takashi   320
Ojala, Jarno   133

Okada, Yusaku   561
Okazaki, Tatsuhiko   85
Okude, Naohito   589
Ono, Kenji   117
Ono, Masaki   573
Onojima, Yusuke   309

Paavilainen, Janne   336
Paiva, Ana   101
Pan, Yupeng   494
Pandey, Anshul Vikram   182
Parsani, Rahul   182
Pereira, André   101
Pereira, Lucas   545
Pinto, Mário   429
Pitrey, Yohann   485
Prada, Rui   101
Próspero dos Santos, Manuel   70

Quintal, Filipe   545

Reidsma, Dennis   477
Roccetti, Marco   437
Rogers, Bill   198
Roman, Xavier   182
Romão, Teresa   1, 352, 473, 553
Rowland, Duncan   445

Saito, Tetsuya   585
Sakakibara, Yoshinobu   44
Sakamoto, Mizuki   549
Sakurai, Sho   453
Salvador, Ricardo   352
Santos, Bruno   553
Santos, Rossana   368
Sato, Chihiro   589
Sato, Munehiko   309
Sato, Yuichi   490
Sawaki, Furi   557
Shahid, Suleman   469, 525
Shin, Kiyoshi   117
Shuto, Keisuke   569
Siio, Itiro   274
Stenfeldt, Liselott   230
Suhaimi, Aisyah   521
Suzuki, Yasuhiro   309
Suzuki, Yu   541
Suzuki, Yuta   561
Sylla, Cristina   565

Tachikawa, Tomoya   569
Tai, Wen-Kai   167
Takahashi, Yoichi   561
Takegawa, Yoshinari   57, 384
Taketomi, Takafumi   589
Tanaka, Jun   320
Tanikawa, Tomohiro   398, 453
Tarumi, Hiroyuki   573
Teixeira, Bárbara   553
Terada, Tsutomu   57, 85, 384
Tewell, Jordan   577
Tiger, Guillaume   151
Topol, Alexandre   151
Toyono, Chiho   569
Tsujino, Yoshihiro   593
Tsukamoto, Masahiko   57, 85, 384

Uchiyama, Hiroko   569
Ueta, Masamichi   453

Urano, Sachi   262, 581, 585
Uriu, Daisuke   589

Vyas, Dhaval   133

Wakama, Hironori   490
Wei, Jun   421

Yaegashi, Rihito   573
Yamamoto, Keiko   593
Yamane, Shinji R.   117
Yasu, Kentaro   406, 557
Yoshida, Shigeo   309
Yoshimura, Sakuji   569
Yoshioka, Hideki   481
Yu, Peichao   581

Zabulis, Xenophon   214
Zhuang, Harry   521
Zhuang, Henry   521